Springer Proceedings in Business and Economics

More information about this series at http://www.springer.com/series/11960

Androniki Kavoura · Damianos P. Sakas
Petros Tomaras
Editors

Strategic Innovative Marketing

5th IC-SIM, Athens, Greece 2016

Springer

Editors
Androniki Kavoura
T.E.I. of Athens
Athens
Greece

Petros Tomaras
T.E.I. of Athens
Athens
Greece

Damianos P. Sakas
Department of Computer Science
and Technology
University of Peloponnese
Tripoli
Greece

ISSN 2198-7246 ISSN 2198-7254 (electronic)
Springer Proceedings in Business and Economics
ISBN 978-3-319-56287-2 ISBN 978-3-319-56288-9 (eBook)
DOI 10.1007/978-3-319-56288-9

Library of Congress Control Number: 2017937285

Printed on acid-free paper

This Springer imprint is published by Springer Nature
The registered company is Springer International Publishing AG
The registered company address is: Gewerbestrasse 11, 6330 Cham, Switzerland

Preface

Aims and Scope of the Conference

The 5th International Conference on Strategic Innovative Marketing 2016 took place in Athens, Greece, during September 23–26, 2016. IC-SIM is an international interdisciplinary conference focusing on the theoretical approach of the contemporary issues evolved in strategic marketing and the integration of theory and practice.

More than 325 pre-registered authors submitted their work in the conference. IC-SIM 2016 finally accepted and hosted 102 original research papers, after a double-blinded peer-review process. During the conference, 14 workshops were held in order to advance and contribute to specific research areas in the field of innovative marketing.

The conference aims at creating a forum for further discussion for a strategic innovative marketing field incorporating a series of issues and/or related organizations that manage marketing in their everyday operations. Therefore, the call for papers was addressed to scholars and/or professionals of the fields of social media and marketing innovation, e-marketing and new technologies, strategic marketing, services and cultural marketing, international and cross-cultural marketing, marketing research and analytics, marketing communications, B2B and B2C marketing. Furthermore, papers focused on issues of consumer behavior and advertising and promotion were also welcomed. IC-SIM provides a common ground for the exchange of insights on strategic issues in the science of innovation marketing, ensuring significant contributions to this field.

The primary objective of IC-SIM is the theoretical approaches of contemporary issues evolved in strategic marketing and the integration of theory and practice. The conference provides a common ground for the exchange of insights on strategic issues in the science of innovation marketing, ensuring significant contributions to this field.

Grouping the emerging technologies in the marketing field together in a close examination of practices, problems and trends, IC-SIM and its emphases on integration and marketing presented the state of the art in the field. This annual event is addressed jointly to academics and practitioners and provides a forum for a number of perspectives, based on either theoretical analyses or empirical case studies that foster the dialogue and the exchange of ideas.

Topics

Marketing of Innovation, Social Media Marketing, Innovations in Online Marketing, Marketing Technological Innovation, Facebook Marketing Strategies, Mobile Marketing, Blogging, Network Analysis, e-branding & Brand Experience Management, Digital Marketing, Marketing and Electronic Commerce, Marketing Analytics, Marketing Research, Marketing Information Systems, Marketing of Emerging Technologies, Sustainable Marketing, Distribution Channel Management, Integrated Marketing Communications, Strategic Marketing Services, Marketing Services, Branding/Online Brands, Benchmarking Strategies, Customer Satisfaction, Emerging Markets, Marketing Management, New Product Design and Development, Creativity Marketing, Sports Marketing, B2B and B2C Marketing, Pricing Strategies in Marketing, Marketing Theory and Applications, Art & Cultural Marketing, Cross-cultural Marketing, Tourism & Destination Marketing, Transport Industry Marketing, Experiential and Sensory Marketing, Customer Relationship Management and Social CRM, Collaborative Marketing, Safety Marketing, Business Economics, Economics of Business Strategy, Accounting Marketing, Global Business Marketing, Finance Healthcare Management, Accounting Education Skills & Competences Higher Education.

Paper Peer Review

More than 245 original researches had been submitted for consideration in IC-SIM 2016. All papers submitted to the conference were reviewed by a double-blind peer-review process. The Conference Scientific Committee composed of competent and expertise reviewers decided about the acceptance of the submitted papers.

Thanks

We would like to thank all members that participated in any way in the IC-SIM 2016 Conference and especially:

- The famous publication house Springer for their communication sponsorship.
- The co-organizing universities and institutes for their support and development of a high-quality conference scientific level and profile.
- The members of the Scientific Committee that honored the conference with their presence and provided a significant contribution to the review of papers as well as for their indications for the improvement of the conference.
- All members of the Organizing Committee for their help, support, and spirited participation before, during, and after the Conference.
- The Session Organizers for their willingness to organize sessions of high importance and for their editorial work, contributing in the development of valued services to the conference.
- Dr. Nasiopoulos Dimitrios, editorial assistant.
- Ms Antonia Veltsista, editorial assistant.

Athens, Greece — Androniki Kavoura
Tripoli, Greece — Damianos P. Sakas
Athens, Greece — Petros Tomaras

The original version of the book was revised. Belated corrections to change the order of First name and Family name of chapter authors have been incorporated.
The erratum to the book is available at 10.1007/978-3-319-56288-9_72

Conference Details

Chair

Damianos P. Sakas, University of Peloponnese, Greece

International Advisory Committee

C.B. Bhattacharya, ESMT European School of Management and Technology, Germany
Sally Dibb, The Open University, UK
Yorgos Zotos, Cyprus University of Technology, Cyprus
Philip Kitchen, ESC Rennes School of Business, France
Michael Belch, San Diego State University, USA
Dimitrios Buhalis, Bournemouth University, UK

Scientific Committee

Fiona Lettice, University of East Anglia, UK
David P. Evans, La Rochelle School of Business, France
Carlota Lorenzo Romero, Universidad de Castilla-La Mancha, Albacete, Spain
Giacomo Del Chiappa, University of Sassari, Italy
Denisa Kasl Kollmannová, Charles University in Prague, Czech Republic
Russell Belk, York University, Canada
Nergis Aziz, Suleyman Sah University, Turkey
Barry Friedman, State University of New York at Oswego, USA
Chris Cooper, Oxford Brookes University, UK
Annette Pritchard, Cardiff Metropolitan University, UK

Organizing Committee

Keynote Speaker

Prof. Peter G.R. Smith
Founder, Stratophase Ltd.,
Covesion Ltd.

Professor Peter G.R. Smith is a Professor in the Optoelectronics Research Centre and Associate Pro Vice-Chancellor International in the Faculty of Physical Sciences and Engineering at the University of Southampton. He graduated from Oxford University with a B.A. in Physics in 1990 and D.Phil. in Nonlinear Optics in 1993. After a year spent as a management consultant he joined the University of Southampton. Peter has worked on a number of areas in optics research ranging from laser spectroscopy to polymer integrated-optics. He has published over 180 journal and conference papers in the fields of periodically poled materials and UV written devices at major conferences, including invited talks at national and international meetings. He was the founder of two spin-outs from Southampton—Stratophase Ltd. in 2003 and Covesion Limited in 2009.

Invited Speakers

Dr. George Kotrotsios
Vice President, Marketing &
Business Development CSEM,
Switzerland

Professor George Kotrotsios is member of the Executive Board of CSEM, a major Swiss R&I facility in microelectronics, nanotechnology and photovoltaics. He is charge of commercialisation of Research and to optimize the usefulness of the R&D for the industry. He is individual member of the Swiss Academy of Engineering Sciences. In 2016 he chairs the Alliance of Fraunhofer-microelectronics, CEA, VTT and CSEM on Smart Systems (HTA). He sits in the Board EARTO (European Association of Research and Technology Organisation) and is member of the Board of Directors of CSEM do Brazil and Femto Engineering in France. His background is in optical fiber sensors, technology and lasers. He holds a Ph.D. Degree in Optoelectronics, Institut National Polytechnique de Grenoble (Fr), an Executive MBA in Management of Technology, HEC —Université de Lausanne/EPFL (CH) and an Electrical Engineering Degree from the Aristotle University of Thessaloniki (Gr).

Dr. Vasilios Gregoriou
Director & Chairman NHRF,
CEO & Founder Advent
Energy Inc.

Dr. Gregoriou is the CEO and cofounder of Advent Technologies Inc, as well as the Director and Chairman of the Board at the National Hellenic Research Foundation (NHRF). Dr. Gregoriou is an internationally known scientist with research positions in both the US (Northeastern, MIT, Polaroid, Princeton) and Greece (FORTH-ICEHT) over his 25 year research career so far. His research activity extends over a wide area of subjects that include the areas of flexible photovoltaics based on organic semiconductors, optically active materials based on conjugated oligomers and polymer nanocomposites. Dr. Gregoriou has more than 20 years of experience in the US market. He has extensive experience in the technical development of new products and in the management of such activities. He holds a Ph.D. in Physical Chemistry from Duke University and he has attended the MBA program at Northeastern University.

Prof. Nikos Stergiopulos
Founder EndoArt SA, Antlia
SA, Rheon Medical SA,
EPFL, Switzerland

Professor Nikos Stergiopulos received his M.S. in Mechanical Engineering from the National Technical University of Athens, Greece, in 1985 and his Ph.D. in Biomedical Engineering from Iowa State University, USA, in 1990. Nikos Stergiopulos holds also a degree in Management of Technology from IMD. He is currently Full Professor and Director of the Laboratory of Hemodynamics and Cardiovascular Technology at the Swiss Federal Institute of Technology in Lausanne, Switzerland. His main research interests are Hemodynamics, Cardiovascular Mechanics and Medical Implant Technology. He has authored more than 160 peer review papers and holds more than 15 patents in medical technology. In 1998 he co-founded EndoArt SA, a medical device start-up company, world leader in telemetrically powered and controlled medical implants for the treatment of congenital heart disease and morbid obesity. He is currently the founder and director of Antlia SA, developer of implantable drug delivery pumps and Rheon Medical SA, developer of an adjustable drainage device for the surgical treatment of glaucoma.

Contents

Part I
Creativity, Innovation and Entrepreneurship Competence in Higher Education

Organized by: Llanos Cuenca, Andres Boza
Business Management, Universitat Politècnica de València, Valencia, Spain

Description

Creativity, innovation, and entrepreneurship are essential aspects for all areas of working and business life. Creativity includes generating ideas, critical thinking, synthesis and reorganization, looking for new opportunities and having the ability to find hidden connections and insights. Innovation means anticipating the needs of the market, offering additional value, and keeping risk and cost under control. Successful entrepreneurs require combination of a creative idea and a broader capacity for execution. Nowadays, higher education is viewing the competences as a discipline that can be learned both theoretically and practically oriented. Training in creativity, innovation, and entrepreneurship competence can be organized as a separate subject or be integrated as a transversal competence into different subjects. Discussion will be organized on, but not limited to, the following elements of impact in this competence: (1) learning outcomes, (2) activities and experiences in higher education, (3) assessment method and evidences of learning, (4) syllabus description.

Transversal Competences as a Medium of Teaching. The Case of Creativity, Innovation and Entrepreneurship

Andrés Boza, Marta Fernández-Diego, Leonor Ruiz, Mariluz Gordo, M.M.E. Alemany, Faustino Alarcón and Llanos Cuenca

Introduction

The incorporation of key competences or similar intended learning outcomes in school curriculum frameworks has been evident for some time. However, it is a necessary but insufficient step towards implementation (Pepper 2011). According to Incode (2012) we can define competence as the complex know-how resulting from the integration, mobilization, and adaptation of capacities and skills to situations that share common characteristics. Competence describes what training participants should be able to do at the end of such training. One competence is acquired through several learning outcomes to be achieved.

This complex know-how must be specified in the design of new curriculums through the set of specific and transversal competencies that students should develop

- Specific competences belong to a specific area of knowledge (in a degree or master) and they are aimed at achieving a specific graduate profile.
- Transversal competences (also named generic competencies and transferable competencies) are generic and transferable in a wide variety of personal, social, academic, and professional contexts throughout life. Therefore, they contribute to a fundamental part of the professional profile and educational profile in all the degrees. These competences include a set of cognitive and metacognitive skills, and, attitudinal and instrumental knowledge, which has a great value to the knowledge society. Transversal competences are not always independent

A. Boza (✉) · M. Fernández-Diego · L. Ruiz · M. Gordo · M.M.E. Alemany · F. Alarcón · L. Cuenca
Business Management Department, Universitat Politècnica de València, Valencia, Spain
e-mail: aboza@cigip.upv.es

A. Kavoura et al. (eds.), *Strategic Innovative Marketing*, Springer Proceedings in Business and Economics, DOI 10.1007/978-3-319-56288-9_1

subjects; they can be a way to enhance learning of specific subjects, which also helps students to develop their new competences.

So, including transversal competences in specific subjects can address these competences and place them into the context of the subject where they can be used to improve specific competences.

In the context of the subject, it is necessary to distinguish two aspects, first how to encourage or promote the ideal environment for the development and achievement of these learning outcomes and second how to evaluate the acquisition of those ones. In order to evaluate the acquisition of the competence a rubric has been defined to bachelor and master degree (Cuenca et al. 2015a, 2016). The development of learning outcomes in classroom should be addressed through lectures, laboratory practices, case studies, etc. Evidence of competence acquisition must be reflected in the design of new curricula.

Competence-based learning requires an effort that it does not only depend on strategies of teaching, but also to know, select, and apply adequate resources for its achievement.

Guide for Selecting Activities

With the aim of incorporating transversal competences into the students' curricula several activities must be defined. It is necessary to establish the relationship between the activity to be done and the learning outcome to be achieved.

These activities should not be an extra work for the students and lecturers but a medium of instruction for the specific concepts using the transversal competences. To do this, it is important to select the unit or theme where the activity will be developed (Fig. 1).

We can find two scenarios

Scenario 1: *Transversal competence activity exists.*
In this case, an activity or list of activities have been previously defined and associated to the transversal competences. These activities are related to a number of learning outcomes of the transversal competence.

Fig. 1 Transversal and specific learning outcomes relationships

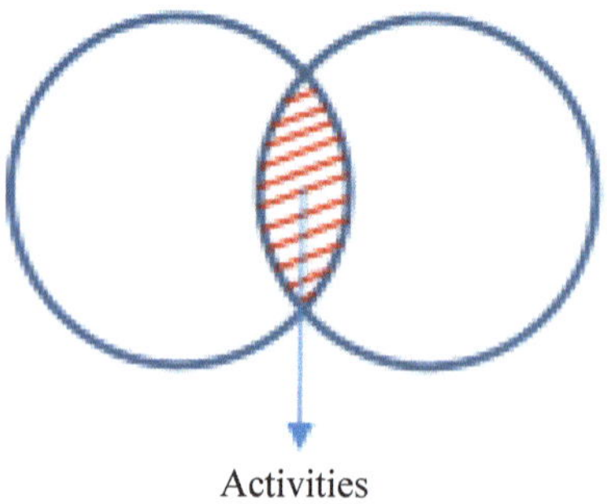

Specific Learning Outcomes (Subject)
Steps

1. Identify the transversal competence to be included in the subject.
2. Select the activity associated with the transversal competence.
3. Identify learning outcomes associated with the transversal competence.
4. Select unit/theme of the subject where the activity will be applied (specific competence).
5. *Adapt the activity to the current context*: *number of students, level, time,* etc.
6. *Identify evidences to be collected*: *colored post-it, videos, photos, documents.*
7. Develop the activity and collect evidences.
8. Assess the competence acquisition.

Scenario 2: *Transversal competence activities have not been identified.*
In this case, although there is not an activity designed, transversal competence includes the learning outcomes associated.
Steps

1. Identify the transversal competence to be included in the subject.
2. Identify and select competence learning outcomes associated with this transversal competence.
3. Select unit/theme of the subject where the learning outcomes can fit (specific competence).
4. Select the assessment method for the competence learning outcomes.
5. Define an activity taking into account what (step 1, 2, and 3) and how (step 4) are we going to assess them.
6. Identify resources needed according to the context: *number of students, level, time,* etc.
7. *Identify evidences to be collected*: *colored post-it, videos, photos, and documents.*
8. Develop the activity and collect evidences.
9. Assess the competence acquisition.

These two approaches help to find an appropriated activity to develop in the classroom with the objective of achieving transversal learning outcomes and specific learning outcomes.

Application to the Creativity, Innovation and Entrepreneurship Competence

According to Boza et al. (2014), creativity, innovation, and entrepreneurship deals with the mindsets and skills associated with creativity and innovation as well as the qualities and practices associated with successful entrepreneurship. For example, entrepreneurship is the individual's ability to translate ideas into action. It encompasses creativity, innovativeness, and risk taking, as well as ability to plan and direct action towards the achievement of goals. It is necessary to consider how to apply these mindsets and skills in their organization/business.

Learning Outcomes Associated to This Competence

The literature review process for learning outcomes related to innovation competence for bachelor degree and master was conducted via Google Scholar (scholar.google.es) and Scopus; also including the preliminary list of learning outcomes of the sciences institute of innovation (ICE 2013) and results of the Tempus project (2014). An extended list of learning outcomes can be found in Cuenca et al. (2015a, 2016).

The assessment of a big amount of learning outcomes results really difficult and complicated for a lecturer in a large classroom. The number of students and the activities to be done in a year must be adequate to assess the competence in an effective and efficient way. Effort and results must be balanced.

In this sense, the preliminary list of learning outcomes have been condensed in order to facilitate the assessment of the entire competence (creativity, innovation, entrepreneurship).

The proposal has been built based on the innovation literature review. The main indicators associated to innovation are: seeking opportunity, generating ideas, execution, and generating value (Cuenca et al. 2015b). These indicators have been divided accordingly to the three education levels (Level 1: first and second year, level 2: third and fourth year, and level 3: master). Each level incorporates more complexity and a growing difficulty.

According to the definitions of creativity, innovation, and entrepreneurship concepts, the competence can be defined as a process with the following activities: environment analysis (opportunity), proposal of creative ideas (generate ideas), deployment or procedure of execution (execution) and finally, risk and benefits evaluation (added value) (Fig. 2).

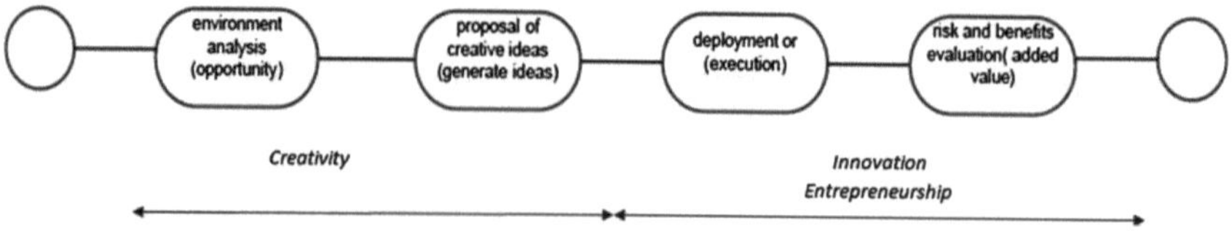

Fig. 2 The simplified process of creativity, innovation, and entrepreneurship

Table 1 Association of learning outcomes and activities in the transversal competence creativity, innovation and entrepreneurship

Creativity, innovation and entrepreneurship competence		Activities							
		Six thinking hats	SCAMPER	6-3-5	Jigsaw	Empathy map	Canvas	Lego serious play	DAFO
Process	*Domain level 1 (1st and 2nd year)*								
Opportunity	(1) Students inquiry the reality	V	V	V	V	V	V	V	V
Generate ideas	(2) Students contribute ideas	V	V	V	V	V	V	V	
Execution	(3) Students formally express ideas		V	V		V	V	V	
Added value	(4) Students identify results							V	
Process	*Domain level 2 (3rd and 4th year)*								
Opportunity	(1) Students identify opportunities and/or areas for improvement	V	V	V	V	V	V	V	V
Generate ideas	(2) Students bring original ideas and approaches	V	V	V	V	V	V	V	
Execution	(3) Students employ strategies and/or creative techniques to formally translate ideas and solutions		V	V		V	V	V	
Added value	(4) Students control results							V	
Process	*Domain level 3 (Master)*								
Opportunity	(1) Students integrate knowledge from other disciplines	V			V			V	V
Generate ideas	(2) Students adopt creative approaches to content and embodiment	V			V			V	
Execution	(3) Students propose an action plan							V	
Added value	(4) Students analyze the value of innovation							V	

Activities Associated to the Competence

Once the main learning outcomes have been defined for the transversal competence, a list of activities has been identified. These activities are oriented to achieve one or more learning outcomes.

The following table shows the association among learning outcomes and activities.

These activities can be used in different subjects to improve the achievement of knowledge and the acquisition of the transversal competence.

Next table shows the case of the subject "IT Governance" at first year in the Master in Computer Science at Universitat Politècnica de València (Spain).

Jointly, with Tables 1 and 2 can be chosen the activities to be applied.

Table 2 Association of transversal competence learning outcomes (competence) and specific learning outcomes (subject)

Learning outcome matrix	Transversal learning outcomes (competence)			
	(1) Students integrate knowledge from other disciplines	(2) Students adopt creative approaches to content and embodiment	(3) Students propose an action plan	(4) Students analyze the value of innovation
Specific learning outcomes (subject)				
Students can communicate their conclusions to specialists and non-specialists in a clear and unambiguous	V	V		
Capacity for integration of technologies, applications, services and systems of computer engineering			V	V
Ability to apply principles of economics and management of human resources and projects, as well as legislation, regulation and standardization of computing			V	V
Capacity for development, strategic planning, direction, coordination and technical and financial management of projects in all areas of Computer Engineering following quality and environmental criteria	V	V	V	V

Conclusions

Transversal Competences as a medium of teaching is a key aspect to facilitate the incorporation of transversals learning outcomes into the subjects at the same time that specific contents are addressed. The acquisition of learning outcomes in the classroom should be addressed through different activities. These activities help lecturers to obtain evidences and assessment of the students' learning. The method proposed in this paper helps them to select the best learning activity according to the transversals and specific learning outcomes.

With the application of this proposal the following benefits have been obtained:

For the lectures, to

- reduce the rejection of transversal competences
- improve coordination among learning outcomes (transversal and specific)
- improve the effectiveness of the activities
- incorporate the activities and transversals and specific learning outcomes into the syllabus.

For the students, to

- improve participation
- recognizes the usefulness of transversal competences in a specific context
- know at the beginning of the subject, the transversal competences tackled and the activities associated.

Acknowledgements This research has been carried out under the project of innovation and educational improvement (PIME/A15) 'DAICE—Design of activities for the Innovation, Creativity and Entrepreneurship Competence' funded by the Universitat Politècnica de València, and the Escola Tècnica Superior d'Enginyeria Informàtica.

References

Boza, A. L. Cuenca, M. Fernández-Diego, L. Ruiz, M.L. Gordo, F. Alarcón, M.M.E. Alemany, and R. Poler. 2014. Innovation, creativity and entrepreneurship competence in higher education. In *Learning objectives and measurement. ICERI2014 proceedings*, 405–411.

Cuenca, L. F. Alarcón, A. Boza, M. Fernández-Diego, L. Ruiz, M.L. Gordo, R. Poler, and M.M.E. Alemany. 2016. Rubric for the assessment the competence of innovation, creativity and entrepreneurship in bachelor degree. *Brazilian Journal of Operations & Production Management* 13 (1).

Cuenca, L. M. Fernández-Diego. M. Gordo, L. Ruiz, M.M.E. Alemany, and A, Ortiz. 2015a. Measuring competencies in higher education. *Sustainable Learning in Higher Education.*

Cuenca, L. P, Bonet, A, Boza, P, Fuentes, N, Lajara-Camilleri, J.A, María-García, M, Peris-Ortiz, and L, Ruiz. 2015b. Innovation, creativity and entrepreneurship learning outcomes in higher education. In *ICERI2015 proceedings*, 3910–3915.

Ice. 2013. Dimensiones competenciales UPV report interno. ICE-Universitat Politècnica de València.

Incode. 2012. Innovation competencies development as integral part of higher education. http://tempus-idea.org.il/idea_wp/.

Pepper, D. 2011. Assessing key competences across the curriculum. *European Journal of Education* 46(3).

Tempus IDEA. 2014. Inter Disciplinary Education Agenda. http://tempus-idea.org.il/idea_wp/.

Using Data Sources, Tools and Applications During Data Mining in Marketing Management of Higher Education

Martina Juříková

Introduction

Higher education is a sector that significantly contributes to the development of society and economics and forms an essential base for sustainable growth. Since 1989, when the political revolution took place in the Czech Republic, the number of students at higher education institutions has grown almost fourfold and higher education institutions have practically become accessible to all those who have successfully completed secondary school leaving examination and are interested in pursuing further studies. The character of higher education institutions has significantly changed and got adapted to unusually high numbers of students with much more varied previous education, profile and background than was usual 10 years ago. However, the transformation has not been completed so far—the necessary profiling and diversification of degree courses have not been carried out; neither the required infrastructure has been created nor the required staff has been recruited. In 2014, Czech higher education arrived at the end of an era of a massive expansion in terms of quantity. Undoubtedly, one of the current biggest challenges is the rapid decline in student numbers as regards the usual applicants caused by the demographic decline and the issue of how to effectively ensure and continually enhance the quality of activities carried out at higher education institutions and reinforce the value and relevance of education for each student.

In the first decade of the twenty-first century, the extension of accessibility to higher education continued in the sphere of Czech higher education. The number of students reached its peak in 2010 and 2011, namely 396 and 392,000 students,

M. Juříková (✉)
Faculty of Multimedia Communications, Tomas Bata University in Zlín,
Zlín, Czech Republic
e-mail: jurikova@fmk.utb.cz

A. Kavoura et al. (eds.), *Strategic Innovative Marketing*, Springer Proceedings in Business and Economics, DOI 10.1007/978-3-319-56288-9_2

respectively. Since then, the student numbers have repeatedly decreased; as of 20 January 2016, 326,909 students studied at higher education institutions in the CR. (Výkonné ukazatele MŠMT 2015, © 2016) One of the major reasons for the current decrease in the number of students is the demographic development. Students born in the second half of 1990s, i.e. in years with low birth rates, progress to the final year of study at a secondary school and, thus, the number of usual applicants for higher education—those who have successfully completed secondary school leaving examination—rapidly decreases. The data provided by the Czech Statistical Office demonstrate that the trend is going to continue. It is estimated that by the end of 2016, the total number of 19-year old in the population will drop from 131,000 (data as of 2011) to 92,000, i.e. by a total of 30%. A reverse tendency, i.e. an increase in the number of applicants who have successfully completed secondary school leaving examination, can be expected only after 2023; in 2028 the high values are supposed to be reattained (approx. 115,000–120,000), even though, apparently, only for a limited period of time. This fact is also the reason why higher education institutions begin to concentrate, besides the quality of education, also on attracting "high-quality" applicants and students, just as in the case of companies that seek efficient and qualified employees.

Data Mining

The Gartner Group defines data mining as "the process of discovering meaningful new correlations, patterns and trends by sifting through large amounts of data stored in repositories and by using pattern recognition technologies as well as statistical and mathematical techniques." The author has refined the notion of data mining for higher education to be a process of uncovering hidden trends and patterns that lend them to predicative modelling using a combination of explicit knowledge base, sophisticated analytical skills and academic domain knowledge. It is producing new observations from existing observations. Or, as explained by Rubenking (2001), "data mining is the process of automatically extracting useful information and relationships from immense quantities of data. In its purest form, data mining doesn't involve looking for specific information. Rather than starting from a question or a hypothesis, data mining simply finds patterns that are already present in the data" (Luan 2002).

Academic analytics is a new field that has emerged in higher education in the aftermath of the widespread use of data mining practices and "business intelligence tools" in business and marketing (Beapler and Murdoch 2010).

This paper is focused on the marketing use of data collected about prospective and actual applicants, not on the enhancement of educational process; that is why it is based more on the questions from the first "business" column applied to the higher education sphere particularly in the Czech Republic.

Methodology

Within this paper, a model will be presented which was prepared using results of research comprising several stages and conducted at the Faculty of Multimedia Communications of Tomas Bata University in Zlín (the Czech Republic) during 3 years. The research involved the following stages:

1. Analysis of the data available (resources, quantity, quality of hard and soft data related to applicants).
2. Qualitative research aimed to identify the decision process used by applicants.
3. Quantitative testing using a sample of 496 applicants for studies at the given faculty.
4. Setting of available software applications intended for the analysis and interpretation of important data.
5. Marketing decisions aimed to reach the target group.
6. Assessment of the first year of application.

Taking into consideration the extent of the study, this paper will briefly deal with the implementation of the first three items—i.e. with results of the analytical stage which may be an inspiration and, to a certain extent, in general applicable for these types of educational institutions in post-communist countries.

Findings

Within the first phase of the research, qualitative interviews were carried out with 12 students in the last year of secondary schools (Please note: In the Czech Republic, a three-level educational system has been introduced: Primary, i.e. 9 years: from 6 to 15 years, secondary—15–19 years, higher—19–24 years) of various specializations as well as of general grammar schools. The aim was, among other facts, to find out about the factors decisive for the selection of a higher education institution, when and from which sources applicants obtain the required information about the educational institution. "Based on interview responses, we may speak about two groups of potential university students. Those who have made their decision and have profiled know what study subject and school they will aspire after, and those who have made their decision to go to university, but have not profiled yet. Both the groups undergo the following information process which at first is passive from their side when they attend presentations and the cooperation with the university, they record achievements and successes of university students and graduates in PR reports etc. Then the 'active' phase follows when they are already interested in communication activities of the particular university." (Jurášková et al. 2015).

It was necessary to quantitatively verify the results of the qualitative interviews; therefore, a questionnaire survey was carried out with 496 FMC applicants.

Respondents were interviewed during their visit to the FMC, namely during the Open Day, or during the admission procedure. They heard about the **FMC for the first time from a friend, who is a FMC student**. This version of a response was given by 185 respondents, which corresponds to **37%** of the total sample (Kocourek 2015). Among other mostly preferred responses the following can be named: The website of the University, attendance at a fair or information received via social networks. The importance of personal recommendation is also evidenced by the fact that the respondents could also mention *another form of the first contact with the FMC* than those listed in the survey. The most frequently given responses included for example: **Positive reference given by a teacher**, **university recommended by an employer or rumours**.

The positive effect of presentation of the University at fairs is evidenced by data obtained from the research surveys, which means that it can be considered one of very important channels. The importance for the FMC is obvious and the opinions of visitors to the fairs can serve to back this statement. The research, conducted every year by the organizers of the Gaudeamus Brno fair, proves that over 50% of attendees to the fairs are grammar school students (Honzík and Mikula 2014 © 2015).

With regard to the relevance of PR activities for applicants, the dependence of the level of prestige of a higher education institution was tested as to whether it is perceived as an institution providing general/specific education. The testing thereof enables us to verify whether it is more appropriate to focus PR activities on more specialized events or to concentrate on building of a general positive reputation. In addition, mainly because of the localization of Tomas Bata University in Zlín, in a relatively small town with a short tradition of higher education in comparison to other towns, the dependence of the perception of prestige of a higher education institution tested as to whether it is perceived as a local (i.e. Czech) or an international university. The testing was carried out using scales from 1 to 5, where 1 = the lowest value, general setting, local orientation of an educational institution, and 5 = the highest level of prestige, specificity of the orientation of an educational institution and its international character (Table 1).

The results indicate dispersion in the responses to the question whether the respondents perceive the FMC as Czech/international. The value of 1.346 was the highest among others. As regards the level of prestige and the variable

Table 1 Statistical tests

	Prestige of HEI	General/ specific	Czech/ international
Mode (most frequent)	4	4	3
OR (ordinal median—middle value)	3.682	3.434	2.811
Dorvar (discrete ordinal variable = dispersion)	1.265	1.276	**1.346**

"general/specific", the middle value was shifted in the direction of "neither—nor" when compared to the most frequent values 4—a rather high prestige/rather international.

$$\text{X}-\text{squared} = 16.8534,\ \text{df} = \text{NA},\ \text{p}-\text{value} = 0.4001$$

The H_0 on the independence cannot be rejected, i.e. the perception of specialization/specificity of education institution is not dependent on the perception of the level of prestige of the given higher education institutions. Since the FMC offers a humanities-oriented degree course in marketing communications (the preferences of the applicants for this degree course were investigated), it is not a higher education institution with narrow specialization (compared to, e.g. medical studies), therefore, it is sufficient to monitor more general coefficients of prestige of the given higher education institution, such as career prospects, etc., with regard to the applicants.

$$\text{X}-\text{squared} = 26.1445,\ \text{df} = \text{NA},\ \text{p}-\text{value} = 0.05519$$

Upon testing the influence of internationality on the level of prestige of the higher education institution, it is possible to state that with the level of importance being 5% the H_0 on the independence of the variables cannot be rejected—the variables are independent in fact. However, with the risk of error being 10%, the independence would be rejected. The result thus reveals that the perception of these values is inconsistent.

Discussion

A model of the collection, analysis and interpretation of data, that would serve to effectively direct marketing activities towards applicants, was made in accordance with surveys conducted within the data mining system setup.

It is possible to acquire hard data—quantitatively processable data from: statistics provided by the Ministry of Education, also from the application for studies (name, surname, email). Google analytics tracking set up for websites and the microsite of the Faculty reveals information related to visit rate, interactivity, newsletter open rate and click rate, database of contacts for the registration for newsletter subscription, etc. It is also important to monitor the interconnection of activities (newsletter—application for a preparation course—application for studies), analysis of Facebook activities (commentaries, involvement of "opinion leaders" from among students, applicants as well as teachers, etc. and their influence on interactivity), portals focused on higher education. Soft data about applicants: their interests, preferences, user-friendliness, web ergonomics, social interaction and social status are no less important for marketing specialists. These can be monitored either on the above-mentioned websites, or they can be interviewed during road shows, fairs and open days.

Testing of hypotheses demonstrated independence between perception of the level of prestige of a higher education institution and perception of its orientation (generally vs. specifically oriented higher education institution), which can be interpreted as the fact that the degree course in Marketing Communications is often selected by students who do not want to study a degree course with narrow specialization. The dependence between internationality of the education institution and its level of prestige is of no importance to them. This means for the marketing specialists that they should focus on an interactive debate with applicants on topics that are attractive to them, to stimulate interest in the degree course among them by means of, e.g. stories about successful graduates, or get them acquainted with the professions that the graduates practise, and avoid providing them with a mere list of specializations, that would not reveal anything about the possible future career of the applicants.

Data mining is a long-term process and the FMC is still at the beginning of the process. Nevertheless, it is important to realize when, what type of data a from where to acquire them, and by means of what kind of tools, which information is primary and which is complementary; how often we will process and evaluate the data, how to plan marketing activities according to the conclusions, etc. which opens up new opportunities for the application of data mining in the sphere of higher education.

References

Baepler, P., and C.J. Murdoch. 2010. Academic analytics and data mining in higher education. *International Journal for the Scholarship of Teaching and Learning* 4 (2): Article 17. http://digitalcommons.georgiasouthern.edu/ij-sotl/vol4/iss2/17.

Honzík, J.M., and P. Mikula. 2014. Evropský Veletrh Pomaturitního a Celoživoního Vzdělávání Gaudeamus 2014, Brno. http://www.gaudeamus.cz/files/gaudeamus14b.pdf. Accessed 25 July 2016.

Jurášková. O., M. Juříková, and J. Kocourek. 2015. Brand building of a university as an integral part of the educational process. *Turkish Online Journal of Educational Technology* 100–105.

Kocourek J. 2015. Charakter značky a její místo v systému marketingových komunikací. PhD thesis. Bratislava.

Luan, J. 2002. Data mining and knowledge management in higher education potential applications. In *Paper presented at the annual forum for the association, for institutional research. 42nd*, Toronto, Ontario, Canada.

Rubenking. N. 2001. Hidden Messages. *PC Magazine*.

Výkonné Ukazatele. 2015. http://dsia.uiv.cz/vystupy/vu_vs_f1.html. Accessed 27 July 2015.

Integration of the Theory and Practice in Continuity with the Development of Key Competencies—One of the Necessary Areas of Solutions for the Czech University Education

Marcela Göttlichová

Introduction

To enhance employability, as well as to sustain the existing strong position of Europe worldwide, the cardinal significance is represented by an efficient system of high-quality education and vocational training. It is the human capital which presents an essential wealth of every society. Especially the high-quality workforce standing in the foreground and capable of participating in the production of top-quality and innovative goods and services, which conditions the success within the competitive environment of the global market.

It is here where one of the most important roles is played by university education in continuity of the close link to the economic as well as social needs. Orientation on the quality and readiness of university graduates with the aim to acquire higher employability chances in the labor market thus become the fundamental need. The most significant task is to ensure the acquisition of the necessary key competencies together with the development of the top degree and attractivity of education and vocational training at universities.

Theoretical Framework

It is education that means the key political component of the Europe 2020: Europe's Growth Strategy, whose primary objectives are in direct continuity with the educational goals of the EU, as the achievement of higher education means more high-qualified workers, thus better employability of these workers, with the

M. Göttlichová (✉)
Faculty of Multimedia Communications, Tomas Bata University in Zlín,
760 01 Zlín, Czech Republic
e-mail: gottlichova@fmk.utb.cz

A. Kavoura et al. (eds.), *Strategic Innovative Marketing*, Springer Proceedings in Business and Economics, DOI 10.1007/978-3-319-56288-9_3

subsequent reflection in poverty reduction. To the given Europe 2020 objectives the following belong: 1. reducing rates of persons finishing education and vocational training to less than 10% (CR/5.5%; 2002/17%—2015/11%), 2. increasing rates of inhabitants aged 30–34 completing university or vocational education to at least 40% (CR/32%; 2002/23.6%—2015/38.7%, out of which 43.3% were women × 34.0% of men) and at the same time, 3. increasing employment to 75% (CR/75%; 2002/66.8%—2015/70.1%) by 2020 (Overview of Europe 2020—Target 2015).

As the figure shows (Table 1), it is the youth (20–29-year-olds) in who we observe a low rate of employment; it is by 8.7% lower in comparison with the overall working-age population. Since the start of the crisis in 2008, the employment rate of the youth has decreased by 4.2%, i.e., from 65.6% (2008) to 61.4% (2015), which reflects their generally weaker integration within the labor market.

The following table (Table 2) presents the fact that the employment rate is generally higher in persons who achieve higher education. In 2015, the employment rate of tertiary education graduates (82.7%) was much higher than was the EU average (70.1%), which was only slightly exceeded in higher secondary or post-secondary non-tertiary education (70.7%). On the other hand, the employment rate in people with primary of lower secondary education represented not only a lower value (52.6%) but at the same time, the group had been most affected by the crisis when a fall by 4.3% was experienced between 2007 and 2015 (Labor market 2016).

Should we look at the resulting values in the Czech Republic from another point of unemployment, we will notice an accord corresponding to the current situation in the EU countries (Table 3).

Increasing the level of achieved education and facilitation of employees with **skills necessary for the knowledge societies** are thus the main focus of the European employment policies of the Europe 2020 Strategy reflecting in the primary goals of the areas of employment and education. The attention is directed

Table 1 Employment rate, by age group, EU-28, 2002-15, (%)

	2002	2008	2015
Age group 20–29	63.4	**65.6**	**61.4**
Age group 30–54	76.7	80.2	79.1
Age group 55–64	38.4	x	53.3
Total (age group 20–64)	66.8	70.3	70.1

Source Göttlichová according to Eurostat online data codes

Table 2 Employment rate age group 20–64, by educational attainment level, EU-28, 2002-15

	2002	2008	2015
Tertiary education (ISCED levels 5–8) (%)	**82.7**	**83.8**	**82.7**
Upper secondary and post-secondary non-tertiary	69.2	71.8	70.7
Less than primary, primary and lower secondary	54.8	56.9 (2007)	52.6

Source Göttlichová according to Eurostat online data codes

Table 3 Employment in the CR according to the level of education and age, 2015 (in print)

Unemployed	Level of the highest achieved education			University education total	
	Primary secondary finished with/without the exam				
Total	**58.7**	**108.5**	**72.1**	**28.7**	**268.0**
15–24 year-olds	13.9	10.3	16.0	**3.4**	43.7
25–29 year-olds	8.5	11.0	10.0	**8.0**	37.5
30–34 year-olds	7.0	15.5	10.2	**2.9**	35.7

Source Göttlichová according to the Czech Statistical Office

towards enhancing the interaction between "the knowledge triangle", so-called the system of science and research, tertiary education, and the area of innovations with the real economic sphere (Europe 2020 Strategy 2010).

Problem Formulation

The problem of the university education, however, remains in the necessity to support the development of transferable skills of university graduates with orientation to the teamwork, presenting and managerial skills, knowledge of enterprise start-up (commercial as well as noncommercial spheres), in the areas of internships and training within educational processes by either integrating employers into the emergence of school educational programs, educational process, internships and practical training, and also of result evaluation, with the share on submitting, supervising as well as opponency of diploma and other theses. It is then an unsatisfactory integration of the theory and real practice reflecting itself in the lack of well-prepared initiative and sufficiently motivated persons, which means the persisting problem preventing enhancing the intensity of innovation processes.

However, it is not exactly express the requirements placed on the level of qualification needed, considering the market volatility, which is the reason for the increasing significance of so-called key competencies. We thus speak of "transferable and universally versatile set of knowledge, skills, competencies and attitudes needed for every individual for their personal fulfillment and development, for integration oneself into the society, and for successful employment" (The definition and selection of key competencies 2005).

Within the project called *Career Consultancy under the Conditions of the Curricular Reform* the attention was focused on ascertaining the requirements of employers in the quaternary (knowledge) sector placed on university graduates and at the same time on the readiness. The knowledge sector is the driving force for innovations in other sectors, particularly the industry and services; it establishes new markets and segments, generates innovative services, products or work methods. It becomes the key to the economic development of the EU countries and of the global society.

The conclusions of 334 completely filled-out forms showed, in the confrontation with the key competencies being pursued (National Institution of Technical and Vocational Education of the Czech Republic), that in the forefront of all requirements considered by employers as absolutely **necessary**/important × unimportant, are: **communication skills**—oral and written communication skills (**87.2**/12.2 × 0.5%), reading and work instructions comprehension (**85.9**/13.0 × 1.0%), the ability to be responsible (**84.4**/14.8 × 0.8%), the ability to solve problems (**84.1**/15.6 × 0.3%), the willingness to learn (78.6/21.1 × 0.3%), the art of dealing with people (77.6/21.4 × 1.0%), the ability to make decisions (77.3/22.1 × 0.5%), the mastery of information handling (72.4/27.1 × 0.5%), the ability to present and express one's own opinion (71.1/27.3 × 1.6%), the mastery of using the IT technologies (68.2/29.2 × 2.6%), adaptability and flexibility (67.4/31.8 × 0.8%), the ability to manage stress (65.9/32 × 2.1%), the ability of teamwork (63.8/**32.6** × 3.6%), the ability to lead (53.6/**38.0** × 8.3%), the mastery of foreign language (43.1/38.6 × 18.3%) (Doležalová 2014). "The ability to communicate efficiently and achieve mutual understanding is often the measure of the success or failure in the development of the company or organization" (Štarchoň et al. 2015).

The survey also showed that the most common forms of cooperation between schools and enterprises (N = 311) are considered by employers to be: evaluated internships and training of students (55%), excursions (40%), unrated internships and training of students (34%), and participation of employees in the educational process, lectures in schools (32%). Other forms of cooperation are less frequent. The knowledge and experience exchange between schools and employers (16%), providing educational materials (16%), and announcing student competitions (15%). 83% of employers admit that they prefer graduates with the experience directly obtained in their company (Doležalová 2014). "When the cooperation is constructed with the effective communication process, the relationship is based on the trust, and it is linked to higher productivity with goods results and qualitative work performance" (Markaki et al. 2012, p. 322).

Problem Solution

According to the results of the national survey, just as requirements directing towards the inevitable setting-out and subsequent orientation on the development of key competencies, it is necessary to provide university students, in connection with the increasing quality for the future professional occupation, with the possibility of a wide range of study subjects reflecting the contemporary demands of the market (of employers) in continuity with the orientation on the **integration of the theory and practice**. It is not only the commercial sphere, but also the noncommercial one, which may extend possibilities of fully fledged employability for university graduates. On the other hand, it is university students who may successfully assist nongovernmental organizations out of the enclosed circle of the lack of human potential and finances reflecting in the inadequate presentation of their activities.

The research survey (the third one within the project called COOPERATION focused on interconnection of the commercial, public, nonprofit, and academic spheres) realized in the form of a questionnaire survey in 263 nongovernmental organizations (NGOs) in the Zlín Region again confirmed the interest of the organizations in cooperation with TBU, but it also proved that 50.2% of the NGOs see the mutual benefit in cooperation of an NGO with the academic world. 8.4% see the benefit in the assistance to the organization itself, 11% in terms of the future profiling of students. 17.5% see no benefit in such cooperation and 12.9% did not respond. From the perspective of future student profiling in marketing communications, a significant finding is proved that marketing and promotion of NGOs still do not correspond to professional level of such services, which opens new possibilities for graduates in the given segment. For 33.1% of NGOs, marketing activities are based particularly on promotional activities of the specific organization, 41.8% run these activities on the basis of intuition. Marketing and promotion in full range and significance are managed by 6.8% of the NGOs, and no marketing activities were discovered in 18.6% of the NGOs. The situation is confirmed also by the fact that only one organization (0.4%) stated that they operate a special marketing department, a qualified person was involved in 20.1%, in 54% of the NGOs marketing and promotion are dealt with by the person with the time to do these activities, in 8.7%, marketing and promotion is not managed at all, and 16.7% did not provide any specific response. 43.5% of the NGOs justified not integrating a marketing specialist by the lack of funding, and 11.6% by the lack of human resources, 39.9% do not perceive any reason to use services of a marketing specialist, and 4.3% of the NGOs did not respond (Göttlichová 2016).

The resulting values showed that "white spots" persist in the area of noncommercial marketing communications, which must be filled in, which means an opportunity for marketing communications students. The Marketing Communications Institute at the FMC TBU in Zlín, in continuity with the Europe 2020 Strategy, thus concentrates its attention on preparing qualified experts with the aim to increase their employability within the labor market.

The students may be introduced to the NGOs activities and operations in their real-life environment and conditions through regular internships and training within NGOs, through student work as volunteers, the selection of the topics for student coursework, bachelor's as well as master's theses oriented on noncommercial communications, particularly through the course called **Projects of nonprofit organizations**; they thus may participate in designing their own as well as submitted projects oriented on marketing activities of the given organization, they learn to be aware of common situations and to perceive them differently and in new contexts, and they especially become acquainted with and try new forms of project management in all its levels. Here, we may speak about the full integrity of the theory and real-life practice with the emphasis on the development of the above mentioned and such essential key competencies, such as for instance: the development of teamwork, presentation and managerial skills, the knowledge of start-up of businesses, the support of the project-managed education—and this in continuity with the inherent development of cooperation between universities and employers, specifically in the nonprofit sphere.

Conclusion

The European cooperation in education and vocational training should not be directed only to achieving a certain percentage of people having university education, but it should be focused on ascertaining appropriate quality of education and employability of graduates within the labor market. The attention must also be paid to project-oriented education focusing on presentation and managerial skills and teamwork, to initiate and motivate students based on the development of key competencies because the labor market may be conquered only by those who can offer more than mere professional skills. And according to the results of the survey, employers will still appreciate those competencies in job applicants that may well be utilized and applied also within the everyday life.

References

Doležalová, G. 2014. *Potřeby zaměstnavatelů a připravenost absolventů škol—šetření v kvartérním sektoru*, 45. Praha: Národní ústav pro vzdělávání.

Europe 2020 strategy. 2010. http://ec.europa.eu/europe2020/index_cs.htm. Accessed 8 Juli 2016.

Göttlichová. M. 2016. *Analýza neziskového sektoru Zlínského kraje*. Projekt Kooperace vysokého školství, veřejné správy, podnikatelského a neziskového sektoru pro socio-ekonomický rozvoj regionu.

Labour market. 2016. http://ec.europa.eu/eurostat/statistics. Accessed 12 Juli 2016.

Markaki. E.N., D.P. Sakas, and T. Chadjipantelis. 2012. *communication management in business. the latent power for career development*. In *Proceedings of the 2nd international conference on integrated information*, Budapest, Procedia—Social and Behavioral Sciences, 319–326.

Overview of Europe 2020—Target. 2015. http://ec.europa.eu/europe2020/. Accessed 12 Juli 2016.

Štarchoň. P., and M. Juříková et al. 2015. *Značky a český zákazník*. Zlín, VeRBuM, p. 104 *The definition and selection of key competencies*, 2005. https://www.oecd.org/pisa/35070367.pdf. Accessed 26 Juni 2016.

Part II
New Ways of Marketing Analytics

Organized by: Tuula Andersson, Nina Helander
School of Business and Services, Tampere University of Applied Sciences, Tampere, Finland

Description

Digitalization changes the ways of marketing. At best, it offers new possibilities for marketing analytics and development of marketing practices. To this workshop we invite both empirical and theoretical research presentations on the theme of how to use different data sources and analytics in marketing. Potential themes for the papers could be for example: (1) measurement of emotions and management of customer experience, (2) value co-creation both in B2B and B2C markets, (3) social media analytics.

Social Media Analytics Empowering Customer Experience Insight

Jari Jussila, Mika Boedeker, Harri Jalonen and Nina Helander

Introduction

From marketing perspective, social media analytics can offer a cost-effective way to gather relevant data and also sophisticated tools to process the data into knowledge that enables making more precise and valuable marketing decisions. It is thus no surprise that the promise of social media analytics is to help companies to improve their reputation and gain increased business performance (Fan and Gordon 2014). According to Zeng et al. (2010), social media analytics is focused on developing tools and methods to enhance collection, monitoring, analysis, synthesis, and visualizing data from social media. In fact, there are several different methods for social media analytics, e.g., trend analysis, topic modeling, social network analysis, and sentiment analysis (Bae and Lee 2012). Of these, sentiment analysis is one of most used ones, as it offers a path to gain understanding of customers' opinions and affective experiences. The aim of sentiment analysis is to identify whether the expressions indicate positive or negative opinions about the given subject (Bae and Lee 2012) providing, for example, the possibility to catch the most unsatisfied customers from social media and preventing them to spread the bad message to

J. Jussila (✉) · N. Helander
Department of Information Management and Logistics,
Tampere University of Technology, Tampere, Finland
e-mail: jari.j.jussila@tut.fi

M. Boedeker
Department of Business Administration and Services,
Tampere University of Applied Sciences, Tampere, Finland

H. Jalonen
Department of Management,
Turku University of Applied Sciences, Turku, Finland

A. Kavoura et al. (eds.), *Strategic Innovative Marketing*, Springer Proceedings
in Business and Economics, DOI 10.1007/978-3-319-56288-9_4

thousands of others in the web (Melville et al. 2009). However, the weakness of this kind of typical sentiment analysis is its inability to capture the deeper contents of the affective experience of the customer—simple positive versus negative categorization of affective experience is not able to reveal how the customer will really act. According to recent research experiment published in Harvard Business Review (Haas 2015), all affective experiences of the customers are not equally valuable for companies, as not all negative experiences lead to unwanted actions by the customer. Instead, the situation can be even vice versa as every negative experience includes also a positive component. It is thus important to understand a variety of different kinds of negative and positive affective experiences and further, the intensity of those.

For this reason, there is a need for a framework and tools that can offer deeper analysis and understanding of affective experiences. The purpose of the study is to present a framework for analysis of affective experiences from social media content.

This paper presents the developed framework and its pilot testing, carried out as part of a wider research process involving two research projects and researchers from three different universities. The paper is structured as following: theoretical base is first opened up and then followed by a description of the research methods and the argumentation of the made choices. After that the developed framework and its pilot testing results are presented. The steps for further research and conclusions of the research end the paper.

Theoretical Bases

The use of the terms of various affective phenomena ("emotion," "feeling," "mood," "preference," "attitude," "emotional," "affective," etc.) both in everyday and scientific concepts is fuzzy (e.g., Bagozzi et al. 1999; Scherer 2005). In this study experience refers to a process of living through an event (Erlebnis) rather than to knowledge and expertise (Erfahrung) (Palmer 2010). Affective experience refers especially to the affective dimension of experience which involves one's affective system through the generation of emotions, feelings, and moods (Gentile et al. 2007), which in turn can further be described according to their features like intensity, duration, cause, awareness, and control (Bagozzi et al. 1999; Beedie et al. 2005; Derbaix and Pham 1991; Scherer 2005). However, in this study the analysis is on the level of affective experience, not making distinction between emotions, feelings, and moods.

Scherer (2005) points out that counting the number of scientific definitions of emotion is hopeless and on the other hand, there is no answer to the question of the number of emotions. Various approaches have been presented, for example ranging from a limited amount of basic dimensions or basic categories to a vast number of discrete or specific affective terms.

There are several dimensional presentations of affective experiences, most of them focusing on the dimensions of valence and arousal resulting in a circumplex structure (see, e.g., Seo et al. 2008). Mehrabian and Russell (1974) suggested that there exists a limited set of basic affective responses to all stimulus situations, independent of the sensory modality involved and this framework has been applied in numerous studies ever since. Variations in pleasure (valence), arousal and dominance (PAD) should universally constitute the common core of human affective states. On a general level, pleasure refers to the degree to which an individual feels for example good, happy, or satisfied. Similarly, arousal refers to the degree to which an individual feels, for example, excited, stimulated, alert, or active. Dominance, in turn, refers to the degree to which an individual feels, for example, in control of, or free to act.

Research Method and the Analytical Framework

How to grasp affective experiences in such manner that they are detected in a sufficient depth and precision but at the same time with a reasonable control over the instrument? Dimensional format is convenient because only two or three general dimensions have to be indicated. On the other hand, the dimensions do not always correspond to the way one naturally talks about affective experiences (Sacharin et al. 2012). Thus, basic level provides more information over and above general dimensions (Laros and Steenkamp 2005), and specific affective terms may

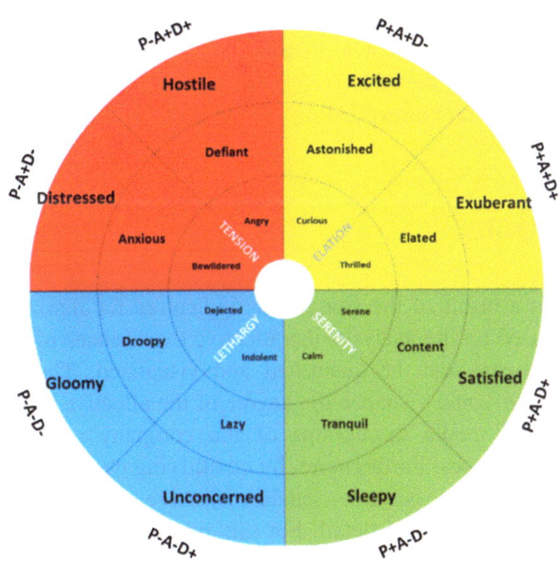

Fig. 1 The framework of affective experiences and affective families

better correspond to the natural way of talking about affective experiences (Sacharin et al. 2012). However, some individuals represent their experiences with a good deal of precision (high granularity), whereas others represent their experiences in more global terms (low granularity) (Feldman Barret 2004; Scherer 2005). Therefore, a practical framework to detect the affective experiences in various degrees of granularity is needed.

In the Fig. 1 the aforementioned, basically three-dimensional "PAD-space" is presented in a two-dimensional pie-type graphic so that each of the four pleasure-arousal combinations (elation, serenity, lethargy, and tension; see, e.g., Seo et al. 2008) are further divided according to dominance to form eight "affective families."

In this way, more than just the superordinate level of positive and negative affect, or the dimensions of pleasure, arousal, and dominance can be detected. Additionally, to make the framework better correspond to the natural way of talking about affective experiences, the affective families are characterized by selecting specific affective terms that represent a larger affective family and refer to a whole range of similar kind of terms. The terms are selected based on circumplex-type presentations like, for example, in Mehrabian and Russell (1974), Seo et al. (2008) and Scherer (2005), and on lists of affective terms like, for example, in Laros and Steenkam (2005).

In Fig. 1, the varying intensity of certain affection is included, e.g., calm—tranquil—sleepy, providing the potential to identify the depth of an emotion and even the so-called weak signals of the customers' perceptions.

In this study, we used NEMO Sentiment and Data analyzer tool (Paavola and Jalonen 2015) to collect data from two software companies in Finland. A total of 2128 tweets were collected during the time period of 22/05/2015–06/10/2015. Each of the 2128 tweets were analyzed by human experts who manually assigned the best matching affective term based on their interpretation to the tweet. To assist in identifying the affective experience of a tweet, a visual representation of affective terms with corresponding affective families was provided (see Fig. 1).

Results

As a result of the study, new indicators for marketing analytics were developed. Based on the analysis, the affective experiences of social media discussions of any company can be quantified and visualized. The introduced method enables to identify and visualize the degree of the affective families that are represented in the social media discussions of the company as high-level indicator of affective experiences. Furthermore, by quantifying each instance of the observed of affective terms it is possible to visualize affective experiences of social media discussions in a higher level of detail. For this purpose, radar chart visualization was employed (Fig. 2).

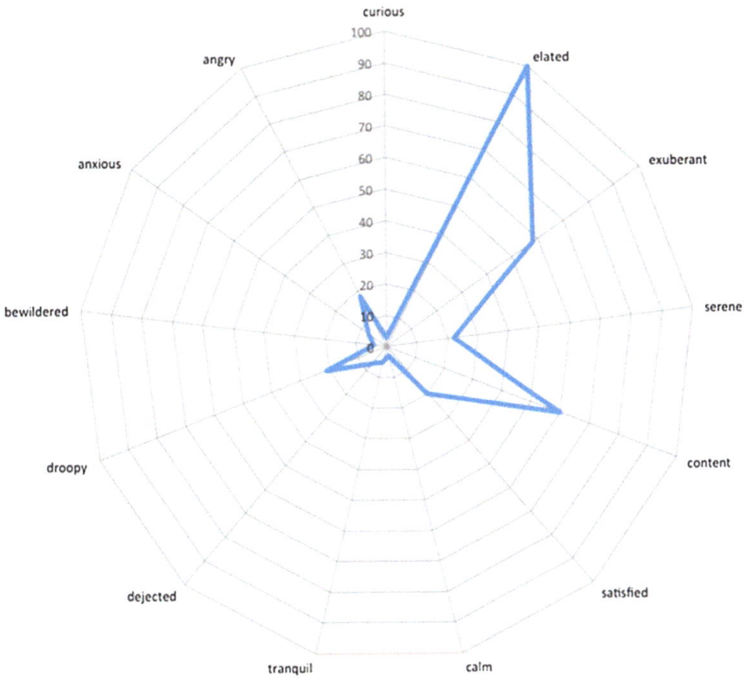

Fig. 2 Radar chart visualization of affective experiences

Conclusions and Discussion

This paper introduced a novel marketing analytics approach for quantifying and visualizing affective experiences. It is recognized that using human experts to analyze the affective experience of social media discussions is neither cost-effective nor a viable option for today's fast paced economy. In this regard, the introduced novel marketing analytics was just a first step in building an automated affective experience analysis of social media content. The next step in the research process is to continue the data gathering and labeling process of the affections, and through algorithm development and machine learning to build the artifact, an automated affection analysis tool, i.e., the "leveraged sentiment analysis tool."

It can be argued that this kind of analysis could replace the traditional customer satisfaction and company climate surveys and provide a real-time window to the affective experiences perceived everyday by the customers and company employees. We also want to underline the importance of having the different intensity levels of the affections in the framework, and suggest these to open up a path for identification of weak signals of the customers' perceptions.

The paper implicitly suggests that, in order to handle affective experiences shared in social media, companies should aim at the ability to map the seeds of negative affective experiences as early as possible. This cannot be done without the help of computers. It is expected that this kind of leveraged sentiment analysis provides organizations with a useful tool to improve their ability to detect symptoms of collective negative affective states—before they become an issue. It can be concluded that social media tools can offer in-depth analytics and knowledge for daily marketing decisions, but a solid integration between the different social media techniques and the traditional marketing models needs to be done. This in turn requires more interaction and shared development activities between marketing experts and the technically oriented experts of social media tools.

References

Bae, Y., and H. Lee. 2012. Sentiment analysis of twitter audiences: Measuring the positive or negative influence of popular twitterers. *Journal of the American Society for Information Science and Technology* 63 (12): 2521–2535.

Bagozzi, R., M. Gopinath, and P. Nyer. 1999. The Role of Emotions in Marketing. *Journal of the Academy of Marketing Science* 27 (2): 184–206.

Beedie, C., P. Terry, and A. Lane. 2005. Distinctions Between Emotion and Mood. *Cognition and Emotion* 19 (6): 847–878.

Derbaix, C., and M. Pham. 1991. Affective Reactions to Consumption Situations: A Pilot Investigation. *Journal of Economic Psychology* 12: 325–355.

Fan, W., and M. Gordon. 2014. The power of social media analytics. *Communications of ACM* 57 (6): 74–81.

Feldman Barrett, L. 2004. Feelings or Words? Understanding the Content in Self-report Ratings of Experienced Emotion. *Journal of Personality and Social Psychology* 87 (2): 266–281.

Gentile, C., N. Spiller, and G. Noci. 2007. How to Sustain the Customer Experience: An Overview of Experience Components that Co-create Value With the Customer. *European Management Journal* 25 (5): 395–410.

Haas, S. 2015. Disappointment makes you more trusting. *Harvard Business Review*.

Laros, F., and J. Steenkamp. 2005. Emotions in Consumer Behavior: a Hierarchical Approach. *Journal of Business Research* 58: 1437–1445.

Mehrabian, A., and J. Russell. 1974. *An Approach to Environmental Psychology*. Cambridge, Massachusetts: MIT Press.

Melville, P., V. Sindhwani, and R. Lawrence. 2009. Social media analytics: Channeling the power of the blogosphere for marketing insight. *Proc. of the WIN* 1 (1): 1–5.

Paavola, J., and H. Jalonen. 2015. An approach to detect and analyze the impact of biased information sources in the social media. In *Proceedings of the 14th European conference on cyber warfare and security 2015: ECCWS 2015*, 213.

Palmer, A. 2010. Customer experience management: a critical review of an emerging idea. *Journal of Services Marketing* 24 (3): 196–208.

Sacharin, V., K. Schlegel, and K. Scherer. 2012. *Geneva Emotion Wheel Rating Study (Report)*. Geneva, Switzerland: University of Geneva, Swiss Center for Affective Sciences.

Scherer, K. 2005. What are Emotions? And How Can They Be Measured? *Social Science Information* 44: 695–729.

Seo, M., L. FeldmanBarret, and S. Jin. 2008. The structure of affect: history, theory, and implications for emotion research in organizations. In *Research companion to emotion in organizations*, ed. N. Ashkanasy, and C. Cooper, 17–44. E. Elgar: Bodmin.

Zeng, D., H. Chen, R. Lusch, and S.-H. Li. 2010. Social media analytics and intelligence. *IEEE Intelligent Systems* 25 (6): 13–16.

Emotion-Gauge: Analyzing Affective Experiences in B2B Customer Journeys

Tuula Andersson, Mika Boedeker and Vilma Vuori

Introduction

The customer travels a certain journey while doing business in B2B encounters. Managing this journey as a whole is important, and may even be more important than concentrating merely on individual touch points. Due to the various affective *experiences* the customer will be "affectively charged" during this journey. There is no doubt of the relevance of the issue in the B2C context but in business relationships the role of affective experiences has not been as salient.

There are various frameworks explaining the sphere of human affective experiences on a certain moment. However, the temporal dimension is not salient in these frameworks. When the aim is to better understand the dynamics of a customer relationship and value creation, it is necessary to develop means to analyze affective experiences throughout the journey.

This paper introduces a novel measuring tool, Emotion-Gauge, for analyzing the affective path a B2B customer travels when encountering various business activities. Emotion-Gauge takes into account both temporal dimension and variations in pleasure, arousal and dominance of affective experiences. The results of applying Emotion-Gauge can assist companies to design their activities in managing the affective path and consequently enhance positive customer experience and value creation. The objective of the research is to test the performance of Emotion-Gauge tool in project-based B2B context. The empirical research uses case study methodology where qualitative interview data is used.

T. Andersson (✉) · M. Boedeker
School of Business and Services, Tampere University of Applied Sciences, Tampere, Finland
e-mail: tuula.andersson@tamk.fi

V. Vuori
Department of Management, University of Vaasa, Vaasa, Finland

A. Kavoura et al. (eds.), *Strategic Innovative Marketing*, Springer Proceedings in Business and Economics, DOI 10.1007/978-3-319-56288-9_5

The paper is constructed as follows. First, theoretical basis is constructed by discussing marketing in B2B context and the significance of affective experiences. Consequently, the PAD framework is introduced and applied to measure affective experiences, added with a temporal dimension. Second, Emotion-Gauge is introduced and explained how it was tested empirically. Finally, the results of the empirical research are presented, and the relevance of findings is discussed.

Theoretical Background

B2B Marketing and Customer Experience

The paper looks B2B context through the lens of relationship marketing philosophy, which incorporates establishing, developing and maintaining of customer relationships (see, e.g. Morgan and Hunt 1994; Gummesson 2011) as well as value co-creation with the customer (Grönroos 2009). In firms that implement relationship marketing, all activities that the customer encounters can be understood as marketing activities, as they affect the customer's perception of the service operations and processes, i.e. customer experience (Clark et al. 2000; Johnston and Clark 2008). Customer experience is formed by the firm's value proposition (e.g. Kaplan and Norton 2006) and its realization, i.e. how and what value the firm promises the customer and how the value is facilitated by the firm (Grönroos 2009; Zeithaml and Bitner 2003). The experienced value can be, e.g. economic, functional, expressive and experiential (Smith and Colgate 2007).

Customer's expectations, encounters with the firm and finally the experienced value are included in the customer journey. This journey consists of several touch points influencing customer's affective experiences. Especially in the B2C context, there are strong claims, and also evidence that understanding and managing the customer journey as a whole is more important than concentrating merely on individual touch points (e.g. Rawson et al. 2013). Additionally, fully (emotionally) connected customers have been found to be 52% more valuable than those who are just highly satisfied (Magids et al. 2015).

These issues should not be overlooked in the B2B context either. It would be deceptive to assume that people leave all their emotions behind when they are acting in the B2B context. (e.g. Tähtinen and Blois 2011; Knight 2012) Also the B2B customer will be "affectively charged" due to the various affective experiences during the journey. These experiences form an affective path, which should be taken into account and managed to enhance value creation.

Analyzing Affective Experiences

The use of the terms of affective phenomena ("emotion", "feeling", "mood", etc.) is fuzzy and confusing (e.g. Bagozzi et al. 1999; Kokkonen 2010; Scherer 2005).

Affective experience involves one's affective system through the generation of emotions, feelings and moods (Gentile et al. 2007). In that sense, affect is conceived as an umbrella and in this study the analysis is on the level of affective experience, not making specific distinction between for example emotions, feelings and moods.

The analysis of the affective experiences in this study is mainly based on the PAD paradigm. Starting from Mehrabian and Russell's (1974) seminal work numerous studies have assumed that variations in pleasure, arousal and dominance (PAD) universally constitute the common core of human affective states. On a general level, pleasure refers to the degree to which an individual feels, for example, good, happy or satisfied. Similarly, arousal refers to the degree to which an individual feels, for example, excited, stimulated or active. Dominance, in turn, refers to the degree to which an individual feels being in control or free to act. In addition to PAD, there are various frameworks explaining the sphere of human affective experiences, ranging from detailed circular or hierarchical models to less detailed dimensional ones (see, e.g. Laros and Steenkamp 2005; Seo et al. 2008). They are useful in explaining the affective state of a person on a certain moment. However, the *temporal dimension is not salient in these frameworks*.

Many frameworks explaining customer experience build on the basis of temporal sequential business processes. For example, customer journey is a sequential diagram depicting the interaction between the customer and the firm (Richardson 2010; Nenonen et al. 2008). Customer journey acknowledges customers' mental models (Nenonen et al. 2008) as well as the temporal dimension, but *the depth of assessing affective experiences is facile*.

In a business context where the customer–supplier processes often are long lasting, the customer's affective state may vary considerably. When the aim is to better understand the dynamics of a customer relationship and the value creation, it is necessary to develop more in-depth means to analyze affective experiences throughout the various processes, i.e. journeys.

Introducing Emotion-Gauge for Sentiment Analysis

Testing Emotion-Gauge by Empirical Study

Emotion-Gauge is a visual scale for all three dimensions of the PAD attached to the phases of a business project. It was developed for research purposes: during an interview the informant can indicate the level of pleasure, arousal and dominance using a numerical scale. Figure 1 illustrates an example of Emotion-Gauge.

The empirical study used extensive case study methodology introduced by Stoecker (1991), where the cases and even individuals are seen as instruments in exploring a specific phenomenon and developing a proposition that could be used to other cases. The data used in testing Emotion-Gauge was collected with personal interviews for customers of a Finnish IT company. Altogether 13 interviews were

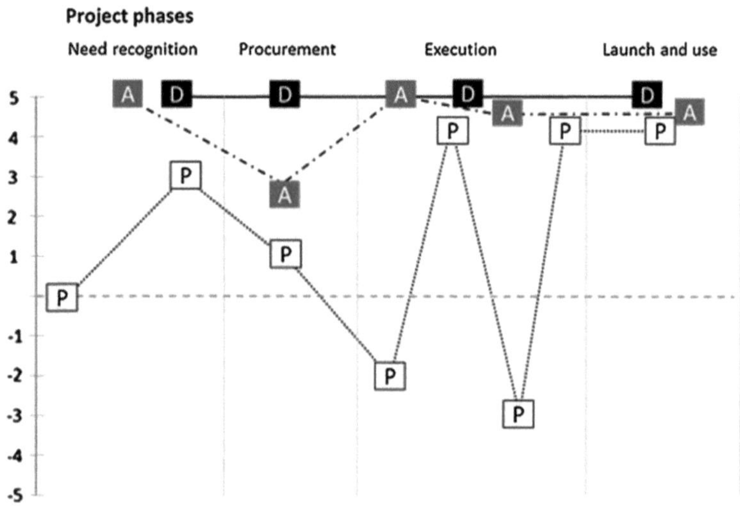

Fig. 1 An example of emotion-gauge of a customer acting as a project manager

conducted between October 2015 and February 2016. All but one interviewees were representatives of big public or government owned organizations.

The interviews followed the steps of an IT project from need recognition to acquisition to execution and finally to launch. The informants were also asked to indicate the value of pleasure, arousal and dominance on a scale from −5 to +5 during each project phase. Connecting the given values in each phase created their emotional path, sort of an emotional 'cardiogram'.

Results

The findings of the study indicate that affective experiences are salient, vary with different phases of the interaction and form unique affective paths. Depending on the customer's previous experience and skills, and the successes or difficulties encountered during the process, all three dimensions could vary from very positive to very negative scale values.

However, that was not always the case. Also more stable affective 'cardiograms' were detected. Some informants remained on a relatively positive level on all three dimensions throughout the whole project. In those cases, they were not personally involved in the daily operations of the project. Another reason was found in the time and length of the project: the interviewee encountered difficulties in remembering his/her emotions from several years back.

When describing their IT projects, the interviewees concentrated mainly on the "facts and figures", i.e. on what actually happened and why. Spontaneous expressions of discrete affective experiences were quite scarce. In the beginning of the project, the experience of enthusiasm was sometimes expressed when the informant felt he/she was about to start something entirely new and meaningful. The pleasure and arousal scores were high even though the feeling of dominance was low. When something very negative had happened, like a considerable time delay or loss of a key person, the informants expressed their affective experiences with distinctive words like 'agony' or 'worry'.

The experience of pleasure generally decreased towards the execution phase and rose again in the end. Nearly all interviewees had faced some difficulties in during the execution phase causing frustration which could be detected from expressions of unpleasant excitement (arousal) or fatigue. But if the supplier was able to manage problematic situations and time delays effectively it gave the customer perception of confidence. So, even if the customer felt he/she was no longer at the helm, the experience of dominance remained positive.

Discussion

Even though most of the interviewees felt it rather easy to indicate their affective experiences with Emotion-Gauge, both the tool and the related interview need further development. Sometimes the dimensions may have been mixed up with each other, especially pleasure and arousal. Sometimes, instead of indicating his/hers own experiences, the interviewee would describe the overall 'feeling' of the project group. Additionally, the dimensions should have been more precisely linked into specific touch points of the customer journey. This was especially difficult if the project had lasted for a long time and the informant had already forgotten the details.

In order to gain better evidence of the functionality of the PAD-dimensions in B2B-relationships, the interview should be developed to encourage the interviewee to express also his/her discrete affective experiences. Now the interviewees maybe concentrated too much on the intensity of the dimensions (the numerical scale values) instead of describing their true experiences, let alone the underlying reasons for their emotions. Yet, Emotion-Gauge proved to be a useful tool in connecting customers' affective path into the whole customer journey.

References

Bagozzi, R., M. Gopinath, and P. Nyer. 1999. The role of emotions in marketing. *Journal of the Academy of Marketing Science* 27 (2): 184–206.

Clark, G., R. Johnston, and M. Shulver. 2000. Exploiting the service concept for service design and development. In *New Service Development – Creating Memorable Experiences*, ed. J.A. Fitzsimmons, and M.J. Fitzsimmons, 71–91. CA: Sage, Thousand Oaks.

Gentile, C., N. Spiller, and G. Noci. 2007. How to sustain the customer experience: an overiview of experience components that co-create value with the customer. *European Management Journal* 25 (5): 395–410.
Grönroos, C. 2009. Marketing as promise management: Regaining customer management for marketing. *Journal of Business & Industry Marketing* 24 (5): 351–359.
Gummesson, E. 2011. *Total relationship marketing*, Routledge.
Johnston, R., and G. Clark. 2008. *Service Operations Management*. Harlow: Pearson Education Limited.
Kaplan, R.S., and D.P. Norton. 2006. How to implement a new strategy without disrupting your organization. *Harvard Business Review* 84 (3): 100.
Knight, L. 2012. Proving the value of emotion in B2B marketing communications. Upshot Agency News.
Kokkonen, M. 2010. *Ihastuttavat, vihastuttavat tunteet*. Jyväskylä: Opi tunteiden säätelyn taito. PS-kustannus.
Laros, F., and J. Steenkamp. 2005. Emotions in consumer behavior: a hierarchical approach. *Journal of Business Research* 58: 1437–1445.
Magids, S., A. Zorfas, and D. Leemon, 2015. The new science of customer emotions. A better way to drive growth and profitability. *Harvard Business Review*, November 2015, pp. 66–76.
Mehrabian, A., and J. Russell. 1974. *An approach to environmental psychology*. Cambridge, Massachusetts: MIT Press.
Morgan, R.M., and S.D. Hunt. 1994. The commitment-trust theory of relationship marketing. *The Journal of Marketing* 58 (3): 20–38.
Nenonen, S., H. Rasila, J.M. Junnonen, and S. Kärnä. 2008. Customer journey—a method to investigate user experience, *Proceedings of the Euro FM Conference Manchester*, 54–63.
Rawson, A., E. Duncan, C. Jones. 2013. The truth about customer experience. *Harvard Business Review*, September 2013, 90–98.
Richardson. A. 2010. Using Customer Journey Maps to Improve Customer Experience, *Harvard Business Review*, 15.
Scherer, K. 2005. What are emotions? and how can they be measured? *Social Science Information* 44: 695–729.
Seo, M., L. Feldman Barret, and S. Jin. 2008. The structure of affect: history, theory, and implications for emotion research in organizations. In *Research companion to emotion in organizations*, ed. N. Ashkanasy, and C. Cooper, 17–44. Bodmin: Edward Elgar.
Smith, B., and M. Colgate. 2007. Customer value creation: a practical framework. *Journal of Marketing Theory and Practice* 15 (1): 7–23.
Stoecker, R. 1991. Evaluating and rethinking the case study. *Sociological Review* 39 (1): 88–112.
Tähtinen, J., and K. Blois. 2011. The involvement and influence of emotions in problematic business relationships. *Industrial Marketing Management* 40 (6): 907–918.
Zeithaml, V.A., and M.J. Bitner. 2003. *Services marketing: integrating customer focus across the firm*. New York: McGraw-Hill.

Customer Perceived Value—A Key in Marketing of Integrated Solutions

Nina Helander, Virpi Sillanpää, Vilma Vuori and Olavi Uusitalo

Introduction

The foundations of successful marketing and sales of integrated solutions are based on deep understanding of how to create value for the customer and help the customer to achieve its goals (Ulaga and Chacour 2001). It is not enough to just to know the customer's current and explicit needs; the secret is in identifying also the hidden and future-oriented needs of the customer. This requires an understanding of value perception. It can be further argued that value perception is consisted of several things, also in the business-to-business marketing. This is especially the case in the context of integrated solutions, where the purchaser needs to evaluate a mix of goods and services, and the overall benefits and costs of the integrated solution (Davies et al. 2006).

For example, it is not easy for a marketer to recognize which are the elements in the total offering that act as the key source of value creation. Furthermore, a complex integrated solution cannot usually be developed and produced by a single company; instead, the system integrator needs to be surrounded by a network of suppliers participating in the creation of the integrated solution (Helander 2004). However, to date little has been written about the role of the supplier organizations, networks and the implications that their participation has on the customer's overall value perception (Brady et al. 2005).

N. Helander (✉) · V. Sillanpää
Information Management and Logistics, Tampere University of Technology, Tampere, Finland
e-mail: nina.helander@tut.fi

O. Uusitalo
Industrial Management, Tampere University of Technology, Tampere, Finland

V. Vuori
Department of Management, University of Vaasa, Vaasa, Finland

A. Kavoura et al. (eds.), *Strategic Innovative Marketing*, Springer Proceedings in Business and Economics, DOI 10.1007/978-3-319-56288-9_6

The aim of this paper is to contribute to this gap. Our special emphasis is on integrated solutions, where the complexity of the offering sets several kinds of challenges for marketing (Davies et al. 2006). In order to examine these problematics, we have conducted a qualitative case study from the industrial automation sector. The case study describes the challenges of developing integrated solutions that are a mix of hardware components, software and services. Increased intelligence in system solutions enables various benefits, e.g., the integration of software to devices and systems makes it possible to improve performance without replacing physical components. However, this new role of software as a highly abstract and intangible element may also raise new kinds of challenges both for the marketer and the customer.

The paper is organized as follows: first we briefly describe the theoretical base of our study building on value creation and integrated solution literature. Then we report our research methods and the case study. Finally, we draw conclusions.

Value and Integrated Solutions

Value is a concept that is commonly used by both academics and actors in the field, but it is often rather unclear what is actually meant by it in different contexts (Lepak et al. 2007, Gummerus 2013, Bourguignon 2005, Ulaga and Chacour 2001, Ford and McDowell 1999). Bowman and Ambrosini (2000) argue that the definition of value is especially unclear in strategic level. In order to understand value in strategy better, they make a division between use value and exchange value, as well as between value creation and capture. Use value is subjectively assessed by customers whereas exchange value is only realized at the point of sale. These relate both to value creation, whereas value capture is determined by the perceived power relationships between buyers and sellers (Bowman and Ambrosini 2000). In this study, we emphasize the viewpoint of value creation, but also the viewpoint of value perception, i.e., the customer's viewpoint.

To build an analytical tool to carry out the empirical study, we will elaborate the concept of value through highlighting three interrelated and supplementary views: the content, process, and context views (Helander 2004). These three angles are used to clarify the rather imprecise discussion surrounding value as a concept.

The *content view to value perception* emphasizes that the concept of value can be regarded as the trade-off between benefits and sacrifices (Walter et al. 2001, Lapierre 2000, Parolini 1999, Slater 1997, Berry and Yadav 1996, Ravald and Grönroos 1996). These benefits and sacrifices can be understood in monetary terms, but they can also be seen as including non-monetary rewards, such as competence, market position, and social rewards (Walter et al. 2001). Non-monetary costs can include, e.g., time, effort, energy, and conflict invested by the customer to obtain the product or service. In this study, value is understood in both monetary and non-monetary terms. Nevertheless, it can still be argued that defining value as the trade-off between benefits and sacrifices offers a content-based view of value as a concept—emphasis is placed on what the customer perceives to be the benefits and sacrifices. In this way, the customer himself/herself defines the content of the value under consideration.

The *process view* emphasizes that value is not merely tied to the actual object of exchange; instead it is dependent on the successfulness of the whole relationship between the customer and the supplier. Thus this view underscores the importance of understanding value creation as a process during which the customer and supplier interact. During the interaction, the goods and related services are exchanged, but also a great deal of interaction occurs between the parties influencing how the customer perceives the total value gained.

The *context view*, for its part, puts forward the notion of differential value: the supplier should be able to create more value than the customer could achieve by choosing some other solution created by another, competitive supplier or by the customer itself. Differential value is very hard to define and measure as the customers' expectations are based on the alternatives available on the market; i.e., the impact of similar or substitute products is remarkable (Parolini 1999). Thus, measuring of differential value always requires also a mapping of other potential solutions and comparison of those with the one under consideration. In the context of integrated solutions this is not, however, an easy task.

The possibility a false perception of value is more likely when there is presence of intangible elements and services; systemic and complex goods; benefits that are not immediate; post-purchase costs and costs of consumables; products and services that are new to the customer; and lastly, infrequently purchased goods (Parolini 1999). Most of these characteristics are present in marketing and sales of integrated solutions (Brady et al. 2005). For this reason it can be argued that integrated solutions are not easily evaluated by the customer in the purchasing situation. As there are so much of complexity related to the integrated solution, it can be argued that the customer sets more weight in the evaluation on the process view of value.

Case Study

We have conducted a qualitative study in order to empirically examine the value perception in a real-life industrial setting. We use a case study, as it is a good method when new perspectives are sought or when there is little knowledge available about the phenomenon under study (Patton 1987). We have examined three deliveries of integrated solutions through the viewpoints of the case company (the solution integrator), the customers of the deliveries and the suppliers participating in producing the deliveries. Our empirical data consists of 14 thematic interviews; 6 interviewees from sellers sales and marketing, 5 customers representing three different projects and three suppliers, representing two different subcontractors.

Our case company is a high-tech company that operates in the industrial automation sector. It provides its organizational customers larger automated production lines based on integration of software programs into electromechanical components; i.e., their offer is a mix of software and hardware. In recent years the case company has started to move from device supplier toward providing entire system solutions, automated production lines. The shift has not been easy, as the employees of the company have not always understood the different business logic that is required in order to be a genuine system provider instead of a device supplier. This has caused several problems in the company's business relationships. Moreover, the transformation has complicated the understanding of what kind of value the company is in fact providing to its customers.

Empirical Findings

The aim of automated production lines delivered by the case company was to create value for the customer by providing more efficient and effective production capabilities. Since the customers were engaged in tough competition, production capabilities played a very important role in the customers' business processes. Customers placed a great value on flexible production processes that enable using a single production line for both mass production and production of customized products. Thus the customers saved both in production line investments and in floor space plus attained shorter production times. This kind of flexibility of a production line required extensive software solutions, thus the role of software was essential in the overall integrated solution.

Most of the benefits of 'more effective production' were easy to measure in monetary terms. However, some potential benefits were hidden and challenging to predict, since the realization of the benefit was not immediate. For example, the benefit of the component-level tracking which was available feature in the integrated solution will not be realized until there is a failure in customer's end products. The case company was able to communicate the general level benefits for the customer, but somehow they missed the opportunities to create customer specific value. In some occasion the marketing and sales people did not realize the potential value creating features, such as component-level tracking, of then-current version of its integrated solution. Such problems identifying the things that customers really value are of course related to the nature of the relationship, the lack of closeness, and also problems in sharing of information between the parties in the relationship.

The customers were expecting the case company to take a more active role in the marketing and after-sales of the integrated solutions, especially related to marketing of its software solution. However, the case company was not active even in contacting those customers to whom they had already delivered an earlier version of the system solution. One reason for the silence could be that some customer deliveries had been so difficult from the viewpoint of the case company that the personnel were a little bit cautious about getting in touch with the customer again.

In addition to direct value in the form of more effective and efficient production, the customers expected also indirect value in the form of consistent and clear service. Especially they would have appreciated to interact only with the case company, from whom they had thought to have a turnkey solution. Instead, several persons from different suppliers were dealing with the matters at the customer's premises. These issues should have been dealt by the case company itself. Thus, the case company was not able to orchestrate its supplier network. Because of this the customers felt disappointed and were troubled by the fact that they did not always know who to contact if problems arise with the production line.

Customers were also dissatisfied with the unclear pricing—in the first place salespersons had promised software upgrades at too low a price, but after the feedback from the persons responsible for the software they tried to raise the price. It seemed that neither the salespersons nor the customers understood the importance and the value of software in the integrated solutions. Everybody seemed to value only physical and tangible equipment. This became evident when the customers wanted to have separate prices for different parts of the integrated solution, but for the software part, they were ready to pay almost nothing.

Conclusions and Discussion

From our case study we can draw up several viewpoints on the marketing of integrated solutions. Next, we will open up these viewpoints and also discuss some of the potential future research needs that we have been able to identify.

As regards the process perspective on value perception, the biggest shortcomings were in the software integration and overall project management phases in our case study. It seems that the separate functions (R&D, marketing, sales and top management) of the case organization did not understand each other well enough. Because of this the role of software was not properly understood. Probably a deep understanding of the customers and their value perception within the case organization would have solved this internal problem. It seems that neither marketing and sales nor top management saw the potential of software in value creation.

From the customers' viewpoint, the most problematic matters were the information sharing and forced interaction with several actors, as their desire was to just interact with the case company. This shows us the importance of the well-performing relationship management and the well-working customer interface, which also facilitates the process of value creation. Customers value the easiness of just interacting with one company. Thus a poorly managed supplier network may cause dramatic decrease in the customer value perception, even though the object of exchange would be of good quality. The process and the interaction around the actual delivery of the integrated solution is thus the key to the overall value perception. When looking the value perception from the context viewpoint, differential value is a key issue, too. In the case of complex integrated solutions it becomes rather difficult for customers to compare alternative solutions and distinguish among them. In such cases, the ability to identify indirect indicators of the value creation capability of the case company would have played an important role. For example, the reference projects of the case company could have acted as indicators of the value creation capability.

Nevertheless, if the case company wants to succeed in future, it needs to pay more attention to such things as its project management competencies and the ability to handle responsibilities and risks. Moreover, it becomes a matter of reputation and trustworthiness; the case company should convince the customer of its value creation capabilities and competencies. These viewpoints of capabilities of the suppliers are interesting avenue for future research to open in more detail. We will continue this study by going into more details of the discussion of supplier value creation capabilities.

References

Berry, L.L., and M.S. Yadav. 1996. Capture and communicate value in the pricing of services. *Sloan Management Review* (Summer), 41–51.

Bourguignon, A. 2005. Management accounting and value creation: the profit and loss of reification. *Critical Perspectives on Accounting* 16: 353–389.

Bowman, C., and V. Ambrosini. 2000. Value creation versus value capture: Towards a coherent definition of value in strategy. *British Journal of Management* 11: 1–15.

Brady, T., A. Davies, and D. Gann. 2005. Creating value by delivering integrated solutions. *International Journal of Project Management* 23: 360–365.

Davies, A., T. Brady, and M. Hobday. 2006. Charting a path toward integrated solutions. *MIT Sloan Management Review* 47 (3): 39–48.

Ford, D., and R. McDowell. 1999. Managing business relationships by analyzing the effects and value of different actions. *Industrial Marketing Management* 28: 429–442.

Gummerus, J. 2013. *Value creation processes and value outcomes in marketing theory: Strangers or siblings*? vol. 13, 19–46.

Helander, N. 2004. *Value-creating networks: an analysis of the software component business*. Acta Universitatis Ouluensis, G Oeconomica 16, Oulu: University of Oulu.

Lapierre, J. 2000. Customer-perceived value in industrial contexts. *Journal of Business and Industrial Marketing* 15 (2/3): 122–140.

Lepak, D., K. Smith, and M. Taylor. 2007. Value creation and value capture: A multilevel perspective. *Academy of Management Review* 32 (1): 180–194.

Parolini, C. 1999. *The value net. A tool for competitive strategy*. Wiley.

Patton, M. 1987. *How to use qualitative methods in evaluation*. California: Sage.

Ravald, A., and C. Grönroos. 1996. The value concept and relationship marketing. *European Journal of Marketing* 30 (2): 19–30.

Slater, S.F. 1997. Developing a customer value-based theory of the firm. *Journal of the Academy of Marketing Science* 25 (2): 162–167.

Ulaga, W., and S. Chacour. 2001. Measuring customer-perceived value in business markets a prerequisite for marketing strategy development and implementation. *Industrial Marketing Management* 30: 525–540.

Walter, A., T. Ritter, and H.G. Gemünden. 2001. Value creation in buyer-seller relationships. *Industrial Marketing Management* 30 (4): 365–377.

Reliability and Perceived Value of Sentiment Analysis for Twitter Data

Jari Jussila, Vilma Vuori, Jussi Okkonen and Nina Helander

Introduction

With the advent of social media, people have become more eager to express and share their opinions on web about corporate and product brands (Jansen et al. 2009). In the marketing literature, customers' opinions and emotions are receiving increasing attention. Many studies have chosen Twitter as a source for collecting data on customers' opinions about brands (e.g., Jansen et al. 2009). One reason for this is that sentiment analysis over Twitter offers organisations a fast and effective way to monitor people's feelings toward their brand, business, and directors (Saif et al. 2012). Sentiment refers in this study to an individual's state of negative or positive feeling that spreads through social interaction, that has an object and that ultimately aims to some kind of action (Jalonen 2014).

Several computational approaches have been proposed to automatically identify and extract subjective information from tweets (Bravo-Marquez et al. 2014). Some of these approaches are applicable to any language, while others are language specific. This study investigates the reliability and perceived value of SentiStrength (e.g., Thelwall et al. 2010, 2012) and Nemo Sentiment and Data Analyzer (Paavola and Jalonen 2015), both tools developed to understand Finnish language. The purpose of this study is to evaluate the reliability and perceived value of these two automatic sentiment analysis tools in contrast to analysis made by human

J. Jussila (✉) · N. Helander
Information Management and Logistics, Tampere University of Technology, Tampere, Finland
e-mail: jari.j.jussila@tut.fi

V. Vuori
Department of Management, University of Vaasa, Vaasa, Finland

J. Okkonen
School of Information Sciences, University of Tampere, Tampere, Finland

A. Kavoura et al. (eds.), *Strategic Innovative Marketing*, Springer Proceedings in Business and Economics, DOI 10.1007/978-3-319-56288-9_7

evaluators. For this purpose, a dataset of tweets from a Finnish software company was collected. For evaluating reliability, Krippendorff's α is computed, which measures the agreement among observers, coders, judges, raters, or measuring instruments (Krippendorff 2007). In order to evaluate the perceived value of these analyses and tools, interviews of the case company representatives were carried out.

Theoretical Background

Social media enables free expression of vast range of sentiments that customers experience when interacting with a company or its products, services, or brand. When a company is, e.g., tagged to an emotionally charged tweet, it may have a significant positive or negative effect on company's brand (e.g., Jalonen 2014) and consequently performance (Luo et al. 2013). Company brand is more and more affected by the way it is on display in social media (Khim-Yong et al. 2013). The simultaneous advantage and disadvantage of social media is that it promotes visibility, and its uncontrollable nature may multiply the implications for a company. The consequences of actions in social media are unpredictable but may be highly visible when going viral. In business setting, this derives a need for making decisions and actions during a limited time span, as especially negative incidents in social media concerning the company require quick actions in order to diminish the risk of losing value (Jalonen 2014). Companies can control the incidents in their external environment only to a certain limit, and therefore their only option is to try to understand these (Stoffels 1994) and adjust their own actions accordingly.

Strategic management literature promotes the idea that a company's every action should be based on conscious decisions and that these decisions should be grounded on fair understanding of the current situation. Competitive intelligence is a process that analyses data and provides a company relevant information about the external environment and thus helps the company gain competitive advantage over other players in the field (e.g., Bensoussan and Fleisher 2007; Vuori 2011). One of the most contemporary competitive intelligence actions aimed to back up decision-making is analyzing data derived from social media. In fact, social media offers a new kind of dimension to competitive intelligence—the social aspect of the masses, providing new kinds of analytics and a path to transform social media content into strategically actionable knowledge (He et al. 2016). For example, understanding how the company brand is perceived by customers and how their sentiments toward it are expressed in social media (Stieglitz and Dang-Xuan 2013) gives the company possibility to take actions to enhance the customer experience and promote brand visibility.

Sentiment analysis software is seen as an efficient way to analyse the masses of social media derived data providing companies understanding of how it is depicted in social media. However, the reliability of sentiment analysis software may be questioned. First, analysis made with sentiment analysis software is based on binary machine logic, where the data is refined by a system lacking serendipity and ambiguity. This may cause the risk of false analysis, as the machine logic may not correctly interpret the content of tweets made by human beings. Non-binary human logic may contain many different truths due to its fuzziness and ambiguity, whereas binary machine logic allows only one, possibly misinterpreted, truth (Vuori and Okkonen 2012). Another noteworthy issue is that while the subject of information may be internal (e.g., the company brand), the sources of the information may be both internal (employees) and external (customers). The company may be tagged in a tweet by an employee, and it is likely that the employees' tweets are more often positively than negatively charged. It is worth of discussion, should these "insider tweets," possibly distorting the data, be extracted from analysis that focuses on customer experience and brand perception. Furthermore, automatic analysis tools are not usually able to take into account the context of the tweet, which may further reveal the target of the expressed emotion. And finally, the automatic analysis tools do not typically understand sarcasm that, e.g., tweets can include. Taking to account these frailties of using software to analyse sentiments, it is fair to ask can it, in fact, understand the sentiments expressed in social media, and, more importantly, Is it safe to base decisions of company's actions on such analysis?

Research Approach

Computational approaches and tools that can understand Finnish language include SentiStrength (e.g., Thelwall et al. 2012, 2010) and Nemo Sentiment and Data Analyzer (Paavola and Jalonen 2015). This study investigates the reliability and perceived value of these two automatic tools, in contrast to human evaluators. Nemo Sentiment and Data Analyzer tool is a cloud-based service that enables both collecting the Twitter data and analyzing sentiment using two separate algorithms: one based on logistic regression (LR) and the other on random forest (RF) classification. SentiStrength algorithm calculates the positive and negative sentiment strength for each tweet on a scale of 1–5. These values were used to compute the classification of the tweet to positive, neutral, or negative. The three algorithm based data classifications are compared to two human evaluator classifications. The working hypothesis is that human evaluators classify tweet data uniformly and are able to extract correct sentiments by human logic.

In order to investigate the reliability and perceived value of automated versus human evaluator evaluated sentiment analysis, we collected Twitter data from a Finnish software company. A total of 509 tweets were collected using Nemo Sentiment and Data Analyzer tool.

The human evaluators independently classified the tweets into one of three categories: positive, neutral, or negative using a spreadsheet processor. The data was imported to SentiStrength and sentiment strength was calculated for each tweet. Krippendorf's α (Hayes and Krippendorff 2007) value was then calculated using SPSS to the human evaluator classified tweets, SentiStrength classified tweets, and Nemo Sentiment and Data Analyzer tool classified tweets. In the process, the evaluations were compared in pairs assuming that human evaluations were the baseline, yet they had distinctive notions on the sentiments. For avoiding misunderstanding and misinterpretations α should have somewhat high value. Social scientists commonly rely on data with reliabilities $\alpha \geq 0.800$, consider data with, $800 > \alpha \geq 0.667$ only to draw tentative conclusions, and discard data whose agreement measures $\alpha < 0.667$ (Krippendorff 2004). In this case, all values of are low as depicted in Table 1.

For the evaluation of the perceived value of the analyses, we carried out a workshop where the results of the analysis were presented to the case company representatives (business unit manager, key account manager, marketing specialist) and their opinions on the analysis and its value for business decisions were asked.

Table 1 Evaluations

	Positive agreement	Neutral agreement	Negative agreement	Krippendorff's α
Human evaluator 1 versus Human evaluator 2	337 versus 171 **166**	146 versus 326 **180**	19 versus 5 **14**	0.1962
Human evaluator 1 versus Nemo LR	337 versus 121 **216**	146 versus 348 **202**	19 versus 20 **1**	−0.0492
Human evaluator 1 versus Nemo RF	337 versus 224 **113**	146 versus 217 **71**	19 versus 13 **6**	0.1787
Human evaluator 1 versus SentiStrength	337 versus 265 = **72**	146 versus 227 **81**	19 versus 10 **9**	0.2700
Human evaluator 2 versus Nemo LR	171 versus 121 = **50**	326 versus 348 **22**	5 versus 20 **15**	0.3266
Human evaluator 2 versus Nemo RF	171 versus 224 **53**	326 versus 217 **109**	5 versus 13 **7**	0.2760
Human evaluator 2 versus SentiStrength	171 versus 265 **94**	326 versus 227 **99**	5 versus 10 **5**	0.3102
Nemo LR versus Nemo RF	121 versus 224 = **103**	348 versus 217 **131**	20 versus 13 **7**	0.4563
Nemo LR versus SentiStrength	121 versus 265 **144**	348 versus 227 **121**	20 versus 10 **10**	0.1821
Nemo RF versus SentiStrength	224 versus 265 **41**	217 versus 227 **10**	13 versus 10 **3**	0.2057

Results

The evaluations are presented in Table 1. On each row evaluations are compared on absolute levels and by Krippendorff's α. The first three columns describe the values difference in assessment as the nominal difference between evaluator is described with bolded figure on each row.

The interviewed company representatives perceived the analysis valuable in general terms, as they were able easily and in visual way to see the distribution of the negative versus positive tweets hashtagged to their company. When taking a closer look to the tweets analysed by the human evaluators, the company representatives found the influence of the context highly relevant. For example, most of the negative tweets were not targeted toward the case company, but instead, e.g., toward the Finnish government making unwise decisions concerning information systems, or even toward the case company's competitors. This important fact was not revealed by the automatic analysis tools, as they were not able to take into account the context of the specific tweet, nor the potential sarcasm behind the tweet.

Conclusions and Discussion

As noted in results section, all pairs failed the test in sense that the hypothesis of human being more powerful and smart algorithms existing should be discarded. Drawn from the data, there are significant variations with human and machine evaluations, yet algorithms provide more uniform analysis. There are several reasons for such variation. First reason for failure is the limited amount of data, there can be structural issue that hinders the tweet classification by the human evaluators. On the other hand, the use of human evaluators is dependent on their subjective experience on the issue and personal attributes. The high variation in classification is due to human evaluators different judgement.

Highest value of α was when compared human evaluator 1 or human evaluator 2 to SentiStrength or Nemo LR to Nemo RF. This provides initial evidence, that elaborated algorithms and human evaluators may succeed, yet it is issue of technical development. On the other hand, Nemo LR and Nemo RF provided highest α, due to common ancestry as they assess the tweets similarly.

Human evaluators provide assessment based on their insight and/or prior knowledge. However in this data the assumption of human sensitiveness or preciseness on sentiments is not supported due to high variation. The study does, however, have several limitations that may impact the results. The human evaluators had little prior experience of performing sentiment analysis and their knowledge of the company and its business was limited. This can, for instance, impact the interpretation on what tweets are actually classified negative toward the company. In addition, the amount of observations was relatively small and not meeting gold standards set for sentiment classification. Further research should include a more extensive set of observations and involve also company employees and more experienced sentiment evaluators performing the classification.

References

Bensoussan, B.E., and C.S. Fleisher. 2007. *Business and competitive analysis: Effective application of new and classic methods*. New Jersey: Financial Times Prentice Hall.

Bravo-Marquez, F., M. Mendoza., and B. Poblete. 2014. Meta-level sentiment models for big social data analysis. *Knowledge-Based System*. Vol. 69, 86–99.

Hayes, A.F., and K. Krippendorff. 2007. Answering the call for a standard reliability measure for coding data. *Communication Methods and Measures* 1: 77–89.

He, W., X. Tian., Y. Chen., and D. Chong. 2016. Actionable social media competitive analytics for understanding customer experiences. *Journal of Computer Information Systems* 56 (2): 145–155.

Jalonen, H. 2014. Negatiiviset tunteet ja sosiaalinen media muodostavat yrityksille vaikean yhdistelmän. *LTA* 2: 14.

Jansen, B.J., M. Zhang, K. Sobel, and A. Chowdury. 2009. Twitter power: Tweets as electronic word of mouth. *Journal of the American Society for Information Science and Technology* 60: 2169–2188.

Khim-Yong, G., H. Cheng-Suang, and L. Zhijie. 2013. Social media brand community and consumer behavior: Quantifying the relative impact of user—and marketer-generated content. *Information Systems Research* 24 (1): 88–107.

Krippendorff, K. 2004. Reliability in content analysis: Some common misconceptions and recommendations. *Human Communication Research* 30 (3): 411–433. doi:10.1111/j.1468-2958.2004.tb00738.x.

Krippendorff, K. 2007. *Computing Krippendorff's alpha reliability*. ASC: Dep. Pap. 43.

Luo, X., J. Zhang, and W. Duan. 2013. Social media and firm equity value. *Information Systems Research* 24 (1): 146–163.

Paavola, J., and H. Jalonen. 2015. An approach to detect and analyze the impact of biased information sources in the social media. In *proceedings of the 14th European conference on cyber warfare and security 2015: ECCWS 2015*, 213. Academic Conferences Limited.

Saif, H., Y. He., H. Alani. 2012. Semantic sentiment analysis of twitter. In *The Semantic Web–ISWC 2012*, 508–524. Springer.

Stieglitz, S. and L. Dang-Xuan. 2013. Emotions and information diffusion in social media—Sentiment of microblogs and sharing behavior. *Journal of Management Information Systems*. 29(4).

Stoffels, J.D. 1994. Strategic issues management: A comprehensive guide to environmental scanning. Pergamon.

Thelwall, M., K. Buckley, G. Paltoglou, D. Cai, and A. Kappas. 2010. Sentiment strength detection in short informal text. *Journal of the Association for Information Science and Technology* 61: 2544–2558.

Thelwall, M., K. Buckley, and G. Paltoglou. 2012. Sentiment strength detection for the social web. *Journal of the Association for Information Science and Technology* 63: 163–173.

Vilma, V. 2011. Social media changing the competitive intelligence process: Elicitation of employees' competitive knowledge. Tampereen teknillinen yliopisto. Julkaisu-Tampere University of Technology. Publication 1001.

Vuori, V., and J. Okkonen. 2012. Refining information and knowledge by social media applications: Adding value by insight. *Vine* 42 (1): 117–128.

Part III
Development and Marketing Strategies in Innovative Technological Enterprises

Organized by: Christos Riziotis
Theoretical and Physical Chemistry Institute (TPCI), National Hellenic Research Foundation (NHRF), Athens, Greece

Description

Technological innovation requires certain steps and efficient strategies for the successful turn into entrepreneurship and the formation of viable enterprises. In this frame, a number of topics are important to be considered for the development and the effective marketing of such enterprises. The workshop seeks to present marketing strategies as well as empirical approaches and real examples of such successful cases of technological innovative enterprises. Topics of interest could be: technology transfer, entrepreneurship, start-ups, spin-off, spin-out, technology protection, patent portfolio formation strategies, market penetration tactics, merging and acquisition, technology adaptability, enterprises development through clustering strategies, venture capital funding, incubation, trademarks, etc. Diversity of represented technological areas could enable an efficient mapping and comparison in the employed strategies, drawing useful conclusions as workshop's outcome.

Measuring the Impact of Burnout on Job Satisfaction and Organizational Commitment

G. Zapantis, M. Skordoulis, M. Chalikias, D. Drosos and A. Papagrigoriou

Introduction

Burnout can be considered as a new disease which affects negatively a large number of employees in developed countries. According to Maslach and Jackson (1982), burnout is a complex psychosomatic phenomenon that can only be analyzed under three different dimensions. The first of these dimensions concerns the feeling of being emotionally overextended, the second concerns depersonalization while the third one concerns the feeling of exhaustion and cynicism, where employees feel less effective in their job and their performance is decreased.

Job satisfaction is in managers' and researchers' spotlight as common understanding dictates a direct connection to a firm's productivity. However, according to various researchers, there is not a strong relationship between these two constructs. On the other hand, other researchers' state that job satisfaction is necessary for a firm's success as they note a major influence on employees' performance. These different views probably derive from the fact that job satisfaction is just one between the various factors that affect a firm's productivity (Bockerman and Ilmakunnas 2010). Employees' satisfaction should be taken into consideration as employees are one of the most important resources for a firm's success (Skordoulis et al. 2014).

According to Meyer and Allen (1991) organizational commitment refers to a psychological condition which both characterizes the relationship between an employee and a firm while it affects an employee's decision to remain at the firm. Organizational commitment consists of three levels; affective commitment, continuance commitment, and normative commitment (Meyer and Allen 1991).

G. Zapantis · M. Skordoulis · M. Chalikias (✉) · D. Drosos · A. Papagrigoriou
Business Administration Department, Piraeus University of Applied Sciences, Egaleo, Greece
e-mail: mchalikias@hotmail.com

A. Kavoura et al. (eds.), *Strategic Innovative Marketing*, Springer Proceedings in Business and Economics, DOI 10.1007/978-3-319-56288-9_8

Lots of researchers have recorded a correlation between job satisfaction and organizational commitment (Knoop 1995; Meyer et al. 2002; Jahangir and Shokrpour 2009). These results show the importance of job satisfaction for organizational commitment.

The aforementioned connection seems to be even more important in periods of economic crisis where firms are trying to minimize their operating costs using means such as wage cuts, while at the same time employees are asked to increase their performance.

The aim of this paper is to measure and analyze the impact of burnout on job satisfaction and organizational commitment of Greek SMEs employees.

Materials and Methods

The research sample consists of 150 employees of Greek SMEs and was selected using random sampling.

The research tool is a structured questionnaire divided into four parts. The first part is based on Meyer and Allen's model (Meyer and Allen 1991) and aims to measure respondents' organizational commitment. The second part is based on Job Descriptive Index and focuses on respondents' job satisfaction measurement. The third part which is based on Maslach Burnout Inventory (Maslach and Jackson 1981) consists of 21 questions and is oriented in burnout measurement. All the questions of these parts are adapted to a five-point Likert Scale. The fourth part of the questionnaire last but not least, the fourth part of the questionnaire consists of six questions relating to respondents' demographic characteristics.

Research Results

Questionnaire Reliability

Using Cronbach's Alpha coefficient, we will measure our questionnaire's reliability (Table 1).

Due to the data in the table above, the rate for organizational commitment is 0.861, for job satisfaction is 0.778 while for burnout is 0.8; these measures are considered reliable as their values are higher than 0.7.

Table 1 Cronbach's Alpha coefficient

	Cronbach's Alpha	No of items
Organizational commitment	0.861	10
Job satisfaction	0.778	8
Burnout	0.800	21

Table 2 Means and standard deviations of burnout scores

	Mean	Std. deviation
Emotional exhaustion	2.594	0.500
Depersonalization	2.568	0.449
Reduced personal accomplishment	3.006	0.449

Burnout Scores

The means and standard deviations of the three burnout subscales are shown in Table 2.

As seen in Table 2, three different scores are calculated: emotional exhaustion score, depersonalization score, and personal accomplishment score. It should be noted that higher degrees of burnout are recorded when the means of emotional exhaustion and depersonalization are high (Genc 2016). Furthermore, reduced personal accomplishment means higher degrees of burnout (Jesse et al. 2015).

Organizational Commitment Scores

The means and standard deviations of the three commitment subscales are shown in Table 3.

Based on the above results, we may conclude that the respondents tend to remain at their positions because they want to (affective commitment). The less important reason for them to remain at their positions is because they feel obligated to the firm (normative commitment).

Examination of the Relationship Between General Burnout Score and General Job Satisfaction Score

Due to the fact that the score variables derived from the sums of the constructs of these factors, they can be considered as scale ones. Furthermore, Kolmogorov Smirnov *p*-values are higher than 0.05 for all the variables. As far as the previous are concerned, we may use Pearson correlation coefficient to examine possible correlations between them.

Table 3 Means and standard deviations of organizational commitment scores

	Mean	Std. deviation
Affective commitment	3.549	0.855
Continuance commitment	3.500	0.841
Normative commitment	2.833	0.492

Table 4 Correlation coefficients

		General job satisfaction score	Emotional exhaustion score	Depersonalization score	Personal accomplishment score
General burnout score	Pearson correlation coefficient	−0.305	0.875	0.515	0.423
	p-value	0.001	0.000	0.000	0.000

Table 5 Correlation coefficients

		General job satisfaction score	Affective commitment score	Continuance commitment score	Normative Commitment score
General organizational commitment score	Pearson correlation coefficient	0.845	0.667	0.801	0.717
	p-value	0.000	0.000	0.000	0.000

A correlation matrix for general burnout score, general job satisfaction score and the scores of emotional exhaustion, depersonalization, and personal accomplishment is shown in Table 4.

Due to the data in Table 4, a negative correlation is confirmed between general burnout score and general job satisfaction score.

Examination of the Relationship Between General Organizational Commitment Score and General Job Satisfaction Score

As in this section we will examine score variables as well, Pearson correlation coefficient will be used in order to examine possible correlations.

Data in Table 5 may confirm that organizational commitment is positively correlated to job satisfaction. This correlation is high. This means that the higher levels of employee satisfaction mean higher levels of committed to a firm as well. As far as it is concerned, firms should try to adopt methods that may lead to higher levels of employee satisfaction.

Conclusions

This research explored the relationships between burnout, job satisfaction, and organizational commitment among employees of Greek SMEs.

According to the statistical analysis carried out, a negative correlation is confirmed between burnout and job satisfaction. Furthermore, a high positive correlation between organizational commitment and job satisfaction is recorded.

As far as it is concerned, job satisfaction, burnout, and organizational commitment have a critical importance for the SMEs. SMEs' managers should seek for ways to improve their employees' attitude in order to gain higher levels of job satisfaction and organizational commitment.

For a future research, it might be quite interesting to investigate the factors that lead in burnout, job satisfaction, and organizational commitment. This can be a useful tool for firms' managers as organizational presence and intervention in these cases may have a great importance for the early diagnosis and treatment of symptoms which associated with reduced job satisfaction and low organizational commitment.

References

Bockerman, P., and P. Ilmakunnas. 2010. *The job satisfaction-productivity nexus: A study using matched survey and register data*. Helsinki: Helsinki Center of Economic Research.

Genc, G. 2016. Learned resourcefulness and burnout levels of English teachers. *International Journal of Psychology and Educational Studies* 3 (1): 1–13.

Jahangir, F., and N. Shokrpour. 2009. Three components of organizational commitment and job satisfaction of hospital nurses in Iran. *The Health Care Manager* 28 (4): 375–380.

Jesse, M.T., M. Abouljoud, and A. Eshelman. 2015. Determinants of burnout among transplant surgeons: a national survey in the United States. *American Journal of Transplantation* 15: 772–778.

Knoop, R. 1995. Relationship among job involvement, job satisfaction and organizational commitment for nurses. *The Journal of Psychology* 129 (6): 643–649.

Maslach, C., and S.E. Jackson. 1981. *MBI: Maslach burnout inventory*. CA: Palo Alto.

Maslach, C., and S.E. Jackson. 1982. *Burn out in health professions: a social psychological analysis in social psychology at health and illness*. Lawrence NJ: Erlbaum Associates.

Meyer, J.P., and J. Allen. 1991. A three component conceptualization of organizational commitment. *Human Resource Management Review* 1: 64–89.

Meyer, J.P., D.J. Stanley, L. Hersovitch, and L. Topolnytsky. 2002. Affective, continuance and normative commitment to the organization: A meta-analysis of antecedents, correlates and consequences. *Journal of Vocational Behavior* 6 (1): 20–52.

Skordoulis, M., M. Chalikias., M. Koniordos. 2014. Students' satisfaction through DREEM and LOT-R. In *Communications in Computer and Information Science. 466: Knowledge-Based Software Engineering: Proceedings of 11th Joint Conference on Knowledge-Based software Engineering—JCKBSE*, eds. Kravets et al., pp. 113–122, Volgograd, Sep 2014, Switzerland: Springer International Publishing.

The Relationship Between Subordinates and Supervisors and the Impact on Job Satisfaction and Efficiency of the Employees

G. Tsitmideli, G. Sidiropoulos, M. Chalikias, D. Drosos and P. Kalantonis

Introduction

Contemporary business environment is becoming more and more competitive, which makes it difficult for any king of business to survive. Many business executives declare that the main factors connected to low employee efficiency deal with the reduction of their personal motivation and the decrease of their mood to work. Human resources are of great importance for modern organizations due to the fact that employees have become an important element of strategies leading them to a competitive advantage (Skordoulis et al. 2015).

Lots of researchers consider that job satisfaction is necessary for the prosperity of a business, while others believe that employee satisfaction is an unnecessary luxury (Valvi et al. 2009). According to Spector (2000), job satisfaction has a major influence on the prosperity of businesses and is presented through the increase of the employee performance.

According to Jewell and Siegall (1990), there is a positive correlation between job satisfaction and employee performance; more specifically, satisfied employees seem to be more productive. On the other hand, work displeasure means job stress and professional exhaustion (DeMato 2004).

Employee satisfaction is a multidimensional term which represents the overall attitude of a person and the feelings for specific aspects of his job (Kreither and Kinicki 2010). Herzberg et al. (1959), found that employee satisfaction is in high

G. Tsitmideli · G. Sidiropoulos · M. Chalikias (✉) · D. Drosos · P. Kalantonis
Business Administration Department, Piraeus University of Applied Sciences, Egaleo, Greece
e-mail: mchalikias@hotmail.com

A. Kavoura et al. (eds.), *Strategic Innovative Marketing*, Springer Proceedings in Business and Economics, DOI 10.1007/978-3-319-56288-9_9

levels in the first years of an employee's job, then declines with a culmination about 20 years of work, while is increased again when it is close to 30 years until the end of the employee's service.

The quality as well as the measurement of the satisfaction levels concerning the offered health care is a powerful evaluation tool for these specific services (Drosos et al. 2015). In healthcare sector, cooperation and balanced relationship between employees impose them to work together and provide high quality nursing services. One of the main healthcare sectors is that of obstetric which consists of clinics that provide obstetric and gynecological services. Nowadays, competition and economic crisis have a big impact on the survival of nursing and obstetric institutions. For this reason, staff must be satisfied from their job in order to be more efficient. The relationship between employees and supervisors is particularly interesting in this sector because high employee performance levels in an obstetric clinic are associated with the best of services.

The purpose of this research is to examine the relationship between supervisors and subordinates of the obstetric clinics sector and its impact on job satisfaction and efficiency.

Materials and Methods

The main aim of the paper is the investigation of those factors which influence job satisfaction and employee performance from the above relation. 130 employees who worked on obstetric clinics have responded to a special questionnaire which has been collected and statistically analyzed. Specifically 100 employees work in the administrative and in the nursing department sector and 30 supervisors are either in administrative or in nursing or in the scientific departments. The percentage of the sample which was extracted from each clinic was analogous to the size of the clinic.

Research Results

The Relationship Between Subordinates and Their Supervisors

The questionnaire responded by the supervisors, was designed to collect data concerning their opinions regarding subordinates' job satisfaction and department's increasing efficiency.

The departments' supervisors were asked if they believe that there is a correlation between job satisfaction and employee efficiency. According to Jewell and Siegall (1990), there is correlation between job satisfaction and employee performance and especially, the most productive employees are more satisfied with their work. 18 supervisors strongly agreed with the fact that there is a correlation between job satisfaction and employee efficiency.

Furthermore, a 50% of supervisors strongly agreed with the fact that job satisfaction is necessary for welfare in a clinic. According to Spector (2000), job satisfaction significantly affects businesses prosperity and is presented through the increased employee performance. It makes sense that a satisfied employee is a productive employee.

Supervisors, who motivate subordinates are aimed to take responsibility, to make efforts for achieving goals. From the responses of subordinates, it was confirmed that 67% of them strongly agree with the fact that a supervisors' role leads in job satisfaction and subordinates' increasing performance. Also, 29 out of 30 departments' supervisors agreed with the fact that subordinates' activation is a concern for senior management and goals achievement depends on the cooperation with human resources.

Ranking of the Main Factors Which Influence the Job Satisfaction and Employee Performance in the Obstetrics Sector

As job satisfaction and employee performance at the clinic are concerned, it was revealed that the main factor affecting them is the relationship developed between senior managers and employees. The factor which affects less these constructs is this of business policies along with the culture of the clinic. The following table shows the factors affecting job satisfaction and employee performance the most (Table 1).

Table 1 Job satisfaction and performance

	Mean	Std. Deviation
Business policies	3.52	1.01
Stress level and daily pressure	3.67	1.01
The feeling that you rewarded fairly	3.7	1.11
A chance for development	3.8	0.92
Job certainty	3.83	1.02
Job description	3.98	0.89
Relationship with the supervisor	4.04	0.98

Table 2 Components matrix for the factors affecting job satisfaction and employee performance

	F1	F2
Business policies	0.788	
Chances for development	0.770	
Job certainty	0.692	
The feeling of being rewarded fairly	0.676	
Job description	0.668	
Stress level and daily pressure		0.833
Relationship with the supervisor		0.679

Factor Analysis on the Constructs Affecting Job Satisfaction and Employee Performance

The subordinates took part in the research were asked to express their views on the extent job satisfaction and performance is affected. A factor analysis is used to order to categorize these constructs.

According to Table 2 data, the examined variables were categorized into two dimensions:

- workplace characteristics and,
- emotional factors developed in the workplace.

Conclusions

According to the statistical analysis carried out, the subordinates' responses show that their job satisfaction and performance are eventually affected by the relationship that is developed between them and their supervisors. Furthermore, the supervisors' responses showed that the achievement of corporate goals and the welfare of the clinic are influenced by the relationship between them and their subordinates as well.

The second conclusion that can be drawn is that the behavioral features of a supervisor may influence the effectiveness of a department. Three are the most important behavioral features with the highest effect namely, the rewards for a great performance, the recognition of an excellent service, and the use of development inspection method by monitoring the work of each employee. Moreover, employees seem to be efficient when they enjoy the favors of their supervisors.

Thus, departments' supervisors should take seriously into account this finding as it is important for the success of their departments.

References

DeMato, D.S. 2004. Job satisfaction of elementary school counselors: A new look. *Professional School Counseling* 7: 236–245.

Drosos, D., N. Tsotsolas., A. Zagga., M Chalikias., and M. Skordoulis. 2015. Multicriteria satisfaction analysis application in the health care sector. In *Proceedings of the 7th international conference on information and communication technologies in agriculture, food and environment—HAICTA 2015*, 737–754, Sep 17–20, Kavala, Greece.

Herzberg, F., B. Mausner, and B.B. Snyderman. 1959. *The motivation to work*. NY: John Wileyand Sons Inc.

Jewell, L.N., and M. Siegall. 1990. *Contemporary industrial and organizational psychology*, 2nd ed. MI: West Publishing Company.

Kreither, R., and A. Kinicki. 2010. *Organizational behavior*, 9th ed. NY: McGraw Hill.

Schultz, P., and E. Schultz. 1994. *Psychology and work today*, 6th ed. NY: McMillan.

Skordoulis, M., M. Chalikias., D. Drosos., and M. Koniordos. (2015). Staff recruitment process and methods: The case of the mobile telephony industry in Greece. Communications in Computer and Information Science, Vol. 535, Switzerland: Springer. In *Proceedings of the 1st international conference on creativity in intelligent, technologies and data science—CIT&DS 2015*, 292–306, Sep 15–17, Volgograd, Russia.

Spector, P.E. 2000. *Industrial and organizational psychology: Research and practice*, 2nd ed. NY: Wiley.

Valvi, A., and K. Frangos. 2009. Is employee productivity associated with job satisfaction? *Review of Job Relations* 53: 83–90. (In Greek).

Vaskova, R. 2006. Gender differences in performance motivation. European observatory of working life. http://www.eurofound.europa.eu/observatories/eurwork/articles/gender-differences-in-performance-motivation. Accessed 12 Sep 2016.

Part IV
6th Symposium on Management Challenges (IANOS): Crisis Kills or Links?

Organized by: Panagiotis Trivellas
Department of Logistics Management, TEI of Central Greece, Lamia, Greece

Description

This symposium attempts to cast light on concurrent advances on the fields of organizational behavior, HRM, innovation and knowledge management, strategic leadership, sustainability, SCM, and higher education. Diverse and modern perspectives on the development and evolution of the relative disciplines on regional and national levels will be discussed and debated. However, does the current crisis impose threats to survival (kills?) or yield opportunities for changes and synergies to growth (links?)? Are the same fundamental cornerstones such as leadership, strategy, knowledge, and innovation produce both excellence and perish? (Knowledge Innovation Leadership Learning Strategy: KILLS?, Leadership Innovation Networking Knowledge Strategy: LINKS?) In the light of the current recession, this symposium aims to track different views, discuss and publish research on the challenges in the field of management which influence societies, cultures, networks, organizations, teams, and individuals. Furthermore, this session will put a special emphasis on the investigation of those business processes fostering innovation and facilitating management transitions from dominant structures to more evolutionary, developmental paradigms.

The Role of Organizational Culture in the Greek Higher Tourism Quality

D. Belias, E. Velissariou, A. Koustelios, K. Varsanis, D. Kyriakou and L. Sdrolias

Introduction

The tourism industry constitutes one of the most important sectors in many local economies in Greece, mainly because of its constant increasing contribution to the income of these regions, but also due to the opportunities offered for further growth (Karakitsiou et al. 2007). Tourism is one of the most dominant industries at a global level that affect the world's economy. On the other hand, quality is related to the customers' satisfaction and to the extent to which organizations meet their customer's expectations. So quality is considered as the main determinant of customer satisfaction, which in turn influences purchase intentions (Spreng and Mckoy 1996).

Organizations seem to adopt a philosophy of continuous improvement in terms of quality. Nowadays the world is a fast paced and rapidly changing environment, where organizational culture of a company plays a huge role in its effectiveness. It turns out to be one of the key components for success and sustainability with a focus on higher quality for customer satisfaction.

D. Belias (✉) · A. Koustelios
Department of Physical Education and Sport Science, University of Thessaly, Trikala, Greece
e-mail: dbelias@pe.uth.gr

E. Velissariou · L. Sdrolias
Department of Business Administration, Technological Educational Institute of Thessaly Greece, Larissa, Greece

K. Varsanis
Department of Business Administration, Technological Educational Institute of Western Macedonia, Kozani, Greece

D. Kyriakou
Department of Economic Sciences, Aristotle University of Thessaloniki, Thessaloniki, Greece

A. Kavoura et al. (eds.), *Strategic Innovative Marketing*, Springer Proceedings in Business and Economics, DOI 10.1007/978-3-319-56288-9_10

Methodology

The methodology that was used in this paper is the critical review of the current literature. Relevant literature selection was derived from popular online bibliographic databases, like Science Direct, Emerald, EBSCO host, and scientific search engines like Google Scholar. Also, general search engines like Google have been used. The types of bibliographic sources included in the research are articles published on scientific journals, books, conference proceedings, company papers and studies, white papers, online sites, and online journals. The selection of these literature sources was made on the basis of relevance to the topic of the paper and it is not exhaustive.

Literature Review

Organizational Culture

The organizational culture of a company consists of the setting of values, rules, and priorities that are followed by the personnel and all the individuals that are involved in it. These values are beliefs and ideas about what kinds of goals members of an organization should pursue and ideas about the appropriate modes or standards of behavior organizational members execute to achieve these goals (Hill and Jones 2001).

Over the years, this system of shared assumptions, values, and beliefs has gained more and more attention to the organization's management. A definition by Schein (1985) states that organizational culture is "a pattern of basic assumptions-invented, discovered or developed by a group as it learns to cope with its problems of external adaptation and internal integration that has worked well enough to be considered valid and, therefore, to be taught to new members as the correct way to perceive, think and feel in relation to those processes". All of the above have a strong influence on the personnel's behavior and dictate the way they behave during their job duties partially or even totally.

Organizational culture provides guidelines and boundaries for the behavior of the members of the company. Some characteristics that deal with the organizational culture are linked with an orientation toward the results and the outcomes. Emphasis on the people of the company is important because they also affect the company through their actions and way of implementing tasks. Denison (1984) highlights the importance of an organization possessing a "strong" culture, by "exhibiting a well integrated and effective set of specific values, beliefs and behaviors, which will lead to a higher level of productivity performance". Sathe (1985) emphasized in "Organizational culture in terms of meanings and understandings with a focus on cognitive aspects. Culture as something being shared, which is distinctive and unique". Efficiency, reflexivity, innovation and flexibility, supervisory support, and quality are among the most salient characteristics that influence the organizational culture of a company and contribute to its performance. These elements are also obtained using simulation modeling of the corresponding processes (Dimitrios et al. 2013a, b).

Greek Higher Tourism Quality

OECD (2009) suggests that “it is essential for attracting investment to continue improving the quality of both the cultural and tourism offer. Convincing residents of the benefits of tourism development is increasingly crucial as they come to form the core of the cultural and creative tourism experience”. It also implies that “whole series of steps need to be taken in order to develop a successful synergy between culture and tourism, and these need an adequate strategy to be established (2009)”. During the last decades, there has been a turn to high quality services concerning tourism industry in Greece. This enables companies such as hotels and restaurants to become more competitive with a focus customer orientation.

Quality matters to a high extent and it is inherently linked with customer satisfaction, performance, and success. For example, hotels survival depends on the satisfaction of the clientèle needs with the high level of customer satisfaction leading to higher loyalty (Lavlak and Right 2003). Despite Greece suffering from the economic crisis, the Greek tourism industry is still developing and opportunities arise. This makes the need for higher quality a necessity and vital to the company’s implementation of strategic planning. Not only it is essential for attracting more customers, but it is also an important tool for the operational effectiveness and efficiency. Quality especially in services based companies is a decisive key component of the overall business operation. The right skilful personnel and the dominant organizational culture contribute to the satisfaction of the customer. Especially in a face-to-face service business, high quality without a doubt coexists with customer and employee satisfaction levels. This practically means that high performance and good communication among staff are creating a well-based infrastructure to increase quality and boost efficiency (Trivellas and Reklitis 2014).

By measuring customer satisfaction, a company can evaluate its current position among rivalry and identify any potential market opportunity. In addition, through understanding the customers’ expectations, a company can realize what needs and desires need to be fulfilled. The expected behavior is also a characteristic that most of the companies within the industry try to predict and be well prepared for. Tourism industry is heavily influenced by a significant number of factors from the external environment. Therefore it is more than necessary to improve the quality of the services that are offered in order to protect competitive advantages and increase customer’s loyalty at a high level Trivellas et al. (2015a, b) and Vasiliadis et al. (2015). After all, customer’s satisfaction is the result of interaction between his experience and the actual expectations he had. This involves characteristics that are linked with accommodation, food consumption, natural and urban environment, hospitality, and entertainment. Furthermore, it should be emphasized that overall satisfaction is strongly related to all three loyalty measures (revisit intention, recommendation, and confirmation of expectations) which is consistent with the relative literature (Grigoroudis and Siskos 2010). All these are necessary for the decision-making process, the positioning of products and services and the market segmentation analysis. Overall, the organizational culture enhances both sides; the effectiveness of the company and the individual's well-being (Dekoulou and Trivellas 2014).

Discussion

As Watson suggests: "an important trend in managerial thinking in recent decades has been one of encouraging managers to try to create strong organizational cultures" (2006). But connoisseurs claim that a stable culture and a seemingly strong culture do not always indicate an efficient and quality oriented culture. Thus, it is not always a common sense that a culture with strongly and commonly shared attitudes, values, and beliefs is able to survive and prosper. This is also due to the fact that goals, beliefs, and attitudes should from time to time be reviewed and changed according to the possible changes that occur within the business environment. If an organization continuously remains stable then endorsing the same beliefs might prove to be cumbersome and not positive to change. It is not only about how strong organizations support their beliefs, but also about the quality of the beliefs that they support. As Schein (2004) states: "the concept of culture is the climate and practices that organizations develop around their handling of people" (2004). It is clear that when organizations ensure employee commitment through culture awareness programs, team-oriented projects, and initiatives then it is more possible to achieve a climate suitable for change that further endorses the relevant culture that is advocated by managers Trivellas and Dargenidou (2009).

Conclusion

The competitive advantage of Greece lies in the tourism industry and it emerges from the fact that it possesses a highly good reputation and fame due to its Mediterranean climate and its natural pristine beauties. As it is mentioned by the National Tourism Organization: "The tourism industry constitutes a vitally important economic sector, occupying the most prominent place in the Greek economy, by contributing to its development. At the same time, the industry is elevating the country to one of the top 10 destinations worldwide" (2012).

Nevertheless competition is intense within the country. Therefore quality expectations rise and companies trust to make their customers more loyal in order to achieve a long lasting relationship that may also affect other people through recommendations or even word of mouth. So an emphasis is given in fulfilling customer's expectations. Managers are aware that they could not achieve this without having a proper organizational culture that will boost effectiveness and efficiency in all levels and aspects. For having an improved performance, companies adopt practices that aim on boosting quality and also try to achieve synergies between it and the organizational culture of the company (Trivellas et al. 2012).

Suggestions for Further Research

Future researches should try to have an insight on how the organizational culture can be directly measured in relations with quality of the service that is provided to customers. Through identifying the organizational climate that dominates a company managers will be able to optimize the overall performance by identifying inherent strengths and weaknesses. They can also exploit the opportunities that are offered and create more competitive advantages that can assist them in avoiding future risks and threats. In addition, variations in perceptions between managers and lower level personnel should be examined in order to identify what are the priorities in common among all employees.

References

Dekoulou, P., and P. Trivellas. 2014. Learning organization in Greek advertising and media industry: A way to face crisis and gain sustainable competitive advantage. *Procedia—Social and Behavioral Sciences* 148: 338–347.

Denison, D.R. 1984. Corporate culture to the bottom line. *Organizational Dynamics* 13 (2): 5–22.

Grigoroudis, E., and Y. Siskos. 2010. Preference disaggregation for measuring and analysing customer satisfaction: The MUSA method. *European Journal of Operational Research* 143 (1): 148–170.

Hill, C.W.L., and G.R. Jones. 2001. *Strategic management*, 5th ed. Houghton Mifflin: Means Business Inc.

Karakitsiou, A., A. Mavrommati, A. Migdalas, and K. Tsiakali. 2007. Customer satisfaction evaluation in the tourism industry: The case of Chania. *Foundations of Computing and Decision Sciences* 32 (2): 111–124.

Lavlak, C., and L. Right. 2003. *Marketing principles and services*. Abolfazl Tajzadeh (trans): Semat Press.

Dimitrios, N.K., Sakas, D.P., Vlachos, D.S. 2013a. Analysis of strategic leadership simulation models in non-profit organizations. *Procedia—Social and Behavioral Sciences*, 276–284.

Dimitrios, N.K., Sakas, D.P., Vlachos, D.S. 2013b. Analysis of strategic leadership models in information technology. *Procedia—Social and Behavioral Sciences*, 268–275.

OECD. 2009. The impact of culture on tourism.

Sathe, V. 1985. *Culture and related corporate realities: text, cases, and readings on organizational entry, establishment, and change*. Homewood: Irwin.

Schein, E.H. 2004. *Organizational culture and leadership*, 3rd ed. San Francisco: Jossey-Bass.

Schein, E.H. 1985. *Organizational culture and leadership: A dynamic view*. San Francisco: Jossey-Bass Publishers.

Spreng, R.A., and R.D. McKoy. 1996. An empirical examination of a model of perceived. Watson, T.J. 2006. *Organising and managing work*, UK: Pearson Education Limited.

Trivellas, P., and D. Dargenidou. 2009. Organisational culture, job satisfaction and higher education service quality. *The TQM Journal* 21 (4): 382–399.

Trivellas, P., N. Kakos., L. Vasiliadis., and D. Belias. 2015a. Sustainability, social marketing & host attitudes about tourism in the city of Larissa. In 2nd international conference on Strategic Innovative Marketing, ICSIM-2015, Sept 24–27, in Myconos, Greece.

Trivellas, P., N. Kakos., L. Vasiliadis., and D. Belias. 2015b. Residents' perceptions toward cultural, social and economic benefits and costs of tourism industry: An empirical survey, second international conference IACuDiT, At Springer proceedings in business and economics, volume: Tourism and culture in the age of innovation.

Trivellas, P., and P. Reklitis. 2014. Leadership competencies profiles and managerial effectiveness in Greece. *Procedia Economics and Finance*, 9(Ebeec 2013), 380–390.

Trivellas, P., P. Ipsilantis, I. Papadopoulos., and D. Kantas. 2012. Challenges for quality manage-ment in higher education-investigating institutional leadership, culture and performance. Quality assurance and management, 103–129.

Vasiliadis, L., P. Trivellas., D. Belias., and J. Meleas. 2015. Cultural tourism revisited: The case of Thessaly, second international conference IACuDiT, At Springer proceedings in business and economics, Volume: Tourism and culture in the age of innovation.

Integrating Total Quality Management Philosophy in the Greek Tourism Sector

D. Belias, E. Velissariou, A. Koustelios, K. Varsanis, D. Kyriakou and L. Sdrolias

Introduction

Quality is about meeting or even exceeding the customers' expectations. Nowadays most of the companies in all kind of industries pay lots of their attention to it because through continuous improvement of their offered products and services; they struggle for becoming better. This strategy is of vital importance in the tourism sector and especially to countries like Greece where tourism has a crucial role in the country's economic sustainability.

The tourism market contributes to a high extent into the endogenous development. Thus an emphasis in improving the quality is a thing to be done by all business units that want to be progressive and respond to challenges effectively.

D. Belias (✉) · A. Koustelios
Department of Physical Education and Sport Science, University of Thessaly, Trikala, Greece
e-mail: dbelias@pe.uth.gr

E. Velissariou · L. Sdrolias
Department of Business Administration, Technological Educational Institute of Thessaly Greece, Larissa, Greece

K. Varsanis
Department of Business Administration, Technological Educational Institute of Western Macedonia, Kozani, Greece

D. Kyriakou
Department of Economic Sciences, Aristotle University of Thessaloniki, Thessaloniki, Greece

A. Kavoura et al. (eds.), *Strategic Innovative Marketing*, Springer Proceedings in Business and Economics, DOI 10.1007/978-3-319-56288-9_11

Methodology

The methodology that was used in this paper is the critical review of the current literature. Relevant literature selection was derived from popular online bibliographic databases, like Science Direct, Emerald, EBSCO host and scientific search engines like Google Scholar. Also, general search engines like Google have been used. The types of bibliographic sources included in the research are articles published on scientific journals, books, conference proceedings, company papers and studies, white papers, online sites and online journals. The selection of these literature sources was made on the basis of relevance to the topic of the paper and it is not exhaustive.

Literature Review

Total Quality Management (TQM)

"TQM is a process-oriented organizational philosophy focusing on quality management and aiming at customer satisfaction through the improvement of product and service quality" (Mehra et al. 2001). As it is commonly accepted, the term quality concerns the ability to meet or exceed what the customer expects. In order to do so, each type of organization needs to be aware of the characteristics that add value to the customer and lead to increased loyalty and satisfaction rates (Evans and Lindsay 2010). These are linked with offering improved quality of goods or services, cost reduction, sustainability, and increase in profits. Another definition of Quality Management was provided by the International Organization for Standardization (ISO). In detail, quality management is seen as the activities which engage in the determination of quality objectives, responsibility, and overall quality policies. The latter are implemented in order to proceed to quality control, quality planning, quality improvement, and quality assurance.

The idea of TQM emerged due to the fact that quality has a rather broad scope and sense. It focuses on people rather than in quality control and aims at the customer satisfaction and the continuous improvement of product and service quality. In order to determine the parameters of the quality, specific components of organizations are useful. In specific, the parameters of quality should involve aspects such as human resource utilization, leadership, planning for quality, information and analysis, quality results quality assurance of products and customer satisfaction. Total Quality Management is a process that involves all employees within an organization at all levels.

After all, the key for future success within a mutable environment is to keep evolving though flexibility and adaption to changes. The process itself not only it involves but also engages the employees to establish procedures and standards in pursuit of fulfilling expectations. This is achieved strategically by giving an emphasis on principles such as good understanding, sharing, and responding to customers through marketing concept and thus achieve a advantage against their competitors.

The Importance of TQM in the Tourism Sector

Nowadays, as Fayos-Sola clearly state the development requirements are considered to be integrated values. Those values depend mostly on tourism quality in all sectors of the respective economy and less on the economies of scale. It is important to note that tourism quality was based up to 1996 on economies of scale. To this end, current tourism-related businesses demonstrate an average product cost reduction orientation.

The main concept of Total Quality Management lies within the integration of the whole supply chain process. It is a management tool that enables organizations to monitor products and services provided from a different point of view which is pretty crucial. The customers' angle can provide a great opportunity to interfere with the planned and systematic procedures and activities that aim in developing customers' experience overall. In order to focus on quality assurance an emphasis should be given on quality control and design, especially during the delivery of the service or good (Evans and Lindsay 2010).

A quality service management system is mainly results-oriented. As Reyad mentions, end-users are mostly interested in service characteristics. Thus, quality service management deals with the providers of those services that have tangible results to demonstrate to their customers. Under this perspective, high quality of service is guaranteed during their stay. Additionally, staff knows how it can commit to the high-quality service provision (2005). Regarding the hospitality sector, the concept of quality is widely discussed concerning delivery of products and guest services. Organizations should decisively perform according to expected standards.

When such offers to customers meet or even exceed their expectations then they are willing to pay more for this extra quality that they received. As Hayes, Ninemeier, and Miller imply service quality is actually an experience for the guests during their stay/visit in lodging units (2011).

When tourism-related organization creates value for its customers then it is more likely to maintain these customers also in the future. This is crucial because experience shows that retaining the same customers can be less expensive and less time consuming that trying to get new customers, Trivellas et al. (2015a, b) and Vasiliadis et al. (2015). Within a highly competitive market like Greece where rivalry is intense, the idea of focusing in quality is increasingly accepted especially by hotel businesses no matter the size. Customers also seem to appreciate this idea and they are becoming more conscious regarding their rights and their anticipations. Soteriadis and Varvaressos also confirm that high service quality has been used by hotels in order to establish competitive advantages. To this end, under this perspective quality management can assist hotel companies to increase their competitiveness (2006). Development can be achieved through stepping into the shoes of customers, consider what their expectations are and carefully design the succeeding procedures. In addition, by empowering the staff and through appropriate training a company can secure the constant implementation of the process and secure it. Furthermore, self-evaluation via measuring tools is very important in order to apply modifications and potential changes. Feedback is necessary and quality standards needs to be updated and keep up with trends.

Discussion

TQM has contributed to the solution of various organizational problems and to the organizational performance improvement (Joiner 2007). Nevertheless, there are strong evidence that the level of its implementation might differ among different organizations and especially hotels. Overall, though, TQM seems to have a positive influence in the performance of those organizations. The results are visible in all levels, from enforcement of teamwork and better reward systems till the empowerment of service details and customer feedback.

Trivellas and Reklitis (2014) also claim that "job satisfaction is directly related to staff's values and opinions about the working conditions and the climate, human relations and communication, security and supervisory support, teamwork and flexibility". Thus enabling the business is becoming more responsive to changes that arise from both internal and external sources. This leads to the mitigation of uncertainty in decision-making process and to the fulfillment of the customers' needs appropriately. TQM and market orientation are related and are both catalysts to the performance of the organization. This is so critical specifically if we consider how mutable factors of the external environment can be and that changes can occur fast. Furthermore, it is logical to pursue quality accreditation under the schemes of EFQM, ISO and Eco-labels.

Conclusion

Tourism is the key element of development for a country like Greece. This can be attributed to its contribution to the country's GDP and GNP, encouragement of investments, increase of employment and development of the economy in a dynamic way. The integration of this development through the focus on quality results in the development of valuable and unique production coefficients in the local economies. Additionally, businesses operating the sector can be clustered according to the needs of niche/specialized markets. Tourism industry, as a service sector appears to be associated closely with the provision of high-level services and to an extent quality. In the long run, TQM provides opportunities that lead to differentiation of products and services provided. This enforces the organization with competitive advantages that benefit the sustainability of the organization. After all, quality assurance is not a short-term process but a long term commitment and cooperation with the customers.

A proper identification and recording of the impact should be implemented in order to reassure the quality and set priorities. There are various mechanisms that aim to deliver quality within the tourism services. They have to deal with the involvement of the customers in the standardization in the quality process that allows them to measure quality. Thus the organization will be able to make improvements and more investments. The most important factors related to businesses' success are related with customers' satisfaction and their retention throughout the years. As it is mentioned earlier it can be much more difficult and costly to attract new customers than try to maintain the customers you have now. This can be achieved by providing incentives that fulfill the customers' expectations or even exceed them. Continuous improvement of quality, regular training of the personnel, as well as, customer orientation is crucial to the organization's sustainability in the long run. These elements are also obtained using simulation modeling of the corresponding processes (Sakas et al. 2014, 2015).

Suggestions for Further Research

Further improvement and excellence in terms of service quality is required for modern tourism businesses. More researches could be made regarding the overall customers' experiences that provide a more comprehensive aspect. Quality might differ depending on the customer's perception and background and this has much to do with culture. So an organization should take into account the different groups of tourists it serves and customize the experience it provides since experiences are rather personal and only exist to one's mind (Pine and Gilmore 1999). Time of responding is crucial nowadays, so organizations should be proactive rather than proactive. For that reason, an insight to the upcoming trends would be necessary; not only at a level of Greece but also at a worldwide level.

References

Evans, R.J., and M.W. Lindsay. 2010. *Managing for quality and performance excellence*. USA: South-Western Cengage Learning.

Fayos-Sola, E. 1996. Tourism policy: A midsummer night's dream? *Tourism Management* 17 (6): 405–412. Elsevier Science.

Hayes, K.D., D.J. Ninemeier, and A.A. Miller. 2011. *Foundations of lodging management*. UK: Pearson Education.

International Standard, Quality Management and Quality Assurance-Vocabulary. ISO 8402:1994 (E/F/R), 2nd ed. 1/4/1994, 16.

Joiner, T.A. 2007. Total quality management and performance: The role of organization support and co-worker support. *International Journal of Quality and Reliability Management* 24 (6): 617–627.

Mehra, S., J.M. Hoffman, and D. Sirias. 2001. TQM as a management strategy for the next millennia. *International Journal of Operations and Production Management* 21 (5/6): 855–876.

Pine, J., and J. Gilmore. 1999. *The experience economy: Work is theatre and every business is a stage*. Boston: Harvard Business School Press.

Sakas, Damianos P., Dimitris Vlachos, and Nasiopoulos K. Dimitrios. 2014. Modelling strategic management for the development of competitive advantage, based on technology. *Journal of Systems and Information Technology* 16 (3): 187–209. doi:10.1108/JSIT-01-2014-0005.

Sakas, Damianos P., Nasiopoulos K. Dimitrios, and Androniki Kavoura. 2015. The development of Facebook's competitive advantage for brand awareness. *Procedia Economics and Finance* 589–597.

Soteriadis, M., and S. Varvaressos. 2006. Quality Service in Hotel Businesses, Centre International de Recherches et d'Etudes Touristiques, Collection Studies and Reports, Série C, Volume C-8, Aix-en-Provence.

Trivellas, P., N. Kakos, L. Vasiliadis, and D. Belias. 2015a. Sustainability, social marketing and host attitudes about Tourism in the city of Larissa. In *2nd international conference on strategic innovative marketing, ICSIM-2015*, Sept 24–27, Myconos, Greece.

Trivellas, P., N. Kakos, L. Vasiliadis, and D. Belias. 2015b. Residents' perceptions toward cultural, social and economic benefits and costs of tourism industry: An empirical survey, second international conference IACuDiT. In *Springer Proceedings in Business and Economics, Volume: Tourism and Culture in the Age of Innovation.*

Trivellas, P., and Reklitis, P. 2014. Leadership competencies profiles and managerial effectiveness in Greece. *Procedia Economics and Finance* 9 (Ebeec 2013), 380–390.

Vasiliadis, L., P. Trivellas, D. Belias, and J. Meleas. 2015. Cultural tourism revisited: The case of Thessaly, second international conference IACuDiT. In *Springer Proceedings in Business and Economics, Volume: Tourism and Culture in the Age of Innovation.*

The Role of Organizational Culture in Greek Higher Education Quality

D. Belias, D. Kyriakou, A. Koustelios, K. Varsanis and L. Sdrolias

Greek Higher Education and Quality Assurance

Higher education in Greece has undergone a process of changes due to recent economic and political conditions of Greece. The economic recession has affected higher education in multiple ways, among which budget reduction is the most important. Higher education institutions have been forced to seek new resources and revise their management practices, in order to adjust to the contemporary situation. Considering the market forces of competition and socioeconomic conditions, the political context and students' learning experiences and expectations, it is legitimate to apply the marketing paradigm in tertiary education (Trivellas et al. 2012). This implies the improvement of higher education quality, namely improvement in the accuracy, clarity and reliability of the delivered services (Trivellas and Dargenidou 2009). Moreover, globalization and international

D. Belias (✉) · A. Koustelios
Department of Physical Education and Sport Science, University of Thessaly,
Trikala, Greece
e-mail: dbelias@pe.uth.gr

D. Kyriakou
Department of Economic Sciences, Aristotle University of Thessaloniki,
Thessaloniki, Greece

K. Varsanis
Department of Business Administration, Technological Educational Institute
of Western Macedonia, Kozani, Greece

L. Sdrolias
Department of Business Administration, Technological Educational Institute
of Central Greece, Psachna, Greece

A. Kavoura et al. (eds.), *Strategic Innovative Marketing*, Springer Proceedings in Business and Economics, DOI 10.1007/978-3-319-56288-9_12

competition have added more issues to be addressed (Denison and Mishra 1995; Dimitrios and Trivella 2015).

Despite large amounts of expenditures on education and the increased number of students in higher education institutions, in comparison with other OECD countries, quality was not a concern, as academic staff was not increased respectively and appropriate procedures were not followed, mainly due to political pressures (Trivellas et al. 2012). Furthermore, autonomy of higher education in Greece is only reflected on educational activities and research projects (Trivellas et al. 2012).

The European guidelines for the improvement of higher education quality draws attention to the adjustment of curricula to the current labor market needs, so that entrepreneurship is promoted (EUR-Lex 2011). In consistence with these European guidelines, national authorities must address the key issues of transparency, diversification, mobility, and cooperation (EUR-Lex 2011). The Greek Law 3374/2005 stresses that quality assurance is a "systematic, structured and continuous commitment to quality", through the establishment of criteria and regular internal and external assessment (Hellenic Quality Assurance).

In Greece, the new reforms require that state intervention is limited and focus is drawn to quality assurance and accountancy (Zeri 2007). Moreover, it is implied that entrepreneurship, innovativeness, and experimentation are values which can promote quality of teaching and administration (Trivellas and Dargenidou 2009). Diversification is also promoted, so that uniformity is substituted by the creation of different strategic planning for each institution. However, there is the risk of great limitations imposed in certain universities, due to the unequal distribution of resources, because of the financial crisis, which may lead to negative evaluations (Zeri 2007).

Attempts to reform the regulatory context of higher education and recent improvements were either rejected by academics or failed to be implemented due to the financial crisis (Trivellas et al. 2012). It is possible that quality assurance systems failed because the staff was unprepared or unwilling for change, which causes instability, and because they might feel additional work load due to the pressure to respond to external scrutiny, bureaucracy, and accountability processes (Trivellas and Dargenidou 2009). According to Zeri (2007), reforms failed due to weak leadership and the existing organizational culture.

The Hellenic Quality Assurance Agency for Higher Education was the benchmark of the introduction of a system of quality assurance in Greek tertiary education. As an independent body, it is responsible for monitoring and supervising, coordinating and supporting evaluation procedures, without, however, controlling or intervening. Its purpose is the creation of a reference point, in the form of a unified quality assurance system, so that the state makes informed decisions about supporting higher education institutions (Hellenic Quality Assurance). However, only half of Greek institutions have followed the procedures guided by the Hellenic Quality Assurance Agency (Trivellas et al. 2012).

Quality in Education

From the numerous definitions of quality, one concludes that it can be described as the conformance to requirements that meet customers' needs and expectations (Prajogo and McDermott 2011; Trivellas et al. 2012). There has been drawn a distinction between higher education customers, as internal customers are the ones who are engaged in the learning process, while external customers are considered to be the future employers and employees, who expect that higher institutions prepare and equip students for their future career (Rinehart 1993, cited in Trivellas et al. 2012).

Trivellas et al. (2012) noticed that higher education universities had focused on a more insular view, by assessing internal resources, based on the conviction that these were the determinants of quality. Moreover, institutions had focused on external customers, rather than internal customers and students' perceptions of service quality, also ignoring employees' views about teaching and administration. However, due to a shift of focus into performance, and therefore, the outcomes of service, rather than the resources, higher education institutions started pursuing quality management. It is widely accepted that quality should be determined by the stakeholders. Students and graduates and their families, academic employees and administration staff, employers, governmental bodies, the local and the wider community should be the assessors of quality, regardless of their diverse perceptions of quality (Trivellas and Dargenidou 2009; Trivellas et al. 2012). As students are regarded to be customers, it is suggested that they should also be educated in what they need by higher education institutions, rather than being satisfied in terms of their desires (Trivellas et al. 2012).

Trivellas et al. (2012) draw attention to the promotion and reinforcement of initiatives that target effectiveness and sustainability, which is also suggested by the Institutional Management in Higher Education (2010) launched by OECD, highlighting the reduction of public funding due to the global crisis. Five years before, UNESCO (2005) had published Guidelines for ensuring quality of international higher education and the provision of high-quality education to the students.

Internationalization is also another issue which should also be addressed (Trivellas et al. 2012) at a national level, but in consistency with EU actions (EUR-Lex 2011). Integrating an international dimension to higher education, research and functions of educational institutions can be interpreted as the way higher education responds to globalization (Knight 1997) and it should, therefore, be considered in terms of quality.

Organizational Culture

As the values of an institution change in order to adapt to requirements of quality, organizational culture is brought into scope (Lagrosen 2003). The relationship between organizational culture and effectiveness is established in the literature

(Denison and Mishra 1995; Prajogo 2008; Prajogo and McDermott 2011). Although no definition is unanimously accepted, most of the attempts to define organizational culture have some common points. The most integrative and consistent explanation seems to be the following: "culture consists of some combination of artifacts (…), values and beliefs, and underlying assumptions that organizational members share about appropriate behavior" (Detert et al. 2000, p. 851, cited in Prajogo and McDermott 2011, p. 713). In the literature, organizational culture is studied in terms of content and strength. The first aspect involves the values and behaviors of the members, while the latter lies in the integration of these values and behaviors among the members (Prajogo 2008; Prajogo and McDermott 2011; Schein 2004).

Schein (2004) explains that culture is interrelated with leadership, as it is affected by leadership behavior, while concurrently it constitutes the essence of leadership. The creation and management of culture in an organization constrain the stakeholders' behavior, but it simultaneously provides stability, cohesion, and meaning. It is essential that a leader manages to identify the limitations and make changes to adapt the organizational culture to contemporary conditions.

Intellectual, managerial, and emotional competencies of leadership have been found to be linked with leadership success in diverse contexts, although different profiles have been related to different circumstances. Therefore, additional competencies are required for a leader to be successful in each environment (Trivellas and Reklitis 2014), but most importantly, leadership should address resistance to change and infuse members with a shared mission.

However, this constantly evolving process includes the creation of group identity and group learning process, so that it is embedded in all the organizational operations and functions. Nevertheless, the importance of the role of the individual is highlighted in the literature, as each organizational member should be taken into consideration both as an agent and as a subject of a system, as individuals influence structures and are concurrently affected by them (Prajogo 2008; Prajogo and McDermott 2011).

The basic concerns regarding organizational culture are the adaptation to external environmental conditions and the integration of the internal processes, which ensures the capacity to adapt. Regarding the first, organizational culture is considered to be an integral part of the process of external adaptation. It includes complex phenomena from group structures to individual behaviors and core beliefs to objective artifacts. It is suggested that there should be a shared mission which provides the basis for the goals that are to be set and attained through agreed upon means. A consensus on the criteria for measurement can provide insight and concrete data for the effectiveness of the organization, as well as the appropriate information for remedial actions to implement, in case a need for correction emerges. As for internal integration, specific issues should be taken into consideration. Common language, group boundaries, power distribution, and peer relationships are interrelated to the quality of performance (Schein 2004). Again, emphasis is drawn to the dynamic nature of culture, which lies on consensus on every step and function of the organization (Schein 2004).

In operational performance terms, Prajogo and McDermott (2011) found that developmental culture is related with product quality, product innovation, and process innovation. Having highlighted the importance of quality and innovation of organizations, in order to achieve high-quality performance, they associated it with different types of organizational culture, in consistence with the literature. Participative culture promotes discussion and pluralistic views about current and future policies, preventing alienation, disappointment, and negative feelings. Institutional culture includes the members' openness to change, inspired by initiatives which promote quality.

Trivellas and Dargenidou (2009) studied the impact of organizational culture on the quality of higher education services and found that specific types of culture are linked with different dimensions of service quality. Based on new knowledge and information, they launch products and services which are innovative, rather than competitive. Thus, the need for systematic upgrade of staff knowledge and integration of novel practices emerges (Dekoulou and Trivellas 2014).

Regarding internationalization, it is essential that a culture encouraging international and intercultural values and promoting related initiatives should be integrated in the overall culture of the institution. However, because national culture influences organizational culture (Lapina et al. 2015), organizational culture cannot contradict the national one, as cultural misunderstandings may lead to problems (Lagrosen 2003). Therefore, it is stressed that failure to protect and maintain the unique characteristics, which form the identity of each institution induces the risk of uniformity and homogenization of institutions (Knight 1997), which contradicts the concept of competiveness. The impact of national culture on organizational or institutional quality management is more evident in multinational firms (Lagrosen 2003) and international institutions. Whether internationalization is a means or an indicator of quality, its contribution to the improvement of the quality of education is unanimously accepted (Knight 1997) and should, therefore be infused in the organizational culture.

Schneider et al. (1996) warn that when there is no strategic planning and no cohesion in the organizational climate and culture, changes and initiatives are more likely to fail. They suggest changes in climate to achieve changes in culture. Changing everyday practices and routines, which influence the beliefs and values of the members, and enhancing effective communication of new ideas and values change the climate and transform the culture. In the same vein, Trivellas and Dargenidou (2009) suggest that leadership should focus on positive interactions and relationships among the staff and their well-being, so that transformation of attitudes is achieved. Having openness, innovativeness, and trust as the core values of the academic community and engaging its members in decision-making processes, a leader can increase the possibilities for substantial cultural change. These elements are also obtained using simulation modeling of the corresponding processes (Dimitrios et al. 2013).

Conclusion

In line with the Greek quality assurance system, comparability, transparency, and accountability are the main goals for higher education (Trivellas et al. 2012). To achieve these goals it is essential that quality management is accepted by students, professors, and administrative personnel and that they are involved in quality assurance procedures regarding cultural change. Organizational culture transformation lies in the capabilities of leadership and the stakeholders' embracing the new quality management systems and institutional culture (Trivellas et al. 2012).

References

Dekoulou, P., and P. Trivellas. 2014. Learning organization in greek advertising and media industry: A way to face crisis and gain sustainable competitive advantage. *Procedia—Social and Behavioral Sciences* 148: 338–347.

Denison, D.R., and A.K. Mishra. 1995. Toward a theory of organizational culture and effectiveness. *Organization Science* 6 (2): 204–223.

Dimitrios, Nasiopoulos K., and L. Trivella. 2015. Knowledge management strategy within the higher education. The case of Greece. Procedia—Social and Behavioral Sciences 488–495. doi:10.1016/j.sbspro.2015.01.1227.

Dimitrios, Nasiopoulos K., Damianos P. Sakas, and D.S. Vlachos. 2013. The role of information systems in creating strategic leadership model. Procedia—Social and Behavioral Sciences. 467–477.

EUR-Lex. 2011. Communication from the Commission to the European Parliament, the Council, the European Economic and Social Committee and the Committee of the Regions Supporting Growth and Jobs—an Agenda for the Modernisation of Europe's Higher Education Systems. Document 52011DC0567. http://eur-lex.europa.eu/legal-content/EN/ALL/?uri=CELEX%3A52011DC0567.

Hellenic Quality Assurance Agency. http://www.hqa.gr/en/index.php.

Knight J. 1997. Internationalisation of higher education: A conceptual framework. In *Internationalisation of Higher Education in Asia Pacific Countries*. European Association for International Education.

Lagrosen, S. 2003. Exploring the impact of culture on quality management. *International Journal of Quality and Reliability Management* 20 (4): 473–487.

Lapina, I., I. Kairisa, and D. Aramina. 2015. Role of organizational culture in the quality management of university. In *20th international scientific conference economics and management-2015 (ICEM-2015)*, 213, 770–774.

Prajogo, D. 2008. The multidimensional relationships between organisational culture and performance. In *22nd ANZAM Conference 2008*, 1–18.

Prajogo, D.I., and C.M. McDermott. 2011. The relationship between multidimensional organizational culture and performance. *International Journal of Operations and Production Management* 31 (7): 712–735.

Schein, E.H. 2004. *Organizational culture and leadership*, 3rd ed. San Fransisco: Jossey-Bass.

Schneider, B., A.P. Brief, and R.A. Guzzo. 1996. Creating a climate and culture for sustainable organizational change. *Organizational Dynamics* 24 (4): 7–19.

Trivellas, P., and D. Dargenidou. 2009. Organisational culture, job satisfaction and higher education service quality. *The TQM Journal* 21 (4): 382–399.

Trivellas, P., and P. Reklitis. 2014. Leadership competencies profiles and managerial effectiveness in Greece. *Procedia Economics and Finance* 9 (Ebeec 2013): 380–390.

Trivellas, P., P. Ipsilantis, I. Papadopoulos, and D. Kantas. 2012. Challenges for quality management in higher education-investigating institutional leadership, culture and performance. *Quality Assurance and Management* 103–129.

UNESCO. 2005. *Guidelines for Quality Provision in Cross-Border Higher Education*. Paris: United Nations Educational, Scientific and Cultural Organization.

Zeri, P. 2007. The university in crisis. *Science and Society* 17: 249–257.

Integrating Total Quality Management Philosophy in Greek Higher Educational Institutions

D. Belias, A. Koustelios, K. Varsanis, D. Kyriakou and L. Sdrolias

Total Quality Management (TQM)

The focus of Total Quality Management (TQM) is on customer satisfaction ad service quality (Talib et al. 2011). Its advocates state that implementation of TQM practices leads to improved quality of products and services, reduction of costs, increase of customer and staff satisfaction, and financial profits (Powel 1995; Talib et al. 2011). However, there is serious argumentation against TQM, especially in terms of costs and other obstacles, such as management time consumption, paperwork, formality, and failure to address the needs of certain organizations (Powel 1995; Talib et al. 2011).

In contrast with past practices which focused on quality control and were result-oriented, TQM is a process-oriented organizational philosophy focusing on quality management and aiming at customer satisfaction through the improvement of product and service quality (Mehra et al. 2001). It is essential that there is a quality culture, so that all stakeholders realize that it is a dynamic, rather than static, process requiring continuous efforts.

D. Belias (✉) · A. Koustelios
Department of Physical Education and Sport Science, University of Thessaly, Trikala, Greece
e-mail: dbelias@pe.uth.gr

K. Varsanis
Department of Business Administration, Technological Educational Institute of Western Macedonia, Kozani, Greece

D. Kyriakou
Department of Economic Sciences, Aristotle University of Thessaloniki, Thessalloniki, Greece

L. Sdrolias
Department of Business Administration, Technological Educational Institute of Central Greece, Psachna, Greece

A. Kavoura et al. (eds.), *Strategic Innovative Marketing*, Springer Proceedings in Business and Economics, DOI 10.1007/978-3-319-56288-9_13

Literature confirms that the main criteria for determining quality in service organizations include leadership, information and analysis, planning for quality, human resource utilization, quality assurance of products and services, quality results and customer satisfaction (Cornesky et al. 1991, p. 76).

After an exhaustive review of studies on TQM practices, Talib et al. (2011) concentrated on the key practices of TQM in service industries. They discuss the positive results which derive from the 49 TQM practices, without failing to highlight organizational performance and service quality. Implementation of TQM was connected with quality of conformance and customer satisfaction, while it was found that organizational knowledge and skills and job satisfaction were related to the engagement of the staff. Similarly, Trivellas and Reklitis (2014) have found that job satisfaction is directly related to staff's values and opinions about the working conditions and the climate, human relations and communication, security and supervisory support, teamwork, and flexibility.

However, several issues emerging during the processes of development of the quality improvement and measurement of the results might hinder TQM successful implementation. According to Talib et al. (2011), the most frequent issues found in the literature are leadership inability and inconsistent organizational culture. Inefficient resources and failure to change organizational culture, lack of training, engagement or commitment, resistance to change and lack of motivation, unrealistic expectations and failure to inform the stakeholders about the programme, lack of strategic planning and structural problems were the main reasons for the failure of TQM in service industries. Beer (2003) has also connected failures of TQM with problems in its implementation, rather than due to the theoretical constructs and methodological issues. He, therefore, highlights the need for high quality management.

According to Cornesky et al. (1991), there are certain conditions, which should be established, before implementing TQM, in consecutive order. The first step is to educate and enhance commitment of administration staff and, then, to educate and establish commitment of the faculty and the academic staff. The next step requires the establishment of trust and pride in the quality of work, while change of institutional culture follows. Trivellas and Dargenidou (2009) have studied the influence of academic and administrative staff's job satisfaction on service quality, as they realized that in higher education the human factor is essential.

Mehra et al. (2001) have found in the literature, 45 factors which are linked with TQM implementation, which they put into five categories. Focus on human resources, management structure, quality tools, supplier support, and customer orientation are found to be the major factors. Within the first category, human resources focus, group-based incentive systems, training, involvement and empowerment of the staff, adoption of reward systems tied to key measures and recognition are vital for the successful implementation of TQM. Regarding management structure, leadership, and organizational culture are the most important elements. Providing adequate information to the staff and prioritizing and coordinating actions are related to quality planning. As for the quality tools, quality planning and reengineering, measurement of key result areas and informed decisions are involved. With respect to the supplier support, it is stressed that supplier involvement and the relationship between the supplier and the buyers are critical issues. Finally, customer orientation includes considering customer satisfaction, benchmarking, and the adoption of a continuous improvement process.

Powell (1995) has found that behavioral, practices such as executive commitment, staff empowerment, and open organization are the more crucial factors which induce effective integration of TQM philosophy than TQM tools and techniques. He, therefore, emphasizes on the need to create an organizational culture that promotes these factors, instead of mere implementation of TQM principles and practices, and explain that a long process of introducing and developing changes in management practices and culture is required (Beer 2003).

The same view is expressed by Prajogo and Fujimoto (2006), who consider culture to be the most important factor that affects the implementation of TQM and identify failure to receive the desired outcomes due to inability or limited ability of human resource management. Customer focus, continuous improvement, and involvement are also essential.

Prajogo and Sohal (2006) have made the connection of quality management and innovation clear in their study. They found that TQM implementation and integration of technology management and Research and Development (R&D) management can predict organizational quality and innovation performance. They state that organizational structure and culture, strategy, and process are to be considered with regard to integrating technology and R&D and TQM in order to attain high innovation performance.

TQM in Greek Higher Education

TQM has been studied and implemented in various service contexts, among which education (Talib et al. 2011). Trivellas et al. (2012) refer to Bonvillan and Dennis (1995) to identify three factors which influence higher education quality. The market forces due to modern socioeconomic changes which require competitive practices, the political context which determines public funding and accreditation and students' expectations. It is students' satisfaction of their learning experience and outcomes that contributes to the reputation of the institution.

Customers in education are distinguished between internal, who are involved in the learning processes, and external, who are the future employers and employees. Although it is not feasible to meet all stakeholders' needs and expectations at the same time, attempts to focus on either internal or external customers are more likely to fail (Trivellas et al. 2012; Dimitrios et al. 2013a, b).

Based on the literature, Trivellas et al. (2012) have identified five types of quality which are not appropriately taken into account within educational contexts. Transcendent quality refers to the educators' expertise and reputation, without, however, taking external factors into account. Manufacturing-based quality focuses on the conformance to customer expectations, counterbalancing the past view of focusing on resources. However, institutions do not consider customer satisfaction and external factors in the service design. Product-based quality is determined by the outcome, which is students' learning. Because it is linked with assessment practices and measurable outcomes, misleading results may occur, as specific metrics fail to assess students' knowledge and skills acquired during their studies. Value-based quality involves the customers' perceived connection between the tuition fees and their salary after graduation, which, within contemporary contexts, cannot be bridged. Finally, user-based quality is strongly related with customers' needs and preferences, which, however, are subjective and idiosyncratic in educational environments.

Although Trivellas et al. (2012) recognize the diversity in quality perceptions, they highlight a major finding in the literature, that stakeholders should be the ones who determine quality. Stakeholders in higher education are the current students and the ones who graduated and their families, the institutional staff, whether academic or administration staff, employers, agencies of the government, the local community and society.

In Greece, quality assurance is materialized by the Hellenic Quality Assurance Agency for Higher Education (HQA 2009), which, since 2006, has been responsible for evaluation procedures, without, however intervening in the function or mission of higher education. Indeed, only half of the higher education institutions in Greece have accepted and implemented these procedures (Trivellas et al. 2012).

The obstacles which are found in the literature to hinder the application of TQM philosophy include lack of constancy of purpose, mobility of top management, focus on short-term results and figures and poor evaluation of performance (Cornesky et al. 1991). In a similar vein, among the various problems that should be addressed in Greek higher education, are the following: ineffective teaching which makes students devalue education, lack of connection between university studies and labor market, poor facilities, disregard of students' and staff's well-being, professor-centered attitudes, ineffective assessment procedures (Mitka and Mouroutsos 2013).

Suggestions

In a highly demanding environment, organizations, and more specifically higher education institutions, are expected to respond to constant changes by developing innovative practices and delivering quality products and services. As quality and innovation are perceived to be sources of competitive advantage (Prajogo and Sohal 2006), the implementation of Total Quality Management (TQM) is suggested in Greek higher education institutions.

First, it is suggested that TQM practices are connected with each specific context, so that both benefits and limitations are better understood. Staff commitment should be ensured and constant feedback and shared information should be the basis for quality improvement, based on the customers' needs and expectations (Talib et al. 2011).

The creation of a quality culture is a prerequisite for the effective implementation of TQM. For the enhancement of service quality, "… *a sustained improvement in the clarity, accuracy and reliability of services delivered under a holistic perspective*" is required (Trivellas et al. 2012, p. 106). Stakeholders' needs and expectations should be met and both internal and external customers should be taken into consideration. Focus on customer and process, innovation and environment are also suggested for the successful implementation of TQM. Constructing knowledge through innovations and strategic management should be emphasized, while both internal processes and external transactions should be carefully planned to achieve global competitiveness (Mehra et al. 2001).

Technology integration and research should be promoted to attract the interest of external customers. TQM should be integrated along with technology management and Research and Development management, so that innovations are promoted and supported (Prajogo and Sohal 2006). Decentralization and diversification, transforming organizational culture, and eliminating obsolete processes are also essential for TQM integration.

Quality of teaching should be related with resources, theoretical and practical knowledge and expertise, positive attitudes, quality curricula, creativity, openness to innovations and willingness to change. Quality in administration should be linked with flexibility, the ability to adapt and proactiveness. Leadership should support and encourage people and facilitate the process of change (Trivellas and Dargenidou 2009).

Effective leadership and employee engagement in decision-making processes, trust and commitment are also needed for TQM integration (Trivellas and Dargenidou 2009). It is important to realize that individual effectiveness of leadership is connected with both leadership competencies and managerial effectiveness (Trivellas and Reklitis 2014). Moreover, higher quality performance should be encouraged by relating staff's capabilities and needs to the organizational context and job demands (Trivellas and Reklitis 2014).

Strategic planning, effective leadership, efficient resources, and systematic assessment procedures are crucial parts of this process. In brief, continuous improvement and quality assurance should be the primary objectives of Greek higher education (Dimitrios et al. 2013a, b).

References

Cornesky, R., S. McCool, L. Byrnes, and R. Weber. 1991. *Implementing Total Quality Management in Higher Education*. Madison: Magna Publications.

Beer, M. 2003. Why Total quality management programs do not persist: the role of management quality and implications for leading a TQM transformation. *Decision Sciences* 34 (4): 623–642.

Hellenic Quality Assurance and Accreditation Agency. HQA. http://www.hqa.gr/en/index.php.

Mehra, S., J.M. Hoffman, and D. Sirias. 2001. TQM as a management strategy for the next millennia. *International Journal of Operations and Production Management* 21 (5/6): 855–876.

Mitka E., and Mouroutsos S.G. (2013). TQM principles in Greek Universities. In *Proceedings of INTED Conference*, 2166–2172, Valencia, Spain.

Nasiopoulos K. Dimitrios, Damianos P. Sakas, and D.S. Vlachos (2013a). The role of open source leadership in developing high technology companies. *Key Engineering Materials, Scientific Net* 543: 402–405 (2013).

Nasiopoulos K. Dimitrios, Damianos P. Sakas, and D.S. Vlachos. (2013b). Analysis of strategic leadership models in information technology. *Procedia—Social and Behavioral Sciences* 268–275.

Powell, T.C. 1995. Total quality management as competitive advantage: a review and empirical study. *Strategic Management Journal* 16 (1): 15–37.

Prajogo, D.I., and A.S. Sohal. 2006. The integration of TQM and technology/R&D management in determining quality and innovation performance. *Omega* 34 (3): 296–312.

Prajogo D., and Fujimoto Y. (2006, January). The role of human resource management in moderating the relationship between organisational culture and TQM adoption. In *Proceedings of the 20th ANZAM (Australian New Zealand Academy of Management) Conference on 'Management: Pragmatism, Philosophy, Priorities*, 6–9.

Talib, F., Z. Rahman, M.N. Qureshi, and J. Siddiqui. 2011. Total quality management and service quality: An exploratory study of quality management practices and barriers in service industry. *International Journal of Services and Operations Management* 10 (1): 94–118.

Trivellas, P., and D. Dargenidou. 2009. Organisational culture, job satisfaction and higher education service quality. *The TQM Journal* 21 (4): 382–399.

Trivellas, P., and Reklitis, P. (2014). Leadership competencies profiles and managerial effectiveness in Greece. *Procedia Economics and Finance* 9: 380–390 (Ebeec 2013).

Trivellas P., Ipsilantis P., Papadopoulos I., and Kantas D. (2012). Challenges for quality management in higher education-investigating institutional leadership, culture and performance. *Quality Assurance and Management* 103–129.

Relationship Between Supervisor's Emotional Intelligence and Transformational Leadership in Hotel Organizations

Tryfon Vasilagos, Panagiotis Polychroniou and Leonidas Maroudas

Theoretical Background

Researchers have developed measures of emotional intelligence (e.g. Salovey and Mayer 1994; Bar-On 1997; Bar-On and Parker 2000; Mayer et al. 2002; Boyatzis and Goleman 2001; Law et al. 2004; Rahim et al. 2006). Gardner's (1983, 1999) concepts of intrapersonal and interpersonal intelligences provided basis for the conceptualization of emotional intelligence. Whereas intrapersonal intelligence is the ability to understand one's own emotions, interpersonal intelligence is one's ability to understand the emotions of others (Polychroniou 2009). Emotional intelligence relates to a number of noncognitive skills, abilities, or competencies that influence a manager's capacity to deal with environmental demands and pressures (Goleman 1995). Emotional intelligence competencies enhance supervisors to understand subordinates' feelings and provide emotional support to team members in order to attain common goals.

Following Burns (1978) and Bass (1985, 1990) transformational leadership is associated with distinct dimensions of idealized influence, inspirational motivation, intellectual stimulation, and individualized consideration (Polychroniou 2009). Transformational leaders have the capacity to motivate inspirationally hotel employees in order to develop engagement. Hospitality organizations should invest in developing extrovert supervisors who exhibit transformational leadership behaviors using emotional intelligence competencies (Zopiatis and Constanti 2012). Transformational leadership influences team and departmental performance through organizational commitment (Patiar and Wang 2016). In addition, hotel supervisors that utilize transformational leadership could help their employees to obtain the creative skills required by increasing their experiences of engaging in creative

T. Vasilagos (✉) · P. Polychroniou · L. Maroudas
Department of Business Administration, University of Patras, Patras, Greece
e-mail: tvasilagos@gmail.com

A. Kavoura et al. (eds.), *Strategic Innovative Marketing*, Springer Proceedings in Business and Economics, DOI 10.1007/978-3-319-56288-9_14

activities developing also an organizational brand climate to distinguish hotel organization from its competitors (Uen et al. 2012; Wang et al. 2014).

Hypotheses

Intrapersonal (self-regulation, self-awareness) and interpersonal dimensions (empathy, social skills, motivation) of emotional intelligence that possessed by a supervisor can have a positive effect on her/his transformational leadership (Goleman 1995, 2001; Gardner 1999; Rahim et al. 2006; Antonakis et al. 2009; Cavazotte et al. 2012). Transformational leaders communicate vision and values, create an atmosphere of change and motivate inspirationally people through idealized influence (Polychroniou 2009; Hur et al. 2011; Follesdal and Hagtvet 2013). A leader who exhibits idealized influence is characterized by having employees who respect and trust them (Avolio and Bass 1995). Power and confidence as part of the idealized influence dimension could be the most visible sign of transformational leadership (Brown and Arendt 2010). Hotel employees are likely to emotionally identify and cooperate with a leader who is willing to provide individualized consideration and improve their job performance (Lee and Ok 2012; Wolfe and Kim 2013). Based on previous contributions we hypothesize the following:

H1. Self-regulation is related positively with hotel supervisor's transformational leadership.
H2. Self-awareness is related positively with hotel supervisor's transformational leadership.
H3. Empathy is related positively with hotel supervisor's transformational leadership.
H4. Social skills are related positively with hotel supervisor's transformational leadership.
H5. Motivation is related positively with hotel supervisor's transformational leadership.

Methodology

The primary objective of this research is to investigate the relationships between hotel managers' emotional intelligence competences and transformational leadership. Participants were 149 employees representing 117 Greek and Cypriot hotel organizations. Sixty five (43.6%) participants were working as human resources/marketing managers and 108 (92.3%) organizations represented four- and five stars hotels. This highlights that the sample is comprised mainly by experienced participants reflecting validation of survey.

In terms of gender, sample is comprised by 62 male (41.6%) and 87 female (58.4%). In terms of age 82 (55%) of the participants were 24–33 years old, 38 (25.5%) were 34–43 years old and 29 (19.5%) were over 43 years old. All respondents had completed undergraduate studies in business administration (34.2%), tourism management (20.8%), economics (11.4%), marketing (10.1%), accounting/finance (10.1%), and other studies (13.4%).

Preliminary data were collected by means of structured questionnaire. Transformational leadership was assessed by subordinates' response to 20 items of the MLQ (Bass and Avolio 1995). Supervisor's emotional intelligence competencies (self-awareness, self-regulation, empathy, social skills, motivation) were measured with 30 items based on EQI (Rahim et al. 2002, 2006).

Results

Groups of variables have been examined on all aforementioned stages measured with the Likert scale (1: I completely disagree—5: I completely agree). The variables were grouped by applying factor analysis, after checking the adequacy of the sample using the Keiser-Meyer-Olkin index and verifying that according to the Bartlett's Test of Sphericity variables' correlations allow for the application of factor analysis. Thereafter, we implemented tests on the reliability of the factors using the coefficient Cronbach-a. To test hypotheses, data analysis proceeded in two stages using S.P.S.S., factor analysis and Pearson correlation.

Exploratory factor analysis (principal component analysis, loading > 40, eigenvalue > 1) on the 30 EQI items supported the five independent dimensions of emotional intelligence (self-awareness, self-regulation, empathy, social skills, motivation. The internal consistency reliability coefficients of the five subscales of the EQI, as assessed with Cronbach α, were 0.948 (self-regulation), 0.905 (self-awareness), 0.939 (empathy), 0.966 (social skills), 0.950 (motivation). We also computed an exploratory factor analysis (principal component analysis, loading > 0.40, eigenvalue > 1) on the 20 items adopted from MLQ. Results confirmed a significant factor representing transformational leadership. The Cronbach α for this scale was 0.968.

Pearson correlation analysis was performed between: (a) self-regulation, self-awareness, empathy, social skills, motivation and (b) transformational leadership. Findings indicate positive associations between hotel supervisor's emotional intelligence competencies and her/his transformational leadership. Correlations between transformational leadership and self-regulation ($r = 0.397$, $p < 0.01$), self-awareness ($r = 0.347$, $p < 0.01$), empathy ($r = 0.357$, $p < 0.01$), social skills ($r = 0.353$, $p < 0.01$), motivation ($r = 0.409$, $p < 0.01$) were significant providing support to H1, H2, H3, H4, and H5.

Conclusions

Transformational leaders have an emotional impact on subordinates. Hotel managers that comprehend the importance of emotional intelligence are in a position to identify the emotional needs of their subordinates, to provide mentoring and individualized consideration and work collectively. In order to understand the emotional needs for effective handling, a leader should have self-awareness and self-regulation. Furthermore, empathy, social skills, and motivation are related positively with transformational leadership. Empathy, social skills, and motivation are interpersonal dimensions of emotional intelligence that if possessed by a hotel manager can have a positive a developing effect on her/his leadership. Empathy and social skills help leaders to perceive team members' feelings and needs, provide emotional support and help others to regulate their emotions with tact and diplomacy. Motivation is also needed to lead a hotel employee to remain focused for attaining common goals and to develop engagement. Intellectual stimulation and supervisor's individualized consideration develop employee quality of work, creativity, and innovative behaviors. Hotel employees are likely to respect a leader who is considerate and is willing to help subordinates to improve job performance and develop human capital. Managerial implications include that hotel supervisors in modern hotel organizations should further develop emotional intelligence competencies and enhance their transformational leadership with focus on human resources development in an unpredictable and ever-competitive environment in Mediterranean hotel industry.

References

Antonakis, J., N. Ashkanasy, and M. Dasborough. 2009. Does leadership need emotional intelligence? *The Leadership Quarterly* 20: 247–261.

Avolio, B., and B. Bass. 1995. Individual consideration viewed at multiple levels of analysis: A multi-level framework for examining the diffusion of transformational leadership. *The Leadership Quarterly* 6 (2): 199–218.

Bar-On, R. 1997. *Bar-on emotional quotient inventory (EQ-i): Technical manual.* Toronto: Multi-Health System.

Bar-On, R., and J.D.A. Parker. 2000. *The handbook of emotional intelligence: Theory, development, assessment, and application at home, school, and in the workplace.* San Francisco: Jossey-Bass.

Bass, B.M. 1985. *Leadership and performance beyond expectations.* New York: Free Press.

Bass, B.M. 1990. From transactional to transformational leadership: learning to share the vision. *Organizational Dynamics* 18 (3): 19–31.

Bass, B.M., and B.J. Avolio. 1995. *MLQ multifactor leadership questionnaire (From 5x-short).* Redwood City, CA: Mind Garden.

Boyatzis, R.E., and D. Goleman. 2001. *The emotional competence inventory*, University ed. Boston, MA: HayGroup.

Brown, A.E., and W.S. Arendt. 2010. Perceptions of transformational leadership behaviors and subordinates' performance in hotels. *Journal of Human Resources in Hospitality and Tourism* 10 (1): 45–59.

Burns, J.M. 1978. *Leadership*. New York: Harper & Row.

Cavazotte, F., V. Moreno, and M. Hickmann. 2012. Effects of leader intelligence, personality and emotional intelligence on transformational leadership and managerial performance. *The Leadership Quarterly* 23: 443–455.

Follesdal, H., and K. Hagtvet. 2013. Does emotional intelligence as ability predict transformational leadership? A multilevel approach. *The Leadership Quarterly* 24: 747–762.

Gardner, H. 1983. *Frames of mind: The theory of multiple intelligences*. New York: Basic Books.

Gardner, H. 1999. *Intelligence reframed*. New York: Basic Books.

Goleman, D. 1995. *Emotional intelligence*. New York: Bantum Books.

Goleman, D. 2001. An EI-based theory of performance. In *The emotionally intelligent workplace: How to select for, measure, and improve emotional intelligence in individuals, groups, and organizations*, ed. C. Cherniss, and D. Goleman. San Francisco: Jossey-Bass.

Hur, Y., P. Van Den Berg, and C. Wilderom. 2011. Transformational leadership as a mediator between emotional intelligence and team outcomes. *The Leadership Quarterly* 22: 591–603.

Law, K.S., C.S. Wong, and L.J. Song. 2004. The construct and criterion validity of emotional intelligence and its potential utility for management studies. *Journal of Applied Psychology* 89: 483–496.

Lee, J., and C. Ok. 2012. Reducing burnout and enhancing job satisfaction: Critical role of hotel employees' emotional intelligence and emotional labor. *International Journal of Hospitality Management* 31: 1101–1112.

Mayer, J.D., P. Salovey, and D.R. Caruso. 2002. *MSCEIT user's manual*. Toronto: Multi-Health Systems.

Patiar, A., and Y. Wang. 2016. The effects of transformational leadership and organizational commitment on hotel departmental performance. *International Journal of Contemporary Hospitality Management* 28 (3): 586–608.

Polychroniou, P. 2009. Relationship between emotional intelligence and transformational leadership of supervisors: The impact of team effectiveness. *Team Performance Management* 15 (7): 343–356.

Rahim, A., C. Psenicka, S.-Y. Oh, P. Polychroniou, J. Dias, Md Rahman, and S. Ferdausy. 2006. Emotional intelligence and transformational leadership: A cross cultural study, current topics in management. *Transaction Publishers* 11: 223–236.

Rahim, A., C. Psenicka, P. Polychroniou, J. Zhao, C. Yu, K. Chan, K. Yee, M. Alves, C. Lee, Md Rahman, S. Ferdausy, and R. Wyk. 2002. A model of emotional intelligence and conflict management strategies: A study in seven countries. *The International Journal of Organizational Analysis* 10: 302–326.

Salovey, P., and J.D. Mayer. 1994. Some final thoughts about personality and intelligence. In *Personality and intelligence*, ed. R.J. Sternberg, and P. Ruzgis. Cambridge, UK: Cambridge University Press.

Uen, J.-F., T. Wu, H.-C. Teng, and Y.-S. Liu. 2012. Transformational leadership and branding behavior in Taiwanese hotels. *International Journal of Contemporary Hospitality Management* 24 (1): 26–43.

Wang, C.-J., H.-T. Tsai, and M.-T. Tsai. 2014. Linking transformational leadership and employee creativity in the hospitality industry: The influences of creative role identity, creative self-efficacy, and job complexity. *Tourism Management* 40: 79–89.

Wolfe, K., and J.H. Kim. 2013. Emotional intelligence, job satisfaction, and job tenure among hotel managers. *Journal of Human Resources in Hospitality and Tourism* 12 (2): 175–191.

Zopiatis, A., and P. Constanti. 2012. Extraversion, openness and conscientiousness: The route to transformational leadership in the hotel industry. *Leadership and Organization Development Journal* 33 (1): 86–104.

Dynamic Combination of Automatic Forecasts for Corporate Budgeting

Sotirios D. Nikolopoulos

Introduction

Probably the most important function of business is forecasting, which is a starting point for planning and budgeting. Traditionally, budgeting is regarded as one of the most important financial and accounting functions (Ekholm and Wallin 2000; Tanlu 2007). In recent years, rapidly changing market conditions have made financial planning tools of increasing importance both for managers and practitioners. However, the use of traditional budgets has been criticized as a management control tool (Hope and Fraser 2003). In the relevant literature, a number of new tools have been proposed as a replacement to traditional budgets, such as rolling forecasts and beyond budgeting (Bergstrand 2009; Bogsnes 2009). The purpose of rolling forecast is to use the most frequent data in order to make more flexible and adaptable organizations that are able to cope with changing environments (Lorain 2010). There is an increased number of companies adopting rolling forecasts as a part of the Beyond Budgeting model (Bogsnes 2009), and the main reason is to become more adaptive and hence can better support company planning and control processes (Hope and Fraser 2003).

Management, typically operates under conditions of uncertainty or risk and one of the fundamental objectives of forecasting is to reduce risk and uncertainty of financial decisions. A variety of forecasting techniques is available for the analyst to choose the most appropriate one. However, in real business life, the number of time series to be forecasted is enormous and the forecasts have to be updated frequently making forecasting modeling an almost impossible procedure. Therefore, automatic

S.D. Nikolopoulos (✉)
Department of Accounting and Finance, TEI of Thessaly, Larissa, Greece
e-mail: s.nikolopoulos@gmail.com

A. Kavoura et al. (eds.), *Strategic Innovative Marketing*, Springer Proceedings in Business and Economics, DOI 10.1007/978-3-319-56288-9_15

forecasts of large numbers of univariate time series are often needed in business (Leonard 2002).

When multiple forecasts are available for a target variable, forecast combination methods provide a simple and effective way to improve the forecasting performance of individual forecasting models. Further, they provide a simple procedure to manage misspecified and unstable forecasters, small sample sizes, and structural breaks in the data (Huang and Lee 2010; Mandel and Sani 2016). Usually, forecast combination methods outperform the best individual forecaster. For example, combination of forecasts has been applied with success, most of the time, in forecasting interest rates (Guidolin and Timmermann 2009), equity premium prediction (Rapach et al. 2010), realized volatility (Patton and Sheppard 2009), stock market return prediction (Nikolopoulos and Papakyriazis 2004), etc. However, most of the existing combination models focus on environments that ignore the complexity of real-world data. Several studies propose combination models capable of adapting to various environments and system instabilities (Aiolfi and Timmermann 2006; Nikolopoulos and Papakyriazis 2002; Smith and Wallis 2009; Tian and Anderson 2014).

In this paper, we apply, in the not trivial problem of forecasting monthly sales and cost of goods sold (COGS) for a manufacturing company, a combination scheme of automatic forecasts, based on a state-space representation where the combination weights are estimated online by means of the Kalman Filter.

Combining Automatic Forecasts

An automatic forecasting system can be used to automatically fit various models (i.e., exponential smoothing models, ARIMA, and dynamic regression models). Automatic forecasts may be used in cases where there is not an experienced forecaster; the number of the forecasts to be generated is large; the frequency of forecasting updates is high; the real model in not known or it is difficult to be identified (Leonard 2002). Combining a number of automatic forecasting models may produce superior forecasts especially out-of-sample. The forecast package (Hyndman 2016) for the R system for statistical computing, implements various automatic forecasting models. In the current work, two general automatic forecasting models are utilized. That is an exponential smoothing state-space model (ETS) and an autoregressive integrated moving average (ARIMA) model (Hyndman and Khandakar 2008; Hyndman et al. 2002). In particular, the ETS model offers 15 methods, such as simple exponential smoothing (N, N), Holt's linear method (Ad, N), etc. (Hyndman 2016; Hyndman and Khandakar 2008; Hyndman et al. 2002).

The automatic ARIMA model identifies a seasonal ARIMA model in the following form ARIMA (p, d, q)(P, D, Q)m. The three components (p, d, q) are the

AR order, the degree of differencing, and the MA order. The other three components are a specification of the seasonal part of the ARIMA model, plus the number of periods per season m. The automatic function in R in order to estimate the (p, d, q, P, D, Q) uses a variation of the Hyndman and Khandakar algorithm, (Hyndman and Khandakar 2008) which combines unit root tests, minimization of the AICc and MLE to obtain an ARIMA model.

For the combination of the forecasts, we propose a state-space representation where a dynamic linear model combines in real time the automatic forecasts. A State-Space model, is composed of an unobservable state: $x_0, x_1, x_2, \ldots, x_t, \ldots$ which forms a Markov Chain, and an observable variable: $y_0, y_1, y_2, \ldots, y_t, \ldots$ which are conditionally independent given the state. A very important class of state-space models is the dynamic linear model, which is specified by three equations. Equation (1), is a normal prior distribution for the p-dimensional state vector at time t = 0, Eq. (2) is called the observation equation and Eq. (3) the state equation or system equation.

$$\theta \sim \mathcal{N}_p(m_0, C_0) \tag{1}$$

$$Y_t = F_t\theta_t + \upsilon_t \qquad \upsilon_t \sim \mathcal{N}_m(0, V_t) \tag{2}$$

$$\theta_t = G_t\theta_{t-1} + w_t \qquad w_t \sim \mathcal{N}_p(0, W_t) \tag{3}$$

where G_t and F_t are known matrices (of order $p \times p$ and $m \times p$ respectively) and $(\upsilon_t)_t$ and $(w_t)_t$ are two independent sequences of independent Gaussian random vectors with mean zero and known variance matrices $(V_t)_t \geq 1$ and $(W_t)_t \geq 1$, respectively. Furthermore, it is assumed that θ_0 is independent of (υ_t) and (w_t) (Petris et al. 2009).

In this form, one can model nonlinear relationships between x and y, structural changes in the process under study, as well as the omission of some variables. For the optimal properties of the algorithm, the interested reader is referred to the following work (Kalman 1960; Gelb 1974; Hamilton 1994; Nikolopoulos and Papakyriazis 2002).

In our work, the dynamic linear regression model that is used to combine the automatic forecasts is described by

$$Y_t = x_t^{'}\theta_t + \upsilon_t \qquad \upsilon_t \sim \mathcal{N}(0, \sigma_t^2) \tag{4}$$

$$\theta_t = G_t\theta_{t-1} + w_t \qquad w_t \sim \mathcal{N}_p(0, W_t) \tag{5}$$

where $x_t^{'} = \lfloor x_{1,t} \ldots x_t^p \rfloor$ are the values of the p explanatory variables at time t. Setting G_t as the identity matrix and W diagonal, correspond to modeling the regression coefficients as independent random walks (Petris et al. 2009).

Application

In this section, we implement the automatic models presented in Sect. 2 and then we combine the forecasts with a simple average model, an unrestricted linear regression model, and our proposed Dynamic Linear Model. In our experiments, we utilize the data of a Greek manufacturing company that belongs to the chemical sector. In particular, we use monthly sales from January 2008 to December 2010 that is 36 observations, for "in sample" model estimation. The monthly sales of 2011 are used for "out of sample" forecast, combination and forecast evaluation. The estimated automatic models for the sales are ARIMA(0, 0, 0)(1, 1, 0)[12] with drift and ETS(M, N, M), while the respective models for the COGS are ARIMA (1, 1, 0) and ETS(M, A, N). The triplet (E, T, S) refers to the three components: error, trend, and seasonality. Thus, the model ETS(M, A, M) has multiplicative error, additive trend, and multiplicative seasonality, while the model ETS(M, N, M) has multiplicative error, no trend and multiplicative seasonality. More information for model description and measures of forecast accuracy can be found in Hyndman (2016) and Hyndman and Koehler (2006) respectively (Figs. 1 and 2).

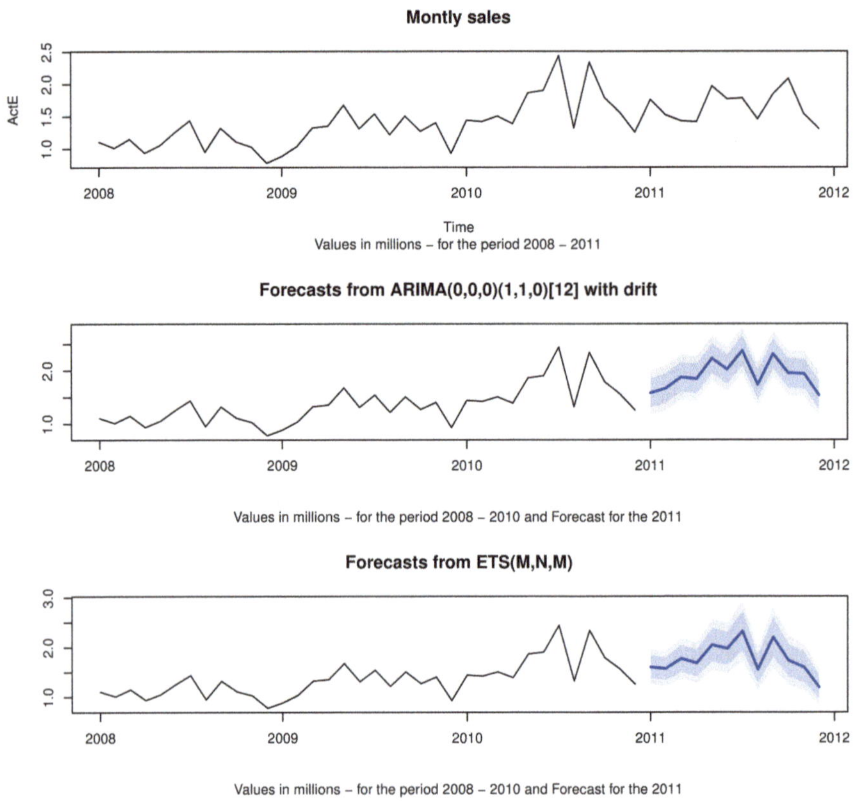

Fig. 1 Actual and forecasted monthly sales

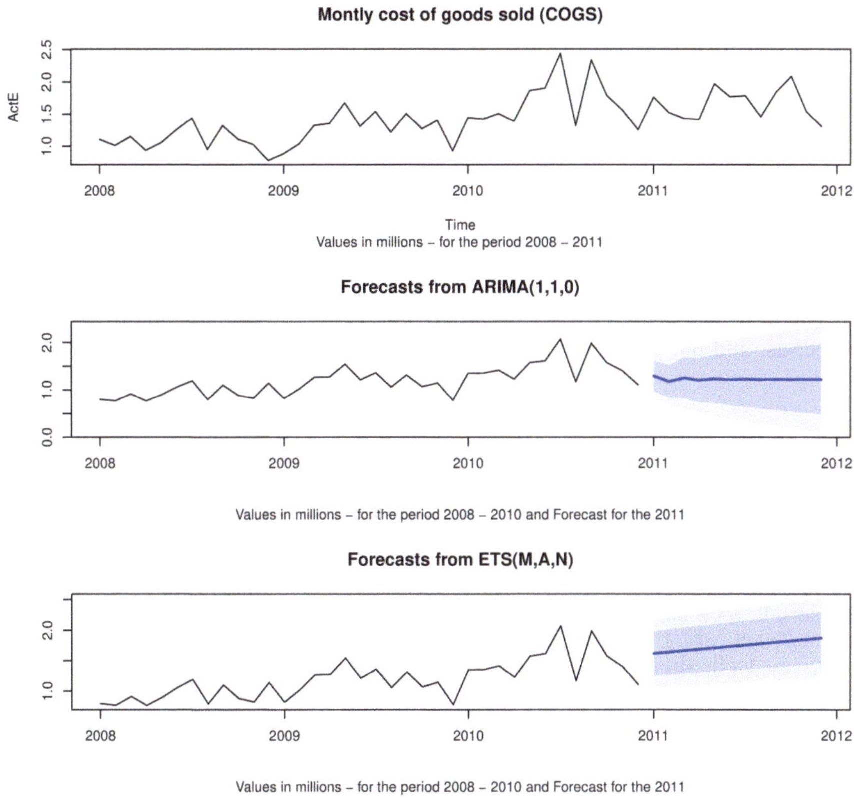

Fig. 2 Actual and forecasted COGS

Conclusions

A dynamic linear model was applied for the combination of monthly sales and COGS forecasts. The combination of forecasts greatly reduced the model selection risk, while the out-of-sample performance of the proposed combination model was better than any other single or combined forecasting model applied in this work. It is noticeable that in terms of RMSE the forecast improves from 1 to 55% points with regard to any other forecasting model (see Tables 1 and 2). We expect the

Table 1 Out of sample accuracy measures for monthly sales forecasts

	ME	RMSE	MAE	MPE	MAPE	ACF1	Theil's U
ARIMA	−0.262	0.344	0.315	−16.678	19.508	−0.133	1.147
ETS	−0.110	0.261	0.216	−6.990	12.857	−0.031	0.855
Average combination	−0.186	0.291	0.256	−11.834	15.444	−0.109	0.966
Linear combination	−0.287	0.389	0.327	−17.697	19.730	−0.080	1.315
Dynamic combination	−0.033	0.251	0.192	−2.949	11.497	−0.009	0.809

Table 2 Out of sample accuracy measures for monthly COGS forecasts

	ME	RMSE	MAE	MPE	MAPE	ACF1	Theil's U
ARIMA	0.113	0.206	0.169	6.888	11.875	0.084	0.860
ETS	−0.407	0.451	0.407	−32.790	32.790	0.028	1.909
Average combination	−0.147	0.231	0.186	−12.951	15.304	0.022	0.994
Linear combination	−0.204	0.272	0.222	−17.269	18.339	0.015	1.168
Dynamic combination	−0.071	0.204	0.175	−7.250	13.841	0.100	0.886

dynamic combination benefits to be higher when we combine more automatic forecasts, and this experiment is left for a future work.

References

Aiolfi, M., and A. Timmermann. 2006. Persistence in forecasting performance and conditional combination strategies. *Journal of Econometrics* 135 (1–2): 31–53.

Bergstrand, J. 2009. *Accounting for management control*. Studentlitteratur.

Bogsnes, B. 2009. *Implementing beyond budgeting: Unlocking the performance potential*. Wiley.

Ekholm, B.G., and J. Wallin. 2000. Is the annual budget really dead? *European Accounting Review* 9 (4): 519–539.

Gelb, A. (1974). *Applied optimal estimation*. MIT press.

Guidolin, M., and A. Timmermann. 2009. Forecasts of US short-term interest rates: A flexible forecast combination approach. *Journal of Econometrics* 150 (2): 297–311.

Hamilton, J.D. 1994. *Time series analysis*, vol. 2. Princeton: Princeton University press.

Hope, J., and Fraser, R. 2003. *Beyond budgeting: How managers can break free from the annual performance trap*. Harvard Business School Press.

Huang, H., and T.H. Lee. 2010. To combine forecasts or to combine information? *Econometric Reviews* 29 (56): 534–570.

Hyndman, R.J. 2016. Forecasting functions for time series and linear models, R package version 7.1. http://github.com/robjhyndman/forecast.

Hyndman, R.J., and Y. Khandakar. 2008. Automatic time series forecasting: The forecast package for R. *Journal of Statistical Software* 27 (3): 1–22.

Hyndman, R.J., and A.B. Koehler. 2006. Another look at measures of forecast accuracy. *International Journal of Forecasting* 22 (4): 679–688.

Hyndman, R.J., A.B. Koehler, R.D. Snyder, and S. Grose. 2002. A state space framework for automatic forecasting using exponential smoothing methods. *International Journal of Forecasting* 18 (3): 439–454.

Kalman, R.E. 1960. A new approach to linear filtering and prediction problems. *Journal of Basic Engineering* 82 (1): 35–45.

Leonard, M. 2002. Large-scale automatic forecasting: millions of forecasts. In *International Symposium of Forecasting*, 156.

Lorain, M.A. 2010. Should rolling forecasts replace budgets in uncertain environments? vol. 20, 177–208. Elsevier.

Mandel, A., and Sani, A. 2016. Learning Time-varying forecast combinations. *Documents de travail du Centre d'Economie de la Sorbonne 2016,* 36. https://halshs.archives-ouvertes.fr/halshs-01317974/.

Nikolopoulos, S.D., and Papakyriazis, P. 2002. On dynamic model combination. In *5th Hellenic-European Conference on Computer Mathematics and its Applications*, 627–638.

Nikolopoulos, S.D., and Papakyriazis, P. 2004. Improved market forecast with optimal dynamic combiners. In *6th Hellenic-European Conference on Computer Mathematics and its Applications*, 774–781.

Patton, A.J., and K. Sheppard. 2009. Optimal combinations of realised volatility estimators. *International Journal of Forecasting* 25 (2): 218–238.

Petris, G., S. Petrone, and C. Patrizia. 2009. *Dynamic linear models with R*. New York: Springer.

Rapach, D., J. Strauss, and G. Zhou. 2010. Out-of-sample equity premium prediction: Combination forecasts and links to the real economy. *Review of Financial Studies* 23 (2): 821–862.

Smith, J., and K.F. Wallis. 2009. A simple explanation of the forecast combination puzzle. *Oxford Bulletin of Economics and Statistics* 71 (3): 331–355.

Tanlu, L. 2007. Does the adoption of rolling forecasts improve planning? An empirical investigation of the consequences of rolling forecasts. *Social Science Research Network*. http://papers.ssrn.com/sol3/Delivery.cfm?abstractid=1004125.

Tian, J., and H.M. Anderson. 2014. Forecast combinations under structural break uncertainty. *International Journal of Forecasting* 30 (1): 161–175.

Financial Text Mining in Twitterland

S.D. Nikolopoulos, I. Santouridis and T. Lazaridis

Introduction

We are living in the "information age", where information is a valuable asset. Information is created by models utilizing data, which most of them are in textual form, and the amount of data in our world has been exploding. The International Data Corporation (IDC), estimated that the total amount of data created and replicated in 2009 was 800 exabytes. Further, they projected that data volume is growing 40% per year, and will grow 44 times between 2009 and 2020 (McKinsey and Company 2011).

Text mining is an emerging research area in accounting and finance that it has many similarities with traditional qualitative analysis (Loughran and Mcdonald 2016). The purpose of text mining is to process, by means of appropriate hardware infrastructure and algorithms, textual data in order to extract meaningful information from the text, and, thus, make the information contained in the text accessible to the various data mining (statistical and machine learning) algorithms. Common terms shared between qualitative analysis and text mining are document summarization, topic modeling, sentiment analysis, etc.

Microblogging is an increasingly popular form of "professional" communication on the web. Twitter is currently one of the best-known microblogging platforms and online social networking service that enables users to send and read short 140 character messages called "tweets". The significant impact Twitter may have on financial markets become apparent on April 23, 2013 when a fake tweet on a

S.D. Nikolopoulos (✉) · I. Santouridis
Department of Accounting and Finance, TEI Thessaly, Larissa, Greece
e-mail: s.nikolopoulos@teilar.gr

T. Lazaridis
Department of Business Administration, TEI of Western Macedonia,
Grevena, Greece

A. Kavoura et al. (eds.), *Strategic Innovative Marketing*, Springer Proceedings
in Business and Economics, DOI 10.1007/978-3-319-56288-9_16

hacked official Twitter account of the Associated Press news agency (@AP account), sent out at about 1:07 p.m. ET, saying "Breaking: Two Explosions in the White House and Barack Obama is Injured." The AP quickly announced it was hacked. However, the market impact was already intense. The Dow Jones Industrial Average plunged more than 140 points and bond yields fell. Within 6 min, the Dow recovered its losses and was trading with triple-digit gains. Reuters estimated that the temporary loss of market capitalization in the S&P 500 alone totaled $136.5 billion (Karppi and Crawford 2015).

Mining microblogging data to model stock market is a very active research topic (Bollen et al. 2011; Groß-Klußmann and Hautsch 2011; Rao and Srivastava 2013; Sprenger et al. 2014; Zhang et al. 2012). In the relevant literature, it is argued that investor sentiment can be used to forecast stock market variables such as prices, returns, volume, trends, etc. For example, several studies have shown that individual's financial decisions are significantly affected by their emotions and mood (Nofsinger 2005; Peterson 2007; Ranco et al. 2015). These findings are in line with recent advances in behavioral and Emotional Finance which provide plausible explanations for market inefficiencies (Fairchild 2012; Malkiel 2003; Raines and Leathers 2011; Tuckett 2011).

Twitter Mining Methodology

The first step in text mining analysis of tweets is to search for relevant tweets and then create a corpus or text database that is a collection of documents/tweets. We search for tweets utilizing the application programming interface (API) provider by the Twitter to obtain a collection of public tweets (Makice 2009). There are various ways or keywords one may use to search information on Twitter. For example, by performing a search by a simple text term (i.e., INTC), or by using hashtag (i.e., #INTC), username (i.e., @INTC), or cashtags (i.e., $INTC). The selection of the search term greatly affect the results. From our experiments in financial text mining, the cashtag is the most appropriate way to search relevant financial information since it can reduce the information noise and the size of the corpus.

The next step is to preprocess the data. Text preprocessing is the process of making clear each language structure and to eliminate as much as possible the language dependent factors (Wang and Wang 2005). We applied standard data cleaning and preprocessing techniques for preparing the Twitter data for the subsequent analysis. That is, removing numbers; converting to lowercase; remove punctuation; removing common words that usually have no analytic value; removing common word endings (e.g., "ing", "es"); stripping white space, to remove white space left over by the previous prepossessing steps; etc. Thus, the tweet:

> RT: $IBM's cloud revenue grew 30% in 2Q, reached $11.6B for the last 12 mos. See what's driving this growth https://t.co/DFn3Tv6h

After the appropriate preprocessing, it is transformed into the following text:

ibm cloud revenue grew reached last what driving this growth

Then, we create mathematical matrices, called document term matrix (dtm) or term document matrix (tdm), describing the frequency of terms/words that exist in a corpus. In a dtm, rows correspond to documents in the collection and columns correspond to terms. These matrices can be used for information retrieval and plotting, clustering and PCA, thematic and sentiment analysis, etc.

Information retrieval is the activity of obtaining relevant information from a corpus. Searches for information on the corpus can be based on full-text or other content-based indexing (Rijsbergen 1979).

Clustering is an unsupervised learning paradigm. Clustering methods try to identify inherent groupings of the text documents so that a set of clusters are produced in which clusters exhibit high intra-cluster similarity and low inter-cluster similarity (Shawkat Ali and Xiang 2010).

In machine learning and natural language processing, topic models represent a class of computer programs that automatically extracts topics from texts. Topic modeling is a frequently used text-mining tool for discovering hidden semantic structures in a text bod. In machine learning and natural language processing, topic models represent a class of computer programs that automatically extracts topics from texts. Topic modeling is a frequently used text-mining tool for discovering hidden semantic structures in a text body. It does that by exploiting the correlations among the words and latent semantic themes. Latent Dirichlet Allocation (LDA) and "Topic Modeling" are often used synonymously, but LDA is a special case of topic modeling. LDA represents documents as mixtures of topics that spit out words with certain probabilities (Bei et al. 2003).

Finally, one important application of text mining is text sentiment analysis. This technique tries to discover the sentiment or polarity of a written text. This can be used to categorize text documents into a set of predefined sentiment categories (e.g., positive or negative sentiment categories), or it can be used to give the text a grade on a given scale. In essence, it is the process of determining the emotional tone behind a series of words, used to gain an understanding of the attitudes, opinions, and emotions expressed within an online mention. We use the positive and negative words dictionary created by Hu and Liu (2004) to create two sentiment indexes. The first sentiment index is created as the difference between positive and negative words in each document and the second by the polarity score of the qdap package (Rinker 2016).

Application

In this section, we apply the methodology described in the previous section for the analysis of mined tweets of the Intel Company. We discovered 1.920 relevant tweets for the Intel stock, searching the Twitter database using as a search string the stock quote for Intel corporation common stock $INTC. The 1.920 retrieved tweets used to create a corpus. Then we created a dtm and from that point, we are able to retrieve useful information from the corpus. For example, in Table 1 all terms that appear more than 50 times are presented. In Table 2 the correlation between the term bearish and other terms of the corpus are presented.

Thus, the terms bearish and doji coexist in all documents of the corpus as indicated by the correlation 1. Therefore, in our corpus the term bearish that is

Table 1 Terms of frequency higher than 50

aal	aapl	Alert	amd	amzn	Apple	bac	Bernstein	Big	Cat
cmg	cop	corp	csco	dis	Dividend	dow	Earnings	epd	ete
Global brand	goog	IBM	Intel	Internet	jnj	Market	msft	nasdaq	New
Next	nflx	nvda	Options	pfe	Poised	Price	pru	qcom	Read
Reporting	sbux	Shares	Stock	Stocks	Tech	Things	Top	Trend	Week

Table 2 Relationships/correlation between the term "Bearish" and other terms in corpus

Doji	Technical	ddd	itw	jns	pbi	pff	pfg	pgx	psec	swingtradebot
1	0.820	0.580	0.580	0.580	0.580	0.580	0.580	0.580	0.580	0.580

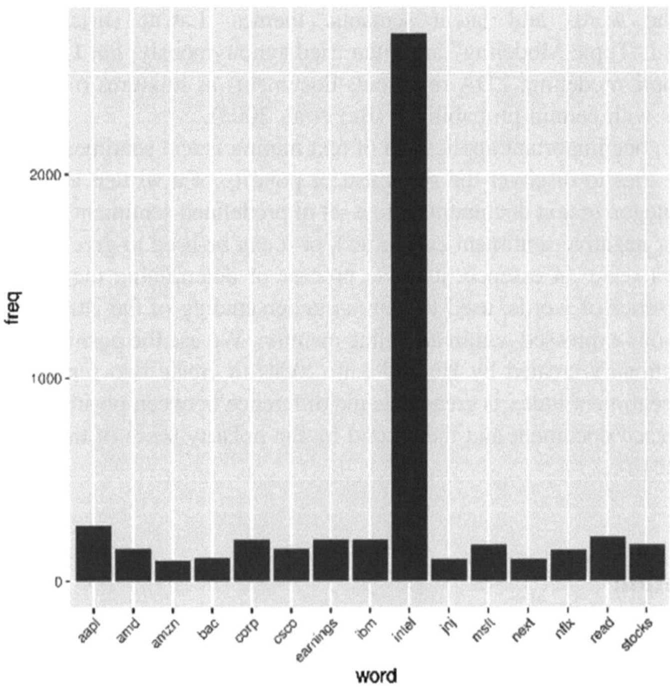

Fig. 1 Words that appear at least 100 times

investors who believe that a stock price will decline is related to companies of NYSE and NASDAQ such as ddd, itw, etc. Further, we can plot words that appear more than specific times or to create a cloud of words (see Figs. 1 and 2).

Then, we create a hierarchical cluster of terms using the ward metric (Fig. 3), and a bivariate cluster plot to visualize partitions of the terms in our corpus (Fig. 4). The Bivariate Clustering Plot (Fig. 4) gives a two-dimensional representation of the objects and the spanning ellipses of the clusters. Note that the boundary of a spanning ellipse always contains several objects. The distance between two clusters is represented as a line connecting the cluster centers. Objects belonging to different clusters are plotted with different characters. At the bottom of both plots, we see that 91.41% of the point variability is explained by the first two principal components.

The next step is to create the topics utilizing the LDA algorithm. The number of topics was identified by trying out different values of topics, to find which value produces the maximum log-likelihood, given the data (Graham and Ackland 2015). Twelve topics were identified but given space constraints of the paper only seven

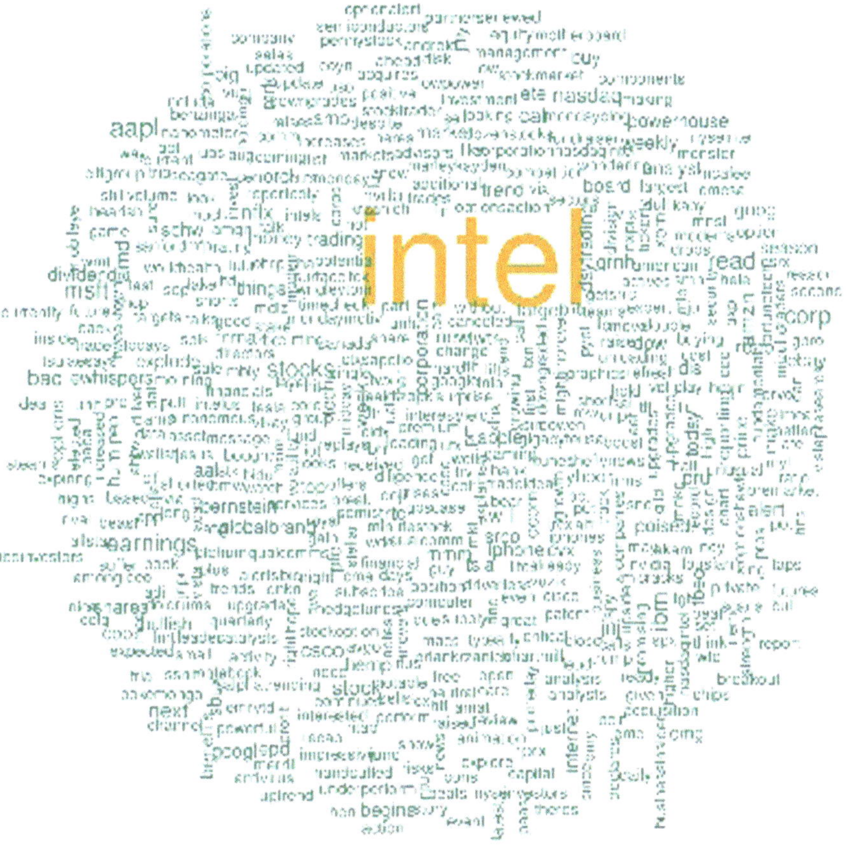

Fig. 2 Cloud plot of 600 most frequent words for Intel stock

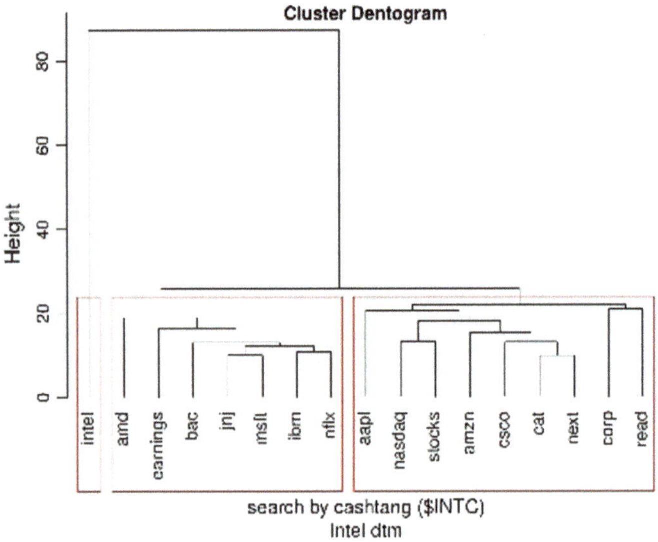

Fig. 3 Hierarchical clustering

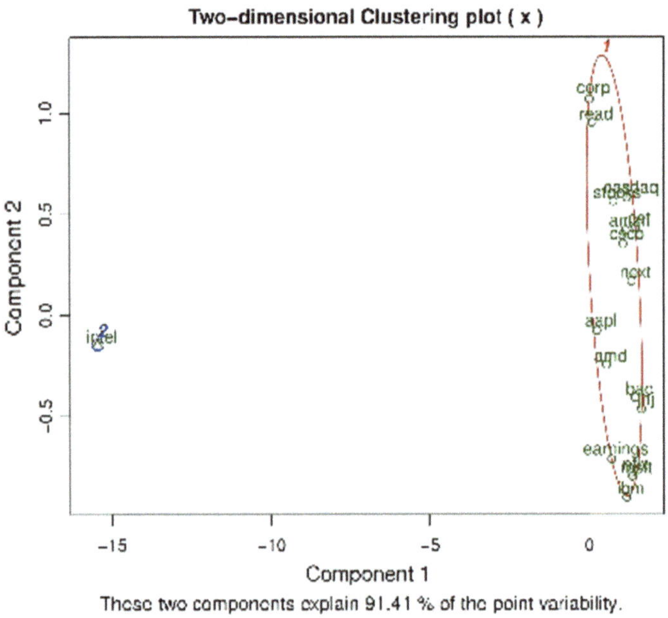

Fig. 4 Bivariate clustering plot

topics are presented in Table 2. Based on those terms, one may perform qualitative analysis but this experiment is left for a future paper (Table 3).

Table 3 Identified topics

Topic 1	Topic 2	Topic 3	Topic 4	Topic 5	Topic 6	Topic 7
Holding	Time	Reporting	Short	Reporting	Going	Explore
Shar	Book	Game	Buying	News	Overvalued	Qualcomms
Notebook	Breakout	Replays	Itunes	Optionsaction	Premarket	cons
Fousfan	Boost	Citigroup	Action	Expert	Another	Declares
Taps	Short	Neutral	Beast	Capital	Reiterated	Negative
mlb	Hits	Tweaktown	Thursday	Raised	slw	Reason
Put	Avastavg	Expiring	coyn	Announces	abc	Action
Semiconductor	Current	Highest	Gaming	Stockoption	adbe	Catalysts
Anavex	Fundamental	Nice	Second	Bought	Boosted	Holding
Division	Interested	Resources	Takes	Canceled	Channel	itus

Finally, we created a sentiment index using the QDAP polarity algorithm. We found strong relationship of the sentiment index and the daily returns of the intel

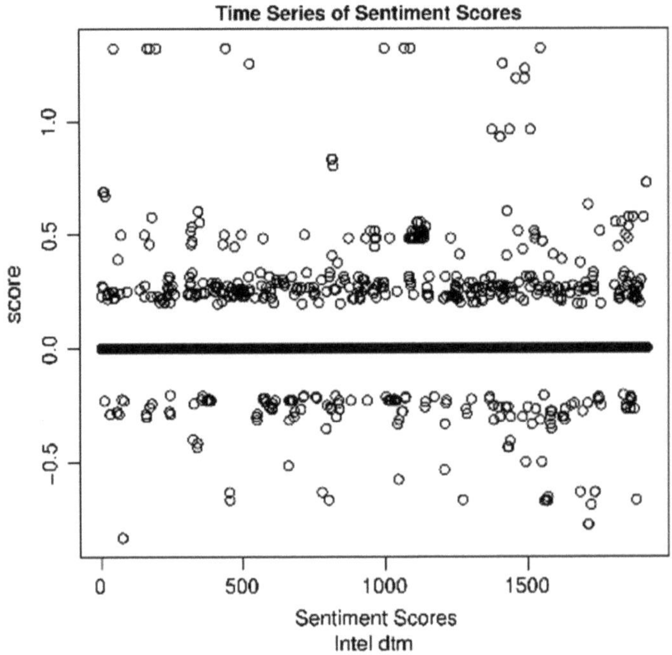

Fig. 5 Time series SI scores per tweet

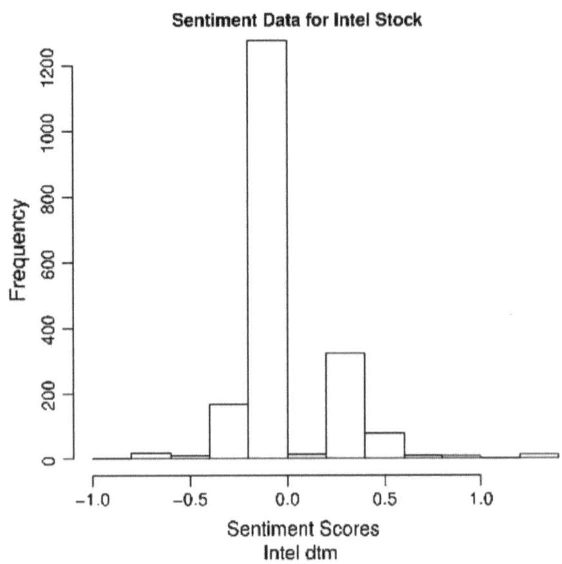

Fig. 6 Histogram of SI scores

stock. However, the results are not shown here because the sample of the experiment is ten days which is very short to draw statistically firm conclusions. Nevertheless, we have shown how to explore relevant for a problem tweets in order to help the decision-making process. In future work, we will apply the techniques presented here in a number of interesting financial and accounting problems (Figs. 5 and 6).

Conclusions

In this paper, we reviewed the current research of text data mining for financial applications. While the results of these applications are promising there are a lot yet to be asked and many issues should be addressed before this type of research becomes main stream. For example, in most of the studies the time period for forecasting stock variables are very short and the created variables (i.e., sentiment indexes) somewhere subjective. Further, while most of the studies make strong arguments against EMY, none of them estimates abnormal returns for a long period of time. Transaction cost is ignored as well as processing information cost which in this case could be quite high. On the other hand, we found promising use of text mining in event studies in order to better understand the factors that take off equilibrium the system (i.e., in structural brakes). We examined most of the available techniques for financial text mining and presented methodological guidelines for the implementation of those techniques through the application of text mining of tweets regarding IBM stock. The value of this methodology/approach is that it enables the researcher to apply a quantitative and objective methodology in handling unstructured or semi-structured data (e.g., annual reports, audit reports). By doing that, the bias of data selection is minimized and the data that derive from the methodology are more eligible by other researchers.

References

Blei, D.M., A.Y. Ng, and M.I. Jordan. 2003. Latent dirichlet allocation. *Journal of Machine Learning Research* 3: 993–1022.

Bollen, J., H. Mao, and X. Zeng. 2011. Twitter mood predicts the stock market. *Journal of Computational Science* 2 (1): 1–8.

Fairchild, R.J. 2012. From behavioural to emotional corporate finance: A new research direction. *International Journal of Behavioural Accounting and Finance* 3 (3–4): 221–243.

Graham, T., and R. Ackland. 2015. Topic modeling of tweets in R: A tutorial and methodology. https://www.academia.edu/19255535/.

Groß-Klußmann, A., and N. Hautsch. 2011. When machines read the news: Using automated text analytics to quantify high frequency news-implied market reactions. *Journal of Empirical Finance* 18 (2): 321–340.

Hu, M., and B. Liu. 2004. Mining opinion features in customer reviews. In 19th *National conference on artificial intelligence*, 755–760.

Karppi, T., and K. Crawford. 2015. Social media, financial algorithms and the hack crash. *Theory, Culture and Society*.

Loughran, T., and B. Mcdonald. 2016. Textual analysis in accounting and finance: A survey. *Journal of Accounting Research*.

Makice, K. 2009. *Twitter API: Up and running: learn how to build applications with the twitter API*. O'Reilly Media, Inc.

Malkiel, B.G. 2003. The efficient market hypothesis and its critics. *Journal of Economic Perspectives* 17 (1): 59–82.

McKinsey & Company. 2011. Big data: The next frontier for innovation, competition, and productivity. Technical Report.

Nofsinger, J.R. 2005. Social mood and financial economics. *The Journal of Behavioral Finance* 6 (3): 144–160.

Peterson, R.L. 2007. Affect and financial decision-making: How neuroscience can inform market participants. *The Journal of Behavioural Finance* 8 (2): 70–78.

Raines, J., and C. Leathers. 2011. Behavioral finance and post Keynesian—Institutionalist theories of financial markets. *Journal of Post Keynesian Economics* 33 (4): 539–554.

Ranco, G., D. Aleksovski, G. Caldarelli, M. Grčar, and I. Mozetič. 2015. The effects of twitter sentiment on stock price returns. *PloS One* 10 (9). doi:10.1371/journal.pone.0138441.

Rao, T., and S. Srivastava. 2013. Modelling movements in oil, gold, forex and market indices using search volume index and Twitter sentiments. In *Proceedings of the 5th annual ACM web science*.

Rijsbergen, C.J.V. 1979. *Information retrieval. Butterworth-Heinemann*, 2nd ed.

Rinker, T.W. 2016. *qdap: Quantitative discourse analysis package*. http://github.com/trinker/qdap.

Shawkat Ali, A., and Y. Xiang. 2010. *Dynamic and advanced data mining for progressing technological development: Innovations and systemic approaches: Innovations and systemic*. IGI Global.

Sprenger, T.O., A. Tumasjan, P.G. Sandner, and I.M. Welpe. 2014. Tweets and trades: The information content of stock microblogs. *European Financial Management* 20 (5): 926–957.

Tuckett, D. 2011. *Minding the markets: An emotional finance view of financial instability*. Palgrave Macmillan.

Wang, Y.W.Y., and X.J.W. Wang. 2005. A new approach to feature selection in text classification. In *2005 International conference on machine learning and cybernetics*, 18–21, Aug 6.

Zhang, X., H. Fuehres, and P. Gloor. 2012. Predicting asset value through twitter buzz. In *Advances in Collective Intelligence 2011*, 23–34. Springer.

Part V
2nd Symposium on Business Modelling

Organized by: Damianos P. Sakas
Department of Informatics and Telecommunications,
University of Peloponnese, Tripoli, Greece

Description

Simulation modeling provides a powerful methodology for advancing theory and research on complex behaviors and systems. This session aims at promoting understanding of simulation methodology and developing an appreciation of its potential contributions to management theory by describing the nature of simulations, its attractions, and its special problems, as well as some uses of computational modeling in management research.

Stuffing Keyword Regulation in Search Engine Optimization for Scientific Marketing Conferences

Ioannis C. Drivas, Apostolos S. Sarlis, Damianos P. Sakas and Alexandros Varveris

Introduction

For the improvement of websites' ranking in the global stage of www the process of Search Engine Optimization (SEO) constitutes one of the main key players. SEO is a necessary function for providing an easy for users access to the appropriate information (Rehman et al. 2013) as this statement refers to the benefits of SEO practices. SEO can be set under the overall framework of the effort to increase the ranking of a website in search results for given target keywords (Moreno and Martinez 2013). In addition, Gandour and Regolini (2011) in their study describe SEO as the process of multiple techniques to increase one's site content, making it more attractive to users as well as crawlers, by implementing changes within the site while focusing the effort on chosen themes and keywords. It can be seen in these two definitions that the presence of keywords have a crucial role in SEO practices. Moreover, for Choudhari and Bhalla (2015) *Keyword Analysis* is the most important part of the optimization and in the same line Al-Ananbeh et al. (2015) point out that appropriate keywords are the first step to build high-rank websites.

According to BlueCaribu Company, there are more than 932 million websites that include SEO practices information, as 3.5 people per second look up on Google for SEO practices. As to these observations and findings, more and more enterprises adopt SEO processes to their websites for the augmentation of their rankings and therefore their presence in the Internet digital world. In this paper, the authors

I.C. Drivas (✉)
Computer Science & Information Technology, Linnaeus University, Växjö, Sweden
e-mail: ioannis.c.drivas@gmail.com

A.S. Sarlis
Computer Science and Technology, University of Peloponnese, Tripolis, Greece

D.P. Sakas · A. Varveris
School of Law, National & Kapodistrian University of Athens, Athens, Greece

A. Kavoura et al. (eds.), *Strategic Innovative Marketing*, Springer Proceedings in Business and Economics, DOI 10.1007/978-3-319-56288-9_17

proceed into a keyword analysis via using specific tools and metrics which indicate the best possible keywords for websites that promote scientific events such as conferences in the field of marketing. Moreover, the authors proceed into the creation of a dynamic simulation model as a decision-making tool that estimates an optimal way of distributing company's resources in proportion with an upcoming total satisfaction regarding this investment.

Using Tools and Indicators

For the extraction of the appropriate keywords that need to be included onto websites that promote conferences on strategic innovative marketing, SEMrush Competitive Data Tool was used (http://www.semrush.com). SEMrush gives the opportunity to observe which are the most commonly used keywords for the under examination websites while it indicates the current position of the website if users type specific keywords. Also, this application estimates keywords difficulty level as an indicator that evaluates if a keyword could be ranked well in organic search results in particular keywords as the higher is the percentage the harder is to achieve high rankings for the specific given keyword.

Keywords in a webpage also related with the Metadata Description, with Alt tags on Images, with the Headings or even with the URL paths that website has. In other words, appropriate usage with the right keywords in the right frequency enables crawlers to index easier the webpage. According to the SEMrush analysis keyword tool, there are more than seven recommended top keywords that websites are using for the promotion of strategic innovative marketing conferences. There are also other relevant keywords related with organizing a scientific conference process such as Proceedings, Registration, Publication Policy, Participants, and so on. However, these relevant keywords can be characterized at least general or even incompatible within the webpage ranking improvement and for that reason they were estimated via SEMrush with high rates of Keyword Difficulty in particularly more than 70%. Therefore, the extracted keywords and the difficulty of them are:

- strategic marketing conference: Keyword Difficulty: 66.98%
- marketing innovation conference: KD: 56.52%
- strategic marketing international: KD: 67.89%
- innovative marketing: KD: 59.73%
- Anchor keyword (conference's acronym + conference): KD: ~45%
- conference marketing strategy: KD: 53.49%
- Other relevant keywords: KD: >70%.

In continuation of the previous keyword analysis, it is noteworthy to refer that this process was implemented into Google.com of US database as it has the highest number of URLs displayed in organic search results for the given keywords related with the strategic innovative marketing conferences. As it can be seen in KD remarks, some keywords have low level of difficulty less than 55%. Rightly someone could think that using only these keywords in the website is a good way for improving rankings. However, stuffing or over using keywords is not a process that evaluated positively by crawlers (Connolly and Hoar 2015; Khana and Vivekanand 2011). For that reason keywords density must be used with prudence by webmasters.

Dynamic Simulation Modeling Process

In this study, a dynamic simulation modeling process via iThink 10.0.2 simulator of iSee Systems was used for estimating the proper way of distributing the resources of an enterprise for the construction of a webpage with the appropriate keywords. The utility of DMS process has already been implemented in other studies that related heavily with the coordination and promotion of scientific conferences in the way that managing and distributing company's resources (Sakas et al. 2016; Plikas et al. 2015; Nasiopoulos et al. 2014). For the construction of the model, iThink software uses stocks and flows, convertors and connectors as a graphical user interface representation. Stocks represent the conglomeration of physical or non-physical resources. Flows represent an activity that fills or reduces a stock. Convertors are responsible of keeping values stable or serve as an external input or converting inputs into results, through user-defined algebraic relations or graphics functions. Lastly, Connectors provide connections and actions between the elements of the model (Fig. 1).

For the construction of a webpage with proper keywords in order to be ranked well by search engines, an enterprise proceeds to the optimal distribution of resources as they depended from the aforementioned Keywords Difficulty (KD) in global ranking and therefore the time for creating content-text and integrating all the keywords in the website. The model is running for 4 weeks since the keywords have specific lifetime value and due to that fact, after the first month, further research and modifications are necessary.

In the model, the available resources of the company are being distributed between seven stocks. Each stock represents each relevant keyword among the keywords that the webmasters of the company's conference website are going to invest (including "Other Keywords" as a stock). The ulterior goal is the raise of the satisfaction points (Total Keywords) of user/visitor increasing webpage visibility and the organic traffic driven to the website in order to have positive ROI. Each Controller, controls the percentage of the resources that company invests to each Keyword. Each Convertor, using a specific algorithm depended on the keywords. The algorithm is based on the KD and the estimate profit according to the available

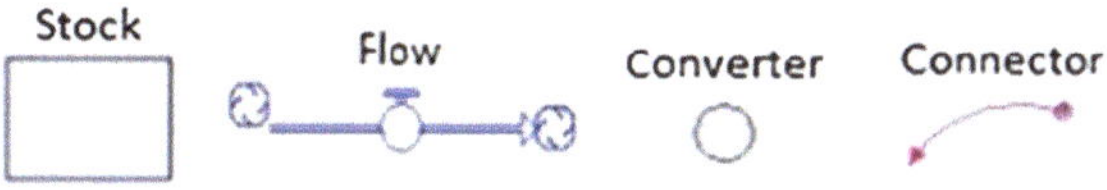

Fig. 1 Graphics and elements of iThink simulator

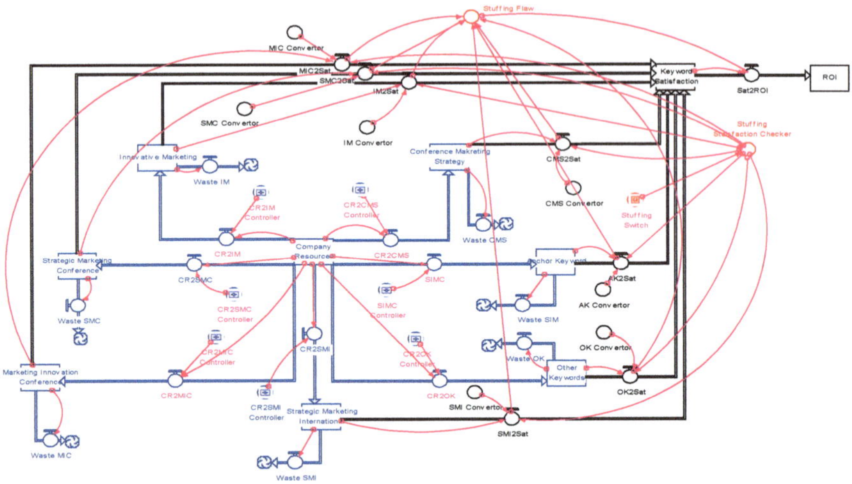

Fig. 2 Dynamic simulation model of the keyword investment and the total satisfaction profit of strategic innovative marketing conferences' webpage

resources producing a unique profit indicator from each keyword investment (profit indicator). The Waste of each keyword is depended solely on the KD (competition). When each keyword fulfills its unique goal, transfers its unique profit to the Total Satisfaction stock. Total Satisfaction stock conglomerates the profit of each separate stock.

On the other hand, Stuffing Satisfaction Checker Convertor (red convertor in Fig. 2), checks for any overflow use of any keyword with the proper algorithm depending the search engine. An overflow will cause the dramatic drop of the satisfaction points of all keywords (drop on ROI), since it will affect the total site visibility (Stuffing Flaw Convertor will affect the ROI). Stuffing Switch will On/Off the Stuffing Satisfaction Flaw Convertor depending the phase of the model implementation. Stuffing switch starts as OFF until the content/keyword implementation is ready and when it is ON it can predict the potential outcome of the investment.

Implementation of the Model

Figure 3 shows the main user interface of the simulation model. It presents the optimum percentage of the resources available in order to have a sustainable model.

The available company resources are 1000 credit points. Those credit points are distributed with specific percentage among each stock. This action represents the resources that company invests for each keyword in order to raise the organic traffic of the webpage (e.g., using keywords in metadata description, alt tags on images

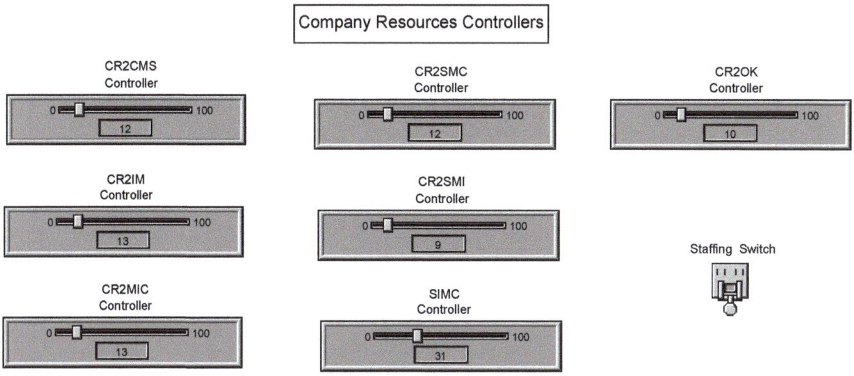

Fig. 3 Interface of the dynamic simulation model

and so on). The resources are being distributed dependently the KD and the goal of the conference's webpage as the website needs specific and relevant ranking according to the conference action and topic.

After the model implementation for 4 weeks, specific results are being presented. As Fig. 4 presents, the Total Satisfaction curve (black curve) is rising every time that each keyword fulfil each unique goal. As being expected, Company Resources (blue curve) are falling over as the resources of the company are being investing in each keyword. *Anchor Keyword* (red curve) seems to provide a great amount of Satisfaction points accordingly to the amount of resources that the decision maker invests regarding the KD and the aim of the conference in order to be ranked with this keyword. On the other hand, Strategic Marketing International keyword (orange curve) seems to be the keyword with the minimum profit and with a high rate of KD as well (Fig. 6).

Figures 5, 6, and 7, indicate the amount of resources that are being invested every week and the amount of profit that each stock-keyword contributes to the ROI of rankings in the global ranks. At the end of the fourth week (from Initial = 0 to 3, ROI points are 1.445) which translated into organic reach satisfaction. It is also

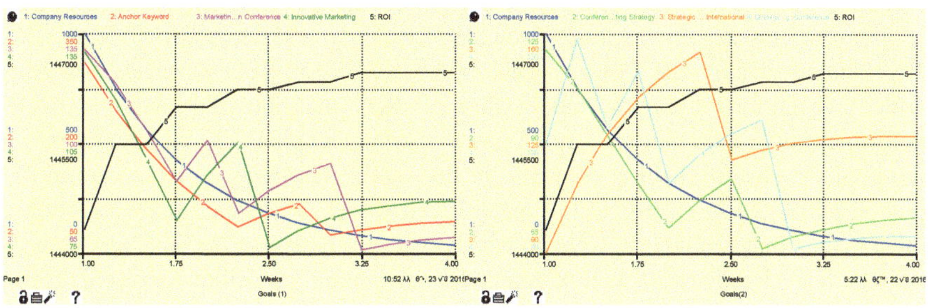

Fig. 4 Graphs of goals of the dynamic simulation model

11:15 ΑΜ 23/9/2016 — Table 1 (Table1)

Weeks	Company Resources	Marketing Innovation Confe	Strategic Marketing Confer	Keyword Satisfaction	ROI
Initial	1.000.00	130.00	120.00	902.50	1.444.315.88
1	316.41	100.75	108.85	134.73	1.445.999.83
2	100.11	93.48	90.93	90.32	1.446.345.48
3	31.68	69.78	94.49	25.07	1.446.466.18

Fig. 5 Table 1 of Goals of the Dynamic Simulation Model regarding the decision maker's ROI based on the keywords "Marketing Innovation", "Conference", and "Strategic Marketing Conference"

11:15 ΑΜ 23/9/2016 — Table 2 (Table2)

Weeks	Company Resources	Anchor Keyword	Conference Makreting	Innovative Marketing	Keyword Satisfaction	ROI
Initial	1.000.00	310.00	120.00	130.00	902.50	1.444.315.88
1	316.41	112.68	62.79	96.22	134.73	1.445.999.83
2	100.11	73.50	59.88	84.32	90.32	1.446.345.48
3	31.68	92.24	66.20	88.87	25.07	1.446.466.18

Fig. 6 Table 2 of Goals of the Dynamic Simulation Model regarding the decision maker's ROI based on the keywords "Anchor Keyword", "Conference Marketing", and "Innovative Marketing"

11:15 ΑΜ 23/9/2016 — Table 3 (Table3)

Weeks	Company Resources	Strategic Marketing Intern	Other Keywords	Keyword Satisfaction	ROI
Initial	1.000.00	90.00	100.00	902.50	1.444.315.88
1	316.41	148.00	106.31	134.73	1.445.999.83
2	100.11	124.88	98.50	90.32	1.446.345.48
3	31.68	127.28	77.64	25.07	1.446.466.18

Fig. 7 Table 3 of Goals of the Dynamic Simulation Model regarding the decision maker's ROI based on the keywords "Strategic Marketing International", and "Other used Keywords"

noteworthy to refer that the low increase of results plus the nonvarying situation of Satisfaction after 3.5 weeks is analogous to the minimal invest of resources.

Conclusion and Future Implications

In this paper, the authors highlighted not only the importance of proper keywords in a conference website that a company has, but also suggested a way of distributing resources for the maximum outcome via using a dynamic simulation model. In addition, the authors implemented a convertor that prevents keywords use from *stuffing-overuse* as other studies indicate (Connolly and Hoar 2015; Khana and Vivekanand 2011). The proper usage of keywords for SEO purposes combined with a dynamic simulation model that predicts the potential outcome of the investment with a certain amount of resources must be placed as an integral part of the total On-site SEO. In conclusion, in this study there was an examination of a crucial point, the keywords utility on SEO. However, a holistic implementation of other issues that probably a website has, constitutes a second decisive step that the authors had already start to implement for an overall modeling representation of SEO practices and the benefits of it, as the chaotic mantle of search engine results threatens.

References

Al-Ananbeh, A.A., B.A. Ata, M. Al-Kabi, and I. Alsmadi. 2012. Website usability evaluation and search engine optimization for eighty Arab university websites. *Basic Science & Engineering* 21 (1): 107–122.

BlueCaribu. How big is the SEO Industry on the Internet? http://www.bluecaribu.com/seo-industry Accessed 10 Sep 2016.

Choudharia, K., and V.K. Bhallab. 2015. Video search engine optimization using keyword and feature analysis. *Procedia Computer Science* 58: 691–697.

Connolly, R., and R. Hoar. 2015. *Fundamentals of web development*. New York, NY: Pearson Education.

Gandour, A., and A. Regolini. 2011. Web site search engine optimization: A case study of Fragfornet. *Library Hi Tech News* 28 (6), 6–13.

Khana, S., and O. Vivekanand. 2011 Concept of search engine optimization in web search engine. *International Journal of Advanced Engineering Research and Studies* 1 (1): 235–237.

Moreno, L., and P. Martinez. 2013. Overlapping factors in search engine optimization and web accessibility. *Online Information Review* 37 (4): 564–580.

Nasiopoulos, K.D., D.P. Sakas, and D.S. Vlachos. 2014. Modeling the scientific dimension of academic conferences. *Procedia-Social and Behavioral Sciences* 147: 576–585.

Plikas, J.H., K.D. Nasiopoulos, and H. Plikas. 2015. Academic conferences promotion process and social media. Modeling of the problem. *International Journal of Strategic Innovative Marketing* 2: 60–71.

Rehman, K., K. Ahmed, and N. Muhammad. 2013. The foremost guidelines for achieving higher ranking in search results through search engine optimization. In *International Journal of Advanced Science & Technology* 52: 101.

Sakas, D.P., D.S. Vlachos, and D.K. Nasiopoulos. 2016. Modeling the development of the online conference's services. *Library Review* 65 (3): 160–184.

Communicating Strategically for Improving Team Effectiveness in ICTs Organizations

I.C. Drivas, D.P. Sakas and C. Riziotis

Introduction

Team Effectiveness can be characterized as one of the basic pillars for improving the overall performance in ICTs organizations. The crucial importance of Team Effectiveness is clearly highlighted in several studies arising in this way the necessity for creating a strategic communicational path that leads an organization to effective communicational channels between decision makers and employees (Verma et al. 2016; Volmer and Sonnentag 2011). It is also noted that each decision maker influence the performance and the coordination of team, hence team effectiveness (Santos et al. 2015). Moreover, according to Kozlowski and Ilgen (2006) several theories are very useful but they appeared with indirect implications about team effectiveness due to the fact that these theories neglect processes that decision makers follow in order to coordinate employees' knowledge and skills.

In previous research approach, team effectiveness factor played a central role to the overall job satisfaction of employees (Drivas et al. 2016a) illustrating in this way the first path for the creation of a strategic communicational model. However, the main goal of this study is to examine if four principles of decision makers practices can be set under the umbrella of team effectiveness. The existence of clear goals and objectives inside the organization, employees' recognition, information sharing between individuals, and the troubleshooting effectiveness are main key

I.C. Drivas (✉)
Computer Science & Information Technology, Linnaeus University, Växjö, Sweden
e-mail: ioannis.c.drivas@gmail.com

D.P. Sakas
Computer Science & Technology, University of Peloponesse, Tripolis, Greece

C. Riziotis
National Hellenic Research Foundation, Athens, Greece

A. Kavoura et al. (eds.), *Strategic Innovative Marketing*, Springer Proceedings in Business and Economics, DOI 10.1007/978-3-319-56288-9_18

points that need to be examined in order to understand if these components can be adopted as cornerstones for the improvement and augmentation of the current teamwork effectiveness.

Clear Goals and Objectives

Progressing into the creation of a communicational model that embraces high collaboration between decision makers and employees in the ICT sector, the existence of clearly defined goals and objectives constitutes a communicational cornerstone. Clear goals are one of the vital few (Tohidi 2011). Furthermore, Bojeun (2014) in his work points out that managers frequently start an effort without clear understanding of goals and objectives or the complexity and the percent of risk that have to take. Although this is not a new assertion, the problematic mantle starts to cover all the individuals and especially employees in ICTs development sector, when they do not know, not only how the new ICT product would finally look like, but also how will they know when they finally achieved organization's goal. In this case, some main pillars for placing the framework of clear goals is the good understanding of organizational policies, the provision of necessary job guidelines, while employees know their specific role in the team, or even the definition of clear goals for the job performance in an overall effort to improve dynamically the efficiency and the effectiveness of the team.

Employees' Recognition

Recognizing employees' effort can be characterized as a difficult multidimensional process in which several influencers took place. Indeed, managers dealing with the challenge to measure the influence that they caused to their employees, and also they probably think wrong that all the kinds of recognitions and motivations have the same outcomes in all the followers (Canós-Darós 2013). In any case, the level of equal treatment from decision makers among employees and the participation of employees in decision-making process probably highlights employees' recognition level. In addition, how much venerable and valuable is an employee to others or the possibility that management recognizes the extra effort employees put into their tasks, are some key elements which always needed to be taken into serious consideration from the decision makers in order to establish a well-structured communicational strategy.

Information Sharing

To begin with, the ICT organizational environment holds the rains of how to deal with the rapidly daily produced information globally. Considering the strategic information collection and management as one of the main capitals which a company has, a clear framework of how employees share and deal with the daily produced company's information must be defined. Measuring the level of exchanging information among individuals, estimating the quantity and the quality of feedback that employees receive, or even observing the motility that team members share their knowledge and expertise to solve upcoming problems, are a few, but surely crucial components that ICTs decision makers must take into consideration. The aforementioned statements come to be strengthened by Gholipour et al. (2011), pointed out that decision makers might take wrong decisions if they are not willing to use appropriate resources or if they do not have a clearly defined strategy for innovation on how to *handle* and *share* the produced knowledge. Moreover, according to Wong (2008) research and the results of it, the distribution of knowledge in teams affects the quality of problem solving.

Troubleshooting Effectiveness

In a working environment which is governed under the spirit of teamwork, the synonym of effectiveness is the efficacy in troubleshooting or problem solving. Even if a group consisted of highly skilled members, the result and the way of dealing with the problematic situation is what truly matters. In other words, if a problematic situation cannot be solved and there is no strategic planning for solving it, then the potential improvement of the organization remains inexistent. Caveleri et al. (2012) mentioned that shifting a team into more active types of collaboration in learning and knowledge processing not only gives the opportunity to deal with problems with greater agility and openness in troubleshooting, but also arise highly qualitative solutions to the upcoming problems. In order to establish a strategic troubleshooting plan, management should always take into serious consideration some axes that related mostly with: decision makers' efforts to help employees solving problems in their job, the periodical meetings and the well facilitation of them, the quality of results with clear agreements and outcomes after meetings sessions and the constructively working persistence on problematic issues until they are resolved.

Having always in mind that team effectiveness plays a central role in decision-making chess game, all the main aforementioned factors including employees' recognition, information sharing, and clear goals and objectives should be examined as to their performance to the troubleshooting effectiveness which is finally related with the overall effectiveness of team. In this way, a positive correlation between these components should shed the lights for the construction of a communicational model that affects drastically the overall effectiveness of a team in an ICT organization. Hence the following hypotheses examined if:

H1 Clear goals and objectives has a positive effect in troubleshooting effectiveness
H2 Employees recognition has a positive effect in troubleshooting effectiveness
H3 Information sharing has a positive effect in troubleshooting effectiveness.

Methodology

A convenient purposively questionnaire was sent via email to 235 employees and managers who were directly associated with ICT organizations, all of them with different positions in their organization. The convenience sampling method has been used to achieve high level of representative sample plus for high availability for data gathering (Drivas et al. 2016b). Survey's content validity was established before the final distribution in a testing-pilot process to 12 pilot respondents. After reminding to them one time, 164 participants anonymously and confidentially agreed to complete the questionnaire (response rate 69.78%) in a seven Likert Scale, minimizing the proclivity of responding in a socially desirable way. The survey was partitioned into four major sections as they described above, giving an additional effort to the encapsulation of demographics of participants illustrating their profile (Table 1).

Table 1 Respondents' profile

Gender	Education	Job experience	Position	Self estimated technological experience
Female: 54.88% Male: 45.12%	Undergraduate studies: **30.49%** Post-graduate studies: **48.17%** Doctorate (PhD): **21.34%**	Up to 1 year: **9.26%** 1–5 years: **21.6%** 6–10 years: **15.43%** 11–20 years: **30.86%** 21 years or more: **22.84%**	Employee: **67.9%** Technical support: **6.79%** Manager: **14.81%** Senior manager: **10.49%**	Very low exp.: **0.61%** Low exp.: **3.07%** Slightly low exp: **1.84%** Medium exp.: **17.18%** Slightly high exp.: **38.65%** High exp.: **32.52%** Extremely high exp.: **6.13%**
Sample size, $N = 164$				

Results

To begin with, before testing the hypotheses, the authors ran a Principal Component Analysis (PCA) which extracted four factors and also excluded variables with statistically insignificant loadings. Thus, one variable of Clear Goals factor (0.021 < 0.05 *sig. level*) and one variable of Employees Recognition factor (0.034 < 0.05 *sig. level*) were excluded from the analysis. The other two factors the Information Sharing and Troubleshooting Effectiveness extracted higher factor loadings above the limit of 0.5 *sig. level.* In the effort to testify the hypotheses regarding the correlations among the factors and also to confirm each factor's construct validity a Confirmatory Factor Analysis (CFA) with oblimin rotation was used. CFA can be used in order to testify if the measures of a factor have parallel indications with a researcher's understanding regarding the nature of the upcoming factor (Kline 2010). Three fit measures were used to evaluate if the strategic

Table 2 Factorial loadings matrix, means, st. deviations, and overall fit of the CFA model

Constructed factors	Items	Mean	St. deviation	Loadings
Clear goals	CG1	4.7	1.621	0.962
KMO: 0.864	CG2	4.62	1.602	0.928
Cronbach's alpha: 0.892	CG3	4.40	1.74	0.957
Var. explained: 89.947	CG4	5.09	1.66	0.919
Sig. bartlett: 0.00				
Employees recognition	ER1	4.42	1.57	0.785
KMO: 0.918	ER2	4.15	1.62	0.905
Cronbach's alpha: 0.942	ER3	4.20	1.71	0.907
Var. explained: 84.743	ER4	5.29	1.49	0.916
Sig. bartlett: 0.00	ER5	5.57	1.46	0.921
	ER6	5.18	1.55	0.940
	ER7	5.43	1.51	0.943
	ER8	5.51	1.29	0.926
	ER9	5.48	1.406	0.902
Information sharing	IS1	4.83	1.5	0.778
KMO: 0.912	IS2	4.22	1.54	0.577
Cronbach's alpha: 0.794	IS3	5.43	1.55	0.967
Var. explained: 81.121	IS4	5.49	1.38	0.855
Sig. bartlett: 0.00	IS5	4.96	1.58	0.942
	IS6	4.91	1.57	0.836
	IS7	4.97	1.66	0.726
Troubleshooting effectiveness	TE1	4.68	1.6	0.740
KMO: 0.859	TE2	4.35	1.63	0.942
Cronbach's alpha: 0.819	TE3	4.38	1.51	0.945
Var. explained: 89.957	TE4	4.45	1.64	0.949
Sig. bartlett: 0.00	TE5	5.32	1.45	0.892
	TE6	5.19	1.44	0.928
Model-fit index		*Statistical values-scores*		
Chi-square/degree of freedom		1.958,32		
Goodness-of-fit index		0.962		
Comparative fit index		0.897		

communicational model fits statistically in order to be adopted: chi-square/degree of freedom (χ^2/d.f), goodness-of-fit (GFI), and the comparative fit index (CFI). Table 2 summarizes the overall variables and the loadings of them plus the overall fit values of CFA model, while all the extracted values appeared with acceptable statistical levels.

Discussion and Future Implications

In this study, the authors tried to designate a strategic communicational model that can be adopted from decision makers in ICTs organizations for the optimization of their communicational channel between them and their followers. Regarding the tested hypotheses, as it can be seen in Table 3, all the three factors have significant statistical correlations with Troubleshooting Effectiveness as an axis that is related heavily with the overall team efficiency and efficacy. In other words, it can be said that if each team solves constructively each problematic situation then it is possessed under highly overall effectiveness.

It is also noteworthy to refer that according to the sample, if decision makers establish clear goals and objectives to their employees', then a more efficient problem-solving process takes place (correlation between factors: 0.484), a fact which related with Hendrix (2004) research paper. In addition, there is an important correlation between information sharing and troubleshooting effectiveness (correlation between factors: 0.168) which not only related with Wong's (2008) results but also arises future implications in order to establish a well-structured framework of strategic information management which helps an ICT organization improve its troubleshooting effectiveness. These elements are also obtained using simulation modeling of the corresponding processes (Sakas et al. 2014).

Table 3 Correlations between factors and hypotheses testing

Factors	Clear goals and objectives	Employees recognition	Information sharing	Troubleshooting effectiveness
Clear goals and objectives	1.000	0.591*	0.131*	0.484*
Employees recognition	0.591*	1.000	0.182*	0.251*
Information sharing	0.131*	0.182*	1.000	0.168*
Troubleshooting effectiveness	0.484*	0.250	0.168*	1.000

Sample size, $N = 164$. *Correlation is statistically significant at the 95% level 2-tailed (i.e., $p \leq 0.05$)

Although a model proposed that embraces clear goals, employees' effort recognition, and information sharing in order to improve troubleshooting effectiveness, it will be very fruitful to design a dynamic simulation modeling process with an actuarial tendency, in order to fully understand the future potential of that model inside an organization as other researchers already constructed in management and decision-making sector (Nasiopoulos et al. 2013). Lastly, the survey of this study was distributed in more than ten countries with different decision-making and leadership cultures in ICTs organizations and indeed these four factors probably play a central role in strategic communication process. However, the multidimensionality of different cultures and how communication process is performed arises and reflects a new era of barriers for the establishment of a lingua franca on communicational planning processes and principles, although the existence of the aforementioned factors as core values of strategic communication process.

References

Bojeun, M.C. 2014. *Program management leadership, creating successful team dynamics*. New York: CRC Press Taylor & Francis Group.

Canós-Darós, L. 2013. An algorithm to identify the most motivated employees. *Management Decision* 51 (4): 813–823.

Cavaleri, S., J. Firestone, and F. Reed. 2012. Managing project problem-solving patterns. *International Journal of Managing Projects in Business* 5 (1): 125–145.

Damianos Sakas, Dimitris Vlachos, and Dimitris Nasiopoulos. 2014. Modelling strategic management for the development of competitive advantage, based on technology. *Journal of Systems and Information Technology* 16 (3): 187–209. doi:10.1108/JSIT-01-2014-0005.

Drivas, I.C., A.I. Damaskinou, and D.P. Sakas. 2016a. Strategic communication process for sustainable entrepreneurial environment in nonprofit organizations. In *International Conference of Strategic Innovative Marketing (IC-SIM 2015) Proceedings in Business and Economics*. Springer.

Drivas, I.C., D.P. Sakas, and G.A. Giannakopoulos. 2016b. Self-other agreement for improving communication in libraries and information services. *Library Review* 65 (3): 206–223.

Gholipour, A., A. Pirannejad, S.F. Kozekanan, and F. Gholipour. 2011. Designing motivation system to produce creativity and entrepreneurship in petrochemical company. *International Journal of Business Management* 6 (5): 137–144.

Hendrix, G. 2004. *The Importance of goals to the success of work teams*. Centre for the study of work teams: University of North Texas.

Kline, R.B. 2010. Principles and practice of structural equation modeling, 3rd ed. New York: Guilford Press.

Kozlowski, S.W.J., and D.R. Ilgen. 2006. Enhancing the effectiveness of work groups and teams. *Psychological Science in the Public Interest* 7: 77–124.

Nasiopoulos, K.D., D.P. Sakas, and D.S. 2013. Analysis of strategic leadership simulation models in non-profit organizations. In *Procedia—Social and Behavioral Sciences* 73: 276–284.

Santos, J.P., A. Caetano, and S.M. Tavares. 2015. Is training leaders in functional leadership a useful tool for improving the performance of leadership functions and team effectiveness. *The Leadership Quarterly* 26 (3): 470–484.

Tohidi, H. 2011. Teamwork productivity & effectiveness in an organization base on rewards, leadership, training, goals, wage, size, motivation, measurement and information technology. *Procedia Computer Science* 3: 1137–1146.

Verma, N., S.N., Rangnekar, and M.K. Barua. 2016. Exploring decision making style as a predictor of team effectiveness. *International Journal of Organizational Analysis* 24 (1): 36–63.

Volmer, J., and S. Sonnentag. 2011. The role of star performers in software design teams. *Journal of Managerial Psychology* 26 (3): 219–234.

Wong, S.S. 2008. Task knowledge overlap and knowledge variety: The role of advice network structures and impact on group effectiveness. *Journal of Organizational Behavior* 29 (5): 591–614.

Part VI
2nd Symposium on Healthcare Services: Special Aspects and Challenges in an Evolving Environment

Organized by: Charalampos Platis
National Center for Public Administration and Local Government, Athens, Greece

Description

This section will accommodate research papers, study of cases, and thorough presentation by reviewing the literature in the field of health policy (Health Systems) as well as at more "technical" issues from everyday healthcare practice. Objectives of the module is the emergence of both, the specificity of Health Care Delivery Systems and from the other the close relationship with the modern trends in Management such as Operation Research, Strategic Planning, Target Setting Procedure, Evaluation Analysis, New Technologies in Management of Human Resources and Financing Management etc.

Improve the Effectiveness of the Provided Healthcare Services and the Efficiency of a Public Hospital in the Light of a Manager

Maria Papadaki and Charalampos Platis

Background

Health, as social good, has been established internationally, either it is being referred to the private or the public sector, and cannot follow the rules of supply and demand that determine the market mechanism (Malliarou et al. 2011). Considering the rapid technological improvement, the increasing demands of citizens for better quality services and the political pressure to rationalize the expenses due to economic recession, it raises the need to restructuring healthcare units (Saltman et al. 2011). The usefulness of a Manager in healthcare units is being recognized nationally (Carter et al. 2011), while a knowledge–skills complex is being appreciated with special value. The internal and external environment analysis of a hospital is necessary to set the goals. Setting specific priorities will lead to the efficient performance of the organization and the supply of quality services. Priority of course will be given to consider and implement selected management tools. In Greece, completed suggestions to embrace the role of a modern Manager in a public hospital were made after the last official call to cover positions Governors and Deputy Governors Hospital (Official call 2015) that were enforced in 2016. In conclusion, the question is which priorities will be set and which management tools will be chosen by the new Manager of the Greek Public Hospital in order to

The original version of the book was revised. Belated corrections to change the order of First name and Family name of chapter authors have been incorporated. The erratum to the book is available at 10.1007/978-3-319-56288-9_72

M. Papadaki (✉)
Postgraduate Course in Healthcare Management Msc, Social Sciences,
Hellenic Open University, Athens, Greece
e-mail: merulio80@yahoo.gr

C. Platis
Collaborating Scientific Personnel at Hellenic Open University, Athens, Greece

A. Kavoura et al. (eds.), *Strategic Innovative Marketing*, Springer Proceedings in Business and Economics, DOI 10.1007/978-3-319-56288-9_19

improve the quality of the provided health services and at the same time the performance of the organization as a business. This assignment is referred to a public Hospital of Crete, Venizeleio Pananeio General Hospital (VPGH).

Review

The Profile of an Effective Manager and the Management Demands of a Public Hospital

Duties–Competencies

In opposition to hospital's social status, comes its business dimension and its goal to reduce the continuously rising running cost and compete in the market (Rekleiti et al. 2012). Maintaining at the same time or even improving the quality of the provided services. Taking into consideration the above parameters, the duties and competences of a manager in a public hospital, define the administrative framework and emphasize on his leadership profile. Studying the content of the law 3329/2005 (2005), someone could categorize the duties as strategic planning-organization, management of financial incomes, leadership-motivating, management of staff, material and building structure and evaluation feedback.

Knowledge–Skills

According to the last official call (Official call 2015) for filling manager positions at Greek public hospitals, it is regarded as essential qualification to possess a degree from a Greek academy or technological educational institution or an analog to a certified degree of a foreign country. Supplementary are evaluated related M.Sc., Ph.D. degrees, recommendation letters, previous experience, educational and social work, participation in voluntary actions, personality through interview and evaluation test.

However, in practice, the effective management of a hospital demands a holistic overview of its functioning, by improving the manager's basic knowledge in technological applications, in theories of health sciences, such as epidemiology, biostatistics, public health, of economic sciences, of medicine, and of social sciences (Theofilou 2011). Beyond acquiring knowledge, the skills of a Manager are all those supplements to achieve the setting goals. They can be categorized as:

- Interpersonal (Leadership, relations)
- Communication
- Analysis. The flexibility of designing–programming comes to a success through the total view of the organization, plus the subtractive conception of the individual parts of it (Pisek and Wilson 2001).

Ways to Improve the Effectiveness of the Provided Services and the Performance of VPGH via SWOT Analysis

In order to improve the effectiveness of the provided services and the performance of VPGH, the analysis of its internal and external environment (Table 1) is necessary.

Proceeding, lays the selection of 3 priority goals for more effective health service providence and best performance of the hospital.

At the level of internal business procedures, the implementation of the model "Total Quality Management" is the guide to plan an efficient function of it. That means to meet the patient's needs considering law expenses with the least cost (Karasoulos 2014). Through the procedure of the quality circle (environment analysis, criteria, standards, instructions and protocols) the improvement of the product health is ensured (Toyntas 2003). The goal is to develop a system of internal check and evaluation of service quality.

Next strategic goal is the financial rationalization. The economic efficiency of the organization depicts the quality of the services and it is affected by the funding methods and the health suppliers (Xenos et al. 2014). Its reduced autonomy according to the institutional framework, the reduce of the annual governmental budget in healthcare expands, the discrepancy of the real cost of services to

Table 1 Description of the internal and external environment of VPGH via SWOT analysis

Strengths	Weaknesses
• Experienced staff • Secured incomes by the annual governmental funding • Positive image of hospital's social work to the community • DRGs • Efficient biomedical equipment	• Absence of a business plan • Reduced performance • Old and inefficient building structure • Loosen control mechanism of performance and health quality • Ineffective internal staff management • Lack of expertise staff to function biomedical equipment applications, nurses, paramedical. • Lack of distinctly aired and widespread form of duties • Law percentages of educational updating • Reduced employee satisfaction • Unpleasant working climate
Opportunities	**Threats**
• Law 3329/2005 to establish managers • Direction 2014/24/EE to change the way of supplying • Funding investment or not programs via European funds • Adopt and implement quality insurance policies • Introduce e-Health (electronic health)	• Economic crisis • Bureaucracy • Lack of investment orientation • Rising morbidity • Intense political interference • Lack of political will to enforce reforms

payments by the insurance fund and the political instability, lead to the necessity of improving funding (Rekleiti et al. 2012).

At labor-intensive services, such as a hospital, the component human resources take a leading role in relation to economic and material resources (Polyzos 2014). Its arithmetic luck, the knowledge deficiency and the indifference of delivering maximum work efficiency need to be planed from the beginning, in order to offer quality services.

Implement Management Tools to VPGH, Based on Priorities

A particularly useful tool is the adoption of a certification system ISO9001:2008 that concerns the fulfillment of predetermined standards. For Greece the State Carrier of the certification is called ELOT (Greek organization of standardization), it is non-hospital and provides the certification after the check and evaluation is completed in predetermined time. In parallel a quality index is recorded (Toyntas 2003). It embraces the principals of Clinical Governance. It creates a framework through functions (Vanu Som 2004), taking advantage of possibilities as:

- Clinical control (Reduce medical mistakes, save time and money from useless tests). Implement DRGs so as to match the real to the demanding.
- Clinical effectiveness. (Evidence-based medicine and practice concerning protocols and instructions of medical and nurse community that already exist).
- Risk management. Create a business plan of anticipation to confront with possible risks or deal with arising problems.
- Benchmarking. A technique for comparative study and data analysis to other organizations with common assets, so as to adopt their techniques (Platis 2015).
- Patientqaul. A service tool measurement for patient satisfaction that reflects quality service necessitating questionnaires and special software (Kostagiolas et al. 2006).
- E-Health. Information management in health to transfer healthcare funds, according to WHO (Sofoy 2014).

The timetable for introducing clinical governance in hospital management through ISO9001/2008 has 3 years overtime. The financing is state because no other funder copes with economic.

Restrictive parameters are the staff's denial to adopt the general plan due to failure to embrace the goals. Moreover, staff's inefficiency to handle new technology and computer network, the incorrect application at specific management tools, the luck of motivation and bureaucracy are additional restrictions (Jakab et al. 2002). To improve the funding methods the chosen tools to be used are:

- Pest analysis.
- Esy-net. Web platform to provide updated data in credibility (incomes, medical expenses and payrolls, patient inflows–outflows). Create a data base by recording economic operations, checks, evaluation and feedback.

- EOPYY (National organization of provision healthcare services)
  - Single computerization.
  - Equalization revenue (social security funds, governmental grants) to hospital bills.
- Fund investment programs by EU, such as the program of energy upgrading by installing photovoltaic.
- DRGs. Reduce the hospital's deficit (Xenos et al. 2014).
- Diagnostic and therapeutic protocols.

The restricts are bureaucracy, modern technology, limited autonomy (initiatives, decision making) (Gogos 2011), specialized knowledge in technology, informatics, specific software, politics based on petty values, indifference of political leadership suspend the application of the legislation (Dikaios et al. 1999). The timetable is 2 years.

Lastly, staffing based on progressive practices, is the evaluation of the current efficiency and the respective needs. The chosen tool is the job outline, based on the prepared guide by the Ministry of Administrative Reform (Guide to design job profiles 2013), where the substantial and typical qualifications are described. There are features of internal allocation such as:

- The ability of the manager to convince the employees about the usefulness of the program.
- Motivation theories (Target and acquired needs by Mc Clelland). Motivate the staff and detect the partners to start a pilot program in one section at first.
- Integrated information systems to manage economic resources (Karvouni 2010).
- Draw up rules of hierarchical staff development.
- Benchmarking.

Labor input features such as European Community programs and voluntary teams in sections or processes of low specialization. Restrictive factors are the institutional framework, loosen political leaderships, consolidated promotion culture, reduced annual government grants, technical informational inadequacy project, and resistance to changes. The timetable is 1 year and the tool evaluate its implementation is the servqual method (Kostagiolas et al. 2006).

Conclusions

Corresponding to the health policy of the country, the goals the Manager of a public hospital sets in strategic and functional level demand the implementation of a business plan, using testing management tools in effectiveness. Quality assurance of the provided services, the financing improvement and management of staffing constitute the priorities for the specific hospital. The chosen tools are practices of modernized management governance in health units. The evaluation of the plan effectiveness is still in early stages due to failure to gather information and results. The restricts coming forward like economic recession, the suffocated institutional framework, the luck of strategic goals and motives, the technological inefficiency and the established interventional policy of the specific administrations, are some of the issues the contemporary manager is asked to cope with. The combination of knowledge and skills make his effort less difficult, acknowledging the abilities to improve the effectiveness of the provided health services and the total performance of the organization.

References

Carter, K., S. Dorgan, and D. Layton. 2011. Why hospital management matters. *Implications, Health International.*

Dikaios, K., M. Koytoyzis, N. Polyzos, J. Sigalas, and M. Chletsos. 1999. Basic management principles of management (management) health services. In Historical and critical weighting healthcare, conclusions on the development of health policy in Greece, ch. 17.5, 543–546, Patra. ISBN: 960-538-050-1.

Gogos, Ch. 2011. Management in public and private hospital in Greece. *Rostrum of Asclepius "To Vima tou Asklipiou" Journal* 10 (1).

Guide to design job profiles. 2013. Ministry of administrative reform and e-government. Directorate General Administrative Organization & Procedures, Directorate Organizational Development. http://www.minadmin.gov.gr/wp-content/uploads/20130508_odhgos_sxed_perigr.pdf. Accessed 28 Mar 2016.

Jakab, M., A. Preker, A. Harding, and L. Hawkins. 2002. The introduction of market forces in the public hospital sector, from New Public Sector Management to Organizational Reform, June 2002, ISBN1-932126-62-7.

Karasoulos, Ch. 2014. Modern approach to the operation of a hospital. *Review Article, Rostrum of Asclepius—"To Vima tou Asklipiou" Journal* 12 (1): 10–11.

Karvouni, P. 2010. Integrated information systems in the health sector and implementation of XDS-MS standard. Institutional Depository University of Patras. http://hdl.handle.net/10889/4100. Accessed 22 Mar 2016.

Kostagiolas, P., H. Platis, and Zimeras St. 2006. A management approach for the public healthcare sector based on user expectations. *Archives of Hellenic Medicine* 23 (6): 603–614.

Malliarou, M., P. Sarafis, K. Karathanasaki, and K. Sotiriadou. 2011. Characteristics of health and inability to impose rules of the free competitive market. *Interscientific Health Care* 3 (2): 38–43.

N 3329/2005. 2005. Newspaper of the Hellenic Republic. Issue 1, 81, Athens, 4 April 2005.

Official Call. 2015. Greek Republic, Ministry of health, division human resources and management support, human resources of legal persons. Call for expressions of interest to cover positions Governors and Deputy Governors Hospital. http://www.moh.gov.gr/articles/newspaper/proslhpseis-diorismoi/3639-prosklhsh-ekdhlwshs-endiaferontos-gia-thn-kalypsh-thesewn-dioikhtwn-kai-anaplhrwtwn-dioikhtwn-nosokomeiwn?fdl=8874.Athens. Accessed 28 Dec 2015.

Pisek, P.E., and T. Wilson. 2001. Complexity, leadership and management in healthcare organizations. *Journal List, BMJ* 323 (7315): PMC1121291.

Platis, Ch. 2015. *The business intelligence as a decision-making system in health units*. Patra: Greek Open University.

Polyzos, N. 2014. Management of the health resources and leadership with emphasis in health. Extract, YpiresYgeias04Dior_Layout 1 8/28/14 10:41 PM Page 193.

Rekleiti, M., M. Tananaki, and P. Kyloudis. 2012. Health expenditure in the Greek healthcare system: An international comparison. *Review Article, Perioperative Nursing* 1 (1): p5.

Saltman, R.B., A. Duran, and H.F.W. Dubois. 2011. Governing Public Hospitals, Reform strategies and the movement towards institutional autonomy. Introduction: Innovative governance strategies in European public hospitals, 1–14, Observatory Studies Series No. 25, published in United Kingdom 2011.

Sofoy, K. 2014. *E-health applications, Quality in health, medical informatics*. http://www.qualityinhealth.gr/. Accessed 8 Apr 2016.

Theofilou, A. 2011. The contribution of social sciences in the evaluation of health—Related quality of life. *e-Journal of Science & Technology (e-JST)* (2): 6. http://e-jst.teiath.gr/issue_20/theofilou_20.pdf. Accessed 24 Mar 2016.

Toyntas, G. 2003. Quality issues in medical practice and in health services. *Archives of Hellenic Medicine* 20 (5): 532–546.

Vanu Som, C. 2004. Clinical governance: A fresh look at its definition. Clinical Governance: 2004:9, 2: ABI/INFORM Global, 87.

Xenos, P., M. Nektarios, N. Polyzos, and J. Yfantopoylos. 2014. Modern methods of hospital funding, competition and financial. *Archives of Hellenic Medicine* 31 (2): 172–185.

The Use of Information System at Public Hospital Pharmacies in Greece: Myths and Reality

Ioannis Karafyllis, Charalampos Platis and George Pierrakos

Introduction

The medicine sales have been increased from 2000 to 2008 in an annual average basis of 19.2%. From 2000 to 2007, the expenses have almost tripled from 442M€ to 1.176M€.

The total pharmaceutical expenses in 2009 was almost 8.5B€ or 3.7% of GDP while the European average was below 1.5%.

There are plenty of Pharmacy Information Systems (PIS) that can be used by the pharmacy of a hospital and that can help to reduce the medical mistakes and the stay of patients at hospital. PIS are especially designed for helping pharmacists to make decisions about patient drug therapies. Their emphasis lies on reducing medical errors, improving communications between nurses and the pharmacy department, and providing integration and interoperability in closed-loop medication administration (Mettler et al. 2009; Enrado 2005). Key features are for example prescription management (e.g. matching of prescriptions to available pharmaceutical products), clinical screening (e.g. monitoring of drug interactions and other medication-related complications, creation of patient drug profiles), Inventory management (e.g. control of stock) and reporting (e.g. generation of reports concerning the medication usage and the costs of the purchased drugs) (Biohealthmatics.com 2006).

I. Karafyllis (✉)
Industrial Management and Technology Department, University of Piraeus, Piraeus, Greece
e-mail: jkaraf@hotmail.com

C. Platis
National Center for Public Administration and Local Government, Hellenic Open University, Athens, Greece

G. Pierrakos
TEI of Athens, Athens, Greece

A. Kavoura et al. (eds.), *Strategic Innovative Marketing*, Springer Proceedings in Business and Economics, DOI 10.1007/978-3-319-56288-9_20

Computerized Physician Order Entry (CPOE) is an electronic ordering system with a proven record of reducing medication errors and patient hospital stays (Adams et al. 2008; Beuscart et al. 2004; Koppel et al. 2005). It is assumed to reduce up to 80% of medication errors, and 50% of errors with serious potential patient harm (Bates et al. 1998). The medicines play a critical role to provide patients with an efficient and effective health cure. The procurement of pharmaceutical products is a basic component of the medicine management while the supply chain provides the critical connection between the medicine producer and the patient. It is incorporated in the medicines management and it has as aim to ensure that the correct medicines are available for the patients in the correct time.

The National Organization for Healthcare Services (EOPYY) theoretically is responsible for defining the primary health budget, the medicines and the hospital care at their members. The budget though is calculated mostly within an historical basis or a horizontal percentage reduction. In reality hospitals a social security institutes deficits cannot be encountered efficiently.

Deficits are covered partially with legislative interventions, without providing an incentive for resources saving of for procedures improvement.

The Ministry of Health and the social security institutes, have exceptionally low potential because of their insufficient power and the lack of a real Integrated Information Systems (IIS) that provide detailed information for the suppliers' activities.

The bigger part of the cost increases due to new, creative, expensive but also necessary new products (Kontozamanis 2001) that are sold more expensively, without having important changes in there drastic element (high price without the relative efficiency). This factor increases the total pharmaceutical expenses of the country. The main responsible though seems to be the uncontrolled volume of medicines that extend due to ageing of the country population, the easier access of the patients to medicines in relation to the past but also because of the discover of new drastic substances.

In addition, the total pharmaceutical expenses in Greece do not interconnect with the increase of epidemiology or the population sickliness since there have not been recorded important changes in these sectors, but not also with the increase of medicines (factor that contributes by 25% to the increase of pharmaceutical expenses).

A similar research that has been presented the increase of antibiotics expenses has revealed that new expensive medicines are prescribed with an absurd, rapid increase (Zintzaras 2003).

The total pharmaceutical expenses in Greece constitute 2.8% of GDP and 1.4% in Eurozone (OECD 2016).

Greece is one the most spending countries after the United States and Japan (over 700 USD). By contrast, Denmark spent less than half the OECD average on retail pharmaceuticals in 2013. In terms of share of GDP, OECD countries spent, on average, around 1.4% of GDP in 2013 on retail pharmaceuticals. Again, there is considerable variation with Greece spending twice that level as a share of GDP, whereas Denmark and Norway spent less than half.

In Greece, pharmaceutical expenditure per capita decreased by close to 10% per year since 2009. This compares with growth of over 11% each year between the period 2005 and 2008.

In Greece, medicine prices were cut twice per year (the last three years) while prices of generics at market entry were gradually reduced from 80 to 32.5% of the originator's price (OECD 2016).

However, pharmaceuticals can also be distributed to inpatients in hospitals and other institutions. The additional pharmaceutical expenditure in the hospital sector ranges from less than 10% on top of retail spending in Canada and Korea to more than 40% in Portugal. On average, this raises the overall pharmaceutical bill by around 20%, resulting in more than one health dollar in five going towards purchasing pharmaceuticals.

The share of the overall pharmaceutical bill accounted for by hospitals has seen a rising trend in many countries. This is partly explained by the proliferation of specialty drugs, which are often delivered in a hospital setting (including in an outpatient department) rather than dispensed via pharmacies (Hirsch et al. 2014).

Another explanation for the growing share of hospital drugs in total pharmaceutical spending is that in some countries cost-containment measures in the post-crisis period tended to focus on the retail pharmaceutical sector, whereas hospital pharmaceutical spending remained more stable or continued to rise (Barros 2012).

Measurement Method

The questionnaire of this study has been divided into four parts. The first one has included the general information for the hospital, the second one the qualitative characteristics of the participant interrogator, providing his anonymity. The third part contained the questions that had to do with information and procurement services. More precisely, it contained questions with respect to the existence or not of any information system at the hospital, the interconnectivity and the familiarity of the personnel with them. Furthermore it contained questions about the use of e-procurement systems and the time required for the competition procedure.

The questionnaire has been sent by post at all the 139 public hospitals, at the office of the Managing Director with a cover letter explaining the objective of the study and the persons addressed to.

Among the 139 hospitals, 26 have answered (18.7%) responsible pharmacists of them, high percentage if someone consider the difficulty of recording the data related to hospitals procurement but also the workload of the staff working to them.

An analysis of the answers has been realized and the answers have been correlated with:

YPE, the number of hospital employees, the number of patients hospitalized per year, the number of beds, the annual amount of money spent for procurement.>

Additionally, a processing has been made according to criteria such as their profile.

The sex, the age, the occupied position, the personnel category, the level of education, the years of work at the hospital.

In the present research has answered a percentage of 20% of the employees in public hospitals pharmacies. The demographic characteristics of the employees are the followed:

40% men and 60% women, 68.2% were pharmacies managers, 4.5% was senior managers and 27.3% pharmacies supervisors, 96.2% was pharmacist and 3.8% was administrative personnel 24% with doctoral studies, 16% with master degree studies and 56% with bachelor degree studies.

In addition, 50% of them had more than 16 years in pharmacy and more than 21 years in hospital. A percentage of 29.4% had more than 5 years that have been working as pharmacists.

Results

The study records the existence or not of Information System in hospitals drugstores, the processes knowledge, the knowledge of supplies/of electronic supplies as well as the way of controlling the reserves in the public hospitals.

In hospital pharmacies there is an Information System for the implementation of electronic procurement in a percentage of 69.2%. In hospitals with more that 1000 employees, the percentage is almost 85.7% while in hospitals employing until 249 employees there is an Information System in a percentage of 25%. In drugstores of hospitals having between 100 and 499 beds there is an Information System in 83.3%, of other with more than 500 beds in 66.7% while those between 0 and 99 beds in a percentage of 20%.

In relation with the number of the persons hospitalized, an Information System for electronic procurement possess 77.8% for hospitals with more than 20,000 annually hospitalized and follows those with 5.000–9.999 annually hospitalized in 71.4% while those with 0–4.999 in a percentage of 33.8%.

An Information System for inventory control (ERP) possesses the 95.8% of hospital drugstores while Information System for economic services have the 75%. Hospital drugstores with employees between 250 and 499 have an Information System in a percentage of 37.5%. In the hospitals that hospitalize 0–4.999, the drugstores state that there is an Information System in economic division in a percentage of 60% while in these that hospitalize 5.000–9.999 the percentage is 40%.

75% of the hospitals use an Information System for patients monitoring. Hospitals with 250–499 employees have in a percentage of 50% while those with beds from 100 to 499 have in a percentage 80% following those with 0–99 beds in a percentage of 66.7% and finally those with more than 500 beds in a percentage of 50%.

Cooperation between IS in hospitals is recorded in a percentage of 75%.

84% of the employees in pharmacies state that are familiarized with Information System. In hospitals with 250–499 employees they state familiarization 75% while in all others is more than 85%.

Among those familiarized with Information System, 50% state that they are very much familiarized, 20% more and 30% are less familiarized.

In hospitals not having Information System, 87.5% of the personnel think that their existence would be necessary.

73.1% of pharmacists state that they are not realizing electronic procurement. It is important that the higher percentage (50%) of those using electronic procurement belong to hospitals with 0–249 employees and follow those with 500–999 employees (34.8%) and finally those with more than 1000 employees (14.8%).

It seems that the hospitals hospitalizing 0–4.999 persons use more electronic procurement methods (34.8%), then those hospitalizing 5.000–9.999 (29.6%) and finally those hospitalizing more than 20,000 patients.

Hospitals of which the amount spent for procurement are between 20 and 50M€ use electronic procurement systems in a percentage of 50% and then those of 0–4.9M€ (27.9%) and finally those with amounts between 5 and 19.9M€.

The expiration date control is done by 69.2% on eye, by 30.8% on the shelve position, by 38.5% empirically and only by 11.5% in an electronic way (scanner, RFID).

In orders it is not marked the budget price in 46.2%, the specification/composition in 65.4%, the managing director's decision in 42.3% and the objective of the procurement in a percentage of 73.1%. Furthermore, it is not marked by 69.2% neither the duration of the procurement nor the justification of the procurement by 65.4%.

It can be assumed that there is a lack of control and programming since basic elements that might help for resources saving in a great percentage are not marked on orders.

On beds basis, hospitals with 0–99 beds the knowledge rate of the procurement legislative framework is almost 75%, in hospitals with 100–499 beds is known by 97.4% while funnily enough in those with more than 500 beds the percentage is only 50%.

With regard to the knowledge of legislative framework for the electronic procurement relating the employees the percentages are as followed: 250–499 at 22.2%, 500–999 at 16.7%, more than 1000 employees at 33.3% while in hospitals employing 0–249 the legislation is not known at all.

Regarding the number of patients hospitalized, the results are: 5.000–9.999 hospitalized at 14.3%, 10.000–19.999 at 25%, more than 20,000 patients hospitalized at 37.5% while in hospitals with 0–4.999 annually hospitalized are not know at all.

In relation to the number of beds, in hospitals offering 0–99 and more than 500 beds the percentage is minimum while in those with beds between 100 and 499 is 27.8%.

In hospitals spending 0–4.9M€, pharmacists are not aware of the legislative framework of electronic procurement, in those spending between 5 and 19.9M€ the framework is known in a percentage of 33.3% and in those spending 20–49.9M€ in 50%.

At YPE level, the 1st and 3rd are aware of the legislation in a percentage of 33.3%, the 7th in 25%, the 6th in 14.3% while the 2nd, 4th and 5th are not well aware of it (low knowledge rate). 83.3% of drugstores order in a frequency of 15 days, 12.5% within 30 days and 4.2% every 3 months. 87.5% of hospital pharmacists are aware of legislative procurement framework while only 20.8% are aware of the relevant electronic procurement framework.

Conclusions

The expenses for medicines and the medical equipment constitute the second higher cost after the salaries of the hospitals personnel. The risk for mal management and corruption in procurement procedures is especially increased in hospitals.

An important management tool for the corruption prevention in hospitals is the implementation of "prescription book", of hospital medicines and the establishment of specialized committees for the definition of new medicines or equipment needs, of supplies auction processes and the implementation of systematic inventories monitoring in all levels. Every management system must define strictly the responsibilities and approvals in decision-making process in order to be located the individual who breaks the law. In addition the existence of an Information System for medicines interconnection is necessary not only for the patient health but also for the fight against the hyper prescription.

Serialization, Bar Coding (or 2D code) and RFID use are more necessary in order for the debit to be per patient and for the medicine card to be informed for the medicines provided but also for the medicine transaction to be recorded automatically and to be found the real hospitalization cost per patient.

Nowadays, in Greece there are three public organizations (EOPPY, IDIKA, EOF) that are keeping records of medicines' consumption. The first two keep records of the values and medicines' volume that are reimbursed by the social security and health system while EOF is recording all medicines' categories (reimbursed or not, hospitals' and parallel exports).

In 2014, in a public hospital of Athens there has taken place an attempt of recording in real time all medicines entering the hospital pharmacy. The effort showed that the medicine's barcode can be cancelled in real time and consumption statistics can be prepared per clinic, department in a daily/monthly/yearly basis. The demo was successful but it has not been implemented until today. As a result, nobody knows the real medicines' consumption in hospitals and no one can predict effectively the next year's orders. As a consequence the excessive spending cannot be spotted and the cuts are made horizontally and not in a rational basis.

The medicines inventories and their stay constitute probably the most difficult and resource requiring job taking that medicines have expiration date or/and need special conditions for their transportation, storing to be provided to the patients. It is more often the phenomenon that medicines expire before their use, as a result having the augmentation of the hospital medicines expenses. With the implementation of supply chain methods the objective is the medicines storing and organization in a way that excludes such phenomenon appearance. The pharmaceutical products could be stored taking account their characteristics:

- Date of arrival in hospital
- Category
- Expiration date
- Maintenance conditions required

It has been counted that 20% of the time of the employees of the pharmacies is spent for the order, rework, invoicing, modifications recording (Karokis et al. 2000).

An efficient politics for the generics can reduce more the pharmaceutical expenses compared with the prototypes′ prices reduction, when the patent of many prototypes medicines expires in the next 2–3 years.

Introduction of new accounting and IS in order to accurately calculate, control and assess every process. It is estimated that from the implementation of the information technology systems the pharmaceutical expenses can be reduced by 30%.

An essential condition for the effective implementation of rationalizing expenses politics is the analysis and assessment of all health expenses per code—cost centre—section—cure category—products and services (KEME 2010).

Control of parallel exports and mainly of the illegal trade of originality authenticity tapes, through the disaster and return of the authenticity tapes and the publication of relevant elements and the use of new technologies.

Establishment of motives for doctors, pharmacists and patients to use cheaper medicines, prototypes and generics.

Exploitation of pharmaceutical and economic evaluation tools with cost analysis and result assessment for the new precise treatments.

Computerization of social security institutes for the accounts automation.

Use of hospital packages and medicines disposal with number of peels contained, etc. in quantity equivalent to the medicine's dose and in a relevant charge.

Guidelines and therapeutic protocols for the right prescription and the direction from the more expensive choices to more economic and efficient solutions.

Better information of doctors for the new medicines.

Publication of similar preparation prices comparing tables and announcement to doctors.

Exploitation of international conclusions/findings for effective cures (p.e. NICE) that must not be recommended or approved. Stricter control of generics' quality.

Configuration of a modern framework for bioequivalence studies implementation with the exploitation of academic and state infrastructures as reference centers (KEME 2010). An easy access to generics' market after patent expiration as it is already foreseen by European guidelines. Concentration of all the medicine responsibilities at the Ministry of Health.

The hospital pharmacists have to be informed for the framework of procurement and its possible changes. It must be adapted consumption/need prototypes per reference unit and a record to be created of approved products and services.

References

Adams, M., D. Bates, and G. Coffman. 2008. *Saving lives, saving money: The imperative for computerized physician order entry in massachusetts hospital*. Boston: Massachusetts Technology Collaborative and New England Healthcare Institute.

Barros, P.P. 2012. Pharmaceutical market reforms in portugal under the memorandum of understanding. *Eurohealth* 18 (1). European Observatory on Health Systems and Policies.

Bates, W.D., L.L. Leape, and J.D. Cullen. 1998. Effect of computerized physician order entry and a team intervention on prevention of serious medication errors. *Journal of the American Medical Association* 280 (15): 1311–1316.

Beuscart-Zephir, C.M., S. Pelayo, and P. Degoulet. 2004. A usability study of CPOE's medication administration functions: Impact on physician-nurse cooperation. *Studies in Health Technologies and Informatics* 107 (2): 1018–1022.

Biohealthmatics.com. 2006. Pharmacy Information Systems. http://www.biohealthmatics.com/technologies/his/pis.aspx. Accessed 15 June 2016.

Enrado, Patty. 2005. *Buyers guide: Pharmacy systems*. http://www.healthcareitnews.com/news/buyers-guide-pharmacy-systems. Accessed 15 June 2016.

Hirsch, B.R., S. Balu, and K.A. Schulman. 2014. The impact of specialty pharmaceuticals as drivers of health care costs. *Health Affairs* 33 (10): 1714–1720.

Karokis, A., A. Christodoulopoulou, T. Tsiaras, and E. Mossialos. 2000. Pharmaceutical price controls and positive drug list effects on total and social insurance pharmaceutical expenditure. In *Proceedings of the 5th Annual ISPOR Conference*, Washington DC.

KEME. 2010. Study of health system economic operation for the reviling of sources of spending and proposals for their confrontation. Research Centre of Health Services, Athens.

Kontozamanis, V. 2001. *The Greek pharmaceutical market*. Athens: Institute for Industrial and Economic Studies. (in Greek).

Koppel, R., P.J. Metlay, and A. Cohen. 2005. Role of computerized physician order entry systems in facilitating medication errors. *Journal of the American Medical Association* 293 (10): 1197–1203.

Mettler Tobias, and Rohner Peter. 2009. E-procurement in hospital pharmacies :an exploratory multi-case study from Switzerland. *Journal of Theoretical and Applied Electronic Commerce Research* 4 (1): 23–38.

OECD. 2016. *OECD pharmaceuticals expenditure and policies: Health working papers no 87*. Paris.

Zintzaras, E., and J.P.A. Ioannidis. 2003. Modelling of escalating outpatient antibiotic expenditures. *Journal of Antimicrobial Chemotherapy* 52 (6): 1001–1004.

Organization Style and Its Effect on Employee Satisfaction and Personal Performance

Charalampos Platis and Emmanouil Zoulias

Introduction

Within this work we try to investigate the impact of Organization style in relation to employee satisfaction and personal performance, which reflects the opinion of employee about their job satisfaction and personal performance in the field of healthcare. Although there are innovative theories and techniques in term of therapeutic methods as well as in health administrative and economical area (Platis et al. 2014), traditional theories that deal with human as an employee and his behavior, satisfaction and performance that are always valuable. Employee satisfaction and personnel performance are among the most important factors highly related to workplace health risks as well as for the patients and for the employees. The ever increasing demand for higher quality health care services, inevitably leads to investigate the therapeutic relationship of patient's life quality and exploration of their views. These issues are particularly important for people possessing managerial roles and requiring management skills of high expertise. On the other hand, job performance is one of the most vital factors providing safety and reliable services of high quality in health care sector (Platis et al. 2014).

The analysis methodology based on modern tools using Data Mining technologies. The field of data mining, like statistics, concerns itself with "learning from data" or "turning data into information but data mining is not a "statistical déjà vu" (Hand 1999). Statistics is the science of learning from data; on the other hand "Data

The original version of the book was revised. Belated corrections to change the order of First name and Family name of chapter authors have been incorporated. The erratum to the book is available at 10.1007/978-3-319-56288-9_72

C. Platis (✉) · E. Zoulias
National Centre for Public Administration and Local Government,
National School, Pireos 211, Tavros, Greece
e-mail: charisplatis@gmail.com

A. Kavoura et al. (eds.), *Strategic Innovative Marketing*, Springer Proceedings in Business and Economics, DOI 10.1007/978-3-319-56288-9_21

mining is the process of exploration and analysis, by automatic or semiautomatic means, of large quantities of data in order to discover meaningful patterns and rules" (Berry M.J.A. et al.). Using data mining methods we can reveal hidden patterns of the data or even unrevealed relationships in data. It combines knowledge and techniques from various scientific fields such as DBM (Data Base Management, Artificial Intelligence, Machine learning. Analysis of trainee's opinion has been applied in various applications even within medical area (Wang et al. 2015; Dimitris et al. 2013).

Pattern recognition techniques have been widely used as a base for developing decision support systems in medicine to assist diagnosis (Leroy et al. 2007). These techniques include Artificial Neural Networks (ANNs) (Haykin et al. 1999), evolutionary algorithms such as genetic algorithms (Goldberg 1989), fuzzy logic (Linkens et al. 2001), various hybrid systems (Papageorgiou et al. 2005), Artificial Immune Systems (AIS) (Timmis et al. 2000), Support Vector Machines (Cristianini et al. 2000), k-NN (Shakhnarovish et al. 2005), Majority vote, considered as one of the simplest and most intuitive methods for combining classifier outputs (Narasimhamurthy et al. 2005; Kuncheva et al. 2004).

Materials and Methods

The field research was conducted in National Centre of Public Administration where public servants came from all over Greece were trained and gaining professional skills. Structured questionnaires were distributed to 300 nurses participating in training programs and 245 valid questionnaires were returned. Response rate is about 73%. Most nurses are female (79%) and the 52.4% of the respondents are between 35 and 45 years old. The 31% of the participants enjoyed from 1 to 5 years of experience in the same department/clinic. Most nursing staff (55.3%) has income ranging from 1,000 to 1,300 euros. The 33.6% of the respondents are working in a department occupying more than 20 employees.

The structured questionnaire was employed to carry out the survey. The measurement instrument was thoroughly evaluated before released. Ten head nurses of the hospitals involved examined it along with two experienced researchers; the instrument's cognitive relevance to the healthcare sector was confirmed prior to data collection. The instrument was developed by adapting existing multi-dimensional scales to capture opinion about leadership and employee job performance by providing respondents with 7-scale Likert scaled questions for each multi-item measure employed. The questioner has 15 questions for employee satisfaction, 8 questions for employee personal performance, and 36 questions for organization type. The aim is to apply data mining methods to reveal any possible patterns on employee satisfaction and employee personal performance answers (targets) based on organization type answers (attributes). Within this application we tries two approaches, the first using all available organization type answers and we do not apply a feature selection technique, the second using the well-known a feature selection method of forward selection (Pudil et al. 1994). The sample was transformed in the following rule, each answer of the 7-scale Likert converted to 0 for answers between 1 and 4 and 1 for 5 and 7. As a result all transformed answers are 0 or 1. This transformation was made taking into account that our aim in this work is to discriminate the answers in a way of in favors and opponents, the sample is rather small to perform 7 categories for the data and the performance of data mining algorithm using 7 categories with such a small sample is rather low as we tested (Kuncheva et al. 2003).

The proposed decision method based on the comparison of four well-known classifiers, Decision Trees, k-NN, Naïve Bayes, and Majority Vote process as an output of the three already used classifiers, the Decision Trees, k-NN, Naïve Bayes. In the present implementation, the performance of the proposed Decision Tree classifier was tested using as splitting criterion gain ratio, max depth of the tree 3, applying pruning, confidence 0.25, minimal leaf size 2, and minimal size for split 4. The KNN algorithm with number of nearest neighbors equal to 9, Mixed Euclidean Distance as measure type as rule used to decide how to classify each sample. The Naïve Bayes uses Laplace correction. Finally according to the methodology of the classification based on the majority vote (called hereafter as MVC—Majority Vote Classification), the three well-known classifiers, Decision Trees, k-NN, Naïve Bayes, were trained using the same training set. After the training phase, a test feature vector **f** was classified using the outputs of the three classifiers according to the majority vote procedure, as shown in Table 1 (Fig. 1):

Results

The application of the above proposed decision methods using a set of data mining techniques illustrates interesting results for the following employee personal satisfaction (SAT8) and personal performance (PR9A) questions:

1. SAT8_01—job physical conditions, using the feature selection (FS) step
2. SAT8_04—management style, using the feature selection (FS) step
3. SAT8_05—freedom in work style, using the feature selection (FS) step

Table 1 Classification of feature vector according to the majority vote procedure—CMV

Decision tree	k-NN	Naïve bayes	Final decision based on majority vote
Class 1	Class 1	Class 1	Class 1
Class 1	Class 1	Class 2	Class 1
Class 1	Class 2	Class 1	Class 1
Class 1	Class 2	Class 2	Class 2
Class 2	Class 1	Class 1	Class 1
Class 2	Class 1	Class 2	Class 2
Class 2	Class 2	Class 1	Class 2
Class 2	Class 2	Class 2	Class 2

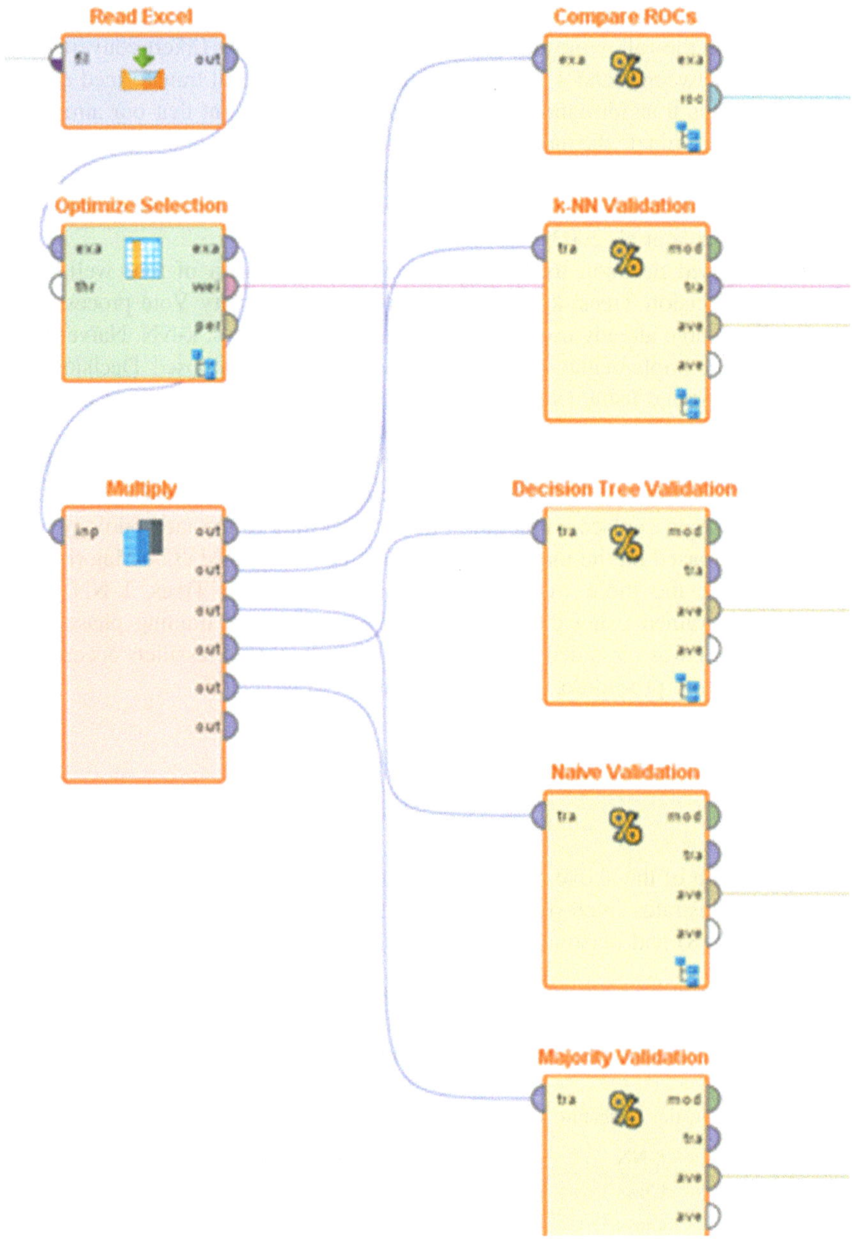

Fig. 1 Data mining algorithm methods

4. SAT8_08—salary and bonus, without using the feature selection (WFS) step
5. SAT8_11—opportunities to use your skills, using the feature selection (FS) step
6. SAT8_13—the attention they give to your suggestions, using the feature selection (FS) step
7. PR9A_2—amount of work, without using the feature selection (WFS) step
8. PR9A_4—working time, without using the feature selection (WFS) step
9. PR9A_6—personal goals achievement, both on using and without using the feature selection (FS—WFS) step
10. PR9A_7—suggestions for improving the quality and productivity, without using the feature selection (FS) step
11. PR9A_8—overall ability of job execution, without using the feature selection (FS) step

Table 2 illustrates the overall performance of each algorithm to predict the answer of a future "subject" on the employee satisfaction and performance questions, based on the object's answers to the organization style questions. The interesting results in Table 2 are those that are bold and Italic. The explanation is that those results have both high overall accuracy as well as adequate specificity and sensitivity. All the other results might have high overall accuracy but they have low or even zero sensitivity or specificity.

The results in Table 2 illustrates that SAT8_01, SAT8_04, SAT8_05, SAT8_11, SAT8_13 reveal valuable results using the Feature Selection step, SAT8_08, PR9A_2, PR9A_4, PR9A_7, PR9A_8 reveal valuable results without using Feature Selection step and PR9A_6 on both cases. In addition to that Decision Trees algorithm proved to be the worst algorithm selection since only one result can be categorized as valuable in SAT8_12, in this case Decision Tree gives the best results. On the other hand k-NN, Naïve Bayes, and Majority Vote are proved to be efficient for SAT8_01, SAT8_04, SAT8_05, SAT8_11. Naïve and Majority Vote

Table 2 Overall accuracy with feature selection (FS) and without feature selection (WFS)

	Decision tree FS—WFS %	k-NN FS—WFS %	Naïve bayes FS—WFS %	Majority vote FS—WFS %
SAT8_01	67.92–67.92	**73.23**–69.95	**73.23**–60.23	**73.13**–66.32
SAT8_04	64.67–61.83	**72.72**–64.63	**73.58**–68.78	**72.35**–65.88
SAT8_05	58.15–58.15	**73.97**–63.00	**73.90**–66.22	**71.90**–66.25
SAT8_08	83.67–93.12	83.25–93.12	63.33–**73.60**	82.07–**92.70**
SAT8_11	60.23–61.40	**71.08**–65.38	**70.75**–65.05	**71.15**–67.88
SAT8_13	55.30–54.90	67.73–61.35	**70.33**–64.20	66.38–65.48
PR9A_2	93.08–93.08	93.08–93.08	93.08–**73.10**	93.08–93.08
PR9A_4	96.33–96.33	96.33–96.33	96.33–**75.55**	96.33–96.33
PR9A_6	79.67–97.67	**72.47–77.58**	79.67–58.43	79.67–**78.05**
PR9A_7	81.30–81.30	81.30–**78.88**	81.30–59.35	81.30–**80.50**
PR9A_8	95.12–95.12	95.12–95.12	95.12–**74.77**	95.12–95.12

Table 3 Confusion matrices for SAT8_01, SAT8_04, SAT8_05, SAT8_08, SAT8_11 SAT8_13

Question algorithm over accuracy	SAT8_01 k-NN and naïve bayes 73.23%		SAT8_04 naïve bayes 73.58%		SAT8_05 k-NN 73.97%		SAT8_08 majority vote 92.70%		SAT8_11 majority vote 71.15%		SAT8_13 naïve bayes 70.33%	
True	1	0	1	0	1	0	1	0	1	0	1	0
1	21	8	135	40	123	44	228	17	42	17	72	34
0	58	159	25	46	20	59	1	0	54	133	39	101

Table 4 Confusion matrices for PR9A_2, PR9A_4, PR9A_6, PR9A_7, PR9A_8

Question algorithm over accuracy	PR9A_2 naïve bayes 73.10%		PR9A_4 naïve bayes 75.55%		PR9A_6 majority vote 78.05%		PR9A_7 majority vote 80.50%		PR9A_8 naïve bayes 74.77%	
True	1	0	1	0	1	0	1	0	1	0
1	174	11	181	4	185	43	196	44	178	6
0	55	6	56	5	11	7	4	2	56	6

have good performance on SAT8_8, k-NN and Majority Vote for PR9A_6 and PR9A_7 Naïve Bayes for SAT8_13, PR9A_2, PR9A_4, PR9A_8. These elements are also obtained using simulation modeling of the corresponding processes (Sakas et al. 2013).

In Tables 3 and 4 we illustrate the confusion matrices of the best overall result, based on the most efficient algorithm and for each personal satisfaction (SAT8) and personal performance (PR9A) question according to Table 2.

Discussion—Conclusions

Using "Forward" as a Feature Selection method Decision we observe that for employee personal satisfaction (SAT8) is more effective and reveals interesting results. On the other hand personal performance (PR9A) questions are more accurate without using any Feature Selection Method. Another finding is that for all algorithms used within this work, Decision Trees, k-NN, Naïve Bayes, and Majority Vote we observe high overall accuracy on various tests but also very high sensitivity and extremely low specificity or vice versa. Those results lead to the result that those methods can predict very well answers signed as one (zero, respectively), in other words answers of 6–7 (1–5) in the 7-scale. As an example for question working time overall accuracy for Naïve Bayes is 96.33% with feature selection and 75.55% without feature selection. In addition to that, sensitivity is 1, 0.76 and specificity is 0, 0.44, respectively (see Table 5). In particular the above mentioned results illustrate that that Naïve Bayes algorithm for working time question although gives very high overall accuracy using feature selection the negative answers cannot predict sufficiently, zero specificity. As a result Naïve

Table 5 Confusion matrices for PR9A_4 using naïve bayes algorithm

Over accuracy	With feature selection 96.33%		Without feature selection 75.55%	
True	1	0	1	0
1	237	9	181	4
0	0	0	56	5

Bayes algorithm for working time question gives adequate overall accuracy without using feature selection and negative answers can predict better, 0.44 specificity.

Furthermore, we can conclude that Decision Trees algorithm is not effective as an algorithm for questions of this work. On the contrary we can propose the use of Naïve Bayes method for the detection and forecasting of possible answers on subjects of Organization style and its effect on employee satisfaction and personal performance regarding samples of particular characteristics followed by k-NN and Majority Vote Algorithm.

As a future application we propose the application of this methodology on other parameters of organizational psychology, like motivation, communication, and group dynamics. Furthermore some technical advancements can take place like the application of various feature selection methods before the application of data mining methods as well as more data mining algorithms.

The model can lead to a series of secure and high reliability conclusions for the opinions, perceptions, and attitudes of employees of health care services and particularly for the rational and expected relation among three top concepts organization style, employee satisfaction, and personal performance. In this way, future manager's decisions can be documented very well regarding health care marketing (employee's satisfaction, patient's satisfaction, organization profile, etc.) as well as health care management.

References

Alimisis, Dimitris, and Zoulias Emmanouil. 2013. Aligning technology with learning theories: A simulator-based training curriculum in surgical robotics. *Interactive Technology and Smart Education* 10 (3): 211–229.

Cristianini, N., and J. Shawe-Taylor. 2000. *An introduction to support vector machines: and other kernel-based learning methods*. New York, NY, USA: Cambridge University Press.

Damianos, P. Sakas, Nasiopoulos K. Dimitrios, and D.S. Vlachos. 2013. The role of information systems in creating strategic leadership model. *Procedia—Social and Behavioral Sciences* 467–477.

David J. Hand. 1999. Statistics and data mining: Intersecting disciplines. In *ACM SIGKDD Explorations*, June 1999, vol. 1, issue 1, 16–19.

Goldberg D. 1989. *Genetic algorithms in optimization, search and machine learning.* Addison-Wesley.

Haykin, S. 1999. *Neural networks: A comprehensive foundation*. Upper Saddle River, NJ, USA: Prentice Hall.

Kuncheva, L.I., C.J. Whitaker, and C.A. Shipp. 2003. Limits on the majority vote accuracy in classier fusion. *Pattern Analysis and Applications* 6: 22–31.

Kuncheva, L.I. 2004. *Combining pattern classifiers: Methods and algorithms*. Chichester: Wiley Inter Science.

Leroy, G., and H. Chen. 2007. Introduction to the special issue on decision support in medicine. *Decision Support Systems* 43: 1203–1206.

Linkens, D.A., and M. Mahfouf. 2001. The intelligent systems in biomedicine laboratory in the department of automatic control and systems engineering at the university of Sheffield, UK. *Artificial Intelligence in Medicine* 21: 171–176.

Narasimhamurthy, A. 2005. Evaluation of diversity measures for binary classifier ensembles. In *MCS 2005,* ed. N.C. Oza, R. Polikar, J. Kittler, and F. Roli. LNCS, vol. 3541, 267–277. Springer, Heidelberg.

Papageorgiou, E.I., and P.P. Groumpos. 2005. A new hybrid method using evolutionary algorithms to train fuzzy cognitive maps. *Applied Soft Computing* 5: 409–431.

Platis Charalampos, and Zoulias Emmanuel. 2014. Impacts of robotic assisted surgery on hospital's strategic plan. In *Procedia—Social and Behavioral Sciences*, 3rd International Conference on Integrated Information (IC-ININFO), vol. 147, 321–326.

Pudil, P., J. Nonovocova, and J. Kittler. 1994. Floating search methods in feature selection. *Pattern Recognition Letters* 15: 1119–1125.

Shakhnarovish, Darrell, and Indyk. 2005. *Nearest-neighbor methods in learning and vision*. The MIT Press.

Timmis, J., M. Neal, and J. Hunt. 2000. An Artificial immune system for data analysis. *Biosystems* 55 (1–3): 143–150.

Wang, H.-F.A, J.-F.A. Jin, X.-Q.A. Feng, X.A. Huang, L.-L.B. Zhu, X.-Y.C. Zhao, and Q.D. Zhou. 2015. Quality improvements in decreasing medication administration errors made by nursing staff in an academic medical center hospital: A trend analysis during the journey to Joint Commission International accreditation and in the post-accreditation era. *Therapeutics and Clinical Risk Management*, 11, 393–406.

A Prospective Evaluation of Health-Related Quality of Life of Cancer Patients Receiving Day and Home Care Services in Greece

George Pierrakos, Dimitra Latsou, Aspasia Goula, John Pateras, John Nikolados, Charis Platis, Markos Sarris and Sotiris Soulis

Background

Over the past decades, the healthcare trend in the care for people with long-term conditions is the de-hospitalization of medical treatment (Mor et al. 1988) and the establishment of primary care networks with emphasis on home care (Bodenheimer et al. 2002). For this reason, the combination of the daily nursing services and home care has been proposed (Igarashi et al. 2014).

In Greece, primary and home care services encounter organizational problems (Adamakidou and Kalokerinou 2010). Thus, the care of cancer patients is primarily hospital-centered, although in recent years the services offered in day clinics are steadily increasing (Pierrakos et al. 2016). Pain clinics operating within hospitals have an important role mainly for palliative support for physical pain while care at home is provided mainly for patients with end-stage disease and is not self-served (Pierrakos et al. 2013). Further to this context, as the quality of life of cancer patients is an important factor associated with the progression of the disease, it is important for health professionals to employ a quality of life measurement tool for cancer patients. The objectives of the present study were: (1) to compare the HRQoL of cancer patients versus the existing Greek normal population scores; and (2) to assess the HRQoL of cancer patients receiving home care versus day care services.

G. Pierrakos (✉) · D. Latsou · A. Goula · J. Pateras · J. Nikolados · M. Sarris · S. Soulis
Faculty of Management and Economics, Health and Welfare Management, Department of Business Administration, Research Laboratory on Social Innovation, Health, Social Protection, Social Entrepreneurship Technological Educational Institute of Athens, Athens, Greece
e-mail: gpier127@gmail.com

C. Platis
National Centre for Public Administration and Local Government, Athens, Greece

A. Kavoura et al. (eds.), *Strategic Innovative Marketing*, Springer Proceedings in Business and Economics, DOI 10.1007/978-3-319-56288-9_22

Methods

Study Design and Participants

This prospective study was conducted from July to August 2011 among cancer patients who received day care or home care services from two specialized hospitals of Attiki (Metaxa and Agioi Anargiroi) which are the only hospitals in Greece offering home care services for cancer patients. Participant selection was based on stratified random sampling and the questionnaires were filled-in with personal interviews. Of the initial sample of 147 patients, 113 were enrolled in our study, leading to a response rate of 76.9%; the remainder, declined participation. Of the participants, 88.5% stated that they are not self-managed and 11.5% self-managed. Finally, the majority of patients (66.4%) received day care in hospital and 33.6% received home care. The patients who received home care were not self-managed. According to the hospitals' protocols, patients receive home care services only if the physicians characterize a patient as "non self-manageable".

All patients completed the SF-36 questionnaire which is an instrument employed to measure the health level of a population. The Greek translation and validation of SF-36 has been successfully tested in repeated surveys (Sarris et al. 2008) and has been applied in similar surveys in the Greek health sector by other researchers (Yfantopoulos et al. 2001; Pierrakos et al. 2011). The key feature of SF-36 is the simultaneous measurement and assessment of both physical and psychosocial health with a grid of 36 scales that are grouped into eight scales: Physical Functioning, (PF), Role Physical (RP), Bodily Pain (BP), General Health (GH), Vitality (VT), Social Functioning (SF), Role Emotional (RE), and Mental Health (MH) (Ware et al. 1992). These eight scales provide the basis for calculating two summary measures, the Physical Component Summary (PCS) and the Mental Component Summary (MCS), in order to summarize the physical and mental state of health. Greek normal population scores (n = 1426) obtained from a previous health survey in (Pappa et al. 2005) were used to generate mean values matched for age and gender. These mean values were used for comparison with mean SF-36 scores from this study.

Ethical clearance was obtained from the Scientific Council of the two hospitals in question. All participants were given in written and oral information about the study and signed an informed consent form.

The hypotheses of this study are

H1 *Cancers patients had lower quality of life than GR normal population*

H2 *Patients, who received home care, achieve a better quality of life than patients who received day care services.*

Statistical Analysis

For the assessment of the questionnaire's internal consistency, the coefficient a Cronbach was used and the questionnaire met the criterion of 0.825 which is considered reliable. Student's t-test was used in order to compare quantitative variables among two groups. Levels of significance were two-tailed and statistical significance was set to P = 0.05. The SPSS22.0 software was used for statistical analysis.

Results

The majority of the respondents were female (61.9%); 36.3% were ≥70 years old; 52.2% were compulsory education level graduates and 31.9% secondary education level graduates. Finally, the majority of participants (58.4%) were retired and 46.9% had monthly household income of 600–1,300€.

Patients suffered from various cancers, described in declining order: 36.3% breast cancer, 18.6% digestive tract, 14.2% blood and lymphatic systemic cancer, 12.4% respiratory tract, 10.6% reproductive system, 3.5% unknown, 2.7% urinary tract and 1.8% bone and articular cartilage. Also, 62.8% had undergone surgery, 36.3% chemotherapy and 0.9% received hormone therapy. The majority of the respondents (75.2%) did not have metastasis and 53.1% had been hospitalized.

Figure 1 shows the mean values of the eight SF-36 scales for the study population, compared to the local population norms. Cancer patients scored significantly worse in all SF-36 subscales compared to the population norm, except for RE.

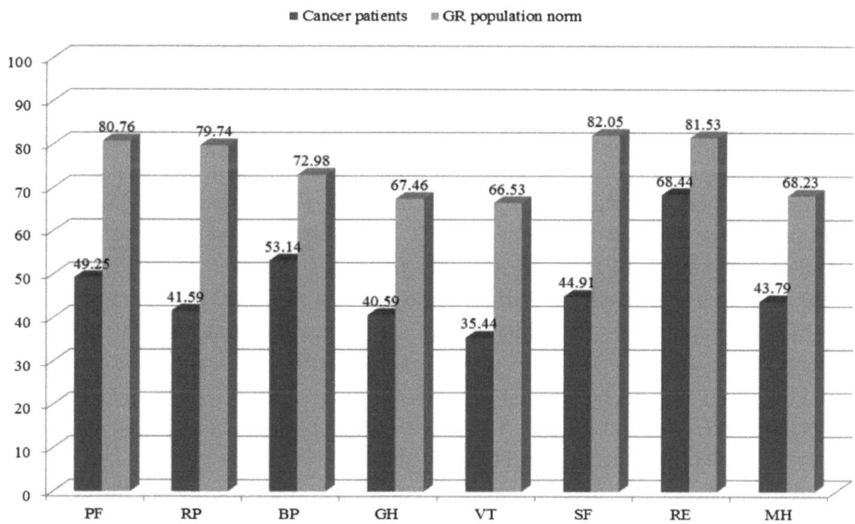

Fig. 1 Study participants' SF-36 scores compared to local population norms

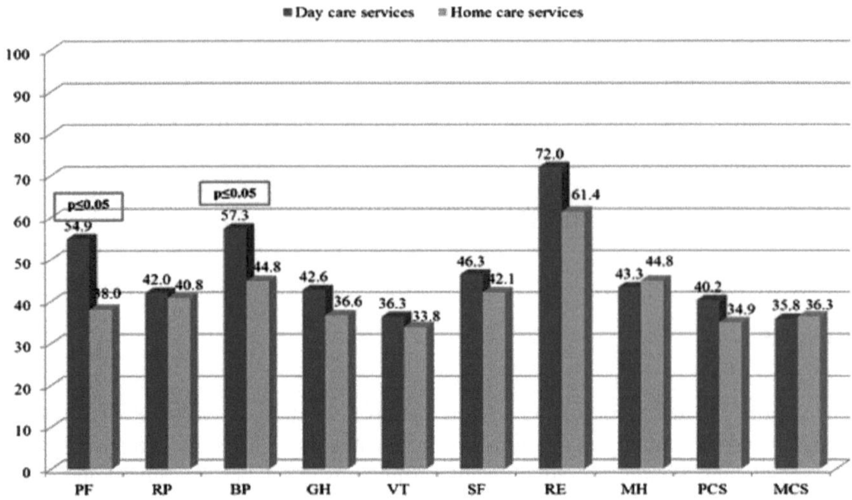

Fig. 2 8 dimensions of SF-36 per type of service

It is noted that patients who received day care had statistically significant higher PCS versus those who received home care (40.3 ± 9.5 vs 34.5 ± 8, respectively; $p = 0.007$). Figure 2 presents the 8 SF-36 scales and the PCS/MCS of day care compared to home care services.

Discussion

The objectives of this study were the comparison of the HRQoLof cancer patients with the Greek normal population and the assessment of HRQoL of cancers patients who receive home care compared to those who receive day care services.

The SF36 instrument is a widely used measure of HRQoL in chronic morbidity. The Greek version of SF36 was chosen for this study because it has been previously validated and GR population norms were available for comparison with a chronic pain population such as the cancer patients. These elements are also obtained using simulation modeling of the corresponding processes (Sakas et al. 2013).

According to our results, all SF-36 scale scores were lower than the norm of the local Greek population. The difference in scores ranged from 20 to 30 points for general health and mental health scales, except for the RE scale score which differed only by 13 points between study patients and population norms. The observed substantial differences in PF, RP, VT, and SF scales between cancer patients and the general population indicate significant disability in the study participants.

Additionally, some findings of this study are consistent with those of the international literature, where in the study of Barrios et al. (2015) highlights that cancer patients had worse physical HRQoL, but same psychological HRQoL than the general population and in other study indicates that cancer occurrence affects less in mental and emotional dimensions (Boini et al. 2004). Also, studies focus on the impact of cancer on mental health, point to that the diagnosis and treatment of cancer may be associated with anxiety and depression (Nosarti et al. 2002; Boini et al. 2004). However, heterogeneous results demonstrate that there are small differences when evaluating quality of life of cancer patients and the norm population (Hammerlid et al. 1999).

Comparing the two groups of patients receiving day care and home care, it was found that patients who received day care services, responded with a higher mean value in Physical Function and Bodily Pain (PF statistically significant $p \leq 0.05$), versus patients who received home care. In contrast, patients who received home care services seemed to have had higher mean value in Mental Health, but the difference was statistically insignificant. The patients who received home care are not self-managed according to the hospital protocol and usually they are end-stage patients. Home care and patient-centered approach care affects positively on cancer patient's quality of life (Tralongo et al. 2011).

Conclusion

Currently, it is generally accepted that with good prognosis and care, cancer can evolve into a chronic disease with a reasonable level of patient's quality of life. The Greek National Healthcare System is oriented to the Hospital as the center for the provision of services. According this study, patients have a lower level of quality of life compared with the norm population, which indicates that the Greek National Healthcare System does not appear to be sufficient for the holistic treatment of cancer disease. There is a need to enhance home care with workforce and inter-sectoral approach to promote treatment strategy for patients with cancer.

Acknowledgements We wish to thank the Health Professionals in hospitals and home care units for their support in this study.

Funding

This study was the result of collaboration between the European Social Fund and the Greek Ministry of Health and the Division of Health and Welfare Management-Technological Educational Institute of Athens.

References

Adamakidou, T., and A. Kalokerinou. 2010. New health policies on primary health care in Greece. *Health Science Journal* 4: 15–23.

Barrios, R., M. Bravo, J.A. Gil-Montoya, I. Martínez-Lara, B. García-Medina, and G. Tsakos. 2015. Oral and general health-related quality of life in patients treated for oral cancer compared to control group. *Health and Quality of Life Outcomes*, 13: 1.

Bodenheimer, T., E. Wagner, and K. Grumbach. 2002. Improving primary care for patients with chronic illness: The chronic care model, Part 2. *JAMA* 288: 1909–1914.
Boini, S., S. Briançon, F. Guillemin, P. Galan, and S. Hercberg. 2004. Impact of cancer occurrence on health-related quality of life: A longitudinal pre-post assessment. *Health and Quality of Life Outcomes*, 2: 1.
Hammerlid, E., M. Ahlner-Elmqvist, K. Bjordal, A. Biörklund, J. Evensen, M. Boysen, et al. 1999. A prospective multicentre study in Sweden and Norway of mental distress and psychiatric morbidity in head and neck cancer patients. *British Journal of Cancer* 80: 766–774.
Igarashi, A., T. Ishibashi, T. Shinozaki, and N. Yamamoto-Mitani. 2014. Combinations of long-term care insurance services and associated factors in Japan: A classification tree model. *BMC Health Services Research* 14: 382.
Mor, V., M. Stalker, R. Gralla, H. Scher, C. Cimma, D. Park, et al. 1988. Day hospital as an alternative to inpatient care for cancer patients: A random assignment trial. *Journal of Clinical Epidemiology* 41: 771–785.
Nosarti, C., J.V. Roberts, T. Crayford, K. McKenzie, and A.S. David. 2002. Early psychological adjustment in breast cancer patients: A prospective study. *Journal of Psychosomatic Research* 53: 1123–1130.
Pappa, E., N. Kontodimopoulos, and D. Niakas. 2005. Validating and norming of the Greek SF-36 health survey. *Quality of Life Research* 14: 1433–1438.
Pierrakos, G., A. Kalokerinou, T. Adamikidou, J. Nikolados, A. Goula, D. Latsou, K. Vourliotou, and M. Sarris. 2013. Pain clinics operation evaluation in Greek national health system. *Hellenic Journal of Nursing* 52: 81–92.
Pierrakos, G., E. Michopoylou, I. Kondili, A. Ganas, and M. Sarris. 2011. Health related quality of life of smokers and non-smokers. *Nosileftiki Journal* 50: 203–213.
Pierrakos, G., G. Tzamalouka, D. Latsou, A. Goula, S. Asonitou, T. Adamakidou, D. Tzamaloukas, J. Pateras, C. Platis, and A. Kalokerinou. 2016. Health professionals' continuing training needs for improving home care services. *International Journal of Strategic Innovative Marketing* 03 (01).
Sakas, Damianos P., N.K. Dimitrios, and D.S. Vlachos. 2013. The role of information systems in creating strategic leadership model. *Procedia—Social and Behavioral Sciences* 467–477.
Sarris, M., A. Goula, B. Gioka, and S. Soulis. 2008. Quality of life of patients and quality of health care after renal transplantation. *Archives of Hellenic Medicine* 25: 201–208.
Tralongo, P., F. Ferrau, N. Borsellino, F. Verderame, M. Caruso, D. Giuffrida, et al. 2011. Cancer patient-centered home care: a new model for health care in oncology. *Therapeutics and Clinical Risk Management* 7: 387–392.
Ware, J.E., and C.D. Sherbourne. 1992. The Medical Outcome Study, 36-item short-form health survey (SF-36): Conceptual framework and item selection. *Medical Care* 30: 473–483.
Yfantopoulos, J., G. Pierrakos, and V. Zanakis. 2001. A Comparative study of the quality of life patients with patients with hepatitis C. *Archives of Hellenic Medicine* 18: 288–296.

The Role of Local Government in the Provision of Social Services in the Third Age. Case Study: The Municipality of Volos

Athanasia Papadimitriou, Charalampos Platis and Emmanouil Zoulias

Introduction

Income is among the major factors as it determines access to health care and is a social welfare index of people. Services that are available by any insurer are limited and characterized by long time wait, resulting to discourage beneficiary (Di Matteo and Martin 2011). The continuous support of aging people in other family members reflects the social values and cultural ethos enjoying the high esteem of the family environment. Simultaneously, ensure an active role in family affairs (Nesami and Shorofi 2014).

The social interaction in living together situations in persons of age 65 years and above is an important communication and active social participation parameter. Losses of nearby persons, such as the death of husband, wife, and friends are regarded as the most stressful life events. The feeling of loneliness restricts contact with the immediate social network and reveals failure on daily events (Newman and Cauley 2012). Depression is common, in persons over 65 years of age and became worst supported by relevant physical and socioeconomic problems. Studies indicate the positive effect of social support to bereaved (Powers et al. 2014).

The original version of the book was revised. Belated corrections to change the order of First name and Family name of chapter authors have been incorporated. The erratum to the book is available at 10.1007/978-3-319-56288-9_72

A. Papadimitriou (✉) · C. Platis
Open University of Greece, Patras, Greece

C. Platis · E. Zoulias (✉)
National School, National Centre for Public Administration
and Local Government, Athens, Greece
e-mail: ezoulias@teemail.gr

A. Kavoura et al. (eds.), *Strategic Innovative Marketing*, Springer Proceedings
in Business and Economics, DOI 10.1007/978-3-319-56288-9_23

The quality of life based on evaluation using human development indicators reflects in the best possible way the mental, physical, and social health of individuals or groups. The main concern of health professionals is the health-related quality of life which turned into a key health indicator. The quality of life related to health can be defined as functionality of physical, psychological, and social aspects and general health perception. Quality of life related to health is a term that tries to embrace WHO definition about health including personal health status and social prosperity during health evaluation procedure. In addition to that used to assess the effects of interventions in health care with a view to continuation of the most efficient and effective treatments to achieve increased longevity, reduced morbidity and well-being of patients (Nakou 2001).

According to Chen (2015), there is a negative reflection of quality of life related to health to aging people who have any mental disorder. Therefore, proposed an increase on health sector resources to maintain cognitive function in the aging. According to Van der Aa et al. (2015), the scalable treatment is a promising way to cope with depression and anxiety in aging people with vision problems. According to Cooper et al. (2015), there were improvements in the use of polypharmacy and reducing unnecessary prescription drugs to interventions suggested in their research.

Goal of home social care services adoption is the addressing of socioeconomic difficulties and health problems associated with this aging group (Aletras et al. 2010). WHO highlights the social and emotional breakdown of health ας major factor for aging beyond the traditional limitations of the biomedical model. The socio-psycho-emotional needs are key factors in determining the state of health (Aleksias 2007).

Material, Population

Within this work, the program *Help at Home* in municipality of Volos is under research. The total area of Volos municipality is 385.614 km^2 being the 7th largest municipality in Greece with 144.449 population. During the last census, definite trends of aging are stated according to National Statistic body in 2011. The municipality of Volos includes nine regions: four urban and five rural.

From March 2016 to April 2016 were selected and collected replies of the research sample of aging individuals who used the health services of Volos hospital and part of it appealed to supportive medical attention by private doctors. The survey involved 100 people from the 138 who were asked to take part. Furthermore, the sample attended at the outpatient clinic of the General Hospital of Volos for various reasons, while the research is sample supported by private doctors conducting in the privacy of the participants.

The first research sample covered only beneficiaries of the program *Help at Home* and the second aging people who did not use those services for improving their health status. A prerequisite for the selection of cases was the age. As indicated in this study, WHO defines aging people over 60 years old. This research focused mainly on aging citizens and included people who stood in the late or middle age. The persons selected to participate in the study ranged in ages from 50 to 94 years.

Research Scope

The orientation of this research is to depict the quality of aging people life who benefit from the provision of social services sectors through the *Help at Home* of Volos Municipality to improve their health as well as people who used the health services of Volos Hospital and private doctors.

The purpose of this work is through the statistical analysis and correlation tests, to highlight the quality of life of aging people using social services of *Help at Home* program and aging people who do not make use of the service. Furthermore, this work investigates whether there is influence of demographic and socioeconomic characteristics in the quality of life of aging. The research questions that were investigated are as follows:

1. Is there significant difference in perceptions of the beneficiaries of the program in comparison to non-beneficiaries?
2. What is the correlation between the perceptions of the aging about their quality of life with demographic and other factors such as: sex, age, education level, marital status, employment relationship, living arrangements, income, and self-reported health problems?

Method

This work tries to investigate the type (positive or negative) as well as the level (high or low) of the effect by various factors on the perceived quality of life of aging. The use of χ^2 statistical method declares only the existence of a statistical significant correlation between two variables, there is neither indication of how the one variable affects the other nor the strength or positive nor negative. In order to come to a result the Spearman method is used, which apart from the statistical significant correlation checks also the statistical significance level. Furthermore, the sign of Spearman's factor assists to understand a negative or positive affection as well as the scale of affection. The affection is declared as more positive if the factor is near 1 and is more negative if the factor is near -1.

The internal consistency reliability is excellent when the coefficient takes values from 0.90 to 0.94 for values greater than 0.94 is considered that the various samples of the questionnaire are similar to each other. In this study, the quality of life scale for the aging people, the coefficient alpha of Cronbach is equal to 0.803, indicating that the scale of research is reliable.

Results

The first sample consisted of 100 participants, 79% were women and 21% men. The age of respondents ranges from 50–54 to 90–94 years, with the majority being in the age group of 80–84 years and expressed in a percentage of 28%, followed by the age group 70–74 and 75–79 years with percentages of 16% and 14% respectively, and the age group ranging from 85 to 89 years with 13%. The age groups of 60–64 and 65–69 years have rates 10% and 9%, respectively, while in the age group 90–94 years the rate is 7%. Finally, the age groups 50–54 and 55–59 were involved in 1% and 2%, respectively. The income of the majority of survey participants 61% ranges from 5,100 to 10,000 € per year, while a significant percentage of 33% does not exceed 5,000 € per year. Just 5% said annual income of 10,100–15,000 and 1% of those with an annual income between 5,100 and 20,000 €.

The respondents state the state diseases that have been diagnosed with a half of the respondents diagnosed with hypertensive disease (50%) and diseases of the joints (48%). The other diseases of Fig. 1 are approximately equally spaced over the sample.

The analysis results show that none of the demographic characteristics tested show statistically significant correlation with the perceived level of quality of life (at a significance level 0.05) and therefore do not appear to be a relevant factor.

Subsequently, similar methodology was employed (nonparametric correlation analysis) to investigate the effect (or otherwise) of diagnosed diseases in the level of quality of life of respondents as they perceive it. The performed statistical analysis reveals that there is a statistically significant relationship between the presence of ischemic heart disease ($p = 0.269$, statistically significant = 0.007) and accidents/falls ($p = 0.353$, statistically significant = 0.000) and the perceived level of quality of life (with a confidence interval of 95%). The results of the analysis are

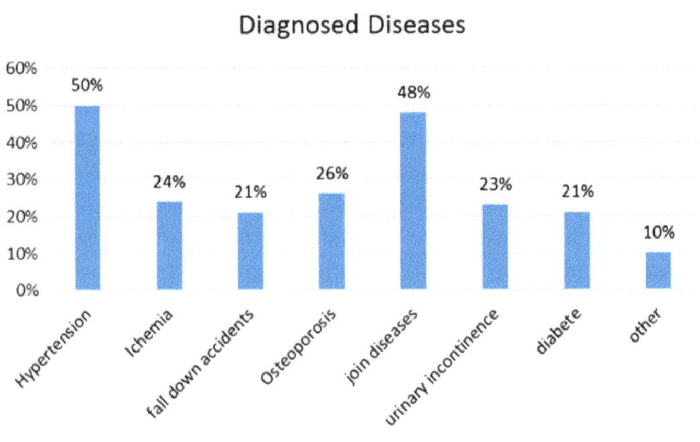

Fig. 1 Diagnosed diseases

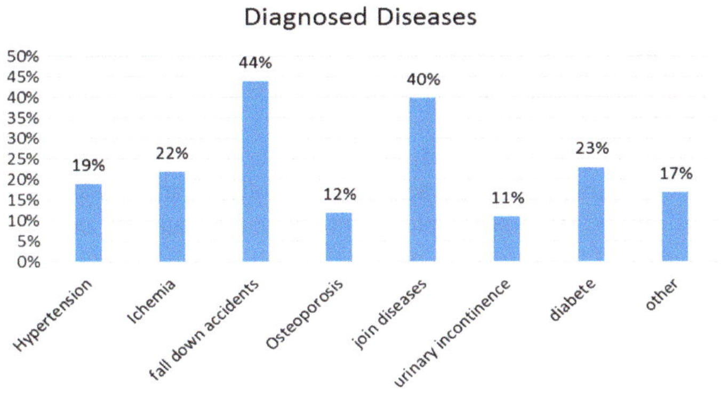

Fig. 2 Diagnosed diseases

that the influence exerted by accidents/falls in perceived quality of life is higher than the effect of ischemic heart disease.

The second sample consisted of 100 aging people who did not use social care service *Help at Home* program. The majority of this sample consists of women and expressed with 62% and men account for 38% of the sample. The age group 85–89 years is 25%, 75–79 years and 80–84 years are found at levels 20% and 18%, respectively, followed by the age group 90–94 years 15%, 70–74 years 12%, 95–99 years 4%, and finally the age groups 60–64 and 65–69 years at a rate of 3% for each. The annual income of the majority (71.72%) ranges from 5,100 to 10,000 €, while from 5,000 € and more than 10,100–15,000 € percentage 14.14%.

Diagnosed diseases of the respondents with a majority of these have fall accidents (44%) and diseases of the joints (40%) Fig. 2.

Discussion

The profile of the respondents who participated in *Help at Home* program was basically women (79%), aging people with the majority belonging to the age group of 80–84 years (28%), low educational level (59.18% knowledge primary education and 26.53% no education), a family widowed (49%), pensioners with income of the vast majority (94%), not to exceed 10,000 € per year. Alongside the 46.46% left alone, while 35.35% lives with husband/wife. Overt comorbidity with half of the respondents has been diagnosed with hypertensive disease (50%) and joint diseases (48%). Then the mapping profile of the respondents who did not benefit of social services *Help at Home* program displays that the majority of the sample consists of women (62%), older people with the majority belonging to the age group of 85–89 years (25%), moderate educational level (41.41% primary education and 43.43% secondary education knowledge), the family situation is balanced between married people and people who have been widowed (47.47% each category), pensioners with the majority of income (85.86%), ranging from 5,100 to 15,000 € per year. While 46% stays with the spouse or their children (44%). Comorbidity characterizes that the second research sample respondents have accident cases (44%) and joint diseases (40%).

According to the parametric analysis of correlations carried out to investigate the effect of various demographic characteristics of both research samples in perceived quality level of life, the first sample is not presented statistical correlation to the perceived quality of life and is not proved to be an identifier agent. In contrast, the second sample shows a statistical correlation with demographic characteristics that express gender, educational level, and marital status. Specifically, the women of the sample did not use the provision of social care services *Help at Home* program, they tend to perceive their quality of life at a higher level than men.

In the present study, we emerged from the main problems of aging limiting mobility and hence the difficulty participating in everyday activities. Improper design of buildings, public transport, and communal spaces are a reality that creates difficulties living independently and movement of persons with disabilities. Successful removal of imbalance will result in the accessibility of structures and their participation in diverse programs and activities in order to avoid social exclusion of this age group and thus to bring about closer ties between the community members.

References

Aleksias, G. Flamou. 2007. Evaluation of social and psychoemotional support of elderly people with health problems, social isolation and exclusion. The case of Help at Home program. *Greek Medical Society Records* 24 (Suppl 1): 37–42 (in Greek).

Aletras, V., A. Kostarelis, M. Tsitouridou, D. Niakas, and A. Nicolaou. 2010. Development and preliminary validation of a questionnaire to measure satisfaction with home care in Greece: An exploratory factor analysis of polychoric correlations. *BioMed Central Health Services Research* 10: 189.

Cooper, J., C. Cadogan, S. Patterson, N. Kerse, M. Bradley, C. Ryan, and C. Hughes. 2015. Interventions to improve the appropriate use of polypharmacy in older people: A Cochrane systematic review. *British Medical Journal Open* 5. doi:10.1136/bmjopen-2015-009235.

Di Matteo, M., and L. Martin. 2011. The process of disease, introduction in health psychology.

Nakou, S. 2001. The evaluation of quality of life in health sector. Applications in pediatric sector. *Greek Medical Society Records* 18 (3): 254–266 (in Greek).

Nesami, M.B., and S.A. Shorofi. 2014. Cultural and socio-economic factors on changes in aging among Iranian women. *Global Journal of Health Science* 6 (3): 145–154.

Newman, A., and J. Cauley. 2012. *The epidemiology of aging*. Netherlands: Spinger.

Powers, S., T. Bisconti, and C. Bergeman. 2014. Trajectories of social support and well-being across the first two years of widowhood. *Death Studies* 38 (8): 499–509.

Van der Aa, H., G. Van Rens, H. Comijs, T. Margrain, J. Twisk, and R. Nispen. 2015. Stepped care for depression and anxiety in visually impaired older adults: Multicentre randomised controlled trial. *British Medical Journal* 531. doi:10.1136/bmj.h6127.

Part VII
Marketing Communications in Online Communities

Organized by: Natalia Rubio
Economics and Business Studies, Universidad Autónoma de Madrid, Madrid, Spain

Description

Information from customer-customer and customer-firm in online communities plays an important role in purchase decision process. The aims of this workshop are understanding: (1) the customer's use of online community for pre-purchase information gathering, (2) the customer's value co-creation with product and service providers through online communities (3) the response of the product and services providers to the customers' participation in online communities and (4) the customers' participation on brand products and services with other customers in different communities, with acquaintances (i.e., on the Facebook) and strangers (i.e., on online brand communities).

Pharmaceutical Marketing STAR

Tiago Costa, Teresa Tiago, Flavio Tiago, Sandra Faria and João Couto

Introduction

The emerging importance of social media in business organizations is raising awareness among the decision makers towards this thematic. Platforms such as Facebook, Twitter and YouTube are now a part of the businesses communication strategies, leading to a dialogue between users/consumers and marketers. In the pharmaceutical industry similar communication strategies are being adopted. However, this industry and specially its marketing department are subjected to intensive regulations due to the healthcare nature of the business, which can suppress a quick adoption of these platforms. Moreover, in the pharmaceutical marketing environment, the lack of official and specific regulations for social media creates uncertainty, which also turns social media implementation process into a difficult path to follow.

This research aims to evaluate the presence of the pharmaceutical industry on social media platforms such as Facebook, Twitter and YouTube, and characterize the types of digital engagement strategies used, considering that the health sector has legal and communication constraints that vary between countries.

To perform this research, a new methodological approach and concept model were developed in order to evaluate the top 20 pharmaceutical companies' presence on the selected social media. This approach includes a descriptive analysis of each social media platform for each pharmaceutical company, followed by a cluster analysis with a characterization of each cluster and highlighting the differences found in terms of social network interaction and value created.

Findings from this study show that not all pharmaceutical companies are present on social media, and some platforms are more used than others. Interestingly the

T. Costa · T. Tiago (✉) · F. Tiago · S. Faria · J. Couto
Economics and Business School, University of the Azores,
Ponta Delgada, Portugal
e-mail: maria.tp.tiago@uac.pt

A. Kavoura et al. (eds.), *Strategic Innovative Marketing*, Springer Proceedings
in Business and Economics, DOI 10.1007/978-3-319-56288-9_24

level of engagement was not linked with the size of the companies and the digital engagement strategies varied between the analyzed social media platforms. Looking at the dimensions of the STAR model (storytelling, triggers, amusement and reaction) digital activity was proven to be quite different among companies (Tiago et al. 2016b). Most pharmaceutical companies have a content-oriented strategy that maximizes the engagement in social media, but the majority of the countries mostly directed to prescribers and not to final users. In this sense, some messages have a compelling storytelling that does not match the triggering and reaction effects.

Background

The subject of social media is a top priority of discussion in the business world (Kaplan and Haenlein 2010). No longer, acting digital is enough. Firms need to be digital if they want to keep pace with their. These authors state that people responsible for taking decisions in companies and also consultants are trying to find ways to increase companies' profitability through social media (e.g. Wikipedia, YouTube, Facebook and Twitter).

However, the search for interaction and establishment of relationships is no longer a novelty. Aghaei et al. (2012) argued that before social media, the internet already allowed a limited user interaction. To them, Web 1.0 (first web generation) could be considered as the "read-only web". This form provided users the possibility of establishing limited interactions and releasing content, but it users could only search and read information (Aghaei et al. 2012; Tiago and Veríssimo 2014). For Rollins and Perri (2013), in the middle of the 90s with the Web 1.0, the increasing people's awareness of the internet provided a new way for them to control the information receive. The Web 2.0 is considered to be the "read-write web" (Rollins and Perri 2013). Aghaei et al. (2012) referred that the technologies associated with the Web 2.0 permitted the creation of groups of people who shared the same interest for social interactions. These authors state that with this Web, the online interaction was based on a two-way communication. According to Rollins and Perri (2013), in the rise of the Web 2.0, the most relevant information was not coming from several media channels but from online users.

Kotler et al. (2015) considered that "social media are a means for consumers to share text, images, audio and video information with each other and with companies and vice versa, encouraging brand engagement at a deeper and broader level than before" (p. 291). Likewise, Kietzmann et al. (2011) advocated that these social media which are composed of seven functional blocks can, through mobile and web-based technologies, allow interaction between users (see, Fig. 1).

According to Kaplan and Haenlein (2010), social networks sites are applications that allow users to interact through online profiles. For Kotler et al. (2015), the business-to-consumer and business-to-business communication can be leveraged through social networks (e.g. Facebook, Twitter and LinkedIn). These authors stated that marketers are still trying to understand what will be the best approach to

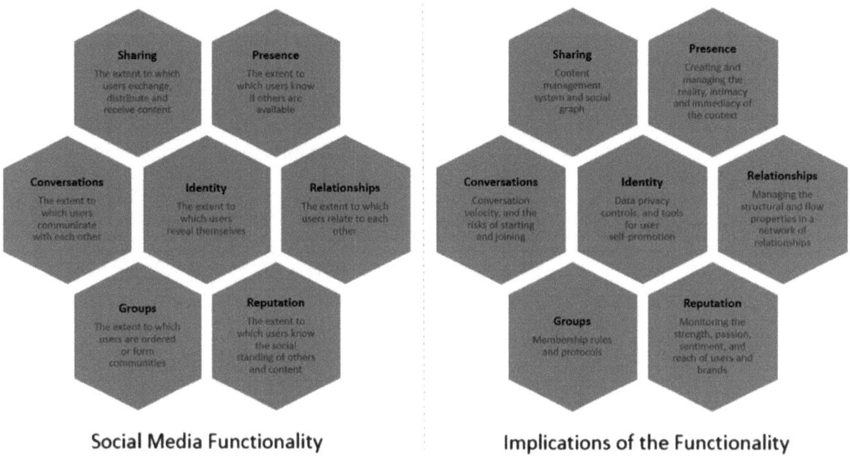

Fig. 1 The "honeycomb" of social media. *Source* Adapted from Kietzmann et al. (2011), p. 243

social networks and their users. They also state that it is sometimes difficult to capture the attention of users and persuade them because social networks are viewed as non-commercial platforms (users want mostly to interact with other users).

Facebook presence has become a must for numerous companies and Twitter can enhance businesses (even for small companies) (Kotler et al. 2015). Bolotaeva and Cata (2010) explained that social networks can leverage brand presence, brand awareness and also they can reduce advertisement costs (especially important in fragile economic situations). However, it is important for companies to be aware of ethic matters (e.g. user privacy; spamming and publicity policies; data mining and legal concerns) (Bolotaeva and Cata 2010).

To Griffiths (2012), social networks allow the exchange of healthcare information associated with symptoms, possible diagnosis and treatments, adverse effects experienced, medical evidence, as well as opinions about their experiences with healthcare providers. This author affirm that in the health care system, there are two sides, namely the patients-side and providers-side that connect with each other through common platforms. In the providers-side there are medical technology companies, pharmaceutical companies, healthcare professionals, managers and professional groups that control patient data, and through it they can influence the shape of health care systems. In the patients-side lays the demand-side, where each single patient acquires information from providers and can find support and advices in their social circle. Online social networking can also be a form of interaction between the two sides. These platforms can be important in the gatekeeping and mediation process and can act as a vehicle for information (Griffiths 2012) (Fig. 2).

Tiago et al. (2016a) stated that the empowerment among patients and providers is increasing and social media is allowing greater control to their users. These

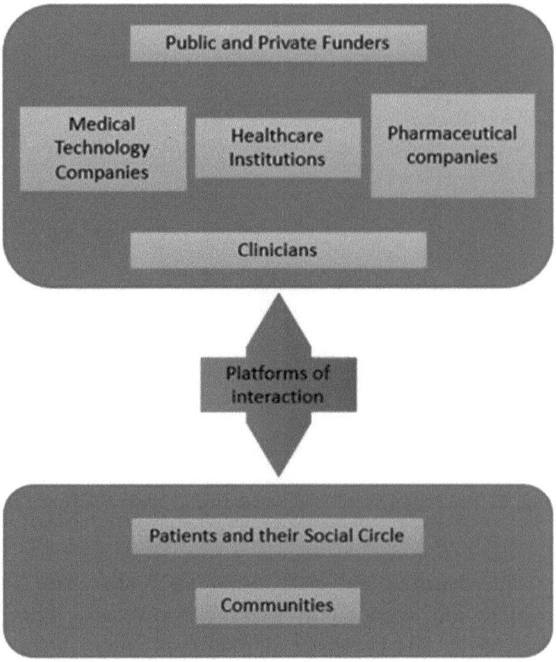

Fig. 2 The health care system as a two-sided network. *Source* Adapted from Griffiths et al. (2012)

empowered audiences will establish connections with the pharmaceutical industry through social media if pharmaceutical companies are trustworthy through their eyes and have something positive to offer (Tiago et al. 2016a; Bakker 2002). According to Rollins and Perri (2013), social media platforms provide wonderful opportunities for pharmaceutical marketers interact with their customers and acquire knowledge of their markets. In order to pharmaceutical marketers effectively manage these platforms, they need to understand how to listen to customers' voices and approach these customers; they need to create optimized messages for each scenario and possess a great ability to adapt to regulatory and technological settings that are in constant mutation (Rollins and Perri 2013). Tiago et al. (2016a) suggested that pharmaceutical companies can gather data through social media platforms that are important for brand monitoring and can also obtain critical information about consumers. For them, these two resources enable pharmaceutical companies to develop innovative marketing strategies and services that could increase brand awareness, customer loyalty, improve patient compliance, as well as respond promptly to information requests from patients and physicians. However, the data such as the user-generated content created and provided by patients and physicians needs to be treated in a secured environment, according to regulations. Regardless gains perceived there still no evidence that pharmaceutical companies can reach and engage customers' through social networks.

Research Methodology and Final Considerations

Acknowledging the relevance of social networks to interact, inform and engage with clients is critical to assess the online activities that promote a higher engagement between pharmaceutical firms and their different publics.

As showed in previous research the interaction on social network can be much more than brands post, incorporating factual data, opinions and promoting interactions (Humphreys et al. 2014), for this reason the research approach used combined the social network analysis and content analysis. With these considerations in mind, a four-dimensional framework: storytelling, triggers, amusement and reaction (STAR) is proposed to leverage social interaction between firms and customers (Fig. 3).

Each dimension will corresponds to its weight as found in previous multidimensional analyses of social media contents (Tiago et al. 2016b).

The sample comprehends the major 20 pharmaceutical firms, extracted from the top 50 pharmaceutical companies (in terms of revenue) elaborated by Pharmaceutical Executive in 2013. The data used was gathered directly from the original social network sites (Facebook, Twitter and YouTube). For data treatment, we used a mix approach combining qualitative and quantitative analyses, starting with a descriptive analysis of traffic, volume and structure of the network, followed by the estimation of the engagement level for each of the social media networks study.

When analyzing social media presence of the top 20 pharmaceutical companies, several conclusions were taken. In this sample, 70% of the companies have a Facebook page (Johnson & Johnson has Facebook page but was not analyzed due to method's restrictions), 90% have a Twitter account, while 15 have a YouTube channel. Both Takeda and Daiichi-Sankyo pharmaceutical companies are completely absent on such platforms. The majority of brand posts were in a form of photo, totalizing 59% posts. In second place are posts with links, with 24% posts. The least frequent form of posting was in a form of status posts and video, with 9% and 8%, respectively. The levels of engagement found were truly low, and only six brands had users' co created contents on it. The STAR model could not be totally assessed since only two dimensions were present in the majority of the firms:

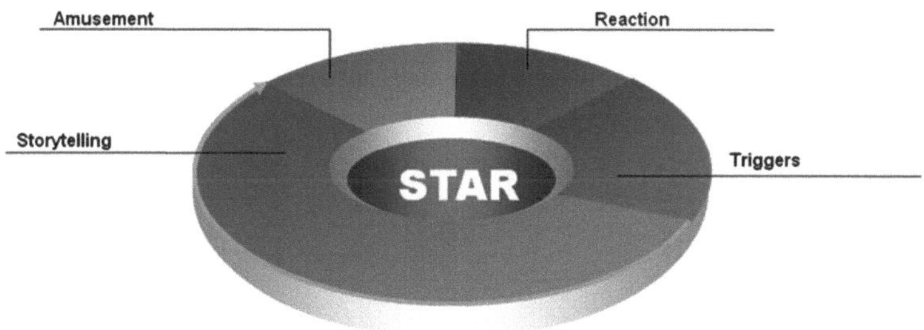

Fig. 3 STAR model

reaction and trigger, implying a diminished use of social media to communicate with general public. However, when analyzing the specific content posted some have a compelling storytelling that does not match the triggering and reaction effects. Therefore, we can infer that pharmaceutical companies ignore the social media trend, and that might be due to ethical and legal issues that surround these platforms. Further research is needed it to confirm this considerations and follow-up this communication phenomenon.

Acknowledgements We gratefully acknowledge Advance Research Centre—ISEG and financial support from "Fundação para a Ciência e Tecnologia" (FCT—Portugal), national funding through research grant (UID/SOC/04521/2013) and CEEApIA.

References

Aghaei, S., M.A. Nematbakhsh, and H.K. Farsani. 2012. Evolution of the world wide web: From WEB 1.0 TO WEB 4.0. *International Journal of Web and Semantic Technology* 3:1.

Bakker, A.R. 2002. Health care and ICT, partnership is a must. *International Journal of Medical Informatics* 66: 51–57.

Bolotaeva, V., and T. Cata. 2010. Marketing opportunities with social networks. *Journal of Internet Social Networking and Virtual Communities* 2010: 1–8.

Griffiths, F., J. Cave, F. Boardman, J. Ren, T. Pawlikowska, R. Ball, A. Clarke, and A. Cohen. 2012. Social networks—The future for health care delivery. *Social Science and Medicine* 75: 2233–2241.

Griffiths, M.D. 2012. Facebook addiction: concerns, criticism, and recommendations—A response to Andreassen and colleagues. *Psychological Reports* 110.

Humphreys, L., P. Gill, and B. Krishnamurthy. 2014. Twitter: A content analysis of personal information. *Information, Communication and Society* 17: 843–857.

Kaplan, A.M., and M. Haenlein. 2010. Users of the world, unite! The challenges and opportunities of Social Media. *Business Horizons* 53: 59–68.

Kietzmann, J.H., K. Hermkens, I.P. McCarthy, and B.S. Silvestre. 2011. Social media? Get serious! Understanding the functional building blocks of social media. *Business Horizons* 54: 241–251.

Kotler, P., K.L. Keller, D. Manceau, and A. Hémonnet-Goujot. 2015. *Marketing management.* NJ: Prentice Hall Englewood Cliffs.

Rollins, B.L., and M. Perri. 2013. *Pharmaceutical marketing*. Jones & Bartlett Publishers.

Tiago, M.T.B., F. Tiago, F. Amaral, and S. Silva. 2016a. Healthy 3.0: Healthcare digital dimensions. *Reshaping Medical Practice and Care with Health Information Systems* 287.

Tiago, T., F. Tiago, S.D. Faria, and J.P. Couto. 2016b. Who is the better player? Off-field battle on Facebook and Twitter. *Business Horizons* 59: 175–183.

Tiago, T., and J. Veríssimo. 2014. Digital marketing and social media: Why bother? *Business Horizons* 57: 703–708.

Comparison Shopping Websites and Their Impact on Consumers' Purchase Intention

Theodoros Kentistos-Rannos and Prodromos D. Chatzoglou

Introduction

Beyond general internet search offered by search engines like Google, Yahoo, Bing, etc., consumers with the use of a Comparison Shopping Websites (CSWs) are able to quickly collate information about numerous vendors along with price information, product information, payment methods, shipping methods and quality indicators with substantially lower search cost compared to a manual search (Moranga-Gonzalez and Wildenbeest 2011).

In Greece, CSWs dealing with products are mainly skroutz.gr and bestprice.gr, offering their services with no cost for consumers, while retailers are charged in a cost-per-click basis, with future plans to become an autonomous channel for retailers to sell their products.

Literature Review

By extending the retail competition models to the Internet, specific problems concerning consumers' lack of research arise. Usually when searching the world wide web for a product or a service, consumers seem unwilling to fully explore the alternatives, even though they are a few "clicks" away (Bailey et al. 2007), a

T. Kentistos-Rannos (✉) · P.D. Chatzoglou
Hellenic Open University, Patras, Greece
e-mail: theodoros.kentistos@gmail.com

P.D. Chatzoglou
Department of Production and Management Engineering,
Democritus University of Thrace, Xanthi, Greece

A. Kavoura et al. (eds.), *Strategic Innovative Marketing*, Springer Proceedings in Business and Economics, DOI 10.1007/978-3-319-56288-9_25

problem that was partially solved with the emergence of the CSWs, dealing in part with small retailers' problem of limited web visibility (Wan et al. 2007).

Providing that consumers actively select the media based on their awareness of their needs, they receive gratification as they explore in an individual context (Sangran et al. 2009). Lim and Ting (2012), in their analysis of the Uses and Gratifications (U&G) theory in online shopping, confirmed the correlation between three of the main dimensions of the underlying constructs of the U&G theory (entertainment and informativeness gratification and the web irritation); and also confirmed a relationship between attitude and intention of online shopping.

As consumers shift their focus toward activities other than shopping, online vendors need to maximize the speed and ease of shopping in order to take advantage of shopping any-time, any-place using the internet, as it is "the foremost driver of overall online shopping convenience" (Jiang et al. 2013).

CSWs familiarize the consumers with the prices of the available products and services, thus increasing competitive pricing pressure on firms (Ronayne 2015). As the information provided by the CSWs is, in most cases, costless (Moranga-Gonzalez and Wildenbeest 2012), consumers are incentivized to take into account all the parameters concerning the sellers of a homogenous product or service and make a well-informed decision based not only on price but other factors as well (Dullek et al. 2011), regarding both their online and offline purchases (Bodur et al. 2015). This is supported by the results of a research conducted in Greece by ELTRUN, where almost a third of the sales in physical stores was made after online research (Doukidis and Fraidaki 2015), indicating that purchase intention created through the use of a CSW is not only directed towards purchasing online but provides insights in price and product (or service) validation in all channels. In general, CSWs create value beyond traffic generation and referrals for the internet retailers, with shopping convenience (Ong 2011a), but since the emergence of these websites, evidence appeared in certain countries of price elevating to encompass the cost of multiple listings (Ronayne 2015).

For online retailers, the different levels of prices and store reviews in CSWs gave out a distinct effect (Bodur et al. 2015); it was crucial for high-priced online retailers to have a favorable rating, especially for consumers that do not use the price-retailer quality heuristic. Reviews and ratings in CSWs play an important role in validating the valuation of a retailer, especially if the retailer is unknown to the consumer. However, there is a personal bias in paying more attention to negative or positive reviews, based on the way they perceived the credibility and helpfulness of the review (Ong 2011b). This indicates that personal preferences can make the difference, with usefulness of CSWs having an effect on user continuing to use that website (Ong 2011a).

Theory Development

Socio-demographic variables are associated with consumer innovativeness and shopping behavior; younger and poorer people are more likely to adopt new technologies or new ways in shopping, in contrast to older people who are less familiarized with the usage of computers and are not time-constrained and, usually, enjoy socializing while shopping. Adoption behavior is also likely to be influenced by education (Dholakia and Uusitalo 2002), since adopters tend to be more educated than non-adopters. Certain psychographics traits also appear to be differentiated between comparison and non-comparison shoppers, such as experience while shopping, shopper role experience, and general personality traits (Mittal 2016).

Furthermore, various factors measuring the experience in terms of years of shopping online and previous shopping experience in buying similar products found to have an effect on the selection process (Jung et al. 2014).

Perceived hedonic and utilitarian benefits as well as perceived stress have an effect on the selection of the channel for purchase, affecting not only search intention but also purchase intention (Dholakia and Uusitalo 2002; To et al. 2007), with stress being lower for comparison shoppers (Mittal 2016) and search and evaluation convenience playing a significant role to the overall perceived convenience of the use of the internet as purchase channel (Jiang et al. 2013).

Finally, preferences in seller selection appear to have an effect in consumers' purchase intention, with price having a greater effect in the selection process, especially in cases involving shortlisting (Ong 2011a; Dullek et al. 2011).

The abovementioned lead to the following hypotheses:

The use of CSWs is positively correlated with...

H1 shoppers of (a) lower age; (b) lower income; (c) higher education level
H2 consumers' psychographic characteristics
H3 internet usage
H4 previous internet shopping experience
H5 perceived benefits (hedonic and utilitarian benefits and stress)
H6 perceived search and evaluation convenience

Purchase intention is positively correlated with...

H7 the usage of CSWs
H8 perceived benefits (hedonic and utilitarian benefits and stress)
H9 search and evaluation convenience
H10 seller selection criteria

Data Collection and Analysis

Online distribution of structured questionnaires was used to gather the necessary primary data to test the validity of the proposed theoretical framework, using a convenience and snowball sampling approach. In order to measure the factors examined, the questionnaire included questions that were adopted from various previous studies (Mittal 2016; Jung et al. 2014; Passyn et al. 2013; Jiang et al. 2013; Ong 2011a; To et al. 2007; Dholakia and Uusitalo 2002). The questionnaire was sent through online channels to friends, co-workers, and students attending the MBA program of the Hellenic Open University. Respondents were also asked to forward the link to the questionnaire to people they know in an attempt to increase the size of the target sample. The survey was conducted in April 2016 and the final sample consisted of 207 responses. Most of them are female participants (58.5%), well educated (undergraduate 37.2%, postgraduate 45.4%), with a mean age of 36.22 years. Additionally, most of them have full-time employment (69.6%), with unemployed representing only 8.7% of the sample and university students another 5.8%. Finally, 52.6% earn less than 1000 €/month, 30.4% between 1000 and 1500 €, while 17% earn more than 1500 €/month.

Descriptive Statistics Analysis

The results indicate that, on average, participants were browsing the internet approximately 4 h and 46 min on a daily basis, while approximately 10% of that time (27 min) was spent on online shopping activities. They have 5.5 years of online shopping experience and an average of 4.1 purchases during the last three months. Additionally, examining the results concerning different dimensions of consumers' psychographics it was revealed that: choice satisfaction plays a huge role in the mindset of the participants since most of them are quite satisfied with the purchasing choices they have made in the past and seem unwilling to change that. Participants consider themselves to be rather conscious that they have a certain budget when shopping. Post-purchase confidence is slightly higher than pre-purchase confidence indicating a positive feedback from their purchases. Most of the participants were most likely to focus on buying something that meets their needs but also have the best deal in purchasing a product. In buying gratification, participants felt gratification being more important than only buying what was needed. Socialization with close friends/relatives is important for participants.

Focusing on the results concerning the interaction with a CSW, participants were more receptive in the concept of using a CSW whether they intended to buy either online or offline. Apart from the intention of buying, participants were rather indifferent in using a CSW and its functions in a daily basis.

Moreover, examining the seller selection criteria, participants were more willing to purchase from a store they had shopped in the past and were happy with, while they also valued purchase safety as the second most important factor. Price and user reviews were valued slightly lower but equally, indicating that they also played an important role in the process of selecting a store. Personal knowledge of a seller seemed to have a lesser effect on the selection than being happy with previous purchases, thus underlying the fact that there are participants who would choose to buy from an unknown store as long as their other criteria of higher value (to them) were satisfied. Participants seemed rather neutral towards selecting a store based solely on the higher quality brands it offered, although perceived product quality is considered as the most important selection criterion.

Structural Equation Modeling (SEM) Analysis

The relations between the factors of the Structural Equation Model (SEM) are presented in the SEM model (Fig. 1) along with the path coefficients and their R^2 values (all path coefficients are significant at a 0.05 level). More specifically, the prediction power (R^2) of the model is 0.49 and 0.28, for purchase intention and CSW usage, respectively, actually suggesting that the independent factors are able to explain a large part of the variation of these two main dependent factors of this model. Looking at Fig. 1, it is concluded that (a) H3, H6, H9, and H10 are supported because both direct and indirect relationships between the factors are found. (b) H5 and H8 are partially supported as stress was not found to be a significant factor and thus excluded in analysis (c) H7 is supported because a direct relationship between the factors is found, and (d) H2 and H4 are supported although only an indirect relationship between the factors is found. As far as H1 is concerned, correlation analysis revealed that only lower age is positively correlated with CSWs usage. It is, therefore, partially accepted. Furthermore, it is evident that internet usage has the strongest (direct and indirect) impact on CSW usage, while perceived benefits have the strongest (direct and indirect) impact on purchase

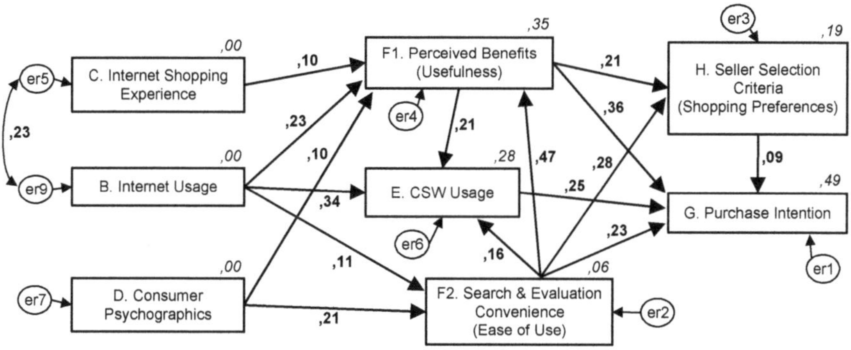

Fig. 1 SEM model

intention. Finally, as can be seen in Fig. 1, the final model includes some more important (and statistically significant) relationships which were not initially examined (mainly between Search and Evaluation Convenience—Perceived Benefits—Seller Selection Criteria).

Discussion and Conclusions

This research presented a model to identify the factors that lead to the use of CSWs in Greece and how this affects the prospect of purchasing. The use of CSWs was found to be highly and positively correlated to the time they spend online. Demographic factors have little to do with the use of the internet and understandably; since the survey was performed online, most of the participants were internet savvy. Comparison shopper psychographics and internet shopping experience did not seem to directly affect the frequency of using a CSW, but they were related in a positive manner with the way internet users perceived convenience and other utilitarian and hedonic benefits from the use of CSWs.

As expected, higher levels of use of a CSW, led to a higher intention to buy, indicating that, for many online consumers, the use of a CSW is a "pit stop" in their buying decision process, with participants that realized a higher level of usefulness and ease of use from a CSW having an even higher intention to purchase.

In addition, in the process of selecting a retailer, consumers take into account previous purchasing experiences as well as other buyer store reviews. Transaction safety was also considered a must for making an internet purchase. However, although lowest price is also considered as very important, it is not more important than the abovementioned criteria (highest seller rating, familiarity, safety).

Concluding, CSWs are a significant channel for both consumers and retailers and, as far as these websites help improve users' experience, will result to an increase of sales, especially when appropriately combined actions from retailers (e.g., to better position themselves amongst their rivals) have taken place.

References

Bailey, J.P., S. Faraj, and Y. Yao. 2007. The road more travelled: Web traffic and price competition in internet retailing. *Electronic Markets* 17 (1): 56–67.

Bodur, H.O., N.M. Klein, and N. Arora. 2015. Online price search: Impact of price comparison sites on offline price evaluations. *Journal of Retailing* 91 (1): 125–139.

Dholakia, R.R., and O. Uusitalo. 2002. Switching to electronic stores: Consumer characteristics and perception of shopping benefits. *International Journal of Retail and Distribution Management* 30 (10): 459–469.

Doukidis, G., and K. Fraidaki. 2015. *Upward trend and maturity in e-commerce, business to consumer [in Greek]*. Athens: ELTRUN, The E-Business Research Center, Athens University of Economics and Business, Department of Management Science and Technology.

Dullek, U., F. Hackl, B. Weiss, and R. Weinter-Ebmer. 2011. Buying online: An analysis of ShopBot visitors. *German Economic Review* 12 (4): 395–408.

Jiang, L., Z. Yang, and M. Jun. 2013. Measuring consumer perceptions of online shopping convenience. *Journal of Service Management* 24 (2): 191–214.

Jung, K., Y.C. Cho, and S. Lee. 2014. Online shoppers' response to price comparison sites. *Journal of Business Research* 67 (10): 2079–2087.

Lim, W.M., and D.H. Ting. 2012. E-shopping: An analysis of the uses and gratifications theory. *Modern Applied Science* 6 (5): 48–63.

Mittal, B. 2016. Psychographics of comparison shoppers. *Journal of Consumer Marketing* 33 (1): 20–31.

Moranga-Gonzalez, J.L., and M.R. Wildenbeest. 2011. *Comparison sites.* Working Paper No. 933 ed. s.l.:IESE Business School.

Moranga-Gonzalez, J.L., and M.R. Wildenbeest. 2012. Comparison sites. *The Oxford Handbook of the Digital Economy*, 224–253. New York: Oxford University Press.

Ong, B.S. 2011a. Online shoppers' perceptions and use of comparison-shopping sites: An exploratory study. *Journal of Promotion Management* 17 (2): 207–227.

Ong, B.S. 2011b. Online shopper reviews: Ramifications for promotion and website utility. *Journal of Promotion Management* 17 (3): 327–344.

Passyn, K.A., M. Diriker, and R.B. Settle. 2013. Price comparison, price competition, and the effects of ShopBots. *Journal of Business and Economics Research* 11 (9): 401–416.

Ronayne, D. 2015. *Price comparison websites.* University of Warwick, Warwick economics research papers series (WERPS) (Number 1056 (version 4)).

Sangran, S., J.A. Siguaw, and C. Guan. 2009. A comparative study of motivation differences for online shopping. *The DATABASE for Advances in Information Systems* 40 (4): 28–42.

To, P.-L., C. Liao, and T.-H. Lin. 2007. Shopping motivations on internet: A study based on utilitarian and hedonic value. *Technovation* 27: 774–787.

Wan, Y., S. Menon, and A. Ramaprasad. 2007. A classification of product comparison agents. *Communications of the ACM* 50 (8): 65–71.

Part VIII
The Role of Branding for Companies and Countries

Organized by: George Avlonitis
Department of Marketing and Communication, Athens University of Economics and Business, Athens, Greece

Description

There is no doubt that brands are companies' most valuable assets, adding both economic and strategic value. In the last few years, brand valuation has been an intensively discussed subject among marketing academics and practitioners. The value of this asset is often referred to a brand equity which is the marketing and financial value associated with a brand's strength in the market or the added value a given brand name provides to a product beyond the functional benefits. Apart from the actual proprietary brand assets, like trademarks and patents, there are some other important elements underlying brand equity, such as brand awareness, brand loyalty, perceived quality, and brand associations. Thus, a major challenge for companies and organizations is to create, maintain, enhance, and assess brand equity and its components. However, in the era of globalization, countries also compete with each other for attention, respect and trust of potential customers, investors, tourists, media, and governments of different and diverge nations. A strong Nation Brand provides a crucial competitive advantage in the international arena. In this workshop, we welcome case studies, review papers, research papers, etc. dealing with all aspects of branding at country, company, and brand levels. The goal of this workshop is to develop a framework for building brand identity in competitive markets involving brand positioning, brand architecture, brand performance, and brand equity.

Influence of Marketing Communication Tools on Brand Building in the Context of Marketing Management and Corporate Prosperity

Olga Juraskova, Martina Jurikova and Romana Cockova

Brand Image

Image is a complex of ideas, feelings, attitudes and opinions that a person associates with particular things, personalities and events. It is a result of the exchange of opinions between an individual and a society, often carried out in a situation of conflict, when the individual is put under pressure which accompanies the process of decision making.

Image is a complex, multidimensional and structured system, which is at the same time expressive and plastic. Its wholeness means more than just a sum of its relevant parts. It comprises objective and subjective, correct and erroneous beliefs, attitudes and experience of an individual or a certain group of people with respect to a particular object. The basic attributes of an image include: quality of the product, corporate communication (use of marketing communication tools), corporate culture (values and attitudes of the company staff), reliability, relationship to customers (customer service, customer-oriented behaviour), innovation of products/products or services offered. Marketing management of companies and institutions is oriented towards profit, towards corporate prosperity (Štarchon and Jurikova 2015, p. 56).

A systematically built image serves to fulfil the marketing aims; it leads to an increase in the profit and ensures long-term competitiveness and prosperity. The corporate image significantly affects the perception of the brand of the product, the

O. Juraskova (✉) · M. Jurikova · R. Cockova
Faculty of Multimedia Communications, Tomas Bata University in Zlín,
Zlín, Czech Republic
e-mail: ojuraskova@fmk.utb.cz

M. Jurikova
e-mail: jurikova@fmk.utb.cz

R. Cockova
e-mail: cockova@fmk.utb.cz

A. Kavoura et al. (eds.), *Strategic Innovative Marketing*, Springer Proceedings
in Business and Economics, DOI 10.1007/978-3-319-56288-9_26

perceived value of the brand affects shopping behaviour of the customers, behaviour of the customers and their attitude towards the brand affects the number of purchases carried out, which generates profit and increases corporate prosperity. The term 'image' expresses a notion, an image that originates and penetrates into bigger picture of marketing communications. Companies are ever-increasingly aware of the need to define corporate culture, as well as of the need to form an image in a planned and systematic manner, that is more and more perceived as an important company management tool. The formation of the image is an integral part of the communication mix. Therefore, it is a part of various forms of marketing communications and is influenceable by these forms (Šula and Banyár 2015, p. 149).

In order to understand the impact of particular forms of marketing communications on the formation of an image, it is necessary to start with the classification of image according to several criteria.

Classification of image:

- according to carriers (internal, external image)
- according to requirements (real, imaginary image)
- according to scope (universal, specific image)
- according to subjects (personal, other persons' image)
- according to objects (image of the company, product, service, store, person, place, idea)

Internal image is created by the objects about themselves. It is usually denoted as "self image". It may be created, e.g. by the producer about himself, about his products, company, but also employees, top management or an individual. This image is affected by the previous experiences, results of the work, position within the company, in a group of people, etc. External image describes how the society perceives us. Many companies as well as persons try to give impression that does not correspond to reality. External image may be intently created by a company or a person by means of advertising and other marketing communication tools. Real image is such an image that is created in the consciousness of the public, in a company, but also in the consciousness of employees, customers, suppliers, distributors and other stakeholders. It is denoted as an acquired image or reputation (Aaker 2003, p. 139). It is often formed only according to what people have heard about the company or what they have been told by others without having personal experience. A company can turn its reputation into its advantage. For example, a company that has a reputation of an expensive but highly qualified institution can expect that its customers will be willing and ready to pay for the products or services more than usual and will anticipate this fact. Imaginary image is created by long-term and ambitious effort of a company or an individual with the help and use of all marketing mix tools (Burnett 2002, p. 134). Each company should have a defined image according to its focus and mission. All factors that form this image then have to conform to this definition. However, when changing the image it is necessary to proceed step by step, because too rapid changes can cause uncertainty, confusion and scepticism in people. Universal image is valid regardless of local peculiarities. The emphasis put on environment protection in case of non-phosphate washing powders can serve as an example, since much attention is paid to this ecological aspect all over the world. Specific image emphasizes a certain peculiarity that is related, e.g. to a territorial location. One's own image or personal image is one of the important factors that influence the position and the role of each individual in an organization, society or family. Other persons' image refers to how we perceive other people, colleagues, partners, relatives, etc.

The image of a company is a complex phenomenon made up of a number of objective and subjective elements. The most significant factors include both material and non-material factors. Non-material factors represent non-material presentation of the company with respect to the public—presentation of the employees of the company in public, employees' clothing, communication style in advertising, sales promotion, direct marketing, presentations at exhibitions and fairs, sponsoring, the level of correspondence, complaints handling, etc. (Breakenridge 2008, p. 168). Non-material presentation focused inward—corporate culture, work atmosphere, management style, dealing with interdepartmental conflicts, etc. also forms an integral part. The material factors include mainly the quality of products and services provided, design of the products, store spaces, buildings, car fleet, design of conference rooms, etc. Positive references, positive information published in the mass media, honourable mention, the use of products by significant persons, celebrities, etc. also have a significant impact on the creation of a positive image.

Image is a sum of activities and proceedings of corporate culture, corporate identity and corporate design that are transmitted by means of corporate communication (Aaker 2003, p. 73)

$$\text{CIm} = (\text{CC} + \text{CI} + \text{CD}) \times \text{CCom}$$

CIm corporate image, *CC* corporate culture, *CI* corporate identity, *CD* corporate design, *CCom* corporate communications.

Methodology

Within the primary research, in accordance with specialized literature search dealing with the issue of a brand image, the criteria that have impact on a brand image in theory as well as in applied corporate environment were defined. The survey examined the general influence of predefined criteria on the image and their influence on the specific corporate image, i.e. how respondents generally perceive particular image criteria in theory, and how they perceive them in a particular corporate environment, in which they work. A total of 75 respondents (n = 75) participated in the survey, out of which 52% were women and 48% men. 55% of the respondents were representatives of a small organization (up to 50 employees), 17%

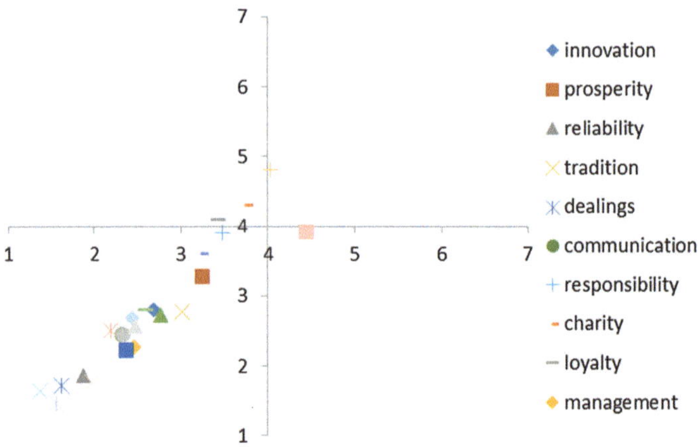

Fig. 1 The dependence of the effect of attributes on the image in general and their influence in corporate environment

representatives of a medium-sized company (51–250 employees) and 28% representatives of a large company (over 250 employees). Regional companies were represented in 35%, local in 40% and global in 24%. The largest group was represented by services (56%), business (19%), state administration (13%), industry (6%) and other spheres without further specification (6%).

The results of the survey suggest that particular criteria for the formation of an image, and that in general terms in comparison to a particular corporate environment, as well as in different specializations and market environments may be perceived differently. The results of the survey are portrayed in a chart showing the dependence of the general impact of the criteria on an image and their influence in the corporate environment (Fig. 1).

If we place in the diagram a linear curve that would demonstrate the situation in which the general and the specific perception of a given attribute is identical, we can then state that the most important attributes of an image are: behaviour towards customers, quality of the product, reliability with respect to negotiation with partners, supply reliability. These conclusions apply generally, regardless of the type of market environment, and are identical with minimum variance from the point of view of general perception as well as the perception of the impact in a particular company.

In the following research the shift in the perception of the general impact of the attributes on the formation of a brand image was measured. Employees of the Czech companies (n = 109) who are in charge of brand building by means of marketing communication tools were interviewed using the CAPI method. The Likert scale demonstrates the results of the survey. The order of the criteria: reliability, rapidity, credibility, corporate culture, quality of management, internal communication, relations, innovation, tradition, events, loyalty programmes, environment, profitability, charity, fairs, size of the company, web, publicity,

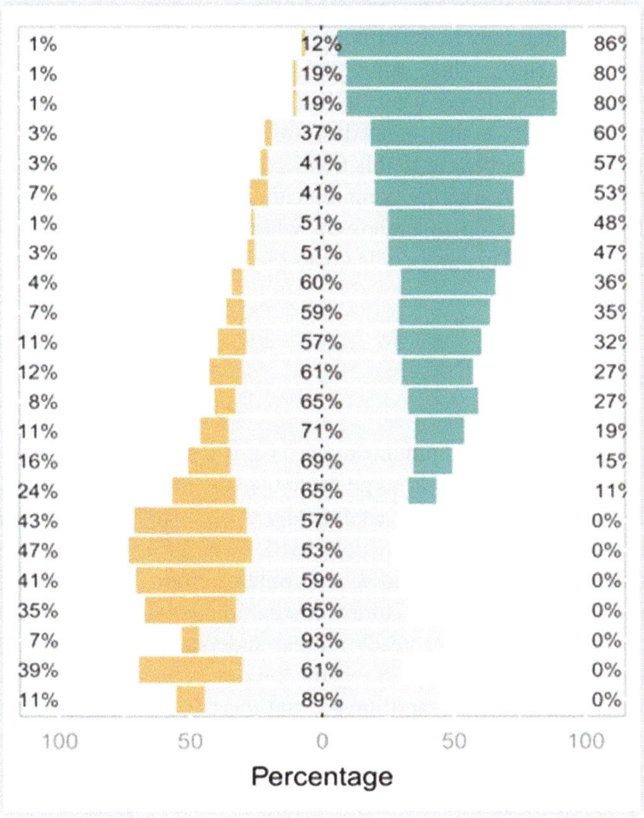

Fig. 2 Likert scale showing criteria importance in the formation of a brand image

corporate presentation, graphic design, employees' behaviour, communication, quality. Graphic illustration in Likert scale: left—crucial importance, centre—medium importance, right—non-important (Fig. 2).

The most important criteria in the formation of a brand image are publicity, presentation of the brand and web presentation. All these criteria form part of marketing communication tools, which suggests that marketing communications are of crucial importance for the formation of a brand image. In view of the fact that the most important criteria belong to the sphere of public relations as one of the forms of marketing communications, relationships and establishing relationships with stakeholders are of crucial importance for the image and are essential for the creation of a love brand.

Formation of an image is a long-term process of marketing management, therefore, consistency of the message and consistent formation of the required image with respect to target groups are vital. The failure to respect the consistency of the formation of an image as a result of changes in the marketing management of the company and institution management is a frequent problem. An image is created by means of benefits that may be functional or emotional. Functional benefits relate to the product parameters, while emotional benefits insert the product/brand in a "world, in which the customer wants to live" (nevertheless, in most cases, s/he does not). A fictitious reality is thus created in the customer's mind, who then classifies products into those that belong to this fictitious reality and those that do not belong there. Effective use of marketing communication tools, and mainly public relations tools, leads to the creation of brands, in which people believe, which they buy, recommend and love. This process leads to the formation of a love brand.

Conclusion

The sphere of marketing communications is a science as well as an art. It is a scientific discipline because a large quantity of information, knowledge and experience and the ability to think analytically is necessary to ensure the effectivity of the marketing communications tools used. It is an artistic discipline because creative thinking, the ability to look at problems from different points of view, courage to communicate and use stories in communication is needed. The ability to communicate effectively and to reach mutual understanding is often considered as the yardstick of success or failure as regards the development of a company; it leads to the creation of a positive brand image, and therefore to corporate prosperity. In the time of modern marketing, with social changes constantly growing in speed and the rapid introduction of information technology, it is necessary for the brands to consciously and effectively build their image with the objective to create a love brand by using marketing communication tools. Customers who have established such a relation to the brand are ranked among the most valuable customers; they are loyal, try new products and mainly recommend the brand to other customers. This is of utmost significance for the brand prosperity. Marketing management of companies should be aimed at enforcing those criteria of a brand image that are essential for the creation of a love brand. The study revealed particular results of the research that deals with this issue, and in accordance with the results of the survey, a model leading to the creation of the brand image was made and it is applicable in theory as well as in practice.

References

Aaker, D. 2003. *Brand bulding*. Brno: Computer Press. ISBN 80-7226-885-6.

Breakenridge, D. 2008. PR 2.0 New Media, New Tools, New Audiences, Pearson Education, New Jersey. ISBN 0-321-51007-0.

Burnett, K. 2002. *Relationship fundraising*. San Francisco: Wiley Company. ISBN 0-7879-6089-6.

Štarchon, P., M. Jurikova, a kol. 2015. Značky a český zákazník. Zlín: VeRBuM. ISBN 978-80-87500-76-7.

Šula, T., and M. Banyar. 2015. Innovative Marketing as a Tool for Building a Positive Image of an Institution of Higher Education and Increasing the Competitiveness of its Graduates—Analysis of the Functional Use of Projects of the Department of Marketing Communications at the Faculty of Multimedia Communications of TBU in Zlín and their Potential for Integration into the Teaching Process. *In Procedia—Social and behavioral sciences,* Elsevier Ltd., 2015, s. 146–153. ISSN 1877-0428.

Current Perception of a Brand in Czech Consumers' Mind

Martina Juříková and Josef Kocourek

Introduction

Karlíček (2016), Aaker (2004), Štarchoň (2015) and other authors emphasize that a brand is, above all, a carrier of a particular meaning which influences the customers' perception of its value and of the value of products and services represented by the brand. Thus, a brand may be a very important competitive advantage, because thanks to such an advantage the customers can perceive the given products, services and/or the entire institution as a more trustworthy and more attractive for them than other brands existing on the market. The author Johnová (2008) agrees with this interpretation as she considers a brand to be an inseparable component part of a product. Particularly as regards services or non-material products, a brand is in her opinion all the more important as the customer does not have an opportunity to view the relevant product. Therefore, a brand itself is a special type of goods bought by the customer. Each brand undergoes its own development which is observed during several essential stages. In order to develop a strong global brand, a long path has to be taken, which for many successful local brands ends halfway. Many elements are decisive for the overall success rate of a brand on the market, which have to produce a synergic effect in case that the brand aims to be successful. Such a strategy is usually referred to as strategic management of a brand, which accompanies the brand throughout the brand's entire life cycle. This strategy creates, manages, measures and maintains the value of a brand. Within assessment of several different brand management strategies, Keller (pp. 73–79) has listed the following four basic steps in this process:

M. Juříková (✉) · J. Kocourek
Faculty of Multimedia Communications, Tomas Bata University in Zlín,
Zlín, Czech Republic
e-mail: jurikova@fmk.utb.cz

A. Kavoura et al. (eds.), *Strategic Innovative Marketing*, Springer Proceedings
in Business and Economics, DOI 10.1007/978-3-319-56288-9_27

1. Identification and determination of positioning and values of a brand
2. Planning and implementation of marketing programmes for the brand
3. Measuring and interpretation of a brand's performance
4. Increase in and maintenance of the value of the brand

At the very beginning, it is necessary to exactly determine and define the position of a brand, the type of product which the brand is supposed to represent and how it is expected to react to competition, i.e. it is indispensable to determine the so-called *positioning* of a brand. The above-mentioned defines it as "a decision on the planned offer and image of the company so that it will occupy a clear and valuable position in the mind of the target consumer". A correctly set positioning is able to persuade the consumer of advantages of the said brand in comparison to the competition, and play down possible disadvantages. Positioning should also include the brand in a specific product category and take this category into consideration when handling the brand.

According to Keller (p. 72), positioning is based on two fundamental pillars—determination of values of a brand and the brand mantra. "The basic values of a brand comprise a set of abstract associations (properties and advantages) which characterize the brand". Thus, it is necessary to determine the desirable brand associations within the values; such associations may take the form of several catchwords, a place, a well-known personality or any other form. Mantra refers to a short expression of three to five words, which should describe the main aspects of the brand and its basic values. Keller compares the brand mantra to DNA and mentions the mantra of the Nike brand as an example: real, athletic, performance. At the first stage, a certain idea which the owners have regarding the brand is produced, i.e. how their brand is expected to be perceived and what its characteristics should be. This idea is then reflected in the awareness (*awareness*) of the customers. The main task of marketing including all its tools is above all to ensure that the customers have awareness of the set identity of the brand. At the second stage, various marketing programmes and activities are in charge of bringing the positioning of the brand in existence. *"The basic premise is about what is necessary to produce the said product or provide the said service, i.e. an organization with certain values, culture, people, programmes, skills and other activities. This characteristic may create a basis for differentiation, for an offer of a value and for a relationship to a customer"* (Aaker 2003, p. 99).

The organization sets out its mission, visions and aims, determines the basic values of the organization, and, thus, the values of the brand as well (Gottlichova 2015). Afterwards, the corporate culture is partially a reflection of the perception of the brand on the market. Suitably selected staff, a positive internal atmosphere and sharing of defined values is a basis for a successful brand of an organization.

The climax of the process of strategic management of the brand is an increase in the brand values. The implementation and maintenance of brand values is the final step which is actually still at its initial stage. Marketing specialist or brand manager, who is in charge of the brand, must continuously assess the money invested, its profit and plan other strategic decisions aimed at an increase in the effectiveness.

"The creation of a brand is an 'art' but it owes a lot to the religion. You could really very easily gain the misleading impression that many brands inherently pretend to be a sort of a mini-religion" (Haig 2006, p. 15). To use religion to declare knowledge, loyalty and faithfulness is a non-standard solution, however, a real one. It is all the more real if we decide to analyze global brands which are present on several markets and are forced to better notice cultural differences between the respective nations. Religion is, principally, also a "global affair". Among the basic prerequisites of correlation between religion and brands, faithfulness can, undoubtedly, be named. Other characteristic features of a brand on the market, which are by Haig confronted with the religion such as faith, omnipresence, the brand gurus (representatives) themselves, welfare, purity, prayer houses, icons and miracles. Aaker also claims that there is "*a set of assets (and liabilities) related to the brand name and symbol, which increases (or decreases) the value provided by the product or service to the customer*" (Aaker 2003, p. 8). Aaker presents a theory which declares that even the actual value of the product is formed by the brand value, which is an economic fact very important to the companies. A valuable and well-known brand is more likely to achieve higher sale and can have more options regarding the price.

The main areas which the company should focus on are, according to Aaker, knowledge, brand faithfulness, perceived high quality, association with the brand and other assets (Aaker 2003, pp. 8–9).

The individual opinions as to the brand value and the creation thereof are very similar and even identical in many regard. Except for Haig, who is rather detached in his attitudes, the descriptions of brand values made by Aaker and Keller are reason-based and reflect a certain knowledge level in customers. If we were to look for common milestones in the theories, we would find plenty of areas where experts share an opinion. Knowledge, faithfulness, association and general awareness can be named among the properties of values which a brand simply must have. In this regard, the theories formulated by all the above-mentioned authors coincide.

Methodology

With funding provided by the IGA project implemented at the FMC and entitled "Support of the Publishing Activity of Research Plans in Excellent Directions at the FMC of TBU in Zlin", a representative survey was conducted in the Czech Republic with the aim of finding out about the attitudes of respondents as regards the influence and importance of the price, quality, country of origin and awareness of the perception of a brand. The research was conducted via face-to-face interviews, using the CAWI technology and through a survey within a selected representative sample in the Czech Republic (1,028 persons). The research quota included age, gender, income and size of a town/village, and the division of these socio-demographic data in the basic set was defined in accordance with data obtained from the Czech Statistical Office. The collection of the data took place in October and November. The principal part of the research comprised 28 Likert scales enabling to find out about customers' preferences and their opinions as to local and foreign brands. A five-level scale was used. The scales took the form of statements, and respondents had an opportunity to give their opinion formulated as follows: Strongly agree/Partly agree/Neither agree nor disagree/Partly disagree/ Strongly disagree.

Descriptive statistics were prepared using the Statgraphics programme and displayed as frequency tables, correlation and a summarized analysis of opinions were carried out using the statistical software entitled R.

The topic of this paper is a detailed analysis of the structure of responses given by a representative sample and shown on a Likert scale, and an assessment of the tool—corrplot (A graphical display of a correlation matrix)—the aim thereof is to analyze the dependences between the individual claims made by Czech respondents.

According to the research originally carried out by the authors of this paper, three quarters of the respondents are willing to look for information about the country of origin of the relevant product, and 59% of them perceive the purchase of a Czech product as a benefit for the Czech economy. Two thirds of the Czechs buy primarily Czech foodstuffs, 54% of them even prefer local foodstuffs. However, the entire sample also comprises almost one third of persons who do not know (or who are not sure of) the quality of Czech products; 24% do not know whether the Czech products are trustworthy, and 23% do not know whether it is possible to find Czech products in the distribution network. Here are the options for government institutions as well as for the Czech producers themselves with the aim of supporting and promoting the high quality of local (national) products.

The lowest number of respondents (23%) agree (completely or partly) with the statement saying that they trust foreign products; 25% of them giving the reason that, according to their experience, foreign products are of a higher quality. Foreign products are more popular with the Czechs as long as the products include consumer goods (electronics but also clothing and shoes) (Fig. 1).

A colour and graphic display of correlation coefficients occurring between all thinkable pairs of questions present the direct/indirect dependence between the individual variables. A colour scale on the right displays the level of the relevant correlation coefficient.

The calculation itself was made based on responses given by respondents on an ordinal scale of 1–5. Although the correlation as a tool was developed with the aim of calculating the strength of the bond between two independent communicating (numerical) values, and these conditions had not been met in this case, several interesting findings can be observed. There are strong dependences between questions which test the perception of brand depending on their origin, the

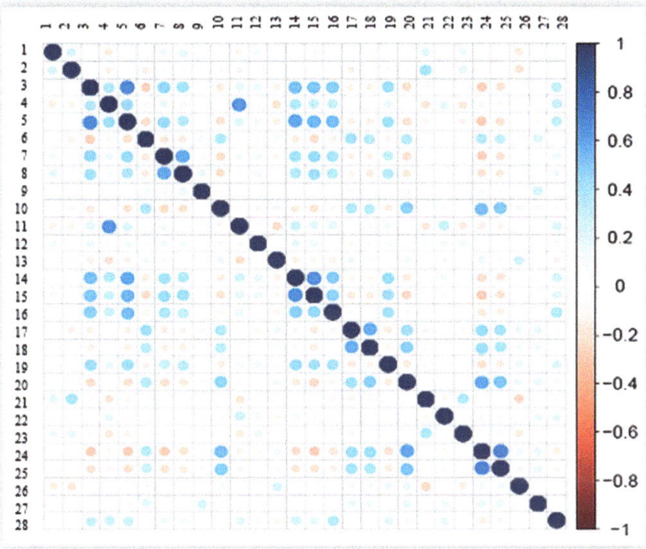

Fig. 1 Corelation matrix: dependences between the individual claims. *1* I buy cheap goods; *2* brand is not important; *3* I prefer CZ products; *4* I am interested in the origin; *5* it is important to buy CZ products; *6* I go to shops offering foreign products; *7* I trust CZ products; *8* high quality of CZ products; *9* foreign products are cheaper; *10* foreign products are of a higher quality; *11* I am willing to find out about the origin; *12* confused by all the options; *13* I have my favourite brands; *14* buying CZ products is good for the Czech economy; *15* I buy CZ products because I like the CR; *16* I buy CZ foodstuffs; *17* I buy foreign shoes, clothing; *18* I buy foreign consumer goods; *19* I am willing to pay a higher price for CZ products; *20* better experience with foreign products; *21* I do not care about the brand; *22* I cannot find CZ products; *23* I have no preferences; *24* I trust foreign products; *25* foreign products are of a higher quality; *26* I am willing to pay a higher price for my favourite brand; *27* foreign products are easier to come by; *28* local foodstuffs

willingness to look for information regarding the products in question and/or to preferably buy Czech/foreign products, brand preferences in spite of the high price, and so on. In the Czech environment, which opened up to global brands only 25 ago, groups of persons have been formed who are strongly focused on the origin of a product and, at the same time, whose price sensitivity has not increased—they are willing to pay a higher price for high quality, and look for information on the required products.

Discussion

A more detailed descriptive and correlation analysis has shown that Czech customers can be segmented depending on their preferences as to the country of origin. It can be stated that strong dependences appear in three segments: First, in questions concerning Czech products. The segment with the working title of "patriots" comprises persons who are aware of the importance of production and consumption of Czech products for the national economy, i.e. it is important to them to buy Czech products which they trust and which they buy (in particular locally produced foodstuffs); such customers are willing to pay a higher price for Czech products. On the contrary, in the Czech Republic a strong group of persons with the working title of "globalists" has distinguished itself, who prefer foreign products because they consider such products to be of a higher quality (this refers in particular to consumer goods but also to shoes and clothing), their experience with such products is better. The third and smallest group is formed by people who do not care about the origin. Such customers mostly do not care about the product brand either, they buy cheap non-branded products, they do not pay much attention to the shopping process, i.e. they do not look for specialized stores, are not able to assess the availability of Czech/foreign products, etc.

Conclusions

This paper is a summarizing overview of basic theoretical starting points for brand building and involves the results of research carried out on this topic in the Czech Republic using a representative sample of 1,028 persons. Based on its results, it can be stated that the Czechs have been developing a stronger focus on brands, they want to be informed about the products' quality and country of origin. If such products are available for them, they often decide to buy Czech foodstuffs, frequently also the local ones. A significant group of consumers, however, prefers foreign products, in particular in the sphere of consumer goods. The market economy and global brands were introduced to the Czech Republic in the 1990s only and, thus, the group of "patriots" continues on distinguishing itself here, who prefer traditional Czech brands and, therefore, for example, the comeback of some "retro brands" showing the original quality and packaging, which was presented by some hypermarket chains last year was a real success (Retro značky a jejich úspěch-proč je Češi milují? 2015, ©2016).

References

Aaker, D.A. 2003. *Brand building*. Brno: Computer Press.
Aaker, D.A. 2004. *Brand portfolio strategy*. New York: Free Press.
Göttlichová, M. 2015. Changes in the legal system of the non-governmental organizations in the Czech Republic and the possibilities for innovation of communication policy in the non-profit sector. *International Journal of Strategic Innovative Marketing*, Greece, Mikonos, pp. 17–31.
Haig, M. 2006. *Království značek*. Praha: Ekopress.

Karlíček, M. 2016. *Marketingová komunikace: jak komunikovat na našem trhu*. Praha: Grada Publishing.

Retro značky a jejich úspěch-proč je Češi milují? http://student.e15.cz/art-de-vivre/retro-znacky-a-jejich-uspech-proc-je-cesi-miluji-1215622. Accessed 27 July 2016.

Štarchoň, P., M. Juříková, a kol. 2015. Značky a český zákazník. Zlín: Verbum.

Generation Z and Religion in Times of Crisis

Aikaterini Stavrianea and Irene Kamenidou

Introduction

Even though the significance of religion on people's life has been well acknowledged over the years, the academic research on the domain is still scarce (Alam et al. 2011; Granger et al. 2014) especially for periods of harsh economic conditions.

Basic aim of the present study is to empirically examine the attitudes and behaviors of Generation Z toward the church and religion. Of primary interest to the research is also the effect of the economic crisis on this generation and specifically on their relationship with the church and religion. This paper is organized as follows. First, we briefly present data about the Greek crisis and we review the literature about religion and church participation, as well as about the generation Z. Second, we present the methodology and the empirical results of the study, and third, we conclude with the discussion and possible implications.

Generation Z

This paper focuses on Generation Z or Gen-Zers, who according to Uta (2012) were born from 1994 to 2009, and which is the youngest adult generation. This generational cohort consists of young people who will have families in the future, thus they are of special research interest. They are the generation of the 320 €; the ones

A. Stavrianea (✉)
Technological Educational Institute of Athens, Athens, Greece
e-mail: kstavrianea@gmail.com

I. Kamenidou
Eastern Macedonia and Thrace Institute of Technology (EMaTTech), Kavala, Greece

A. Kavoura et al. (eds.), *Strategic Innovative Marketing*, Springer Proceedings in Business and Economics, DOI 10.1007/978-3-319-56288-9_28

that the economic crises has a direct impact on their future for leaving the country and for creating a family. Generation Z or Gen-Z'ers is also acknowledged amongst others as the generation with great expertise toward technologies, smartphones, and social media. As Kaplan (2012) reports (they) "don't read newspapers (which is why newspapers will likely disappear in the near future), don't watch regular TV (at least not without passing it through a TiVo), and are surrounded by their personal mobile devices most of the time (which makes it nearly impossible to reach them through billboards or radio). But the fact that social media have always been part of their lives—Facebook was founded in 2004, YouTube in 2005, and Twitter in 2006—makes them perfect candidates for mobile social media applications". Additionally, Williams and Page (2011) assert that people belonging in Generation Z are traditionalists, value the family, and are more responsible. These elements are also obtained using simulation modeling of the corresponding processes (Dimitrios et al. 2015; Nasiopoulos et al. 2017)

The Financial Crisis

The great recession that Greece is facing since the end of 2009 has without any doubt affected the lives of a vast majority of the population with adjustments such as cuts in pension and wages as well as lowering public expenditure and social security benefits (Stavrianea and Siomkos 2016). Official Data denote that by May, 2016 unemployment rate reached 23.5% and the same rate reached 50.3% for the year group of 15–24 years old (Hellenic Statistic Authority 2016). Data show that for the year 2015 a 35.7% of the population lives under the risk of poverty or social exclusion (Hellenic Statistic Authority 2015).

Religion and Church Participation

Religion undoubtedly has a strong influence on people's attitudes values and behaviors both at a personal and at a social level (Mokhlis 2009; Alam et al. 2011). The research on this area though is scarce (Alam et al. 2011; Granger et al. 2014). One can refer to religion as a set of beliefs that are taught since the very early stages of childhood and people overtime commit more to them; as they grow older they are more capable to better comprehend these teachings. In that sense religion has therefore the ability to form a person's behavior (Kotler 2000; Alam et al. 2011) and may influence buying decision (Kotler 2000). Religion is an important cultural factor. Belonging to a certain religion group also provides a personal and cultural identity for a person (US Religion Landscape 2008).

As far as the relationship between religiosity and consumer behavior we should not forget that religion can influence and shape the attitudes toward goods, services, brands, and advertising messages (Fam et al. 2004) and may influence the importance that material goods have for people. In addition, there are examples of religion that may even forbid the use of goods or services (Alam et al. 2011). Still the influence of religion on consumer behavior is not adequately researched (Granger et al. 2014).

Belonging to a religion community or a spiritually based community (Mankowski and Rappaport 2000) bonds its members with common values and ideals and these communities can provide strong social and financial advantages through contributions and philanthropic work. In the last decades it is observed both in Europe and in the U.S. a decline in the participation and membership of religions (Olson and Beckworth 2011; Granger et al. 2014), primarily in the youngest ages (Lee 2010) who do not show the same interest or prefer other activities in their leisure time.

Limited research has examined church membership or the mechanism with which religion can influence buying behavior but it has been scarcely examined in the context of the youngest adult generation and even more in an economic crisis environment. In this limited research context, Chen (2010) found that an economic shock can cause religion intensity. Even though, in some countries the church is still a central point and active participant in both the private and public arena, still a better comprehension is needed of the factors that make people more willing to allocate their time and resources for church purposes (Granger et al. 2014). Religiosity but also other needs such as philanthropic participation and contribution (Parboteeah et al. 2004), as well as the desire to interact socially with other members of the community (Graig-Lee et al. 2008), may play an integral role for the young adults as far as church participation is concerned.

Methodology

A structured questionnaire was developed exclusively for this reason based on literature review and extensive qualitative research. Data was collected via web-based self-administered online questionnaire (Google docx forms), engaging a non-probability, mixed sampling method approach to subjects belonging in Generation Z (1994+) by Facebook messages. Data analysis included frequencies, percentages, means, reliability, factor, cluster analysis, and ANOVA test.

Results-Discussion

Sample Profile

From the 115 gen-Z'ers participating in the study, the majority were women (67.0%), 20 years old (29.6%), single (92.0%), students (66.0%), equality existing regarding urban and rural area of residence; with 11.3% of the respondents having no family member with a job and 36.7% answering that at least one family member was fired from their jobs due to the economic crisis.

Economic Crisis and Generation Z

Gen Z'ers were asked to state the extent to which the economic crisis and the situation in the Mediterranean influenced their lives (psychological-fear, economic, etc.). Results revealed that the economic crisis has a large or very large impact on the vast majority of Gen Z'ers (78.2%), while the situation in the Mediterranean had a large or very large impact on 57.4% of Gen Z'ers. Both of these results are notable, due to the young age of this cohort, since youngsters are usually carefree. Additionally, Gen Z'ers were asked up to what year, they believe that the economic crisis will last in Greece and to identify which year they consider as the worst for Greece due to the economic crisis. The vast majority considers that the economic crisis will last up to 2020 (56.5%); and that the worst year has passed, pointing out years between 2010 and 2015 (60.9%).

Economic Crisis and Church

Subsequently, Gen Z'ers were asked if they go or not to church. Forty-six percent goes rarely or never goes to church; 30.4% goes sometimes; and 23.6% goes frequently or very frequently. The extent in which the economic crisis affected Gen Z'ers attitude and behavior toward church was rated on a 7-point Likert scale. About one half (46.5%) of Gen Z'ers stated that the economic crisis had no impact or a small impact on their visit to church, a 21.7% stated a neither small nor big impact, and a 31.8% stated a quite big to very big effect. As regards the hours spend in church per month by Gen Z'ers; 33.1% indicated that they do not go to church at all (0 h/month); 35.7% spend 1–4 h/month; 18.2% spend 5–9 h/month; and 13.0% spend more than 10 h per month in church.

Gen-Z'ers attitudes toward church during economic crisis were rated using 14 statements produced by extensive qualitative research and literature review on a 7-point Likert scale (1 = completely disagree up to 7 = completely agree). These statements were: Faith generates solidarity among people; Faith in any religion helps psychologically people in times of crisis; I believe in the prophecies the Elder Paisius; I believe in the prophecies of the great fathers; The relationship with the church helps us withstand the economic crisis; I believe in the prophecies of Kosmas Aitolos; I believe that Church is the prop when people go through difficult situations; I believe that after the economic crisis people go more often to the Church or believe more; We have to go to church; I believe that after the economic crisis people believe more in God; In the Church I find what I need; The economic

Table 1 Segmentation based on attitudes toward church and faith

Factors of attitudes based on church and faith	1st cluster, n = 39	2nd cluster, n = 50	3rd cluster, n = 26	ANOVA F	Statistics (p)
F1: "Prophecies and solidarity"	**4.63**	**5.14**	1.99	92.314	0.000
F2: "Fulfillment of esoteric needs"	2.60	**4.69**	1.81	108.794	0.000
F3: "Psychological empowerment"	3.39	**4.86**	2.83	43.267	0.000
F4: "Religiosity and crisis"	2.48	3.71	1.86	27.037	0.000

Source The Authors

crisis is a crisis of values and can be solved by the world turning to church; Monasticism is a solution when there is an economic crisis or war; The economic crisis affected my faith in God.

Results revealed that no statement has mean score (MS) > 6. One statement has MS > 5: "Faith generates solidarity among people" (MS = 5.11), and three statements MS ≥ 4.00; with the statement "Faith in any religion helps psychologically people in times of crisis" (MS = 4.56), being the highest of the three MS. The statement that has the lowest MS is "The economic crisis affected my faith in God" with MS = 2.26.

Factor Analysis

Factor analysis was continuously employed on the 14 statements in order to reduce the items into fewer ones and proceed to further analysis. Factor analysis regarding Gen Z'ers attitudes toward church and faith, and economic crisis produced four factors (KMO = 0.812; BTS = 797.913; df = 91; p = 0.00) accounting for 68.2% of total variance (T.V.). These factors were "Prophecies and solidarity;" "Fulfillment of esoteric needs;" "Psychological empowerment;" and "Religiosity and crisis". The four factors derived were continuously treated as new variables in order to precede to segmentation based on Gen Z'ers attitudes. Cluster analysis with these four variables produced three segments (Table 1). ANOVA statistics revealed that all four factors contributed in the statistically difference of the three clusters' behavior.

Conclusion

The Greek Church has become more people oriented and played a prominent role in the years of the financial crisis. There is no doubt that this young generation feels involved and embraced by the church. For the majority of the participants in the research it seems that the church acts like a protective shelter in this era of great financial uncertainty. As results show, apart from the beliefs, and teachings about the religion—especially dominant for one group of the participants—the need for emotional and social support in such a hazardous economic environment is central in the relationship that the Gen Z'ers have with the church. Values such as solidarity and support of the weaker socio economic groups are extremely important for the Gen Z'ers and that is also an important element of information for the marketing practice of both the non-profit and profit organizations who want to enhance relationships and build trust with this generation—e.g., by employing practices such as donations. As more research is conducted, the relationship of people of all age groups with the church in periods of crisis will be high lightened.

References

Alam, S.S., R. Mohd, and B. Hisham. 2011. Is religiosity an important determinant on Muslim consumer behaviour in Malaysia? *Journal of Islamic Marketing* 2 (1): 83–96.

Chen, D.L. 2010. Club goods and group identity: Evidence from Islamic resurgence during the Indonesian crisis. *Journal of Political Economy* 118 (2): 300–354.

Dimitrios, Nasiopoulos K., Damianos P. Sakas, and Androniki Kavoura. 2015. The development of Facebook's competitive advantage for brand awareness. *Procedia Economics and Finance* 589–597.

Fam, K.S., D.S. Waller, and B.Z. Erdogan. 2004. The influence of religion on attitudes towards the advertising and controversial products. *European Journal of Marketing* 38 (5/6): 537–555.

Hellenic Statistic Authority. 2015. http://www.statistics.gr/documents/20181/f5f875ea-5cc8-4901-8ce4-6d98b30c6ec0. Accessed 3 Sept 2016.

Hellenic Statistic Authority. 2016. http://www.statistics.gr/el/statistics/-/publication/SJO02/2016-M05. Accessed 3 Sept 2016.

Graig-Lee, M., J. Harris, and W. Lau. 2008. The role of dispositional, organizational and situational variables in volunteering. *Journal of Nonprofit and Voluntary Sector Marketing* 19 (2): 1–24.

Granger, K., V.N. Lu, J. Conduit, R. Veale, and C. Habel. 2014. Keeping the faith! Drivers of participation in spiritually-based communities. *Journal of Business Research* 67: 68–75.

Kaplan, A.M. 2012. If you love something, let it go mobile: Mobile marketing and mobile social media 4x4. *Business Horizons* 55 (2): 129–139.

Kotler, P. 2000. Consumer market and consumer behavior. *Principles of marketing,* 8th ed. Upper Saddle River, NJ: Prentice-Hall.

Lee, S. 2010. Marketing through sport: A case of a religious organization. *International Review on Public and Nonprofit Marketing.* 7 (1): 87–96.

Mankowski, E.S., and J. Rappaport. 2000. Narrative concepts and analysis in spiritually based communities. *Journal of Community Psychology* 28 (5): 479–493.

Mokhlis, S. 2009. Relevancy and measurement of religiosity in consumer behavior research. *International Business Research* 2 (3): 75–84.

Nasiopoulos, Dimitrios K., Theodora Papadopoulou, and Dimitrios S. Vlachos. 2017. Merchandizing IT products via social networks. modeling and simulation of the procedures. In *Springer Proceedings in Business and Economics*, pp. 507–513.

Olson, P.J., and D. Beckworth. 2011. Religious change and stability: Seasonality in church attendance from the 1940s to the 2000s. *Journal for the Scientific Study of Religion* 50 (2): 388–396.

Parboteeah, K.P., J.B. Cullen, and L. Lim. 2004. Formal volunteering: A cross-national test. *Journal of World Business* 39 (4): 431–441.
Stavrianea, A., and G. Siomkos. 2016. Crisis Marketing: Effects on the consumers' behavior and their materialistic values. Paper presented at the ICCMI 2016, 4th international conference on contemporary marketing issues, June 22–24, 2016, Heraklion, Greece.
Williams, K.C., and A.R. Page. 2011. Marketing to the generations. *Journal of Behavioral Studies in Business* 3 (4): 1–17.
US Religion Landscape Survey. 2008. Washington, DC: Pew Forum on Religion and Public Life, Pew Research Center.
Uta, I.A. 2012. The impact of the new technology of teaching and learning on the higher education. *Economy Informatics* 12 (1): 42–53.

Consumer-Brand Relationship Development Process in the Context of Online Booking Services: The Role of Cognitive and Affective Drivers

A.N. Giovanis, P. Athanasopoulou and S. Mamalis

Introduction

Along with the growth of information and communication technologies, the internet continuous to gain importance in the tourism industry in general and in the area of online booking in particular (Buhalis and Law 2008; Mouakket and Al-hawari 2012). As a result, traditional travel agencies face lower market shares than online booking service providers. However, despite the rapid expansion of online booking services worldwide, online service providers face a lot of challenges including the development of appropriate customer retention mechanisms (e.g., Mouakket et al. 2012). The main reason for this is that competition is one-click away and consumers may not even need to make multiple clicks to find a service provider that offers a better option.

Moreover, the increasing competition that characterizes online services markets has increased the importance of branding in this context in order to differentiate from competitors (e.g., Ozturk et al. 2016). More specifically, the use of branding to differentiate a company from its competitors has been proved to be the most effective strategy towards the development of sustainable competitive advantage (Sreejesh and Roy 2015). Previous studies on consumer-brand management find that one of the ways consumers differentiate brands is based on the relationship they develop with them (Fournier 1998). Also, De Chernatony and Dall'Olmo Riley

A.N. Giovanis (✉)
Department of Business Administration, Technological Educational Institute of Athens, Athens, Greece
e-mail: agiovanis@teiath.gr

P. Athanasopoulou
Department of Sport Management, University of Peloponnese, Sparta, Greece

S. Mamalis
Department of Business Administration, Technological Educational Institute of Eastern Macedonia and Thrace, Kavala, Greece

A. Kavoura et al. (eds.), *Strategic Innovative Marketing*, Springer Proceedings in Business and Economics, DOI 10.1007/978-3-319-56288-9_29

(1997) recognize the role of brands as relational tools for service providers and consider the brand as much more than a source of identity or differentiation. Since the development of strong consumer-service brand relationships is expected to positively affect consumers' behavioral responses, service providers are trying to find ways to strengthen the ties with their customers by continuously improving the level of brand relationship quality (BRQ) (Tsai 2011; Nyffenegger et al. 2014; Ozturk et al. 2016).

BRQ is an indicator, developed by Fournier (1998), representing the strength and depth of the relationship between a person and a brand and it reflects six cognitive and affective relationship building concepts. Also, Nyffenegger et al. (2014) empirically validate that the cognitive and the affective/emotional beliefs of customers about service brands have a distinct influence on several brand loyalty manifestations. They also argue that this two-dimensional BRQ conceptualization has important implications in better understanding the role of BRQ in establishing and developing strong consumer-brand relationships.

Finally, another important issue in service branding is the role of BRQ on what customers perceive that the brand is doing for them. Brand theory and practice suggest that brand evidence, representing the service brand dimensions contributing to customers' brand evaluation, is used by customers to evaluate the perceived level of BRQ (e.g., Grace and O'Cass 2005; Nyffenegger et al. 2014; Sreejesh and Roy 2015). Therefore, if service providers manage brand evidence effectively, they will be able to develop more favorable associations among their brands and their customers.

Thus the purpose of the study is to propose a conceptual model that considers separately the cognitive and the affective aspects of BRQ of online service brands and then empirically investigate their mediation effects on the link between brand evidence and brand loyalty. The proposed modeling framework is expected to be beneficial for online service providers in developing differentiated service brands and creating a sustainable competitive advantage (Fournier 1998; Sreejesh and Roy 2015).

Theoretical Background and Hypotheses

Cognitive and Affective Aspects of BRQ

BRQ is a higher order construct, proposed by Fournier (1998), reflecting six cognitive and emotions driven relationship building dimensions. Following Nyffenegger et al. (2014), BRQ can be considered as a two-dimensional construct where these two BRQ components are defined along these cognitive and affective relationship building elements. The first BRQ component is called cognitive BRQ (CBRQ). Nyffenegger et al. (2014, p. 91) define CBRQ as "the strength and depth of a consumer's beliefs in and evaluations of service brand performance." They used two concepts from the relationship marketing field to conceptualize CBRQ: relationship satisfaction and brand trust. *Satisfaction* (SAT) with the relationship expresses the accumulated positive versus negative emotions that one party experiences with the other party in a relationship (e.g., Aaker et al. 2004). *Brand trust* (TR) is defined as consumers' willingness to rely on the ability of the brand to perform its stated function (Chaudhuri and Holbrook (2001, p. 82)). The second BRQ component is called affective/emotional BRQ. Nyffenegger et al. (2014, p. 91) define ABRQ as "the strength and intensity of a consumer's personal connection and closeness with the brand based on the positive feelings the consumer develops for that brand." Following the theory of brand love, they use commitment, intimacy and passion as the three facets of ABRQ. *Commitment* (COM) reflects the free will of customers to maintain the relationship with a service brand and is based on emotions such as the feeling of belonging or respect for the other party; *intimacy* reflects the emotional closeness to the brand, and finally *passion* (PAS) refers to a primarily affective, extremely positive attitude toward a specific brand that leads to emotional attachment with the service brand and a feeling of incompleteness in case of brand absence (Fournier 1998; Nyffenegger et al. 2014).

Antecedents of BRQ Components

Grace and O'Cass (2005, p. 128) define brand evidence as "the set of service brand associations experienced by the consumer during the pre-purchase and consumption stages." In other words, brand evidence includes all the brand dimensions of a service that are used by customers to evaluate the brand. In the context of offline services they use service quality (core service, servicescape, and employee service); perceived value, and self-image congruence as defining components of brand evidence. Nyffenegger et al. (2014) also consider partner quality and self-image congruence as antecedents of BRQ. In this study we adapt the above mentioned brand evidence dimensions in the online services context. To assess partners' quality, service quality and brand value offered by online booking platforms will be used. Furthermore, e-service quality is considered as one of the key determinants of companies' performance in the online context. In this study the scale proposed by Mouakket and Al-hawari (2012) will be used to measure e-SQ. This scale is composed by five components: efficiency (EFF); reliability (RLB); responsiveness (RSP); privacy (PRV), and contact (CNT). E-SQ will be conceptualized as a higher order formatively measured construct for three reasons. First, customers in the online environment tend to judge their transaction experience as a whole rather than evaluating each single sub-process separately (e.g., Sousa and Voss 2012). Second, the six dimensions of e-SQ do not necessarily share a common theme and third, changes in any of these are expected to cause changes in E-SQ (Sousa and Voss 2012). Brand value (BV) is considered as the second aspect of brand evidence. BV is conceptualized as a multi-dimensional construct derived from customers' perceptions of the benefits provided by a service brand. This study divides BV in two dimensions, the utilitarian and the hedonic (Chaudhuri and Holbrook 2001). Utilitarian value (UV) is determined by the rational and economic valuations of consumers. The hedonic value

(HD) is more subjective and emotional, and results more from fun and entertainment during consumption. Following the suggestions of Lin et al. (2005), the aggregation/summation of the proposed BV dimensions that exert various effects on global BV (formative approach) is the most appropriate structure for BV representation. The formative approach is preferable when the objective of the study is to confirm the interrelationships among BV and other constructs in a nomological network and because the BV components are distinct in nature, and are not interchangeable. The final element of brand evidence is self-image congruence (SIC). SIC refers to the cognitive match between consumers' self-concept (e.g., actual self, ideal self) and the personality of a service brand (e.g., Sirgy et al. 1997). Nyffenegger et al. (2014, p. 92) justifies the importance of SIC for the brand relationship development process using the quote of a marketing manager saying that "marketing research show us that consumers use and especially love brands that they can identify with."

Nyffenegger et al. (2014) find that partner quality and perceived similarity positively affect ABRQ since perceived similarity between customer's personality and brand personality and the customers' tendency to like those who like them and treat them appropriately increase the chances of brand relationship development. Moreover, previous research has shown that brand quality (Aaker et al. 2004) and self-image similarity (e.g., Nyffenegger et al. 2014) positively affect CBRQ, since both increase the level of relationship satisfaction and brand trust. Hence the following hypotheses are proposed:

H_1 CBRQ is positively affected by (a) e-SQ, (b) BV and (c) SIC

H_2 ABRQ is positively affected by (a) e-SQ, (b) BV and (c) SIC.

Brand Loyalty

The proposed model considers brand loyalty (BL) as the outcome of the service brand relationship development process. Oliver (1999, p. 34) defines brand loyalty as "a deeply held commitment to rebuy or repatronize a preferred product/service consistently in the future, thereby causing repetitive same-brand or same brand-set purchasing, despite situational influences and marketing efforts having the potential to cause switching behavior." Following the findings of previous studies that both BRQ components positively affect BL (Nyffenegger et al. 2014) and at the same time enhance the impact of brand evidence on BL (e.g., Tsai 2011), the current study investigates the mediation effect of BRQ components on the effects of e-SQ, PV, and SIC on BL. Based on the above the following are hypothesized:

H_3 BL is positively affected by (a) ABRQ, (b) CBRQ, (c) e-SQ, (d) PV, and (e) SIC

H_4 Both ABRQ and CBRQ mediate the relationship among e-SQ, PV, SIC, and BL.

Research Methodology

The proposed model was tested with data collected during the first quarter of 2015, using a convenient sample of online booking users in Greece. Using the mall-intercept methodology, potential respondents were asked to complete a self-administered questionnaire. The scales used to operationalize the concepts of the proposed model were adopted from different sources to suit the study. All items were measured on a seven-point Likert scale ranging from 1 "strongly disagree" to 7 "strongly agree." Of the 1,000 completed questionnaires, 29 questionnaires were eliminated due to incomplete data, leaving 971 questionnaires for data analysis.

Results

The majority of participants were female (54%). Thirty two percent (32%) of respondents were less than 25 years old, 38% were in the 25–34 age group, 20% were in the 35–44 age group and only 10% were more than 44 years old. In terms of educational background, 62% of respondents had a university degree.

Data were analyzed with PLS–PM and data analysis involved a two-phase approach. The first phase includes the analysis of the measurement model, while the second phase examines the structural relationships among latent constructs. The test of the measurement model involves the estimation reliability; convergent validity, and discriminant validity of the model's first-order constructs (Hair et al. 2011). The reliability of all constructs was examined using the Cronbach's Alpha (CA) and Composite Reliability (CR) measures. Hair et al. (2011) suggest that a value of 0.70 provide adequate evidence for internal consistency. CA and CR values of all measures included in the study exceed 0.78 and 0.87, respectively, suggesting that all measures were good indicators of their respective components. The average variance extracted (AVE), which indicates the amount of variance that is captured by the construct in relation to the variance due to measurement error, was used to assess convergent validity. AVE values for all constructs exceed 0.65, which is much higher than the recommended cut-off value of 0.50 (Hair et al. 2011), suggesting satisfactory convergent validity. Discriminant validity was assessed by comparing the square root of AVE extracted from each construct with the correlations among constructs. The findings provided strong evidence of discriminant validity among all first-order constructs as the square roots of AVE for all first-order constructs (the diagonal entries of the intercorrelations matrix) are higher than their shared variances (Hair et al. 2011).

The repeated indicator approach was used to approximate the second-order reflective/formative factors. In this study, ABRQ and CBRQ are modeled as second-order reflective constructs. CR and AVE measures of both higher order constructs are used to assess higher order's reliability. CR and AVE for CBRQ equal 0.95 and 0.69, respectively, and for ABRQ 0.92 and 0.62, respectively, which are well above the recommended thresholds of 0.70 and 0.50, respectively, providing evidence of reliable second-order constructs. Finally, all loadings of the second-order constructs on the first-order constructs exceed 0.88 for CBRQ and 0.90 for ABRQ loyalty and are significant at $p = 0.001$. All the above suggest that CBRQ and ABRQ reflect customers' perception of their pre-specified sub-dimensions. The measurement quality of the formative second-order constructs (e-SQ, BV) was tested following the suggestions by Diamantopoulos and Winklhofer (2001). First, the correlations among the first-order constructs of e-SQ and BV were examined. The absolute correlation among the components of e-SQ and BV is 0.54 and 0.44, respectively. These correlations indicate that e-SQ and BV are better represented as formative rather than reflective second-order constructs since both usually exhibit extremely high correlations (≥ 0.8) among their first-order factors. Moreover, all first-order e-SQ-related and BV-related components were found to have significant path coefficients at $p = 0.001$ in forming customer perception about e-SQ and BV. Finally, the variance inflation factors (VIF) were computed for first-order trust dimensions to assess multicollinearity. All VIF values were found to be less than 10 suggesting that multicollinearity is not a concern for e-SQ and BV components.

The significance of the paths included into the proposed model was also tested with PLS–PM using a bootstrap resample procedure. In assessing the PLS model, the squared multiple correlations (R^2) for each endogenous latent variable were examined and the significance of the structural paths was evaluated. The PLS–PM results are illustrated in Fig. 1 that also includes the results from the assessment of second-order constructs.

Results indicate that among the e-SQ components, reliability, responsiveness, and efficiency are perceived as more important by online booking services customers followed by privacy and contact. Among the BV components the importance of UV is greater than that of HD. The effects of all brand evidence elements on CBRQ is statistically significant at $p = 0.001$ explaining 62% of its variance. E-SQ is the most significant driver of CBRQ followed by BV and SIC. These results confirm H_{1abc}. Moreover, H_{2abc} are also confirmed, since the effects of all brand evidence elements on ABRQ are statistically significant at $p = 0.001$ explaining 44% of its variance. Now, BV is the most significant driver of ABRQ followed by SIC. The effect of e-SQ on ABRQ, though statistically significant, is very low. The two BRQ components have the biggest contribution in the formations of customers' intentions to retain their online service provider. Among the elements of brand evidence only BV directly affects BL, while the effects of e-SQ and SIC on BL were found statistically insignificant. Based on these results, H_{3abd} were confirmed, while H_{3ce} were not and the three significant antecedents of BL explain 64% of its variance. To test the mediation effects of BRQ components, the significance of the relevant indirect effects of brand evidence on loyalty were evaluated. Results confirm H_{4abc}, since the indirect effects of e-SQ (b = 0.15; t = 4.12); BV (b = 0.35; t = 7.00), and SIC (b = 0.15; t = 3.58), through the two BRQ components, on BL are statistically significant at $p = 0.05$, meaning that

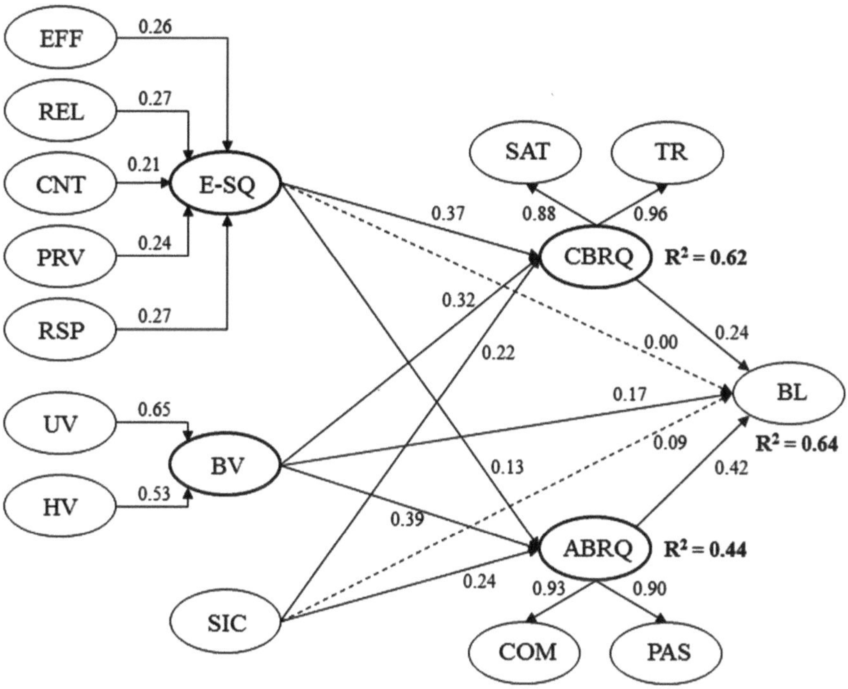

Fig. 1 Structural model's results

BRQ partially mediates the BV–BL link and fully mediates the e-SQ-BL and SIC-BL links.

Conclusions

This study enhances knowledge on how consumers relate to online service brands by proposing a modeling framework that explains the interrelationships among brand evidence and BRQ as they all affect BL. The results confirmed the findings of previous studies, that BRQ has two components that differently affect online brand loyalty. More specifically, loyal online booking services' users develop mostly affective/emotional relationships with a service brand, while their brand relationships that are based on cognitively related aspects operate at a second level. Thus, for online booking service providers aiming to retain their valuable customers, gaining their satisfaction and trust is not enough to succeed. They have to develop emotional ties with them, while they will use any cognitive ties as supporting tools. As far as the role of brand evidence is concerned, all brand evidence elements can be used to develop cognitive brand relationships, while only BV and SIC can be used to develop emotional ties with customers.

References

Aaker, J., S. Fournier, and S.A. Brasel. 2004. When good brands do bad. *Journal of Consumer Research* 31: 1–16.

Buhalis, D., and R. Law. 2008. Progress in information technology and tourism management: 20 years on and 10 years after the Internet—The state of eTourism research. *Tourism Management* 29: 609–623.

Chaudhuri, A., and M.B. Holbrook. 2001. The chain of effects from brand trust and brand affect to brand performance: The role of brand loyalty. *Journal of Marketing* 65: 81–93.

Diamantopoulos, A., and H. Winklhofer. 2001. Index construction with formative indicators: An alternative to scale development. *Journal of Marketing Research* 38: 269–277.

Fournier, S. 1998. Consumers and their brands: Developing relationship theory in consumer research. *Journal of Consumer Research* 24: 343–353.

Grace, D., and A. O'Cass. 2005. Service branding: Consumer verdicts on service brands. *Journal of Retailing and Consumer Services* 12: 125–139.

Hair, J.F., C.M. Ringle, and M. Sarstedt. 2011. PLS-SEM: Indeed a silver bullet. *The Journal of Marketing Theory and Practice* 19: 139–152.

Lin, C.H., P.J. Sher, and H.Y. Shih. 2005. Past progress and future directions in conceptualizing customer perceived value. *International Journal of Service Industry Management* 16: 318–336.

Mouakket, S., and M.A. Al-hawari. 2012. Examining the antecedents of e-loyalty intention in an online reservation environment. *The Journal of High Technology Management Research* 23: 46–57.

Nyffenegger, B., H. Krohmer, W.D. Hoyer, and L. Malaer. 2014. Service brand relationship quality hot or cold? *Journal of Service Research* 18: 90–106.

Oliver, R.L. 1999. Whence consumer loyalty? *Journal of Marketing* 63: 33–44.

Ozturk, A.B., K. Nusair, F. Okumus, and N. Hua. 2016. The role of utilitarian and hedonic values on users' continued usage intention in a mobile hotel booking environment. *International Journal of Hospitality Management* 57: 106–115.

Sirgy, M.J., D. Grewal, T.F. Mangleburg, J.O. Park, K.S. Chon, C.B. Claiborne, J.S. Johar, and H. Berkman. 1997. Assessing the predictive validity of two methods of measuring self-image congruence. *Journal of the Academy of Marketing Science* 25: 229–241.

Sousa, R., and C. Voss. 2012. The impacts of e-service quality on customer behaviour in multi-channel e-services. *Total Quality Management and Business Excellence* 23: 789–806.

Sreejesh, S., and S. Roy. 2015. A new consumer-brand relationship framework. In *Consumer brand relationships*, ed. M. Fetscherin, and T. Heilmann, 165–197. Palgrave-Macmillan: New York.

Tsai, S.P. 2011. Fostering international brand loyalty through committed and attached relationships. *International Business Review* 20: 521–534.

Fashion Brands, Social Media, and Consumers' Exposure to Marketing Messages

Artha Sejati Ananda, Ángel Hernández-Garcia and Lucio Lamberti

Introduction

Consumers' perception of marketing messages has a strong meaning because messages cannot change consumer behavior unless consumers acknowledge the existence of these messages (Yoo et al. 2000). *Social media marketing* (SMM) studies mostly take managerial (e.g., Tsimonis and Dimitriadis 2014) or social media data content analysis (e.g., He et al. 2013) approaches. Current research devotes little attention to whether consumers perceive and acknowledge the existence of the different marketing messages on social media in the same way that companies actually deploy their SMM strategy. The study addresses this issue, and has two main objectives: first, to confront the N-REL framework for fashion brands' SMM actions with consumers' perceptions of such actions; second, as a by-product of the first objective the research also aims to generate and refine specific dimensions of social media marketing activities. The study builds on the concept of consumers' exposure to marketing stimuli, and poses the following research question:

RQ: *Do consumers' perceived type and frequency of fashion brands' SMM activities match the actual type and frequency of those activities?*

A.S. Ananda (✉) · Á. Hernández-Garcia
Departamento de Ingeniería de Organización, Administración de Empresas y Estadística, Universidad Politécnica de Madrid, Madrid, Spain
e-mail: artha.ananda@tige.ior.etsit.upm.es; arthasejati.ananda@polimi.it

A.S. Ananda · L. Lamberti
Dipartimento di Ingegneria Gestionale, Politecnico di Milano, Milan, Italy

A. Kavoura et al. (eds.), *Strategic Innovative Marketing*, Springer Proceedings in Business and Economics, DOI 10.1007/978-3-319-56288-9_30

Theoretical Background

Fashion Brands and Social Media Marketing Activities

Fashion brands use social media to communicate with the consumers, while consumers use them for lifestyle expression. Ananda et al. (2015) provide an initial classification of SMM actions applicable to luxury fashion brands, and Ananda et al. (2016a) propose a more comprehensive framework (*N-REL*) that identifies and classifies social media marketing strategic actions. N-REL differentiates between active—*representation* and *engagement*—and passive—*listening-in*—SMM strategic actions. *Representation* actions deliver marketing communications about the company profile and information about products; *engagement* covers actions that focus on interaction with customers, add value, and generate benefits for the company; and *listening-in* refers to market intelligence. From N-REL, Ananda et al. (2016b) propose a list of SMM strategic actions and test the framework in SME fashion brands.

Consumer Perceptual Process

The perceptual process is the means by which individuals select, organize, and interpret physical sensations—sight, hearing, smells—into a meaningful whole (Solomon and Rabolt 2009). Factors that determine the stimulus that an individual perceives are the *exposure* to the stimulus—frequency or intensity, the *attention* it generates, and the individual's *interpretation* of the stimulus (Solomon and Rabolt 2009).

In marketing research, it is common to use consumer's perceived frequency or intensity to different marketing stimuli—brands, labels, logos, marketing actions—to measure variables associated with firms' or marketers' activities. Besides, marketing and consumer behavior research may use perceived frequency of exposure to marketing stimuli to measure consumer attitudes and behaviors. For example, Yoo et al. (2000) measure perceived advertising spending, in terms of how frequently consumers see advertising campaigns, and price promotion as the perceived relative frequency of price deals presented for a focal brand.

Design/Methodology

Conceptual Framework and Research Design

The empirical approach proposes an initial list of 36 SMM actions from the results of Ananda et al. (2015, 2016b). The research framework only considers active actions because those are the only ones that consumers may experience in social media. The unit of analysis of the research is consumers who are member of at least one fashion brand's social media "official" community. This choice ensures that participants have been exposed to marketing actions of fashion brands in social media. The study does not consider specific types of products (e.g., luxury or non-luxury), company size, or country of the fashion brand.

Data Collection and Analysis

Data collection includes two different surveys to reduce common method bias. The two surveys are online self-administered questionnaires posted on social media and distributed by email to respondents. Seven-point Likert-type scales measure all the items about perception of exposure to SMM contents, with anchors of 1 = never and 7 = all the time. The first questionnaire (Q1) incorporates text to describe the SMM actions, while the second questionnaire (Q2) incorporates stimuli examples taken from real brands' social media public posts. The final set includes 45 respondents and 43 respondents for Q1 and Q2, respectively. Each survey was conducted among different groups of individuals in various countries—mainly from Indonesia, Spain, Italy, and France.

The data analysis includes two steps. The first one involves calculation of means of perceived exposure to the different SMM actions. The second step encompasses a nonparametric test of means, by calculating Spearmann's rho correlation to check the similarity of the two pairs of data: items of SMM actions by brands—from the results of Ananda et al. (2015, 2016b), and perceived frequency of actions by consumers—from Q1 and Q2. Spearmann's correlation coefficient (r_s) is preferable when the assumption of normal distribution is not tenable (Artusi et al. 2002). The method transforms the relative magnitudes of paired variables into ranks. An identical relationship between the original variables occurs when $|r_s| = 1$.

Results: Consumers' Perceptions of Fashion Brands' SMM Actions

Table 1 summarizes SMM actions by fashion brands in Ananda et al. (2015, 2016b) with ranks provided by (1) Ananda et al. (2016b) from their social media content analysis, (2) perceived frequency of social media content types by consumers from Q1, and (3) same as the previous one, but with Q2. Calculation of Spearman's rho between the two groups—consumers and brands—yields a value of $r_s = 0.702$ ($p < 0.01$) for Q1 (1–2) and $r_s = 0.654$ ($p < 0.01$) for Q2 (1–3). Comparison between both methods (Q1 and Q2, 2–3) yields a Pearson's correlation of 0.759 and $r_s = 0.700$. These coefficients indicate a moderate to high strong positive correlation

Table 1 SMM actions by fashion brands (Ananda et al. 2015, 2016b)

Id	Action	Rank		
		(1)	(2)	(3)
4	Product promotion (e.g., pictures and videos of products)	2	1	2
2	Providing access/link to e-commerce/shop	1	2	3
5	Contents on brand's expertise, values, and culture	4	3	18
28	Upcoming product sneak-peeks	8	4	6
13	Providing exclusive campaign previews	10	4	10
32	Reporting or sharing events about product, offline stores, or other offline promotional events (e.g., live streaming of fashion weeks)	3	6	10
14	Casual socialization and greetings contents	13	7	5
22	Publishing corporate contents on achievements, news, results, or success stories	13	8	23
8	*Posting contents about personalities, celebrities, or influencers*	*5*	*9*	*4*
21	*Sharing/retweeting/liking personalities', celebrities' or influencers' (e.g., blogger's posts or endorsements)*	*12*	*10*	*17*
1	Brand profile and corporate information	18	11	12
36	Offering free product or price discount for customers on social media	16	12	1
20	Contents not directly related to the brand's field of expertise but are associated with brand's culture and value	7	13	15
17	Promoted posts or ad banners	20	14	8
29	Customer appreciation (e.g., thanking customers for the purchases, feedbacks, or being members of the community)	19	15	12
26	*Showcasing customers' positive reviews about the brands*	*24*[a]	*16*	*20*
34	*Answering customers' inquiries about brand and its products*	*24*[a]	*16*	*23*
15	*Encouraging and engaging customers to share their brand experiences in social media*	*11*	*18*	*12*
31	*Applications related to a special event or theme (e.g., games)*	*21*	*19*	*20*
23	*Responding to customers' complaints*	*24*[a]	*20*	*28*
9	Inviting customer to offline social gathering events	6	21	30
12	*Product giveaway promotions or contests (encouraging winners to share their experiences on social media)*	*13*	*23*	*7*
6	Location-specific deals (e.g., through "check-ins" or other location-sharing applications)	24[a]	24	21
35	*Encouraging regular customers to participate in the review process*	*24*[a]	*24*	*25*
18	*Following/joining competitor´s social media account*	*24*[a]	*24*	*34*
10	*Addressing issues raised by customers about products or services*	*24*[a]	*25*	*20*
30	Retailers'/business partners' news or activity contents	9	26	16
16	*Applications to allow mass product/experience customization*	*24*[a]	*27*	*29*
3	*Polling or posting questions to get customer feedback*	*24*[a]	*28*	*25*
19	*Providing a specific Q&A session or applications about the brand and its products*	*24*[a]	*28*	*27*
24	*Inviting positive reviewers to become brand advocates/ambassadors*	*24*[a]	*30*	*34*
7	Publishing customers' purchases to encourage others	17	31	9

(continued)

Table 1 (continued)

Id	Action	Rank		
		(1)	(2)	(3)
27	*Engaging customers to participate in CSR campaign*	*24*[a]	*32*	*31*
25	*Crowdsourcing tactic in gathering ideas for product design or companies' profile*	*21*	*33*	*35*
33	*Apologies to customers*	*24*[a]	*35*	*18*
11	*Sharing competitors' social media contents*	*23*	*36*	*36*

[a]No actions registered (sharing last rank). *Italic rows* indicate engagement actions

between brands' and consumers' views, and only slight differences between both methods. Therefore, there is a reasonable good match between consumers' perceptions of fashion brands' social media marketing actions and brands' marketing intensity. Additionally, a Mann–Whitney test shows no differences across both samples for most of the items—27 actions—while the median test—more appropriate for small sample sizes and ordinal variables—returns significant differences only in seven actions: product promotion; brand's expertise, culture and values; publishing customer's purchases; sharing competitor's social media contents; brand achievements and success stories; sharing offline events; and apologies to customers. Note that, in terms of ranking, only brand's expertise, publishing customer's purchases, brand achievements, and apologies to customers differ much between both methods.

Discussion

The results suggest that marketing messages for which consumers' exposure is bigger—i.e., most frequent actions—relate to social shopping activities: product promotion and links/access to the brand's online shop. Social shopping, or social commerce, involves the use of Internet-based media to allow the participation of consumers in the marketing, selling, comparing, curating, buying, and sharing of products and services (Stephen and Toubia 2010). The results also show that consumers are mostly aware of the presence of representation actions, but not so much of engagement actions. These findings confirm the findings from Ananda et al. (2016b), but from a consumer-centric approach.

The fact that exposure to representation actions exceeds by large consumer's exposure to engagement actions has important implications. Because there are two paths to fashion purchasing behavior in social media marketing—through fashion involvement and online brand engagement (Smith et al. 2016)—fashion brands may be missing an opportunity to reach a wider audience, by favoring involvement—with representation actions—over brand engagement—with engagement actions.

Table 2 Item proposition to measure fashion brands' SMM actions

Type of action	Highly recommended[a]	Require further testing[a]
Representation	• Providing access to the brand's e-commerce or e-shopsites • Providing product promotion contents (e.g., picture or videos about products) • Providing contents on upcoming product sneak-peeks • Providing exclusive campaign previews • Reporting or sharing events about product, offline stores, or other offline promotional events	• Providing contents on brand's expertise, values, and culture • Publishing customers' purchases • Publishing greeting contents • Publishing promoted posts or ad banners • Providing contents associated with brand´s culture and value, but not directly related to the brand's field of expertise • Showcasing brand achievements, results, innovation, news, or success stories • Customer appreciation contents • Providing and sharing activities and news of retailers/business partners • Posting contents on brand profile and corporate information • Offering free products or price discounts for customers' purchase
Engagement	• Posting contents about personalities, celebrities, or influencers	• Encouraging customers to share their brand experiences • Sharing/retweeting/liking personalities', celebrities' or influencers' post • Employing promotional giveaways or contests

[a]In no particular order

The results Table 2 clearly highlight the adequacy of the six actions that rank consistently high—among the top ten in all cases—as potential relevant indicators to measure SMM activities. Thirteen items show a poorer match between brands' and consumers' perspectives and rank in the middle interval in all cases, requiring further testing. Finally, the results suggest the removal of the seventeen items that are rare/infrequent from both brand and consumer perspectives—omitted in Table 2.

From a methodological standpoint, the different results for some actions between Q1 and Q2 are also thought provoking. Because the selection of the different sample posts sought to avoid any ambiguity—i.e., the possibility that the content might fit more than one SMM action, the results suggest that availability of examples of each SMM action may influence, albeit slightly, the different responses to the questionnaire, which can indicate that the exact formulation of some actions require further revision and/or clarification.

Acknowledgements This research is conducted within the framework of European Doctorate in Industrial Management (EDIM), funded by the Education, Audiovisual and Culture Executive Agency (EACEA) of the European Commission under the Erasmus Mundus Action 1 Programme.

References

Ananda, A.S., A. Hernández-García, and L. Lamberti. 2015. Social media marketing in Italian luxury fashion. In *5th annual international workshop on luxury retail, operations and supply chain management*, 25–27 May, Milan, Italy.

Ananda, A.S., Á. Hernández-García, and L. Lamberti. 2016a. N-REL: A comprehensive framework of social media marketing strategic actions for marketing organizations. *Journal of Information and Knowledge,* Advance Online Publication. doi:10.1016/j.jik.2016.01.003.

Ananda, A.S., Á. Hernández-García, and L. Lamberti. 2016b. SME fashion brands and social media marketing: From strategies to actions. Manuscript Submitted for Publication.

Artusi, R., P. Verderio, and E. Marubini. 2002. Bravais-Pearson and Spearman correlation coefficients: Meaning, test of hypothesis and confidence interval. *International Journal of Biological Markers* 17 (2): 148–151.

He, W., S. Zha, and L. Li. 2013. Social media competitive analysis and text mining: A case study in the pizza industry. *International Journal of Information Management* 33 (3): 464–472.

Smith, D., Á. Hernández-García, Á.F. Agudo-Peregrina, and J.F. Hair Jr. 2016. Social network marketing: A segmentation approach to understanding purchase intention. In *2016 International conference on social media and society*.

Solomon, M.R, and N.J. Rabolt. 2009. *Consumer behavior in fashion,* 2nd ed. New Jersey: Pearson Prentice Hall.

Stephen, A.T., and O. Toubia. 2010. Deriving value from social commerce networks. *Journal of Marketing Research* 47 (2): 215–228.

Tsimonis, G., and S. Dimitriadis. 2014. Brand strategies in social media. *Marketing Intelligence and Planning* 32 (3): 328–344.

Yoo, B., N. Donthu, and S. Lee. 2000. An examination of selected marketing mix elements and brand equity. *Journal of the Academy of Marketing Science* 28 (2): 195–211.

A Report on Museum Branding Literature

Zoe-Charis Belenioti, George Tsourvakas and Chris A. Vassiliadis

Introduction

Belonging to NPOs' world, today museums face several challenges deriving not only from economic downturn (Cole 2008), such as reduction of financial support, need for reliance to private sector, growing competition both within NPOs industry and leisure FPOs industry (Cole 2008), but also from social and technological variables (Kolb 2013; Cole 2008; Griffin 2008; Kawashima 1998; McLean 1995a) emerged the marketing and branding orientation as the only means to achieve viability (Sargeant and Wymer 2007).

Despite the importance of branding in museums, according to Belenioti and Vassiliadis (2015), "scholars have paid far too little attention to brand equity models and customer based equity models" (2015:2). Moreover, no previous research has categorized the available literature for museum branding. This is the first paper that enhances our understanding by serving as a starting point for researchers in such area. Based on a literature review analysis we identify that the available studies by 2016 in museum branding emerge the following streams:

- Harnessing the branding notion within NPOs and museum industry
- Success factors, drivers and impediments of museum branding

Z.-C. Belenioti (✉) · G. Tsourvakas
Department of Journalism and Mass Communications, Aristotle University of Thessaloniki, Thessaloniki, Greece
e-mail: zoibelenioti@gmail.com; zbele@jour.auth.gr

Z.-C. Belenioti · C.A. Vassiliadis
Department of Business Administration, University of Macedonia, Thessaloniki, Greece

A. Kavoura et al. (eds.), *Strategic Innovative Marketing*, Springer Proceedings in Business and Economics, DOI 10.1007/978-3-319-56288-9_31

Review: The Current State of Knowledge

Harnessing the Branding Notion Within the Museum Industry; To Brand or Not to Brand?

Recently, museums have redefined their activities harnessing branding tools. Precisely, to Vassiliadis and Belenioti, "the growing competition within NPOs and FPOs leisure industry, the financial squeeze along with the need for a more customer focus orientation (Cole 2008), the need for broadening the museum's audience (Kawashima 1998) and the technological advances have compelled museums to include active experience shifting to the experiential notions of edutainment, artetainment and Disneyfication" (2015:6).

However, branding has been a controversial issue in this sector. On the one hand, brand enthusiasts view branding as a beneficial cycle sources of resources (human, financial, social) that leads to build new partnerships and boost the viability (Kylander and Stone 2012). Especially, vast researchers call for the need to brand the culture (Rentschler and Osborne 2008; Griffin 2008; Kotler et al. 2008; Bradburne 2001). Vassiliadis and Belenioti (2015) also praise the multidimensional benefits of branding in terms of financial performance, enhancement of the audience attachment, enrichment of educational process and the social role of museums, expansion of audience in line with the branding supporters (Bradburne 2001; Byrnes 2001; Caldwell 2002; Kawashima 1998; 1995; Rentschler and Osborne 2008; Ames 1988; Kotler and Kotler 2000; Kolb 2013; King 2015; Williams 2011; Griffin 2008; Cole 2008). In the same vein, Ciasullo et al. (2015) and Commission (2016) extol the beneficial role of ICT tools and the internet towards the digital preservation of museums. Europeana project exemplifies the above initiative presenting a major contribution of Greece (Commission 2016).

On the other hand, brand skeptics express their disregard and ethical concerns towards the marketing orientation (Byrnes 2001; Mitchel 2004; Kylander and Stone 2012). Sargeant (2008) based on Liao et al. (2002) ends this debate by presenting the modest solution, the compromisers' view; although marketing and branding is indeed applicable it should be eliminated when it becomes the only and one reason d'etre.

In our opinion, marketing is indeed the backbone of museums' sustainability and branding is the heart of the future museum. The advantages of branding appear to overcome the disadvantages. Nevertheless, due to the specific attributes of museums managers urge to apply brand strategies always showing diligence. As noted by Williams (2011), branding is definitely a catalyst of museum performance. Likewise, Vassiliadis and Fotiadis (2008) confirm the contribution of segmentation to the successful museum branding.

Components, Drivers and Models of Museum Brand Orientation

According to Bridson and Evans (2007), "Brand orientation is defined as the degree to which the organization values brands and its practices are oriented towards building brand capabilities'' (2007:2). A number of scholars have explored the brand orientation (Bridson and Evans 2007; Bridson et al. 2009; Evans et al. 2012; Caldwell and Coshall 2002; Kotler and Kotler 2000; Massi and Harrison 2009; Rentschler and Osborne 2008; Williams 2011). First, Caldwell and Coshall (2002) confirmed that although museums adopt slowly brand orientation they lag in creating strong brand identity and associations. Then, Bridson and Evans (2007) conclude four criteria of a museum's brand orientation. Moreover, they accentuate the reciprocal benefits of branding, both for the museum and the audience. All dimensions are explained analytically in the Table 1.

As regards the drivers of museum orientation, Evans et al. (2012) list various factors such as the increasing demand of commercial and curational assemblage management for the sake of museum viability, the leadership style, the intrinsic need of museum for bigger recognition and brand uniqueness. As regards the barriers of museum brand orientation, a number of scholars agree that disregard towards branding and limited financial resources are the main impediments of branding. (Bridson and Evans 2007; Evans et al. 2012). Some years later Evans et al. (2012) add the funding perspective as another important barrier. Vassiliadis and Fotiadis (2008) also acknowledge the importance of segmentation to the successful museum branding.

Relating to the conceptualization models of museums' brand orientation, the literature emerges two models. Evans et al. (2012) introduce a six-dimensional model that treat museums brand "as an organizational culture and compass for decision-making and four brand behaviors (distinctiveness, functionality, augmentation and symbolism)" (2012:13). Internal and external variables are the moderator factors that will establish the notion of brand first at the philosophical level and then at the whole brand museum behavior level. Given this model, Evans et al. (2012) discover that a strong curational orientation decreases the brand

Table 1 The four criteria of museum brand orientation based on Bridson and Evans (2007)

Distinctiveness	The ability of a brand oriented museum to be perceived as unique cultural assets, to be differentiated from its competitors by adding a competitive advantage and serving as a decision-making factor for visitors
Functionality	To which extent a museum communicates, attaches visitors with the artifacts and enhances the museum experience via additional feature
Augmentation	To which extent a museum delivers a long term relationship with its audience and communicated a superior brand image
Symbolism	To which extent a museum brand effects the audience perception of their selves and boost their social identity. To which degree the museum is established as a distinctive cultural icon

orientation due to the implied suspicion and disregard of leadership style. Conversely, as a link between the commercial and curational management a strong commercial orientation boosts the brand orientation and improves the museum experience.

Furthermore, Massi and Harrison (2009) show important differences in branding application—in terms of consistency—between Italian and Australian museum managers. Their study depicts two different approaches of branding: The classic model (applied in Europe) and the modernist model (applied in Australia). Within classic model cultural brand is mainly associated with the renowned history and heritage of the museum. In this case, the brand has been already built via the unique heritage. Museums perceive branding rather as a secondary enhancing tool because museum experience is cultural driven and non-entertainment driven. Hence, branding process is limited, traditional and implicit and managers show a very low degree of consistency and coherence in their branding. On the contrary, modernist model perceives branding as the second raison d'etre of museum. Here, museums usually built the identity on a story instead of history. Thus, branding is applied to its full potential and consistency is the backbone of the museum's viability.

In addition, Kotler and Kotler (2000) recognize the need for managers to improve the museum experience via branding but without distorting the core mission of museums, its curational role. Similarly, Bridson et al. (2009) urge managers to strive for the combination of curational and commercial orientation to achieve a distinct brand that will entail to financial boost. To Bridson et al. (2009) and Massi and Harrison (2009) consistency across all functions of the museum is the critical success factor. Moreover, Tsourvakas et al. (2016) conclude that marketing innovations indeed boost NPOs' financial performance but they still have a limited influence on the NPOs' cultural performance.

Discussion and Conclusions

Drawing on a review of 33 papers this paper extends our knowledge by classifying the available bibliography in two main strands. First, although branding offers vast benefits to museums at financial and societal level, museum branding is still a neglected and controversial issue. Second, the study revealed that the curational orientation should merge with the branding orientation. For each of these aspects the study reveals scant literature in empirical studies. This may be explained by the infancy of branding adoption in museums stemming from the differences between FPOs and NPOs.

Overall, his study provides valuable theoretical and practical implications. The principal theoretical implication of this study is that it will provide a valuable theoretical starting point for researchers in such area by the classification of the current the state of museum branding literature. Moreover, this is the first study that categorizes the most important aspects of museum branding literature. Overall, this study strengthens the importance and necessity of branding application in NPOs and precisely museums. Consistent to the brand advocates, we view branding as a driver for both NPOs and museums' sustainability and growth. In terms of practical implication, as branding is a structural element of viability especially within the today's perpetual financial instability, we firmly encourage museum practitioners to deploy branding tactics to assure sustainability. Therefore, a key policy's priority should be to combine carefully the commercial and curational perspective to enhance museum experience and boost museum identity, image and recognition.

Limitations and Further Research

These findings may be somewhat limited by the literature review analysis. Furthermore, as several questions remain unanswered at present the present study warmly welcomes further research in this field. Finally, there is abundant room to explore the influence of social media and integrated marketing communications (Belch 2008) further use in museum branding.

References

Ames, P.J. 1988. A challenge to modern museum management: Meshing mission and market. *International Journal of Museum Management and Curatorship* 7 (2): 151–157. doi:10.1080/09647778809515116.

Belch, G.E., and M.A. Belch. 2008. Advertising and promotion: An integrated marketing communications perspective. In *Learning*, 4th ed., 668.

Belenioti, Z.C., and C. Vassiliadis. 2015. Branding in the new museum era. In *Proceedings of the 4th international conference on strategic innovative marketing*. Forthcoming, Mykonos 2015. Springer.

Bradburne, J.M. 2001. A new strategic approach to the museum and its relationship to society. *Museum Management and Curatorship* 19 (1): 75–84. doi:10.1080/09647770100701901.

Bridson, K., and J. Evans. 2007. Don't tate us! The impediments and drivers of branding museums. In *ANZMAC 2007: 3 Rs, reputation responsibility relevance*, 430–436. University of Otago, School of Business, Dept. of Marketing.

Bridson, K., J. Evans, and R. Rentschler. 2009. How brand oriented are museums and galleries? An exploratory investigation across three countries. In *How brand oriented are museums and galleries? An exploratory investigation across three countries, and galleries?*.

Byrnes, W. 2001. *Management and the arts (review)*. Focal Press. doi:10.1353/tj.2001.0039.

Caldwell, N., and J. Coshall. 2002. Measuring brand associations for museums and galleries using repertory grid analysis. *Management Decision* 40 (4): 383–392. doi:10.1108/00251740210426376.

Ciasullo, M.V., M. Gaeta, G. Monetta, and L. Rarità. 2015. E-Cultural value co-creation. A proposed model for the heritage management. In *Palermo: 18th Toulon-verona conference "excellence in services"*, 139–158.

Cole, D. 2008. Museum marketing as a tool for survival and creativity: The mining museum perspective. *Museum Management and Curatorship*. doi:10.1080/09647770701865576.

Commission, E. 2016. Digitisation and online accessibility of Europe's cultural heritage and digital preservation. http://www.worldcat.org/oclc/870633257.

Commission, E., I. Of, T.H. Recommendation, E. C., Digitisation0, O. N., Accessibility, O., Material, O. F. C., and D. Preservation. 2016. Progress report, 2013–2015.

Evans, J., K. Bridson, and R. Rentschler. 2012. Drivers, impediments and manifestations of brand orientation: An international museum study. *European Journal of Marketing* 46 (11): 1457–1475. doi:10.1108/03090561211259934.

Griffin, D. 2008. Advancing museums. *Museum Management and Curatorship* 23 (1), 43–61. doi:10.1080/09647770701757167. 2015.

Kawashima, N. 1998. Knowing the public. A review of museum marketing literature and research1. *Museum Management and Curatorship*, 17 (1), 21–39. doi:10.1080/09647779800301701.

King, B.A. 2015. Branding, legitimation and the power of museums : The case of the Louvre Abu Dhabi. *Museum and Society* 13 (3), 322–341. August.

Kolb, B. 2013. *Marketing for cultural organisations.*

Kotler, N.G., P. Kotler, and W.I. Kotler. 2008. *Museum marketing and strategy: Designing missions, building audiences, generating revenue and resources.* http://books.google.com/books?id=nQgTAQAAMAAJ&pgis=1.

Kotler, N., and P. Kotler. 2000. Can museums be all things to all people?: Missions, goals, and marketing's role. *Museum Management and Curatorship* 18 (3) 271–287. doi:10.1080/09647770000301803.

Kylander, N., and C. Stone. 2012. *The role of brand in the nonprofit sector,* February.

Laidler-Kylander, N., and B. Simonin. 2009. How international nonprofits build brand equity. *International Journal of Nonprofit and Voluntary Sector Marketing* 14: 57–69. doi:10.1002/nvsm.

Massi, M., and P. Harrison. 2009. The branding of arts and culture: An international comparison. *Deakin Business Review* 2 (1) 19–31. http://dro.deakin.edu.au/view/DU:30023943.

McLean, F. 1995a. A marketing revolution in museums? *Journal of Marketing Management* 11 (6) 601–616. doi:10.1080/0267257X.1995.9964370.

McLean, F. 1995b. Future directions for marketing in museums. *International Journal of Cultural Policy* 1 (2) 355–368. doi:10.1080/10286639509357991.

Mitchel, R. 2004. Edutainment ? No thanks. I prefer playful learning. *Associazione Civita Report on Edutainment* 14.

Rentschler, R., and A. Osborne. 2008. Deakin research online. marketing artertainment: Are museums jumping on the brandwagon? *In 3Rs, reputation responsibility relevance.* Otago University, School of Business, Dept. of Marketing, 2007. http://dro.deakin.edu.au/eserv/DU:30019106/dejong-editors-2008.pdf.

Sargeant, A. and W. Wymer. 2007. *The Routledge companion to nonprofit marketing.* London: Routledge.

Tsourvakas, G., M. Prodromos, G. Ioanna, and D. Paraskevi. 2016. The contribution of marketing innovations on art organization performance: Cases from the biggest art organizations in Greece. *International Journal of Nonprofit and Voluntary Sector Marketing* 3–12. doi:10.1002/nvsm.

Vassiliadis, C. and Z.C. Belenioti. 2015. Museums and cultural heritage via social media: An integrated literature review. *Tourismos: An International Multidisciplinary Journal of Tourism* (forthcoming) (in press).

Vassiliadis, C., and T.A. Fotiadis. 2008. Multiple museum construct motivators: A multivariable analysis with repertory grid analysis (RGA) approach. *Tourismos: An International Multidisciplinary Journal of Tourism* 3 (1) 2–35.

Williams, E. 2011. Branding the art world. *Creative Review* 52–56.

“Greek Breakfast”: A New Tourism Brand Name for an Age-Long Gastronomy Tradition

Alexios-Patapios Kontis and Aristeidis Gkoumas

Introduction

Although tourism is one of the most important factors of economic development in Greece, the dominant model of growth which has been selected for several years in the majority of Greek destinations is that of mass organized leisure tourism (Tsartas et al. 2014); a development model of low performance and competitiveness. Since the 1970s, when the absence of appropriate administrative structures (central and regional) for planning and management of an effective national tourism development strategy and the rapidly “industrialization” of the tourism product began, tourism in Greece has acquired standardized and homogenized characteristics; this has not allowed the differentiation of the country’s product throughout the years (Lagos 2005). At the same period, increasing international tourism competition set new rules in the global tourism market, looking for new innovative and imaginative tourism products. As a result destinations focus on distinctiveness of place by using local attributes in the launching of innovative, new products and brands, which can help establish a more unique selling proposition (Haven-Tang and Jones 2006); since tourists are no longer satisfied only with traditional services and instead seek something that they did not have a chance to experience elsewhere (Ritchie and Crouch 2003). Nowadays tourists seek more and more experiential experiences, expect to learn more about the history, culture, environment and society of the area they visit searching for active and interactive activities in their travel. Hence,

The original version of the book was revised. Belated corrections to change the order of First name and Family name of chapter authors have been incorporated. The erratum to the book is available at 10.1007/978-3-319-56288-9_72

A.-P. Kontis (✉) · A. Gkoumas
Country Department of Business Administration, University of the Aegean, Chios, Greece
e-mail: alexis.kontis@gmail.com

A. Kavoura et al. (eds.), *Strategic Innovative Marketing*, Springer Proceedings in Business and Economics, DOI 10.1007/978-3-319-56288-9_32

demand for novel experiences has become a major trend in the tourism industry and a good alternative to homogenization of mass commoditization of tourism services. From the marketing point of view, a nexus of primary and secondary tourism products are key elements for attracting tourists to particular destinations. “The diversification, intensification and linkage of these products can be crucial for the competitiveness and sustainable development of destinations” (Benur and Bramwell 2015).

Competitiveness is a crucial factor for traditional destinations such as Greece, particularly if we consider that there are plenty new emerging competitors who offer products and services with, in many cases, similar characteristics (Tsartas et al. 2013). An overall comparison of the Greek case with other European countries shows that diversity, quality and re-branding of tourism product are issues of major importance for the overall viability of the destination (Costa et al. 2014; Papatheodorou and Arvanitis 2014).

The challenge for Greek tourism authorities and businesses is to create innovative products, in order for the country to become a successful player in the global tourism market and to provide long-lasting solutions for structural problems of sustainable tourism development. The “Greek Breakfast” project is an initiative applied by the Hellenic Chamber of Hotels (HCH) which utilizes the cultural—gastronomic wealth of the country to connect tourism, local communities and local production, in order to enrich tourist experiences, diversification hotels’ product and achieve multiple positive social and economic benefits in all sectors.

Gastronomy and Tourism

Nowadays food has gained recognition as an integral part of the tourism product, and as a mean of destinations differentiation. The combination of food and tourism generates a lot of benefits for all local stakeholders (Hall and Mitchell 2006; Boyne et al. 2002; Hashimoto and Telfer 2006). Local food is a vital element for the construction of a “sense of place” by promoting local identity and destination appeal (Haven-Tang and Jones 2006), while local products add authenticity to the tourist experience and provides motivation for increasing tourism flows (Sims 2009). Local foods producers are benefited both by tourism-related spending on local economy, as well as by the additional sales outlet that tourism provides (Boyne et al. 2003). It is fairly certain that tourism/food connection provides opportunities for local food producers to add value to their products by creating a tourist experience centered on raw materials, while “gastronomic experiences can add value to tourists with a link between local culture, landscape and food, by creating an ‘atmosphere’ which will generate a memorable holiday experience” (Hjalager and Richards 2002, p. 224). According to Howard, “the linkage of the food with tourism industries has the potential to increase the number of visitors to a region, extend the length of visitor stay, and increase revenue generation.” (2001, p. 3).

Acknowledging the role of food in tourism as a vehicle in experience economy (Sidali et al. 2013), tourism literature reveals plethora of tourism destinations (countries and regions) which address to gastronomic tourism as a means for destination differentiation and also a critical competitive advantage. "Food became a stimulator for attracting new niche markets, supporting regional identities, developing quality tourism and sustainable tourism. Food has therefore developed from being a basic necessity for tourist consumption to an essential element of regional culture." (Jones and Jenkins 2002, p. 115). Several European destinations of France, Italy, and Spain or countries such as Scotland, Wales, the United Kingdom, and Germany have incorporated food tourism as an important component of their development or promotion strategies by capitalizing on their food/wine reputation to increase tourism expenditure (du Rand and Heath 2006; Boyne et al. 2003).

"Greek Breakfast" Project

Breakfast is an integral part to a destination's cultural heritage and heavily influences and at the same time is influenced by the local farming landscape and environment, which play a crucial role to the construction of the unique character, identity and authenticity of each destination, while promoting local cultural values, increasing tourist satisfaction and providing opportunities for visitors to explore other cultures and different ways of life. "Local food" has been identified as a distinguished tourist attraction and forms a major component of local economy, destination promotion strategies, tourism decision-making and competitiveness. Although it is accepted that breakfast constitutes an integral part of travel and tourism experience, there is a lack of established national breakfast patterns or types by other competitive destinations.

Contemporary concerns on food quality and healthy diet have led global consumers towards healthier lifestyles and food consumption (Slow Food Movement[1]). Current trends indicate a general shift towards fresh and organic products as consumers seek alternatives with no hidden additives and a minimal farming, to table cycle (e.g., 100 Mile Diet[2]). Mediterranean diet identified internationally as a modern nutritional model inspired by the traditional dietary patterns of some of the countries of the Mediterranean basin (particularly Greece and Southern Italy) that are characterized by high consumption of olive oil, fruit and vegetables, bread, wheat, fish, and red wine and is often cited as a extremely beneficial one. According

[1]Rediscover the flavors and savors of regional cooking, banish the degrading effects (inter alia homogenization) of Fast Food and develop taste rather than demean it.

[2]Eating meals prepared from scratch (nothing out of a box) made from the freshest organic food ingredients that had traveled the shortest possible distances from their production and eaten or preserved at their seasonal peak.

to UNESCO the Mediterranean diet was declared "intangible cultural heritage of mankind".

Based on the trends of the international tourism market, Hellenic Chamber of Hotels proceed on the development of a new distinct tourism product and a powerful brand name capable to provide multiple benefits to Greek economy. The construction of a strong national brand name alone, it is a rather complicated and ambitious task which demands the participation and collaboration of different and diverse organizations, institutions, groups and stakeholders.

"Greek Breakfast" project follows an integrated approach for the creation of a cohesive network of certified business (hotels and local producers), encouraging the direct cooperation among different actors, in order to offer new and traditional tastes of Greek cuisine based on authentic recipes and local gastronomy customs of each destination. Particularly, Hellenic Chamber of Hotels, by the "Greek Breakfast", aimed to enrich breakfast offered by Greek hotels with local traditional dishes and products.[3] The ultimate objective was to assist Greek hoteliers to move from mass tourism to more alternative and sustainable oriented experiences to create quality products for hotel guests through familiarization with local products and cuisine from Greek destinations.

"Greek Breakfast" project based on a multilevel study of the current situation analysis about of breakfast types offered by Greek hotels, recent international trends in breakfast consumption, local productivity portfolios for every region of the country (tangible and intangible goods related to food), recording also possible strengths, weaknesses, opportunities and threats. General culinary data from each destination (culinary history, products, foods, recipes, producers, literature, cooking patterns, etc.) were selected. Furthermore, information and training for hoteliers about Greek Breakfast philosophy, promotional activities, familiarization trips, etc., were put into action in order to support multiplex inbound and outbound marketing activities. Depending on availability, the implementation of multiple actions, such as local events across Greece for engaging local stakeholders, dissemination of information regarding the project to local and national media, was also undertaken.

From the beginning an emphasis was given to the development of communication strategy for the effective promotion of the new product and the promotion of the "Greek Breakfast" as a strong tourism brand with powerful and easily identified logo. The brand of "Greek Breakfast" is simple, comprehensive and memorable, combined geographical identity (Greek) with contextual description (Breakfast). The new brand demonstrates a highly competitive identity, represents the core essence and unique characteristics of the product which stands out from the competition. "Greek Breakfast" is an illustrative example of sound interaction between destination's values and assets with visitors' perceptions.

[3]E.g. Protected Designation of Origin (PDO) products, Protected Geographical Indication (PGI) products, Traditional Specialties Guaranteed (TSG) products, traditional and organic products.

"Greek Breakfast" logo developed upon the extensive and multiple uses of wheat and olives. In particular, bread and olive oil are two of the basic ingredients of the Greek land, since the ancient times and still today play a significant part of daily dietary customs. Beyond their historical continuity, bread and oil remain among the first savory choices for visitors, highly correlated with Greek landscape and nature. The unique taste as well as the symbolic value of wheat and olive transformed them to a trademark of Greek cuisine and a metonymy of Greece itself for the majority of tourists. By using this international recognition "Greek Breakfast" project aims to create a world-established logo that is a symbol which after consistent usage over time gets acceptance and recognition and in the future will be a synonym of Greek hospitality.

Another priority of the "Greek Breakfast" project was the synthesis of local products and different models of breakfast for each destination across the country. Next step was to create a critical mass of hotels which offer "Greek Breakfast", in order for the project to achieve practical usage and integrated capacity. Therefore "Greek Breakfast" communication strategy addressed mainly to domestic b2b participants. These enterprises obliged to display the "Greek Breakfast" logo in a visible place whereas a special labeling for products and foods should be explicitly mentioned on the breakfast menu of hotels.

After completing most of its deliverables and goals the project has established already a unique tourism product for the Greek hospitality sector, aiming to receive acceptance and recognition of "Greek Breakfast" at national and mainly international levels. The communication strategy predicts all the necessary corrective actions not only for the enterprises (B2B) but also for tourists/consumers (B2C). The dissemination of information regarding the project will use extensively digital technology, internet and social media (website, mobile applications, social media campaigns, etc.) in order to raise awareness of "Greek Breakfast" and increase the competitiveness of the destination as a whole.

The intangible nature and the versatile content of the "Greek Breakfast" call for continuous mentoring so that to ensure the quality characteristics and values of its brand name. For this reason an integrated web based system has been designed for the constant evaluation of the implantation process by collecting and analyzing primary and secondary data. The ultimate goal of the project is to secure the quality of the provided services related with brand "Greek Breakfast" across the country—the most valuable asset with economic and strategic value- and above all to introduce into domestic and international tourism market a well-accepted product of exquisite quality.

All in all as a core element of destination marketing, the 'Greek Breakfast' exploits productively the Greek culinary tradition to promote the wealth and authenticity of local agricultural products and traditional gastronomy based on mutual cooperation between hoteliers and local producers. Under these circumstances "Greek Breakfast" will act as a "pull" factor that stimulates visitors' loyalty and satisfaction.

Conclusions

It is generally agreed that "Greek Breakfast" did not even exist as a concept before the Hellenic Chamber of Hotels built it as a new brand name (Skordili and Melissourgos 2015). According to the recent research on the effects and acceptance of "Greek Breakfast" by Greek hoteliers, the initial results indicate substantial recognition in a very short time. Specifically, 93.7% of the respondents believed that "Greek Breakfast" contributed much or very much to the promotion of local products and cuisine of each destination. Also, 91.8% of the respondents recognized the importance of the project to the promotion and advertising of the country's culinary heritage and identity. Similarly, 90.9% underlined that project enhanced the diversification and enrichment of the Greek tourist product in general, whereas 88.2% pointed out its significance to the exploitation of the cultural gastronomic wealth of Greece (Trihas et al. 2015).

Reviewing national and local press unveils several obstacles and opportunities as perceived by different participants during the implementation of the project. Potential benefits were quickly acknowledged by the businesses involved. Hoteliers realized that the competitive edge stemming from the use of authentic local products, and added-value services, will create loyal customers attracting visitors with higher income and move away from cost competitiveness (Karayiorgos 2013).

Finally, "Greek Breakfast" can be used as an innovative tool for food companies to generate demand for culinary tourists who seek for authentic, quality Greek food products, while simultaneously extracting multiple socioeconomic benefits from direct (local) and indirect (exports) consumption.

References

Benur, A., and B. Bramwell. 2015. Tourism product development and product diversification in destinations. *Tourism Management* 50: 213–224.

Boyne, S., D. Hall, and F. Williams. 2003. Policy, support and promotion for food related tourism initiatives: A marketing approach to regional development. In *Wine, food and tourism marketing*, ed. C.M. Hall, 131–154. New York: Haworth Hospitality Press.

Boyne, S., F. Williams, and D.R. Hall. 2002. On the trail of regional success: Tourism food production and the Isle of Arran Taste Trail. In *Tourism and gastronomy*, ed. G. Richards, and A.M. Hjalager, 91–114. London: Routledge.

Costa, C., E. Panyik, and D. Buhalis (eds.). 2014. *A comparative approach to European tourism planning and organization systems: An introduction in European tourism planning and organization systems: The EU member states*. Bristol: Channel View Publications.

du Rand, G., and E. Heath. 2006. Towards a framework for food tourism as an element of destination marketing. *Current Issues in Tourism* 9 (3): 206–234.

Hall, C.M., and R. Mitchell. 2006. Gastronomy, food and wine tourism. In *Tourism business frontiers: Consumers, products and industry*, ed. D. Buhalis, and C. Costa, 137–148. London: Butterworth Heinemann.

Hashimoto, A., and D. Telfer. 2006. Selling Canadian culinary tourism: Branding the global and the regional product. *Tourism Geographies* 8 (1): 31–55.

Haven-Tang, C., and E. Jones. 2006. Using local food and drink to differentiate tourism destinations through a sense of place. *Journal of Culinary Science and Technology* 4 (4): 69–86.

Howard, D. 2001. Creating your destination's competitive advantage: Your regional identity. In *Paper presented at the 2nd New Zealand food and wine tourism conference.*

Jones, A., and I. Jenkins. 2002. A taste of Wales—Blas Ar Gymru: Institutional malaise in promoting Welsh food tourism products. In *Tourism and gastronomy*, ed. A. Hjalager, and G. Richards, 115–131. London: Routledge.

Karayiorgos, L. 2013. Greek breakfast becomes a world known brand name. Naftemporiki, 25 June, 13 [in Greek].

Lagos, D. 2005. *"Tourism economics" (in Greek).* Athens: Kritiki Publications.

Papatheodorou, A., and P. Arvanitis. 2014. Tourism and the economic crisis in Greece- regional perspectives. *Région et Développement* 39: 183–203.

Ritchie, J., and G. Crouch. 2003. *The competitive destination: A sustainable tourism perspective.* Cambridge: CABI Publishing.

Sidali, K.L., E. Kastenholz, and R. Bianchi. 2013. Food tourism, niche markets and products in rural tourism: Combining the intimacy model and the experience economy as a rural development strategy. *Journal of Sustainable Tourism.*

Sims, R. 2009. Food, place and authenticity: Local food and the sustainable tourism experience. *Journal of Sustainable Tourism* 17 (3): 321–336.

Skordili, S. and Y. Melissourgos. 2015. *Connecting tourism and the agro-food sector: The Greek breakfast initiative and the case of Santorini.* Harokopio University: Department of Geography

Stavrinoudis, Th., P. Tsartas, and A. Papatheodorou. 2013. Business environment and accommodation policies in Europe. In *Trends in European tourism planning and organisation,* ed. C. Costa, E. Panyik, and D. Buhalis, 175–188. Clevedon: Channel View Publications.

Trihas, N., A. Kyriakaki, and S. Zagkotsi, 2015. Local cuisine and agricultural products as a means of enhancing tourists' gastronomic experiences in Greece. In *IMIC 2015: 1st international conference on experiential tourism,* Santorini, Greece, 9–11 Oct 2015.

Tsartas P., A. Papatheodorou, and M. Vasileiou. 2014. Tourism development and policy in Greece. In *European tourism planning and organisation systems: National case studies* (Volume III), ed. C. Costa, E. Panyik, and D. Buhalis, 295–316. Clevedon: Channel View Publications.

Part IX
User Generated Content and Marketing

Organized by: Nga Ho-Dac
Marketing Department, San Francisco State University, San Francisco, USA

Description

The aim of the session is to explore the impacts of user-generated content (UGC) on marketing theories and practice. With the proliferation of social media, lots of content has been created by users. This changes the landscape of marketing where traditionally the content was created by marketers only. Now marketers cannot control the content anymore but instead just a part of a web of content creators. The impacts of UGC on marketing are twofold: impact on consumers and impact on marketers. Consumers nowadays rely not only on marketers' content but also on UGC to make their decisions. On the other hand, UGC provides marketers with useful information to improve their marketing practice. User-generated content (UGC) includes customer reviews, forum discussion, social media content created by users, etc. This session includes but not limited to these topics: impacts of UGC on consumer decision-making, sales, branding, product development, and public relation.

Cliff Diving in Virtual Communities

Teresa Tiago, Flavio Tiago, Sandra Faria and João Couto

Introduction

Beginning in the late 1990s, the concept of tourism related to sports emerged and has since been defined by Standeven and Deknop (1999) as "all forms of active and passive involvement in sporting activity, participated in casually or in an organized way for non-commercial or business/commercial reasons that necessitate travel away from home and work locality." As in many other tourism domains, tourists often search online for peer group opinions when choosing their travel experiences (Williams et al. 2015). Online interactions and offline experiences both influence the selection of events and social media interactions become an important part of the fan and event experience. Within these social networks, the communication is quite extensive often allowing for more contact between sport figures and fans. The increased interaction before, during and after an event enriches the overall experience at the sporting events. From a sponsor's perspective, these ongoing social interactions challenge organizations to customize their offerings and integrate tools and features that enhance communication processes among all (Kavoura 2014). The content created tends to reflect the relational commitment and satisfaction points of the sports tourist. Thus, detailed monitoring of social media can be extremely important for brands and destination marketing organizations (DMOs—organizations that promote the development and marketing of a destination) that want to promote sports tourism events (Stavrianea and Kavoura 2014).

This insight compels us to analyze tourist/fan activities on different social networks for Red Bull cliff diving events. In the support of this effort, we used a combination of social network analysis and content analysis of data from Facebook and Instagram related to two cliff diving events located in distinctive destinations.

T. Tiago (✉) · F. Tiago · S. Faria · J. Couto
Economics and Business School, University of the Azores,
Ponta Delgada, Portugal
e-mail: maria.tp.tiago@uac.pt

A. Kavoura et al. (eds.), *Strategic Innovative Marketing*, Springer Proceedings
in Business and Economics, DOI 10.1007/978-3-319-56288-9_33

The goal of our inquiry was to better understand the underlying social media domain by either validating past conceptual constructions or reshaping our view using new information. As highlighted in previous research, the interaction on social networks related to tourism experiences can be extensive including factual data, opinions, and recommendations. (Humphreys et al. 2014; Van Rheenen et al. 2016). For this reason, the research approach utilized in this study analyzed both social networks and content. Specifically, the four-dimensional framework that considers storytelling, triggers, amusement, and reaction (STAR) was leveraged to assess both events and destinations present on social media (Tiago et al. 2016).

The results of the social network analysis (SNA), that in the case used the graph theory including structural and locational properties of the network, suggest that in the case of the Red Bull diving event in Denmark both the event itself and the destination influenced the composition of the social network and its activities. In this sample, the new and/or active fans shared similarities to each other based on one of two elements: geographic location or event-information. However, other results show that this pattern is not the same for other events promoted by Red Bull.

Background

"Ego-involvement" is a common reference found in the literature regarding people's involvement with sports and athletes. Ego-involvement was presented by Allport in 1945, who explained that involvement is only present when an activity is valued from the individual's perception and composes a blend of hedonic value, symbolic value and a core component for individual's life (Beaton et al. 2011). Despite this definition, there continue to be questions surrounding motivations for involvement and interest in various sports. When looking at sports as events that attract people to a specific location and for a specific period of time, the notion of sports tourism arises (Van Rheenen et al. 2016). However, as mentioned previously, not everyone feels the same level of ego-involvement as it relates to sporting events thus creating different experiences for different tourists (Bosnjak et al. 2016).

Hvass and Munar (2012) noticed that digital marketing influences on tourist experiences increased over time, challenging firms and DMOs to follow a similar approach used in other industries to adopt an active and interactive online presence (Tiago and Veríssimo 2014).

As discussions of and research on social media and its implications for the tourism and hospitality industries have grown over the last two decades, some researchers have focused on new strategies and advances made by companies and DMOs (Hays et al. 2013; Liu 2000; Hvass and Munar 2012) Others have concentrated on tourist use of digital platforms (Zhang et al. 2014; Goodyear et al. 2014; Litvin et al. 2008; Xiang and Gretzel 2010; Neuhofer et al. 2014). However, as noticed by Van Rheenen et al. (2016), there is still an opportunity to better define

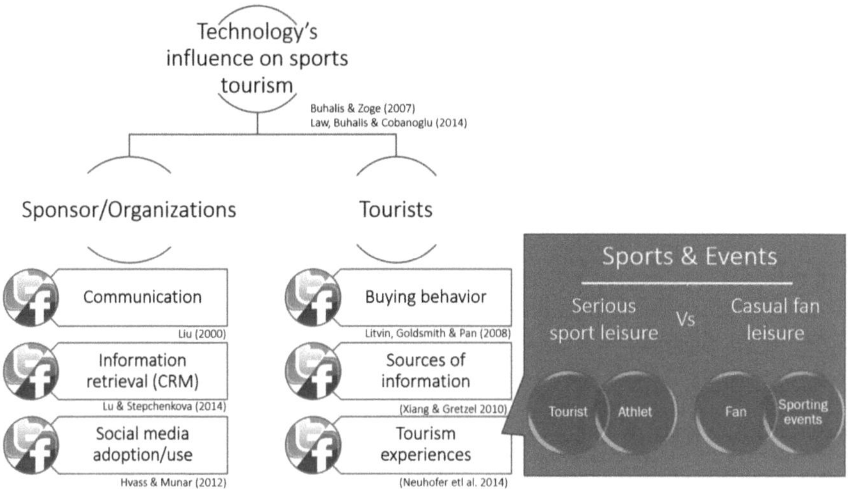

Fig. 1 Technology's influence on sports tourism

the boundaries of sports tourism and the impact of technology on the behavior of sports tourists—both the serious sports enthusiasts and the casual sports fans (Shipway and Jones 2007) (Fig. 1).

Starting with web 2.0, social media interactions have become a part of the event experience for fans and online and offline experiences both tend to drive interest regardless of how closely people follow the sport (Tiago et al. 2016). So, social media have considerably improved fans, sport figures and organizations interaction dynamics. Social media networks are dynamics arenas where communication increases (Filo et al. 2014). Currently, reputation and online engagement are key to the success of any sports-related brand, athlete, or event. Social media sites play an increasingly larger role in the lives of sports fans around the world, allowing for before, during and after event interactions with players and other fans.

In order to make the fan experience unique across social media and other channels, marketers need to start thinking like fans and assess what they value. The content tends to reflect their level of involvement and satisfaction. Monetizing social media is a real opportunity for brands and DMOs that want to promote sport tourism events. Evidence from literature suggests that sports events can promote a destination through online electronic word-of-mouth (eWoM) on social media at the same time promoting the event itself. Nonetheless, the nature of these effects is not completely understood.

Emotion and practical values of content have already been debated as factors that would positively influence fan engagement. In addition, researchers have acknowledged that people travel to watch or participate in sports events. However, what makes them choose one sporting event instead of another? Moreover, what makes them willing to share and comment on their experiences?

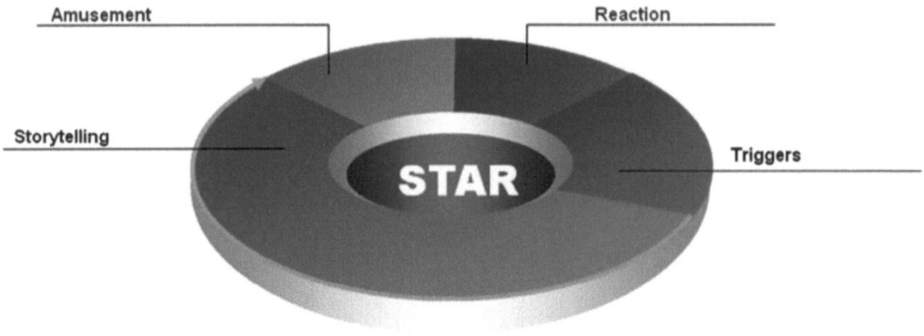

Fig. 2 STAR model

Research Methodology

As highlighted in previous research, the interactions on social networks related to tourism experiences can be much more than simple advertising impacts. Also involved are reviewing factual data, sharing opinions, and promoting additional interaction (Humphreys et al. 2014). For this reason, the research approach used in this work combined both social network analysis and content analysis. A four-dimensional framework is proposed to best understand the impact from activities tied to brands and destinations, which includes storytelling, triggers, amusement, and reaction dimensions (STAR model).

Figure 2 shows how each component of the STAR model is weighted based on its relative contribution as determined in previous multidimensional analyses of social media content (Tiago et al. 2016).

Data collection, performed during the weeks before and after the events of 2015 and 2016, focused on the content created on two social networks—Facebook (http://www.facebook.com) and Instagram (https://www.instagram.com). Historically, researchers have preferred to analyze data from Twitter since the content is public and therefore easily accessible. As our focus was the analysis of sports tourism behavior at specific events (Red Bull cliff diving), these two social networks were instead chosen due to their popularity among the cliff diving fans from the two countries where the events took place (Denmark and Portugal). To profile the fans of each event the social structures were analyzed using graph theories. Afterwards, the content was analyzed and a level of engagement was estimated.

Final Considerations

The results obtained from the SNA suggest that in the case of the Red Bull event in Denmark both the event and the destination influenced the composition of the network and its corresponding activity. New and/or active fans were closely linked to each other based on one of two elements: geographic location or event-information. The outcome at the Portuguese diving competition was quite different, reflecting the strategy of adopting the official Red Bull cliff diving page as the event page instead of a local web alternative. The sports fans that commented on the event were geographically diverse and linked most closely by their involvement in the sport.

The quantitative and qualitative analyses validated the use of the STAR model and the results reinforced the notion that the level of engagement reflects the messenger's capacity to integrate in a balance way these four dimensions. In the case of the Red Bull cliff diving event in Denmark, more photos were posted but it was the videos that proved to be the most engaging content. Consequently, the trigger dimension received a relative weight that was much higher than recorded in previous studies. Similar results were found in the case of the Portuguese event with local photos also triggering a significant number of comments and shares. Besides the videos, the content posts that promoted an increased level of engagement among fans focused on the personal stories of Red Bull team members. This finding confirms that ego-involvement is present and is reflected in the storytelling. However, in this context the storytelling should be understood as a nonstop and mostly improvisational phenomenon, made up of interlinked content that generates a positive feeling of belonging between fans, athletes and brands. Finally, amusement and reaction were discovered in the sports tourists' ability to share, comment, and have fun in the social domains. Interestingly, the two network nodes showed different preferences in terms of type of content. The location-based node shared more event videos that contained local landscapes while the event-driven node focused on detailed sport images and videos.

In general, our results prove that a community of varying interests can be created and managed around a sporting event. Location and the type of event are varying factors as are the different profiles of users/fans. In order to enhance the engagement level, the content shared should have an underlying theme that connects people and creates a story that fans want to follow, regardless of the location of the event. Otherwise, the community will include only strangers and will not generate positive eWoM for either the destination or the sports tourism event.

Regardless of the main differences found between this study and previous analyses conducted with sport figures, it has been shown by using the STAR model that high levels of engagement can be reached by establishing a virtual community of fans and followers.

Based on this research, the practical implications for sports tourism events content is to create it and enhance it through the STAR model. Even considering that the four dimensions are not required, their well-adjusted use can enhance the engagement levels on social media pages related to sports events.

Acknowledgements We gratefully acknowledge the Advance Research Centre—ISEG, financial support from "Fundação para a Ciência e Tecnologia" (FCT—Portugal), national funding through research grant (UID/SOC/04521/2013) and CEEAplA.

References

Allport, G.W. 1945. The psychology of participation. *Psychological Review* 52: 117.
Beaton, A.A., D.C. Funk, L. Ridinger, and J. Jordan. 2011. Sport involvement: A conceptual and empirical analysis. *Sport management review* 14: 126–140.
Bosnjak, M., C.A. Brown, D.-J. Lee, B.Y. Grace, and M.J. Sirgy. 2016. Self-expressiveness in sport tourism determinants and consequences. *Journal of Travel Research* 55: 125–134.
Filo, K., D. Lock, and A. Karg. 2014. Sport and social media research: A review. *Sport Management Review*.
Goodyear, V.A., A. Casey, and D. Kirk. 2014. Tweet me, message me, like me: Using social media to facilitate pedagogical change within an emerging community of practice. *Sport, Education and Society* 1–17.
Hays, S., S.J. Page, and D. Buhalis. 2013. Social media as a destination marketing tool: Its use by national tourism organisations. *Current Issues in Tourism* 16: 211–239.
Humphreys, L., P. Gill, and B. Krishnamurthy. 2014. Twitter: A content analysis of personal information. *Information, Communication & Society* 17: 843–857.
Hvass, K.A., and A.M. Munar. 2012. The takeoff of social media in tourism. *Journal of Vacation Marketing* 18: 93–103.
Kavoura, A. 2014. Social media, online imagined communities and communication research. *Library Review* 63: 490–504.
Litvin, S.W., R.E. Goldsmith, and B. Pan. 2008. Electronic word-of-mouth in hospitality and tourism management. *Tourism Management* 29: 458–468.
Liu, Z.H. 2000. Internet tourism marketing: Potential and constraints. *Tourism and Hotel Industry in Indo-China and Southeast Asia: Development, Marketing and Sustainability* 34–51.
Neuhofer, B., D. Buhalis, and A. Ladkin. 2014. A typology of technology-enhanced tourism experiences. *International Journal of Tourism Research* 16: 340–350.
Shipway, R., and I. Jones. 2007. Running away from home: Understanding visitor experiences and behaviour at sport tourism events. *International Journal of Tourism Research* 9: 373–383.
Standeven, J., and P. Deknop. 1999. *Sport Tourism*. Champaign: Human Kinetics.
Stavrianea, A. and A. Kavoura. 2014. Communicating the sense of belonging to an 'imagined community' of a destination for advertising its proposed experiences and the creation of brand loyalty. In *2nd international conference on marketing and management issues*, Athens, 18–20.
Tiago, T., and J. Veríssimo. 2014. Digital marketing and social media: Why bother? *Business Horizons* 57: 703–708.
Tiago, T., F. Tiago, S.D. Faria, and J.P. Couto. 2016. Who is the better player? Off-field battle on Facebook and Twitter. *Business Horizons* 59: 175–183.
Van Rheenen, D., S. Cernaianu, and C. Sobry. 2016. Defining sport tourism: A content analysis of an evolving epistemology. *Journal of Sport & Tourism* 1–19.
Williams, N.L., A. Inversini, D. Buhalis, and N. Ferdinand. 2015. Community crosstalk: An exploratory analysis of destination and festival eWOM on Twitter. *Journal of Marketing Management* 31: 1113.
Xiang, Z., and U. Gretzel. 2010. Role of social media in online travel information search. *Tourism Management* 31: 179–188.
Zhang, Z., Z. Zhang, and R. Law. 2014. Positive and negative word of mouth about restaurants: Exploring the asymmetric impact of the performance of attributes. *Asia Pacific Journal of Tourism Research* 19: 162–180.

Attitude Toward Change: Factors Affecting Hospital Managerial Employees' Resistance to Change

Vasiliki Amarantou, Stella Kazakopoulou, Prodromos Chatzoglou and Dimitrios Chatzoudes

Introduction

Within an organization, applying changes is an inevitable practice in order to ensure its viability and alter its initial condition (Agboola and Salawu 2011). Employees' effort to preserve the status quo and avoid duty changes is defined as resistance to change.

In the context of the present study, when it comes to organizational changes, researchers essentially refer to business process reengineering efforts. However, previous studies have proven that most of BPR initiatives tend to fail (Buick et al. 2015), mainly due to resistance to change (Wittig 2012; Georgalis et al. 2015).

The management of resistance to change is an issue which has attracted researchers' attention. However, many of the studies seem to have several limitations as well as many research gaps. More specifically, many researchers investigate the effect of specific factors on resistance to change, while the relationship between resistance to change and other acknowledged factors is often omitted (Bhattacherjee and Hikmet 2007; Georgalis et al. 2015). Moreover, a lot of the existing empirical surveys collect data from only one organization/company (Bhattacherjee and Hikmet 2007; Hanif et al. 2014; Georgalis et al. 2015; Ming-Chu and Meng-Hsiu 2015), while other distribute questionnaires via mail, which means that there is a lack of direct contact between researchers and respondents (Hanif et al. 2014). This complicates the communication between researchers and participants and, therefore, the understanding of the actual situation. So it is obvious that in such cases generalization of the results is not possible or meaningful (Ming-Chu and Meng-Hsiu 2015).

V. Amarantou (✉) · S. Kazakopoulou · P. Chatzoglou · D. Chatzoudes
Department of Production and Management Engineering,
Democritus University of Thrace, Xanthi, Greece
e-mail: biki89.amar@gmail.com

A. Kavoura et al. (eds.), *Strategic Innovative Marketing*, Springer Proceedings in Business and Economics, DOI 10.1007/978-3-319-56288-9_34

The present research studies the attitude toward change of managerial employees who work for Greek public hospitals. The motivating factor for dealing with this subject was the current condition of the Greek healthcare sector, which just like in many other countries requires immediate change.

In the context of the present survey, an original research model investigating the dynamics among eight (8) different factors was created and empirically tested. Six (6) of these factors are independent (personality traits, perception of BPR, job perception, management–employee relationship, disposition toward change and the anticipated impact of change), while the other two factors "Attitude towards Change" and "Resistance to Change" constitute the main dependent factors.

Literature Review

Oreg (2006) refers to employee resistance to change, as a three-dimensional phenomenon (cognitive, affective, and behavioral resistance) which are influenced by different factors. He proved that, depending on the type of resistance to change, there will be a corresponding effect on employees work reality (Oreg 2006).

Ming-Chu and Meng-Hsiu (2015) underlined that the Management should focus at managing employee resistance to change, since it obstructs the proper implementation of change programs. Furst and Cable (2008) proved that when employees feel that the required assistance is provided to them and their wellbeing is something top management is concerned with, indicating organizational support, then they have a more positive psychology toward their job. This makes them being more receptive toward the imminent change and thus, reduces their resistance (Ming-Chu and Meng-Hsiu 2015).

Conceptual Framework

The proposed conceptual framework is the result of an extensive literature review and incorporates some of the most important factors that affect managerial employees' (ME) attitude and resistance toward change (RtC). These factors are: personality traits—PT (Stanley et al. 2005; Mayer et al. 2010; Wittig 2012), perception of BPR (Stanley et al. 2005; Peccei et al. 2011; Mlay et al. 2013), job perception—JP (Kwahk and Lee 2008; Peccei et al. 2011; Mlay et al. 2013), Management-employee relationship—MER (Oreg 2006; Mlay et al. 2013), disposition toward change—DtC (Oreg 2006; Kwahk and Lee 2008) and anticipated impact of change—AIC (Oreg 2006; Kwahk and Lee 2008).

Managerial employees' personality traits include their defensive mechanisms, irrational thoughts, as well as, their disposition toward cynicism (Stanley et al. 2005). Employees who have the above characteristics will probably have a negative attitude toward change and they will most likely resist to a possible change.

Management personnel's perception of BPR plays a significant role in the way that they react to change usually when a BPR is considered as beneficial, the resistance will be rather low (Mlay et al. 2013). Moreover, if employees feel comfortable in the new environment, after the implementation of a change program, then they will most likely have a positive attitude toward change.

In addition, the intrinsic rewards and the satisfaction managerial employees gain from their job affect their attitude toward change. If the administrative staff is pleased with the working conditions and their position within the hospital, it may want to preserve the current situation which will be threaten by the proposed changes.

Managerial employees' perception about the management–employee relationship is of great importance. More specifically, the better the management–employee relationship, the less the expressed resistance and the more positive the attitude toward change will be (Stanley et al. 2005).

Further, managerial employees' disposition toward change refers to the tendency they have for change. Of course, the inclination people have for accepting or rejecting change differs from one another (Oreg 2006). Employees who have positive disposition toward change, will likely have a positive tendency thus, they will not resist change implementation (Oreg 2006; Kwahk and Lee 2008).

Respectively, influenced by their attitude toward change (AtC), managerial employees are likely to express less or greater resistance to change (Wittig 2012). If they have a positive attitude toward change, then it is expected that they will show less resistance (Wittig 2012).

Finally, if the anticipated impact of change is thought to be negative, then it is reasonable that managerial employees will create a negative perception toward change (Kwahk and Lee 2008; Peccei et al. 2011) and, it is likely that they will resist its implementation (Oreg 2006).

Hypothesis 1 ME personality traits are positively related to their AtC.

Hypothesis 2 ME perception of BPR is negatively related to their AtC.

Hypothesis 3 ME perception of their job is positively related to their AtC.

Hypothesis 4 MER is negatively related to managerial employee AtC.

Hypothesis 5 ME disposition toward change positively affects their AtC.

Hypothesis 6 ME disposition toward change is positively related to RtC.

Hypothesis 7 ME attitude toward change positively affects their RtC.

Hypothesis 8 AIC positively affects managerial employee AtC.

Hypothesis 9 AIC is positively related to their RtC.

Research Methodology

The total sample of the survey is consisted of 134 employees who work at the administration departments of six hospitals. In order to measure each factor of the research model, multiple items (questions) were used to create a structured questionnaire. The items included in the questionnaire were drawn from the global scientific literature and they were fully adjusted, as to respond to Greek reality.

More specifically, personality traits were measured using 4 items (Oreg 2006), perception of BPR with nine items (Mlay et al. 2013; Al-Ameri 2013), job perception with 5 (Oreg 2006), management–employee relationship with four (Stanley et al. 2005), attitude toward change with four (Peccei et al. 2011) and disposition toward change, resistance to change and anticipated impact of change with 15 in total items (Peccei et al. 2011). The five-point Likert scale was used for the measurement of all factors.

The survey was conducted during September–November 2015. The sample is consisted mainly by women (71.6%), aged 41–55 years (58.2%), or 25–40 years (29.9%), with high level of education, with more than 16 years of experience in Hospital (46.8%), who are mainly office employees (83.6%) or department directors (13.5%).

Results

Factor Analysis

To evaluate the proposed research model, factor analysis was initially performed in order to examine the validity of the structure of the questionnaire and the factors of the proposed conceptual framework. All relevant indicators, for all factors, are within limits, according to the statistical theory (KMO > 0.6, TVE > 60.00, Factor Loadings > 0.6, Cronbach a > 0.6) (Dimitriadis 2010).

Hypothesis Testing

The evaluation of the conceptual framework and the testing of the research hypotheses were conducted using Structural Equation Modeling/SEM (Joreskog and Sorbom 1996). Many indices have been used to evaluate the overall fit of the model (Dimitriadis 2010). These indicators are the Normed $X^2(X^2/df)$ (acceptable values 1–5), the RMSEA (Root Mean Square Error of Approximation) (acceptable values < 0.1), the CFI (Comparative Fit Index) and GFI (goodness of fit Index) (acceptable prices > 0.9) and the RMR (root mean square Residual) (acceptable values < 0.05).

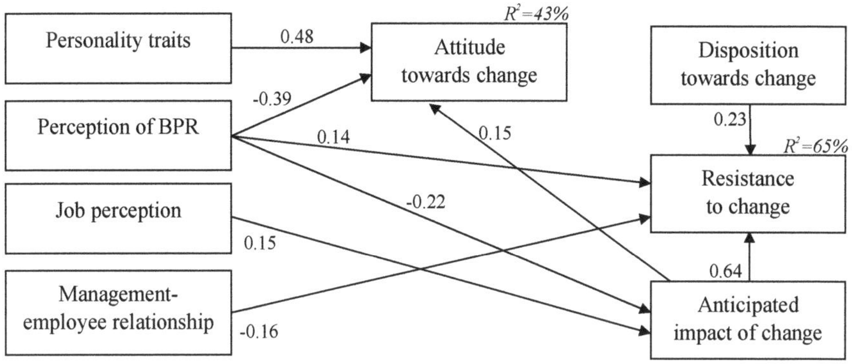

Fig. 1 Final model (SEM)

The actual results concerning these indices support our claim that the model is a valid model with acceptable overall fit (X^2/df = 0.503, CFI = 1, GFI = 0.971, TLI = 1, RMR = 0.027, RMSEA = 0). The use of SEM methodology resulted in a new model, which is illustrated in Fig. 1.

The interpretative and predictive power of the final model is highly satisfactory. More specifically, the included independent factors are able to interpret 43% of the variations of the dependent factor "Attitude towards Change" and 65% of the variations of the other dependent factor "Resistance to Change." From the initial hypotheses five are accepted (1, 2, 6, 8, 9), while four are rejected (3, 4, 5, 7). Further, four new relationships are proposed. All path coefficients presented in Fig. 1 are statistically significant at 0.05 level.

Conclusions

Managerial employees' personality traits and their perception of BPR are the factors that mostly affect their attitude toward change. Furthermore, the anticipated impact of change also affects their attitude. Regarding management personnel's resistance to change, seems to be strongly affected by the anticipated impact of change, too. Moreover, managerial employees' disposition toward change, their perception of BPR and management–employee relationship is also related to the appearance of such behavior (resistance). In conclusion, the fact that the relationship between managerial employee's attitude and resistance to change was not proved does not mean that it does not exist. It is reasonable that managerial staff's attitude toward change would influence their behavior, but it is possible that an intermediate factor, not examined in the present study, plays a significant role.

Management should ensure that employees are properly informed, in order to understand that change is necessary (Wittig 2012). Moreover, it is necessary for the smooth and successful implementation of change programs to establish and maintain good relationship (trust, feedback, etc.) between its members and leadership. As many researchers highlight, such a relationship is significant for the restriction of the phenomenon "resistance to change" (Stanley et al. 2005; Oreg 2006; Yue 2008; Boohene and Williams 2012; Georgalis et al. 2015). Therefore, Management should be interested about employees' welfare and should aim at the creation and preservation of a pleasant working environment. Such an environment would promote solid relations within the organization and, consequently, reduce employees' resistance to change.

References

Agboola, A.A., and R.O. Salawu. 2011. Managing deviant behavior and resistance to change. *International Journal of Business and Management* 6 (1): 235–242.

Al-Ameri M. 2013. Assessing resistance to technological change for improved job performance in the UAE (Public sectors), Doctoral dissertation, University of Salford: UK.

Bhattacherjee, A., and N. Hikmet. 2007. Physicians' resistance toward healthcare information technology: A theoretical model and empirical test. *European Journal of Information Systems* 16 (6): 725–737.

Boohene, R., and A.A. Williams. 2012. Resistance to organisational change: A Case Study of Oti Yeboah Complex Limited. *International Business and Management* 4 (1): 135–145.

Buick, F., D.A. Blackman, M.E. O'Donnell, J.L. O'Flynn, and D. West. 2015. Can enhanced performance management support public sector change? *Journal of Organizational Change Management* 28 (2): 271–289.

Dimitriadis E. 2010., *Statistical applications with the use of S.P.S.S 17 and LISREL 8.7*. Kritiki Publishing: Athens (in Greek).

Furst, S.A., and D.M. Cable. 2008. Employee resistance to organizational change: Managerial influence tactics and leader-member exchange. *Journal of Applied Psychology* 93 (2): 453–462.

Georgalis, J., R. Samaratunge, and N. Kimberley. 2015. Change process characteristics and resistance to organizational change: The role of employee perceptions of justice. *Australian Journal of Management* 40 (1): 89–113.

Hanif, M., Y.S. Khan, and A. Zaheer. 2014. Impact of organizational resistance to change on BPR implementation: A case of state bank of Pakistan. *European Journal of Business and Management* 6 (4): 186–196.

Joreskog, K.G., and D. Sorbom. 1996. *LISREL 8: Structural equation modeling with the SIMPLIS command language*. Chicago: Scientific Software International.

Kwahk, K.-Y., and J.-N. Lee. 2008. The role of readiness for change in ERP implementation: Theoretical bases and empirical validation. *Information & Management* 45 (7): 474–481.

Mayer, P.H., M. Yaron, and S.R. Lowenstein. 2010. Impact on length of stay after introduction of emergency department information system. *Western Journal of Emergency Medicine* 11 (4): 329–332.

Ming-Chu, Y., and L. Meng-Hsiu. 2015. Unlocking the black box: Exploring the link between perceive organizational support and resistance to change. *Asia Pacific Management Review* 20 (3): 177–183.

Mlay, S.V., I. Zlotnikova, and S. Watundu. 2013. A quantitative analysis of business process reengineering and organizational resistance: The case of Uganda. *The African Journal of Information Systems* 5 (1): 1–26.

Oreg, S. 2006. Personality, context, and resistance to organizational change. *European Journal of Work and Organizational Psychology* 15 (1): 73–101.

Peccei, R., A. Giangreco, and A. Sebastiano. 2011. The role of organisational commitment in the analysis of resistance to change. *Personnel Review* 40 (2): 185–204.
Stanley, D.J., J.P. Meyer, and L. Topolnytsky. 2005. Employee cynicism and resistance to organizational change. *Journal of Business and Psychology* 19 (4): 429–459.
Wittig, C. 2012. Employees' reactions to organizational change. *OD Practioner* 44 (2): 23–28.
Yue, W. 2008. Resistance, the echo of change. *International Journal of Business and Management* 3 (2): 84–89.

Part X
Innovations on Shipping Management and Marketing

Organized by: Aristotelis Alexopoulos
BCA, Shipping, Transport and Logistics, Athens, Greece

Description

Generally what applies to management theories its cut out for shipping as well—objectives are the same as in any other business. Management skills, tools, and disciplines are used where needed in shipping no matter what the terminology, staff titles, rules, or objectives are. It is realized that the ship is part of the total company organization and not to isolate it in order to be effective. Ship management is both shore-based and ship-board management related to the safe operation of the vessel on a daily basis to ensure compliance with regulations and customer's needs in a cost-effective way. Shipping marketing or more precise marketing of shipping companies is quite active in modern times becoming a necessity in both the tramp and the liner markets. It focuses on the satisfaction of the customer's needs (he can either be a charterer/shipper/consignee) by transporting the goods to their destination and earning a reward. This is done through a thorough investigation of the market so that the customer's transport needs can be forecasted and at the same time all necessary means must be well-organized, planned, and controlled. A specialized symposium in the shipping sector hosted by the 5th International Conference on Strategic Innovative Marketing consists of a number of specialized papers focusing on the related fields of logistics, strategic shipping management, safety and environmental management, and marketing shipping services.

Are Greek Tanker Operators Aware of IMO's Sustainable Maritime Transportation System and Willing to Follow Its Goals and Actions?

Athena Parsotaki and Aristotelis B. Alexopoulos

Introduction

Research Context

This paper investigates the level of sustainability incorporation into everyday practice of shipping with particular focus on oil tanker operators of the Greek shipping industry. Sustainable targets and actions that have recently proposed by IMO are analyzed and evaluated.

In 2012, the UN Conference on Sustainable development held in Rio de Janeiro and known as Rio+20, (UN Rio+20) witnessed intense negotiations that resulted in the outcome document, entitled "The Future We Want." The document calls for a wide range of actions and also commits Governments to working toward a transition to a "green economy." This should evolve around the three, equally important, dimensions of sustainable development, i.e., the economic, social and environmental dimensions. Most importantly, at Rio+20, Governments agreed that the UN General Assembly should launch a process to establish a set of specific Sustainable Development Goals (SDGs), together with a strategy to finance their implementation. SDGs had to be action-oriented, concise and easy to communicate, limited in number, global in nature, and universally applicable to all countries while taking into account different national realities and respecting national policies and priorities.

The contribution of IMO to SDGs was made in the symposium on a sustainable maritime transportation system (SMTS), during the World Maritime Day (September 26, 2013). This event provided an opportunity for a discussion on a global agenda of the (SMTS) and resulted in an official statement of IMO about it.

A. Parsotaki (✉) · A.B. Alexopoulos
Shipping, Transport and Logistics Department, Business College of Athens, Athens, Greece
e-mail: athinapar@yahoo.gr

A. Kavoura et al. (eds.), *Strategic Innovative Marketing*, Springer Proceedings in Business and Economics, DOI 10.1007/978-3-319-56288-9_35

The SMTS document therefore was announced with the intention to provide a meaningful input to sustainability issues of maritime transportation. This document calls for a wide range of actions from the various maritime industry stakeholders and also invites Governments to begin working toward a transition to a "green economy." The (SMTS) proposes sustainable goals and actions in specific areas, such as safety culture and environmental protection, energy efficiency, maritime security, energy supply for ships and maritime traffic support providing an opportunity for IMO member-states and policy makers directly involved in maritime industries to consider the (SDGs) in achieving desired objectives. The consideration of sustainability goals occurs regardless time and location (Chatzinikolaou and Ventikos 2011). These elements are also obtained using simulation modeling of the corresponding processes (Sakas et al. 2014; Dimitrios et al. 2013)

This approach was expressed in informal basis, in order to ensure that the SMTS will not impinge on the formal intergovernmental process of the UN toward the development of sustainable development goals (The Open Working Group was established on January 22, of 2013 by decision 67/555 A/67/L.48/rev.1 of the General Assembly).

Research Questions

The main question which arises is if tanker operators in Greece are aware of the SMTS and to what extent are they prepared to adopt its goals and actions. Particular objectives of this research are presented below:

1. Emphasize the perception of tankers operators in Greece about sustainability and their alertness to implement sustainable goals and acts.
2. Highlight the perceptional difficulties of SMTS implementation.
3. Contribute to the discussion of sustainability issues with Greek tanker operators.

Historical Background

Sustainability Definition

The idea of sustainability dates back in the 1970s. It was a key theme of the UN Conference on the Human Environment in Stockholm in 1972. The concept was shaped explicitly in order to suggest that it was possible to achieve economic growth without affecting negatively the environment (IUCN 2006). As an official concept, sustainability and sustainable development were introduced in 1987 by the World Commission on Environment and Development (WCED). Even though there is no consensus on a globally accepted definition for sustainability or sustainable development (Jeon 2005), the most renowned definition for this concept is the one introduced by WCED in the so-called "Brundtland" Report (WCED 1987): "Sustainable development is development that meets the needs of the present without compromising the ability of future generations to meet their own needs."

As a result, a variety of interpretations have extended the concept to include mainly institutional and political dimensions or various aspects of life and life systems. Inevitably, the concept of sustainability has become to mean different things to different people. These have made the terms of sustainability and sustainable development, to a large extent, subjective, and user-defined (Keiner 2004).

The 2005 World Summit on Social Development identified sustainable development goals, such as economic development, social development, and environmental protection (UN 2005). These three goals are forming the so-called three pillars of sustainability. A fashionable way of expressing these three pillars is known as people, planet, prosperity (PPP or P3), where People represent the social pillar, Planet the environmental pillar, and Prosperity the economic pillar. Prosperity has replaced the term Profit (decision made at the World Summit on Sustainable Development in Johannesburg 2002), to reflect that the economic dimension covers more than the company's profit.

The concept of IMO on a "Sustainable Maritime Transportation System"

In response to Rio+20 agreements, IMO began to work on identifying and setting sustainable development needs and goals for the maritime transport industry together with strategies to finance their implementation. IMO presented at the Symposium on (SMTS) at the World Maritime Day on September 26, 2013, its view as regards the maritime transportation system and the role of the organization in achieving objectives toward this direction. The document "a concept of a SMTS" reflects the latest outcome of the internal mechanism's considerations and expands on the idea of a SMTS. According to this document: *"the Sustainable Maritime Transportation System must deliver safe, secure, efficient and reliable transport of goods across the world, while minimizing pollution, maximizing energy efficiency and ensuring resource conservation."*

The official document of IMO aspires to cover the demand set by Rio+20 on specific goals and targets toward a SMTS. IMO on the pathway to a SMTS has started working on the following areas around which sustainable maritime development goals could be set:

- Safety Culture and Environmental Stewardship.
- Education and Training in Maritime Professions and Support for Seafarers.
- Energy Efficiency and Ship-Port Interface.
- Energy Supply for Ships.
- Maritime Traffic Support and Advisory Systems.
- Maritime Security.
- Technical Cooperation.
- New Technology and Innovation.
- Finance, Liability, and Insurance Mechanisms.
- Ocean Governance.

Methods and Tools

The work was carried out in two pathways: a historical background study and a questionnaire study. The findings of these two studies will be jointly presented in the final phase. Other input for information will be also provided from the interview process with an expert in this field Mr. Stefanos Chatzinikolaou, Research Engineer in the Laboratory for Maritime Transport of the National Technical University of Athens.

The Survey

The group of tanker operators in Greece was selected from the Greek-Cypriot Maritime Guide and Marine Information services (MIS). The exact numbers refer to 187 shipping management companies that operate 1.429 tanker vessels. 51 out of 187 questionnaires were received and catered for statistical analysis through IBM SPSS statistical package.

Results and Findings

The historical background main findings are summarized below:

1. The IMO's SMTS document constitutes the first introduction of sustainability in the official agenda of the international shipping industry.
2. Some sustainability activities (mainly technological and operational solutions for improving energy efficiency) are applied. Large companies are more active in this respect.
3. High on the agenda is the issue of energy efficiency. Some sustainability issues covered by the SMTS are well accepted and observed by the industry, e.g., issues of safety.

The questionnaire main findings are summarized below:

1. The respondents (oil tanker operators located in Greece) accepted the SMTS document as a sound initiative toward sustainability.
2. They believe that the introduction of sustainability into maritime transport practice calls for active participation by all stakeholders of the sector.
3. Responds showed that Greek operators are strongly interested in safety and environmental awareness areas of the (SMTS) and have some interest in other areas also, e.g., security reasons.
4. Energy efficiency is considered a sound goal for operators in order to enhance sustainability. It is noted that the SMTS clearly states that the target should be also efficiency beyond the ship, addressing the ship-shore interface.

5. Air emissions reduction strategies are generally accepted and alternative fuels are also considered as promising solutions.
6. It is shown from the analysis per company size that those with larger fleets seem to be more interested in the SMTS.
7. Statistical tests (T-TEST) have shown that tanker operators that use management systems in one area are more positive in accepting a sustainability goal in that area.

The main conclusions from the interview phase are:

1. Sustainability is a sound concept but with many uses and different interpenetrations. There is no consensus on how to define, measure, and assess the sustainability performance of transport systems.
2. The IMO document covers some important sustainability issues of the sector. The IMO initiative on sustainability is sound; however, a key issue will be in the future the creation of understanding and cooperation in these matters between different players of the industry.
3. Many Greek shipping companies are well prepared for moving toward sustainability goals and have experience in working with management systems that observe important areas of sustainability (e.g., safety, environmental awareness, energy efficiency, etc.).

Conclusions-Recommendations

IMO remains the main international regulatory body of the industry. In this sense the proposed SMTS that has already been launched in an informal basis might initiate the diplomatic discussions within the IMO framework. It is acknowledged though, that the collaboration of governments, class societies and other private bodies and initiatives is necessary for the effective spreading of (SMTS) goals and actions in the entire area of international maritime industry. The specific survey for the perception of Greek tanker operators in Greece about the SMTS actions and goals has revealed that this particular segment shows willingness in cooperating with other linked stakeholders for the effective implementation of sustainability goals and actions.

Apart from shipping companies there are also other important stakeholders (such as charterers, shipyards, governments, class societies, ports, etc.), who will have to accept the values and goals of the (SMTS) and be able to cooperate in order to achieve its goals. In addition, if these stakeholders will be in favor to introduce sustainable goals and actions then the creation of an international (SMTS) might represent an effective future project of IMO.

There is also evidence that consumers of goods that are transported all over the world tend to become more sensitive to the environmental and social impacts of products and goods they buy and use. As a result some big charterers have recently released statements saying they will not allow their goods to be shipped on F- and G-rated ships (Carbon War Room.com). It is therefore possible that if the demand side enhances its awareness in sustainability issues the attention will be also transmitted to other stakeholders of maritime industry.

References

Bruntland, G. 1987. *Our common future: The world commission on environment and development*. Oxford: Oxford University Press.

Carbon war room.com. 2015. https://carbonwarroom.com/sectors/transport/shipping/operation-shippingefficiency. Assessed May 2015.

Chatzinikolaou, S.D., and N.P. Ventikos. 2011. Sustainable maritime transport: An operational definition. In *Sustainable maritime transportation and exploitation of sea resources, (IMAM 2011)*, vol. 2, 931–939. CRC Press.

Dimitrios, Nasiopoulos, K., Damianos P. Sakas, and D.S. Vlachos. 2013. The role of open source leadership in developing high technology companies. *Key Engineering Materials, Scientific Net* 543:402–405.

http://www.liu.xplorex.com/csr_shipping.htm. Accessed 12 April 2015.

http://www.un.org/womenwatch/ods/A-RES-60-1-E.pdf. Accessed 17 March 2015.

IMO. 2014. SMTS. http://www.imo.org/MediaCentre/HotTopics/SMD/Pages/default.aspx. Accessed 12 May 2015.

IUCN. 2006. The Future of Sustainability Re-thinking Environment and Development in the Twenty-first Century Report of the IUCN Renowned Thinkers Meeting, 29–31 Jan 2006. http://cmsdata.iucn.org/downloads/iucn_future_of_sustanability.pdf. Accessed 28 Apr 2015.

Jeon, C.M., and A. Amekudzi. 2005. Addressing sustainability in transportation systems: Definitions, indicators, and metrics. *Journal of Infrastructure Systems* 11(1).

Keiner, M., C. Zegras, W. Schmid, and D. Salmerón. 2004. *From understanding to action: sustainable urban development in medium-sized cities in Africa and Latin America*. Springer ISBN 978-1-4020-2921-9.

Sakas, Damianos, Dimitris, Vlachos, and Dimitris, Nasiopoulos. 2014. Modelling strategic management for the development of competitive advantage, based on technology. *Journal of Systems and Information Technology*, 163:187–209. doi:10.1108/JSIT-01-2014-0005.

United Nations General Assembly. 2005. 2005 World Summit Outcome, Resolution A/60/1, adopted by the general Assembly on 15 Sept 2005.

World Summit on Sustainable Development Johannesburg, South Africa, 2002 Report. http://www.unmillenniumproject.org/documents/131302_wssd_report_reissued.pdf. Accessed 11 March 2015.

Strategies in 'Shipping Business Management'

Alexandros M. Goulielmos

Shipping Tactics and Strategies, 2010–2016

Shipping Strategies: Survival Versus Looking After Opportunities?

Shipping tactics and strategies are clearer within a current economic and business environment. We identified first the depression that hit the dry cargo sector, which started in 2010. In a depression, ship-owners' main strategies are: to survive, and to look after 'opportunities.' This last strategy presupposes a 'liquidity[1] strategy' during the previous boom (2003–2008)...Current statistics support this strategy under the title 'looking after opportunities.' Greeks,[2] e.g., spent \$2.30b in 2015–2016 to buy used tonnage (165 units; \$13.94 m average price), followed by Chinese (\$575 m).

Worth noting is that \$65b of ship values were gone in the market in 2015 due to depression, while the very low prices emerged in 2016 for the first time since 1999 (Clarkson R S). The strategy: 'buy cheap and operate cheap', provided owners a 27% p.a. increase in revenue (Clarkson R S).

[1]Banking finance also may be available; but own liquidity is also required for either laying—these ships-up or operate them at a loss or in case banks do not provide liquidity.
[2]The following 6 companies spent the indicated amounts for buying used ships (\$1.049 m): 'Anangel' \$379 m (36%); 'Seanergy' \$167 m; 'East Med' \$165 m; 'Diana' \$129 m; 'Thenamaris' \$106 m and 'Sea Traders' \$103 m (~46%).

A.M. Goulielmos (✉)
Maritime Division, Business College of Athens, Athens, Greece
e-mail: agoulielmos@bca.edu.gr

A. Kavoura et al. (eds.), *Strategic Innovative Marketing*, Springer Proceedings in Business and Economics, DOI 10.1007/978-3-319-56288-9_36

In addition, certain owners' strategy is to sell older and smaller ships; Greeks sold 105 units for 1.17b ($11.14 m average price), followed by Japanese,[3] who sold 104 units for $1.20b ($11.54 m average price). Greeks paid $2.8 m more per ship they bought, on average, vis-à-vis those sold, supporting our argument that ships obtained by Greeks were younger and larger. This characterizes exactly the Greek 'fleet renewal strategy.'

Now, visiting the 'internet sites/company reports' of 17 shipping companies in August 2011—we saw that 11 of them lost about $270 m during the 2nd quarter of 2011. Certain of these companies adopted mainly tactics, under the pressure of losses and of falling profits. This is the reactive strategy we have talked about. The initial fear was the end—2008 depression, but shipping recovered in 2009, and this misled shipowners that depression was not coming…

The Freight Rate Markets in 2016

Freight rates fell at levels covering only fuel costs! According to 'Fearnley's' (Feb. 2016), a Cape earned from $5,100 to $5,300/day[4] (one year t/c); a Panamax $4,500, and a Supramax $5,000. Their full costs were from $14,000 to $23,000/day for a Cape; $10,000 to $15,000 for Panamax; and $9,000 to $14,000 for Supramax. The newbuilding Cape required $9,000/day more. This is the *competitive disadvantage* of obtaining ships from newbuilding market. This justifies one past exclusive 'strategy of Greeks to avoid newbuilding.'[5]

Do We Have Obstacles to Shipping Companies' Growth?

Shipping companies are obviously victims of their ill-timed 'growth strategy'! According to Fig. 1, a total of 753 m dwt had been, (or will be), delivered by 2017 (and since 2000). But this tonnage, albeit, will be not needed![6]

---

[3]Greeks *sold* ships at a lower average price than Japanese, i.e., $400,000 less. Presumably Greek ships were older/smaller… Japanese are the regular sellers since 1970s. Greeks are the regular buyers since 1830. Japanese know better how to build ships. Greeks know better how to operate ships. Apparently, there is a different strategy between Japanese and Greeks. Greeks create a competitive advantage via sale and purchase; Japanese create a competitive advantage via new-building. Who is more right?

[4]The figures vary according to whether the ship is newbuilding, resale, 5 years of age or 10 years.

[5]It is interesting that in the early history of Greek shipping, shipowners who ordered new-buildings were characterized as "adventurers." This is the "old times wisdom."

[6]It is expected, for the world dry cargo fleet, to reach 850 m dwt in 2016, adding an extra only of 50 m dwt by 2017!

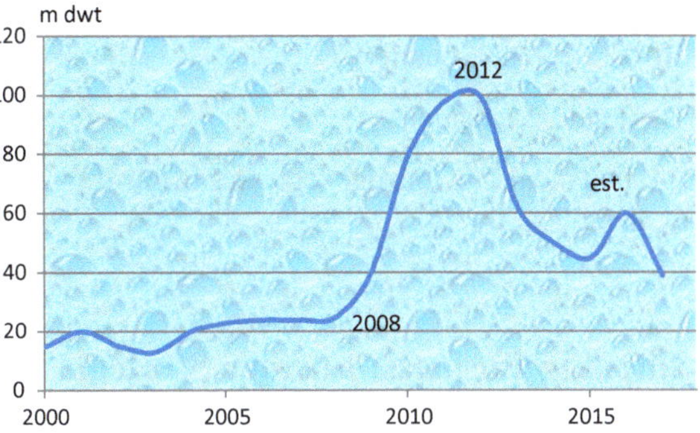

Fig. 1 Deliveries of Dry Cargo ships, 2000–2017. *Source* 'Fearnley's', 2016

As shown, deliveries reached, in 2012, the unbelievable level of 100 m dwt. This of course was sustained by China's growth; but now China, and India—though different economies—decided to slow down their growth!

Regret to say that a 'forecasting strategy' is absent from shipping, because the 2016 slowdown/depression was clearly not anticipated.

Scrapping: The Dream of Every Ship-Owner for Survival

When in a depression, shipowners dream a recovery from 'scrapping'! Scrapping, however, is a slow process; one expects 85 m dwt to be scrapped, between 2016 and 2017, against deliveries of 100 m... Thus 15 m dwt will be round seeking employment... From 2000 to 2015, scrapping removed 224 m dwt, amounting to *1/3 of tonnage delivered...* Hopes thus for a recovery based on scrapping means 3-years waiting; and this on the condition that *laid-up tonnage* is *zero,* which is not (Fig. 2 shows about 2 m dwt to be round seeking for employment in 2013; this is expected to rise sharply in 2016 and thereafter as signs of massive laid- up have been noted in Greek anchorages like 'Elefsina' port). Worth noting is the stop in

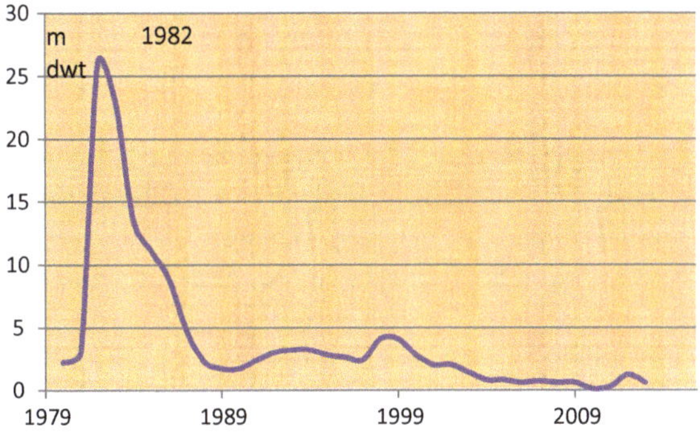

Fig. 2 Global Laid-up tonnage of dry cargo tonnage, 1980–2013. (*Source* Data from 'Japan's Shipbuilders Assoc.', 2014.)

orders, which has been noticed, forced by the *realized* losses, we reckon, during 2010–2016 (first quarter).

The Laid-up situation

As shown, laid-up tonnage regresses below 4 m dwt since 1987, with a rise in 2013 to about 2 m dwt.

Shipping Business: Further Strategic Issues

Do You Want to Be a Shipping Manager? Become First a Strategist or a General!

According to literature, *everything now is strategic* leading, controlling, planning and organizing are now *strategic*. Always research tried to know' the reasons for certain companies' excess profitability and exceptional market success...put in the form of a question: 'why certain shipping companies make money and other do not'? This is an essential question for all industries and for shipping (which has to be answered by Academia...).

We saw Greek shipping companies' strategies to imitate other larger and more successful companies in their actions/investments. We saw also a concentration of shipping companies' activities on what they did best, and this acted as an 'attractor' to an even *higher concentration*. What are or should be shipping companies' strategic aims? Strategic aims are next shown (Fig. 3). A shipping company has (or has to have) a mission, (plus a vision); company's strategy takes into account both company's *environment* and *competitors;* strategy is built on firm's *advantages*[7] and *competencies*; strategies are better, if implemented; important and priority strategies are those leading to company's timely *growth* and *survival.*

Be Careful: You Are Now Entering in a Competitive Environment

The framework of shipping is competitive. Shipping—by the majority of its economists—is considered a *perfect competitive paradigm*. Shipping is characterized by: high degree of transparency, high connectivity, high capital intensity, intense cyclicality, *volatility,* and *unpredictability*. These six ingredients make an *explosive mix* for shipping manager. Moreover, there is the bad reputation of forecasting in addition, the 'opinions differ about the predictability of cycles and on

[7]Large clever Greek shipping companies have a long list of all possible ways to save money/cut costs during operations under a depression.

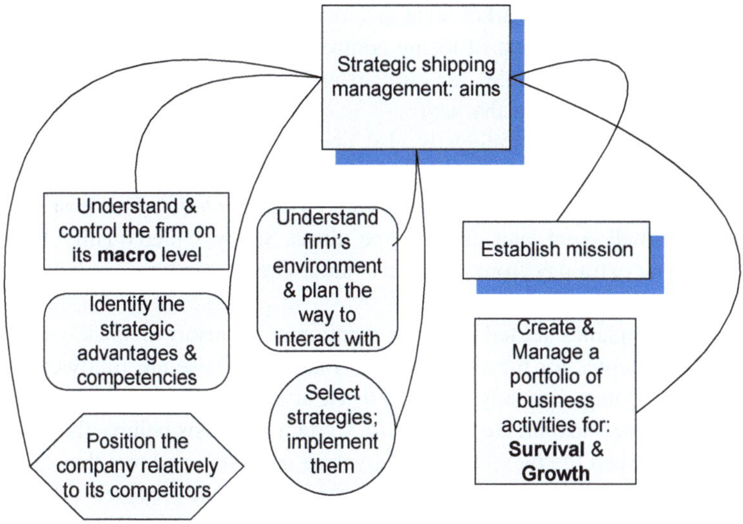

Fig. 3 Aims of strategic shipping management

the reliance that can be placed on forecasting'. One secret of competitive markets that few economists declare is that price can be determined in any place in the Supply and Demand quadrant.

Separation of Shipping Strategies in 'Traditional' and 'Modern'

Shipping strategies can be distinguished in: *traditional* and *modern*. The first, seeks to maximize *the number of ships and/or the amount of tonnage owned*. Ships are obtained mainly from the second hand market (but not exclusively). In addition, the strategy is to obtain[8] *larger* and *younger* ships, at rock bottom prices, if possible above the 5 years of age. The dominant strategy behind the above is surely the '*provision of services at the lowest cost possible*[9] ("*cost-leadership*"), using also timing' ('*timing of the decisions*'[10]). Here-in also we classify *the 'family-run' shipping companies.*

As a rule, traditionalists operate their tonnage 'in-house,' caring *personally* about crewing, maintenance, storing, provisioning, insurance, chartering and post

[8]This does not mean that these companies do not consider types, sizes and markets unknown to them hitherto like product carriers, VLCCs, ULCCs, LNGs, LPGs, and large Containerships.

[9]This is primarily sought after through lower *capital cost*, which covers from 30% to 50% of total cost.

[10]Goulielmos and Goulielmos (2009) have shown *that right timing* means *right forecasting*....

fixture. They also have a 'market identity', meaning a feel on freight markets and at the same time having the fear of losing control over the destiny of their ships. This fear keeps shipping companies far away from stock exchanges, where ownership can be lost from an hour to the next.

The 'Asset-playing'[11] strategy is also applied within the renewal strategy of companies (including 'asset-playing' with new buildings using the 'option orders'). As a result, the *strategy to compete is by the 'cost advantage'*. This cost strategy is attributed to 'small-sized' and 'family-type' firms. Safety, called quality, has also to be offered at no extra pay from charterers' side. Greek shipping, we believe, is the best archetype of the above strategy.

Shipping companies started also—as mentioned- to resort to stock exchanges.[12] We call the strategies for these companies 'modern.' These are followed by those who want a shipping company *publicly listed* and *managed by professionals*; and having *no focus on maximizing ownership*. Certain scientists believe that there is an *antagonism* between the two—traditional versus modern—and that the second tries to replace the first. We believe that there is room for all, provided they can beat competition. The modern is supposed to create larger companies, superior competitive advantages, accessibility to new capital, integrity,[13] timeliness, financial accuracy and reporting, higher profitability, and higher success…

[11]'Asset playing' per se cannot be easily distinguished from 'speculation.' Certain maritime economists use the time duration an asset is kept in-house before she is sold as the criterion of genuine asset-playing… Asset-playing has a different substance among different types of vessels and over time: for an LNG e.g. (147,000 cm) the price rose from $190 m to 218 in 2 years (2004–2006); for a Panamax (dry bulk) it was $34 all along. The first is only prone to asset-playing. This means that values must fluctuate to be suitable for asset playing.

[12]From 30,000 shipping companies only about 200 are listed, if our calculations are correct (data from 'Tradewinds').

[13]Many characteristics of these are due to the fact that the company is listed.

How Do Dry Bulk Freight Levels Affect Minor Dry Commodity Trade and Shipping Marketing During Economic Recession Periods?

Konstantina Athanasiou

Introduction

The aim of this research project is to explore in which manner and at what degree dry bulk freight levels affect minor dry commodity parcel sizes and shipping marketing during periods of economic recession.

This is when every enterprise, regardless of economic sector, is trying to minimize costs and maintain competitive advantage. In this context, enterprises with more robust financial standing may be able to maintain or even increase trade volume and subsequent parcel size, so as to benefit from economies of scale. Thus, apart from their own means and microeconomic decisions, could the reduced freight rates lure traders to increase parcel size and overall trade volume, shift mode of transport, and develop new requirements for the carrier?

Data Sources and Methodology

In order to explore how dry bulk freight levels affect commodity parcel sizes and shipping marketing during economic recession periods, attempts of establishing strong correlation between the two coefficients will be made, targeting to validate the empirical hypothesis that attractive freight rates would contribute to an extend in shipment size augmentation that ensures economies of scale. Data collected refer to parcels of the aforementioned commodities shipped by P Group, a commodity trading group of companies, during the last eight (8) years (2008–2016) of involvement in a high shipping density sector, with non-randomized samples

K. Athanasiou (✉)
Shipping, Transport and Logistics Department, Business College of Athens, Athens, Greece
e-mail: keathanasiou@hol.gr

A. Kavoura et al. (eds.), *Strategic Innovative Marketing*, Springer Proceedings in Business and Economics, DOI 10.1007/978-3-319-56288-9_37

facilitating quantitative analysis. As of marketing section, data are yielded by a non-randomized questionnaire distributed to the personnel of Freight Trading Dept. All data are distributed by consent of the Board of Directors and Freight Trading Department senior management.

Data Discussion

Nature of Demand

As an empirical observation, the frequency of orders for a soft trading house would remain practically stable, and the only changeable factor would be the parcel size, as a result of lower total demand. In the same context, and also due to specific requirements of these niche trades, the trade routes have remained more or less unchanged through the years, contributing to uniform lead times and cost distribution between orders placement.

Notwithstanding the above constant frequency of the trade, the initial response of the commodity traders was to develop a Just In Time policy, with smaller and more frequent parcels, as the purchasing and stocking ability had decreased anyway, and the freight market had been in historically low levels, making exposure to it less costly than exposure to inventory maintenance. Also, this system seemed more convenient in markets with low potential of demand forecasting as a result of high product diversification and variability.

Parcel Size as Per Combes Model and Internal Economies of Scale

Indeed, crisis seemed to prolong, and many commodity buyers seemed to make relevant adjustment to their logistic and financial policies. Also, the slump in storage spaces values as real estate and the lowering of warehousing services asking prices made again higher exposure to freight market a not so attractive choice. Contributing to this need for change of strategy has always been the fact that even in turbulent freight markets; the cost of transportation for commodities with specific handling requirements is generally higher. Also, possibly positive outlook of freight market could make overall freight rates increase. Additionally, a Just In Time order policy needs an in-depth design, feedback, troubleshooting, and a Total Quality System in order to avoid variability and subsequent errors that create a greater need for safety stock. If all the above are taken into account, it is yielded that up to a point, which is up to every individual company to decide and calculate, the cargo transportation expenses are disproportional to the value of shipment. As an extension to Combes model, economies of scale dictate that the cost of transportation is—in theory—inversely proportional to the parcel size. The above statement may in fact affect the whole fiscal and logistics incurred costs, and if economies of scale are not achieved, companies cannot take advantage of the difficult market conditions as said in the literature. So, as a result of the trade-off between inventory and freight costs, parcel size should increase.

The Role of Discounted Freight Rates

Determining the optimum parcel size can be very challenging, as the actual optimum points of internal economies remain obscure. Deviations occur by unexpected circumstances and subsequent costs, such as claims, failure in demand prediction and client satisfaction, seasonality of traded goods, etc. However, discounted freight rates are regarded as an immediate, tangible solution for costs reduction for traders. These, mostly due to the carrier's economies of scale, are mostly evident if mode of transport changes, as depicted below (darker shades containerized, lighter bulk): (Figs. 1, 2, 3).

If distributions are observed closely, it is clear that most shipments exceed vessel load. Even a higher freight asked for full deadweight capacity exploitation and/or dangerous cargo handling can be 95% cheaper per ton on average for the three

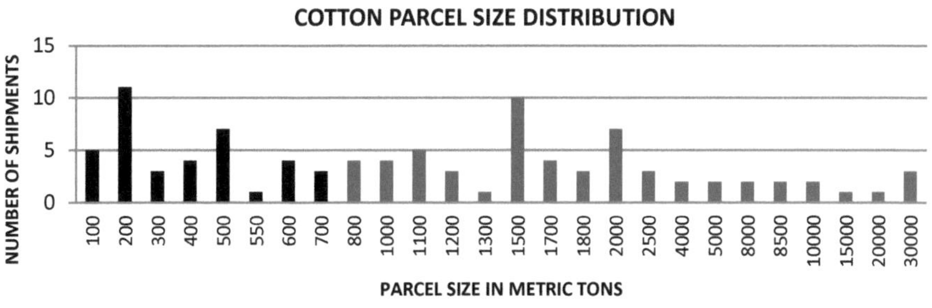

Fig. 1 Cotton PSD (2008–2016)—(*Source* P Group, compiled by the author)

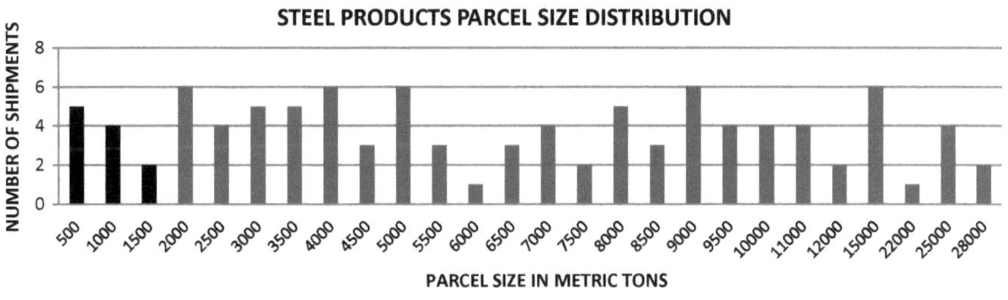

Fig. 2 Steel products PSD (2008–2016)—(*Source* P Group, compiled by the author)

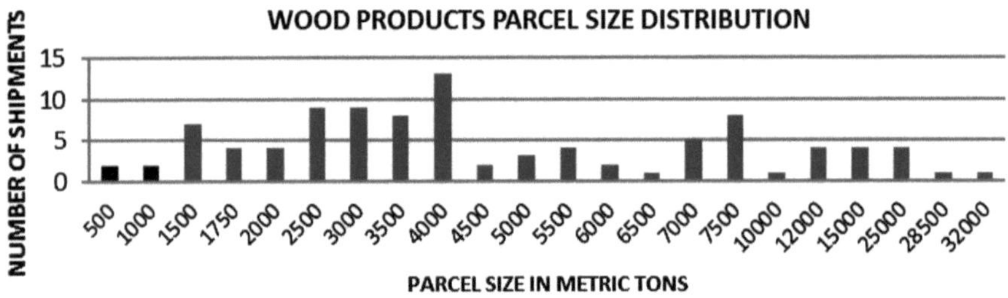

Fig. 3 Wood PSD (2008–2016)—(*Source* P Group, compiled by the author)

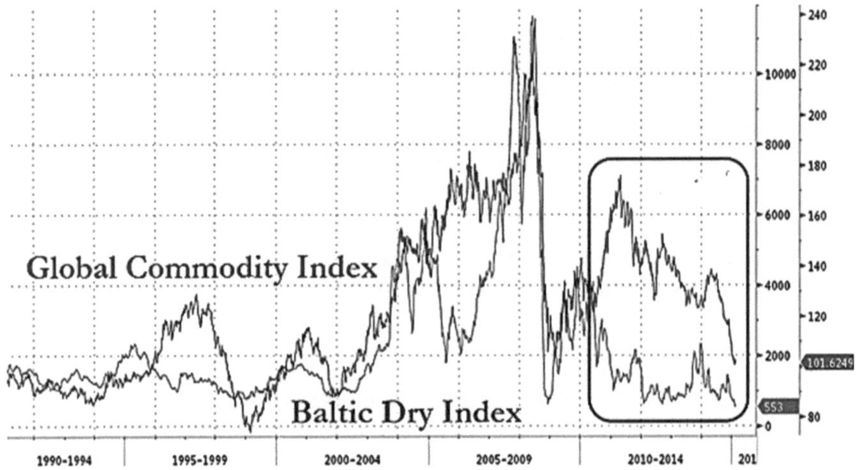

Fig. 4 BDI outgrows global commodity index (*Source* P Group, market research, 2016)

commodities, compared to that transported with a container. Cotton, as a Class 4 IMDG Cargo, is a typical example, as provided by P Group fixtures database: *For containerized transport, from port A to port B, cost has been about $6.000,00 per metric ton. For bulk transport, for the same route, from port A to port B, freight can range from $50,00 to $10,00 per ton, depending on the market condition, vessel size, and stowage factor* (Fig. 4).

This disproportional fall of the freights may also be well attributed to the oversupply of tonnage that continues to exist, making BDI and subsequently, vessel earning, to plunge even further. This results in the Global Commodity Index (that takes into account trade volume and prices of commodities) to outgrow BDI, making trade growth and value disproportional to increase in freight rates.

The above diagram signifies that dry bulk freight rates can actually be much lower than expected. P Group reports freights to be around 60% below the forecasted levels, especially since 2010 up until nowadays.

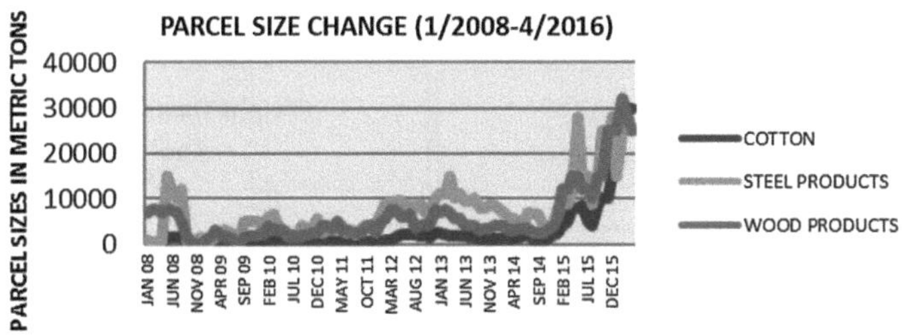

Fig. 5 Parcel size change (2008–2016)—(*Source* P Group, compiled by the author)

A Case of Strategic Parcel Size Augmentation

Looking further to P Group example, given the discounted freight rates, it deemed reasonable that, even under a tight budget, some extra costs could be worth defraying for maintaining larger stock and subsequent facilities. It is not only because of the estimated lower logistics and transportation cost per unit to be achieved in long term, but also the 60–70% lower commodity prices that may yield profits if sold higher in the future, as well as the stable to positive freight rate outlook within the next 2 years, till 2018, are leading the group to desire more exposure to private depreciated/amortized assets than to volatile freights. Toward this direction, P Group made a strategic decision to gradually augment parcel sizes and overall trade volume (Fig. 5).

The chart depicts an uninterrupted parcel size increase trend from the last quarter of 2008 until April 2016 that reached almost 94% from the average low point to the maximum.

Costs Numerical Illustrations

To sum up, the P Group case clearly validates the Grammenos approach that not only freight rates impact commodity parcels sizes, but also tend to contribute to their augmentation during the periods of worldwide economic recession. In pie chart, there is a breakdown of the total freight reduction, which as stated earlier, it reached 92.85%. If 100% is the initial estimated freight budget, then cost distribution is as follows: (Table 1).

If total savings are deployed 100% for purchasing commodity, the above-stated parcel size augmentation is justified. It is also of particular importance that freight rate reduction and subsequent internal economies of scale jointly triggered a 29% decrease in total costs, which was strategically decided to be exploited for parcel size augmentation, meaning that if deemed appropriate, a reduction in freight rates (=1) can result in up to approximately 2, 3 times increase in parcel size, for minor commodity trades.

Table 1 Costs reduction analysis—(*Source* P Group, compiled by the author, 2016)

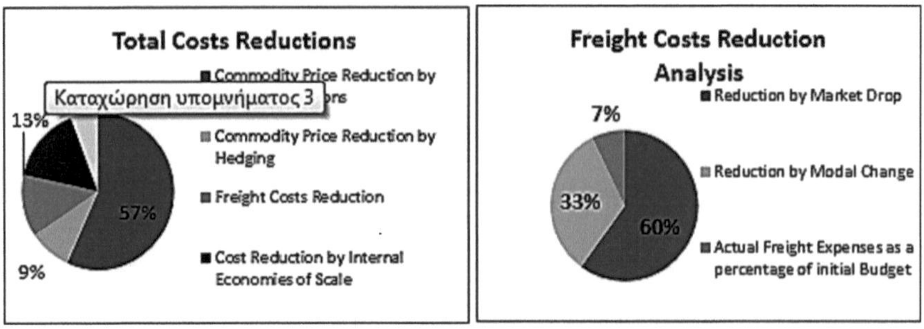

Impact in Shipping Marketing

The concept of marketing has been mostly disregarded by researchers. This is because, especially during economic boom periods or in relation with certain, major commodity, non-niche trades (e.g., Ores, coal, grain), this main deem is unworthy to spend resources on. However, minor commodities transportation requires the increased speed, personalized handling and reliable tracking of containerized transport, combined with cost and space efficiency of bulk transport. As inferred by a questionnaire, in exchange for a freight or hire that corresponds to a niche trade, the expected performance of a bulk operator is of higher standards than average. Being reachable, reliable, and informative, as well as acting as a core component of a supply chain, are the pillars of a modern perception of shipping marketing.

Conclusions

Throughout this research project, it has been validated that minor commodity parcel sizes not only are impacted by the dry bulk freight levels, but can also trigger their increase during periods of recession, by luring commodity traders to utilize savings toward purchasing greater quantities. Also, the impact of this fact on the shipping industry marketing has been examined, shedding light to an underestimated component of the global transportation industry.

Reference

P Group Market Research and Freight Trading Depts. Databases (2008–2016) reconsidered. *Review of International Economics* 7(2), 219–227.

The Process of Employing Greek Ship Officers Onboard Greek Ships: A Proposal for a New Recruiting Tool

Aristotelis B. Alexopoulos and Panagiotis Karagiannidis

Introduction

Greek shipping has a prominent position internationally and its merchant fleet is one of the largest in the world, amounting to 15.9% of the world tonnage, and almost 50% of the EU fleet. It obtained its competitive advantage due to the possession of specialized know-how at operational management level and the ability to operate its ships competitively by focusing on cost control and cost effective technical management. However, a significant part of this success was and continues to be the human resources, both for office and onboard personnel (McLaughlin 2012; Caesar 2015). Even today, elements, like the specific knowledge, the experience, the loyalty, the commitment, well training, and motivation are what characterize the Greek ship officer and make him so valuable to the Greek shipping industry (Progoulaki and Theotokas 2010).

This paper presents a new effective recruitment model that is capable to hire newcomers in order to ensure a constant flow of seafarers to meet the needs of the industry. A dynamic database is designed to encompass all data referring to Greek seafarers having as a target the maximum productivity with the highest levels of safety. The purpose is to identify the hard and soft skills of the personality of each candidate in order to find out whether he/she is fit for the job. To perform this task, a survey among 12 of the largest Greek-owned shipping companies that manage 772 vessels, was conducted (this is more than one-third of all vessels operated by all Greek-owned shipping companies). The survey was based on personal face-to-face

A.B. Alexopoulos (✉)
Marine Environmental Law and Maritime Policy, Business College of Athens, Athens, Greece
e-mail: abagr@yahoo.com

P. Karagiannidis
Shipping, Transport & Logistics Department, London Metropolitan University, London, UK

A. Kavoura et al. (eds.), *Strategic Innovative Marketing*, Springer Proceedings in Business and Economics, DOI 10.1007/978-3-319-56288-9_38

interviews or through telephone conversations with crew managers or managing directors that were responsible for hiring new personnel. A questionnaire was developed that aimed at examining the recruitment practices, what hiring tools are used during the procedure and the attitudes and opinions that the shipping companies hold, in respect of the selection for their applied recruitment practice.

This research is based on the questions set below:

- Which were the usual recruitment procedures by Greek shipping companies in the past?
- What were the problems met during the hiring process regarding the safe manning of vessels?
- What was the behavior and reaction of Greek shipping companies to new recruitment methods?
- How can we improve the methods of hiring seafarers that will meet the current needs of a shipping company?

Literature Review

For the past several years manpower updates, published by the International Shipping Federation (BIMCO/ISF 2010), have reported a marked decline in the number of officers each year, especially in qualified officers from OECD countries. The employment levels of Greek seafarers have declined substantially. The growing size of maritime trade makes them even more important and the shortage of seafarers became a serious issue for the shipping industry.

A lot of factors have affected the seafarers' employment levels in the Greek maritime industry. It is a complex problem with many and different causes. In the recent years, the Greek seamen have refocused their career perspectives. The Greek seafarer nowadays remains for a shorter period at sea. The imbalance between retired seafarers and newcomers is an important issue as well. Concurrently, the Greek shipping industry is experiencing the phenomenon of a gradual leakage of students from the Greek Marine Academies (GMA). Even today most of the personnel working ashore are ex-officers that are transferred to shore-based offices after a successful career on sea or retention. Technological changes have affected seamen's specialties and their relative importance on the ship's production procedure. In parallel, specific operational cost-cutting survival strategies were applied by shipping companies in order to get sustainable competitiveness in seafarers' wages and the high wages of the Greek seafarer due to institutional factors are playing a serious role in their substitution by cheap foreign seafarers. Progoulaki (2007) argues that shipping companies are not socially responsible. They are not focusing enough on welfare of all (shore and sea based) personnel with respect to human rights and for the protection of the marine environment. The fact is that the shipping industry is not so attractive any more to potential workforce, especially to the younger generation. Well-known reasons as bad reputation due to hazards and accidents, heavy workload, long periods away from home and family are becoming familiar through social media to the young people, so the latter, if they have the choice, prefer to work at shore.

On the other hand, Human Resources (HR) makes the competitive advantage of shipping companies sustainable. Consequently, the company must invest in maintaining its hiring policies, its systems and the relationships with its employees by focusing on their value and managing the human element in an optimum manner. In order to keep its HR, the company needs to apply its best efforts to offer a secure environment, to motivate and support seafarers' skills so that they feel as an important part of the company. Selecting personnel is a complex procedure. The hiring methods and tools used by shipping companies should be effective and able to recruit the right seafarers. Therefore, many shipping companies due to long experience have developed and implemented their own HRM systems and hiring processes (Mitroussi 2008). The industry had acknowledged inadequacies in institutional and organizational levels that led to the phenomenon of the global shortage of ship officers. So far the recruitment methods have been proven inefficient contributing to the problem. It is recommended to address issues and to take measures that hinder effective recruitment.

It is evident from the above that the shortage in the numbers of officers does not provide any tolerance in making mistakes during the recruiting process. Although shipping companies continue to outsource some of their basic tasks, the security levels have not improved (Progoulaki and Roe 2011). It has been acknowledged that hiring seagoing personnel based on low-cost criteria is too risky, due to the possibility of causing a maritime incident either related to ship or company. Effective recruitment means not only to attract newcomers, meet the career expectations, and give them a realistic preview of working onboard ships, but also to have the right tools to distinguish even the last potential candidate. The importance matter is not only to persuade the newcomer, but also not to lose him by any wrongful evaluation, i.e., if one seafarer has left his last employer, this does not necessarily mean that he is not fit for a post in another shipping company. There can be a lot of reasons why a seafarer left his former employer. The crew manager must be able to gather and evaluate the importance of all information, sometimes through the contact between companies in order to take the final decision. However, it is considered an illegal process that has been confirmed by all crew managers. Therefore, it is essential to develop recruiting tools that will assist crew managers during the hiring process.

Methodology

The aim of this paper is to examine the recruitment process of Greek officers by Greek shipping companies. Especially, the way a crew manager has conducted an interview, the tools he used for his assistance, how effective were these tools according to his opinion, what were the difficulties and failures he had been facing during the procedure and if he would have changed anything through the used process. The issue of the recruiting process was initially approached with an extended literature review, and further enriched with primary data that was collected by conducting a survey among Greek shipping companies in a 2-month span. The analysis focuses on 12 of the 40 largest (based on tonnage). Our preference was on merchant vessels (tramp shipping and containers), since this environment is substantially different to passenger and cruise shipping. The sample consisted of 12 Greek-owned shipping companies that managed a number of 772 vessels out of a total of 2092 vessels. All the shipping companies chosen were large sized with fleets over 24 vessels each, employing Greek ship officers, having offices in Greece, operating globally, and having at least one vessel flying the Greek flag.

For the requirements of the survey, no distinction was made between ship management and ship-owning companies. The collected data from this sample allowed us to get a good picture of the practices that Greek shipping companies adopt in their recruitment process. The methodology followed included the development of a questionnaire that was used in a structured interview. The survey was based on personal face-to-face interviews with crew managers or managing directors that were responsible for crew management issues or through telephone conversational interviews. The questionnaire aimed at examining the recruitment practices, what hiring tools they used during the procedure and the attitudes and opinions that the shipping companies held, regarding the selection of their applied recruitment practice. We have created a dynamic database that will be regularly updated based on data such as seafarers' personalities in order to gain maximum productivity with the highest safety level. Having in mind different kinds of constants and variables, the development of a flowchart will assist the crew manager during the recruiting process of personnel. The purpose is to identify the hard and soft skills of the personality of each candidate, so as to examine whether he/she is fit for the job, because in the past the usual recruiting methods were too simple for the selection of seafarers. Below we present our model (Fig. 1). These elements are also obtained using simulation modeling of the corresponding processes (Sakas et al. 2014; Dimitrios et al. 2015).

Limitations of the Research

We have come in contact with all major shipping companies for distributing the questionnaire and asked for their recruiting tools and programs, but they denied giving us more information due to companies' policies about private matters. Generally, we observed that the recruiting process is treated as a secret issue between companies, and so only a few companies were willing to share information.

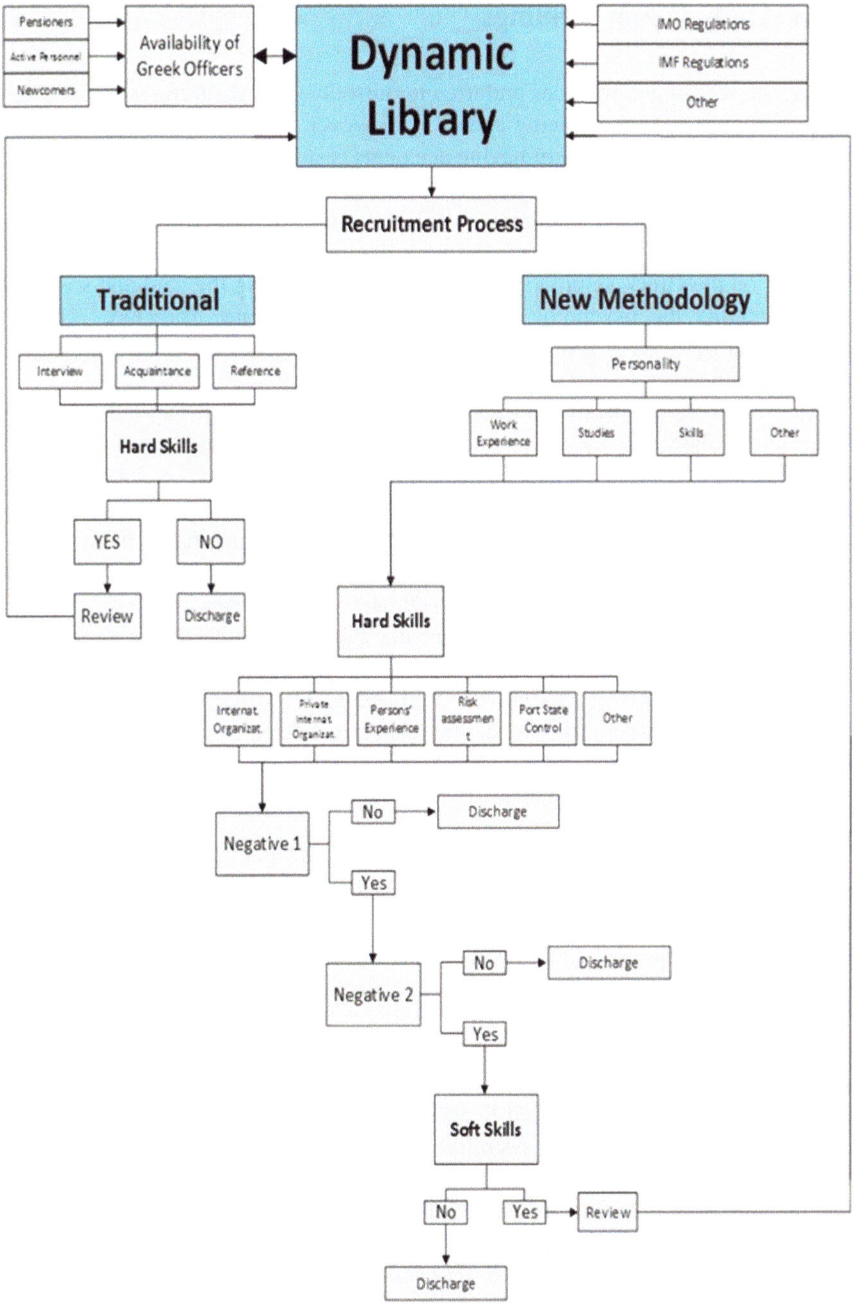

Fig. 1 Dynamic library flowchart

Data Analysis and Findings

So far, the shipping companies preferred to outsource the recruiting process relying on the adequacy of the manning agencies. However, security levels have not been improved and the possibility of having accidents is still high. In our research, we are focusing on cost reduction through more effective proactive evaluation measures during the hiring process. In other words, by taking tailor made measures that aim at satisfying safety levels, we have created a decision support system (DSS) model focusing on the Greek shipping officers and by highlighting the hard and soft skills and evaluating the psychological profile of the candidate. Therefore, we have conducted a survey that showed almost all crew managers follow the same path of recruiting officers.

The Greek ship officer approaches the shipping company through references from other colleagues, by acquaintances or presenting himself to the company by providing his CV. After the first contact, if he is an experienced seafarer he will be interviewed by the crew manager and later by the relevant department manager. The decision will be taken by the crew manager based on the outcome of the interview, on the CV and appearance of the candidate and on the opinion of the relevant department manager. If he is a new cadet, he will be interviewed by the crew manager based on some typical questions, like the reason of becoming a seafarer, if it is his first choice of occupation, family tradition, health problems, etc. A positive outcome is followed by a familiarization procedure. However, the final decision for both will be taken after a trial travel with experienced and trusted officers onboard. In other words, the decision is more based on the experienced eye of the crew manager and the general hard skills, rather than on data that refer to the candidate's personality.

More specifically, in our research we have found that due to the insufficient recruiting process and lack of data, many crew managers do not recruit from manning agencies and prefer references from other officers that they trust or even better have worked with. But most of the shipping companies prefer to recruit cadets directly after graduation, under special circumstances first-year cadets are hired, i.e., one shipping company recruits almost 90% of cadets for their crew and according to the crew managers, with this safety policy the cadets are learning their duties long before they are promoted to officers and only if they are sure that they are fit for the job. This approach is perfectly expressed by building bonding relations with the cadet who becomes familiar with company's culture and family-oriented policies; whereas the shipping company from her side must ensure that the employee will remain so as this investment will not be lost. Some shipping companies were aiming at long-lasting work relations with their employed Greek seafarers and offering different kind of benefits and compensations to motivate hem and improve their performance.

Another interesting issue stemming from the survey was that Greek shipping companies employ Greek seafarers not only for ships that fly the Greek flag (ownership), but also on foreign-flagged vessels (with Greek interests), despite the fact that their wages are much higher compared to their foreign colleagues because the Greek seafarer has to pay his insurance obligations by himself. This shows the trust they have in them.

Through the survey we came across varying situations, i.e., one crew manager has developed and used his own questionnaire, another crew manager is using a computer-based software to confirm job competence before confirmation of employment (program named 'seagull'), another company has developed its own computer-based software and another company is supported by a professional external recruiting company (by providing questionnaires, conducting tests, making psychological profiles of the cadets). However, most of the Greek shipping companies rely on the personal interviews taken by the experienced crew managers who usually are ex-shipmasters of the same company and performing their duties for many years.

In addition, crew managers during the hiring process have no information about the candidate there are about to recruit (the only information they have are summarized on the CV of the candidate and the interview). The evaluation is usually based on the external outfit, his behavior, and his answers. They usually get information about the potential recruits off the record, from a colleague crew manager that hired him the last time, and who is usually also an ex-ship master too, but because they know each other so well, getting references unofficially is not always specific and accurate whatsoever. It is noted that, during the hiring process they said, that the first impression plays a great role to the evaluation, i.e., the first thing being observable is their outfit.

By all means, situations such as alcohol-addicted, being dishonest and/or arrogant, having bad temper, lacks knowledge of the basics, lack of communication especially in English, were rejected. However, nowadays due to shortage of seafarers (in numbers) the criteria are getting more elastic, i.e., looking more for personnel that acquire basic knowledge according to their rank and the type of ship and cargo and at least having safety and environmental awareness.

Another case was the approach of recruiting by not posing many personal questions during the interview and making the candidate feel uneasy that will end up in avoiding the company for future hiring. Therefore, we have created a new methodology, a new hiring tool that is based on many and different kinds of data putting emphasis on the hard and soft skills of the candidate, allowing the crew manager to have a more concrete picture about the person he is about to hire. The new recruiting process will be based on the personality of the seafarer. In the beginning, his work experience and studies will be checked and, if he passes the first stage, he will be further evaluated on his soft and hard skills.

The hard skills are the skills that are tangible and can be measured with tests and interviews. All the special characteristics and requirements of the profession and all hard skills required by officers and ratings are defined in detail by the related international conventions, transnational and national policies, joint working agreements (ISM, STCW, SOLAS, OPA, ISPS, etc.), but he will also be evaluated by his professional work experience, his knowledge about risk assessment, port state control requirements, and other issues that a company might think important.

If it happens during evaluation to come up with some minor negative characteristics, a second (or third) evaluation could take place to evaluate the specific issues. After that, a positive evaluation leads to the next level of soft skills evaluation. The soft skills are the psychological and emotional competence that the person has to deal with the challenges in his professional life. These skills are very important when it comes to ship officers, because they characterize the quality of the crew (Harris 2000). The soft skills of a potential officer and rating in our case are defined as: decision-making, problem solving, critical thinking, creative thinking, effective communication, interpersonal relationship skills, self-awareness, empathy, coping with emotions, coping with stress, etc. Obviously, the final decision will be taken on board after a trial voyage, but we believe by providing all these data to the crew manager, we are minimizing to a great extent the hiring of a person that could become a potential danger to the ship, crew, and company.

Conclusion

The field survey revealed that most of the shipping companies are using almost none or primitive hiring tools. In essence, the hiring tool is the crew manager himself. Most of them are retired ex-ship masters having good experience in choosing the new seafarers, but it cannot be proved that crew managers are experts or have vast knowledge in the field of human resources; they are more empirical learning from their mistakes, creating in time their own database of seafarers through references and personnel that have passed the evaluation in test trips, with any risk that this policy implies to safety to crew and ship. Consequently this recruiting tool, although it is not possible to evaluate at every detail a candidate, having in mind that many risks related to personnel may have substantial costs to the ship owner, can offer better information and other details regarding the personality of the seafarer.

References

BIMCO/ISF. 2010. BIMCO/ISF manpower update: The worldwide demand for and supply of seafarers. Dalian Maritime University and Institute for Employment Research. University of Warwick.

Caesar, D.L. 2015. Training seafarers for tomorrow: The need for a paradigm shift in admission policies. *Universal Journal of Management* 3 (4): 160–167.

Dimitrios, K. Nasiopoulos, Damianos P. Sakas, D.S. Vlachos, and Amanda Mavrogianni. 2015. Simulation of generation of new ideas for new product development and IT services. In *AIP (American Institute of Physics) Conference Proceedings*, vol. 1644, 60.

Harris, M. 2000. *Human resource management—A practical approach*, 2nd ed. USA: The Dryden Press, Harcourt College Publishers.

McLaughlin, H.L. 2012. Seafarers and seafaring. In *The Blackwell companion to maritime economics*, ed. W.K. Talley, 321–332. Oxford, UK: Wiley-Blackwell.

Mitroussi, K. 2008. Employment of seafarers in the EU context: Challenges and opportunities. *Maritime Policy* 32 (6): 1043–1049.

Progoulaki, M. 2007. Dealing with the Culture of the Maritime Manpower in a Socially Responsible Manner. Scholar of PENED Programme and 'Propondis' Foundation, University of the Aegean, Department of Shipping, Trade and Transport.

Progoulaki, M., and I. Theotokas. 2010. Human resource management and competitive advantage: An application of resource-based view in the shipping industry. *Maritime Policy and Management* 34 (4): 383–403.

Progoulaki, M., and M. Roe. 2011. Dealing with multicultural human resources in a socially responsible manner: A focus on the maritime industry. *WMU Journal of Maritime Affairs* 10: 7–23.

Sakas, Damianos P., Dimitris Vlachos, and Dimitrios K. Nasiopoulos. 2014. Modelling strategic management for the development of competitive advantage, based on technology. *Journal of Systems and Information Technology* 16(3): 187–209. doi:10.1108/JSIT-01-2014-0005.

Evolution of Logistics Centers and Value-Added Services Offered in Port Areas and the Importance of Marketing

Afroditi-Anastasia Menegaki and Aristotelis B. Alexopoulos

Introduction

The shipping industry dates back millenniums and consequently, so do the ports and harbours where ships would drop anchor and load or unload their cargoes. Through the years the ports had developed and moved from one port generation to another and along with them, the demands of the port users for cargo handling and further services increased as well, until the logistics centres and services provided became one of the key factors in nominating a particular port instead of another. The ports realised that in order to gain a competitive advantage over the global competition, they had to meet the demands of the port customers through the development of logistics centres and by providing value-added services.

We examine the emerging of logistics centres and value-added services walking the same time the path of port generations to present, examining what might be lying in the future services offered in port areas and how can a competitive advantage be achieved through marketing practices adopted by ports.

A.-A. Menegaki (✉) · A.B. Alexopoulos
Shipping, Transport and Logistics Department,
Business College of Athens, Athens, Greece
e-mail: dauntless96@windowslive.com

A. Kavoura et al. (eds.), *Strategic Innovative Marketing*, Springer Proceedings in Business and Economics, DOI 10.1007/978-3-319-56288-9_39

Ports, Logistics Centers and Value-Added Services—A Parallel Evolution

Logistics Centres and Value-Added Services—An Insight Look

The Logistics Centres are areas usually located near or connected to a port, where operations and procedures regarding cargo transportation, logistics and cargo distribution take place by several operators. These areas need to be fully equipped with the necessary facilities (e.g. storage places and warehouses, etc.) and linked by several means of transportation (e.g. rail, highways, air and sea) so as to perform multi-modal transportation of cargoes. Multi-modalism is actually the procedure of using more than one means of transportation for a cargo (e.g. truck–ship–aeroplane) without affecting its unitised form throughout the conveyance, going from one destination (e.g. warehouse) to another (warehouse or final destination).

The Logistics value-added services, on the other hand, are services that exceed the main logistics facilitations such as storage in warehouses and shipping. The value-added services practically increase the initial value of the cargo shipped, thus benefiting the proprietor of the cargo and stimulating the efficiency of the supply chain (Koch 2006).

The logistics centres and the value-added services offered in the port areas had evolved along with the ports. As the customers' demands for further services other than those of the basic port facilities increased, the ports had to adapt, expand and consequently, give birth to the new generation of logistics. Several factors played a key role such as the globalisation and the vast competition that arose amongst the ports around the world. The logistics value-added services provided by a port have become one of the key elements that will attract, maintain and increase the number of customers of a particular line. Yet the question remains; at which point did the logistics centres and the value-added services become a major factor that would determine the number of customers choosing a particular port over another? To answer this question, we need to turn back to the evolution of ports and keep track of the gradual changes on the port users' needs as time elapsed.

A Brief Historical Approach

Port history can be divided into generations, according to the United Nations Convention on Trade and Development (UNCTAD). These generations are characterised by the evolution of the ports in terms of cargo handling, cargo types, port facilities, structure and activities, logistics and services provided. UNCTAD marked the beginning of these generations right after the World War II.

Before the 1960s, where the first generation of the ports began (UNCTAD 1992), the ports would offer only basic services, limited to the handling and storing of cargo, along with some navigational help for the customers with the latter having relations on an informal basis with the port. Back then, the ports were the place where the land met the sea and the cargoes can change their means of transportation. Cargo movements were anything but swift and investments were made solely for the port facilities in terms of cargo handling yet neglecting technological advances. At that time, the value-added services were almost fully neglected by both the port users and the investors.

Things began to change during the next two decades. The ports belonging to the second generation could now accept more types of cargo, and offered commercial services to their customers, whilst efforts were made so as to build long-term relations with the port users (UNCTAD 1992). According to Beresford (2004), such services increased the value of the cargoes. It was then that the value-added services began to appear and the logistics centres started to operate with basic functions being the receiving, storing, palletizing, labelling, documenting and shipping of cargoes. Industrial services, and thus facilities, were developed close to the port area, dealing mainly with products of iron, steel, chemicals, fertilisers, sugar and other "agro-food activities" (UNCTAD 1992).

The third-generation ports were those built from the 1980s until the end of the century. With the rate of transportation of containerised cargoes increasing and the emerging of multi-modalism, the ports started to include logistic activities and formed terminals and centres of distribution, in order to fully meet the customers' needs. The competition amongst the ports is based not only on the prices or the port location as it was before but also on the available logistics services and value-added services provided. The logistics centres evolved and expanded their activities into bonding, cross-docking, receiving, storing, packing, palletizing, labelling, marking, unitising, documenting, transporting of cargoes (Bolten 1997).

Competition and Challenges in Modern Times

Nowadays the logistics centres and the value-added services provide activities that add value to the goods under transportation. Some of the newest such services are the management of materials and inventory, the negotiations regarding the freight, the audits as to safety, the performance evaluation and others (Bolten 1997). Another service provided by the logistics centres is that of Assembly; a semi-manufacturing service that has lately become the reason for the development of the "manufacturing type warehouse" logistics centres.

It is clear that the importance of VAS in the supply chain management has been comprehended to a greater extent. However, according to Professor John Mangan, the competition has incomparably increased along with the global needs for cargoes' transportation, and became multidimensional. There is competition amongst ports in terms of location, either in the same country or around the world; there is also competition amongst the logistics centres themselves and the ones who provide services and facilities in the port. Last but not least, there is competition amongst the different options available for cargo transportation. Ports are now strategically chosen by their users, based on their providing services, and the ones that have fully updated logistics centres are preferred by the customers.

Logistics centres can be found in various types and sizes. In Asia, e.g. a well-known logistics centre is that of the Port of Singapore that deals with huge volumes of cargo on a daily basis. Its advanced equipment and facilities along with logistics services provided to the customers, offer the basic logistics activities yet with limited manufacturing. On the other hand, ports in Taiwan primarily invest on the offers of manufacturing services amongst the rest of their logistics activities. In Japan, the value-added services of logistics are highly appreciated and owing to this, the ports are formed and developed accordingly. One of the best ports in terms of quality logistics centres and services provided, is deemed to be the port of Rotterdam.

It has been argued that at some point, as the logistics centres develop gradually, the value-added services that were considered previously will become simple logistics services. Some suggest that in the near future, the competition amongst the ports and the shippers will give its place to the competition amongst "total logistics chains", thus giving birth to the fourth generation of ports.

Discussion—The Role of Marketing in the Competition Amongst Ports

Wang (2011) argues that both customer value and supply chain value, can be increased to a maximum through marketing of port logistics that are based on supply chain management, with the latter being a type of management that focuses on the customers and achieves swift response to the market through the strategy of cooperative partnership within the supply chain.

Investing on a Marketing Concept that Is Based on Customer Relationship

Focusing on the customers, this type of marketing, also referred to as *Relationship Marketing*, creates strong and long-lasting bonds with important customers and colleagues within the supply chain (e.g. suppliers), so as to meet the demands of each client and maintain them whilst attracting new ones to create such long-term relationships.

Yet positive relations should also be kept in the heart of the firm (personnel, colleagues, competition, government agencies, etc.), so as to achieve a spherical competitive advantage by establishing long-term loyalty of its clients and its internal environment. So, how do we establish such marketing processes at a Port?

Satisfied Customers Equals Loyal Customers

Supply chain management is based on the preservation of long-term relationship amongst the firm and its customers and this can be achieved through continuous customer satisfaction. In the case of a Port, that could mean the need of constant update of the Port's facilities or value-added services so as to keep up with both the international competition and the needs of its customers.

Competition Amongst Port Partners

In a constantly competitive and increasing global market, the firms who compete on their own have less chance of surviving in relation to those who create alliances not only with their competitors but with their partners who play a major role in their firm's smooth operation. Such competition increases both the market share and the ability to adapt to the market fluctuations or customer requirements. Thus, ports could follow the same pattern in order to keep up with the customer expectations, in terms of quality and quantity of services provided as well as value-added services which lead to the satisfaction of the clients.

Satisfied Employee Equals Loyal Employee

The heart of each firm, or in our case of a port, is the personnel; without which none of the operations or aims of the firms would ever be met. Investing on long-term relationships with the port's employees and earning their trust, assures the smooth operation and increased quality of services of the port, as well as the port's relations with its clients. Thus, ports should invest on maintaining a high moral amongst their personnel and increased satisfaction through reasonable actions benefitting the employees.

Conclusions

The logistics centres and the value-added services evolved along with the port operations in order to meet the customers' needs and demands for swift and cost-efficient transportation of cargoes around the world. With the increase in the volumes of cargoes transported worldwide throughout the last two decades, the logistics centres play a key role in the port selection by shippers and the competition amongst the ports of the world.

Logistics centres are expected to develop even more in the future, changing radically the traditional image and functions of the ports, thus turning the port-to-port competition that previously existed, into a competition amongst supply chain systems, in which ports are only a link. To keep up with the customer requirements and the increased competition, the ports have less chances if operating in their traditional way rather than investing on the cooperation and competition. In such way, they can increase their market share by adapting easier to the fluctuations of the market and the customers' quality and operational requirements. These elements are also obtained using simulation modelling of the corresponding processes (Sakas et al. 2014; Nasiopoulos et al. 2015).

References

Bolten, E.F. 1997. *Managing time and space in the modern warehouse*. New York: AMACOM Div American Mgmt Assn.

Koch, U. 2006. Logistic potentials for value added services in port-located areas. http://www.logvas.com/fileadmin/Logvas/Final_Reports_06/3_VAS_in_port_areas_and_derived_effects.pdf. Accessed 1 Sept 2016.

Nasiopoulos, Dimitrios K., Damianos P. Sakas, D.S. Vlachos, and Amanda Mavrogianni. 2015. Simulation of generation of new ideas for new product development and IT services. In *AIP (American Institute of Physics) conference proceedings*, vol. 1644, 60.

Sakas, Damianos P., Dimitris Vlachos, and Dimitros K. Nasiopoulos. 2014. Modelling strategic management for the development of competitive advantage, based on technology. *Journal of Systems and Information Technology* 16 (3): 187–209. doi:10.1108/JSIT-01-2014-0005.

UNCTAD. 1992. Port marketing and the challenge of the third generation port. http://unctad.org/en/PublicationsLibrary/tdc4ac7_d14_en.pdf. Accessed 1 Sept 2016.

Wang, L. 2011. Study on port logistics marketing under the environment of supply chain. *International Journal of Business and Management* 6 (3).

The Role of Marketing in the Shipping Industry in Case of Accidents

Anastasios Georgakis and Aristotelis B. Alexopoulos

Introduction

The main goal of this project is to investigate the accident of Gino (1979), examine what were the environmental, economic and political/social consequences and what were their effects on the shipowning company, and present the alternative scenarios the company could have followed, so as to better manage its operations and at a second phase its reputation. The questions set are as follows:

- What were the impacts (economic/environmental/social/political/company) of the accident?
- What were the company's actions before, during and after the accident, so as to be able to argue that their business conduct is of high quality and, therefore, effectively promote the company's image toward the industry and all the stakeholders?

Methodology

For the purposes of this research project, all literature review is embodied in the data analysis section with appropriate citation. Initially, the methodology of environmental impact analysis (EIA) was used, through a Leopold Matrix (LM). After the EIA was showcased, the company's actions were investigated and compared to an alternative approach that the company could have used in order to better implement the marketing theory in its actions with respect to such accident. Data

A. Georgakis (✉) · A.B. Alexopoulos
Shipping, Transport and Logistics Department, Business College of Athens, Athens, Greece
e-mail: tasosgeorgakis@gmail.com

A. Kavoura et al. (eds.), *Strategic Innovative Marketing*, Springer Proceedings in Business and Economics, DOI 10.1007/978-3-319-56288-9_40

used for the project were of both primary and secondary nature. Primary information was obtained by the author through direct communication with data sources regarding the Gino accident (Liberian Registry, Cedre, EMSA, IOPC funds). Data regarding marketing theory and its applications were of secondary nature. During the creation of this paper, a major limitation was the availability of data for the Gino accident. Information existing proved scarce and, unfortunately, many authorities did not have or have not shared (up to the time of submission) any extra data. Data regarding the impact of cleaning operations were difficult to obtain and cross-referenced (Tables 1 and 2).

Table 1 LM damage caused by Gino accident and cleanup operations

magnitude / significance	Accident spill (bunkers/hull)	Cargo spill	Cleaning operations	Average values
Seawater	4 / 2	0 / 0	2 / 2	2 / 1,3
Air	0 / 0	0 / 0	1 / 1	0,3 / 0,3
Land	0 / 0	0 / 0	0 / 0	0 / 0
Seabed	0 / 0	0 / 0	0 / 0	0 / 0
Flora	2 / 1	0 / 0	0 / 1	0,6 / 0,6
Fauna/fisheries	2 / 1	0 / 0	0 / 1	0,6 / 0,6
Ornitho-fauna	2 / 1	0 / 0	1 / 1	1 / 0,6
Landscape	0 / 0	0 / 0	0 / 0	0 / 0

Table 2 LM for Gino accident

Economy	1 / 0	0 / 0	0 / 0	0 / 0
Legislation	0 / 0	0 / 0	0 / 0	0 / 0
Social outcry	0 / 0	0 / 0	0 / 0	0 / 0
Social health	0 / 0	0 / 0	0 / 0	0 / 0

Data Analysis

Accident Description and Data Collection

Tanker Gino collided with another tanker the Team Castor in the early morning of April 28, 1979 off the coast of France. The vessel sunk at some 130 m deep with its cargo of 32.000 tons of carbon black feedstock, left in her intact (Cedre 2007) and another 1650 tons of bunker oil being spilled after the collision. Team Castor was the giveaway vessel in the crossing situation and was obliged to keep well clear of Gino, according to the regulations of the IMO's convention regarding collisions at sea (COLREG). Some early inspections to the wreck recommended no actions to secure the cargo off the vessel (Hooke 1997), and therefore, it was left within the tanks.

Environmental Impact Assessment

Following the gathering of the data, the LM was constructed in order to quantify the findings and allow for their evaluation. We see that, at the time of occurrence, Gino was not a considered a threat to the environment. The bunkers spilled were quickly cleaned by the action of 17 French Navy vessels and further research at the place of the wreck showed some limited contamination to the seabed affecting flora and fauna. As a result, France decided not to commence cargo collection operations, releasing the owner of any liability regarding the accident and therefore not claiming for the IOPC funds' liability amount of 3 million USD.

The accident caused no heavy consequences to the environment, nor did it cause any social, political/regulatory, or economic reactions. It was conceived as a non-dangerous event and Gino's wreck was left to lie at the 130 m depth seabed at a distance of 30 nm from Ushant Island (Hooke 1997). However, could the company have done something in order to avoid the accident, or right after the accident in order to more efficiently resolve the situation and at the same time, promote a good image towards its customers? Undoubtedly, if it had occurred nowadays, global outcry would have fallen upon the company. So what is the correct approach in a marketing perspective for a company toward the issue of safety of navigation?

Marketing in the Shipping Industry

Existing Regulations

According to IMO's MARPOL convention and the US law OPA 1990, shipping companies should take operational precautions when it comes to transportation of cargoes that are dangerous for the environment in case of an accident. Such measures include the company's and coastal states' proactive preparations in an event of an accident, in a proactive way—by setting construction standards, on board safety routines, traffic separation schemes, crew training for both the everyday activities on board, as well as, in case of emergencies. In addition, in the event of oil pollution due to operational issues, specific requirements have been introduced (oily water separator for the discharges of bilge water, etc.) in order to reduce to the minimum such pollution. In case of marine pollution due to a maritime accident, the IMO's OPRC convention of 1990 provides a framework designed to facilitate international cooperation and mutual assistance in preparing for and responding to major oil pollution incidents and requires states to plan and prepare national contingency systems (NCS) for pollution response in their respective countries, and by maintaining adequate capacity and resources to address oil pollution emergencies. Such a tool, not only provides for each state to prepare for a maritime accident but also enhances cooperation between different states and promotes the creation of bilateral and multilateral agreements to secure cooperation in such an event.

Apart from individual States, though, shipping companies have the obligation not only to comply with MARPOL, STCW, COLREG, and other IMO conventions' requirements, but should be prepared to act—when needed—in a prompt reliable and efficient manner. In the case of the Gino accident, the operating company (Maritime overseas Corporation) had no reaction to the event of the collision with the other tanker (Team castor). What was worth-founding through research, was that the collision proved to be the result of human error originating from both vessels, i.e., the Team Castor had ignored COLREG regulations and took no action to avoid the collision) and regarding Gino the second officer did not alert the master on time and took no measure as to proactively protect the vessel from the collision. Also the vessel was heading for the Ne lane in the Ushant Traffic separation scheme, which should not have been the correct lane according to the cargo she was carrying (see Annex1 App1 cargo). After the collision, neither the crew nor the top-level management of the company had contacted the relevant authorities of France or UK (following the distress message sent by Gino's radio officer, the French Navy in collaboration with British authorities, sent 17 vessels with chemicals to treat the fuel oil remaining in the surface, while a submarine was ordered to research the wreck of Gino).

Taking into consideration that the accident occurred in 1979, only 1 year after the major disaster, in terms of quantity of oil lost, of the Amoco Cadiz (1978), that raised global concerns, the company could have implemented such procedures, in order to be ready in case one of her vessels being involved in an accident (as it happened) and dealing with it under a professional and prudent way that could be set as an example to follow by showing a good will from the company.

Using Marketing Tools During and Before an Accident

Placing Gino's accident in our days, one may realize that, in order for a company to comply with the existing regulations, as well as attract new customers and keeping a good accident record, specific actions can be used. According to empirical information as presented by Plomaritou (2006) "The largest tanker companies know that the charterers' requirements are orientated towards safety and so they have adopted the philosophy of social marketing," which is interpreted, according to Kotler (2001) as the adoption, by the company, of the duty to investigate its clients' needs and fulfill them in a higher degree than the competition, always paying attention to the environment. Taking the above into consideration, we can propose the following two categories of actions to be adopted by the company's social marketing.

The first category is the proactive actions. Such actions are the ones that the company needs to incorporate into its everyday operations and management practices, so as to make sure that everyone is well trained, educated, and prepared to handle such maritime accidents and create a safeguarding procedure that evaluates risks of operations and improves them in order to minimize such risk. Therefore, in order for a company to proactively promote safety into its operations, the use of risk management is suggested. That way, near miss situations are evaluated and lessons are learned in order to avoid such occurrences in the future. In addition, vessel maintenance should be of major importance, in order to guarantee the seaworthiness of vessels and its safety standards.

Human error is one of the most common causes of maritime accidents. In order for this to be countered, companies should focus on educating and training seafarers for both normal onboard operations as well as emergency situations and crisis management. Companies should establish detailed emergency plans and train their crews to be able to handle extreme situations (fire, collision, etc.). Such plans and training shall be tested by external and internal audits in order to make sure that in case of need, the company, the vessel and the crew will know what to do, and actually do it correctly. In order for a company to proactively face the risk of a maritime incident, they shall establish cooperation with local response teams and antipollution service providers, preferably within the territorial limits of their operation.

Having information regarding available resources, i.e., response teams, contact details and having cooperated with them in the creation of contingency plans, is the major prerequisite for the prompt response in case it is needed. Furthermore, companies can broaden their levels of cooperation, not only locally, but also to a broader degree. Establishing channels of communication with port state control authorities will provide not only for the gathering of important information regarding safety requirements and procedures but also for a smoother cooperation between the company and the port state authorities both in normal and emergency conditions.

The second category is the company's reactive actions. Here, the role of training and beforehand preparation is important. If an accident has occurred, all the internal procedures need to be followed in a timely manner. Communication should be fast and accurate both internally (between vessel and company) and externally (between company and response teams or between crew and authorities). The important thing during the course of an accident is that everything is handled safely and timely. The next step is when the company shall investigate the consequences of the accident and make all the appropriate adjustments to their safety management system (SMS) so that similar events do not occur in the future (Parsotaki and Alexopoulos 2016).

Conclusion

It is acknowledged that, in the event of a maritime incident, especially in the case of serious oil pollution, social pressure, usually through media coverage, is put against shipping companies. Such conditions may result in a company's brand name and reputation to suffer great damages. In addition, the clients of tanker companies (rather a small number in this market, i.e., oil companies) consider the elements of safety and green shipping as of major importance. There is no doubt that, by using the social marketing philosophy, shipping companies try to keep their safety standards at a maximum level, in order to maintain their client numbers and at the same time comply with the existing legislative framework. These elements are also obtained using simulation modeling of the corresponding processes (Nasiopoulos et al. 2013; Sakas et al. 2013).

References

Cedre. (2007). Gino/Team Castor. http://wwz.cedre.fr/en/Our-resources/Spills/Spills/Gino-Team-Castor. Accessed 12 Aug 2016.

Dimitrios, Nasiopoulos K., Damianos P. Sakas, and D.S. Vlachos. 2013. The contribution of dynamic simulation model of depiction of knowledge, in the leading process of high technology companies. *Key Engineering Materials, Scientific Net* 543 (2013): 406–409.

Hooke, N. 1997. Maritime casualties 1963–1996, 2nd ed., 244. London: LLP.

Kotler, P. 2001. *Marketing management, millennium edition*, 10th ed., 107. New Jersey: Pearson Custom Publishing.

O'Sullivan, A. 1978. The Amoco Cadiz oil spill. *Marine Pollution Bulletin* 9 (1): 123–128.

Parsotaki, A., and A.B. Alexopoulos. 2016. Are Greek-Tanker operators aware of IMO's sustainable maritime transportation system and willing to follow its goals and actions? In *5th international conference on strategic innovative marketing, IC-SIM*, 23–26 Sept 2016.

Plomaritou, E. 2006. The key stages of marketing implementation in shipping companies: An empirical research of marketing implementation in the largest tanker and liner companies in the world. http://citeseerx.ist.psu.edu/viewdoc/download?doi=10.1.1.126.6816&rep=rep1&type=pdf. Accessed 30 Aug 2016.

The Commercial and Economic Effects of Fuel Additives in the Maritime Industry in a Heavily Environmentally Regulated Market

Jason Merkouris–Stylopoulos and Aristotelis B. Alexopoulos

Introduction

Today, in the era of global environmental awareness, major instability in fuel costs and unpredictability of regulations, the shipping industry seems to be on the verge of drastically changing directions. However, due to the difficulty of such legal action (ignoring or even denying IMO's legislation), shipowners today have found themselves in a position, where they are forced to make blind choices in relation to compliance with upcoming regulations and be ready for the future. International and national regulations are starting to push owners to reduce the limits of vessels' air pollution but at the same time creating more costs in an already collapsed market that is still not showing any clear signs of recovery.

These changes became very rapid let alone that there are several, still uncertain or experimental choices, of how to cope with these requirements, the shipping industry seems to be unable to move towards one solution that can be viable. The last decade has seen up to present two types of tiers of engines for new-buildings (IMO 2016), two reductions of sulfur emissions in a global scale (IMO 2016) and two reductions in ECA zones (IMO 2016) with intervals of change of almost 1 per year, as well as many changes in local regulations. For less consumption in fuel and thus limiting emissions in recent years, the shipping industry saw the introduction of the shaft generators (MAN Desel & Turbo 2013), the so-called "ECO ships" with more sophisticated aerodynamic and hydrodynamic design (BIMCO 2016), LNG

J. Merkouris–Stylopoulos (✉)
Shipping, Transport and Logistics Department,
Business College of Athens, Athens, Greece
e-mail: jasonmercury@gmail.com

A.B. Alexopoulos
Marine Environmental Law and Maritime Policy,
Business College of Athens, Athens, Greece

A. Kavoura et al. (eds.), *Strategic Innovative Marketing*, Springer Proceedings in Business and Economics, DOI 10.1007/978-3-319-56288-9_41

powered vessels (DNV GL 2016) as well as many other solutions that are still in an experimental stage.

With fuel prices fluctuating heavily, a market condition that barely gives OPEX revenues and none of the above-mentioned innovations being able to guarantee any return in the excess value of the investment, shipowners are very reluctant in making any long-term investments and this even more narrows the whole industry's will and ability to invest in research and development, creating a vicious cycle that is also responsible, along with other factors, of this prolonged and deep recession. However, apart from the long-term solutions presented right above, in recent years we have also noticed a major increase in the fuel additives market that has begun to focus more and more in making the existing fleet more efficient, more economical, and more environmentally friendly. This emerging market in global shipping is offering a brief breath of hope for some shipowners to economically survive a bit longer until the industry's direction becomes clearer (Parsotaki and Alexopoulos 2016).

This research paper aims to clearly address current and upcoming regulations in relation to commercial and economic effects of fuel additives in the shipping industry, quantify the costs that will be imposed to shipowners and charterers (mainly maintenance costs, fuel consumption, sludges, and emissions), and ultimately measure the benefits of using such additives in commercially marketing the vessel.

Literature Review

MARPOL Annex VI

One of the major conventions that is rapidly changing emission standards for vessels is the MARPOL in Annex VI. The changes to this Annex aim to a progressively reduction in emissions of SOx, NOx, and particulate matter at a global level and with the introduction of emission control areas (SECAs) to reduce emissions of those air pollutants further in designated sea areas (IMO 2016). Under the revised MARPOL Annex VI, the global sulfur cap will be reduced from the current 3.50 to 0.50%. This will be effective from January 1, 2020. The limits applicable in ECAs for SOx and particulate matter have already been reduced to 0.10%, from 1 January 2015 against the previous limit of 1.00% (IMO 2015). Currently, the SECAs established under MARPOL Annex VI are: the Baltic Sea; the North Sea; the North American (covering designated coastal areas off the United States and Canada); and the United States Caribbean Sea (around Puerto Rico and the United States Virgin Islands) (IMO 2015) (Table 1).

Apart from the limits imposed by Annex VI the 0.1 standard is already enforced by local regulation in port limits even if such ports are outside SECA areas (ABS 2011).

Table 1 Annex VI sulfur emission limits

Year	Sulfur limit in fuel (% m/m)	
	SECA (%)	Global (%)
2000	1.5	4.5
2010	1.0	
2012		3.5
2015	0.1	
2020		0.5

Source IMO (2015), compiled by Authors

Compliance with MARPOL Annex VI

For vessels to meet these requirements, they must use low-sulfur fuel oil such as marine gas oil. Under the provisions adopted in 2008, ships may meet the SO_x requirements by using approved methods, such as an apparatus or piece of equipment, such as an Exhaust Gas Cleaning Systems or "scrubbers," which clean the emissions before releasing them into the atmosphere (Bureau Veritas 2012). In such case, the equivalent arrangement must be approved by the vessel's flag State that is state party to MARPOL Annex VI (IMO 2015).

Fuel Problems

Diesel engines are built with a set range of viscosities over which the engine can be operated with a minimum and maximum viscosity that applies to the fuel at the fuel injection pumps in running condition. For heavy fuels with high viscosity, the required one is achieved by heating the fuel and for distillate fuels, the fuel at room temperature normally has a viscosity within the specified limits (ABS 2011). Low-sulfur fuels tend to have viscosity near or at the lower limits of allowed viscosity. The main issue is whether they are below that lower limit considering the temperature of the fuel at the injection pumps as such limits vary significantly depending to the type of each vessel's engine. Low-sulfur fuels apart from the lower viscosity also have lower lubricity due to the process that reduces the sulfur which also reduces their lubricating properties. Also another major issue is that the combustion of low-sulfur fuels has an increased content of catalytic fines that can damage the engine (Gard 2007). These facts alone increase the natural wear and tear of the engines but also a common cause of problems is the change over from HFO to low sulfur as the fuels are often incompatible.

Fuel Additives

Bearing in mind that all information presented above have created several expenses to shipowners, such as higher fuel costs, increased maintenance, additional equipment, and fines in the case of noncompliance, due to the big variety of engines' specifications and the inability of creation of fuels specified for the needs of every engine, the fuel additive market is rapidly expanding in the maritime industry creating products that blend with the fuels available in the market and customizing the composition as to better suite individual needs. Such additives increase the efficiency of combustion thus lowering consumption, lowering damages to the engine by increasing lubricity in the fuel, and lowering the catalytic fines by preventing incompatibility of the fuels as well as lowering significantly the production of sludges, something that is becoming a major issue and cost for shipowners and charterers (Innospec 2014).

Methodology

To determine the actual usefulness of such products from an economic point of view, the actual benefits of the use of such additives will be quantified. The difference in consumption will be measured, the rate of machinery deterioration, the percentage of sludge production and the emissions produced. These results will be compared with values prior to the use of the additive as to determine the difference. A cost-benefit analysis will be conducted to determine the economic benefit of its use and at the end the usefulness to the charterer will be determined as to be able to use these features to better market the vessel. These elements are also obtained using simulation modeling of the corresponding processes (Sakas et al. 2014; Dimitrios et al. 2013).

Data Analysis and Discussion of Findings

Experimental research found improved efficiency with consumption ranging from 1 to 3% that the percentage of sludges produced decreased from 1.2 to 0.4%. Also there were improvements in the condition of the engine. To quantify these improvements and translate them to costs and savings, Table 2 bellow shows the calculations of fuel and money saving based on a "worst-case scenario" for a typical 180DWT Capesize bulk carrier as described by the Baltic exchange in the BCI (BDI 2016).

Table 2 Cost comparison

	No additive	With additive	Fuel savings	Additive cost	Net savings
Laden					
Consumption	62 MT	61.38 MT		3.1	
Speed	14	14			
Consumption per mile	0.18452 MT	0.18268 MT	0.00185 MT	0.00923 L	
Cost per mile	$46.13	$45.67	**$0.46**	$0.0005	**$0.46**
Cost per mile in SECA	$86.73	$85.86	**$0.87**	$0.0005	**$0.87**
Cost per day	$15,500.00	$15,345.00	**$155.00**	$0.1550	**$154.85**
Cost per day in SECA	$29,140.00	$28,848.60	**$291.40**	$0.1550	**$291.24**
Ballast					
Consumption	62	61.38		3.1	
Speed	15	15			
Consumption per mile	0.1722 MT	0.1705 MT	0.0017 MT	0.00861 L	
Cost per mile	$43.06	$42.63	**$0.43**	$0.1206	**$0.31**
Cost per mile in SECA	$80.94	$80.14	**$0.81**	$0.0004	**$0.81**
Cost per day	$15,500.00	$15,345.00	**$155.00**	$0.1550	**$154.85**
Cost per day in SECA	$29,140.00	$28,848.60	**$291.40**	$0.1550	**$291.24**

Source Author

Baltic Capesize Description

- 180,000 MT dwt on 18.2 m SSW draft
- Max age 10 years
- 198,000 cbm grain
- LOA 290 m Beam 45 m
- 15 knots ballast/14 knots laden on 62 MT fuel oil (380 cst), no diesel at sea.

The efficiency increased 1%, the bunker prices are at historical lows $250/MT IFO 380 and $470/MT LSMGO and the cost of the additive $21 per liter. Additional discounts given in real case scenarios where not taken into account.

To put these improvements and saving into perspective, in a typical voyage charter in the Route C2 Tubarao to Rotterdam net fuel savings are calculated to be as follows.

The voyage is has a total distance of 5004 miles where 4567 miles burning IFO and 437 miles burning LSMGO. Total saving in the sea voyage are $4567 \times 0.13 + 437 \times 0.81 = \$2481.01$. For a full and complete cargo utilizing maximum DWT the fuel saving are equivalent to more than 1.37 cents per ton. To take into account the savings from sludge removals the following are calculated for this voyage.

Total consumption with no additives is 923.36 MT and the percentage of sludges produces is 1.2% producing 11.08 MT of sludges. Total consumption with additives is 914.12 MT and the percentage of sludges produces is 0.4% producing 3.65 MT of sludges. This is a total difference of 7.43 MT. With a specific gravity of 1.387 this is equal to 10.3 m^3. Facilities in Rotterdam charge €200 + €15 per m^3 of sludges and with today's EUR/USD rate this is equal to \$240 + \$18 per m^3. Savings from the less volume of sludge created is equal to \$185.4 and also it must be taken into account that once one-third of sludges is produces that is one-third of the need to empty the sludge tanks thus the fixed cost of \$240 is calculated one every tree voyages making the average savings \$160. A total of \$345.4 of average savings in discharging operations bringing down that average cost per ton an additional 0.19 cents.

Short Conclusion

From the time charterers point of view such improvements make the vessel more appealing as it consumes 0.62 MT of fuel per day. In a TCT, where there is often an argument on who's account sludge removals are going to be, the shipowner, can be less reluctant to undertake such costs with asking a small additional premium on the rate making both parties happier.

References

ABS. 2011. Fuel switching advisory notice.

BDI. 2016. A history of the Baltic indices. Retrieved from Baltic Exchange, Sept 2016 https://www.balticexchange.com/dyn/_assets/_pdfs/documentation/History_Baltic_Index.pdf.

BIMCO. 2016. What is an "eco" ship. Retrieved from BIMCO https://www.bimco.org/Education/Seascapes/Questions_of_shipping/2013_09_19_What_is_an_ECO_ship.aspx.

Bureau Veritas. 2012. Exhaust scrubbers. http://ntst-aegean.teipir.gr/sites/default/files/forum/exhaustscrubbers_ld.pdf.

Dimitrios, Nasiopoulos K., Damianos P. Sakas, and D.S. Vlachos. 2013. Analysis of strategic leadership simulation models in non-profit organizations. *Procedia—Social and Behavioral Sciences* 276–284.

DNV GL. 2016. LNG as ship fuel. Retrieved from DNV GL: https://www.dnvgl.com/maritime/lng/index.html.

Gard. 2007. Marpol Annex VI—New risks and challenges for owners and charterers. Guard.

IMO. 2015. Sulphur limits in emission control areas from 1 Jan 2015.

IMO. 2016. Prevention of air pollution from ships. Retrieved from IMO http://www.imo.org/en/OurWork/Environment/PollutionPrevention/AirPollution/Pages/Air-Pollution.aspx.

Innospec. 2014. Pre-combustion additives. *Marine Specialties* (5).

MAN Desel & Turbo. 2013. Shaft generators for low speed main engines. MAN.

Parsotaki, A., and A.B. Alexopoulos. 2016. Are Greek-Tanker operators aware of IMO's sustainable maritime transportation system and willing to follow its goals and actions? In *5th international conference on strategic innovative marketing, IC-SIM*, 23–26 Sept 2016.

Sakas, Damianos P., Dimitrios Vlachos, and Dimitrios K. Nasiopoulos. 2014. Modelling strategic management for the development of competitive advantage, based on technology. *Journal of Systems and Information Technology* 16 (3): 187–209. doi:10.1108/JSIT-01-2014-0005.

Part XI
2nd Symposium on Business Informatics and Modelling

Organized by: Damianos P. Sakas, Nasiopoulos K. Dimitrios
University of Peloponnese, Tripoli, Greece

Aims and Scope

The symposium aims to promote the knowledge and the development of high-quality research in business informatics and modeling fields that have to do with the applications of other scientific fields and the modern technological trends that appear in them, such as business informatics, simulation modeling, and business modeling.

Topics

Business Modelling, Business Informatics, Business Model Innovation, Simulation Modelling, E-Business, E-Learning, Business Process Engineering, Enterprise Architecture, Enterprise & Conceptual Modelling, Modelling Methods, Collaborative (Enterprise) Modelling, Business Management, Enterprise & Business Transformation, Methodologies for Business Transformation, Service Innovation, Business Data Engineering, Knowledge Integration, Knowledge Management, Data Science, Business IT, Business Value, Business Analytics, Social Networks Analysis, Social Computing, Tools for Monitoring Risk, Human Computer Interaction, E-Market, Mobile Computing, Service-Oriented Computing, Machine-to-Machine Communications (M2M), Smarter Planet, Information Technology, Computer Science, Business Processes in Cloud (BP-Cloud), Cloud Computing, Security & Compliance in Business Processes, Emerging Technologies, Business Process Modeling, Workflow Management, Model Driven Architecture (MDA), IS Modelling, Open Source, Business Process Management, Modeling Process Architectures, Business Rules Management, Modelling Methods, Languages & Tools, Enterprise Modelling, Business Model & Service Innovation, Data & Knowledge Integration, Model-Driven Computing, Business Economics, Economics of Business Strategy, Global Business, Social Informatics, Business Informatics Security, Management Systems, Social Media Marketing

Main Workshops

1. Business Modelling

Organized by: Damianos Sakas, University of Peloponnese, Department of Informatics and Telecommunications, Greece
Description: Simulation modeling provides a powerful methodology for advancing theory and research on complex behaviors and systems. This session aims at promoting understanding of simulation methodology and developing an appreciation of its potential contributions to management theory by describing the nature of simulations, its attractions, and its special problems, as well as some uses of computational modeling in management research.

2. Smart e-learning

Organized by: Yulia Taratuhina, Higher School of Economics, Business and Management, Russian Federation
Zinaida Avdeeva, National Research University Higher School of economics, Innovation and business in IT, RUSSIA
Description: (1) Cross-cultural multimedia didactics (2) Massive Open Online Courses (MOOC) (3) The principles of the mapping of the personal study pathway in electronic educational environments (4) Best worldwide practices on smart e-learning (5) The problem of choice of appropriate multimedia technology and teaching methods in e-learning for different culture groups (6) Smart e-learning pedagogy (7) Smart e-learning environments in different cultures (countries) (8) Hardware and software systems, portals, and platforms for smart e-learning (9) Smart e-learning: concepts, strategies, and approaches (10) Smart e-learning teaching strategies.

Keynote Speaker

Prof. Dr. Jan Jürjens
Compliance Innovation Lab,
Fraunhofer Innovation Center
for Logistics and IT

Jan Jürjens is Professor, leading the Research Group for Software Engineering at the Institute for Software Technology IST within the Faculty for Computer Science of the University Koblenz-Landau (Koblenz, Germany). He is also Director Research Projects at the Fraunhofer Institute for Software and Systems Engineering ISST (Dortmund, Germany). Previous positions include a Professorship for Software Engineering at TU Dortmund, a Royal Society Industrial Fellowship at Microsoft Research Cambridge, a non-stipendiary Research Fellowship at Robinson College (University of Cambridge), where in 2009 he was appointed as Senior Member, and a postdoc position at TU München. Jan holds a PhD in Computing from University of Oxford and is author of “Secure Systems Development with UML” (Springer, 2005; Chinese translation 2009) and other publications mostly on software engineering and IT security.

Software Protection and Piracy Focusing on the 2008 Crisis: A Comparative Study and Simulation Modeling Regarding the Case of Greece, Germany, and England

John Hlias Plikas, Nasiopoulos K. Dimitrios, Panagiotis Delis and D.S. Vlachos

Introduction

A recent global economic event blocked the path of an economic pillar that strived to advance and sustain our everyday lives and caused a sudden breakdown. That phenomenal crisis is the well-known 2008 global economic crisis that stemmed through America with great negative effects, such as dumping of merchandise and unemployment rate expansion (Bronner and de Hoog 2013). This crisis flood affected the very heart of economic sustainability, forcing a huge amount of businesses to close (Daryanto et al. 2013).

Other scale factors have not gone unaffected. Software protection was not equivalent with the 2008 global economic recession, which supported the florescence of software piracy. Countries with lesser economic power were spotted to be affected the most by software piracy than others. Greece belongs to this category, whereas England and Germany belong to countries sustaining their economic variance in stable levels during that crisis (Gimenez et al. 2015).

Simulations are well known for information and communication technology usage. A real procedure can be simulated, with no real resources needed and no fear of loss. Anylogic 7.2 University is a well-known tool used for this purpose (Dimitrios et al. 2013). E-Views 8 and Regression analysis technique is used in a given sample window spectrums to locate and record certain variables and, eventually, clarify their importance (Jara-Bertin 2015).

J.H. Plikas (✉) · N.K. Dimitrios · D.S. Vlachos
Department of Informatics and Telecommunications, University of Peloponnese, 22100 Tripolis, Greece
e-mail: giannishliasplikas2@gmail.com

P. Delis
University of Peloponnese, Economical Analyses, 22100 Tripolis, Greece

A. Kavoura et al. (eds.), *Strategic Innovative Marketing*, Springer Proceedings in Business and Economics, DOI 10.1007/978-3-319-56288-9_42

There have been only two studies regarding software protection, piracy, and simulation modeling. At the same time, no other study has been conducted so far that shows the association between those factors, combining simulation modeling and regression analysis for the case of Greece, Germany, and England, making this paper one of a kind (Deepdyve 2016). Thorough research through this paper showed that Greece was the country having increased piracy ratings during this crisis, comparing with Germany and England.

Variables that Affect Piracy Rates During the 2008 Economic Crisis and Data Sources

GDP

The level of economic development, Real GDP, shows the possibility of people to demand. GDP Economic Activity is controlled by GDP Nominal and GDP Current. Among software protection dependencies is the financial empowerment which means the greater a country's worth the better the software rights protection (Daryanto et al. 2013). GDP is negative related to piracy rates. GDP per capita in purchasing power is taken from data indicators coming from the World Bank's World Development (World Bank 2016).

Education Level Measured in Years

This variable represents a measurement of a countries potential to adopt a new technology. Years of education is strongly related to education itself, thus the key factors of education are Previous Student Attainment, the Socio Economic Status, Cultural Status, Intellectual Level, Collaboration Adoption Level, and Perception or Insight. A negative relation appears between this factor and piracy rates (Barro 2001). Data were obtained as well from the World Bank's World Development database (World Bank 2016).

Research and Development

A negative relation appears in this factor too, because countries with higher Research and Development (R&D) levels tend to protect in a stronger manner intellectual property rights. In order for R&D to be implemented, Entrepreneur Thinking Adoption must be adopted. In a second stage, innovation will take place giving New Improved Tech and Competitive Advantage (Kumar and Phrommathed 2005). R&D expenditures are taken from the same data as GDP per capita (World Bank 2016).

Software Protection Index

Other known as software trademark index and a combination of civil and criminal codes, Law Protection, and the Level of Quality are strongly related. A positive effect is indicated between this factor and piracy rates (Andrés 2006). Information about software protection index comes from the other known as World Intellectual Property Organization (WIPO), UNESCO which stands for United Nations Educational, Scientific, and Cultural Organization and the WTO, the World Trade Organization (WIPO 2016; UNESCO 2016; WTO 2016).

Dependent, Independent Variables and Monte Carlo Simulation

Piracy rate is the dependent variable. The Business Software Alliance holds national software piracy rates in yearly measurement for eight countries since 1994 (BSA 2011). The independent variables of our model are the software protection index which represents the trademark application variable, GDP per capita in purchasing power, Research and Development expenditures, and education level in education years (Chin 2003). The data that were searched and collected in the databases as explained before.

In Fig. 1, we can see these variables as regarding the three nations that will be analyzed; Greece, Germany, and England, in time window of 1994–2010. Piracy rates is the dependent variable as explained before, Research and development

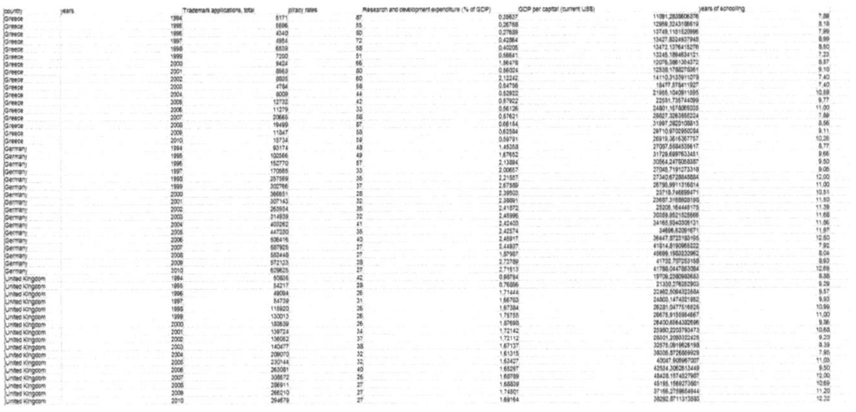

country	years	Trademark applications, total	piracy rates	Research and development expenditure (% of GDP)	GDP per capital (current US$)	years of schooling
Greece	1994	5171	87	0,35637	11091,2838606376	7,89
Greece	1995	5596	55	0,26768	12959,3243188619	8,18
Greece	1996	4340	60	0,27639	13749,1181520996	7,99
Greece	1997	4954	72	0,42864	13427,8324937945	8,99
Greece	1998	6839	58	0,40205	13472,1376415276	8,50
Greece	1999	7200	51	0,56641	13245,1894634121	7,23
Greece	2000	9424	66	1,56478	12076,3861364372	8,87
Greece	2001	8863	80	0,56024	12538,1788276361	9,10
Greece	2002	8835	60	2,12242	14110,3133911078	7,40
Greece	2003	4784	58	0,54756	18477,578411927	7,40
Greece	2004	8009	44	0,52922	21955,1040911595	10,59
Greece	2005	12732	42	0,57922	22551,735744099	9,77
Greece	2006	11279	33	0,56136	24801,1578065035	11,00
Greece	2007	20665	58	0,57621	28827,3263556224	7,89
Greece	2008	19499	57	0,66154	31997,2820108813	8,56
Greece	2009	11847	58	0,62584	29710,9702950284	9,11
Greece	2010	15734	59	0,59791	26919,3616367757	10,26
Germany	1994	93174	48	1,45358	27087,5584535617	8,77
Germany	1995	102566	49	1,67652	31729,6997633451	9,66
Germany	1996	152770	57	2,13894	30564,2475058387	9,50
Germany	1997	170585	33	2,00657	27045,7191273318	9,05
Germany	1998	257569	35	2,21587	27340,6728845884	12,00
Germany	1999	302766	37	2,67589	26795,9911316014	11,00
Germany	2000	366851	28	2,39503	23718,746699471	10,51
Germany	2001	307143	32	2,39891	23687,3168928195	11,50
Germany	2002	263924	35	2,41872	25205,164448175	11,39
Germany	2003	314939	32	2,45996	30359,9521525666	11,68
Germany	2004	403262	41	2,42403	34165,9340306131	11,86
Germany	2005	447230	35	2,42574	34696,62091671	11,97
Germany	2006	506416	40	2,45917	36447,8723183195	12,50
Germany	2007	587925	27	2,44937	41814,8190965222	7,92
Germany	2008	583448	27	1,87987	45699,1983232962	8,04
Germany	2009	572123	28	2,72789	41732,707253158	8,93
Germany	2010	629625	27	2,71913	41785,0447883084	12,69
United Kingdom	1994	60835	42	0,98794	19709,2380983653	8,88
United Kingdom	1995	54217	28	0,76856	21330,276252903	9,29
United Kingdom	1996	49094	26	1,71444	22462,5094323584	9,57
United Kingdom	1997	54739	31	1,66763	24803,1474321952	9,93
United Kingdom	1998	115920	26	1,67384	26281,0477516825	10,99
United Kingdom	1999	130013	26	1,75755	26675,915598467	11,00
United Kingdom	2000	182639	26	1,87698	26400,6564332696	9,98
United Kingdom	2001	139724	34	1,72142	25980,2203793473	10,68
United Kingdom	2002	136062	37	1,72112	28301,2083322425	9,20
United Kingdom	2003	140477	35	1,67137	32675,0919626198	8,39
United Kingdom	2004	209070	32	1,61315	38306,8726889929	7,95
United Kingdom	2005	230144	32	1,63427	40047,905967007	11,03
United Kingdom	2006	263081	40	1,65297	42534,3062813449	9,50
United Kingdom	2007	308672	26	1,68789	48428,1574527987	12,00
United Kingdom	2008	286911	27	1,68339	45195,1569273861	10,69
United Kingdom	2009	266210	27	1,74801	37166,2759654944	11,20
United Kingdom	2010	294679	27	1,69164	38292,8711313583	12,32

Fig. 1 Dependent and independent variables and Greece, Germany, and England for the years 1994–2010

expenditure (% of GDP), GDP per capita (current US$), Trademark applications, total and years of schooling are the independent ones.

Some information values were missing. Monte Carlo simulation method was used in order to close the missing variable gap by multiplying and fill those missing variables with random ones, varying between the highest and lowest value range of each specific variable.

Econometric Model Specification and Analysis Steps

C(1), C(2), C(3), C(4), C(5), will be estimated with C(1) being the constant variable.

$$\begin{aligned}\text{PIRACY\_RATES} = {} & C(1) + C(2) * \text{GDP\_PER\_CAPITA\_CURRENT} \\ & + C(3) * \text{RESEARCH\_AND\_DEVELOPMENT} \\ & + C(4) * \text{TRADEMARK\_APPLICATIONS} + C(5) * \text{YEARS\_OF\_SCHOOLING}\end{aligned}$$

Panel data econometric analysis is used, which explains the chronological perspective of the three nations as shown in Fig. 1 and Table 1. Empirical analysis is carried out to run a simple panel fixed effects regression, selecting the variables using the famous method of Least squares (Chin 2003).

Table 1 Regression results from panel data analysis using least squares estimation method

	Coefficient	Std. error	t-Statistic	Prob.
c(1)	84.30559	12.78404	6.594599	0.0000
c(2)	−0.000583	0.000268	−2.172696	0.0350
c(3)	−13.36137	3.957176	−3.376491	0.0015
c(4)	9.20E-06	2.00E-05	0.461358	0.6467
c(5)	−0.617765	1.369085	−0.451225	0.6539
Mean dependent var	43.43137			
S.E. of regression	12.34089			
Sum squared resid	7005.683		S.D. dependent var	17.89106
Log likelihood	−197.8935		Akaike info criterion	7.956607
Deviance	–		Schwarz criterion	8.146001
Avg.log likelihood	–		Hannan-Quinn crit.	8.028980
Obs with Dep = 0	–		Restr. deviance	–
Obs with Dep = 1	–		Total obs	51

Empirical Analysis of Simple Panel Fixed Least Squares Regression

In Table 1, the importance of a variable factor is analog to the minimization of Prob. Value. The lesser the value, the highest the importance of a variable. According to this, Research and Development factor affects Piracy Rates the most comparing to the other values. Consequently, the negative sign in C(3) factor indicates the negative correlation between R&D and Piracy Rates.

Dynamic Model of the Simulation System

Our dynamic model consists of stocks, flows, converters and connectors. Each of these elements is further described in this section: A Stock represents the accumulation of physical or nonphysical quantity. A Flow represents an activity that fills or reduces a pool. The arrow indicates the direction of positive flow, in or out. A Converter can keep values stable or serve as an external input to the standard or convert inputs into results, through the user-defined algebraic relations or graphics functions. Connectors provide connections between the elements of models. Continuous cable is an action connector and the dotted wire is an information connector (Dimitrios et al. 2013).

Identification and Explanation of the Dynamic Simulation Model

First, t-Statistics were multiplied with "Company_Resources" value to provide the appropriate resources needed to implicate each variable factor (Candelon et al. 2012). In Fig. 2 "Company_Resources" stock, supply the four Stocks around it which represent the independent variables and how they could be fulfilled by a hypothetical company. With a percentage given in "Entrepreneur_Thinking_Adoption" "Innovation" is triggered. A percentage of "Company_Resources" is given in the "Economic_Activity_Control" Stock through the CR2EAC flow. Coming to the "Trademark_Application_Factor." In order to be implemented, "Company_Resources" are given first in "Law_Protection" Stock via CR2LP flow and next resources are given in "Consistent_Level_Of_Quality" through the LP2CLOQ flow. Last but not least, the "Education" Stock. A percentage of "Company_Resources" is being given too. All the previous converge in a certain satisfaction level, presenting a negative relation with the "Piracy_Rates" Stock according to the theory. The "Piracy_Rates" Stock is negatively related to the "Company_Resources" Stock. That can be seen through the red flow color. That indicates negative relation between a certain amount of resources and the piracy rates level. The higher the second the lower the first and vice versa.

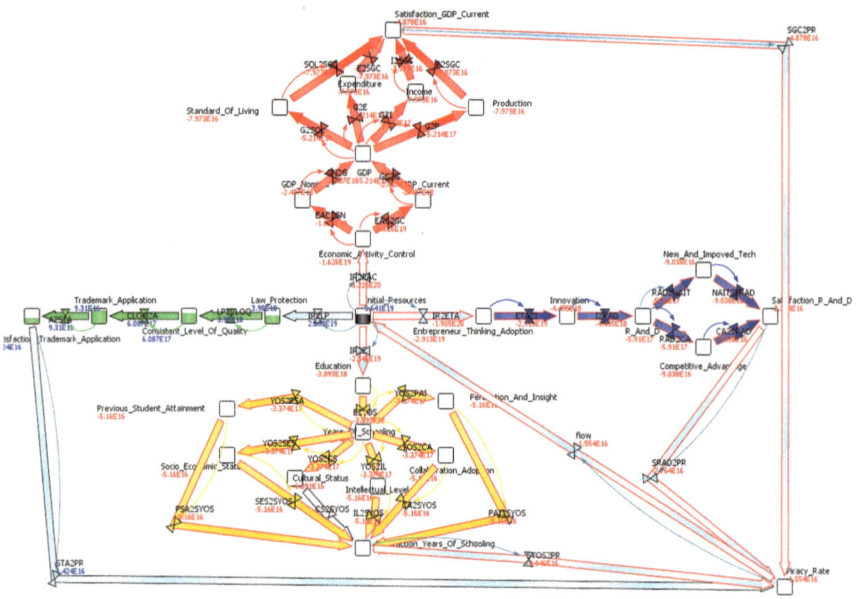

Fig. 2 Dynamic simulation model analysis

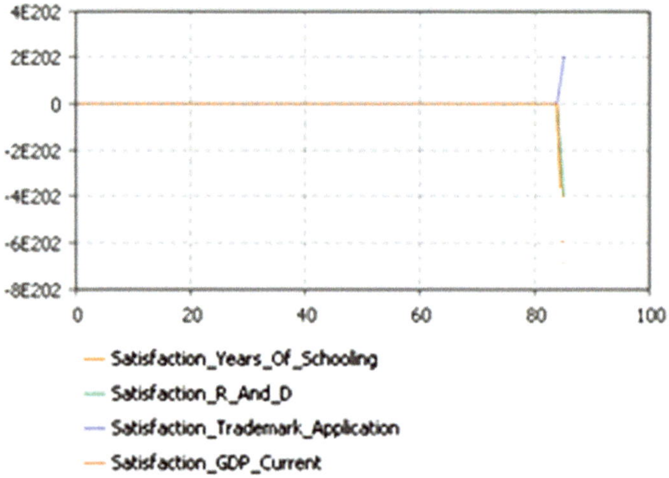

Fig. 3 Time-chart and pie-chart: Satisfaction_Years_Of_Schooling, in conjunction with Satisfaction_R_And_D, in conjunction with Satisfaction_Trademark_Application, in conjunction with Satisfaction_GDP_Current

Figure 3 shows that the satisfaction percentage as regarding all four leading factors is raising significantly during the first months and then they gain stability. Results agree with empirical statistics, showing that Research and Development factor affects with higher negative extend the Piracy Rates factor.

Conclusions

In this research, an attempt was made to simulate the connection between Software Protection and Piracy focusing on the 2008 Crisis, using Anylogic 7.2 University and E-Views 8, and conducting a comparative study and simulation modeling regarding the case of Greece, Germany, and England. The nature of the variables examined is dynamic. Regression analysis is used to calculate the statistical importance and depict it in dynamic modeling. This article attempts to steer the reader to the right direction concerning the influence between Software Protection and Piracy, on the basis of the 2008 economic crisis, using the cases of Greece, Germany and England as a benchmark, by measuring the appropriate satisfaction levels (Dimitrios et al. 2013). Extensive research, statistical analysis and simulation modeling through this paper revealed that R&D has the biggest negative impact in Piracy Rates. The second biggest negative impact is given by GDP Current levels per Capita variable, comparing to the rest of the leading factors. Further research could be conducted on a given software product, the company's objectives and size, as well as the limitations of the firm.

References

Andrés, A.R. 2006. The relationship between copyright software protection and piracy: Evidence from Europe. *European Journal of Law and Economics* 21 (1): 29–51.

Barro, R.J. 2001. Human capita and growth. *The American Economic Review* 91 (2): 12–17.

Bronner, F., and R. de Hoog. 2013. Economizing on vacations: the role of information searching. *International Journal of Culture, Tourism and Hospitality Research* 7 (1): 28–41.

BSA Global Software Piracy Study. 2011. Shadow Market. http://globalstudy.bsa.org/2011/downloads/study_pdf/2011_BSA_Piracy_Study-Standard.pdf. Accessed Oct 9 2016.

Candelon, B., E.I. Dumitrescu, C. Hurlin, and F.C. Palm. 2012. Multivariate dynamic probit models: an application to financial crises mutation.

Chin, W.W., B.L. Marcolin, and P.R. Newsted. 2003. A partial least squares latent variable modeling approach for measuring interaction effects: Results from a Monte Carlo simulation study and an electronic-mail emotion/adoption study. *Information systems research* 14 (2): 189–217.

Daryanto, A., H. Khan, H. Matlay, and R. Chakrabarti. 2013. Adoption of country-specific business websites: The case of UK small businesses entering the Chinese market. *Journal of Small Business and Enterprise Development* 20 (3): 650–660.

Deepdyve. 2016. ICT businesses simulation. https://www.deepdyve.com/search?query=software+protection+piracy+simulation. Accessed Oct 16 2016.

Dimitrios, Nasiopoulos K., Damianos P. Sakas, and D.S. Vlachos. 2013. Analysis of strategic leadership models in information technology. *Procedia—Social and Behavioral Sciences* 73: 268–275.

Gimenez, C., V. Sierra, J. Rodon, and J.A. Rodriguez. 2015. The role of information technology in the environmental performance of the firm: The interaction effect between information technology and environmental practices on environmental performance. *Academia Revista Latinoamericana de Administración* 28 (2): 273–291.

Jara-Bertin, M., F. Lopez-Iturriaga, and C. Espinosa. 2015. Is there a corporate diversification discount or premium? Evidence from Chile. *Academia Revista Latinoamericana de Administración* 28 (3): 396–418.

Kumar, S., and P. Phrommathed. 2005. *Research methodology*, 43–50. US: Springer.

UNESCO—United Nations Educational, Scientific and Cultural Organization. 2016. http://www.uis.unesco.org/Pages/default.aspx. Accessed Oct 9 2016.

WIPO—World Intellectual Property Organization. 2016. http://www.wipo.int/portal/en/index.html. Accessed Oct 9 2016.

World Bank. 2016. http://data.worldbank.org/indicator. Accessed Oct 9 2016.

WTO–World Trade Organization. 2016. Accessed Oct 9 2016 https://www.wto.org/english/res_e/res_e.htm.

Decision Support Systems and Strategic Information Systems Planning for Strategy Implementation

Fotis Kitsios and Maria Kamariotou

Introduction

The latest developments in Information Technology (IT) allow firms to reduce uncertainty since they can obtain decision-making information not only quickly but effectively as well. A central message of the research literature, which is universally accepted, is that the technology itself is unlikely to be a source of sustainable competitive advantage (Leidner et al. 2011; Peppard and Ward 2004).

Decision Support Systems (DSS) are systems which endorse decision-making in planning, problem-solving and decision tasks.

Previous researchers have presented different approaches in DSS, analyzing the phases of the implementation of DSS (Alalwan et al. 2014; Alyoubi 2015; Applegate et al. 1986; Yoo and Digman 1987).

Strategic decisions are typically associated with issues such as the long-term direction of an organization, the mission of an organization, the competitive advantage, as well as the strategic fit with the business environment, the business's resources and competences (Johnson et al. 2008; Dimitrios et al. 2013a, b).

Some main business goals are the reduction of costs, the increase of revenue, the improvement of administrative efficiency, as well as the improvement of service quality, the supply of products and services on time, the increase of competitive advantage and the increase of productivity. Information Systems objectives are needed information in order to facilitate the attainment of organizational objectives, to develop control systems and to improve the flow and availability of information for managers. Furthermore, information is needed to develop applications in light of the systems approach principle, to transfer easier data among applications and to develop systems using most advanced technologies. Other information is needed to

F. Kitsios · M. Kamariotou (✉)
Department of Applied Informatics, University of Macedonia, Thessaloniki, Greece
e-mail: tm1367@uom.edu.gr

A. Kavoura et al. (eds.), *Strategic Innovative Marketing*, Springer Proceedings in Business and Economics, DOI 10.1007/978-3-319-56288-9_43

create corporate common data base in the entire organization to produce accessibility to organizational data base, to confirm data security and confidentiality, and to develop local applications for departmental units (Zviran 1990).

Strategic Information Systems Planning (SISP) is a process of finding opportunities through IT that will add value to the organization, aligning business goals with IT (Zviran 1990). It helps businesses to innovate, create new products, reduce costs, and enhance their relationships with their customers (Lederer and Sethi 1988; Dimitrios et al. 2013a, b).

This study proposes a framework that combines the SISP process and DSS systems in the current changing environment. The specific model is based on previous literature on SISP and DSS and specifies phases that are related to managers making the appropriate strategic decisions. The paper conduces to DSS literature in terms of recommending a model that takes into consideration the phases of SISP and change management, which affects the process of making decisions so that the objectives of the business can be achieved.

The structure of this paper is the following: after a brief introduction to the importance of DSS and SISP, the need for an approach based on this link is presented. Next section includes the description and the implementation of the literature review methodology which was followed in order to highlight the issues which are discussed in this paper. Then a theoretical and conceptual framework based not only on the DSS approach but also on the recommended methods for implementing SISP process, is suggested, whereas the final section concludes the paper.

Literature Review

Literature Review Searching

The steps, based on Webster and Watson methodology, are: Searching, which includes the selection of keywords, databases, topics and timeframe of papers; Backward search, which involves searching of references of the papers; and Forward search, which contains the searching of citations (Webster and Watson 2002).

Searching was done in databases Scopus, Science Direct, Web of Science, and ABI/INFORM using a combination of keywords which were SISP, phases, stages, models, success, innovation, firm performance, competitive advantage, Information systems strategy and business strategy alignment, DSS, change management.

Articles are only in English and are published in scientific journals or conferences, not in books.

Having searched all databases, titles and abstracts of the relevant publications were scanned and the citations and references of the residual articles were then reviewed. A total of 116 articles results consist the final sample.

Search was completed when resulted in common articles from all databases and different combinations of keywords. It was then that the critical mass of relevant literature sources was considered as having been collected.

Articles were classified in three categories according to their concept. These categories were SISP, DSS and change management. Results of the articles supported the creation of the implementation model.

Proposed Decision Support System Model for Strategic Information Systems Planning

Businesses need information for plenty of reasons. Managers utilize information in order to set goals for the business, to formulate suitable strategies and policies to meet specific objectives, as well as to report on the results of operations of the business and to pay taxes in conformance with law. Also, they need information to inform the public of selected policies of the business, to inform employees of various matters as well as to prepare long-range plans. Furthermore, they need information to understand new opportunities and treats, to allocate capital resources, in order to be businesses competitive, to exercise the necessary control in business operations, as well as to define product price and to make decisions about retained situations, when they arise and to learn about competitors (Sakas et al. 2014).

A computer-based system that is used to support decision making is named DSS (Waxlax 1993).

DSS in strategic management includes environmental analysis of gathering internal external information, definition of goal settings such as mission purpose, goals, and objectives and the architecture of DSS such as data base, application programs, and data models. It also contains the strategy formulation, the strategy evaluation and choice, and the strategy implementation planning and control (Alalwan et al. 2014).

This model provides four categories of subsystems, which are environmental analysis subsystem, goal determining subsystem, DDS subsystem, and SISP subsystem. The model combines SISP phases and the DSS subsystems.

The first category includes the definition of the problem or the need, in respect of which a business has to make decisions. The situation analysis is the first phase of the process. In this phase, current business, organizational, and information systems are analyzed. Also, external IT and business environment are analyzed, to determine new trends in information technology.

In the second subsystem, the second phase of SISP is included. In Strategic awareness, key planning issues and objectives are determined and the team which will participate in the implementation of the process is organized. Top managers participate, support, encourage, and control the process.

Next, DSS includes data base, data model, and application programs. This subsystem takes the information from the previous two subsystems and produces an output which is used as an input for the next subsystems. In this subsystem, managers can collect, store, and use the needed information about external and internal environment, in order to make alternative scenarios. Then, they will evaluate them and they will choose the best choice, which will be implemented in the following subsystem. Data can be saved for further elaboration and sensitivity analysis. They can also be organized in external files if further processing is necessary. The user interface is a combination of menus and question/answer dialogues (Zviran 1990).

The last subsystem includes the last three phases of SISP. Strategy conception involves the definition of significant IT objectives and objectives for implementation. The organizing team evaluates them, in order to be supported by technological strategy and to implement them in the next phase. Strategy formulation contains the definition of new IT architectures, processes, projects, and the priorities over them. All these decisions regard on the output of decision support subsystem. Last, in SISP, change management process, action plan, its evaluation and control are defining. As far as change management is concerned, it concerns after decision-making the implementation of the opportunities, objectives, plans, and new processes. The aim of this process is the understanding of the transformation in business processes or the introduction of information systems. The process of change management includes the next steps: the understanding of the need, the definition of the goals in the team, the contact and sharing of change, the delegation of the residence in change, and the distribution of resources. Managers create the redesign plan, in order the vision to be achieved. The last steps include the

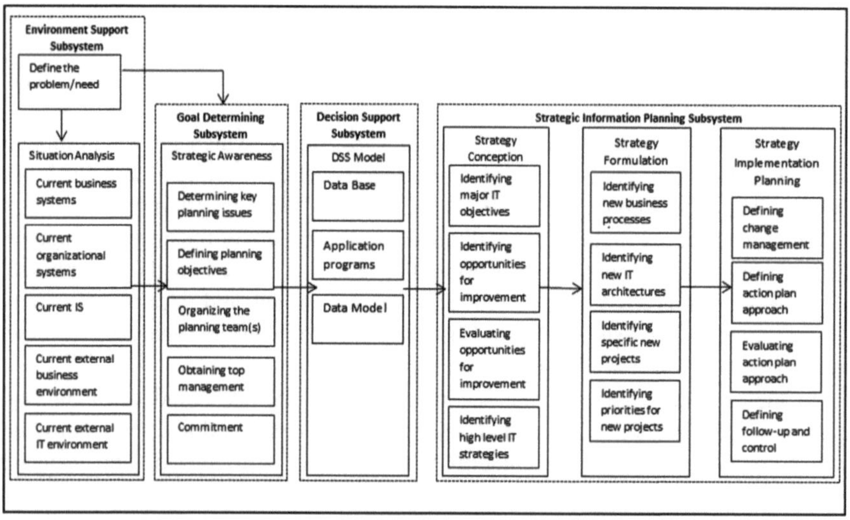

Fig. 1 Proposed model for strategic information systems planning using DSS

implementation and the evaluation of the redesign plan (Brown 2004, 2010; Dooley and O'Sullivan 1999; Malek and Yazdanifard 2012; Maharaj and Brown 2015; Mentzas 1997; Mirchandani et al. 2014; Newkirk and Lederer 2006; Newkirk et al. 2008; Pollack and Pollack 2015; Teng et al. 1996).

The proposed model can be previewed in Fig. 1.

Thus, a DSS with SISP can support strategic management and can be successfully implemented without much resistance if top management support is provided (Yoo and Digman 1987).

Conclusions

So far limited academic studies are concentrated on a holistic approach which combines SISP, change management, and DSS, in order to support managers to make decisions more effectively. This study proposes a framework to suggest a number of stages that combines the SISP process and DSS systems in the current changing environment. The specific model is based on previous literature on SISP and DSS and specifies phases that are related to managers making the appropriate strategic decisions. Therefore, through the introduction of the model and the phases, this paper bridges the gap in the literature regarding the correlation between SISP process and DSS and concurs to the development of a new successful model for decision-making.

A limitation of the model stems from the fact that it has not been tested yet. Nevertheless, the results of an exploratory study will be summarized in an improved conceptual model for further research.

References

Alalwan, J.A., M.A. Thomas, and H.R. Weistroffer. 2014. Decision support capabilities of enterprise content management systems: An empirical investigation. *Decision Support Systems* 68: 39–48.

Alyoubi, B.A. 2015. Decision support system and knowledge-based strategic management. *Procedia Computer Science* 65: 278–284.

Applegate, L.M., B.R. Konsynski, and J.F. Nunamaker. 1986. Model management systems: Design for decision support. *Decision Support Systems* 2: 81–91.

Brown, I. 2010. Strategic information systems planning: Comparing espoused beliefs with practice. In *Proceedings of 18th European conference on information systems (ECIS)*, 1–12.

Brown, I.T.J. 2004. Testing and extending theory in strategic information systems planning through literature analysis. *Information Resources Management Journal* 17: 20–48.

Dimitrios, Nasiopoulos K., Damianos P. Sakas, and D.S. Vlachos. 2013a. Analysis of strategic leadership models in information technology. *Procedia—Social and Behavioral Sciences* 268–275.

Dimitrios, Nasiopoulos K., Damianos P. Sakas, and D.S. Vlachos. 2013b. The role of information systems in creating strategic leadership model. *Procedia—Social and Behavioral Sciences* 467–477.

Dooley, L., and D. O'Sullivan. 1999. Decision support system for the management of systems change. *Technovation* 19: 483–493.

Johnson, G., K. Scholes, and R. Whittington. 2008. *Exploring corporate strategy: Text and cases*, 8th ed. London: Prentice Hall.

Lederer, A.L., and V. Sethi. 1988. The implementation of strategic information systems planning methodologies. *MIS Quarterly* 12: 455–461.

Leidner, D.E., J. Lo, and D. Preston. 2011. An empirical investigation of the relationship of IS strategy with firm performance. *Journal of Strategic Information Systems* 20: 419–437.

Maharaj, S., and I. Brown. 2015. The impact of shared domain knowledge on strategic information systems planning and alignment: Original research. *South African Journal of Information Management* 17: 1–12.

Malek, R., and R. Yazdanifard. 2012. Overview of change management and its implementation, in business, economics. In *Financial sciences, and management*, 149–153. Berlin, Heidelberg: Springer.

Mentzas, G. 1997. Implementing an IS strategy—A team approach. *Long Range Planning* 30: 84–95.

Mirchandani, D.A., and A.L. Lederer. 2014. "Less is More:" Information systems planning in an uncertain environment. *Information Systems Management* 29: 13–25.

Newkirk, H.E., and A.L. Lederer. 2006. The effectiveness of strategic information systems planning under environmental uncertainty. *Information & Management* 43: 481–501.

Newkirk, H.E., A.L. Lederer, and A.M. Johnson. 2008. Rapid business and IT change: Drivers for strategic information systems planning? *European Journal of Information Systems* 17: 198–218.

Peppard, J., and J. Ward. 2004. Beyond strategic information systems: towards an IS capability. *Journal of Strategic Information Systems* 13: 167–194.

Pollack, J., and R. Pollack. 2015. Using Kotter's eight stage process to manage an organisational change program: Presentation and practice. *Systemic Practice and Action Research* 28: 51–66.

Sakas, Damianos P., Dimitrios Vlachos, and Dimitrios K. Nasiopoulos. 2014. Modelling strategic management for the development of competitive advantage, based on technology. *Journal of Systems and Information Technology* 16 (3): 187–209. doi:10.1108/JSIT-01-2014-0005.

Teng, J.T., V. Grover, and K.D. Fiedler. 1996. Developing strategic perspectives on business process reengineering: From process reconfiguration to organizational change. *Omega* 24: 271–294.

Waxlax, J. 1993. An object-oriented DSS for strategic management. *Computers & Industrial Engineering* 25: 573–576.

Webster, J., and R.T. Watson. 2002. Analyzing the past to prepare for the future: Writing a literature review. *MIS Quarterly* 26: 13–23.

Yoo, S., and L.A. Digman. 1987. Decision support system: A new tool for strategic management. *Long Range Planning* 20: 114–124.

Zviran, M. 1990. ISSPSS: A decision support system for information systems strategic planning. *Information & Management* 19: 345–359.

Modeling and Simulation of Promotion Procedures for IT Companies Through Facebook

Tsiavos G. Panagiotis, Pachtiti E. Foteini, Nasiopoulos K. Dimitrios, Damianos P. Sakas and D.S. Vlachos

Introduction

E-commerce is a modern method of product promotion and services with rapid development in the Internet. During recent years, many companies have a exclusively presence online (Pereira Correia et al. 2014). IT companies create an elegant website, which contain detailed information about the products and services they offer, overcoming in this way the need for investment in offices, professional meeting rooms, shops, etc. The promotion of a successful and profitable e-shop can be done in ways that target the lowest possible cost and to maximize their profitability. One of these promotional methods seems to be the use of social media (e.g., Facebook), which on a daily basis visiting million users. In order to check the success rate or not of such a promotional form used a dynamic simulation model.

Methodology—Tools

All possible factors needed by the company for the promotion and commercialization of applications through Facebook (Lilley et al. 2012) follow a modeling methodology. For each basic variable of the model studied and developed those elements that would help in the future to present profits for the company.

This procedure was implemented through the dynamic simulation model, which allows modeling and simulation of a business idea (Aversa et al. 2015). Essentially, the program allows the development of a model drawing as parameters the results of the studies conducted for the construction of a business that promotes products

T.G. Panagiotis (✉) · P.E. Foteini · N.K. Dimitrios · D.P. Sakas · D.S. Vlachos
Department of Informatics and Telecommunications, University of Peloponnese, Tripoli, Greece
e-mail: tsiavospan29@gmail.com

A. Kavoura et al. (eds.), *Strategic Innovative Marketing*, Springer Proceedings in Business and Economics, DOI 10.1007/978-3-319-56288-9_44

(applications) via social media in order to study whether the business idea has the ability to develop or not.

Identification and Development of Variables

This research carried out to identify those variables related to e-commerce, which is implemented through the Facebook, came in four variables that are following to their respective components and are inextricably linked with the initial fund of the company.

These variables are the following:

Market Research: Market research is any organized effort to gather information about target markets or customers. It is a very important component of business strategy. Market research is one of the key factors used in maintaining competitiveness over competitors. Market research provides important information to identify and analyze the market need, market size, and competition (Krush et al. 2016). Market research techniques encompass both qualitative techniques such as focus groups, in-depth interviews, and ethnology, as well as quantitative techniques such as customer surveys, and analysis of secondary data (Zimmerman et al. 2000). Market research is the systematic gathering and interpretation of information about individuals or organizations using statistical and analytical methods and techniques of the applied social sciences to gain insight or support decision-making (Patino et al. 2012).

Facebook Page: The idea of creating a page on the Facebook social networking tool came from the tendency of many companies to have exclusive presence on the Internet. Consequently, the creation of a thorough website, where there will be detailed information about the products and services they offer, disproves the need for investment in offices, professional meeting rooms, shops, etc. The promotion of products is achieved through advertising and various video presenting product.

E-commerce: By the spread has nowadays e-commerce deemed necessary the setup and the integration of an electronic shop (e-shop) on the website of a company (Brengman et al. 2012). Specifically, the purchase was selected from an e-commerce platform, which includes all the features required for a company to facilitate the electronic exchange, and the incorporation of an e-shop in the existing corporate site. The second choice is based on the idea that most companies build and manage websites through a content management system (CMS) (Goodwin et al. 2006).

Applications: Each media creation that can stand in the market as a source of revenue for a business is acceptable. The creation has to follow the flow and evolution that is open to the consumer market in the context of globalization that exists nowadays. The impact of such an integral part of our everyday life, therefore their usability and their quality must be very good to be in every smartphone, tablet, etc.

Analysis of the Simulation Model

The analysis of the model will begin with sharing of principal on four components mentioned in the previous paragraph (Fig. 1).

The orange part of the model relates to the Market Research. We invest 20% of the company resources in this segment and, in turn, it provided satisfy (Satisfaction of MR) through the IF command (Satisfaction_of_MR <65) THEN (0) ELSE (Satisfaction_of_MR * (Percent__of_SMR2CMR/100)) will promote this profit (Counterpoise of MR) with the flow (CMR2A) in the application.

The green part of the model relates to the application and hence the creation. Here, we have two inputs. One of these originates from Counterpoise of MR and the other by the company resources at a rate of about 35%. On their turn will be divided into two levels which will go to the designers (60%) and programmers (40%) who are responsible for the design and implementation of the application. If satisfied or not this process will be examined by the Satisfaction of Application (IF (Satisfaction__of_Application <60) THEN (0) ELSE (Satisfaction__of_Application * (Percent_of_SA2CA/100)) which will give the corresponding gain in Counterpoise of A through flow (SA2CA) performing the relation of (Satisfaction_of_Application * Percent_of_SA2CA) and in turn on the e-commerce and on the object that we are investigating.

The light blue component used in our model is the creation of Facebook Page. From the capital of the company (Company Resources) giving % on the purchase rights relating to the advertising and videos of our application. How goes equally from 50% in Adds and Videos and satisfaction of page (Satisfaction of FP) depends on the IF (Satisfaction__of_FP <55) THEN(0) ELSE (Satisfaction__of_FP * (Percent__of_SFP2CFP/100)). The profit will be transferred via the flow

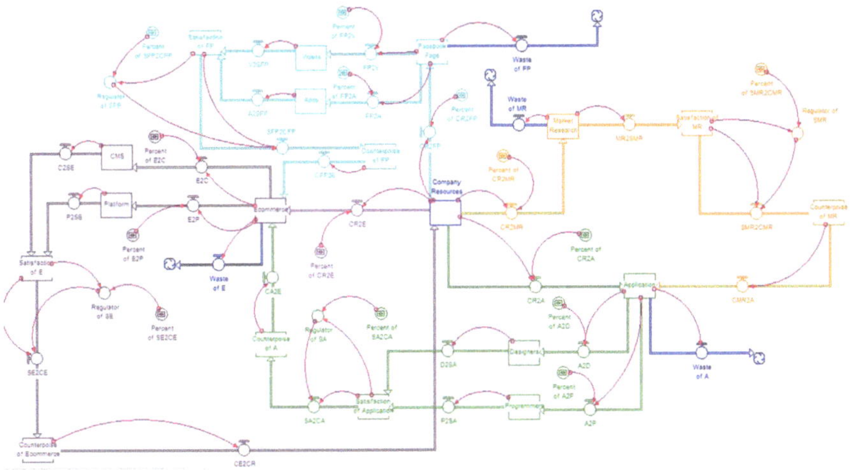

Fig. 1 Model

(SFP2CFP) who performs the Satisfaction_of_FP * Percent_of_SFP2CFP in Counterpoise of FP, which will be a source of inputs for e-commerce.

The purple section analyzes the e-commerce that takes resources as the Counterpoise of A, the Counterpoise of FP as a percentage of the initial capital (company resources). For e-commerce, we distributed equally our resources for the purchase of the platform (Platform) and the content management system (CMS). Their satisfaction (Satisfaction of E) is the only and therefore most important source of revenue for the company and is subject to the condition IF (Satisfaction__of_E <60) THEN (0) ELSE (Satisfaction__of_E * (Percent__of_SE2CE/ 100)) present in the regulator of SE and promote profit in Counterpoise of E-commerce via flow SE2CE in which we put the relationship (Satisfaction_of_E * Percent_of_SE2CE).

Implementation of the Dynamic Simulation Model

To create the models, the modeling software tool iThink, from iSee systems, was used. iThink creates stock and flow diagrams to model and simulate processes. It presents you the results of specific defined by the user inputs and connects the interrelationships between procedures and functions. Outputs can be displayed in the form of graphs and tables. The results of the dynamic simulation model are shown in tables and figures that we provide (Table 1).

Figure 2 indicated that the satisfaction percentage, as regarding all the four factors, is rising significantly during the first months and then those satisfactions

Table 1 Table results

Months	Company resources	Satisfaction create official site	Satisfaction Facebook E-commerce	Satisfaction information material	Satisfaction create application
Initial	100.00	0.00	25.00	15.00	60.00
1	31.64	0.00	49.86	29.13	94.02
2	10.01	2.75	71.03	37.85	97.50
3	5.82	16.61	77.71	41.93	86.10
4	6.70	43.41	70.40	43.84	71.34
5	9.30	65.12	74.46	45.14	63.21
6	17.18	73.74	70.09	46.47	64.04
7	23.13	71.92	72.70	48.46	64.88
8	25.01	65.19	69.17	51.35	62.42
9	26.59	57.83	73.86	54.82	67.86
10	24.97	52.08	72.38	58.61	64.54
11	22.23	49.07	71.27	62.33	67.58
12	18.95	48.27	70.02	65.77	64.94

gain stability. Market research as regarding the contribution of social media in the management of social relations with customers give successful and satisfied results.

Also, Fig. 2 shows that company resources in the beginning, given in the four leading factors, lead to company resources replenishment in a steady rate, and the four factors are eventually tending to stabilize their resources.

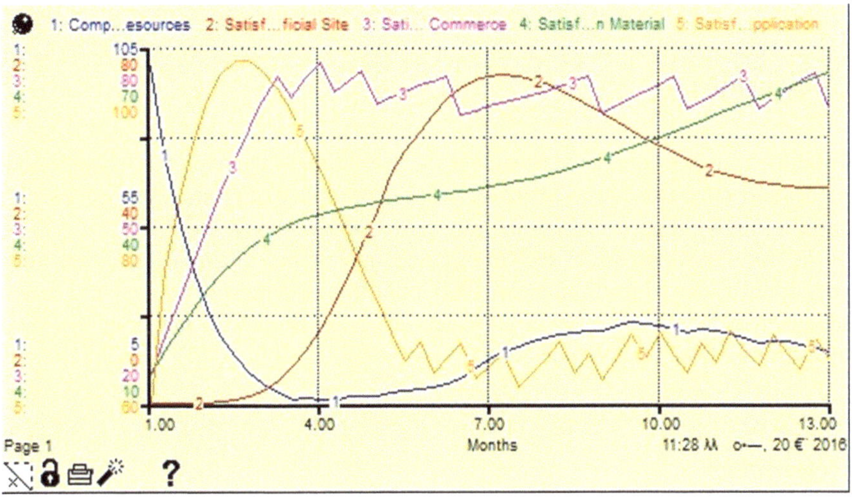

Fig. 2 Graphical results

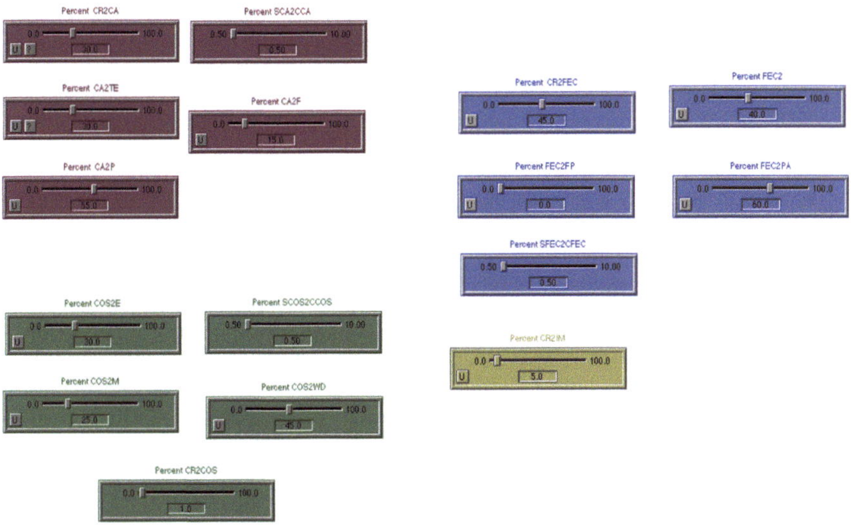

Fig. 3 User interface

Support for Decision Makers

There is need to create the interface of the dynamic simulation model, to enable the user to change the values that the factors can get, studied in the research we have done. Figure 2 shows the main user interface of the simulation model. There are four main sections on this user interface: Market research, Facebook page, E-commerce, and applications (Fig. 3).

Conclusions

From the research conducted as well as the resolution of the exported from the chart model and price lists shows that there is the possibility of promoting technological applications through social media, especially the Facebook.

As the developments of technology and other types of applications are rapid, very soon it will be useful and even essential to new setups to control and thus to see whether the promotion was positively evolving or have to integrate new types of instruments to achieve our goals.

References

Aversa, Paolo, Stefan Haefliger, Alessandro Rossi, and Charles Baden-Fuller. 2015. From business model to business modelling: Modularity and manipulation. In *Business models and modelling* (Advances in Strategic Management), vol. 33 ed. Charles Baden-Fuller, and Vincent Mangematin, 151–185. Bingley: Emerald Group Publishing Limited.

Brengman, Malaika, and Farhod P. Karimov. 2012. The effect of web communities on consumers' initial trust in B2C e-commerce websites. *Management Research Review* 35 (9): 791–817.

Goodwin, Susan, Nancy Burford, Martha Bedard, Esther Carrigan, and Gale C. Hannigan. 2006. CMS/CMS: Content management system/change management strategies. *Library Hi Tech* 24 (1): 54–60.

Kluemper, Donald H., Arjun Mitra, and Siting Wang. 2016. Social media use in HRM. In *Research in personnel and human resources management*, vol. 34, ed. M. Ronald Buckley, Jonathon R.B. Halbesleben, and Anthony R. Wheeler, 153–207. Bingley: Emerald Group Publishing Limited.

Krush, Michael T., Raj Agnihotri, and Kevin J. Trainor. 2016. A contingency model of marketing dashboards and their influence on marketing strategy implementation speed and market information management capability. *European Journal of Marketing* 50 (12): 2077–2102.

Lilley, Stephen, Frances S. Grodzinsky, and Andra Gumbus. 2012. Revealing the commercialized and compliant Facebook user. *Journal of Information, Communication and Ethics in Society* 10 (2): 82–92.

Patino, Anthony, Dennis A. Pitta, and Ralph Quinones. 2012. Social media's emerging importance in market research. *Journal of Consumer Marketing* 29 (3): 233–237.

Pereira Correia, Pedro A., Irene García Medina, Zahaira Fabiola González Romo, and Ruth S. Contreras-Espinosa. 2014. The importance of Facebook as an online social networking tool for companies. *International Journal of Accounting & Information Management* 22 (4): 295–320.

Zimmerman, Alan S., and Michael Szenberg. 2000. Implementing international qualitative research: Techniques and obstacles. *Qualitative Market Research: An International Journal* 3 (3): 158–164.

Modeling and Simulation for the Development of Innovative Ideas for Video Games in Smartphones

Tsomis Konstantinos, Koukouris Georgios, Damianos P. Sakas, Nasiopoulos K. Dimitrios and D.S. Vlachos

Introduction

In a society addicted to technology and its every aspect, the importance of innovative ideas (Abdel Aziz and Rizkallah 2006) is undoubted. Even in the video game (Zackariasson et al. 2010) industry, it can constitute a major issue. The smartphones' (Castro Soeiro et al. 2016) uprising has created a demand for video games compatible with those devices. That is why it is important to understand what a company of this sort is necessary to do, to become viable and competitive in this market section. Proving the importance of those innovations and the factors that affect them is going to be the main focus of this paper, as seen and analyzed below.

Methodology

After the theme was chosen (modeling and simulation for the development of innovative ideas for video games in smartphones), the necessary research on the Internet was conducted, in order to identify the factors that constitute and influence a company of this sort and the correlations between them. Subsequently a model was made, using the simulation modeling software (Hunecker 2009) and it was constructed in such a way that the majority of the factors and percentages used in it would be easily accessible and altered. Finally, the simulation turned up some conclusions.

T. Konstantinos (✉) · K. Georgios · D.P. Sakas · N.K. Dimitrios · D.S. Vlachos
Department of Informatics and Telecommunications, University of Peloponnese, Tripoli, Greece
e-mail: kontsomis@yahoo.com

A. Kavoura et al. (eds.), *Strategic Innovative Marketing*, Springer Proceedings in Business and Economics, DOI 10.1007/978-3-319-56288-9_45

Both the model construction process, and the conclusions, can be found in the following sections.

Main Factors' Analysis

Internet Connection and Database Access

The first main factor that was considered is the Internet connection and database access. The company's staff has to be able to search in the Internet for new trends and the demand associated with them. They also have to be sure that their idea has not already been copyrighted. After taking these steps, they should have access to relevant databases so as to conduct research and procced with coming up with an innovative idea.

Staff Training and Seminars

As technology progresses ceaselessly, so should the employees' knowledge. They must always be up to date for new advancements in their field, which can be accomplished through constant training and seminars. That is why this is considered to be a main factor in the model.

Game Testers

The importance of the game testers cannot be denied. Although their role may seem easy or even unimportant, they are charged with the responsibility of testing their coworkers' ideas. When an idea may seem great in development, it main fail to deliver when it comes to gaming experience, so it is up to the Game Testers to try out these ideas and give feedback to be taken into consideration.

Users' Feedback Validation Staff

An idea or innovation could keep on improving, even after its release to the public. That's where the users' feedback comes in. They are given the ability to criticize the game and its features and suggest additions and adjustments, which the Users' Feedback Validation Staff takes into consideration and, if important and manageable, includes them in the game.

Data Mining Staff

As mentioned above, an idea may look good in paper but fail to pass game experience tests or cannot even be programmed correctly into the game. As time goes by, video games change and new programming methods and languages come up making these ideas more suitable in playstyle and easier to import. That is where data mining (Jun Lee and Siau 2006) Staff comes in. These employees are responsible for either searching in data bases, or on official web pages and blogs or forums, or even in social media and finding ideas such as the ones described above. This is very important because it can bring huge changes into the video games that could not be done in the past.

Dynamic Simulation Model

Every company needs its resources and the one in this simulation is no exception. As seen above, in Fig. 1, the resources are feeding into two factors, Infrastructure and Staff. The Infrastructure, in turn, divides the resource that were received into two sub-factors, Buildings & Maintenance (B&M), and Internet Connection & Database Access (IC&DA). The B&M sector includes all the expenses regarding the premises of the company, such as acquiring them, fitting them with the necessary equipment, and maintaining them. The IC&DA sector refers to the expenses that the company makes to obtain their employees access to all the indispensable information, needed for developing innovative ideas. This factor is further analyzed above.

The second factor is Staff. It includes four sub-factors, three of which are responsible for the company's profit. These factors are Staff Training (Dirani 2012)

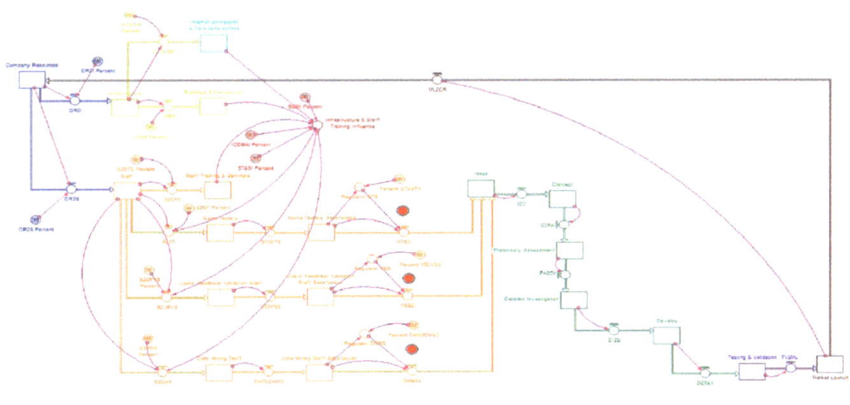

Fig. 1 Dynamic simulation model

and Seminars (ST&S), Game Testers (GT), Users' Feedback Validation Staff (UFVS), and Data Mining Staff (DMS).

The latter three are responsible for returning profit in the form of innovative ideas, but for them to produce any results, the must first be satisfied. Each sector's satisfaction (Martin Cruz et al. 2009) can be altered by any user of the model, through the interface.

The innovative ideas that the staff produces are going through many stages, before they are approved to be included in a new game. Between those stages, there

Table 1 Resources flow

Months	Initial	1	2	3	4	5	6
Company resouroes	100.00	41.43	23.03	36.07	61.72	108.49	180.96
Infrastructure	20.00	15.48	9.38	7.10	8.58	13.83	23.47
Buildings & maintenance	16.00	31.24	41.60	48.17	54.07	62.26	75.91
Internet convection a data base access	4.00	7.31	10.40	12.04	13.52	15.58	18.98
Staff	80.00	0.00	0.00	0.00	0.00	0.00	0.00
Staff training and seminars	8.00	11.29	11.65	11.94	12.35	13.07	14.32
Game testers	78.64	58.35	37.16	30.34	37.92	61.71	104.99
Game testers' satisfaction	73.64	53.66	30.22	0.00	27.39	0.00	62.30
Users' feefibaoe validation staff	78.64	53.23	17.91	5.67	1.79	0.57	0.18
Users' feedback validation staff satisfaction	78.64	53.66	23.91	36.16	48.03	41.28	41.65
Data mining staff	78.64	42.32	13.39	4.24	1.34	0.42	0.13
Data mining staff satisfaction	78.64	52.56	18.35	27.51	30.40	31.32	31.61
Ideas	13.554.26	13.316.37	10.271.36	7.580.47	5.549.62	4.127.65	3.021.8.3
Concept	5.586.28	8.537.26	9.568.30	9.444.17	8.713.90	7.697.07	6.615.03
Preliminary assessment	1.889.88	3.084.55	4.687.32	6.000.16	8.853.97	7.247.00	7.252.24
Detailed investigation	500.96	953.07	1.698.30	2.648.61	3.648.24	4.558.53	5.286.69
Develop	150.29	286.47	538.35	948.35	1.511.41	2.184.42	2.902.98
Testing & validation	45.09	85.94	163.54	304.33	534.12	866.22	1.296.00

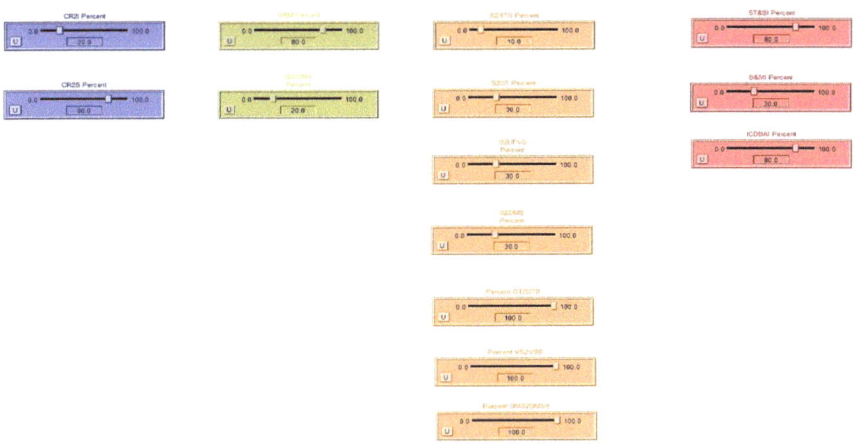

Fig. 2 Resources and satisfactions

Table 2 Resources flow

Months	7	8	9	10	11	12
Company resources	281.28	407.49	553.78	711.54	370.85	1.022.00
Infrastructure	38.18	58.24	83.20	111.94	142.82	173.97
Buildings & maintenance	98.77	135.00	188.80	263.80	362.54	486.19
Internet connection & data base access	24.69	33.75	47.20	65.95	90.64	121.55
Staff	0.00	0.00	0.00	0.00	0.00	0.00
Staff training seminars	16.36	19.48	23.91	29.84	37.35	46.45
Game testers	171.08	261.26	373.62	503.14	642.45	783.10
Game testers' satisfaction	0.00	39.97	0.00	0.00	0.00	0.00
Users'' feedback validation staff	0.08	0.02	0.01	0.00	0.00	0.00
Users' feedback validation staff satisfaction	41.77	41.81	41.82	41.82	41.62	41.83
Data mining staff	0.04	0.01	0.00	0.00	0.00	0.00
Dots mining staff satisfaction	31.70	31.73	31.74	31.74	31.74	31.74
Ideas	2.361.11	1.847.09	1.622.02	1.518.37	1.550.22	1.687.40
Concept	5.577.36	4.653.38	3.866.68	3.238.58	2.762.00	2.429.12
Preliminary assessment	8.968.82	6.494.13	5.913.40	5.295.02	4.690.49	4.136.03
Detailed investigation	5.788.07	6.056.76	6.113.32	5.993.77	5.741.12	5.398.91
Develop	3.600.35	4.220.11	4.722.46	5.085.66	5.304.33	5.386.22
Testing & validation	1.802.26	2.352.48	2.909.43	3.437.15	3.905.28	4.291.67

is a quality control checkpoint, with a set of criteria that the product must pass to reach the next stage. Those stages will be explained below.

The employees are coming up with ideas, but not all of them are suitable to be included in a product. The ones that are clever and original, proceed to the next stage, which is the Concept (Jalonen et al. 2016) The Concept stage performs a quality check and decides which concepts will proceed for Preliminary Assessment, where they will be evaluated from an economic standpoint. Concepts that pass both evaluations get the necessary budget to be developed. Finally, the developed ideas are going through testing and validation and those that see it through, are produced from the company. In the Market Launch stack can be found, only the ideas that passed through all the stages successfully, and they are the ones to bring the company profit.

As can be seen in Table 1, regarding the Company's Resources, during the first 4 months, there is a loss. On the fifth month, the resources are about the amount they were in the beginning and from the sixth month until the end of the simulation, a profit can be seen. In the end, the resources are 10 times the initial company budget.

Taking into consideration both, Table 1 and Fig. 2, it is safe to come up with the ascertainment that since the company is able to achieve its employees' satisfactions, it is able to keep a steady idea producing pace. Those ideas are, in turn, evaluated and the best ones are developed and launched in the market, bringing the company profit (Table 2).

In Fig. 3 can be seen the interface for this dynamic model. From there the user can decide the percentages of the company's resources that are provides to each factor. Each flow is colored the same as the stack it draws funds from, so the blue sliders are referring to the flows coming straight from the Company Resources stack, feeding into the Infrastructure and Staff factors, while the yellow ones draw

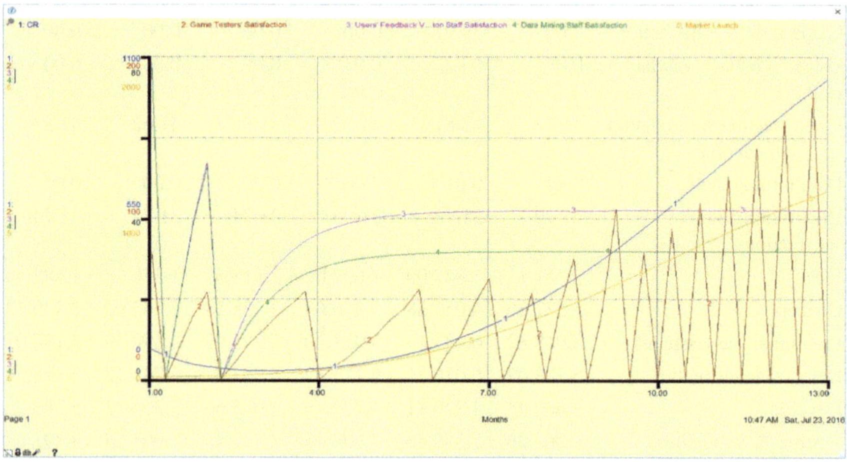

Fig. 3 Interface

funds from Infrastructure and divide them between the Buildings and Maintenance and Internet Connection and Database Access sub-factors. The orange sliders are not only arranging the percentage of the funds that each Staff sub-factor receives from the Staff stack, but also the amount of resources that need to be received from the GT, UFVS, and DMS for them to be satisfied and begin producing innovations. Lastly, the red sliders are used to set the amount of influence the Internet Connection and Database Access and the ST&S exercise upon the Staff's sub-factors, affecting their productivity.

Conclusions

While studying about the "Modeling and simulation for the development of innovative ideas for video games in smartphones," after extensive research and with the help of the Dynamic Model and the Simulation analyzed above, while there is always room for further analysis, there has been reached a conclusion regarding the main factors responsible for the success or failure of a company that operates on this technology field. Such factors were found to be the Internet Connection and Database Access as also ST&S which give the company's staff the ability to conduct research and stay up to date regarding upcoming breakthroughs in technology and provides them the means necessary to exploit them in order to come up with new ideas. Given these tools, the GT, UFVS, and DMS produce innovations, some of which will fulfill the requirements and reach the market. For a company of this instance, the importance of having a steady flow of ideas cannot be denied, as its survival depends on it.

References

Abdel Aziz, Hadia Hamdy, and Ashraf Rizkallah. 2006. Effect of organizational factors on employees' generation of innovative ideas: Empirical study on the Egyptian software development industry. *EuroMed Journal of Business* 10 (2): 134–146.

Castro Soeiro, Filipe, Mariana Santos, and José Alves. 2016. Network-based innovation: The case for mobile gaming and digital music. *European Business Review* 28 (2): 155–175.

Dirani, Khalil M. 2012. Professional training as a strategy for staff development: A study in training transfer in the Lebanese context. *European Journal of Training and Development* 36 (2/3): 158–178.

Hunecker, Felix. 2009. A generic process simulation-model for educational simulations and serious games. *On the Horizon* 17 (4): 313–322.

Jalonen, Meri, Päivi, Ristimäki, Hanna, Toiviainen, Anneli, Pulkkis, and Mika Lohtander. 2016. Between product development and mass production: Tensions as triggers for concept-level learning. *Journal of Workplace Learning* 28 (1), 33–48.

Jun Lee, Sang, Keng, Siau. 2006. A review of data mining techniques. *Industrial Management & Data Systems* 101 (1): 41–46.

Martin Cruz, Natalia, Ana Isabel, Rodriguez Escudero, Juan, Hernangomez Barahona, and Fernando, Saboia Leitao. 2009. The effect of entrepreneurship education programmes on satisfaction with innovation behaviour and performance. *Journal of European Industrial Training* 33 (3), 198–214.

Zackariasson, Peter, Timothy L., Wilson. 2010. Paradigm shifts in the video game industry. *Competitiveness Review: An International Business Journal* 20 (2): 139–151.

Mobile Commerce and Success Factors. Simulation and Modeling of the Problem

Aristotelis Chantzaras, Nasiopoulos K. Dimitrios and D.S. Vlachos

Introduction

Mobile commerce (m-commerce) is one of the fast growing commercial websites based on mobile technologies (Chan and Yee-Loong Chong 2013). M-commerce is an IT-supported business innovation (Lu 2014), and offers business opportunities through Internet access without geographic constraints, as well as personalization and location-based service (Hong 2015).

Although m-commerce system has been regarded as an extension of electronic-commerce (e-commerce) (Chu 2015), which trades the goods, services, and information, the pattern of m-commerce is different from that of e-commerce in terms of interaction styles, usage patterns, and value chain (Chu 2015). Also m-commerce system has moved beyond the PC/TV's static terminal to anytime, anywhere use of mobile devices (Hong 2015).

M-commerce has much more potential compared to e-commerce due to its characteristics such as ubiquity, personalization, and flexibility, so that m-commerce can cover not only transactions of money and goods, but also other entertainment activities. Also m-commerce is superior to e-commerce to provide location-, customer-, personalization-, presence-, and context-based services (Choi et al. 2008).

A BI Intelligence report states that by 2020, m-commerce will make up 45% of total e-commerce, equaling $284 billion in sales. That is more than 3 times what is expected for 2016: BI Intelligence predicts mobile commerce will hit 20.6% of overall e-commerce, or $79 billion (Fig. 1).

After bibliographical and article—paper research, it can safely be assumed that the most important factors concerning the success of m-commerce are:

A. Chantzaras · N.K. Dimitrios (✉) · D.S. Vlachos
Department of Computer and Telecommunications, University of Peloponnese, Tripolis, Greece
e-mail: dit13159@uop.gr

A. Kavoura et al. (eds.), *Strategic Innovative Marketing*, Springer Proceedings in Business and Economics, DOI 10.1007/978-3-319-56288-9_46

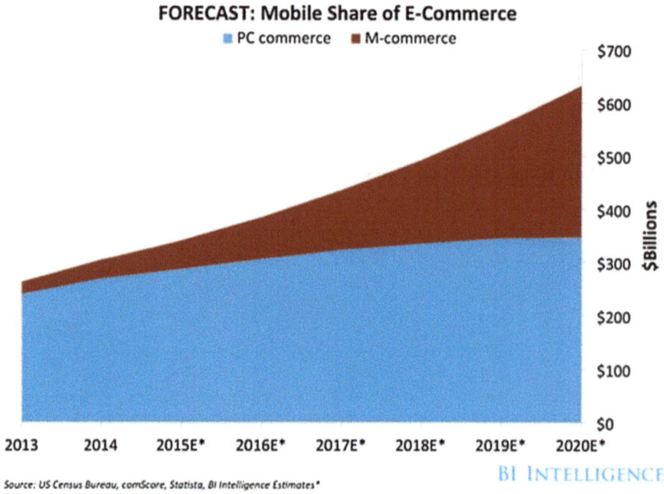

Fig. 1 BI intelligence graph that predicts future m-commerce share

1. Security—Trust
2. Personalization—Localization
3. Convenience.

Security—Trust

Security and the sense of trust it provides to the customer is probably the most important factor for an individual to make the decision of buying an m-commerce promoted product. M-commerce involves great uncertainty and risk (Zhou 2011). There is absolutely no customer that would willingly give his/her personal information for transactions with a website that is not trusted and is not considered of high credibility, which derives from the fact that trust is considered a major obstacle in initiating customer relationships (Shao Yeh and Li 2009). On the other hand, a customer that trusts the website will not have second thoughts and concerns about a purchase and is more likely to buy right away because if it is established, trust has a significant and positive relationship in adoption of m-commerce (Yadav et al. 2016) and is central to the success of personal relationship building (Shao Yeh and Li 2009).

Personalization—Localization

Users need to be able to define how they shop and what they see but moreover the detail content needs to be wrapped around them. Suggested products that are close to user's interests, preferences, and previous purchases are more likely to get their attention. Within personalization, we can merge the localization factor which modifies the promoted to the user content adding high rated and visited products that users in his/her demographic area have purchased—suggested (local trends) and/or products that correspond to the local needs and conditions.

Convenience

Convenience refers to the extent to which m-commerce makes easier for customers to conduct transactions (Khalifa and Ning Shen 2008). A user that is not satisfied by this factor is more likely to abandon the purchase he could possibly make. Although being able to buy products anytime, anywhere is quite convenient, the levels of convenience can increase dramatically by these factors:

1. Speed: The website should be light and easy for the browser to project, because otherwise the user's patience could run out and leave.

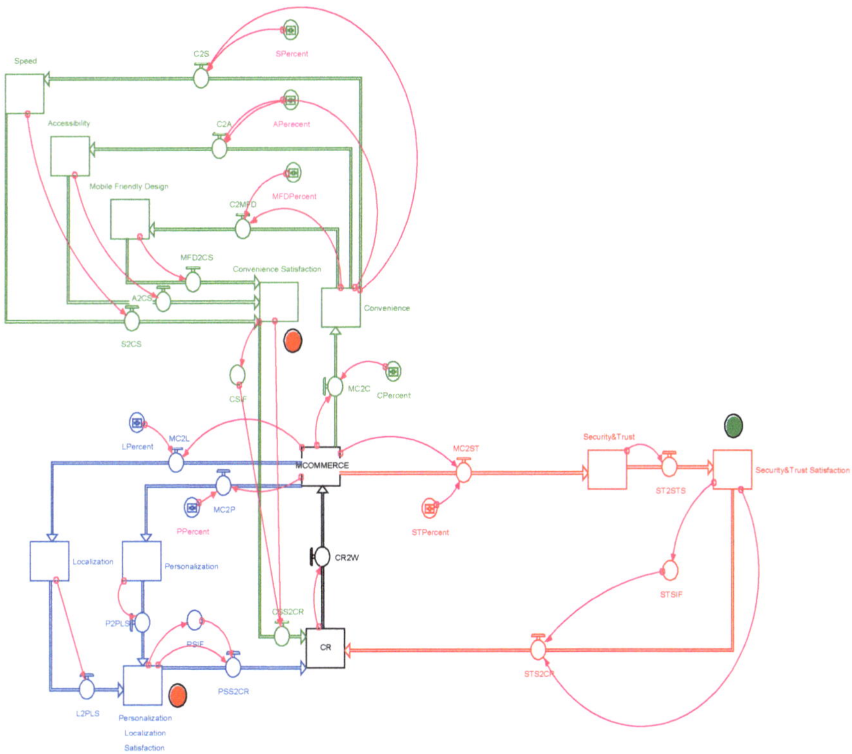

Fig. 2 Simulation model of the problem

2. Accessibility: The site should be easily accessed and an understandable and handy navigation through the different choices should be provided to ease the customer.
3. Mobile Friendly Design: Many websites have problems adjusting to mobile devices and lead the users to frustration. Users should not be tired but on the contrary be fascinated by the design patterns (Fig. 2).

Simulation Model

The company's resources (stock CR) are flowing to the m-commerce stock so they can be distributed to the other stocks that represent the factors. To the down-left side the resources are given to the localization and personalization stocks. When the personalization–localization satisfaction is more than 50% satisfied, resources are returned to the CR. On the down-right side, resources are invested to the Security and Trust stock. When security and trust satisfaction is more than 70% satisfied resources return to the CR. On the upper left side of the model, resources are given to the convenience stock. Then they are shared appropriately to the stocks: speed, accessibility and mobile friendly design. When the convenience satisfaction is more than 60% satisfied, resources are returned to the CR (Figs. 3 and 4).

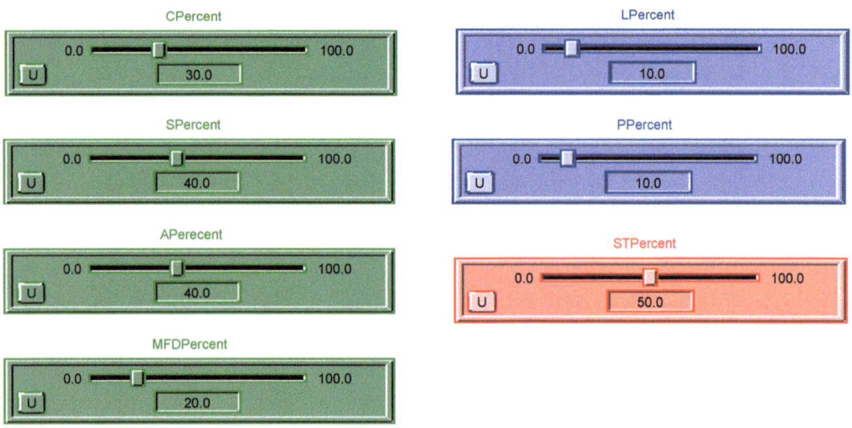

Fig. 3 Interface of the values that are used in the simulation model

Months	CR	Convenience	Speed	Accessibility	Mobile Friendly Design	Convenience Satisfacti
1.00	100.00	30.00	12.00	12.00	6.00	30.00
2.00	45.70	28.48	11.95	11.95	5.98	60.00
3.00	78.16	23.35	10.87	10.87	5.43	55.96
4.00	70.77	21.56	9.49	9.49	4.74	66.05
5.00	77.51	21.68	8.88	8.88	4.44	57.25
6.00	67.49	22.48	8.84	8.84	4.42	63.65
7.00	91.29	22.41	8.91	8.91	4.46	53.85
8.00	83.27	22.24	8.92	8.92	4.46	59.89
9.00	89.09	22.08	8.87	8.87	4.43	50.73
10.00	78.59	22.36	8.91	8.91	4.46	57.45
11.00	69.90	22.44	8.94	8.94	4.47	64.01
Final	81.60	22.23	8.93	8.93	4.46	54.18

Fig. 4 Results of CR, convenience, speed, accessibility, mobile friendly design, convenience satisfaction, throughout the simulation

Tables—Graphs

It can be seen that throughout the whole simulation, the convenience satisfaction is relatively steady. This steady rate is due to the easy adjustment of the users, from the very first months (Fig. 5).

About the personalization–localization satisfaction, some time is needed so that the content can be adjusted completely to the user's preferences and local needs-trends and then the satisfaction is stabilized to satisfactorily levels. About the security and trust satisfaction, after 1 month, the users are convinced for their data-transactions safety and the satisfaction ranges in high and satisfactorily levels (Fig. 6).

Months	Personalization	Localization	Personalization Localizat	Security&Trust	Security&Trust Satisfac
1.00	10.00	10.00	10.00	50.00	50.00
2.00	9.49	9.49	29.92	47.46	81.05
3.00	7.78	7.78	47.54	38.92	67.53
4.00	7.19	7.19	49.56	35.93	66.30
5.00	7.23	7.23	50.62	36.13	64.75
6.00	7.49	7.49	52.62	37.47	64.52
7.00	7.47	7.47	41.73	37.35	64.86
8.00	7.41	7.41	43.38	37.06	64.94
9.00	7.36	7.36	45.44	36.81	64.75
10.00	7.45	7.45	47.09	37.27	64.89
11.00	7.48	7.48	49.31	37.41	65.05
Final	7.41	7.41	50.94	37.06	65.07

Fig. 5 Results of personalization, localization, personalization–localization satisfaction, security and trust, security and trust satisfaction, throughout the simulation

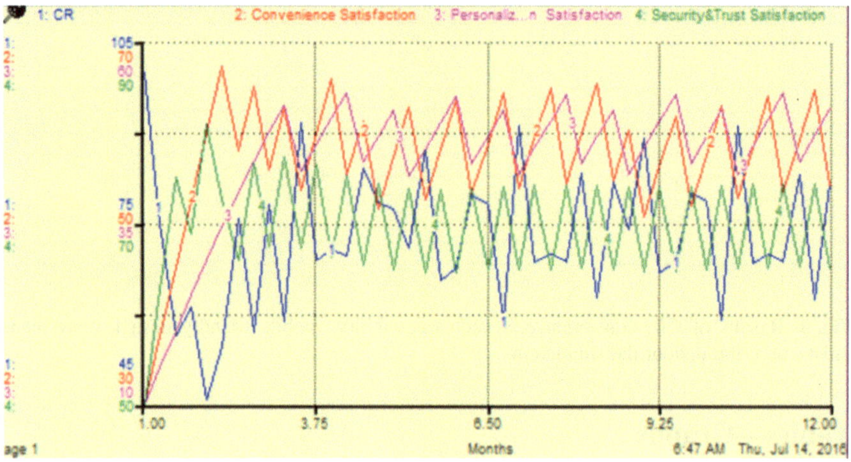

Fig. 6 Graphical display of the results of CR, convenience satisfaction, personalization-localization satisfaction, security and trust satisfaction throughout the simulation

Conclusions

With the right distribution of resources and the ideal circumstances, this simulation model produces high rates of satisfaction to all the crucial factors for the success of m-commerce.

It is concluded that the most important factor for the success of m-commerce security and trust, because it is what the user will certainly check before proceeding to actually buy a product and as soon as he/she is convinced-satisfied, the satisfaction values remain higher than any other factor (always greater than 64.52%) throughout the whole simulation.

References

BI Intelligence report on Mobile Commerce presented at http://digiday.com/brands/mobile-commerce-going-2016/.

Chu, Phuong Anh. 2015. Factors influence customer satisfaction in mobile commerce—A research on Vietnamese mobile users, Bachelor's Thesis.

Chan, Felix T.S., and Alain Yee-Loong Chong. 2013. Analysis of the determinants of consumers' m-commerce usage activities. *Online Information Review* 37 (3): 443–461.

Choi, Jeewon, Hyeonjoo Seol, Sungjoo Lee, Hyunmyung Cho, and Yongtae Park. 2008. Customer satisfaction factors of mobile commerce in Korea. *Internet Research* 18 (3): 313–335.

Hong, Hyun Gi. 2015. Success factors of mobile-commerce system 8 (S7): 630–637.

Khalifa, Mohamed, and Kathy Ning Shen. 2008. Explaining the adoption of transactional B2C mobile commerce. *Journal of Enterprise Information Management* 21 (2): 110–124.

Lu, June. 2014. Are personal innovativeness and social influence critical to continue with mobile commerce? *Internet Research* 24 (2): 134–159.

Shao, Yung Yeh, and Yung-Ming Li. 2009. Building trust in m-commerce: Contributions from quality and satisfaction. *Online Information Review* 33 (6): 1066–1086.

Yadav, Rajan, Sujeet Kumar Sharma, and Ali Tarhini. 2016. A multi-analytical approach to understand and predict the mobile commerce adoption. *Journal of Enterprise Information Management* 29 (2): 222–237.

Zhou, Tao. 2011. Examining the critical success factors of mobile website adoption. *Online Information Review* 35 (4): 636–652.

The Simulation Model of Supply Chains on the Macroeconomic Level is the Tool to Control the Economic Development of the Region

Natalia Lychkina, Elena Molodetskaya and Yulia Morozova

Introduction

Recently, the attention of researchers and business representatives has been focused on the dynamic supply chains, on clusters and complexes (Steger 2009). This position represents a shift from the mechanistic concept of genuine industrial organization operating in the market and consisting of a group of companies, producing uniform output material flows to more complex sets of interconnected and interdependent markets and companies. Analysis of the region's industry has been traditionally focused on the sectors, including groups of companies with similar characteristics, similar production process, producing similar goods, or providing similar services and occupying similar positions in the market. The industrial methodology deals with the performance of business enterprises, structures, and effects of the market behavior (pricing policy, restrictions on freedom of competition, innovation) and looks into the organization of companies. The most significant elements of the market structure in these models are relevant to the nature of the demand, the existing power of distribution among the competitors, entry, and exit barriers in the market, government intervention, and the physical structure of the relationship (horizontal and integrated interaction).

However, the implementation of the region's development strategy needs a comprehensive cross-industry supply chain research. It is necessary to find tools to analyze and predict the economic condition of the region, to evaluate the number of scenarios and solutions to manage the economic development of the region in order

N. Lychkina · Y. Morozova
Faculty of Business and Management, National Research University Higher School of Economics, Moscow, Russian Federation

E. Molodetskaya (✉)
Graduate School of Corporate Management, The Russian Presidential Academy of National Economy and Public Administration, Moscow, Russian Federation
e-mail: helenkorobko10@hotmail.com

A. Kavoura et al. (eds.), *Strategic Innovative Marketing*, Springer Proceedings in Business and Economics, DOI 10.1007/978-3-319-56288-9_47

to choose the most efficient one, balanced in different directions and ensuring the achievement of stable macro-controlled system (Lychkina 2016). To solve this problem, we used a simulation method. The Simulation modeling of supply chain systems allows us to consider the economic condition of the region, in cooperation with a lot of its economic entities, as a living system, lining up the interaction between the participants, which are elements of a single supply chain system. This approach to the analysis and decision-making provides for the coherent development coordinated by various industry trends as well as socioeconomic development of the regions as opposed to the current practice of fragmented production decisions based on the analysis of changes of selected indicators, and local sector-oriented management decisions.

Conceptual Model of the Region's Supply Chain

As an object of management the region is characterized by a complex, interrelated, and interdependent subsystems which possess certain properties, including groups of companies and industries with similar characteristics, combined in similar manufacturing processes that produce similar goods or services and occupy similar positions. Each region has its own index of demography, in other words—has human resources, which are characterized by the level of the relations in the social aspect, and the inter-organizational aspect, that is, has a certain amount of organizations, knowledge, and technology. The driving force of any supply chain is in such basic components as human and material resources and technology. Depending on the qualitative and quantitative status of these three factors the status of polysyllabic interrelated interdependent systems of supply chains changes, thus influencing the development not only of the companies and industries, but also of the region as a whole system.

The levels of management of systems and subsystems in the organization of the supply chain are defined as follows: the basic level is a simple linear supply chain, the integrated level is the sectoral integration of supply chains (complexes or clusters), the inter-industry level implies macro-integration of different supply chains.

Based on the analysis of the structure of the Gross Regional Product the main industries were chosen for the modeling process, manufacturing products that make up the main bulk of the GRP, namely agriculture, machinery, manufacturing (for different regions the sectors of industries may vary). Also in the structure of GRP a large proportion belongs to such sectors as transport, communication and information, finance—these industries provide services. The industries providing services play an important role in the integration of supply chain systems and enhancing closer interaction.

Each industry providing either products or services includes elements of at least a basic supply chain: suppliers, manufacturers, distributors, and retailers. Irrespective of their place in the supply chain, supply chain participants create jobs for people, have the production capacity or the conditions for their use and provide access to material resources (own or borrowed). For each of the supply chain enterprises, there are indicators of input and output material flows. The aggregation process of enterprises within one industrial sector can form a cluster for which also have their input and output parameters of the material flow.

The output of the material flow always requires a certain kind of services and performance of storage operations, transportation, distribution, which is usually the responsibility of the transport infrastructure providing ways for the movement of goods. All participants of the supply chain experience the demand for transport infrastructure in order to deliver their products to the end user.

The region's population is the work force and the driving force of the supply chain as well as the necessary resource for each of the participants in the supply chain. The quality of the labor force affects the development of markets, trades, sales, quality and level of production, the creation of new markets, etc.

Each company has production capacity, which depends on the volume of fixed assets and labor resources and affects the volume of production industries.

A separate question concerns investments made in the development of the transport and logistics infrastructure in the region. The model should include arrangements governing the direction and the amount of the investment in the development of basic and additional industries in the region.

The main indicator of the economic development of the region is the contributions to the budget of all enterprises, population dynamics, income, availability of health services, education, quality of education, and quality of life, etc. Integrated economic efficiency of the region can be estimated at the business level, at the industry level and at the regional level. At the business level the effectiveness criteria are the profit, the level of services, the number of customers, sales, logistics costs. At the industry level the effectiveness criteria are the interactions of participants in supply chains and supply chains themselves, their process of integration at the level of inter-branch industrial structure. The aim of the industry is the increase of the volume of products, the manufacturing capacity or upgrading production facilities, using such efficiency criteria as profit, production volume, and sales volume. At the level of the region the effectiveness of the system of cross-sectoral integration of supply chains is considered. The goal of the region is to improve the quality of life for the population and the efficiency criteria indicators include GRP, population dynamics growth, income of population.

The Implementation of a Simulation Model of the Region's Supply Chain

The simulation model of the region's supply chain system is implemented in the AnyLogic simulation system based on the system dynamics methods and represents a set of interrelated sub-models "Population," "Agriculture," "Manufacturing," "Transport".

The sub-model "Population" describes the dynamics of the three age groups (younger, middle, and high), as well as the dynamics of employment in the region's main industries—agriculture, manufacturing, and transport industry. The model takes into account the migration of the population, depending on the economic situation of the region, in particular the availability of jobs. The key indicator is unemployment at the sub-model level.

The sub-model "Agriculture" (see Fig. 1) and "Manufacturing" describe the movement of material flows in the process of production and distribution of finished products, as well as the related financial flows in the respective industries. Part of the produced finished products of each industry is available in retail. The volume of sales depends on the size and income of the population. The second part of the

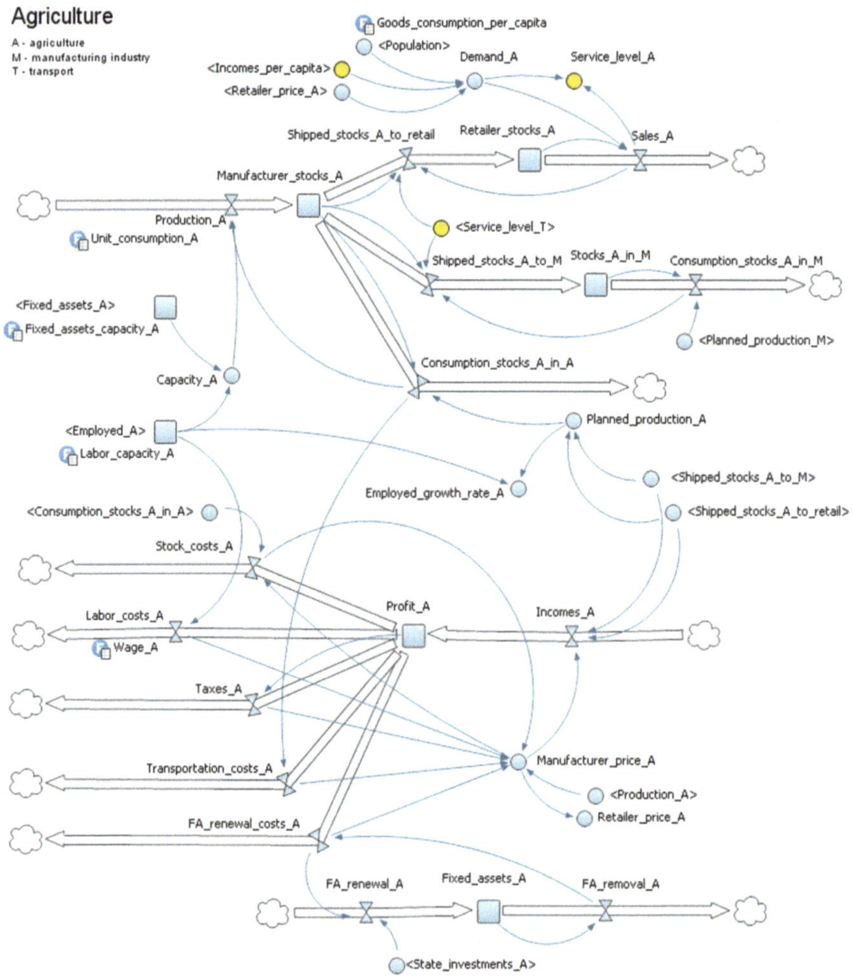

Fig. 1 Fragment of the system flow chart "Agriculture"

production sector comes to another industry as raw materials, the third part of the products is used mostly by producing industry. Thus, the output is affected by the amount of available labor resources and capital assets, as well as by the availability of raw materials. The ability of the industry to meet the demand for finished goods determines the level of service. As a result, sales of products to the population and other sectors of the industry generate revenues that are spent on the purchase of raw materials, labor costs, payment of taxes, and replacement of fixed assets. As a tool of state regulation the model reproduces the state investment mechanism stimulating the renewal of the industry's fixed assets.

Sub-model "Transport" (see Fig. 2) defines and describes the dynamics of the state of transport infrastructure in view of investment in transport infrastructure. Indirectly, it estimates the effectiveness of investments in the development of regional transport infrastructure, as well as how indicators of output streams of supply chain industries such as agriculture and manufacturing industries depend on the state of the transportation infrastructure providing the way, speed of delivery, and better delivery service to the final consumer and, therefore, access to new markets for enterprises.

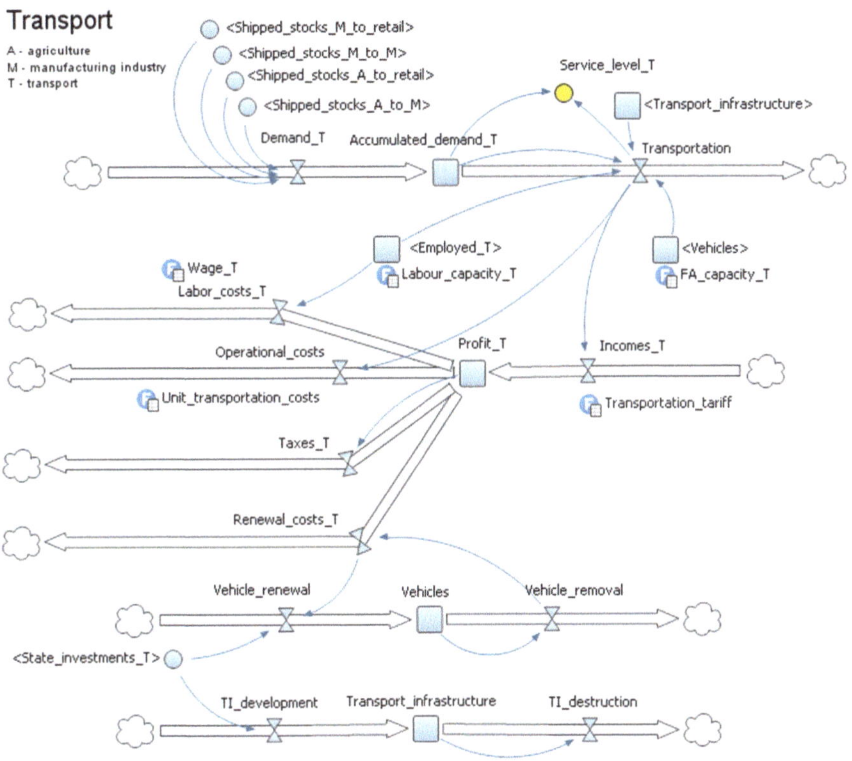

Fig. 2 Fragment of the system flow chart "Transport"

Base data and indicators in the region have been made into one database, enabling us to practically apply simulation for the tasks of strategic development of a certain region to analyze its economic state, predict the region's development, and evaluate a set of scenarios and solutions for the management of the economic development of the region, in order to select the most effective and balanced one in various fields, ensuring the achievement of stable macro-controlled system.

The study of the simulation model of the regional supply chain systems allowed us to identify the cyclical nature and interdependence of the effectiveness of key sectors and their mutual influence on each other at the cross-sectoral level. At the macroeconomic level, the simulation model allowed us to determine the point of imbalance and the impact of the main driving forces: the presence or absence of resources (human and material), the state of production facilities, and the implementation of innovation and technology for socioeconomic development of the region and its economic growth. The simulation model shows the development not only at the regional level, taking into account microeconomic indicators of GRP and the dynamics of industry growth, it also predicts living standards of the population, which are influenced by the level of industries providing services and the quality and volume of products that affect the prices and availability of goods.

Conclusions

As the result of the analysis of the possible outcome based on the created simulation model of the region's development on the example of a particular region of Russia, recommendations have been formulated on the main directions of its activities such as formation of cooperation ties and partnership models both rigid and flexible; the development of several levels of suppliers for major industries; the development of more compact and technologically advanced transport infrastructure of the region as the auxiliary industry for the development of the supply chain system and to maintain the basic engineering and agricultural industries.

The created simulation model is universal and can be filled with data on specific regions, applicable as an effective tool for managing the development of the macroeconomic system with its own regional logistics and transport infrastructure.

References

Lychkina, N.N. 2016. Synergetics and development processes in socio-economic systems: Search for effective modeling constructs. *Business Informatics* (1): 66–79.

Steger, M.B. 2009. *Globalism: The new market ideology*, 3rd ed. Rowman & Littlefield.

Calculating Handling of Business Resources for Establishing a Successful Information's Technology Project

Christos Chaldezos, Damianos P. Sakas, Nasiopoulos K. Dimitrios and Despina S. Giakomidou

Introduction

A major theme of a leader in Information's Technology projects is that he depends on persons in order to achieve his goal, which is no other than delivering on time a successful project. As a result, the importance of hiring stakeholders with specific characteristics is crucial for establishing a successful team throughout he will achieve his goal (Kauer et al. 2007). A skillful project manager has to know which is the key for motivating and organizing his team and never loosing the real motive (Weiss and Hoegl 2016). Without a doubt, leaders should understand that are capable of influencing their team members but not manipulate them. The more a leader manipulates an employee, the less he will gain from him.

When project managers understand their stakeholders, the leadership of a project becomes easier. They do not need to use negative tactics to force people to make an impact (Rezania and Lingham 2009). Using approvable tactics, they synchronize their members with their tasks, matching their personalities, talents, and skills in order to establish a cohesive group. When this happens, members obtain self-confidence, responsibility and they develop a sense of response for their project (Joslin and Müller 2016).

However, leaders should never forget the human factor, if they want to deliver the project on time, not to overcome business budget and to develop a successful project. Some circumstances are common, some can deal with them and some not. A common factor that a leader has to deal with is the dominance of negative feelings, like fear, anger, and disappointment. These kinds of feelings road people

C. Chaldezos (✉) · D.P. Sakas · N.K. Dimitrios
Department of Informatics and Telecommunications, University of Peloponnese, Tripoli, Greece
e-mail: xaldezos@gmail.com

D.S. Giakomidou
Registry Department, Athens Chamber of Commerce and Industry, Athens, Greece

A. Kavoura et al. (eds.), *Strategic Innovative Marketing*, Springer Proceedings in Business and Economics, DOI 10.1007/978-3-319-56288-9_48

in bad performance with the result to make again and again the same parts of the project and not to deal well with time. Furthermore, a great negative factor in a project is without a doubt a conflict. A negative conflict is always the biggest fear of a leader and the greatest threat of a project (Gonçalves et al. 2016).

Model

The model of this theory consists of four parts. The first part contains the basic characteristics that a new employee should have; and his manager must synchronize with his coworkers, in order to be part of successful team. These characteristics are personalities, talents, and skills (Arnatt and Beyerlein 2014).

Since finding the wright personality that will suit the team is not the easiest procedure, and because people are able to display an approvable personality in the hiring procedures, the percentage of the company resources that we choose to provide for finding the suitable personalities comes up to 11%. Hence, because the incoming personality may not match with the whole team and due to the human factor and the possibility of mistake from the human resources team, the waste of personalities is really high, around 40%.

As for the talents, a company should dispose a big amount of resources, since talents are able to make the difference in a project team and give business a great competitive advantage. For that reason, the percentage of the company resources rises up to 23%. We needed more, but finding talented employees in a small amount of time is not the easiest procedure. Also, because talents most of the time need a different approach from the leader in order to be effective, we have a waste of 20% from them.

The last characteristic that a team member should have is his skills. A person with skills will not need a lot of training, and moreover will give a great effort in a small amount of time. So the percentage of company resources that should be provided is 39%. The waste of them is really low—5%—because skills are deducible knowledge.

These factors are filling positively the stock of success, with the amount of resources that stay in them, after subtracting the percentage of waste. Unfortunately, the stock of success is influenced negatively from the controversial factors that are represented in the second part of the model. These factors are fear, anger, disappointment and conflicts. The responsible for these feelings of the members is mainly the project manager when he is unable to manage his team, synchronize their skills and personalities and waste their talents. Also conflicts are a result of those un-synchronizations, lack of goals, and bad time handling (Smith et al. 2011).

Since conflicts are the greatest hazard in a project, the amount of influencing the success is the biggest of all the negative factors and rises to 40%. The other three factors, influence negatively with same amount the success (20%). We could not see any difference between them, because are emotional feelings; therefore imponderable factor. It is crucial to mention that in our model we put a switch between these negative factors and the success, for controlling their influence. This switch is manually opened when a conflict rises or a negative feeling wakes up after a lack of leadership. When everything goes well in a project the switch remains closed.

It is generally known that a company is not able to exploit the entirely success of the project manager. A small amount of it wastes and it rises up to 10%.

The third part of the model shows the benefits of the project manager success. After the wright matching of members, synchronization of their talents and skills and effective repel of conflicts and emotional feelings, the team members acquire self-confidence, responsibility and a sense of response for the project.

The amount of the resources from the stock of success that fills the member's self-confidence is 30%. The waste of it is only 0.05%, since researches shows that when this emotion is achieved, rarely loosed inside the life cycle of the project.

The biggest percentage of the resources from success—40%—goes to the stock of response. This is because, as the time passes and the life cycle of the project goes to its end, the members feel that are part of the project and they have the response to successfully deliver it. Some members may not feel the same for the project, so an important amount of resources will lost (10%).

The remaining resources—20%—will go to the responsibility of the members. Response and responsibility may seem the same, but are totally different factors which influence in common the project life cycle. Since the members will not show the same responsibility, an amount of 10% will lost.

Subtracting the remaining resources from these stocks from their wastes, they fill the project success with non-varying percentages. This stock represents the

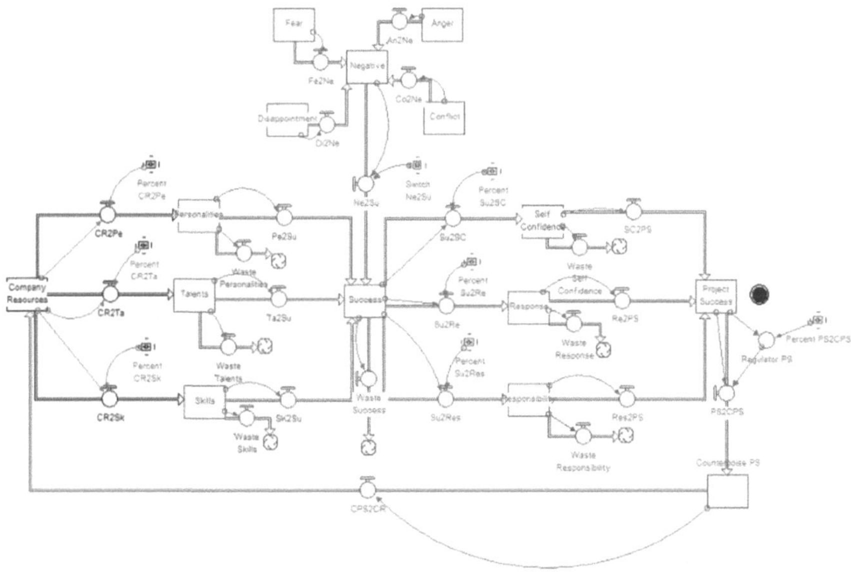

Fig. 1 Model of successful project

successful and on time as well as in budget delivery of a project. For that reason, we place an indicator which shows the satisfaction or not in real time of our goal. When the goal is satisfied, it can return throughout a regulator some resources to the company, for being used in the future in the same or in other procedures. The importance of regulator is really crucial, since it shows the achievement of the optimization of the model and its factors.

The returning is taking place through the regulator, the percentage of it and the Counterpoise_PS stock. The regulator is programmed to allow resources to fill the Counterpoise_PS when the goal is achieved (over 85%). The amount of the returning resources is defined from the Percent_PS2PCS (Fig. 1).

Simulation

The optimum scenario achieved when we returned to the company 0.30% of the resources of project success. As mentioned in the table and the diagram, the project retains its success throughout its yearly project life and the company does not been evacuated. Hence, from the second to fifth month, we managed an accomplishment greater than the expectation. For that reason we managed to return an acceptable amount of resources to the company (Table 1).

Project success is influenced from the leader and from team members. The graph represents the normality of the project. We could achieve continuously rising of the project success, but this would mean that no resources would return to the company (Fig. 2).

Table 1 The company resources to project success (monthly)

Months	Company resources	Project success
1	45.77	92.52
2	32.53	111.76
3	37.00	115.88
4	44.28	110.45
5	47.71	102.35
6	46.73	95.85
7	43.42	92.09
8	39.84	90.28
9	36.99	89.18
10	34.98	87.92
11	33.52	86.23
12	32.23	84.23

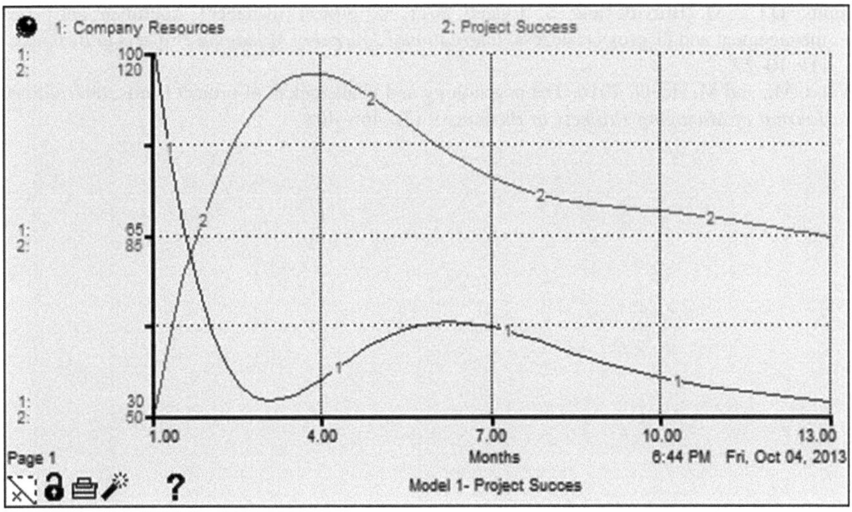

Fig. 2 The graph of company resources and project success in 1-year period

Conclusion

The careful distribution of resources leads to positive effects on the company. Project success is totally influenced both from the leader and the team members. The leader throughout his tactics, skills, and techniques is able to choose the appropriate stakeholders, synchronize the members and leads the project to success, returning some resources to the company. However, the effective project team and its characteristics are really crucial and does not modeled in total in this paper.

References

Arnatt, M.J., and M.M. Beyerlein. 2014. An empirical examination of special operations team leaders' and members' leadership characteristics. *Policing: An International Journal of Police Strategies & Management*, 37 (2): 438–453.

Gonçalves, G., M. Reis, C. Sousa, J. Santos, A. Orgambídez-Ramos, and P. Scott. 2016. Cultural intelligence and conflict management styles. *International Journal of Organizational Analysis* 24 (4): 725–742.

Joslin, R., and R. Müller. 2016. The impact of project methodologies on project success in different project environments. *International Journal of Managing Projects in Business*, 9 (2): 364–388.

Kauer, D., Tanja C. Prinzessin zu Waldeck, and U. Schäffer. 2007. Effects of top management team characteristics on strategic decision making: Shifting attention to team member personalities and mediating processes. *Management Decision* 45 (6): 942–967.

Rezania, D., and T. Lingham. 2009. Coaching IT project teams: a design toolkit. *International Journal of Managing Projects in Business* 2 (4): 577–590.

Smith, D.C., M. Bruyns, and S. Evans. 2011. A project manager's optimism and stress management and IT project success. *International Journal of Managing Projects in Business*, 4 (1): 10–27.

Weiss, M., and M. Hoegl. 2016. The psychology and management of project teams. *International Journal of Managing Projects in Business* 9 (2): 466–468.

Calculating Handling of Company Resources for Establishing an Effective Project Team

Christos Chaldezos, Damianos Sakas, Nasiopoulos K. Dimitrios and Despina S. Giakomidou

Introduction

As the majority of Project Managers mention, the establishment of an effective project team is crucial for achieving the goals ant the purposes of a project (Pina et al. 2008). However, few of them manage to achieve this establishment. Most project teams act as a committee, the members are making some conferences, delivering their tasks and leaving. The synergy and partnership are the great absentees (Senaratne and Samaraweera 2015).

There are many definitions for the project team. The most of them are deficient from our point of view. From our perspective, among all of the approaches that we have read, the most suited is that a team is a small cohesive group, consists of members with supplementary skills which are adhered to achieve a common goal and everyone is responsible for it (Gustavsson and Hallin 2015). Hence, a project team is the basic unit of performance, showing the interaction among skills, talents, experiences and opinions. In other words a project team is neither a committee nor a group of people, is more adaptive and effective than any other group, since it has common purposes leading it to the best performance.

The development of a project team is not an easy procedure. It needs team work, which is the ultimate key for different people to achieve a common goal and a leader who inspires the members. Without a leader it is really unusual for an effective team to been established (Curran et al. 2009). The project managers must act as leaders and do the following actions in order to establish a successful project team:

C. Chaldezos (✉) · D. Sakas · N.K. Dimitrios
Computer Science and Technology, University of Peloponnese, Tripolis, Greece
e-mail: xaldezos@gmail.com

D.S. Giakomidou
Registry Department, Athens Chamber of Commerce and Industry, Athens, Greece

A. Kavoura et al. (eds.), *Strategic Innovative Marketing*, Springer Proceedings in Business and Economics, DOI 10.1007/978-3-319-56288-9_49

- They try to create a cohesive group, in order each member to feel part of something greater and more important than him.
- They inherit synergy among the members.
- They create a collaborative environment.
- They treat each member with respect and they cultivate the mutual respect.
- They balance their needs with team needs, achieving the team members' satisfaction (Berg and Karlsen 2014).

However, when a team lacks of team spirit and faces problems, there are some common characteristics which signify them. The leader must deal with these signs in order protect his team. These problems are:

- Negative conflicts, which are really dangerous and capable of destroying any team.
- Distrust. The mutual respect is disappeared both in actions and thoughts.
- Unclear goals. Each member has their own goals and not a common, with result of loosing synergy among them.
- The team lacks energy. The passion and the encouragement are lost.
- Lack of leadership, either because of the leader or because of the members. If that happens the team is guided from the circumstances and as a result the efficiency is rare (Joslin and Müller 2016).

If the leader manages to balance the negative factors and face them, there are some indicators that prove that the establishment of the project team is successful and the team is going to be effective, producing projects with high yield. The majority of effective project teams show their performance not only from the delivery of a successful project on time, but from many factors during the project life cycle. These factors are:

- The team dynamic
- The collaboration
- The commitment
- The team progress (Rolstadås et al. 2014)

Model

All the factors are represented by stocks in the model of Fig. 1. The percent units define the amount of resources that passes to the stocks. The regulators are interacting between the tactics of the leader and the negative factors, managing the amount of their negative influence on the team. The wastes represent the percent of the resources that we can not deposit from the stocks. The indicators show the satisfaction, or not during the simulation in the project life circle and the Counterpoise Project team controls the resources that are returning to the company.

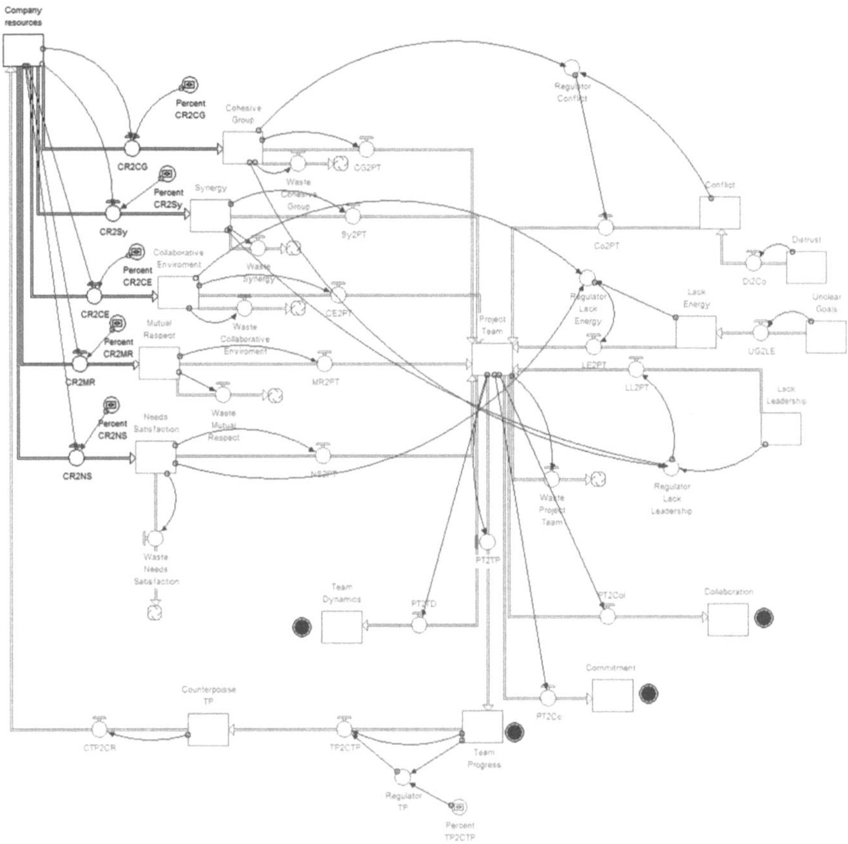

Fig. 1 Effective's team model

It is crucial to mention how the regulators work. After a lot of research we defined the factors and the amounts which leads to the rising of the negative factors. The regulators are running continuously, checking the amount of resources that exist to the stocks. Using complex IF statements, the regulators control the spigots by opening them when the IF statements are satisfied and closing them in the opposite case. Under this situation the model is running independent and trustworthy, without the need of our participation by closing and opening switches.

It has great importance to mention that we manage to satisfy all of the four indicators. This indicates that after many experimentations and approaches we succeeded in the optimization of all of the factors and of the model in general.

Table 1 The company resources and the affect to the effective project team factors (monthly)

Month	Company resources	Team progress	Team dynamic	Commitment	Collaboration
1	31.64	57.77	33.01	24.76	49.52
2	10.01	80.11	45.78	34.33	68.67
3	3.17	99.54	56.88	42.66	85.32
4	1.00	120.09	72.76	54.57	109.14
5	8.40	122.15	87.00	65.25	130.50
6	16.52	119.52	98.17	73.63	147.26
7	18.65	120.53	107.25	80.44	160.88
8	17.64	119.60	115.01	86.25	172.51
9	14.16	116.43	121.68	91.26	182.52
10	13.02	118.85	127.28	95.46	190.93
11	11.32	119.60	131.90	98.92	197.84
12	9.49	118.81	135.66	101.74	203.48

Simulation

After a lot of scenarios and case studies, we introduce the best scenario of monthly reconstruction in a period of one year of the company resources management. In this case, the satisfaction of all the indicators achieved and we manage to return an acceptable amount of resources to the company for reproducing this model, or dispose them for other company's needs.

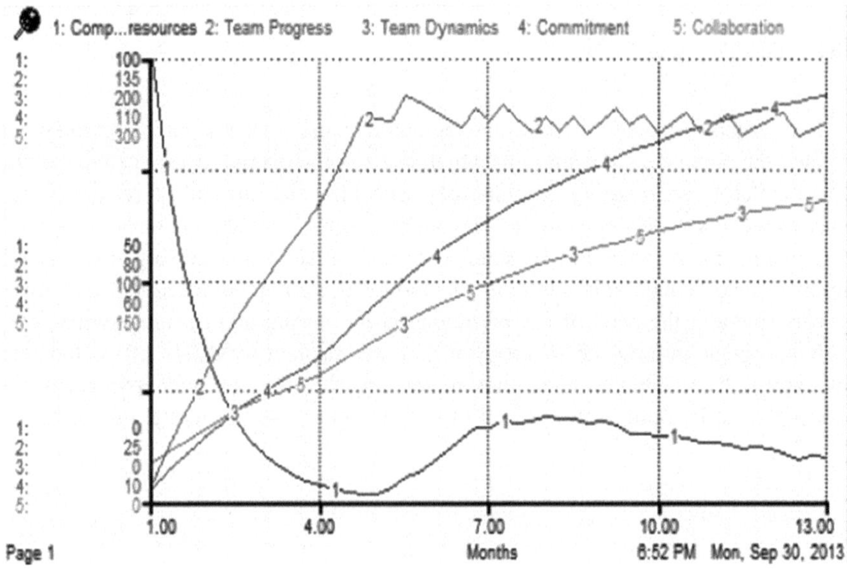

Fig. 2 Company resources and team factors diagram

Specifically, since the indicator of team progress satisfied from the third month, we return 0.2% of its resources to the company. In this way, team dynamic achieved from the seventh month, collaboration from fourth and commitment from sixth. All of the indicators stay satisfied until the end of the project (Table 1).

The smoothness of the diagram shows the effectiveness of the team. Albeit, the team progress stays stable, returning the extra resources to the company (Fig. 2).

The resources of the company are getting fewer until the fourth month. From the fifth to eight month they are on the rise, due to the refund of the resources from the team progress. Until the end of the project, the company continues to obtain resources—around 10% of the initials—amount significant and capable of maintaining the effectiveness of the project team.

Conclusion

The establishment of an effective project team is of paramount significance in the life cycle of a project. The project manager is responsible to develop these skills and techniques in order to become a leader and produce yielding teams for delivering successful projects on time. The model that we developed is a guide for it, however, we strongly believe that can be streamlined, refunding a bigger amount of resources in the company. This is possible by changing the returning procedure, evolving the commitment, collaboration and team dynamic to the returning progress.

References

Berg, M.E., and J.T. Karlsen. 2014. How project managers can encourage and develop positive emotions in project teams. *International Journal of Managing Projects in Business* 7 (3): 449–472.

Curran, C.S., B. Niedergassel, S. Picker, and J. Leker. 2009. Project leadership skills in cooperative projects. *Management Research News* 32 (5): 458–468.

Delgado Piña, M.I., A. María Romero Martínez, and L. Gómez Martínez. 2008. Teams in organizations: a review on team effectiveness. *Team Performance Management: An International Journal* 14 (1/2): 7–21.

Gustavsson, T.K., and A. Hallin. 2015. Goal seeking and goal oriented projects – trajectories of the temporary organisation. *International Journal of Managing Projects in Business* 8 (2): 368–378.

Joslin, R., and R. Müller. 2016. The impact of project methodologies on project success in different project environments. *International Journal of Managing Projects in Business* 9 (2): 364–388.

Rolstadås, A., I. Tommelein, P.M. Schiefloe, and G. Ballard. 2014. Understanding project success through analysis of project management approach. *International Journal of Managing Projects in Business* 7 (4): 638–660.

Senaratne, S., and A. Samaraweera. 2015. Construction project leadership across the team development process. *Built Environment Project and Asset Management* 5 (1): 69–88.

Businesses: The Association Between Their Export Performance and Information and Communication Technology Adoption

John Hlias Plikas, Nasiopoulos K. Dimitrios, Eleni-Karveli Glynou, Damianos P. Sakas and D.S. Vlachos

Introduction

Businesses, the wheel of economic sustainability and a very important variable of a firm's profitability are characterized by their ability to export, the export activity (Daryanto et al. 2012). Through the years, mankind used technology, constantly seeking new ways to survive leading to the creation of the very base of every day's lives, social and economic interactions, information and communication, a linkage to the heart of economy, businesses (Bronner and de Hoog 2013). Greek economy has been a pole of study in the scientific world as it shows different variations in times of crisis and economic unsustainability (Vlamis 2014).

Simulations are used in information and communication technology with great success to simulate a real procedure with no fear of loss. Anylogic 7.2 University is a well-known tool used for this purpose (Dimitrios et al. 2013). Regression analysis is used in specific sample spectrums to identify the importance of specific variable assessments and to clarify importance (Frowd et al. 2015).

There have been 57 previous studies as regarding information and communication technology adoption of businesses and simulation modeling but no other study has been conducted so far that shows the association between businesses' export performance and information and communication technology adoption for a rare sample of 3500 Greek business firms using simulation modeling combined

J.H. Plikas (✉) · N.K. Dimitrios · D.S. Vlachos
Department of Informatics and Telecommunications, University of Peloponnese, 22100 Tripolis, Greece
e-mail: giannishliasplikas2@gmail.com

E.-K. Glynou
Msc in Economical Analyses, University of Peloponnese, 22100 Tripolis, Greece

D.P. Sakas
University of Athens, 18534 Piraeus, Greece

A. Kavoura et al. (eds.), *Strategic Innovative Marketing*, Springer Proceedings in Business and Economics, DOI 10.1007/978-3-319-56288-9_50

with regression analysis with the Anylogic 7.2 University and E-Views 8 tools and that is what makes this paper unique (Deepdyve 2016). Thorough research through the paper showed that information and communication technology adoption from Greek businesses lead to exponential export performance and activity.

Related Literature Review and Variable Assessment

This paper is based on an answered questionnaire of Greek businesses. Exports Intensity, Employee Internet usage, E-Procurement, ICT Production Integration, E-Sales, Human Capital ICT Expert Knowledge, Absorptive Capacity R&D, Technology Monitoring are the variables used representing each yes or no questionnaire answer.

Exports Intensity

Garrido et al. (2008), modelized how firm export performance is led by its competencies and showed that production, marketing and sale ones and informational competencies, lead to strategic competitiveness that gives financial and strategic performance.

Employee Internet Usage

Mathews et al. (2015) proved that Internet marketing capabilities can lead to information availability and international strategic orientation, international network and to international strategic orientation and international capabilities.

E-Procurement

Garrido et al. (2008), also believed that internet tools like size, functional areas, hierarchical level and participation, lead to efficiency and efficacy and categorized them in Intranet, Extranet, Web pages, E-mail, Videoconference and Discussion groups.

ICT Production Integration

Jung et al. (2013) collected annual statistics in ICT capital and labor productivity, during 1994–2007 searching the contribution of ICT capital in labor productivity.

ICT usage, ICT production and Non ICT capital production were the variables used. Eventually, they indicated the ICT capital been lost as regarding the labor productivity.

E-Sales/E-Commerce

Internet marketing capabilities give export information and business network relationships. Online advertising, online sales, online after sale service, market research and purchasing/procurement are part of internet marketing capabilities factors (Bianchi and Mathews 2016).

Human Capital ICT Expert Knowledge

Stucki (2016), braked the Founders' human capital term in general and specific and continued in education and experience and specific in field-specific with division in business and technical and export-specific with division in education and experience. The export-specific part is breaking in the start-up experience, industry experience, large firm experience and international experience.

Absorptive Capacity R&D

Kaynak and Kuan (1993), linked the strategy factors, export activity and firm's economic performance with others that lead to both export intensity and firm's economic performance. Exponential company growth and market value lead to innovation strategy and innovation and eventually to an exponential export activity and performance.

Technology Monitoring

Kaynak and Kuan (1993) also introduced a high–low performer model, with characteristics as export-related R&D expenditure divided in the percentage of export sales from patented products and the export sales from new products. New knowledge from R%D, give export-related R&D expenditure, then export sales from patented products export sales from new products, thus giving export intensity.

Empirical Strategy

The Dependent variable is Exports Intensity in binary numbers. The variables presented in the theory are the independent ones. Binary Probit method is used for binary numbers analysis. C(1), C(2), C(3), C(4), C(5), C(6), C(7), C(8), will be estimated with C(1) being the constant variable.

$$\begin{aligned}\text{EXPORTS\_BINARY} = \mathbf{C(1)} + \mathbf{C(2)} * \text{D10\_ABSORPTIVE\_CAPACITY\_R\_AND\_D} \\ + \mathbf{C(3)} * \text{ICT\_PRODUCTION\_INTEGRATION} \\ + \mathbf{C(4)} * \text{TECHNOLOGY\_MONITORING} \\ + \mathbf{C(5)} * \text{EMPLOYEE\_INTERNET\_USAGE} \\ + \mathbf{C(6)} * \text{ESALES} + \mathbf{C(7)} * \text{E\_PROCUREMENT} \\ + \mathbf{C(8)} * \text{HUMAN\_CAPITAL\_ICT\_EXPERT\_KNOWLEDGE}\end{aligned}$$

In Table 1, we indicate the regression results of the model analysis using Binary Probit method. Positive C(7) and E-Procurement has probability lesser than the other variables. This variable affects Exports_Binary the most, whereas C(4) and Technology_Monitoring has the second biggest positive impact in Exports_Binary variable.

Table 1 Regression results

	Coefficient	Std.Error	z-Statistic	Prob.
C(1)	−0.221635	0.114477	−1.936064	0.0529
C(2)	0.013084	0.017624	0.742375	0.4579
C(3)	0.027275	0.024466	1.114802	0.2649
C(4)	0.045525	0.023537	1.934217	0.0531
C(5)	−0.044563	0.020267	−2.198744	0.0279
C(6)	−0.011018	0.026871	−0.410024	0.6818
C(7)	0.046304	0.024477	1.891761	0.0585
C(8)	−0.024875	0.023046	−1.079354	0.2804
Mean dependent var		0.492716		
S.E. of regression		0.497795	**S.D. dependent var**	0.500161
Sum squared resid		287.2003	**Akaike info criterion**	1.384317
Log likelihood		−799.749	**Schwarz criterion**	1.419019
Deviance		1599.498	**Hannan-Quinn crit.**	1.397407
Avg.log likelihood		−0.685303	**Restr.deviance**	1617.558
Obs with Dep = 0		592	**Total obs**	1167
Obs with Dep = 1		575		

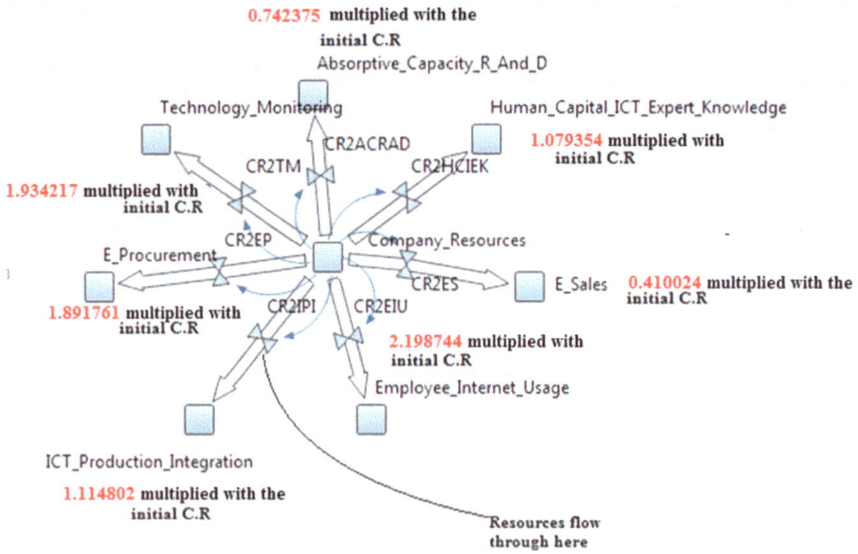

Fig. 1 Exact numbers of resource percentage given from the firm for each variable implication

Implementation of the Dynamic Simulation Model and the Importance of z-Statistic

Anylogic 7.2.0 University is used to modelize our simulation dynamically with empirical analysis and simulation modeling. All previous research connects to this paper, closing the gap with the z-statistic. It measures the null hypothesis of a given sample data. Z is stored as a percentage and is multiplied by the initial resources given to each variable.

Stocks, flows, converters and connectors consist of the model. A stock shows the concentration of a quantity. A flow fills or depletes a stock. The arrow points the direction of a flow in a stock. Connectors are action links or dashed wires, information links. A converter converts inflows into outflows through user-defined algebraic or graphical functions (Dimitrios et al. 2013) (Fig. 1).

Identification and Explanation of the Dynamic Simulation Model

Theoretical research is applied, by using the Dynamic Simulation Model (Dimitrios et al. 2013). Resources are supplied from the basic counterpart "Company_Resources" stock subsection to "E_Sales" stock, "Human_Capital_ICT_Expert_Knowledge" stock, "ICT_Production_Integration" "E_Procurement",

"Technology_Monitoring", "Absorptive_Capacity_R_And_D", "Employee_Internet_Usage" Subsections. "Exports_Intensity" combines the satisfaction levels of the other independent variable factors and in the same time counteracts the initial resources lost. Figure 2 presents this combination.

Figure 3 shows that the satisfaction percentage as regarding all seven leading factors is raising significantly during the first months and then they gain stability. Exports Intensity eventually stabilizes too and gives very satisfied results. Pie chart shows that the amount of Exports gained back, is approximately four times higher than the initial Company Resources lost.

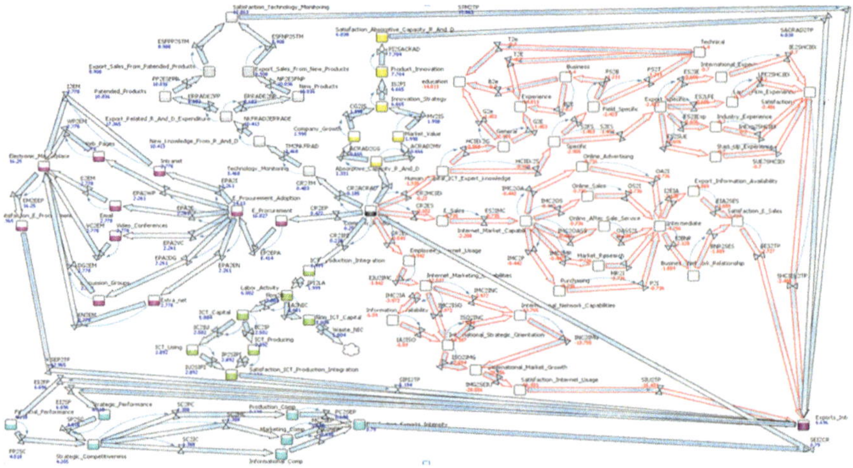

Fig. 2 Implication of the simulation model using Anylogic 7.2 University

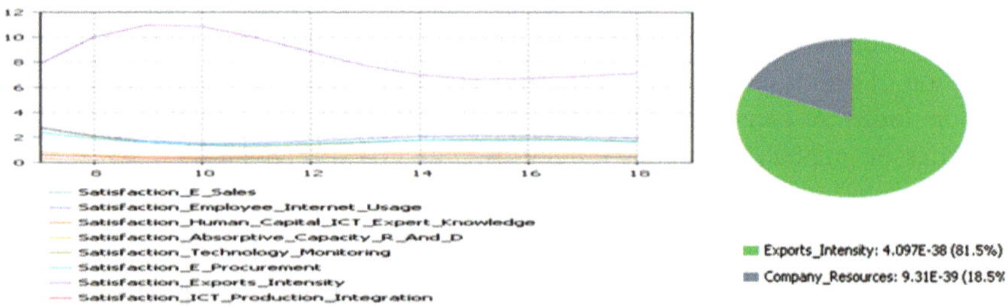

Fig. 3 Time Chart and Pie Chart: Satisfaction E_Sales, in conjunction with Satisfaction_ Internet_Usage, Satisfaction_Human_Capital_ICT_Expert_Knowledge, Satisfaction_Absorptive_Capacity_R_And_D, Satisfaction_Technology_Monitoring, Satisfaction_E_Procurement_ Exports_Intensity and Satisfaction_ ICT_Production_Integration. Pie Chart: Company Resources in conjunction with Exports_Intensity

Conclusions

In this research was made an attempt to simulate the association between their businesses' export performance and information and communication technology adoption for a sample of 3500 Greek business firms by modeling a regression analysis using Anylogic 7.2 University and E-Views 8. The nature of the variables examined is dynamic. Regression analysis and is used to calculate the statistical importance and depict it in dynamic modeling. This article attempts to steer the reader in the right direction about the influence of the export intensity factor in Greek businesses by measuring the appropriate satisfaction levels. Thorough research, statistical analysis and simulation modeling through this paper revealed that E-Procurement has the biggest positive impact in export performance and intensity of the Greek firms. Further research could be conducted on a given IT product or service, the company's objectives, its size and limitations of the firm.

References

Bianchi, C., and S. Mathews. 2016. Internet marketing and export market growth in Chile. *Journal of Business Research* 69 (2): 426–434.

Bronner, F., and R. de Hoog. 2013. Economizing on vacations: the role of information searching. *International Journal of Culture, Tourism and Hospitality Research* 7 (1): 28–41.

Daryanto, A., H. Khan, B. Candelon, E.I. Dumitrescu, C. Hurlin, and F.C. Palm. 2012. Multivariate dynamic probit models: An application to financial crises mutation.

Deepdyve. 2016. *ICT businesses simulation*. https://www.deepdyve.com/search?query=ICT+businesses+simulation. Accessed 9 Oct 2016.

Dimitrios, N.K., D.P. Sakas, and D.S. Vlachos. 2013. Analysis of strategic leadership models in information technology. *Procedia—Social and Behavioral Sciences* 73: 268–275.

Frowd, C.D., W.B. Erickson, J.M. Lampinen, F.C. Skelton, A.H. McIntyre, and P.J. Hancock. 2015. A decade of evolving composites: regression-and meta-analysis. *Journal of Forensic Practice* 17 (4): 319–334.

Garrido, M.J., A. Gutiérrez, and R. San José. 2008. Organizational and economic consequences of business e-procurement intensity. *Technovation* 28 (9): 615–629.

Jung, H.J., K.Y. Na, and C.H. Yoon. 2013. The role of ICT in Korea's economic growth: Productivity changes across industries since the 1990s. *Telecommunications Policy* 37 (4): 292–310.

Kaynak, E., and W.K.Y. Kuan. 1993. Environment, strategy, structure, and performance in the context of export activity: An empirical study of Taiwanese manufacturing firms. *Journal of Business Research* 27 (1): 33–49.

Mathews, S., C. Bianchi, K.J. Perks, M. Healy, and R. Wickramasekera. 2015. Internet marketing capabilities and international market growth. *International Business Review*.

Stucki, T. 2016. How the founders' general and specific human capital drives export activities of start-ups. *Research Policy* 45 (5): 1014–1030.

Vlamis, P. 2014. Greek fiscal crisis and repercussions for the property market. *Journal of Property Investment & Finance* 32 (1): 21–34.

Modelling the Process of a Web-Based Collaboration Tool Development

Nasiopoulos K. Alexandros, Sakas P. Damianos, Nasiopoulos K. Dimitrios and Vlachos S. Dimitrios

Introduction

Most online collaboration tools share the same operation mode. A user creates a message in the collaboration tool, which is called client and the message is delivered to the collaboration server which conveys the message to other clients. The message can be an e-mail, a chat message, a vote in a poll or even a frame in videoconferencing (Dobre 2006) (Fig. 1).

In the following chapters we will simulate the process of a collaboration tool development, from a web design company, from scratch. This means that the company should acquire all the necessary resources for the development of such a tool.

Company Resources Allocation

The main purpose of every healthy enterprise is to create a competitive product or service in order to make profit. To accomplish that, the business managers should explore ways to reduce the resources required to perform various activities (Cooper et al. 1991) and then appropriately distribute the available company resources to obtain the necessary resources for the creation of the product or service. For the purpose of this paper, the necessary resources are the technological resources and human resources for the creation of the final product, the collaboration tool.

N.K. Alexandros (✉) · S.P. Damianos · N.K. Dimitrios · V.S. Dimitrios
Department of Informatics and Telecommunications, University of Peloponnese, Tripoli, Greece
e-mail: pcst15014@uop.gr

A. Kavoura et al. (eds.), *Strategic Innovative Marketing*, Springer Proceedings in Business and Economics, DOI 10.1007/978-3-319-56288-9_51

Fig. 1 Client–server relationship and most popular collaborative tools

Technological resources refer to the required technological equipment to effectively create a product or service. In our case they include:

- A personal computer
- An operating system
- A code editor
- A web hosting provider

Human resources are the most significant in any organization. With the machines, materials and even the money, nothing gets done without man power (Olaniyan et al. 2008). Human resources include (Mathis et al. 2003), among others;

- Staffing is a process of hiring and or positioning in an organization (Heneman III et al. 2005).
- Staff Training is a systematic development of the knowledge, skills and attitudes required by employees to perform adequately on a given task or job (Olaniyan et al. 2008).
- Staff Motivation is the enthusiasm and persistence with which a person does a task. Ngu (1998) contends that the two most important variables explaining employee performance are motivation and ability.

The main goal of the project is the development of a competitive web application, which, in our case, is the collaboration tool. In order to characterize an application as "competitive", certain conditions must met:

- Functionality refers to all the functions that the application should do, according to its purpose.
- Design is about minimizing the complexity of an application while designing a good-looking, easy-to-use, high-performance application.
- Responsive web design makes an application look good on all devices; desktops, tablets and phones.
- Security goals are authentication, authorization, auditing and confidentiality, integrity and availability (Salini et al. 2012).

Collaboration is an interactive process in which human interact to achieve common goals, by sharing knowledge, learning and building consensus (Lomas et al. 2008). A collaboration tool is a tool that enables remote collaboration. A good collaboration tool should:

- Promote communication
- Share a photograph, paper, diagram and similar objects
- Allow natural interactions (Lomas et al. 2008)

Dynamic Simulation Model System Analysis

Since the main factors of the model and its sub-categories, were analyzed, we can create diagrams and tables dynamically (Richardson 2013). To achieve that we made use of iThink software, by isee^{TM} systems. Using this software, we can simulate the influence of each factor to the system, as time passes by (Sakas et al. 2014).

The "Company Resources" stock represents the available human, technical and economical resources for the specific project (Fig. 2). Using flows and converters, company resources are shared for the acquisition of the necessary technological resources and human resources through "CR2TR" and "CR2HR" flows, which are controlled by "Percent CR2TR" and "Percent CR2HR" respectively. The percentages we used are shown in Fig. 3.

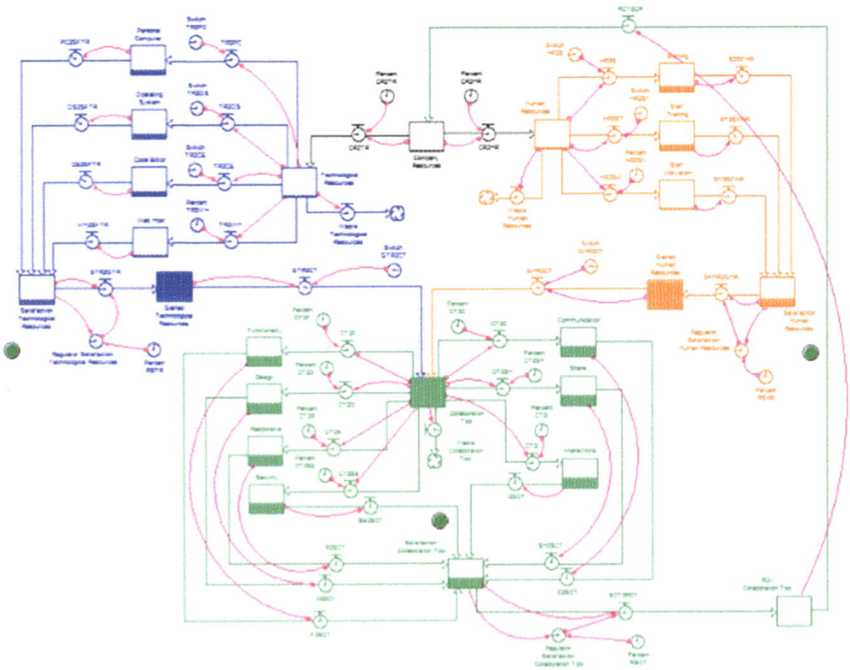

Fig. 2 Dynamic simulation model

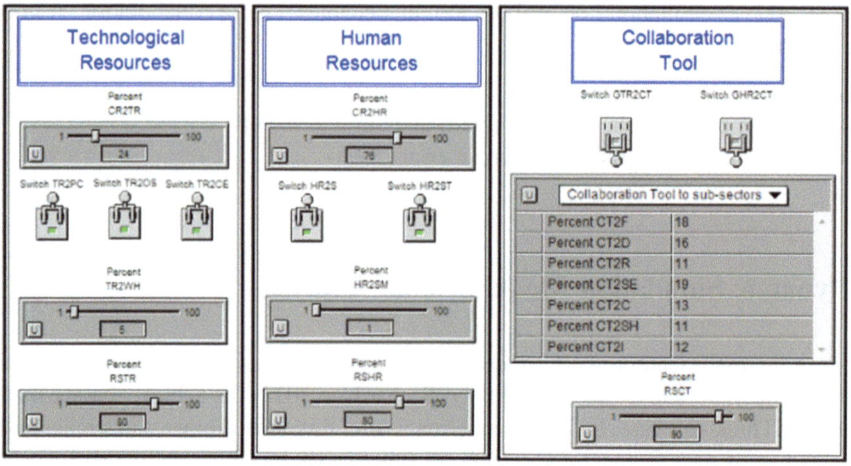

Fig. 3 Administrative interface

"Technological Resources" are shared, for the acquisition of a "Personal Computer", an "Operating System", a "Code Editor" and the "Web Hosting Provider". When these are obtained, resources move to the "Satisfaction Technological Resources" stock which gets full and the adjoining lamp becomes green. Then resources move to "Gained Technological Resources" stock, until the opening of "Switch GTR2CT", which will allow the beginning of the "Collaboration Tool" development.

Human resources are shared to "Staffing", "Staff Training" and "Staff Motivation". Then resources move to the "Satisfaction Human Resources" stock, which when gets full the adjoining lamp becomes green and resources move to "Gained Human Resources" stock, which is controlled from "Switch GHR2CT".

After opening the "Switch GTR2CT" and "Switch GHR2CT", resources move to the "Collaboration Tool" stock. From there, they are shared for the collaboration tool "Functionality", "Design", "Responsive", "Security", "Communication", "Share" and "Interactions". Then, resources are gathered to the "Satisfaction Collaboration Tool" stock which gets full and the adjoining lamp becomes green. After that, resources move to "ROI from Collaboration Tool" stock which represents the "Return of Investment" from the collaboration tool. Finally resources return to the initial "Company Resources" stock.

Running the Model

We run the model with switches "TR2PC", "TR2OS", "TR2CE", "HR2S", "HR2ST" turned on and switches "GTR2CT" and "GHR2CT" turned off, as shown in Fig. 3. That represents the anticipation of the collaboration tool development

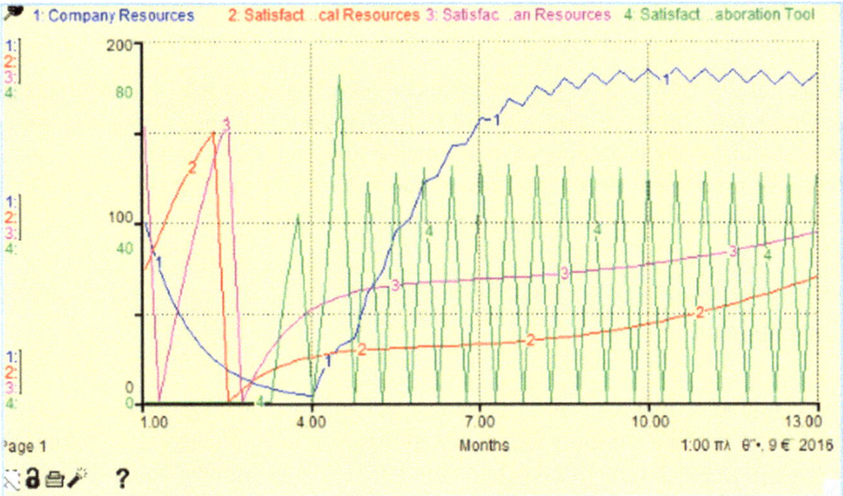

Fig. 4 Graph of company resources, satisfaction technological resources, satisfaction human resources and satisfaction collaboration tool, in one year

beginning, until the acquisition of the necessary technological and human resources.

After the acquisition of the necessary technological and human resources, around third month on Fig. 4, we paused the running, we closed switches "TR2PC", "TR2OS", "TR2CE", "HR2S", "HR2ST" and we opened switches "GTR2CT" and "GHR2CT". Results are shown in Figs. 4 and 5.

1:00 πμ 9/12/2016 Table 2

Months	Company Resources	Functionality	ROI Collaboration Tool
Jan: Initial	100.00	0.00	0.00
Jan	31.64	0.00	0.00
Feb	10.01	0.00	0.00
Mar	3.17	2.52	79.27
Apr	61.01	3.30	104.78
May	121.79	3.52	135.99
Jun	157.28	3.58	150.36
July	175.13	3.55	155.58
Aug	182.73	3.52	156.71
Sep	185.11	3.49	156.17
Oct	185.07	3.46	155.00
Nov	183.97	3.42	153.59
Dec	182.43	3.39	152.11

Fig. 5 Table of company resources, functionality and ROI collaboration tool, in one year

Results

As we can see from Fig. 4, the available company resources fell from one hundred to almost zero, until the acquisition of technological and human resources, around third month. At the beginning of fourth month, they started a constant rising, as the Return of Investment (ROI) from collaboration tool began to rise (Fig. 5), for their final stabilization to almost two times their initial value.

Conclusions

The continuous evolution of 21st century technology, forced companies environment to become increasingly dynamic and organizations to constantly looking for new ways to stay on top of evolution (Buur et al. 2011). Simulation modelling is a business tool, which allows a safe representation of real life conditions for making decisions quick and without suffering from the consequences of a wrong decision (Jansen-Vullers and Netjes 2006).

In this paper we simulated the process of a collaboration tool development. For this purpose, we gathered all the main factors that affect both a web application and a collaboration tool development. After that we made a model of the system, we run the model and we changed some parameters dynamically, for the optimization of the results.

References

Buur, J., and R. Mitchell. 2011. The business modelling lab. In *Participatory innovation conference*.

Cooper, R., and R.S. Kaplan. 1991. Profit priorities from activity-based costing. *Harvard Business Review*.

Dobre, L. 2006. Aspects of collaboration tools in E-learning. *Seria Matematică - Informatică - Fizică* LVIII (1/2006): 51–56.

Heneman III, H., and T.A. Judge. 2005. *Staffing organizations*. USA: McGraw-Hill. ISBN 0-07-298722-7.

Jansen-Vullers, M.H., and M. Netjes. 2006. Business process simulation—a tool survey. In *Proceedings of the seventh workshop and tutorial on practical use of coloured petri nets and the CPN tools*. Denmark: University of Aarhus.

Lomas, C., M. Burke, and C.L. Page. 2008. Collaboration tools. *Educause Learning Initiative*.

Mathis, R.L., and J.H. Jackson. 2003. *Human resource management*. Thomson.

Ngu, S.M. 1998. *Motivation theory and workers compensation in Nigeria*. Zaria: ABU Press.

Olaniyan, D.A., and L.B. Ojo. 2008. Staff training and development: A vital tool for organisational effectiveness. *European Journal of Scientific Research* 24 (3): 326–331. ISSN 1450-216X.

Richardson, G. 2013. System dynamics. *Encyclopedia of Operations Research and Management Science* 1519–1522.

Sakas, D.P., D.S. Vlachos, and D.K. Nasiopoulos. 2014. Modelling strategic management for the development of competitive advantage, based on technology. *Journal of Systems and Information Technology* 16 (3): 187–209.

Salini, P.A., and S.B. Kanmani. 2012. Security Requirements Engineering Process for Web Applications. doi:10.1016/j.proeng.2012.06.328.

Comparing Scrum and XP Agile Methodologies Using Dynamic Simulation Modeling

Nasiopoulos K. Alexandros, Damianos P. Sakas, D.S. Vlachos and Nasiopoulos K. Dimitrios

Introduction

It has been fifteen years since the articulation of agile manifesto in 2001, which brought great changes in software application development (Dingsøyr et al. 2012). According to the Manifesto for Agile Software Development (agileAlliance.org), agile methods value "(1) individuals and interactions over processes and tools, (2) working software over comprehensive documentation, (3) customer collaboration over contract negotiation, and (4) responding to change over following a plan" (Wadhwa and Sharma 2015; Salo and Abrahamsson 2007; Mushtaq and Qureshi 2012).

Agility is the ability to detect and address the business perspective to remain inventive and aggressive in a labile and rapidly changing business environment. The continuous evolution of twenty-first century technology forced companies' environment to become increasingly dynamic and organizations to constantly modify their software requirements to adjust with the new environment (Moniruzzaman and Hossain 2013).

Scrum Methodology

Scrum methodology is a method that tries to keep things simple in a constantly shifting business environment. Scrum is composed of short, strenuous daily meetings of the project team, in order to deliver quality software in 24-h short-time periods called "sprints".

N.K. Alexandros (✉) · D.P. Sakas · D.S. Vlachos · N.K. Dimitrios
Department of Informatics and Telecommunications, University of Peloponnese, Tripoli, Greece
e-mail: pcst15014@uop.gr

A. Kavoura et al. (eds.), *Strategic Innovative Marketing*, Springer Proceedings in Business and Economics, DOI 10.1007/978-3-319-56288-9_52

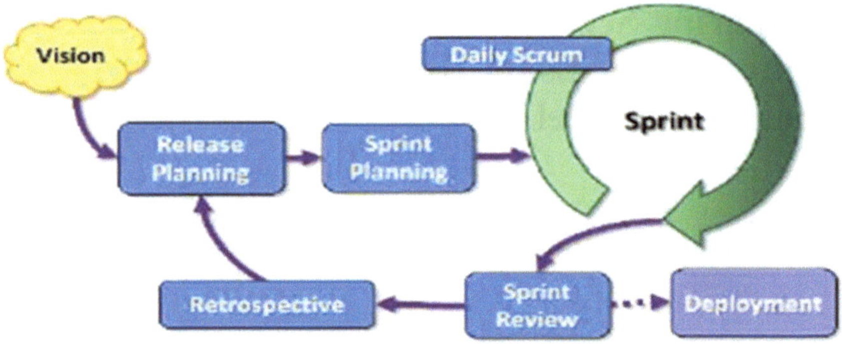

Fig. 1 Scrum methodology process flow (Mahalakshmi et al. 2013)

The key principles of Scrum methodology are the following:

- Small working teams for better communication and less expenses;
- Adaptability to changes in order to produce quality software;
- Daily software "builds" that can be tested, documented and used for further implementation;
- Distinct work segmentation and assignment to teams;
- Constant documentation and testing of the produced product;
- Ability to characterize a product as "finished" whenever required (Yadav 2015) (Fig. 1)

XP Methodology

XP methodology focuses on the constant interaction of customer, manager, and programmer and clearly defines the role each one has. In XP methodology small releases are produced periodically and tested, in order to maintain customer satisfaction through the life cycle of the software development (Fig. 2).

The key principles of XP methodology are as follows:

- Customers should participate actively in the whole process;
- Small releases are produced periodically and tested to gain early feedback from the customers;
- XP team is planning the work for the next release to reach the goals from the customers, within specific time and funds;
- Each member of the team must have full acknowledgment of how the entire product works and own the skills to improve it;
- Code must be continuously inspected for simplicity, refactoring, and tested for integration and errors (Yadav 2015).

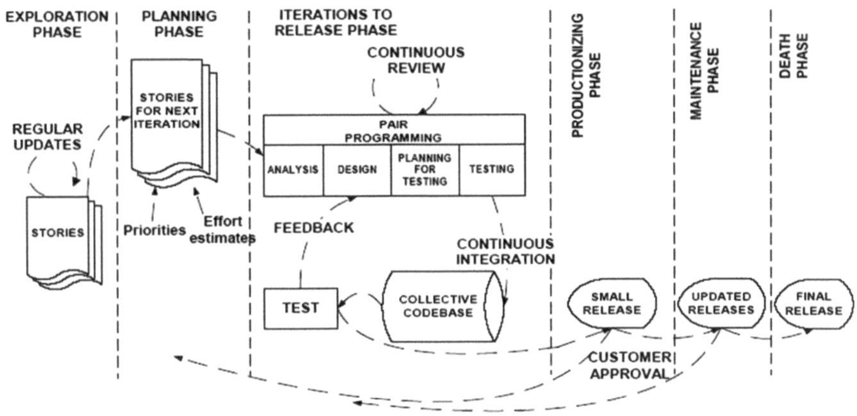

Fig. 2 XP methodology process flow (Al-Saleem et al. 2015)

In the next chapters we will proceed to the simulation and modeling of the two procedures, in order to compare them for finding the most appropriate to be applied in the case of collaboration tools.

Dynamic Simulation Model System Analysis

Since we analyzed the key principles of each methodology, we can create diagrams and tables dynamically (Richardson 2013; Sakas et al. 2014). To achieve that we made use of iThink software, by isee™ systems, using this software, we can simulate the influence of each factor to the system, as time pass by (Sakas et al. 2014; Jansen-Vullers et al. 2006).

The available company resources for this project, represented by “Company Resources” stock, are moved to “Working Teams”, through “CR2WT” flow (Fig. 3). Then they are shared through flows and converters to “Work Segmentation” and “Changing Adaptability”. The distribution of resources has been chosen so as to provide the best results to the procedure of implementing the collaboration tool. After satisfaction of these factors occurs, the lamps become green, the resources of “Work Segmentation” and “Changing Adaptability” are gathered to the “Daily Software”. The next stage is the procedure of “Documentation and Testing” which after being satisfied leads to the software development (Fig. 4).

Figure 5 represents the graphical results for 12 months for five stocks, “Satisfaction Work Segmentation”, “Satisfaction Changing Adaptability”, “Satisfaction Documentation and Testing”, “Satisfaction Product”, and “Company Resources”.

When simulating the XP methodology, “Company Resources” are moved to the “Team”, through “CR2T” flow and are distributed to the “Team Regroup” and “Release” (Fig. 6). “Customers” also give resources to the “Team Regroup” and

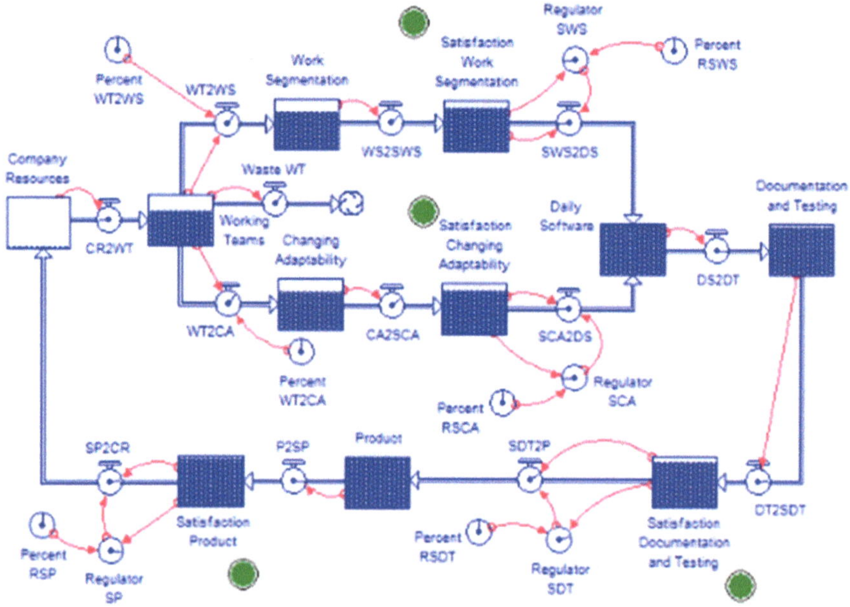

Fig. 3 Scrum methodology dynamic simulation model

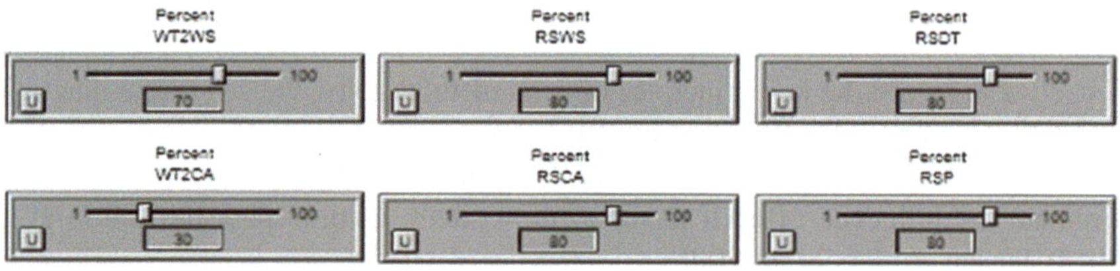

Fig. 4 Scrum methodology simulation converters percentages

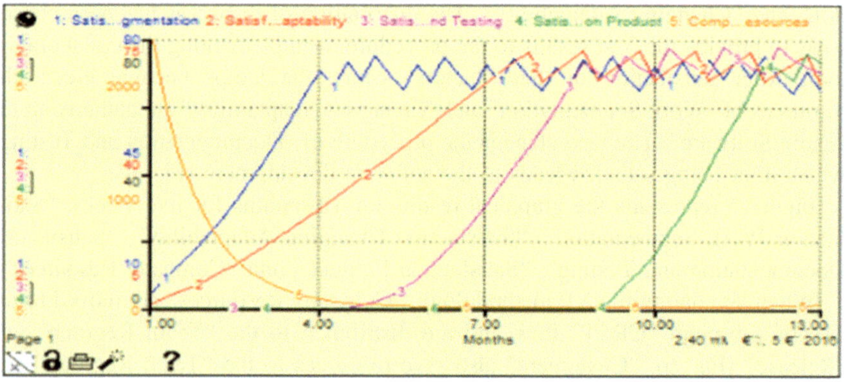

Fig. 5 Scrum methodology simulation graphical results

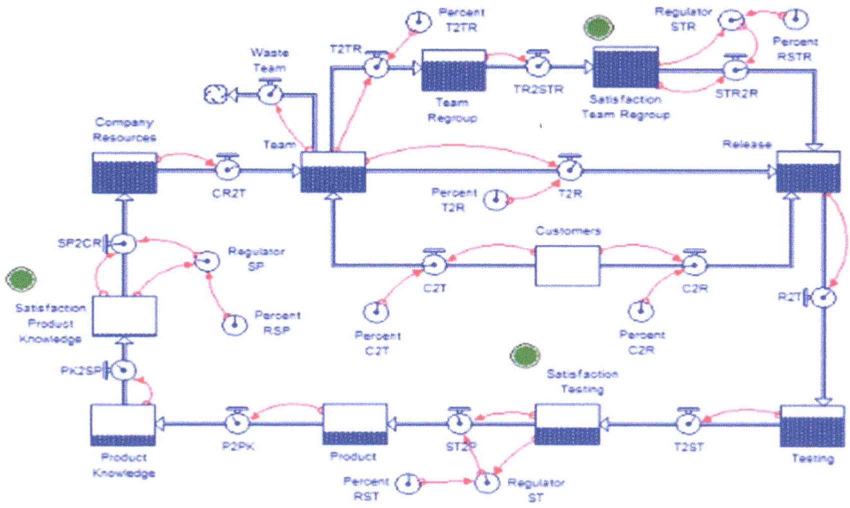

Fig. 6 XP methodology dynamic simulation model

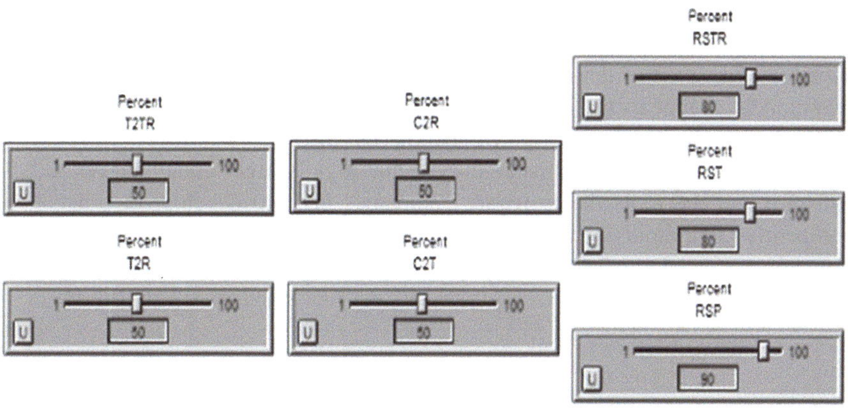

Fig. 7 XP methodology simulation converters percentages

"Release", according to the principles of XP methodology. After "Satisfaction of Team Regroup" occurs, resources are also given to "Release". Next follows "Testing", "Satisfaction of Testing", and the software development in "Product". Then the team acquires knowledge of the product and "Satisfaction Product Knowledge" occurs.

Figure 7 represents the graphical results for 12 months for four stocks, "Satisfaction Team Regroup", "Satisfaction Testing", "Satisfaction Product Knowledge", and "Company Resources" (Fig. 8).

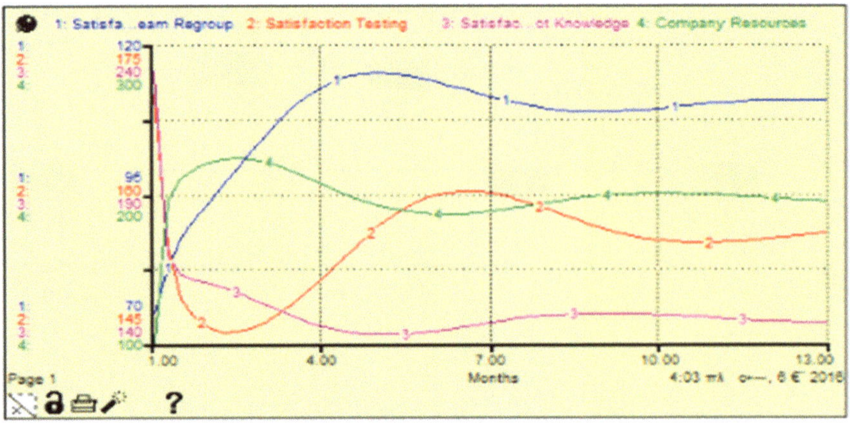

Fig. 8 XP methodology simulation graphical results

Conclusions

The comparison of the results from the simulation modeling of Scrum and XP methodologies shows that the outcomes of the use of Scrum methodology are superior in the case of developing collaboration tools. From the comparison of the two models, it appears that, in XP methodology, we do not achieve methodologies' factors satisfaction, for the case of collaboration tools.

The evolution of twenty-first century technology brought great changes to both software and the tools that software companies need to develop, in order to be competitive in a rapid changing environment (Buur et al. 2011). It is imperative to test software development methodologies in order to check their appropriateness for these new demands.

References

Al-Saleem, S.M., and H. Ullah 2015. A comparative analysis and evaluation of different agile software development methodologies. *International Journal of Computer Science and Network Security*. 15 (7).

Buur, J., and R. Mitchell. 2011. The business modelling lab. In *Participatory innovation conference*.

Dingsøyr, T., S. Nerur, V. Balijepally, and N.B. Moe. 2012. A decade of agile methodologies: Towards explaining agile software development. *Journal of Systems and Software*. 85 (6): 1213–1221.

Jansen-Vullers, M.H., and M. Netjes. 2006. Business process simulation—a tool survey. In *Proceedings of the seventh workshop and tutorial on practical use of coloured petri nets and the CPN tools*. University of Aarhus, Denmark.

Mahalakshmi1, M., and M. Sundararajan. 2013. Traditional SDLC vs scrum methodology—a comparative study . *International Journal of Emerging Technology and Advanced Engineering* 3 (6).

Moniruzzaman, A.B.M., and S.A. Hossain. 2013. Comparative study on agile software development methodologies. *Global Journal of Computer Science and Technology*. 13 (7) Version I.

Mushtaq, Z., and R.J. Qureshi. 2012. Novel hybrid model: Integrating scrum and XP. *Information Technology and Computer Science* 6: 39–44.

Richardson, G. 2013. System dynamics. *Encyclopedia of Operations Research and Management Science* 1519–1522.

Sakas, D.P., D.S. Vlachos, and D.K. Nasiopoulos. 2014. Modelling strategic management for the development of competitive advantage, based on technology. *Journal of Systems and Information Technology* 16 (3): 187–209.

Salo, O., and P. Abrahamsson. 2007. An iterative improvement process for agile software development. *Software Process: Improvement and Practice* 12 (1): 81–100.

Wadhwa, M., and N. Sharma. 2015. Review of agile software development methodologies. *Advances in Computer Science and Information Technology*. 2 (4): 370–374.

Yadav, A. 2015. AGILE: Software development model. *International Journal of Engineering and Technical Research* 3 (3).

The Development of New Ideas for IT Products, Through Social Media

Pachtiti E. Foteini, Nasiopoulos K. Dimitrios, Damianos P. Sakas and D.S. Vlachos

Introduction

The development of new ideas from a business starts when the need for a new product appears or when new technology becomes available (Awwad et al. 2016). The decision of development and, therefore, the actualization of new ideas constitute one of the most significant decisions, which will be taken by a business, because it is directly linked with the business' progress.

With the term social networking (Indrupati and Henari 2012) or social media, we refer to media for the interaction of groups of people through network communities. More specifically, a business is given the opportunity to "communicate" with its staff and the people related to it. Facebook, as a major representative constitutes a category in social media, and due to its versatile uses, makes it easier for the businesses to fulfill their goals. For example, the creation of a page in Facebook and its enrichment with all the information, which is necessary for its visitors as well as its proper formation, are actions, which any business can perform, and therefore promote its ideas (Ho 2014).

Methods for the Development of New Ideas—Generally

The development of new ideas in a business can be achieved in various ways, each of which has its own value (Wennberg and Berglund 2006). For example, through research and development (R&D) in which departments in a company deal with the research into new technologies (Rudall 2011), follow the latest developments in

P.E. Foteini (✉) · N.K. Dimitrios · D.P. Sakas · D.S. Vlachos
Department of Informatics and Telecommunications, University of Peloponnese, Tripoli, Greece
e-mail: claire.pachtiti@gmail.com

A. Kavoura et al. (eds.), *Strategic Innovative Marketing*, Springer Proceedings in Business and Economics, DOI 10.1007/978-3-319-56288-9_53

issues that interest them and keep up-to-date with what is new in the market. In addition, another way to create an idea is from the staff itself, as they interact with other people, express opinions, exchange ideas, propose improvements and, as a consequence, a new idea can be developed. These elements are also obtained using simulation modeling of the corresponding processes (Papadopoulou et al. 2017; Plikas et al. 2017; Plessias et al. 2017; Sakas et al. 2015).

Social Networking

If we focus on Facebook (Maiz et al. 2016), we will notice some secondary ways, which contribute to the creation of an idea.

Drawing ideas: Facebook includes pages, many of which have been created for business purposes. Consequently, the opportunity to draw information for business purposes through these pages is given to the staff of a business. In addition, through Facebook, visitors are referred to hyperlinks, which helps with the gathering of more data (Shao et al. 2015).

Exchange of ideas: thanks to Facebook (Kucukemiroglu and Kara 2015), workers in various businesses can communicate with each other, exchange ideas and data and, as a result, each business separately broadens the scope of information it has gathered for the conception and, later, the actualization of a new idea in the field of technology.

Covering of new needs: the businesses, after collecting all the necessary information, can improve the idea they have formed and desire to promote locating, at the same time, the gaps in the market and filling those by incorporating them in their original idea. In order to achieve this goal, Facebook is crucial, because the collection of information as well as the monitoring of the progress in the market can be done through that (Facebook).

Creating new partnerships: communication among the staff, thanks to the features offered by Facebook, can lead to the creation of new partnerships and to the 'promotion' of collective work (Radclyffe-Thomas et al. 2016). This is especially important in the field of businesses since collectivity constitutes a crucial prerequisite for their survival and progress.

Simulation Model

Based on the results of our research, it allows us to be able to ascribe values to the dynamic simulation model parameterized all those involved in our research. The conjunction between generation of new ideas through social media, new product development and IT services, is dynamic.

As seen from the dynamic simulation model in Fig. 1, the results change when changing the provision of resources to agents. Depending on the sources that

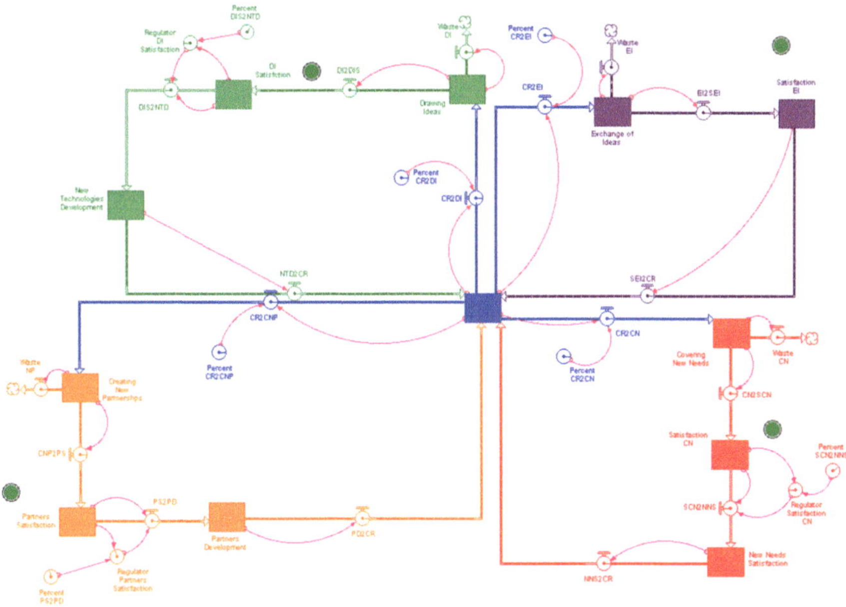

Fig. 1 Model

provided by the Company Resources, involving Drawing ideas, Exchange of ideas, Covering of new needs and Creating new partnerships sections, changing the percentage of new ideas generation from the use of information technology services, through social media.

Implementation of the Dynamic Simulation Model

To create the models, the modeling software tool iThink, from iSee Systems, was used. Simulation model creates stock and flow diagrams to model and simulate processes. It presents you the results of specific defined by the user inputs and connects the interrelationships between procedures and functions. Outputs can be displayed in the form of graphs and tables. The results of the dynamic simulation model are shown in tables and figures that we provide (Table 1).

Figure 2 indicates that the satisfaction percentage, as regarding all the four factors, is rising significantly during the first months and then those satisfactions gain stability. The development of new ideas as regarding the contribution of social media regarding IT products gives successful and satisfied results.

Also, Fig. 2 shows that company resources in the beginning, given in the four leading factors, lead to company resources replenishment in a steady rate and the four factors are eventually tending to stabilize their resources.

Table 1 Table results

4:12 PM 1/10/17 Table 1 (Company Development)

Months	Satisfaction CN	Waste CN	Percent CR2CN	New Needs Satisfaction
Initial	27.00		6.00	0.00
1	53.64	2.96	6.00	0.00
2	77.30	2.63	6.00	0.00
3	80.14	2.22	6.00	17.14
4	80.20	1.95	6.00	22.88
5	79.52	1.83	6.00	24.39
6	78.84	1.79	6.00	24.50
7	78.27	1.77	6.00	24.24
8	77.78	1.75	6.00	23.90
9	93.31	1.73	6.00	7.56
10	91.16	1.70	6.00	9.74
11	89.51	1.66	6.00	10.09
12	86.86	1.64	6.00	12.97

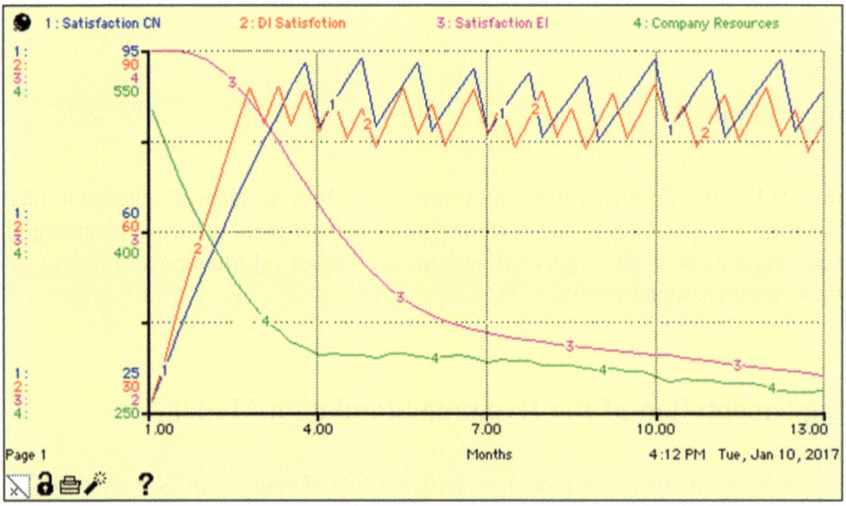

Fig. 2 Graphical results

Support for Decision-Makers

There is need to create the interface of the dynamic simulation model, to enable the user to change the values that the factors can get, studied in the research we have done. Figure 2 shows the main user interface of the simulation model. There are four main sections on this user interface: Drawing ideas, Exchange of ideas, Covering of new needs, and Creating new partnerships sections (Fig. 3).

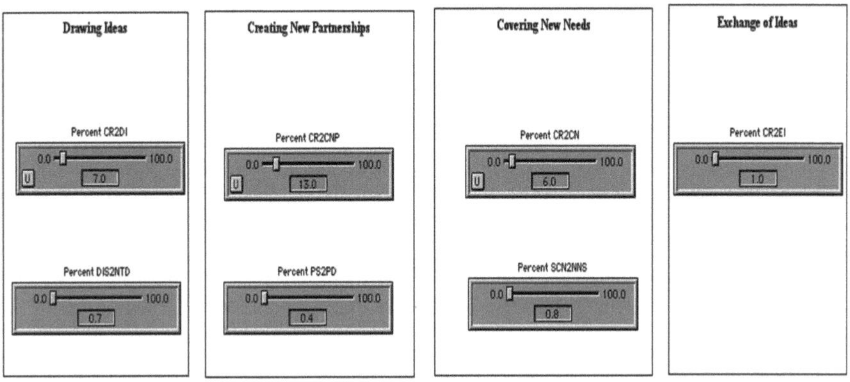

Fig. 3 User interface

Conclusions

New product creation still remains the higher challenge for companies. Most companies have knowledge of the important role new products must play in their production and quest for prosperity: companies are continuously searching for ways to refresh, modify, and redesign their new product development orders and procedures for maximum results.

This standard suggests that to achieve productivity, new product development companies should have a specific and well-designed product policy. These companies should have determined new product target markets along with a lot of confidence, with clear targets. Winning businesses and groups of new product development have devotion toward the choice of the customer. It is important that company should collect as many concepts as possible and most should come from clients so that the company can be in a situation to plan and develop new better products.

This paper investigates and resolves the generation of new ideas for new product development processes through social media and attempted to acknowledge fields in which companies can upgrade their implementation when present new products, mostly through the research of points that are crucial to success. These points were highlighted through an extensive study of the experience and implementation of successful companies presented in the new product development bibliography. The critical success factors which have been presented in the bibliography are generally determined for the complete development process, in order to especially addressing each section. To face this problem, this paper search crucial success agents for each step of the process.

References

Awwad, Abdulkareem, and Mamoun N. Akroush. 2016. New product development performance success measures: An exploratory research. *EuroMed Journal of Business* 11 (1): 2–29.

Ho, Ching-Wei. 2014. Consumer behavior on Facebook: Does consumer participation bring positive consumer evaluation of the brand? *EuroMed Journal of Business* 9 (3): 252–267.

Indrupati, Joel, and Tara Henari. 2012. Entrepreneurial success, using online social networking: evaluation. *Education, Business and Society: Contemporary Middle Eastern Issues* 5 (1): 47–62.

Kucukemiroglu, Setenay, and Ali Kara. 2015. Online word-of-mouth communication on social networking sites: An empirical study of Facebook users. *International Journal of Commerce and Management* 25 (1): 2–20.

Maiz, Ander, Nieves Arranz, and Fdez. de Arroyabe, Juan Carlos. 2016. Factors affecting social interaction on social network sites: The Facebook case. *Journal of Enterprise Information Management* 29 (5): 630–649.

Papadopoulou, Theodora, Dimitrios K. Nasiopoulos, and Dimitrios S. Vlachos. 2017. Merchandizing IT products via social networks. In *Modeling and simulation of the procedures, Springer proceedings in business and economics*, 507–513.

Plessias, Alexandros A., Dimitrios K. Nasiopoulos, and Despina S. Giakomidou. 2017. Modeling of market segmentation in social networks and media. In *Springer proceedings in business and economics*, 523–529.

Plikas, John Hlias, Dimitrios K. Nasiopoulos, and Despina S. Giakomidou. 2017. The contribution of social media in the management of social relations with customers. In *Modelling and simulation of the problem, Springer proceedings in business and economics*, 515–521.

Radclyffe-Thomas, Natascha, Anne Peirson-Smith, Ana Roncha, and Adrian Huang. 2016. Creative cross-cultural connections: Facebook as a third space for international collaborations, In *University partnerships for academic programs and professional development* (*Innovations in higher education teaching and learning*), vol. 7, ed. Patrick Blessinger, Barbara Cozza, 243–266. Emerald Group Publishing Limited.

Rudall, B.H. 2011. Research and development: Current impact and future potential. *Kybernetes* 40 (3/4): 581–584.

Sakas, Damianos P., Nasiopoulos K. Dimitrios, and Androniki Kavoura. 2015. The development of Facebook's competitive advantage for brand awareness. *Procedia Economics and Finance* 589–597.

Shao, Wei, Mitchell Ross, and Debra Grace. 2015. Developing a motivation-based segmentation typology of Facebook users. *Marketing Intelligence and Planning* 33 (7): 1071–1086.

Wennberg, Karl, and Berglund Henrik. 2006. Social networking and the development of new ventures. In *Innovation through collaboration* (*Advances in Interdisciplinary Studies of Work Teams*), vol. 12, ed. Michael M. Beyerlein, Susan T. Beyerlein, and Frances A. Kennedy, 203–225. Emerald Group Publishing Limited.

Multicriteria Assessment of Alternative Policy Scenarios for Achieving EU RES Target by 2030

Ioannis Papadogeorgos, Aikaterini Papapostolou, Charikleia Karakosta and Haris Doukas

Introduction

The "2030 Climate and Energy Policy Framework" was adopted by the European Council on 23/24 October 2014 (EC 2014), deciding on a revised set of targets by 2030. Its main axis is the establishment of binding targets for domestically reducing GHGs by 40% by 2030 compared to 1990 levels and increasing the share of renewables to 27% in gross final energy demand, along with indicative improvement of energy efficiency by at least 27% compared to prevailing projections of future energy demand (COM/2014/15). Contrary to 2020 policy portfolio, the framework "will be fulfilled through MS contributions guided by the need to deliver collectively the EU target" (EU 2015). National policy makers are indulged in supporting the RES target, while sharing the overall 27% target among individual entities.

Multiattribute decision-making problems like this are involved in a large volume of research projects, expressed in fuzzy conditions (Chen et al. 1992; Pei 2013). Fuzzy set theory and hierarchical structure analysis, in conjunction with the multicriteria decision-making method (MCDM), have been extensively used for uncertainty management, incorporating both qualitative and qualitative factors (Wu et al. 2011). Popular multicriteria methods adopted for problem-solving are AHP

I. Papadogeorgos (✉)
Department of Electrical and Computer Engineering, National Technical University of Athens, Athens 15780, Greece
e-mail: ioannispapa@yahoo.com

A. Papapostolou · C. Karakosta · H. Doukas
Decision Support Systems Laboratory, Energy Policy Unit,
Department of Electrical and Computer Engineering, National Technical University of Athens, Athens 15780, Greece

A. Kavoura et al. (eds.), *Strategic Innovative Marketing*, Springer Proceedings in Business and Economics, DOI 10.1007/978-3-319-56288-9_54

(Analytic Hierarchy Process), ELECTRE (Elimination Et Choix Traduisant la REalité), TOPSIS (Technique for Order Preference by Similarity to Ideal Solution) and PROMETHEE (Preference Ranking Organization METHod for Enrichment Evaluations).

Defining the Problem

The main issues of the framework revolve around methods to achieve effort-sharing among the MS, options to secure enhanced deployment of renewable energy across the EU, and their appliance in each MS or in regions. In light of these challenges, alternative scenarios and evaluation criteria are determined for the successful adherence to the agreed EU-wide energy framework (Held et al. 2014).

Four criteria were selected to highlight the best, which incorporate the diversity of policies, regulations and priorities of MS (IRENA 2014; Hood 2011). Static efficiency (C1) refers to the minimization of total system cost. Flexibility (C2) refers to the freedom of each MS to determine its own philosophy on reducing GHGs. Applicability (C3) expresses how measurable a goal is in terms of results. Political and social acceptance (C4) indicates the target's political and social attractiveness.

The selected effort-sharing strategies are assessed within the achievement of the joint binding RES target. "Binding national RES targets (A1)" includes legally compulsory goals, broken down into MS targets according to a fixed formula, including flat rate and GDP-dependent components. "Binding national RES targets through pledging (A2)" allows MS to accept a suggested benchmark, which are obliged to state how their pledges will be achieved through action plans. "Binding regional targets (A3)" indicates MS grouping. MS may act according to their own preferences, being jointly responsible for target achievement of their region. "Indicative national RES targets (A4)" breaks down the RES target to MS according to a fixed formula. Target trajectories are monitored through "naming and shaming". "Indicative national RES targets with incentives for over commitment (A5)" is a polycentric target allocation. Supercredits can be applied to the amount pledged above the benchmark target. "Indicative regional targets (A_6)" merges national targets into a regional one. Each regional group states how it intends to achieve the indicative target. "Binding national RES targets through free pledging (A_7)" allows MS to commit to a RES target determined by them under free pledging. Iteration rounds are followed to negotiate higher targets with MS. "Binding regional RES targets through free pledging (A_8)" includes both formation of regions and iteration rounds to negotiate higher targets and close the EU gap. "RES target on EU level (A_9)" sets a target financed through a EU-wide harmonized instrument. These elements are also obtained using simulation modeling of the corresponding processes (Dimitrios et al. 2013a, b).

Fuzzy TOPSIS Method

An appropriate multicriteria method is necessary for solving multidimensional decision-making problems in fuzzy numbers environment (Chen 2000; Chen et al. 1992). Fuzzy TOPSIS method is performed to identify the best policy scenario and extract conclusions based on final rankings. Firstly, a group consisted of K decision-makers is set. Linguistic variables are selected for evaluating alternatives and criteria (e.g., Low, Middle, and High) and thus, decision-makers' outlook is linguistic. Aggregate performances Xij of alternatives Ai and total weights Wj of criteria Cj are calculated. The fuzzy decision matrix is constructed and normalized based on linear scale transformation. The weighed normalized matrix V is also obtained.

$$\tilde{x}_{ij} = \frac{1}{K}[\tilde{x}_{ij}^{1}(+)\tilde{x}_{ij}^{2}(+)\ldots\tilde{x}_{ij}^{K}(+)], \tag{1}$$

$$\tilde{w}_{j} = \frac{1}{K}[\tilde{w}_{j}^{1}(+)\tilde{w}_{j}^{2}(+)\ldots\tilde{w}_{j}^{K}(+)] \tag{2}$$

$$\tilde{D} = \begin{bmatrix} \tilde{x}_{11} & \tilde{x}_{12}\cdots & \tilde{x}_{1n} \\ \tilde{x}_{21} & \tilde{x}_{22} & \tilde{x}_{2n} \\ \vdots & \ddots & \vdots \\ \tilde{x}_{m1} & \tilde{x}_{m2}\cdots & \tilde{x}_{mn} \end{bmatrix}, \tag{3}$$

$$\tilde{W} = [\,\tilde{w}_1 \quad \tilde{w}_2\cdots \quad \tilde{w}_n\,] \tag{4}$$

$$\tilde{R} = [\,\tilde{r}_{ij}\,]_{mxn} \quad \mathrm{i} = 1, 2, \ldots, \mathrm{m}; \mathrm{j} = 1, 2, \ldots, \mathrm{n} \tag{5}$$

$$\tilde{r}_{ij} = \left(\frac{a_{ij}}{c_j^*}, \frac{b_{ij}}{c_j^*}, \frac{c_{ij}}{c_j^*}\right), \mathrm{j} \in \mathrm{B} \text{ and } c_j^* = \max_i c_{ij}, \text{if } \mathrm{j} \in \mathrm{B} \tag{6}$$

$$\tilde{V} = [\,\tilde{v}_{ij}\,]_{mxn}, \text{where:} \quad \tilde{v}_{ij} = \tilde{r}_{ij}(\cdot)\tilde{w}_j, \mathrm{i} = 1, 2, \ldots, \mathrm{m}; \mathrm{j} = 1, 2, \ldots \mathrm{n} \tag{7}$$

The distance between two triangular fuzzy numbers $\tilde{m}$ and $\tilde{n}$ from FPIS and FNIS (Zhu et al. 2015) is calculated as follows:

$$A^* = [\tilde{r}_1, \tilde{r}_2, .., \tilde{r}_n], \tag{8}$$

$$A^- = [\tilde{r}_1, \tilde{r}_2, .., \tilde{r}_n] \tag{9}$$

$$d(\tilde{m}, \tilde{n}) = \sqrt{\frac{1}{3}[(m_1 - n_1)^2 + (m_2 - n_2)^2 + (m_3 - n_3)^2]} \tag{10}$$

The relative closeness coefficient of each alternative is calculated and the preference order is ranked. All the possible values belong in the interval (0, 1).

$$CC_i = \frac{d_i^-}{d_i^* + d_i^-}, \mathrm{i} = 1, 2, \ldots, \mathrm{m} \tag{11}$$

Case Study

Setting 7-stage transformation scales for criteria weights and alternative rankings, linguistic terms can be transformed into fuzzy numbers (Wang 2014; Table 1). Decision-makers assess criteria weights and alternatives, as depicted in Tables 2 and 3.

Applying Eq. (1) to (11) of the proposed methodology, and based on closeness coefficients, the rankings are defined for achieving the EU RES target (Table 4).

Table 1 Linguistic terms and fuzzy numbers for evaluating alternatives and criteria

Linguistic terms for criteria importance		Linguistic terms for alternatives' ranking	
Very low (VL)	(0.0, 0.0, 0.1)	Very poor (VP)	(0, 0, 1)
Low (L)	(0.0, 0.1, 0.3)	Poor (P)	(0, 1, 3)
Medium low (ML)	(0.1, 0.3, 0.5)	Medium poor (MP)	(1, 3, 5)
Medium (M)	(0.3, 0.5, 0.7)	Fair (F)	(3, 5, 7)
Medium high (MH)	(0.5, 0.7, 0.9)	Medium good (MG)	(5, 7, 9)
High (H)	(0.7, 0.9, 1.0)	Good (G)	(7, 9, 10)
Very high (VH)	(0.9, 1.0, 1.0)	Very good (VG)	(9, 10, 10)

Table 2 Linguistic assessments for the criteria weights by the decision-makers

Decision Maker	Criterion weights			
	C_1	C_2	C_3	C_4
D_1	MH	ML	VH	M
D_2	H	M	VH	ML
D_3	H	H	VH	M

Table 3 Linguistic assessments for the alternatives by the decision-makers

Di	Criteria	Alternative policy strategies								
		A_1	A_2	A_3	A_4	A_5	A_6	A_7	A_8	A_9
D_1	C_1	MP	MP	MG	P	F	MG	P	MG	VG
	C_2	P	F	MP	MG	MG	G	MG	MG	P
	C_3	VG	G	VP	G	G	P	MG	VP	P
	C_4	VP	MP	P	MP	MP	F	F	MP	F
D_2	C_1	F	F	MG	MP	F	G	MG	MG	G
	C_2	VP	MP	F	MP	MP	G	G	MG	P
	C_3	VG	G	MP	G	VG	P	F	P	MP
	C_4	P	F	P	F	G	F	MG	P	MP
D_3	C_1	MG	G	G	MP	F	MG	P	G	MG
	C_2	VP	MP	P	F	MG	G	G	G	P
	C_3	VG	G	MP	F	F	P	F	MP	VP
	C_4	VP	P	P	MP	F	F	F	F	F

Table 4 Calculation of closeness coefficient and ranking of the nine alternative policy strategies

Rank	Ai	Alternative policy strategy	CCi
1	A_5	Indicative national RES targets with incentives for over-commitment	0,476
2	A_2	Binding national RES targets through pledging	0,447
3	A_7	Binding national RES targets through free pledging	0,428
4	A_6	Indicative regional targets	0,413
5	A_4	Indicative national RES targets	0,389
6	A_8	Binding regional RES targets through free pledging	0,379
7	A_1	Binding national RES targets	0,377
8	A_3	Binding regional targets	0,331
9	A_9	RES target on EU level	0,310

Sensitivity Analysis

Through sensitivity analysis, parameters with uncertainty specifications are restricted, improving significantly the model's efficiency (Saltelli et al. 2008). Twenty experiments stand for twenty combinations of criteria weights (Table 5). Offsetting individual alternatives' rankings, the final ranking is extracted.

In Exp. (1) to (7) all criteria weights are equal. In Exp. (8) to (11) the weight of one criterion is set to the maximum possible value (VH), and the rest receive the minimum possible (VL). The reverse is true in subsequent experiments Exp. (12) to (15). In Exp. (16), (17) two of the weights are set in the maximum value and the rest in the minimum. Exp. (18), (19), (20) consist of random weights values (Fig. 1).

Table 5 Results of sensitivity analysis for 20 experiments

No.	CC_1	CC_2	CC_3	CC_4	CC_5	CC_6	CC_7	CC_8	CC_9
1	0,407	0,536	0,378	0,486	0,615	0,579	0,583	0,509	0,429
2	0,376	0,498	0,357	0,456	0,566	0,534	0,539	0,473	0,402
3	0,319	0,426	0,309	0,391	0,482	0,456	0,461	0,405	0,345
4	0,241	0,326	0,238	0,301	0,369	0,350	0,354	0,311	0,265
5	0,163	0,224	0,165	0,208	0,252	0,240	0,243	0,214	0,183
6	0,092	0,127	0,095	0,119	0,143	0,136	0,138	0,122	0,104
7	0,030	0,042	0,032	0,040	0,047	0,045	0,046	0,040	0,034
8	0,151	0,174	0,208	0,105	0,167	0,220	0,126	0,216	0,230
9	0,051	0,131	0,108	0,156	0,177	0,238	0,227	0,211	0,074
10	0,246	0,235	0,086	0,207	0,221	0,084	0,176	0,082	0,076
11	0,058	0,141	0,083	0,154	0,211	0,194	0,213	0,139	0,167
12	0,291	0,412	0,210	0,428	0,504	0,416	0,510	0,344	0,244
13	0,388	0,455	0,307	0,378	0,494	0,399	0,413	0,349	0,395
14	0,197	0,353	0,328	0,328	0,450	0,547	0,462	0,473	0,392
15	0,383	0,447	0,332	0,381	0,463	0,442	0,429	0,420	0,306
16	0,266	0,321	0,161	0,321	0,349	0,274	0,354	0,250	0,115
17	0,177	0,270	0,256	0,217	0,327	0,364	0,289	0,311	0,357
18	0,322	0,408	0,274	0,384	0,452	0,416	0,444	0,378	0,264
19	0,183	0,295	0,165	0,312	0,373	0,332	0,387	0,269	0,210
20	0,300	0,317	0,168	0,275	0,321	0,199	0,265	0,180	0,190

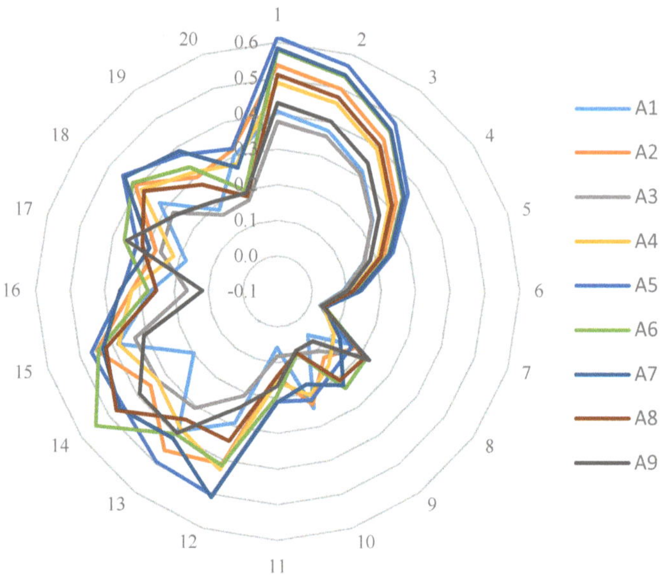

Fig. 1 Sensitivity analysis results in radar chart

Conclusions

Fuzzy TOPSIS method has been a reliable tool against uncertainties, offering a calibrated ranking for the alternatives for achieving the EU RES target by 2030. Sensitivity analysis verified the results' consistency, given that the best strategies remained relatively unchanged with respect to variations of criteria weights. The most influential factor was the applicability of strategies, preventing the declination from the target agreed. "Indicative national RES targets with incentives for over commitment" and "Binding national RES targets through free pledging" received the highest rankings, confirming that non-binding targets at national level enjoy broad MS support, while binding targets enhance alternatives' efficiency. MS may negotiate the target requirements, making strategies flexible and politically acceptable. "RES target at EU level" was the least desirable. Frontrunners hesitate to work with unambitious MS, making the option less applicable and flexible. For further improvement of the decision model, there could be more decision-makers, criteria and alternatives, while a larger transformation scale could quantify linguistic variables more accurately. Conducting more experiments upon sensitivity analysis, with random combinations of weights, could extract more impartial conclusions.

References

Chen, S.J., and C.L. Hwang. 1992. *Fuzzy multiple attributes decision making: Methods and applications*. New York, N.Y.: Springer.

Chen, C.T. 2000. Extensions of the TOPSIS for group decision-making under fuzzy environment. *Fuzzy Sets and Systems* 114 (1): 1–9.

Dimitrios, Nasiopoulos K., Damianos P. Sakas, and D.S. Vlachos. 2013a. Analysis of strategic leadership models in information technology. *Procedia—Social and Behavioral Sciences* 268–275.

Dimitrios, Nasiopoulos K., Damianos P. Sakas, and D.S. Vlachos. 2013b. The contribution of dynamic simulation model of depiction of knowledge, in the leading process of high technology companies. *Key Engineering Materials, Scientific Net* 543 (2013): 406–409.

European Commission. 2014. A policy framework for climate and energy in the period from 2020 to 2030. Communication, COM(2014) 015 final, Brussels: European Commission.

European Council. 2014. Conclusions, Secretariat of the Council, No. 5, General, EUCO 169/14, Brussels, 23/24 October 2014.

European Union. 2015. Council conclusions on the governance system of the Energy Union, General Secretariat of the Council, Press Release 869/15, Brussels, November 26.

Held, A., M. Ragwitz, and G. Resch. 2014. Implementing the EU 2030 Climate and Energy Framework. Towards 2030-Dialogue on RES Policy Framework for 2030, No. 2.

Hood, C. 2011. Summing up the parts—combining policy instruments for least-cost climate mitigation strategies. International Energy Agency, France, September 2011.

IRENA. 2014. *Handbook on renewable energy nationally appropriate mitigation actions*, 2nd ed. International Renewable Energy Agency, December 2014.

Pei, Z. 2013. Rational decision making models with incomplete weight information for production line assessment. *Information Sciences* 222: 696–716.

Saltelli, A., M. Ratto, T. Andres, F. Campolongo, J. Cariboni, and D. Gatelli. 2008. *Global sensitivity analysis: The primer* 277–278. Chichester: Wiley.
Wang, J. 2014. *Encyclopedia of business analytics and optimization*, 1101–1102. Hershey, USA: Business Science Reference.
Wu, C., and D. Barnes. 2011. A literature review of decision-making models and approaches. *Journal of Purchasing and Supply Management* 17 (4): 256–274.
Zhu, Q., and A.T. Azar. 2015. *Complex system modelling and control through intelligent soft computations*. Studies in fuzziness and soft computing, Switzerland, 202–203.

Mechanisms of Management Process Improvement of an Educational Institution

Omarova Naida Omarovna, Omarov Omar Alievich and Ivanova Yelena Vladimirovna

Introduction

Within the frame of complex education modernization it is necessary to develop the mechanism which provides with the upgrade of educational and administrative technologies in the innovative system of continuing professional education in cultural regions (Abdullaev et al. 2013; Asaul and Kaparov 2007).

The competitive market of educational services is creating on the basis of intensive adoption of innovative techniques including distance learning. One of the urgent problem is the export of Russian education (Dzhakhparaeva et al. 2013; Ivanova et al. 2013). For these purposes it is necessary to increase and improve the quality of education. Its forms and content have to meet the requirements, i.e. availability and democracy of education excluding all the forms of discrimination in education. Herewith the requirement of the citizens' learning continuity must be followed during the whole life.

The main goals of the regional higher education can be formulated as follows:

Satisfaction of personal needs in an intellectual, cultural and moral development, in professional education on the basis of broad general humanities and fundamental training;

Provision of region's needs with specialists of different types and qualifications capable to implement progressive social and economic transformations, national and cultural development and spiritual renovation of peoples within the frame of the unified All-Russian informational and educational, scientific and cultural space;

Elimination of training duplication which does not correspond to an educational institution.

O.N. Omarovna (✉) · O.O. Alievich · I.Y. Vladimirovna
Federal State Budgetary Educational Institution of Higher Professional Education
Dagestan State University, Gadzhiev Str., 43-a Makhachkala,
Republic of Dagestan 36700, Russia
e-mail: n.omarova@yandex.ru

A. Kavoura et al. (eds.), *Strategic Innovative Marketing*, Springer Proceedings in Business and Economics, DOI 10.1007/978-3-319-56288-9_55

Modelling the Business Processes of an Educational Institution

For the last two decades all the industries of Russian economy have been undergoing changes. Processes of liberalization and globalization touched upon the educational services sphere. Educational process modernization and optimization are the only ways for Russian universities to survive due to the tough competition in the outer educational space. Offered by D. Norton and R. Kaplan "The Balanced Scorecard" is an efficient mechanism of mission achievement and strategy organization. Largest Russian companies are using the BSC to achieve their goals and this method can be used to organize the operation of budgetary social organizations, educational institutions.

The BSC is the mechanism of mission realization and organization strategy. To realize that it is necessary to formulate a mission, strategy, "the tree of aims" of a university, as well as projected results and clear definition of what have to be done to achieve them. While creating the BSC at a public educational institute on the clients or population are distinguished as the main link of the strategy. Clients of institutions of higher education can be divided into sponsors and recipients. Sponsors' interests (tax payers) are expressed by government structures, such as State Duma of the RF, the Ministry of Education. Recipients are applicants, future diplomaed specialists who are supposed to be in demand by the society and business. Strategic goals must be formulated for each group of "clients". According to Ivanova and Omarova (2014) the mission of an institution of higher education must answer the following questions:

In what measure a university corresponds to legislation of the RF, aims and tasks stated by the Ministry of Education and Science of the RF;

Entrance competition at a university to different professions, graduates-on-demand in the society and business;

Main business processes: at an educational institution the following business processes can be distinguished as teaching, scientific and educational;

Improvement of main business processes. In accordance with the world standards and society requirements the level and quality improvement of the educational process is connected with the change of the functional university management orientation to the process oriented approach. An example of the educational business process is turnout of specialists in a certain profession and form of training (Kaplan Robert 2009). To model the business process it is necessary to determine all the participants and broads of this process and external environment. The external environment is legislative authorities of the RF, the Ministry of Education and Science (have direct "tough" mechanisms of influence on the teaching process); the list of regional organizations and businesses interested in graduates. The participants of teaching process are university administration, deans of departments, heads of chairs, professors, colleagues. At the beginning of this process there are applicants and at the end of it—graduates of certain professions. If this process is considered in the form of "black box" so the training process is a system of innovative transformations, as a result of which applicants make qualified graduates for a fixed term. Figure 1 shows the model "University position on the market of educational services" on example of FSEI HPE DSU.

A higher educational institution can have the following strategic goals:
Competitiveness on the market of educational services;
Cost minimization for specialist training;
Provision of financial structures support.

To achieve these goals it is necessary to optimize the main business processes, the educational process in particular. The aims of teaching process as in the case of Dagestan State University are shown in Fig. 2.

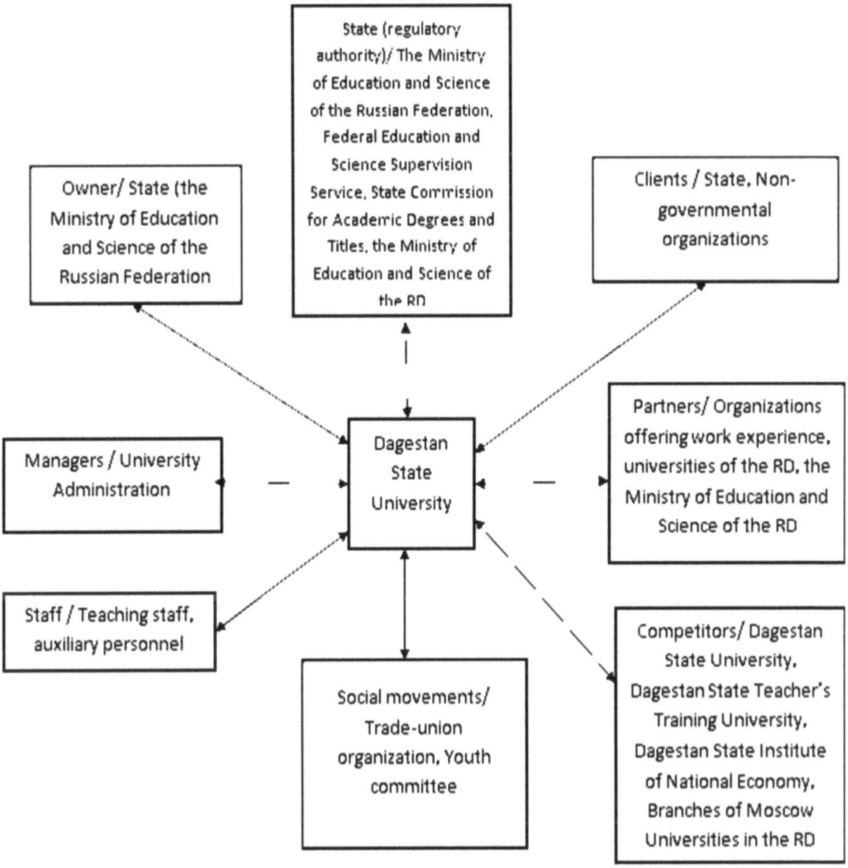

Fig. 1 Model "university position on the market of educational services"

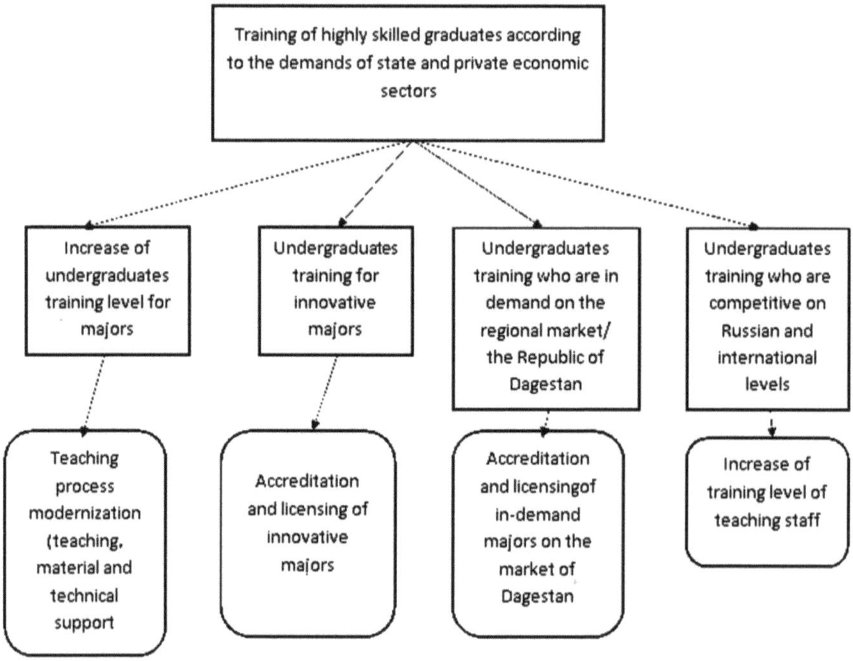

Fig. 2 Diagram of goals of Dagestan State University

Conclusion

Goal achievement of educational process is analysed by the Balanced Scorecard introduction into the process. The BSC outlines four groups of the organization efficiency indices:

Financial indexation;
Indices of internal business processes;
Indices of clients' amount;
Indices of personnel training and promotion.

Dagestan State University is a budgetary institution; correspondingly its financial indexation mainly depends on the non-financial indices of the rest three groups. These are the indices of modernization and innovative teaching programmes implementation, indices of customers' satisfaction, indices of market survey of required specialists, indices of train-the-trainer and retraining.

The Ministry of Education and Science of the RF considered the following indices of universities efficiency in 2014 http://минобрнауки.

The USE average grade of students accepted by the results of the USE on the full-time course of study, bachelor-level and specialist training programmes using budget funds of the Russian Federation with the payment of costs of inputs for education of individuals and legal persons;

The volume of RAD per a research and educational worker;

The share of amount of foreign students from far and near (CIS) abroad countries;

University income from all the sources per a research and educational worker;

Total area of rooms per a student (given student body) possessed by the university and fixed on the operating control basis.

We suggest completing the list with following indices:

The share of innovative directions of undergraduates training in the curriculum of the university;

The interest of employed graduates by their specialities;

Rating of retraining and further training of teaching staff in the leading Russian universities and centres and international retraining centres.

References

Abdullaev, G.S.H., O.A. Omarov, and N.O. Omarova. 2013. Pedagogical and ergonomic basis of electronic learning resource development for economic students realized on the basis of ICT. *Vestnik DSC RAE* №. 3, 61–66.

Asaul, A.N., and B.M. Kaparov. 2007. University management under the conditions of innovative economy. Gumanistica Publisher: 280.

Dzhakhparaeva, D.Yu., O.A. Omarov, and N.O. Omarova. 2013. Factors intensifying youth's extremist mood in social and intensive environment. *Pedagogika* №. 9.

Ivanova, Ye., O.A. Omarov, and N.O. Omarova. 2013. Modern innovative technologies in higher professional education. *Scientific Notes IIE RAE*: 25–31.

Ivanova, Ye. V., N.O. Omarova. 2014. University education process optimization on the basis of the balanced scorecard: Modern problems of mathematical modeling and information technologies in science, education and business (Makhachkala, may 14–15, 2014), 104–108.

Kaplan Robert, S., and P. Norton David. 2009. The strategy-focused organization. In: *How balanced scorecard companies thrive in the new business environment*, 416. Moscow: Olimp-Biznes Publisher.

Activity monitoring performance of federal state higher educational institutions and their branches. http://минобрнауки.

Part XII
6th Symposium on Integrated Information

Organized by: Damianos P. Sakas
University of Peloponnese, Tripoli, Greece

Aims and Scope

The symposium promotes the knowledge and the development of high-quality research in the field of information. It aims to bring its participants the very best analysis and discussion in the developing and interdisciplinary field of the field of information management and integration. It covers a wide field from diverse areas of practice and settings including culture, business, health, education, and government.

Information is critical for the survival and growth of organizations and people. The challenge for information management is now less about managing activities that collect, store and disseminate information. Rather, there is a focus on managing activities that make changes in patterns of behavior of users and organizations and also on information that leads to changes in the way people use information to engage in knowledge-focused activities.

Topics

Integrated Information, Information Management, Knowledge Management, Records/Document Management, Conceptual and Organizational Perspectives of Knowledge, Communication Records/Document Management, Data Management, Health Information, Digital Libraries, Electronic Archives, Data Mining, Digital Collections (repositories, j stors, e-scholarship), Semantics Semantic Web, Software Copyright Electronic Publishing Development of New Metrics, Conservation Management, Digital Preservation, Management of Nonprofit Organizations Cultural Heritage Management, Advocacy, Networking and Influencing Managing, Change in Information, Organizations, Financial Management for Excellence in Information, Organizations, Human Resources, Management in Information, Organizations Conceptual and Organizational Perspectives of Knowledge, Communication, Distance Learning, E-Learning and the Contribution of Information, Organizations E-research, E-science History of Collections, History of Information, Organizations History of Writing and Writing Technologies.

Main Workshops

1. Digital libraries and crowdsourcing

Organized by: Mathieu Andro, Institut National de la Recherche Agronomique, Délégation à l'Information Scientifique et Technique, France

Description: How digitization programs and digital libraries may use volunteer visitors, crowdsourcing, gamification or crowdfunding?

2. Ontology-based Sentiment Analysis

Organized by: Nick Bassiliades, Aristotle University of Thessaloniki, Department of Informatics, Greece

Efstratios Kontopoulos, Center for Research and Technology, Hellas (CERTH), Informatics and Telematics Institute (ITI), Greece

Athena Vakali, Aristotle University of Thessaloniki, Department of Informatics, Greece

Description: Sentiment analysis, a research area with rapidly increasing popularity, involves a set of processes and approaches aiming at identifying and extracting subjective information (i.e., the attitude of a speaker or a writer onsome topic) out of source materials (text, images, videos, etc.). A wide range of applications in various domains and contexts exploit sentiment analysis for various important tasks and decision making (e.g., in product and services reviews assessment, in sales predictions, in investor's choices and in politics formation). The underlying methodologies typically involve machine learning and statistical paradigms, which, however, demonstrate several shortcomings that mostly derive from the lack of semantics. Examples of these drawbacks include the need to deal with noise in text from online social media, with the evolving and unpredicted data threads produced, as well as detecting attitudes (such as irony, sarcasm, etc). The emergence of the semantic web and the relevant semantically rich ontology-based representations may deliver novel approaches and toolsets which can tackle the previous challenges. Therefore, this workshop investigates the deployment of ontology-based techniques, as well as of semantically rich frameworks and tools towards a more fine-grained sentiment analysis of content of any type.

3. Intelligent Methodologies and Technologies for e-Learning Systems, IMTeLS'16

Organized by: Abdel-Badeeh M. Salem, Ain Shams University, Faculty of Computer and Information sciences, Egypt

Description: Intelligent methodologies and machine learning techniques give e-learning systems added computing capability, allowing them to exhibit more intelligent behavior. On the other side, the convergence of artificial intelligence, data science, educational technology and web science is enabling the creation of a new generation of web-based intelligent e-learning systems. The objective of IMTeLS'16 workshop is to bring together scientists engaged in educational technology, computational thinking, web technology, knowledge management, and artificial intelligence. It will provide a forum for identifying important contributions and opportunities for recent research on the different intelligent methodologies and techniques for developing intelligent e-learning systems.

4. Next Generation Information Management Systems

Organized by: Emmanuel J. Yannakoudakis, Athens University of Economics and Business, Department of Computer Science, Greece

Description: Information management constitutes a process related with three core values: (a) the information collection from multiple of sources, (b) the organization and the archiving, (c) the distribution and the dissemination of information to the stakeholders. Libraries and information centers have the key role to information management sector. This can be seen through the rapid development of libraries management systems via relational databases mindset in the last two decades. In the last decade the rapid development in the technology of information and communications have lead to noteworthy changes to operations and structures of libraries related with the services that they provide to their users. Printed information start to lose their domination, while users feel free and convenient to use simple methods to search and retrieve information via the libraries' services. It can be said that automated library systems have not changed significantly in the last two decades, and therefore libraries in order to respond to the new challenges have to adopt heterogeneous systems such as search engines and database of full texts, information link resolvers, services of digital libraries and so on. All the plurality and dimensionality of these services, brings confusion and complexity to users and to the library staff as well, in order to manage and complete daily tasks and activities. From the aforementioned thoughts it can be highlighted a mandatory need for the creation of new a generation of information management systems. The aim of this workshop is the examination of the structure and operationalization of these next generation management systems. Including the following key questions: Which may be the core values and characteristics of next generation information management systems? Is it possible for the current database systems to become the core of those next generation systems? Which may be the most important difficulties that need to be treated for the successful adoption of the new systems?

5. Data Exploration Techniques

Organized by: Kostas Stefanidis, University of Tampere, School of Information Sciences, Finland

Description: Data exploration is related with the efficiently to extracting knowledge from data even if the user does not know exactly what he is intended to looking for. In this workshop, we analyze several data exploration issues and techniques in order to gather the best possible information, creating in this way the knowledge and therefore the wisdom which is needed for the best possible decision making. The emerging area of databases and the rapid evolution of information systems that produce automatically data tailor the data exploration strategic planning as a mandatory field of movement. Thus, we discuss new ideas on how to gather-mine and access data and how the new challenges of data management influence several sectors, such as information science and business analytics.

6. Knowledge Management & Information Systems in the era of the Knowledge Society

Organized by: Miltiadis D. Lytras, The American College of Greece/Deree College, Editor: Int. J. on Semantic Web and Information Systems/Int. J. on Knowledge Society Research, Greece

Description: The purpose of this workshop is to demonstrate how knowledge management (KM), through the fusion of the human-centered approach and Information Systems (IS) function within daily strategies and activities of organizations. Moreover, this workshop tries to illustrate how the implementation of a strategy that combines the Knowledge Management and the Information Systems approach could contribute maximally in any kind of problematic situation inside the walls of an institution plus to any kind of decision making process. How and with what methods Information Systems support the decision making process for an organization? What are the probably rewards in place regarding the sharing of Information and other core values that constitute the meaning of KM and IS? Which maybe the "state of the art steps" for constructing a strategic plan for implementing KM via using IS solution? With what methods the scientific community indicates and measures if the KM process is in the right order for an organization? These are—but not limited to—some of the main key discussions for this workshop that relies heavily in the values of the new era Information Management and in the meaning of Knowledge Society.

7. Institutional Repositories. The State of the Art Best Practices and Best Policies

Organized by: Patrick OBrien, Montana State University, Library, United States

Description: Institutional Repositories (IR) have become a core function of the academic community's dissemination of new ideas across research disciplines. Information quality and quantity in the form of publications, research data, and metadata are among the key aspects that establish well-structured repositories. It is crucial organizations responsible for IR designate policies, strategies and technical approaches that constitute the state of the art. Academic libraries tend to manage IR at most research institutions, and they are well-positioned to maximize the value of IR for research and administration stakeholders. Discoverability of IR content is crucial as it can lead to greater access and citation of publications. IR content discoverability, use, and impact depend heavily on the practices, policies, and technologies implemented. To fulfil the promise of IR, information scientists and librarians must empower themselves with knowledge and expertise of the new practices, standards, and software enabling well-structured IR for use by humans and machines. This workshop aims to bring together information scientists and librarians in order to discuss and promote new practices and policies for institutional repositories.

8. How to deal with semantic heterogeneity in cross-domain information retrieval?

Organized by: Peter Mutschke, GESIS—Leibniz Institute for the Social Sciences, Department of Knowledge Technologies for the Social Sciences, Germany

Description: Due to the growing complexity of examined phenomena scientific progress is increasingly achieved at the boundaries of the established sciences and by cross-discipline cooperation. However, the way to interdisciplinary research is often hindered because of the difficulty of many researchers to understand a foreign language of science. By its nature, this problem affects cross-discipline information retrieval as well. A still challenging issue therefore is to improve search accuracy by understanding the contextual meaning of search terms in cross-domain information seeking scenarios. The workshop aims at bringing together researchers from different scientific application fields to discuss scenarios, approaches, applications, test beds, and new ideas.

9. Bioinformatics and Smart Data

Organized by: Papadopoulou Paraskevi, Deree-The American College of Greece, Department of Science and Mathematics, Greece

Description: The latest developments in bioinformatics require that we move from data management organization culture to learning organization culture where the collection and exploitation of data is meaningful only when it is used to optimize and automate solutions and solve problems. Big data as a concept is defined around four aspects: data volume, data velocity, data veracity, and data value. Veracity and value aspects of big data deal with the quality and the usefulness of big data making management a major challenge for most enterprises in terms of quality. The decisive criterion here is not necessarily the amount of (big) data, but valuable content (smart). Smart data analysis (focusing on veracity and value) is to filter out the noise and hold the valuable data, which can be effectively used to solve for example business problems or improve healthcare operations and opens new avenues to optimize computing capacities, explore molecular biology, genomics and proteomics and health informatics applications and implications. Researchers should be in the position to study entire systems of data in parallel using a variety of tools and methods asking for an integration with biological, biomedical data or business related big data hoping to improve the operations of various molecular biology subdisciplines, medicine, healthcare systems and businesses. The purpose of this workshop is that through lectures and panel discussions on bioinformatics and smart data analysis, an overview and solutions to some of these challenges in the fields of genomics, proteomics, medicine and health informatics will be discussed. Researchers, for example, need to design better collaboration models in healthcare and ask new questions on physiological and pathological clinical actions leading to real-time assistance in disease prevention, prognosis, diagnostics, and therapeutics. Turning this data from big to smart is the challenge that needs to be addressed today in order to lead to real-time assistance hoping to improve medicine and provide better more personalized treatment.

10. Smart cities for sustainable and inclusive development

Organized by: Christina Marouli, Deree—American College of Greece, Department of Science and Mathematics/Director—Center of Excellence for Sustainability, Greece

Description: The smart cities concept has been proposed as a guiding principle for urban development. Smart cities aim to maintain a good quality of life for its inhabitants while increasing resource and energy efficiency, with the use of innovative, cutting-edge technologies. The effectiveness of smart urban applications can be assessed in many different ways: e.g., 'smart economy', 'smart energy', 'smart mobility', 'smart governance', and 'smart neighborhoods'. But smartness, as it provides new opportunities and improved efficiencies, also poses new challenges and vulnerabilities at both the collective and individual levels. This workshop aims to provide a multidisciplinary forum for academics, researchers, practitioners, local government representatives in order to explore questions like: How do smart solutions contribute to high energy efficiency, effective mobility, resource-efficient, and low carbon cities? How can smart urban approaches promote better—good quality of life for all? How can smart cities promote the city as an integrated, balanced (eco)system, promoting social cohesion and justice? How can innovative, integrated technologies help cities become more connected, compassionate and sustainable? We invite submissions on theoretical approaches, research findings and case studies that highlight good practices and challenges related to smart urban solutions/smart cities for sustainable and inclusive development.

11. Information Technology and Environmental Studies

Organized by: Anastasia Misseyanni, Deree—The American College of Greece (ACG), Department of Science and Mathematics, Greece

Description: Environmental studies worldwide use an interdisciplinary approach in their study of the environment, promoting significant strategies towards sustainable development. Their integration with leading edge and streamline technologies is a key value proposition for the big challenges of our times. The objective of this workshop is to promote the scientific dialogue for the enhancement of policies related to environmental management, environmental protection, sustainability and innovative technology intensive services and applications. Five general areas describe the context for contributions for this workshop: Priority 1: Innovative startups for environmental management. The emphasis is given to solutions and real world services promoting various aspects of environmental sustainability. Priority 2: Strategies and frameworks for the new role of environmental studies in the global economy. The main focus is on theoretical works analyzing how environmental studies contribute to the wealth and prosperity in our times. Priority 3: Pilot projects and case studies. Project presentations and case studies discussions are invited with main emphasis paid on lessons learnt and best practices. Priority 4: Emerging technologies for environment management. Works related to the contribution of big data, cloud computing, recommendation systems, learning management systems, and open source technologies are invited. Priority 5: Visioning the future. Vision articles related to the future trends in the domain are invited.

Keynote Speakers

Prof. Abdel-Badeeh M. Salem
Faculty of Computer
and Information sciences
Ain Shams University
Cairo, Egypt

Prof. Dr. Abdel-Badeh M. Salem is Professor Emeritus of Computer Science since September 2007 till now. He was a former Vice Dean of the Faculty of Computer and Information Sciences at Ain Shams University, Cairo-Egypt (1996–2007). He was a professor of Computer Science at Faculty of Science, Ain Shams University from 1989 to 1996. He was a Director of Scientific Computing Center at Ain Shams University (1984–1990). His research includes intelligent computing, expert systems, medical informatics, and intelligent e-learning technologies. He has published around 350 papers in refereed journals and conference proceedings in these areas. He has been involved in more than 400 conferences and workshops as an Int. Program Committee, organizer and Session Chair. He is author and co-author of 15 Books in English and Arabic Languages. He was one of the founders of the following events, First Egyptian Workshop on Expert Systems 1987, Int. Cairo Conference on Artificial Intelligence Applications in 1992 and Int. Conf. on Intelligent Computing and Information Systems 2002, and one of the main sustainers of annual Int. Romanian Internet Learning Workshop Project (RILW), 1997. In addition he was Secretary of Egyptian Computer Society (1984–1990), Member of National Committee in Informatics—Academy of Scientific Research and Technology (1992–2000), Member of Egyptian Committee in the Inter-Governmental Informatics Program, IIP-UNISCO, Paris (1988–1990) and Coordinator of the Annual International Conference for Statistics, Scientific Computing, and Social and Demographic Research (1983–1990). In addition he was a partner of a MEDCAMPUS Projects on Methodologies and Technologies for Distance Education in Mediterranean (1993–1995). He is a member of the Editorial Board of many international Journals. He is a member of Int. Scientific Societies: American Association of Artificial Intelligence (AAAI), USA; British Computer Society, Expert Systems Specialist Group (SGES), Int. Neural Network Society (INNS), USA; Association for the Advancement of Computing Education (AACE), USA; Int. Society for Computers and their Applications ((ISCA), NC, USA, Dec. 95); Int. Society for Telemedicine & eHealth ISfTeH,, Switzerland; Member of Int. Federation for Information Processing (IFIP) Technical Committee WG 12.5, Knowledge-Oriented Development of Applications, Austria (2000 till now), Member of Int. Association for Science and Technology for Development (IASTED), TC on AI and Expert Systems, Int. Association for Science and

Technology for Development, Canada, (2000 till now). Elected member of Euro Mediterranean Academy of Arts and Sciences (EMAAS), September 25, 2015, Athens, Greece. Member of Alma Mater Europaea of the European Academy of Sciences and Arts, Belgrade, January 2016.

Prof. Peter Mutschke
GESIS Department, Germany

Peter Mutschke is the acting head of the GESIS department "Knowledge Technologies for the Social Sciences" (WTS) since March 2010. His research interests include information retrieval, network analysis and Science 2.0. He worked in a number of national and international research projects such as the DFG-funded project "Value-Added Services for Information Retrieval" (IRM) and the EU-funded project "Where eGovernment meets the eSociety" (WeGov). Currently, he is involved in the EU projects "Data Insights for Policy Makers & Citizens" (SENSE4US), "Open Mining Infrastructure for Text and Data" (OpenMinTeD) and "TraininG towards a society of data-saVvy inforMation prOfessionals to enable open leadership Innovation" (MOVING) as well as in major national und European research networks such as the COST action "Analyzing the dynamics of information and knowledge landscapes" (KNOWeSCAPE) and the research alliance "Science 2.0" of the German Leibniz Association. For both research networks Peter Mutschke serves as a member of the management committee.

Prof. Nick Bassiliades
Aristotle University
of Thessaloniki

Nick Bassiliades received his M.Sc. in Applied Artificial Intelligence from the Computing Science Department of Aberdeen University, in 1992, and his Ph.D. degree on parallel knowledge base systems from the Department of Informatics at the Aristotle University of Thessaloniki, Greece, in 1998, where he is currently Associate Professor. He currently also serves as an academic coordinator at the School of Science & Technology of the International Hellenic University, where he also teaches knowledge management in the web. His research interests include knowledge-based and rule systems, multiagent systems, ontologies, linked data and the semantic web. He has published more than 180 papers in journals, conferences, and books, has co-authored four books and co-edited eight volumes. His published research has received over 2200 citations (h-index 25). He was the Program Chair of eight conferences/workshops, he has been member of the program committee of more than 100 and on the organizational committee of six conferences/workshops. He has been involved in 32 R&D projects leading 9 of them. He has been the general secretary of the Board of the Greek Artificial Intelligence Society; he is a director of RuleML, Inc., and also a member of the Greek Computer Society, the IEEE, and the ACM.

Prof. Kostas Stefanidis
University of Tampere

Kostas Stefanidis is Associate Professor at the School of Information Sciences of the University of Tampere, Finland. Prior to that, he was a research scientist with the Information Systems Lab of ICS-FORTH, Greece, and a postdoctoral researcher at the IDI Department of NTNU in Norway and the CSE Department of CUHK in Hong Kong. He got his Ph.D. on personalized data management from the University of Ioannina, Greece. Kostas's research interests include the intersection of databases, information retrieval and the web, and include personalized and context-aware data management systems, recommender systems, keyword-based search, and information extraction, resolution and integration. He has been involved in several international research projects and co-authored more than 40 papers in peer-reviewed conferences and journals, including ACM SIGMOD, IEEE ICDE, and ACM TODS. He is also actively serving the scientific community. Currently, he is the General co-Chair of the Workshop on Exploratory Search in Databases and the Web (ExploreDB), the Web & Information Chair of SIGMOD/PODS 2016 and the Proceedings Chair of EDBT/ICDT 2016.

The Cooperative Role of Marketer and Programmer on SEO Strategies in Scientific Journals

Apostolos S. Sarlis, Ioannis C. Drivas and Alexandros Varveris

Introduction

In the new era of digital marketing advertising, web positioning in combination with high visibility constitutes a decisive component for each company in order to reveal and notify its business scope. Enterprises embrace major strategic objectives in optimizing their presence in the web such as Search Engine Optimization (SEO) strategies for generating qualified traffic or achieving respective higher ranking of company's website among its competitors. To begin with, SEO related with the process of trying to rank highly in search engines in a given webpage or domain for specific keywords (Evans 2007). In addition, SEO constitutes a set of techniques and strategies used by web developers to get better indexed by search engines (Gandour and Regolini 2011).

However, the competitiveness among enterprises for the achievement of highly web rankings in search engines creates a potential requisiteness in order to implement SEO processes in the website via a specific amount of resources investing. In addition, stimulates the query on how and in what way the company's resources should be distributed for achieving an optimal organic reach augmentation. In this

---

The original version of the book was revised. Belated corrections to change the order of First name and Family name of chapter authors have been incorporated. The erratum to the book is available at 10.1007/978-3-319-56288-9_72

A.S. Sarlis (✉)
Computer Science & Technology, University of Peloponnese, Tripolis, Greece
e-mail: sarlisapostolos@gmail.com

I.C. Drivas
Computer Science & Information Technology, Linnaeus University, Växjö, Sweden

A. Varveris
School of Law, National & Kapodistrian University of Athens, Athens, Greece

A. Kavoura et al. (eds.), *Strategic Innovative Marketing*, Springer Proceedings in Business and Economics, DOI 10.1007/978-3-319-56288-9_56

research paper, the authors proceed into a potentially fruitful combination of SEO processes. Moreover, a strategical adoption of an actuarial Dynamic Simulation Modeling (DMS) takes place in order to identify the optimal dissemination of company's resources in its website for achieving higher rankings and therefore higher web positioning and visibility. The body of this study is organized as follows: first the authors adopt practices that other studies recommend for the augmentation of search engine rankings in a plurality of websites related with the promotion of scientific journals in marketing sector.

An estimation of the overall SEO score before and after the recommended implementations takes place in order to estimate the potential improvement. In continuation, a keyword analysis for the encapsulation of appropriate keywords takes place, as the keyword density and stuffing possibility is estimated in these websites in order to avoid Black Hat SEO tactics and therefore be penalized by Google search engine (Connolly and Hoar 2015). Subsequently, an implementation of a dynamic simulation model takes place in order to indicate an optimum way of company's resources dissemination after multiple tests via iThink simulator builder of iSee Systems as a commonly accepted simulator of other studies (Sakas et al. 2016; Sakas and Sarlis 2016; Nasiopoulos et al. 2014).

Adoption of Practices

For the under examined websites related with the promotion of scientific journals of marketing the overall SEO score was calculated via using SEOSiteCheckUp tool as most of the examined websites assessed from 58/100 to 66/100 overall score. Taking into serious consideration the statements and the findings of the scientific community for the improvement of search engines rankings, four major recommended solutions were adopted. According to Al-Ananbeh et al. (2015) and Gennaro (2015) *Keywords Analysis and Selection* constitute one of the most important factors for SEO process. For the selection of the appropriate keywords SEMrush Competitive Data Tool was used as this tool gives an advantage to observe the most commonly by visitors used keywords for the under examined websites. *Title-Tags* creation correlated with the selected keywords was another important recommendation that other studies pointed out (Connolly and Hoar 2015). Missing *Alt-Tags* on images was another one suggestion as if web developers do not provide a written description on images, then crawlers might ignore the indexing process (Jones 2010). Additionally, for Google's Inc. (2010) SEO guide, the *simplification of URLs* converting them into friendly for crawlers, constitutes a crucial rectification for improving website ranking and visibility. Regarding the last one suggestion, *Meta Description* that is in proportion with selected appropriate keywords related with one of the most important indicators for improving website's visibility (Searchmetrics 2015; Google Inc. 2010).

On the flip side, the completion of all these recommendations need to be implemented by three major entities into the digital business environment, the digital marketing specialist team, the programming team and the expert in target group specification team, as the coordination of the first two is a vital one. The digital marketing specialist related mostly with the adoption and implementation of tools and indicators for extracting what needs to be done in a website for improving its organic reach and therefore the visibility of it (keywords analysis, directories listing, etc.). The programming team is responsible for implementing several recommended rectifications (sitemap creation, 404 error pages, etc.). Lastly, the target group expert team is responsible for the specification of potential customers that will be interested for websites and the services of them related with the promotion of scientific journals in marketing topic.

Systems Dynamics Modeling

In this study, iThink simulator 10.0.2 was used for estimating an optimal way of distributing resources in order to achieve higher organic reach into an enterprise's webpage related with the promotion of marketing scientific journals. In Fig. 1, the conglomeration of company's resources encapsulated into *CR* stock.

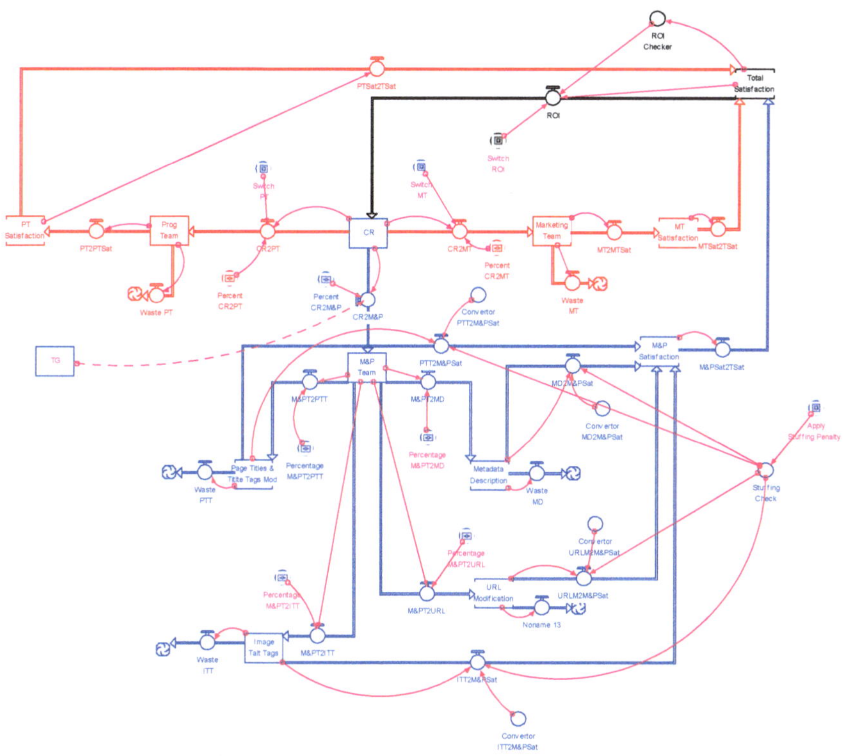

Fig. 1 Cooperation of marketer and programmer on SEO processes for website visibility improvement

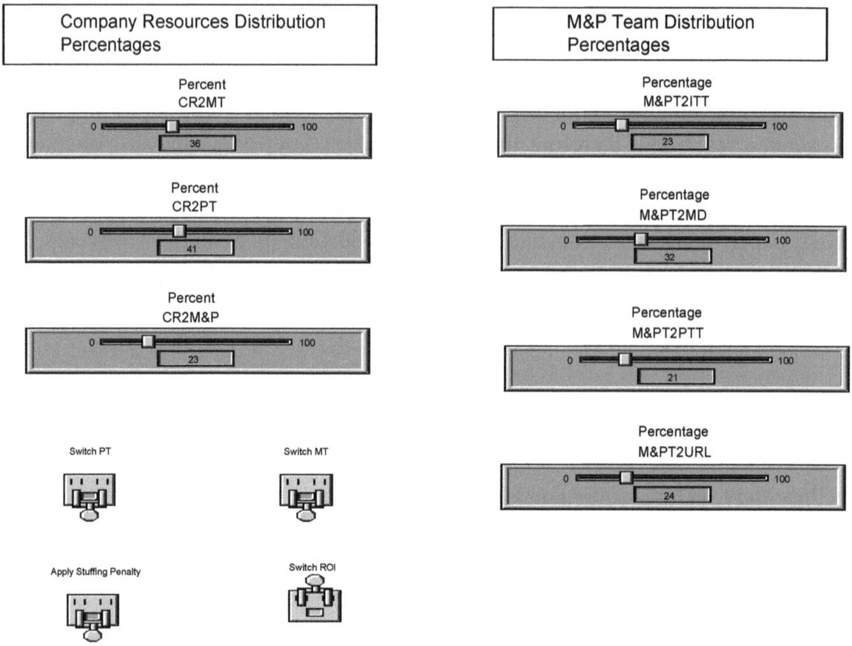

Fig. 2 Interface of the dynamic simulation model and optimal dissemination of resources

In continuation, it is really important to refer that all the actions that need to be done from the Marketing and Programming team sub-models respectively had already been implemented separately for each one of teams and this is the reason why the switchers are in Off-mode as it can be seen in Fig. 2. However, the cooperation of these two entities is a vital one, as it depicts multiple processes that need to be implemented. Target Group (TG) tank represents the amount of resources that the company has already invest in order to find the proper target group through the strategies of the literature review and serves as an external input of the model. Company's resources (CR) are distributed into marketing and programming team sub-model in order to implement four major rectifications adopted from the aforementioned literature review, the *Page Titles and Title Tags*, *Meta Description*, *URLs modification* and *Image Alt-Tags* and therefore they can be illustrated in the model.

Each of these stocks (the *Page Titles and Title Tags*, *Meta Description*, *URLs modification* and *Image Alt-Tags*) has its unique waste, which is the percentage of resources that are being spent without bringing any result as resources. On the other hand there are flows that direct from each stock to the stock *Marketing and Programming Satisfaction*. Each of these stock provides a unique profit to the *M&P Satisfaction* stock which depends to the unique algorithm that each Convertor has (each Convertor is connected to each flow that fills up the *M&P Sat.* stock). As the keywords stuffing possibility always entails risks into the website in order to be characterized with *Black-Hat SEO* tactics, a stuffing regulator as a convertor is placed in order to avoid high keyword usage and percentage of density regarding the four major rectifications (Title Tags, Meta Description, URLs modification, Image Alt-Tags). The *Apply Stuffing Penalty* convertor penalizes each of these flows (therefore impact in the end *Total Satisfaction* stock) if there is stuffing indication at least one stock. Moreover, all the resources that harvested after these implementations into the *Total Satisfaction* stock returned the analogous ROI into the *Company's Resources* stock as they can be disseminated into other future potential company's processes. In Fig. 2 the dissemination of resources for each one of the rectifications takes place.

The available company resources are 12,000 credit points for this specific improvement of the website's visibility as this model *"runs"* for 12 months as each one of the process has a specific percentage of distribution among each stock. It is also fairly important to refer that this specific way of investing company's resources in an optimal way as can be seen in Fig. 3, is exported after multiple trial and error tests into the iThink simulator that the model was built up. While observing Fig. 3, *CR* is decreased after the second when company invests resources, and increased before reinvestment when company earns ROI. Total Satisfaction curve starting to stabilize at second month. *Marketing Team* and *Prog Team* (Programming Team) are a straight line to zero since the Switcher to these investments are currently OFF. Also, *M&P Team* provides its resources to the *Total Satisfaction* stock when the criteria are fulfilled.

Consequently, differentiation into the way of distributing resources extracts different results into the *Total Satisfaction* stock and total *Return on Investment* that could be potentially returned and conglomerated into the *Company's Resources* stock in order to optimize the maximum profit without any penalization. As Fig. 4 numerically presents, the initial Company Resources for the total SEO investment are 12,000.

Fig. 3 Graph of goals of the dynamic simulation model

8:35 AM 7/10/2016 Table 1 (Goals)

Months	CR	M&P Satisfaction	Total Satisfaction	MT Satisfaction	PT Satisfaction
Initial	12.000.00	2.929.19	5.858.38	0.00	0.00
1	15.151.41	1.393.07	3.837.22	0.00	0.00
2	15.503.77	1.280.04	2.565.90	0.00	0.00
3	14.886.19	1.368.53	2.289.86	0.00	0.00
4	14.272.03	1.416.65	2.320.43	0.00	0.00
5	13.832.82	1.405.90	2.349.48	0.00	0.00
6	13.493.62	1.370.09	2.323.90	0.00	0.00
7	13.182.53	1.331.71	2.269.41	0.00	0.00
8	12.873.53	1.296.99	2.209.84	0.00	0.00
9	12.521.94	1.265.26	2.207.38	0.00	0.00
10	12.220.87	1.232.74	2.165.83	0.00	0.00
11	11.880.83	1.200.62	2.175.02	0.00	0.00
12	11.596.91	1.168.88	2.136.26	0.00	0.00

Fig. 4 Table of goals as regards the cooperation of marketer and programmer on SEO strategies

Satisfaction Tables of Marketing and Programming Teams are stuck to zero since the investment for those optimizations are OFF. In M&P Sat. table and Total Satisfaction, the profit of this investment each month is being showed. After the end of the second month the company has its highest profit where at the end of the month the company resources start to decrease. In the end of 12th month, there are still more than 11,500 resources.

Conclusions and Future Implementations

In this paper the authors proceed into the adoption of several major processes that practitioners implement for the augmentation of website's visibility using SEO techniques and tools. Implementing these rectifications into the under examination websites that related with the promotion of scientific journals of marketing resulted an increase into the overall SEO score ranged from 7 to 3 points as these metrics extracted via using SEOSiteCheckUp before and after the implementations. After the agreement of the editorial board, one of the lowest optimizations of the under examination journals' website of SEO ranking is presented in Fig. 5. In continuation, the authors proceeded into a dynamic simulation modeling process in order to estimate the proper dissemination of a specific amount of resources in order to

Fig. 5 SEO ranking difference before and after the implementations

achieve higher rankings and organic reach into the website while using keyword stuffing regulator that contributes maximally to avoid Black-Hat SEO characterization.

From a future implementation point of view, it will be very useful to proceed in an overall identification of problematics that websites have, related with the promotion of scientific journals', in order to design a dynamic model which entails a holistic confrontation of on-site SEO.

References

Connolly, R., and R. Hoar. 2015. *Fundamentals of web development*. New York, NY: Pearson Education.

Evans, M.P. 2007. Analysing google rankings through search engine optimization data. *Internet Research* 17 (1): 21–37.

Gandour, A., and A. Regolini. 2011. Web site search engine optimization: A case study of Fragfornet. *Library Hi Tech News* 28 (6): 6–13.

Gennaro, S. 2015. Brevity and clarity: Titles, keywords, and search engine optimization. *Journal of Nursing Scholarship* 47 (3): 195–196.

Google Inc. 2010. Google search engine optimization starter guide. www.google.com/webmasters/docs/Fsearch-engine-optimization-starter-guide.pdf. Accessed 12 Sept 2016.

Jones, K.B. 2010. *Social media optimization, search engine optimization your visual blueprint for effective internet marketing*, 2nd ed. Crosspoint Boulevard, Indianapolis: Wiley Publishing Inc.

Nasiopoulos K.D., D.P. Sakas, and D.S. Vlachos. 2014. Modeling the scientific dimension of academic conferences. *Procedia-Social and Behavioral Sciences* 147: 576–585.

Sakas D.P., and A.S. Sarlis. 2016. Library promotion methods and tools modeling and simulation on Twitter. *Library Review* 65 (6/7).

Sakas D.P., D.S. Vlachos, and D.K. Nasiopoulos. 2016. Modeling the development of the online conference's services. *Library Review* 65 (3): 160–184.

Searchmetrics. 2015. Search ranking factors 2015: Understand how the deck is stacked. www.searchmetrics.com/knowledge-base/ranking-factors/. Accessed 12 Spet 2016.

Implementation and Dynamic Simulation Modeling of Search Engine Optimization Processes. Improvement of Website Ranking

A.S. Sarlis, I.C. Drivas and D.P. Sakas

Introduction

The global entrepreneurial environment has already begun to deeply understand that one of the first dynamic steps for introducing the new era of marketing and advertising is taking part on top of the lists in search engines (Yalçın and Köse 2010). In simplicity, Search Engine Optimization is the process which enables a page to appear in top of the lists of search engines while users typing specific keywords. Alternatively, SEO is a set of techniques and strategies used by web developers to get better indexed by search engines (Gandour and Regolini 2011). In other words, it can be said that even if a website has high quality and quantity of content, SEO process increases its recognition and legibility in the global stage of rankings in a plurality of search engines, otherwise the chaotic mantle of searching results will cover the website.

Mutually, the global reduced financial flexibility arises the pressure for companies spending their resources in the right time, with the right quantity, hence with the appropriate return on investment regarding their website ranking. In this paper, the authors proceed in a plurality of sequential processes that embraces SEO techniques and strategies with a dynamic simulation modeling method applied in a website operated in global conference organizing and more specifically in the scientific field of Strategic Marketing.

The dynamic actuarial modeling process not only reduced the risk of uncertainty regarding the upcoming resources expenses, but also highlights the percentage of

A.S. Sarlis (✉) · D.P. Sakas
Computer Science and Technology, University of Peloponnese, Tripolis, Greece
e-mail: sarlisapostolos@gmail.com

I.C. Drivas
Computer Science & Information Technology, Linnaeus University, Växjö, Sweden

A. Kavoura et al. (eds.), *Strategic Innovative Marketing*, Springer Proceedings in Business and Economics, DOI 10.1007/978-3-319-56288-9_57

improvement in website's global rankings after SEO indicated implementations. More specifically, at first glance, the authors submitted the aforementioned website to the SEO SiteCkeckUp, a basic free SEO analyzing tool and the results of it indicated several recommendations for augmenting website's rankings. The analyzing tool indicated six recommended programming changes that increase website's visibility in the global stage ranking and accordingly these recommendations implemented. After the implementations, simulation modeling process takes place via iThink^{TM} system software as a model builder on instinctive icons-based and graphical interfaces.

Recommendations of SEO Analyzer

To begin with, the analyzer indicated an overall SEO score of 52/100, including categories of common SEO issues, speed optimizations, server and security recommendations and mobile usability efficacy. The first error that analyzer indicated has to do with the rectification of Metadata Description that was missing as a tag that provides a brief description of the page that can be used by search engines. The second error related with the Keywords usage as a crucial point that influence the indexing process of crawlers and therefore the identification of the topic of the website by search engines. The third error has to do with the Headings Status as Headings help search engines and crawlers to describe the subtopic of webpage. Missing Alt Tags-Attributes on Images as the fourth error was indicated. Alt title tags on images strengthen the message toward search engine crawlers augmenting website's potential accessibility and visibility. The fifth error related with unfriendly URL paths of the website which mostly affect the indexing process of the crawlers. Lastly the final sixth error related with the missing addition of Google Analytics in the website as an important factor that detects the circulation of users on it.

Systems Dynamics Modeling for SEO

The multidimensional utility of Dynamic Simulation Modeling (DMS) covers not only simulations in the IT and digital marketing sector that SEO is part of. DMS processes also indicate their importance and efficacy to the handling of resources in other topics such as strategic management and leadership (Sakas et al. 2014; Nasiopoulos et al. 2013), or even in business environment in an effort to highlighted the organizational cultural change (Trivellas et al. 2007). In an overall framework, according to Ball (2011) modeling refers in an action of generating a process as an abstract representation of some real-world entity or system. To implement the model that encapsulates the expenses of resources regarding the SEO Analyzer recommendations, the modeling software tool iThink 9.0.2, from iSee Systems, was used as a commonly accepted simulator in other studies (Sakas et al. 2016; Tan et al. 2010). iThink software uses diagrams of tanks and flows to model and simulate in a graphical way all the processes and scenarios, and also represents the outcomes of certain inputs that can be defined by the user of the application. In specific:

□: A Tank represents the conglomeration of physical or either nonphysical quantities. For example in this model the *Total Satisfaction ROI* or *Company Resources* are some of them.

: A Flow represents an activity which fills up or evacuates the Tank. Also the arrow indicates the direction of positive flow into or out of a Tank.

○: A Converter is responsible for holding the values of constants. The Convertor also serves as an external input to the model or converts inputs into outputs through user-defined graphical functions or algebraic relationships.

: The Connectors provide the links associations between models elements. On the one hand the solid wire is an action Connector, on the other hand the dashed wire is an information Connector.

In Fig. 1 the dynamic simulation model takes place and enrolls all its functions. To begin with, the blue tank *Company Resources* and the black Tank *Total Satisfaction—ROI* constitutes the core values of the modeling process. The first one controls and distributes the available resources and the second one estimates the final satisfaction of a decision-maker regarding this investment and the return of it. The other tanks represent the missing points or the errors that the SEO Analyzer tool was recommended and therefore the upcoming spending of company's resources for the rectification of them. However, the important key point of this

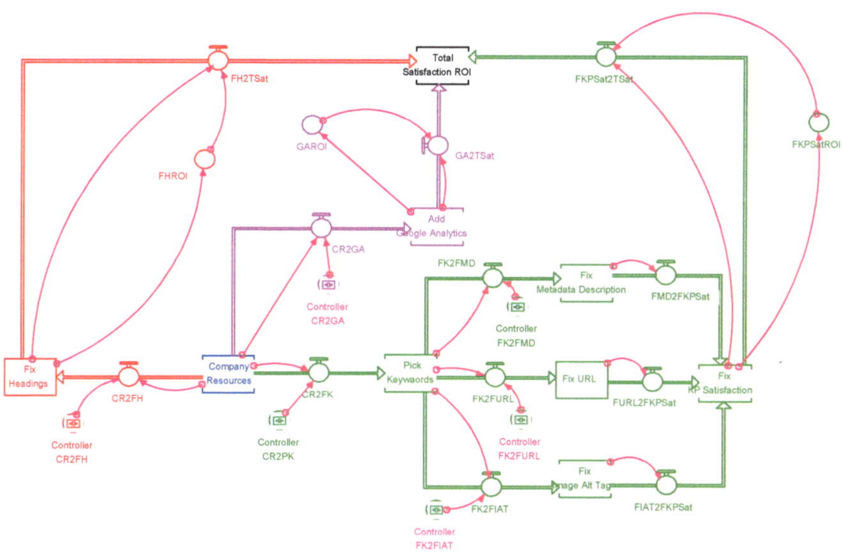

Fig. 1 Modeling the SEO process for the augmentation of search engines rankings

model related with the Converters which are responsible for the final reckoning of the *Total Satisfaction of ROI* as they algebraically calculate the possibility to augment the satisfaction.

Implementing the Recommendations of SEO Analyzer

Figure 2 shows the main user interface of the simulation model. There are two sections on this user interface. Every section represents the % of the resources that provided through sliders in every action.

In the *Company Resources Controllers* section, the amount of company resources distribution percentage is presented. The available resources are 100 credit points for the improvement of search engine rankings at the website. 20% of credits are distributed for fixing of Headings (CR2FH) and other 20% credits are distributed to the prosthesis of Google Analytics (CR2GA). For the selection of keywords and other suggested rectifications 60% of credit points are spent. The last one distribution is higher than the other two fixings CR2FH and CR2GA and this happened due to the fact that is a process that it needs much more working hours from the SEO specialist. In the *Pick Keywords Controllers* section, the amount of Pick Keywords Tank distribution percentage is presented. A total of 40% of the

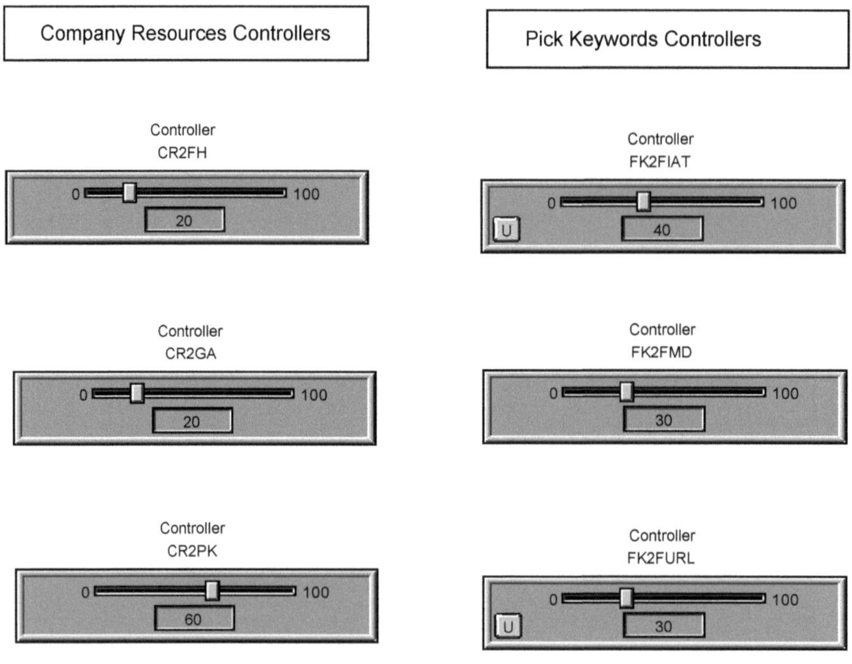

Fig. 2 Interface of the dynamic simulation model

available resources need to be invested into fixing the metadata deception Tank, 30% into fixing URLs (into a more user friendly form) and the rest 30% need to be invested into fixing the Alternative Tag of Images.

As it can be seen in Fig. 3, the implementation of this dynamic simulation model *runs* for 8 h. During of 8 h, all the suggested rectifications that SEO SiteCkeckUp indicated were fixed from the SEO specialist and each recommendation gave a surcharge of the *Total Satisfaction of ROI*. Therefore during of 8 h, the blue line (*Company Resources*) gradually starts to be decreased as more and more resources are invested. However, the diagram shows that the black line (*Total Satisfaction of ROI*) has a gradual and steady augmentation compared with the inversely proportional reduction of Company Resources.

In other words, the decision-maker is fully satisfied regarding the way he spent his resources as the total satisfaction for the return on investment has finally highly increased. Conversely, if the simulation model predicted and therefore extracted a lower *Total Satisfaction of ROI* than this one, then the decision-maker should be very cautious and mindful for this investment as it can be characterized as a perilous one.

Having always in mind the consistent augmentation of *Total Satisfaction of ROI*, Fig. 4 represents numerically the gradual increase of ROI while resources are spent for each implementation strengthening in this way decision-maker's movements and decisions. As it can be seen, in a period of 8 h, (from Initial = 0 to 7) *Company Resources* reasonably reduced (8th h 0.10) while *Keywords Satisfaction*, *Google Analytics* and *Headings* have an augmenting improvement (138.71, 37.31 and 64.52). It is also noteworthy to refer that the low increase of results plus the non-varying situation of ROI in the last 3 h (5, 6, 7) is analogous with the minimal spent of resources, as minimum spend of resources indicates low changes and increases.

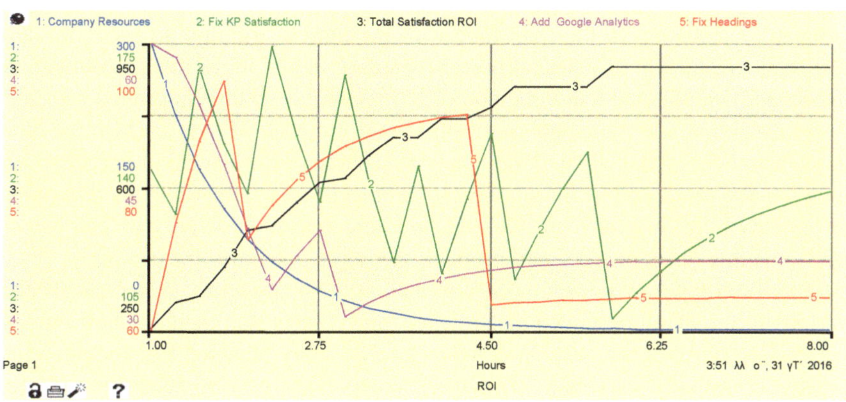

Fig. 3 Graph of goals of the dynamic simulation model

3:51 AM 31/8/2016 Table 1 (Model Table)

Hours	Company Resources	Fix KP Satisfaction	Add Google Analytics	Fix Headings	Total Satisfaction ROI
Initial	300.00	144.00	60.00	60.00	253.20
1	94.92	138.28	40.65	72.61	492.72
2	30.03	167.35	31.33	85.59	621.32
3	9.50	118.66	35.43	89.69	768.84
4	3.01	129.25	36.73	63.94	845.63
5	0.95	113.96	37.14	64.35	893.85
6	0.30	130.66	37.27	64.48	893.85
7	0.10	138.71	37.31	64.52	893.85

Fig. 4 Table of goals of the dynamic simulation model regarding the decision-maker's total satisfaction of this return on investment

Conclusion and Future Implications

In this study the authors first ran an SEO analyzing tool for the identification of issues and problems that a website probably has. The analyzer not only ranked icsim.net with 52/100 overall SEO rating but also indicated some recommendations for rectification. Second, the authors started to rectify each of the recommendation in order to estimate (a) the time spent to complete each one (b) to estimate the difficulty of each one which is related with the spending time, in order to distribute in a proper way company's resources while implementing the DMS. After the completion of all the recommendations the authors reran the analyzer and SEO SiteCkeckUp ranked this time the website with 62/100 overall SEO rating achieving a growth of 10 points.

The third step of this paper related with the construction of a DMS which supports a decision-maker's choice to invest resources for the improvement of company's website in order to increase its visibility with SEO digital marketing strategies and techniques. The model highlighted not only a proper way to spent company's resources in the right time with the right distribution of them, but also that total satisfaction of decision maker regarding the return of this investment has increased. One the one hand, the completed recommendations improved website's visibility giving and increment of 10 point in the overall SEO rating. On the other hand the model predicted that if company's resources will be spent in that way, then the expected result will be the augmentation of satisfaction regarding the investment at SEO ranking improvement plus the minimization of proclivity to take wrong decisions that leads to risky and probably negative outcomes for company.

This prototype as a useful decision-making tool, provides to decision-maker various forms of support such as Switchers and Sliders that facilitate him through the decision-making process. In conclusion, this study depicted that the modeling process contributes maximally to manage complexity, making substantiated decisions based on the well understood and explicitly formulated essentials of the modeled situation. A modeling process which studies and manages the overall framework of on-site SEO improvement needs to be examined as it constitutes a crucial factor for decision-makers' digital marketing promotional success.

References

Ball, P. 2011. Dynamic modelling for supply chain management: Dealing with front-end, back-end and integration issues. In *Production Planning & Control,* ed. Adolfo Crespo Marquez.

Gandour, A., and A. Regolini. 2011. Web site search engine optimization: a case study of Fragfornet. *Library Hi Tech News* 28 (6): 6–13.

Nasiopoulos, D., D. Sakas, and D. Vlachos. 2013. Analysis of strategic leadership simulation models in non-profit organizations. *Procedia—Social and Behavioral Sciences* 73: 276–284.

Sakas, D., D. Vlachos, and D. Nasiopoulos. 2014. Modeling strategic management for the development of competitive advantage, based on technology. *Journal of Systems and InformationTechnology:* 187–209.

Sakas, D., D. Vlachos, and D. Nasiopoulos. 2016. Modeling the development of the online conference's services. *Library Review* 65 (3): 160–184.

Tan, K.S., M. Daud Ahmed, and D. Sundaram. 2010. Sustainable enterprise modeling and simulation in a warehousing context. *Business Process Management Journal* 16: 871–886.

Trivellas, P., P. Reklitis, and N. Konstantopoulos. 2007. A dynamic simulation model of organizational culture and business strategy effects on performance. *American Institute of Physics (AIP)* 963 (2): 1074–1078.

Yalçın, N., and U. Köse. 2010. What is search engine optimization: SEO? *World Conference on Learning, Teaching and Administration Papers Procedia—Social and Behavioral Sciences* 9: 487–493.

Instagram Company Page Creation Modeling and Simulation

A.S. Sarlis, D.P. Sakas, D.P. Vlachos and A. Antoniou

Introduction

Instagram application belongs to the general category of social media platforms. Social media platforms can be defined as a team of applications based on the Internet, as they have been developed and manufactured in the ideological and technological frameworks of Web 2.0. Early twentieth century marketers created a product and then struggled to contrive innovative campaigns and methods to distribute and market the product (Schultz et al. 2011). Web 2.0 allows the creation and exchange of user-generated content (Kaplan and Haenlein 2009) as opposed to early marketers. Today's dominant marketing point of view related mostly with the meaning of social media services governed of the well-known 4Cs of marketing, while they are quite different from 4Ps (Jantsch 2010).

Several research approaches highlighted that the size in the social media is not mandatory to be related with the augmenting interaction. This allegation comes to be strengthened while L2 Think Tank shows that Instagram has the widest interaction among the media (McCarthy 2015). More specifically, comparing the most populated media until December 2014 the Facebook (Statista.com 2014), the rate of interaction in posts from 249 brands was 15 times higher on Instagram rather than Facebook (Emarketer.com 2014). Thus, in the general framework of products promotion and services, as the main goal is the brand to be adjacent to the customer, Instagram application should be an integral part of the advertising campaign.

Instagram is a media which has a highly augmented interaction among the users and constitutes a very crucial media of communication between the company and the user–customer. For this reason it is mandatory to highlight the efficiency of each action in this specific media aiming in this way in the optimization of its utility.

A.S. Sarlis (✉) · D.P. Sakas · D.P. Vlachos · A. Antoniou
Department of Informatics and Telecommunications,
University of Peloponnese, Tripolis, Greece
e-mail: sarlisapostolos@gmail.com

A. Kavoura et al. (eds.), *Strategic Innovative Marketing*, Springer Proceedings
in Business and Economics, DOI 10.1007/978-3-319-56288-9_58

Observing the current optimization practices, the most common of them related with split tests of posts intending to find the optimal material that will be uploaded in the optimal time (in posts that are related with the brand). This specific method, although is indispensable, incompletes for two main reasons. The first one is that each time it is mandatory to repeat from the first step every trial of efficiency for each product, as the recording of previous actions in previous similar situations may be lost in the huddle of information overloading. Hence, resources are wasted inefficiency while with the appropriate provision of possible unfortunate result would have been invested elsewhere. The second main reason is the plethora of actions that must be done in specific time dependent on the provisioned resources in order to optimize the result. In other words, if it is worthy to spent resources in an action, in the specific time, with the analogous result.

For that reasons, a necessity arises for the creation of a dynamic simulation model (Dimitrios and Vlachos 2013). Dynamic simulation models have the ability of predicting a result with specific data. A dynamic simulation model of promoting the company's page on Instagram could be a useful tool for predicting interaction (Followers, Likes and Comments) depending on the provided resources. Therefore, a company would be aware of the quantity of resources that should invest in order to achieve the optimal result or what the result would be, according to the available company's spending resources. Practically, this means that the company has the advantage to test situations or operations without spending resources. The first part of this simulation model is the creation of the company's account on Instagram, which is constructed in the current research approach (Nasiopoulos et al. 2014).

Page Promotion on Instagram

Summarizing the first chapter, the goals on Instagram for a company are:

1. Acquiring new Followers
2. The augmentation of Likes on images and videos
3. The augmentation of Comments on images and videos.

Steps that Should Be Followed for the Construction of the Page

To begin with, for the creation of the dynamic simulation model of promoting the company's page on Instagram, it is necessary to clarify the steps for the construction of it. The first goal is the creation of the page in that specific media. The second step is the maintenance and the augmentation of followers plus the interaction with them in this specific account.

For the account optimization and usage of a company on Instagram, it is recommended to follow specific steps during the construction of it. Company creates the account as a simple user using the same handle (the identifier @example) just as other social media platforms such as Twitter or the same Company's name that has on platforms such as Facebook. That happens in the framework of unification of social media campaign in order for the users not to confused/disorientated from others, finding with an easy way the company in each media.

Subsequently, a profile image needs to be added. The image should be differentiated depending on the goals of a company, such a logo, an offer or an image that informs customers about the company. Additionally, a link with a page that the company has the complete control of it (for example, the homepage of it) should be added. Lastly, Facebook company's account should be connected with Instagram (with the choice that is provided) in the framework of the totally unified campaign in social media networks.

After the account creation, the user (in that case the company) should start adding images. Company's images, representing optically the current of the forthcoming products/services, expected to strengthen the digital Web 2.0 presence of the company in a plurality of search engines. Furthermore, the digital marketing promotion of products would provide to customers an image of products/services improving the relations between customers and company, creating in this way a digital community. It must be taken into serious consideration that the user (company) should be very attentive in order not to "frazzle" the follower with no relative images, but to inform him with regularity.

Lastly, the company should start selecting people for Following, either regarding with the sector of the company, or either inserts calls of contacts from Facebook/Twitter or other media. It is worth noting to refer that the quality of the followers that the company should follow has more essence from the quantity of followers as it is very useful to be relative with the sector that the company operates and not to be naturally famous or simple users. In this way the company starts with a strategical way to modulate its community with specific characteristics, or in other words creating its target group. Then it is important not only to maintain the interest of the followers but also to find new. However, for this specific research, the first step is unfolded and therefore modeled in a simulated way.

Modeling the Process of Construction Company's Page on Instagram

In the third chapter, the construction of the homepage on Instagram will be modeled for the company's needs. The simulated modeling process will be implemented via the editor iThinkTM. Before the construction of this specific dynamic simulation model, some of the tools that iThinkTM provide will be described.

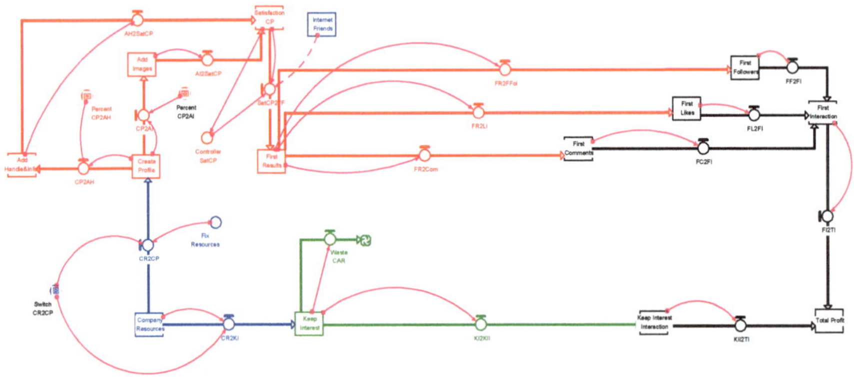

Fig. 1 Modeling the construction of the personal homepage on Instagram

This specific dynamic simulation model depicts the steps that need to be done in order to create a business account on Instagram with an optimal result and the less cost regarding the current situation of the company (company size, available resources). On Instagram the first step that a user needs to do is the creation of the personal homepage either as company or either as a single user.

First, company offers resources for the construction of the personal homepage (as it is illustrated in Fig. 1). These resources could be specific independently from the amount of resources that company would spend. Subsequently, these resources channeled in the decision of company's handle, in the addition of information and also in the addition of an image or even other specific images.

After the fulfillment of these two criteria, then supporters of the company can be called via email, other social media platforms or using other actions. These supporters will constitute the first followers as they will induce Likes and Comments in the posted images as this situation will cause an inaugural interaction of company's page. After the implementation of the aforementioned steps, the efforts focused in the augmentation of followers to maintain the number of them and therefore to improve the level of interaction among the users.

Implementation of Instagram Marketing Model (Page Construction)

In the fourth chapter of this research the interface of the simulated model will be presented (Fig. 2). After that, the results of the model after the process of the implementation will be presented.

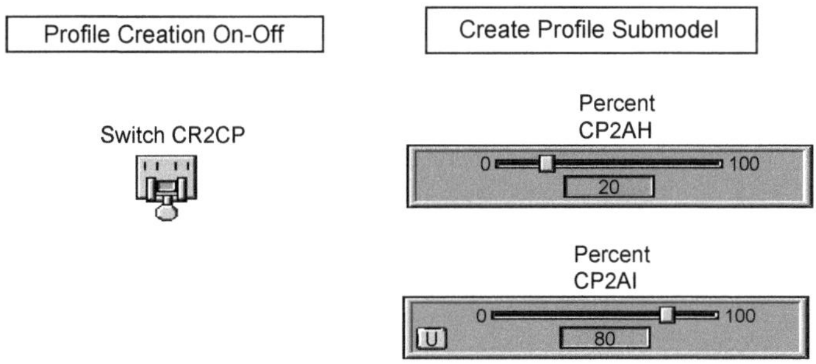

Fig. 2 Interface of the dynamic simulation model

Model Interface

The Profile Creation section shows the Switch which controls the flow of Company's Resources to each submodel. When this Switch is on, the Company provides resources to the Profile Creation submodel. When, the Profile Creation is completed, the decision-maker of the model turns this Switch off. After that action, the resources provision the Profile Creation is stopped and the resources provision to Keep Interest submodel begins.

The Create Profile Submodel section allows the decision-maker to determine Create Profile submodel resources' distribution to any action that can take place via the Profile Creation. These actions are Add Handle&Info and Add Images. The resources provision is controlled through the proper slider.

Instagram Model Implementation

Primarily, for the needs of the simulation some data of the situation must be considered. The first basic data is that the company provides 500 amount of points and these credits translated into half-hours or 250 h per year. The second data is the "Internet friends" of the company, accounted into 100 (in this case for a very small company). With the current presence of these data and particularly the choices of the decision-maker, the invested resources generate specific results. This specific dynamic simulation model will be implemented in a period of 12 months, as it will simulate the situation of the advertising campaign of a company on Instagram for this specific time.

As it can be seen in Fig. 3, the Total Profit increases as the interest of users maintained, or in other words, the followers are increased and therefore the interaction among them. In addition the first results can be seen from the first month that resources were invested.

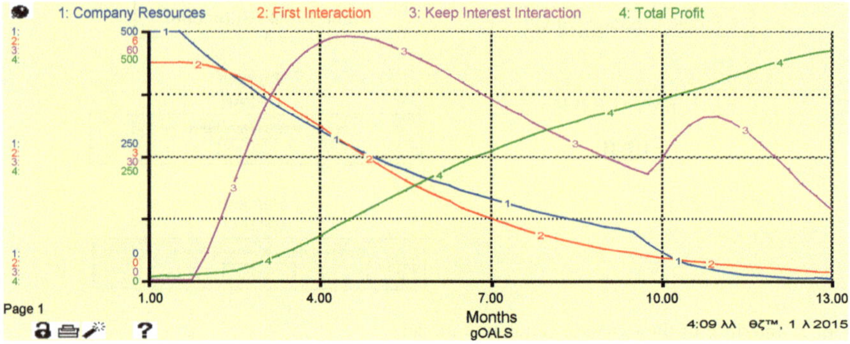

Fig. 3 Graph of goals of the dynamic simulation model

4:09 λλ 1/10/2015 Table 1 (Goals)

Months	Company Resources	First Interaction	Keep Interest Interaction	Total Profit
Initial	500.00	5.25	0.00	5.25
1	451.11	5.17	6.25	10.49
2	367.44	4.58	40.97	35.33
3	299.28	3.69	57.33	88.34
4	243.76	2.80	57.76	150.00
5	198.55	2.05	51.51	208.19
6	161.72	1.47	43.63	258.58
7	131.72	1.05	36.14	300.64
8	107.29	0.74	29.65	335.19
9	54.47	0.52	29.06	363.38
10	17.23	0.36	39.30	398.52
11	5.45	0.25	29.97	435.51
12	1.73	0.18	17.24	460.74

Fig. 4 Table of goals of the dynamic simulation model

In Fig. 4, the results are presented in a numerical way regarding the actions that were implemented. More particularly, the tank First Interaction fills up in the first month and then progressively empties providing the profits in tank Total Profit. The tank Keep Interest Interaction fills up gradually from the second month, while culminates in the fourth month. After the fourth month it starts to be decreased until the 10th month as is increased radically (probably a “reheating” of relations among the users of Instagram), and therefore it starts to decrease its momentum once more.

Conclusion and Further Research

The proper usage of Instagram with the combination of this simulation model would be a dynamic way for the optimization of profits for each company. The presence of dynamic simulation models contribute maximally for handling the complexity of a situation, while the main goal is the creation of a sustainable solution, preventing in this way unfavorable and negative situations. A sustainable model on Instagram is the model that could predict with preciseness the results and the revenues regarding the data and the goals of the management decision-makers. A future decisive effort should be given in order to model the overall process of promoting company's actions on Instagram (after page construction), and therefore on other social media platforms, as this can be happened in the overall framework of digital marketing of an organization. Finally, it must be taken into serious consideration that the algorithm of Instagram evolves with high rapidity, and for that reason, multiple updates should be implemented in the model not only to keep pace with Instagram updates, but also to improve model's efficiency and precision.

References

Don, E. Schultz, Charles H. Patti, and Philip J. Kitchen. 2011. *The evolution of integrated marketing communications: The customer-driven marketplace*. 2 Park Square, Milton Park, Abingdon, Oxon Ox14 4RN: Roultedge.

Emarketer.com. 2014. *Instagram captures higher interaction rates than facebook*. http://www.emarketer.com/Article/Instagram-Captures-Higher-Interaction-Rates-than-Facebook/1010627. Accessed 28 Dec 2015.

Jantsch, J. 2010. *Let's talk: social media for small business*. Duck Tape Marketing. http://www.ducttapemarketing.com/socialmediaforbusiness.pdf. Accessed Dec 2014.

Kaplan, A.M., and M. Haenlein. 2009. Users of the world, unite! The challenges and opportunities of social media. *Business Horizons* 53 (1): 61.

McCarthy, J. 2015. Instagram registers 15x more engagement than facebook: L2. https://www.luxurydaily.com/instagram-registers-15x-more-engagement-than-facebook-l2/. Accessed 27 Dec 2015.

Nasiopoulos, K. Dimitrios, Damianos P. Sakas, and D.S. Vlachos. 2013. Analysis of strategic leadership models in information technology. *Procedia—Social and Behavioral Sciences* 268–275.

Nasiopoulos, K. Dimitrios, Damianos Sakas, Dimitris Vlachos. 2014. Modelling strategic management for the development of competitive advantage, based on technology. *Journal of Systems and Information Technology* 16 (3): 187–209. doi:10.1108/JSIT-01-2014-0005.

Statista.com. 2014. Leading social networks worldwide as of December 2014, ranked by number of active users (in millions). http://www.statista.com/statistics/272014/global-social-networks-ranked-by-number-of-users/. Accessed 27 Dec 2015.

Two Years on—Developing Metrics for Crowdsourcing with Digital Collections

Tuula Pääkkönen

Introduction

In the digital collections of the National Library of Finland (NLF), there are digitized materials from newspapers, journals and ephemera starting from the year 1771. In the public web service the material is available until the year 1910. Anything that is published more recently, after it has been digitized, is made available at the six legal deposit libraries all over Finland. Beyond that, some materials have been opened for research and education via contracts, which allow wider usage permissions.

Crowdsourcing in NLF started in 2014 when a new version of the presentation system was launched. The crowdsourcing features enabled users to do clippings from interesting articles, advertisements or anything else. When creating a clipping as shown in Fig. 1, the area is selected, and simultaneously, the user should add a title and a category and optionally also an article type and keywords.

Why Crowdsourcing?

NLF has started developing crowdsourcing in order to allow all users to do more with the digital materials. Even today family researchers, local historians are the most common user segments, (Hölttä 2016) and it was hoped that crowdsourcing could generate interest and create a platform itself, which would reward of participation (Bremer-Laamanen 2015). In a way, that has occurred, as some of the more recent researcher generations have taken the clippings into use in their research data col-

T. Pääkkönen (✉)
National Library of Finland, University of Helsinki, Mikkeli, Finland
e-mail: tuula.paakkonen@helsinki.fi

A. Kavoura et al. (eds.), *Strategic Innovative Marketing*, Springer Proceedings in Business and Economics, DOI 10.1007/978-3-319-56288-9_59

Fig. 1 Creation of a clipping in at http://www.digi.nationallibrary.fi service

lection phase. In addition, we have seen new kinds of interest in the materials from so-called citizen science practitioners—clippings are shared across social media services and web sites ranging from the communities of local history researchers to flea market sites. Internally, NLF also wanted to see if crowdsourcing could help in finding new and interesting topics from the contents. In that sense, crowdsourcing has also opened eyes towards the materials and to all of the information needs different user segments have. Newspapers shine light to the current events and discussions of the past, which make them good source also for current reader.

One benefit is that that avid users are also helping us at the NLF by notifying us of occasional errors in the metadata or content pages. In fact there are many reasons to utilize crowdsourcing, where Holley (2010) lists a few mentioning, for example, improving the quality of library data, adding value to the data, and encouraging the sense of public ownership of digital materials. The latter has risen especially later on, when people feel that newer materials should be made available as it is the question of a nationally important asset.

First Year of Crowdsourcing Experiences

We analyzed the crowdsourcing metrics after the first year of experiences. The new presentation system version had changed so much, that actually crowdsourcing was not even the most advocated feature in the beginning. Despite that, already in the first 6 months, we started to see the trend where the work of the most enthusiastic users, made big impact to the collection of clippings (Pääkkönen 2015).

During the first year, there were also quite a few queries on the overall functionality and purpose of the crowdsourcing features, based on the feedback received. For this purpose we added video guidance, which shows how a clipping is made and explained how all of the clippings are visible for all users, which creates a sense of community ownership. In addition our customer service gave detailed answers to the specific questions of different users, be it from the effective usage of the search, clippings to managing the sets of clippings.

Brief Overview of Crowdsourcing in Libraries

In some libraries, crowdsourcing has existed for nearly 10 years. One of the most famous cases is the Australian Newspaper Digitisation program, where the text correction is the main focus, reporting over 6000 volunteers within first years (2008–2009), (Holley 2010). In NLF, the first crowdsourcing case was the 'Mole game' (Myyräpeli) in 2011–2012, where via playing a game people inadvertently could help in fixing the OCR (optical character recognition) errors (Bremer-Laamanen 2015). Besides the clippings, nowadays NLF also has a project called Fenno-Ugrica, where crowdsourcing was used for fixing text recognition errors, with help of local language experts (Hakkarainen 2016).

There seem to be many approaches to crowdsourcing in requested tasks and how users are encouraged to join. There are various games, where the user might not even realize participation in crowdsourcing tasks of a library. This is the case of the Biodiversity Heritage Library, where via playing a game participants fix text recognition (Rose-Sandler et al. 2015), although they also have another platform enabling finding, tagging and describing illustrations manually. The China America Digital Academic Library (CADAL) utilizes existing user behaviour and user-given rankings in order to create recommendations for the next books (Yang et al. 2009). In University College London, the Transcribe Bentham project works with manuscript transcription (Moyle et al. 2011) as does the Ensemble @ Yale, with theatre programmes ("Ensemble @ Yale|Yale University Library" 2016) and restaurant menus in the "What's on the menu?" service of the New York Public Library ("Whats on the menu?" 2016) as some examples.

Metrics for Crowdsourcing

The crowdsourcing metrics of the NLF have been followed from the beginning. The metric we wanted was designed to be easy for the data gathering and straightforward to monitor. The target was to get answer to the question of "How much crowdsourcing is used"? For this our metric of choice was the amount of clippings, which the participants have created, as it is the core outcome of being an active participant. That requires that the person has browsed or searched the collections, created an account and taken the time to pick the interesting area, to add metadata and to save the clipping. Creation of a clipping takes from one to 5 min, but when user has a few hundred clippings that show already commitment by the time spent with the digital materials.

Table 1 Summary of user-made clippings

Clippings data	1st year	2nd year
Amount of clippings	19,666	35,345
Top-5 (%)	46	35
Top-10 (%)	64	49
Mean	44.49	40.91
Maximum	2811	3550

Amount of Clippings Over the First Two Years

After the first year the profile of main part of the users with regard to clippings is illustrated in via the red dotted line. The minimum amount of clippings created at this point was 1 and maximum 2811. Due to the few hyperactive users, the mean was 44.49. The five users who created most of the clippings were responsible for 46% of all of the clippings. When extending to the top 10, that covered nearly 64% of all of the work done. In Table 1 there is a brief summary of the data containing the first and second year situation. The mean of the data at the point of second year is 40.91 and median 3.00. The hyperactive top users are still significant part of the creation of the clippings, where top 5 is responsible of the 35% of all of the clippings—however, the impact of the top users is anyhow leveled slightly.

In Fig. 2 the amount of clippings the second year clippings amount is described as a solid blue line. The overall amount of clippings is higher. After the second year it can still be seen that there are even more users who have made one clipping, but there is some increase in the top 10 and top 20 of users.

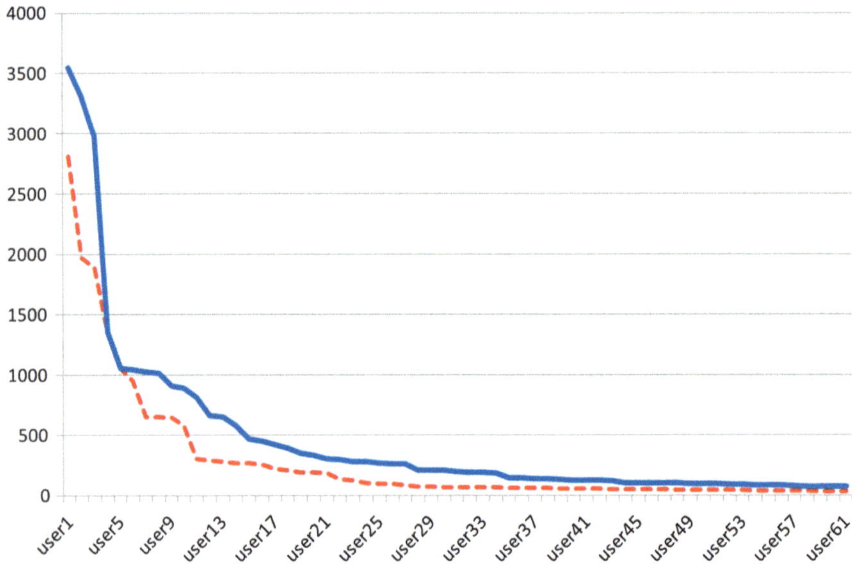

Fig. 2 Clippings quantity comparison first to second year

One caveat, which this calculating of quantities has, is that the user's place can shift as new people join in and create their own sets of clippings. On the other hand, this is one way to ensure anonymity of the users, as the aim is that anyone can utilize the material they see valuable. Quantity alone does not tell all about the value of the material to the user. For an individual user, one clipping can be as valuable as collection of several is for another.

Conclusions

Based on the initial 2 years the top 5 and top 10 of users do the most of the contributions. However, it is good to remember that the majority of the users of the http://digi.kansalliskirjasto.fi service are those who browse, search and read the materials and do not commit beyond that to digitized newspaper collection. Besides digital collections it is also good to remember that the original paper materials are also available for viewing at the NLF and nowadays also the born-digital newspapers end up to the collections of the web harvesting.

Crowdsourcing features have got steady increase over the 2-year period. Counting the quantity of clippings is a simple and to-the-point metric, which is easy to gather and follow-up. With improved communication and extending the content available, we feel that there is a possibility to increase usage even more from the organic growth. In addition, we hope that with collaboration projects, like in Aviisi, we can grow new users for crowdsourcing together with researchers and buildup a community where citizens can help researchers in locating source material. Participants for these citizen science projects should find interesting project, launch them with ease and get started fast (Yadav and Darlington 2016) after which it is possible to get continuous participation.

Recent focus areas in our development projects have been in reporting, access control and improving the search capabilities. However, even if those features have been initiated mainly based on the feedback of various kinds of researchers, we hope that the existing and possible new users of crowdsourcing will find benefits in them and continue participating. The crowdsourcing metrics will require further study to evaluate possible existing metrics from similar kinds of situations and we expect to evolve as new data needs arise.

Acknowledgements This work was funded by the EU commission through its European Regional Development Fund and the program Leverage from the EU 2014–2020 via Aviisi project —the golden century of newspapers to new use.

Big thanks to Mika Koistinen for hinting about a couple of crowdsourcing projects.

References

Bremer-Laamanen, M. 2015. In the spotlight for crowdsourcing. *Scandinavian Library Quarterly*. http://slq.nu/?article=volume-47-no-1-2014-11.

Ensemble @ Yale|Yale University Library. http://web.library.yale.edu/dhlab/ensemble.

Hakkarainen, J.-P. 2016. Introduction to Our Project|Fenno-Ugrica. Fenno-Ugrica Blog Minor. Lang. Proj. – Natl. Libr. Finl.

Holley, R. 2010. Crowdsourcing: How and Why Should Libraries Do It? *LIB Magazine* 16. doi:10.1045/march2010-holley.

Hölttä, T. 2016. Digitoitujen kulttuuriperintöaineistojen tutkimuskäyttö ja tutkijat. http://urn.fi/URN:NBN:fi:uta-201603171337.

Moyle, M., J. Tonra, and V. Wallace. 2011. Manuscript transcription by crowdsourcing: Transcribe Bentham. *Liber Quarterly* 20: 347. doi:10.18352/lq.7999.

Pääkkönen, T. 2015. Crowdsourcing metrics of digital collections. *Liber Quarterly* 25: 41. doi:10.18352/lq.10090.

Rose-Sandler, T., W. Ulate, M. Seidman, M. Flanagan, G. Belknap, V. van Hyning, and V. O'Donnell. 2015. Engaging the citizen scientist in content enhancement for BHL.

Whats on the menu? 2016. http://menus.nypl.org/about.

Yadav, P., and J. Darlington. 2016. Design guidelines for the user-centred collaborative citizen science platforms. arXiv:160500910 Cs.

Yang, C., B. Wei, J. Wu, Y. Zhang, and L. Zhang. 2009. CARES: a ranking-oriented CADAL recommender system. In *Proceedings of the 9th ACM/IEEE-CS Joint Conference on Digital Libraries, JCDL '09*, pp. 203–212. New York, NY: ACM. doi:10.1145/1555400.1555432.

Ethics and Medical Research

Kotsori Ioanna Soultana

During the last 30 years medical science has progressed by leaps and bounds, but oddly enough, never before has human life been threatened so much and so directly from this progress. It is the first time that scientists have not realized so tragically their responsibilities arisen from a thoughtless disperse of medical methods, which could eventually put the subsistence of the human beings itself into jeopardy. Both in an international level and a national one, medical unions, states and governments seek for a code of ethics in medical behavior which is generally accepted, avoiding any kind of dogmatism that would immerge from ideological, philosophical, political, or religious thoughts on behalf of the doctors, as well as their consequent parameters which is propaganda, fanaticism, and enforcement.

In other words there is a demand for an ethical direction in science with the best possible minimalism, so that its directions do not insist on minor problems of inferior or disputable correctness but focus major and more serious problems that common conscience of obligation leads every person to enlisting for a common target.

Modern achievements of Medicine are spectacular, like those of biotechnology and genetic engineering. Unfortunately, not only in personal but also in societal level, modern ethics is in a state of crisis. The apparent progress in the sector of medicine has already created the frame of new perspectives in fields like life expectancy, dealing or totally eradicating diseases that would be incurable during past centuries as well as the potential through medical research to provide with revolutionary solutions in matters like reproduction, study, analysis even interventions, or alternations in human genome, in other words DNA.

However, at the same time it is obvious that through all this progress that there are some ethical dilemmas arising according to which society is wondering if and to which level it is legal and feasible medical research to cross some boundaries.

K.I. Soultana (✉)
University of Peloponnese, Tripoli, Greece
e-mail: ioannakotsori@gmail.com

A. Kavoura et al. (eds.), *Strategic Innovative Marketing*, Springer Proceedings in Business and Economics, DOI 10.1007/978-3-319-56288-9_60

These boundaries have been obviously set based on some commonly used ideas and worldviews which inmost till today, in the technological and scientific progress era, seem to imbue the common subconscious with a nexus of traditional ethic codes. For instance religious codes, however, regressive they may appear nowadays.

In this case, there is an obvious effort on behalf of nations nowadays to set a total code of rules according to which the deontology issue in case of medical research can be adjusted. Today, we examine this very thinking, which is the need for medical deontology to exist. "What is medically amazing doesn't necessarily mean it is ethically accepted" (Alachiotis 2004).

Medical Deontology Code

First of all, it should be noted that The Medical Deontology Code was published on November 28, 2005, while the first one can be located in the work of Hippocrates (Jones 1868). Specifically in Unit 7 titled "Scientific Research" and in articles 24–27 there is a reference on the preconditions for medical research in humans, for clinical research in new medicines or modern curing and diagnostic methods, for non-remedial biomedical research and finally for the publicity of the discoveries.

The research that has human beings as its objective (experimental subject) should have its dominant aim the prevention of diseases, the preservation and the furtherance of health and generally the amelioration of human life and the society (Politis 2006).

Ethics should rely on three basic principles:

- respect for human personality
- science propulsion with legitimate means
- avoidance of desiring reckless profit and any kind of human being exploitation

According to these principles, human being focused research should be driven by respect for genetic identity of a human being, the right of explicit consent and confidentiality of personal data, the exclusion of any kind of human body exploitation even it means organs or cell genome, either for financial reasons or patent actualization purposes. Researchers should pay respect and protect human rights as well as citizen rights and therefore neither taking part in illegitimate inequitable and segregative practices deliberately, nor convincing at them.

From the previous it is obvious that some dilemmas arising directly as far as the medical research ethics is concerned, as well as to "when it can be moral or not."

For instance, in the case of stem cells research (actually they are fetal cells at their primary phase of their development, 4–5 days); there were plenty of controversies from the beginning, especially in the USA, with the mindset that the dominant, but not the unique, source of stem cells are embryos coming either from vitro insemination (Vidalis 2013) or abortions. At the heart of these dilemmas, there are some perceptions on human life protection, therefore fetus' life. Some points of view with metaphysical background have been supported, according to which "human life is absolutely protected by the time of its first existence."

Through several perceptions with metaphysical essence, there is a basic skepticism accruing on the possibility of usage for medical research: can we destroy several types of life (human) even if we have to do with the simplest of these lives like, for example, in the case of a fertilized ovum?

In case of cloning there is undoubtedly the relevant legislative adjustment both abroad and Greece according to which human cloning is forbidden. In our opinion, correctly enough, the idea lies to the fact that there is a danger of some conditions and eugenic genetics to accrue, in terms of personal and ideological targets and resultants. The last one has been connected with some relevant researches that several German scientists have conducted during the Nazi dominant period in Germany. Those researches, abiding to the ideological tenacities of the Nazi theories, were related with the effort to produce human beings by order through genetics, which would eventually meet the Nazis' evolutionary supermen expectations.

Surely, the thought and the potential of having a baby by order which could very well carry genetic elements that you would prefer personally (for instance hair color or eye, body construction characteristics or physical power, etc.), can be undoubtedly very attractive for a lot of people. Nevertheless, it is a case that "surpasses the limits of right to reproduction, aiming at replica production of those who has it, in order either to satisfy his narcistic tendencies or the absolute control of the clones' life": in the name of a misinterpreted right, the human dignity is being underestimated by the time the "clone" is being used as a simple "medium" for other purposes.

At the same time cloning puts a limit on the genetic variety of the human species. By this way, if it spreads it is quite possible that human will be deprivated of his capability of adjusting to the process of evolution, and consequently this will lead to his biological degeneration step by step. Cloning, by means of sex and other features consists a eugenic method, which will lead to illegitimate social discriminations in a society of equality.

The knowledge of predetermination of features encumbers the "clone's" personality crucially and continuously. On the one hand he is an equal subject of the human value—so he is independent "by nature"—on the other hand he carries the burden to prove in his whole life the difference from the "prototype". In other words this method fillips every single person's "uniqueness", which is the necessary precondition of his practical enjoyment of his autonomy.

As far as the deontology in other sectors of medical research is concerned, like in several pharmaceutical products, it is obvious that in case that they are about to be tested on human beings, there is a necessity for the consent on behalf of the person who is about to be used as a guinea pig actually. Apart from consent, doctor has the obligation to indicate any possible side effects of the tested medicine (Vidalis 2013).

Conclusions

Recent progress in field of medical research (with prevailing fields like this of genetics) leaves us speechless by all means but at the same time it creates a series of speculation even objections on how they can be held and where they can aim sometimes.

Clinical research conduction in humans—either it concerns medicine or other therapeutic means—and biomedical research that includes edition of biological specimens of people or editing biological personal data, requires today the austere compliance of certain ethical standards, for the protection of anyone who participates. From the guarantees for the compliance to these standards, the funding by public carriers depends (ex. EU) but also the wide publication of the results of a research (something that concerns any research that is privately funded). So ethics in a research has an impact on the scientific reliability itself. The control of the deontology should be efficient: to guarantee the protection of the participating persons' rights, offering suitable solutions so as the research to carry on integrally.

Based on the Christian ethics (Pellegrino and Gray 1994), a person's internal value is considered to be valuable and non-negotiable as an ambiguous, unrepeatable, priceless and unique species on earth. The recognition of this fundamental principle unstrainly equals to every human's right to enjoy respect and honor for his life and his human dignity. This right is absolute and is a safe guide to every initiative that has human and his health as its main topic. Consequently, human life is an inviolable and totally respected good, that is why the right to life always precedes to the physical integrity, which should be observed especially in cases like transplants, which criteria must be objective and absolutely clear. Otherwise there is a danger to abuse the living donor, if he is a defenseless person. Acceleration of this death or misleading certificate must be avoided.

Of course the general direction here is that through revolutionary medical researches humanity has got the capability to cope up with disease that would remain incurable during the past and that generally there is a chance given to the human life expectancy and to forward some programs that would be of benefit to the population's health.

In some cases these medical researches can be the springboard for the planning and interests promotion, with personal, political, ideological or simply financial aspect, which will eventually lead to human beings and societies to suffer damages in the long run. The suggested solutions to bioethical problems are related to everybody's metaphysical beliefs (Koumantos 2003).

Medical research is neither unlimited nor uncontrolled. It is true that medicine progress has been based upon research that has to do with human experimentation. But this research either for curing the particular disease or for aiming to the advance of science has to take into account the ethic and spiritual principles as they were experienced and are experienced today in the European space, and especially humans' respect to the human person and his dignity. Bioethics is not coming to put a halt on progress; on the contrary it is coming to prove those safeguards that will ensure the respect for human dignity, autonomy, and meritocratic living (Dragona 1989).

Bioethics purpose is not to put limits on science but show new roads. These roads define, not restrict. Its purpose is not to issue consensus or prohibitive prescriptions for every serious problem, but notify about the basic bioethical principles, inform for any consequences that human consent may have in a new technology, making then human responsible for his decisions toward new generations.

That is the reason why it is necessary for a deontology frame to exist, by which some limits and inviolable rules would be set; the spirit of the rules will be dripped in every stakeholders (doctors, researchers, studiers, genetic material donor, etc.) In this point the legal frame contribution could be considered as extremely important, as well as the corresponding state intervention, so that this deontology to be officially grounded but protected too.

We should remember that it is not enough for someone to be a good doctor, but a nice colleague instead.

The protection of human life, health, and dignity precedes the interests of science or society.

References

Alachiotis, S.N. 2004. *Bioethics*. Athens: Greek Letter.

Dragona-Monachou, M. 1989. *Ethics and bioethics*. Athens: Science and Society.

Jones, W.H.S. 1868. *Hippocrates collected works, I*. Cambridge Harvard University Press.

Koumantos, G. 2003. *Bioethical problems*. Athens, Polis.

Pellegrino, E.D., and R.A. Gray. 1994. Character, virtue, and self-interest in the ethics of the medical profession: Part ii: Toward the restoration of virtue ethics. *Reference Services Review* 22 (2): 41–52.

Politis, C. 2006. *Medical deontology code*. Athens: Pan-Hellenic Medical Club.

Vidalis, T. 2013. *Medical ethics*. Athens: Sakkoulas.

Is the Market Value of Software Vendors Affected by Software Vulnerability Announcements?

Georgios Spanos, Lefteris Angelis and Kyriaki Kosmidou

Introduction

A software vulnerability is a bug, a hole or a flaw that one or more threats can exploit to harm the confidentiality, the integrity and the availability of computer systems (Schiffman and CISCO 2005; Mell et al. 2007). A plethora of recent research studies concerning the problem of vulnerabilities (Armando et al. 2013; Scholte et al. 2012; Yang et al. 2010) show their significance in IT management. A major issue for the IT security community is the characterization and prioritization of the ever-increasing number of vulnerabilities. As a result of this situation, vulnerability scoring systems were devised to help prioritize the vulnerabilities (Schiffman and CISCO 2005; Mell et al. 2007; Liu and Zhang 2011; Liu et al. 2012; Wang and Yang 2012; Spanos et al. 2013; Spanos and Angelis 2015).

The market impact of events related to IT security (Spanos and Angelis 2016) constitute an evolving research area that is also of great importance for the business world. The methodology that is used in literature from late 1960s to study the impact of events to the market value of firms is the *event study methodology* (Fama et al. 1969).

The purpose of this paper is to answer to the question if the Software Vendors' Market Value is affected by Software Vulnerability Announcements. Additionally, ways to investigate this impact and to interpret it using vulnerability severity according to two scoring systems are presented in the results.

G. Spanos (✉) · L. Angelis
Department of Informatics, Aristotle University of Thessaloniki, Thessaloniki, Greece
e-mail: gspanos@csd.auth.gr

K. Kosmidou
Department of Economics, Aristotle University of Thessaloniki, Thessaloniki, Greece

A. Kavoura et al. (eds.), *Strategic Innovative Marketing*, Springer Proceedings in Business and Economics, DOI 10.1007/978-3-319-56288-9_61

Experimental

The event study methodology was used in this paper to examine the reaction of the stock market to the software vulnerability announcements. The basic principal of the event study methodology is the fact that when an event occurs the stock price return of the relevant firm will be abnormal.

In this study, three different estimation models, belonging to one-factor model family, were used to estimate the normal return of a stock price. The Market Model, the Market-Adjusted Model and the Mean-Adjusted Model were used as in the related work of Telang and Wattal (2007). Furthermore, the Four-Factor Model was used, which constitutes a more complete model in comparison with the one-factor models (Kothari and Warner 2007); it combines the Fama–French three-factor model (Fama and French 1993) and the momentum factor (Carhart 1997).

The NASDAQ market index was used in the present study, which is appropriate for technology firms. Additionally, the estimation window in the present event study contains 160 days, starting 160 days before the event and ending one day before the event. Also, the event window contains 2 days: the announcement day of the vulnerability and the following day. The 2 days event window [0 to 1] keeps the advantages of short event windows (Brown and Warner 1980; Dann et al. 1977; Mitchell and Netter 1989) but also captures the case that an event is announced after the closing of the stock market.

In order to test the significance of results, the parametric student one sample t-test was used and also two nonparametric one-sample tests, i.e. the Wilcoxon Signed Rank Test and the Sign Test. The selection of the market index, the estimation window, the event window and the statistical tests follow the lines of previous studies in the literature (Cavusoglou et al. 2004; Telang and Wattal 2007; Pirounias et al. 2014).

The dataset used in the present study was collected from the website of the United States Computer Emergency Readiness Team (US-CERT) and covers a short and relatively recent period between May 2014 and November 2014. Finally, according to the practices followed in related literature (Cavusoglou et al. 2004; Telang and Wattal 2007; Pirounias et al. 2014), the vulnerability dataset was filtered against confounding events.

Theory

The growth of the discovered vulnerabilities has led the IT Security community to devise scoring and rating systems to prioritize vulnerabilities in an appropriate way. Two representing vulnerability scoring systems are: The Common Vulnerability Scoring System (CVSS) (Mell et al. 2007) and the Weighted Impact Vulnerability Scoring System (WIVSS) (Spanos and Angelis 2015).

The publication of the vulnerabilities may threaten the reliability and generally, the image of the corresponding software vendors and this could lead to a decrease in the turnover of these companies. Additionally, the fixing of software vulnerabilities by developing the corresponding software patches has cost and especially in the case where the software has already been released, the cost is even higher. Hence the first research question in the form of the null hypothesis is:

H_{01} *There is no impact of software vulnerability announcements to the stock prices of the software vendors*

CVSS and WIVVS scores reflect the severity of the software vulnerabilities according to their particular characteristics. Hence, the greater the score is, the more severe the software vulnerability is, regarding the easiness of its exploitation and the impact that could cause in the affected information systems. A vulnerability can be qualitatively rated as *Low*, *Medium* or *High* depending on its score (either CVSS score or WIVSS score). The next null hypothesis is related to the scoring of vulnerabilities:

H_{02} *The impact of software vulnerability announcements to the stock prices of the software vendors is not associated to the qualitative ratings of the vulnerabilities.*

Results

The application of the event study methodology to the vulnerability dataset shows that the impact of these events to the stock market is negative but not statistically significant (Table 1). These findings reflect that the software vulnerability announcements affect the stock market negatively, but this impact is neither strong nor statistical important. The nonexistence of statistically significant impact is also depicted in Fig. 1, where the mean abnormal returns of the 75 events for the Four-Factor Model are shown for a time interval including 15 days before the event and 15 days after the event. Hence, H_{01} *hypothesis cannot be rejected.*

Finally, to test hypothesis H_{02}, the **Four Factor Model** is used. More precisely, the comparison of means of the cumulative abnormal returns (CAR) is conducted using the analysis of variance (ANOVA), for the qualitative ratings (Low, Medium, High) of the two scoring systems (CVSS and WIVSS). It is obvious from the results (Table 2) that H_{02} *also, cannot be rejected.*

Table 1 The results of the event study methodology

	Mean value	Median	Percent less than zero
Market model	−0.1% (0.39)	−0.1% (0.31)	53.4% (0.64)
Market-adjusted model	−0.3% (0.14)	−0.3% (0.17)	56% (0.355)
Mean model	−0.3% (0.24)	−0.2% (0.38)	54.7% (0.4887)
4 factor model	−0.2% (0.43)	−0.1% (0.42)	52% (0.8176)

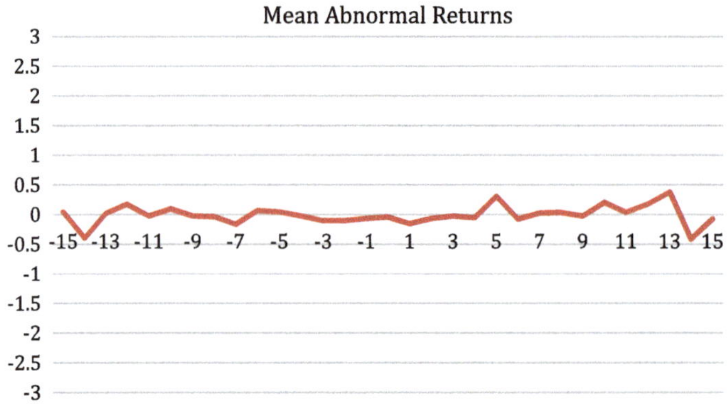

Fig. 1 The mean abnormal returns of the events

Table 2 The results of the ANOVA

	Degrees of freedom	Sum of squares	Mean square	F value	p-value
CVSS qualitative rating	2	0.76	0.3808		
Residuals	72	140.49	1.9512	0.195	0.823
WIVSS qualitative rating	2	7.68	3.838		
Residuals	72	133.57	1.855	2.069	0.134

Conclusions

The results that were described in the previous section show that the software vulnerability announcements have a negative impact to the stock price of the firms, but this impact is slight and also not statistically significant. Moreover, the vulnerability severity as reflected by two vulnerability scoring systems (CVSS and WIVSS) is not associated with the stock market impact. Hence, considering the aforementioned, the answer to the question: "*Is the Market Value of Software Vendors affected by Software Vulnerability Announcements?*" is probably negative.

References

Armando, A., A. Merlo, M. Migliardi, and L. Verderame. 2013. Breaking and fixing the android launching flow. *Computers & Security* 39: 104–115.

Brown, S.J., and J.B. Warner. 1980. Measuring security price performance. *Journal of Financial Economics* 8 (3): 205–258.

Carhart, M.M. 1997. On persistence in mutual fund performance. *The Journal of Finance* 52 (1): 57–82.

Cavusoglu, H., B. Mishra, and S. Raghunathan. 2004. The effect of internet security breach announcements on market value: Capital market reactions for breached firms and internet security developers. *International Journal of Electronic Commerce* 9 (1): 70–104.

Dann, L.Y., D. Mayers, and R.J. Raab. 1977. Trading rules, large blocks and the speed of price adjustment. *Journal of Financial Economics* 4 (1): 3–22.

Fama, E.F., L. Fisher, M.C. Jensen, and R. Roll. 1969. The adjustment of stock prices to new information. *International Economic Review* 10 (1): 1–21.

Fama, E.F., and K.R. French. 1993. Common risk factors in the returns on stocks and bonds. *Journal of Financial Economics* 33 (1): 3–56.

Kothari, S.P., and J.B. Warner. 2007. *Econometrics of event studies*. Handbook of Corporate Finance: Empirical Corporate Finance. B. Espen Eckbo.

Liu, Q., and Y. Zhang. 2011. VRSS: A new system for rating and scoring vulnerabilities. *Computer Communications* 34 (3): 264–273.

Liu, Q., Y. Zhang, Y. Kong, and Q. Wu. 2012. Improving VRSS-based vulnerability prioritization using analytic hierarchy process. *Journal of Systems and Software* 85 (8): 1699–1708.

Mell, P., K. Scarfone, and S. Romanosky. 2007. *A complete guide to the common vulnerability scoring system version 2.0*. https://www.first.org/cvss/v2/guide.

Mitchell, M.L., and J.M. Netter. 1989. Triggering the 1987 stock market crash: Antitakeover provisions in the proposed house ways and means tax bill? *Journal of Financial Economics* 24 (1): 37–68.

Pirounias, S., D. Mermigas, and C. Patsakis. 2014. The relation between information security events and firm market value, empirical evidence on recent disclosures: An extension of the GLZ study. *Journal of Information Security and Applications* 19 (4): 257–271.

Schiffman, M., and C. Cisco. 2005. *A complete guide to the common vulnerability scoring system (cvss)*. http://www.first.org/cvss/v1/guide.

Scholte, T., D. Balzarotti, and E. Kirda. 2012. Have things changed now? An empirical study on input validation vulnerabilities in web applications. *Computers & Security* 31 (3): 344–356.

Spanos, G., and L. Angelis. 2015. Impact metrics of security vulnerabilities: Analysis and weighing. *Information Security Journal: A Global Perspective* 24 (1–3): 57–71.

Spanos, G., and L. Angelis. 2016. The impact of information security events to the stock market: A systematic literature review. *Computers & Security* 58: 216–229.

Spanos, G., A. Sioziou, and L. Angelis. 2013. WIVSS: A new methodology for scoring information systems vulnerabilities. In *Proceedings of the 17th Panhellenic Conference on Informatics*, pp. 83–90. ACM.

Telang, R., and S. Wattal. 2007. An empirical analysis of the impact of software vulnerability announcements on firm stock price. *IEEE Transactions on Software Engineering* 33 (8): 544–557.

Wang, Y., and Y. Yang. 2012. PVL: A novel metric for single vulnerability rating and its application in IMS. *Journal of Computational Information Systems* 8 (2): 579–590.

Yang, S.S., H. Choi, and H. Joo. 2010. Vulnerability analysis of the grid data security authentication system. *Information Security Journal: A Global Perspective* 19 (4): 182–190.

Conceptual Search Algorithms for FDB Databases

E.N. Petraki, E.J. Yannakoudakis and C.A. Kapetis

Introduction

The goal of information retrieval is to identify documents which best match user needs (Gauch et al. 1999). In Database Management Systems information retrieval is often based on free text techniques and users apply queries to the database via query languages like SQL (Structured Query Language). This technique requires users to have knowledge of the database schema and use a query language to search information; this search model is complicated for most ordinary users (Liu et al. 2006). Queries using keywords is the most widely used form of querying today while it is used to search documents on the Web (Gaurav et al. 2001). Search techniques through keywords use ranking mechanisms in order to rank more or less relevant (to the keywords) answers. This type of utility is missing from most database management systems today and all the records or tuples retrieved have the same significance. Keyword search in a database is easy and flexible because it does not require from the user to know details about the underlying schema.

In databases searching utilizes string matching techniques to identify groups of records on the basis of a set of words contained within each record, ignoring any conceptual information. Since a term (concept) can be expressed in several ways, a significant number of records are ignored by the free text techniques. This is the case with SQL and other query languages, query that use string matching and free text techniques. The FDB (Frame DataBase) model (Yannakoudakis et al. 1999) provides more efficient and intelligent retrieval techniques which automatically expand user queries with conceptually related words.

E.N. Petraki (✉) · E.J. Yannakoudakis · C.A. Kapetis
Department of Informatics, Athens University of Economics and Business, Athens, Greece
e-mail: epetraki@aueb.gr

A. Kavoura et al. (eds.), *Strategic Innovative Marketing*, Springer Proceedings in Business and Economics, DOI 10.1007/978-3-319-56288-9_62

The purpose of the current paper is to present the FDB search algorithms which exploit the information provided by the structure of the model, which allows the definition of one or more multilingual thesauri, in order to expand user queries applied to any FDB database with relevant terms derived from the thesaurus. FDB supports dynamically evolving database environments and allows the definition of any multilingual database in the same universal schema; the thesaurus is part of the FDB universal schema and is dynamically defined using appropriate metadata (Petraki 2015). A multilingual thesaurus specifies relations between terms as well as the equivalence terms in each of the languages chosen. Standardized relation types are used to display and identify clearly every relation between thesaurus terms. A multilingual thesaurus allows the definition of conceptual correlations/ equivalences between terms selected from different natural languages.

There are two basic categories of relations among terms, the a priori and the a posteriori (Kapetis 1995). The a posteriori relations are used to identify the subject of a document. It is obvious that query languages use the a posteriori relations between terms in the sense that they use only the specific terms provided by the users and the a priori relations are ignored (Petraki et al. 2013). The adoption of a thesaurus provides for a priori semantic relationships between terms, enabling the extension of user queries on databases using multilingual thesaurus relations. Thus, the set of retrieved records grows because more terms, including related terms, synonyms, narrower terms, etc. and equivalent or similar terms in several languages derived from the thesaurus can be used during the retrieval process.

The algorithms presented in the current paper extends the user queries applied to FDB databases by using the information provided by monolingual or multilingual thesauri, while data retrieval from any FDB Database is also carried out using the conceptual relationships among terms. Increased flexibility is provided on data retrieval as the user can choose from a variety of parameters which define the search process. User choices could be differentiated form one search to another, a fact that provides even greater flexibility to the whole model.

The FDB Model

FDB is an integrated set-theoretic model for database systems that forms a framework for defining a structure that eliminates completely the need for reorganization at the logical level (Yannakoudakis et al. 1999, 2007). FDB provides a universal model which allows the definition of any multilingual database and thesaurus by specifying the appropriate metadata without requiring any changes to the underlying schema. The FDB model, amongst other utilities, allows the administration of multilingual databases at both data and interface levels, the definition of variable length objects (records in the traditional sense), etc. Any changes that may be necessary at the data level do not affect the universal database schema but simply the identification of the appropriate metadata. Conceptual Universal Database Language (CUDL) provides simple statements which allow accessing the information from an FDB schema (Yannakoudakis et al. 2006). The FDB universal schema can be used to define one or more multilingual thesauri and provides, besides traditional keyword search, conceptual searches through one or more multilingual thesauri (Petraki et al. 2013). Different algorithms have been proposed which implement the linking of each frame object (records in the traditional sense) with the underlying thesaurus terms automatically, enrich an existing thesaurus with terms derived from the data base, and create the core for a new thesaurus with terms derived from an FDB database (Petraki et al. 2014).

Basic elements of the model are based on the mathematical theory of unordered sets and consist of the following sets: (a) entities: the unordered set of registered entities that participate in the logical schema, (b) tags: the set of attributes describing each entity, (c) subtags: the set of simple atomic attributes which constitute existing complex tags, (d) domains: the set of all data domains, etc. (Yannakoudakis 1987). The database administrator can create any database under the same FDB schema by defining the appropriate metadata.

More than one language can be supported for both database records and multilingual thesaurus terms: FDB supports multilingual data since the database administrator can define many different languages. Respectively, a thesaurus may be defined in FDB in all supported languages; the thesaurus administrator can define all different types of relations in all supported languages. The reverse relationship can be defined for each type of relationship between thesaurus terms; when a new relation between terms is established the reverse relationship can be automatically created. Moreover, in FDB it is possible to associate a thesaurus term in a language with the corresponding equivalent terms in one or more other languages. The opposite term relationship is also defined in order to identify all the opposite terms for each thesaurus term (Petraki et al. 2013).

The architecture of the FDB enables the utilization of domain independent thesauri; this knowledge offers a powerful search tool when retrieving records from a database. When the user applies queries on the database, the system can use the conceptual relationships derived from the usage forward and backward of the hierarchical structure of the multilingual thesaurus. Relationships like *Broader Term*, *Narrow Term*, etc., can be used in queries for any FDB database to enrich searching with more keywords; this gives rise to the identification of more database frame objects related to the search criteria set by the user. The opposite term relation is a new type of relation introduced in the FDB model. An opposite term provides additional information about each term which, if exploited properly, can be used to reject irrelevant database records (Petraki et al. 2013).

Evidently, a database record/tuple can contain words from more than one language, making it rather complicated for a user to define retrieval criteria. The FDB model utilizes multilingual thesauri to enable multilingual queries to be easily specified and actualized, since the thesaurus metadata form part of the model itself (Petraki et al. 2013).

Conceptual Search Algorithms for FDB

The information provided by multilingual thesauri is used to extend user queries with terms derived from one or more different languages. The adoption/utilization of the information provided by the FDB thesauri in data retrieval from FDB databases enables the usage of the a priori conceptual relations between terms. Search algorithms exploit the structure of the FDB model, enabling users to submit both traditional queries to the database with keywords or to apply conceptual searches in any FDB database using the information provided by one or more multilingual thesauri (Petraki et al. 2015). The conceptual algorithms allow the user to define several different search parameters, as for example (Petraki et al. 2015):

- Opt for searches with the traditional way by typing specific keywords as search criteria, without the use of the thesaurus.
- Opt for conceptual searches using the underlying thesauri. In this case, the user may also select one thesaurus (*t*) or a set of thesauri *T* to be used during the search.
- Opt for one (*l*) or more languages (*L*) to be used in the data retrieval.
- Opt for the fundamental thesaurus relationships (e.g. the use of narrower terms, broader terms, synonyms, etc.) that will be used in the search process.
- Opt for opposite terms provided by an FDB thesaurus in order to eliminate the corresponding result set.

The basic conceptual algorithm works by using two different sets, the *Opposite_terms* and the *All_keywords*. At the beginning of the algorithm both sets are empty. Firstly, the algorithm puts all the keywords defined by the user in the *All_keywords* set. Then, it adds the synonyms, the broader and narrower terms and the related terms in the same set according to the user's options. Similarly, the algorithm puts all opposite terms of each keyword in the appropriate set. In the second part, the algorithm checks all the data frame objects to determine whether one or more terms of the set *All_keywords* exist in the set of important data tags. If one or more terms exist then the specific data frame object will be in the result set. The basic steps of the conceptual search algorithm are the following:

- The user identifies all the keywords that will form the search criteria.
- All thesaurus terms that will be used in the conceptual search are defined.
- Query is extended to include thesaurus terms; all thesaurus terms of the previous step are added in the All_Keywords set.
- Frame objects that include at least one keyword are selected from the FDB database.
- The Result_set is defined for the user.

Improved Conceptual Search Algorithm for FDB

The improved conceptual search algorithm applies conceptual search in any FDB database, it represents a brief and concrete proposal that exploits the advantages provided with the use of one or more multilingual thesauri during data retrieval (Petraki 2015). It also exploits the advantages and innovation of the FDB model. It is an improved algorithm compared to the previous one that offers users advanced flexibility while it enables them to choose different search parameters as different thesaurus relation types for each keyword *k*. The most important advantages of the algorithm are:

- Exploits the integrated structure of the FDB model which contains multilingual databases and thesaurus in the same unified schema.
- Exploits the information provided by the LTAG (linking tag) which is used to correlate each data frame object (record in a traditional database) with one or more thesaurus terms.
- Enables the users to use one or more different multilingual thesauri in the same search.
- Implements multilingual search; It enables the users to adopt one or more different languages for each search.
- Provides advanced flexibility through many different search parameters.
- Enables the usage of each thesaurus in a different level through different search parameters for each keyword.
- Exploits the information provided from the opposite term relation type in order to reduce the number of irrelevant records retrieved.
- Provides advanced flexibility to programmers for implementation of the algorithm.

Conclusions

FDB provides a universal schema that allows the definition of one or more multilingual databases at both data and interface levels in the same underlying schema. Its structure also allows the definition of one or more multilingual thesauri under the same universal schema. Different algorithms have been proposed in order to automatically correlate each data frame object with one or more thesaurus terms, to enrich any existing thesaurus with terms derived from the FDB database and for the creation of the core of a new thesaurus using terms derived from the database. Conceptual search algorithms have been specified to exploit the information provided by the thesauri within any existing FDB database. The conceptual search algorithms allow end users to opt for alternative parameters while searching an FDB database.

The algorithms offer advanced flexibility. The user can associate for each keyword all related thesaurus terms (narrower terms, broader terms, synonyms etc.) in a completely personalized manner. All these keywords are searched in the database tags; when a keyword is found in a tag then the specific data frame object is included in the result set. It is obvious that the search condition identified by the algorithm binds all the keywords with the logical operator OR. The implementation of the specific algorithm, depending of the programming environment, will use different structures to hold (store) the All_keywords set and the data frame objects. However, the interface should also give users the option to adopt the AND logical operator in order to bind the keywords selected. This will not affect the logic of the algorithms introduced in this paper, since the logical operator AND will only be used when the final condition of the search criteria is formed.

Finally, the thesaurus is used as an additional tool that is connected with the existing database. Furthermore, each data frame object can automatically be linked with one or more thesaurus terms. The algorithm presented here can be expanded and improved by including a weighting method in order to avoid query extension with wrong terms, increasing further recall and precision in data retrieval.

References

Fang Liu, Clement Yu, Weiyi Meng, Abdur Chowdhury. 2006. Effective keyword search in relational databases. In *Proceedings of the ACM SIGMOD International Conference on Management of Data*, pp. 563–574.

Gauch, S., J. Wang, and S.M. Rachakonda. 1999. A corpus analysis approach for automatic query expansion and its extension to multiple databases. *ACM Transactions on Information Systems* 17 (3): 250–269.

Gaurav, Bhalotia, Hulgeri Arvind, Nakhe Charuta, and Chakrabarti Soumen. 2001. Keyword search in databases. *Bulletin of the IEEE Computer Society Technical Committee on Data Engineering* 24 (3): 22–32.

Kapetis, C.A. 1995. Multilingual thesaurus automated system: A dynamic tool for information retrieval and documentation. In *1st Greek Technical Chamber Conference: Info Society*, Athens 4–6 December 1995, pp. 591–597.

Petraki, E.N., C.A. Kapetis, and E.J. Yannakoudakis. 2013. Conceptual database retrieval through multilingual thesauri. *Computer Science and Information Technology* 1 (1): 19–32. doi:10.13189/csit.2013.010103.

Petraki, E.N., C.A. Kapetis, and E.J. Yannakoudakis. 2014. Automated thesaurus population and management. In *6th Qualitative and Quantitative Methods in Libraries*, May 27–30 2014, Istanbul, Turkey.

Petraki, E.N., C.A. Kapetis, and E.J. Yannakoudakis. 2015. Conceptual data retrieval from FDB databases. In *7th Qualitative and Quantitative Methods in Libraries*, May 26–29 2015, Paris, France.

Yannakoudakis, E.J. 1987. An efficient file structure for specialised dictionaries and other 'lumpy' data. *International Journal of Information Processing & Management* 23 (6): 563–571.

Yannakoudakis, E.J., and M. Nitsiou. 2006. A new conceptual universal database language (CUDL). In *2nd International Conference From Scientific Computing to Computational Engineering*, Athens, Greece.

Yannakoudakis, E.J., and P.K. Andrikopoulos. 2007. A set-theoretic data model for evolving database environments. In *Proceedings of the International Conference on Information & Knowledge Engineering*, IKE 2007, Las Vegas, Nevada, USA.

Yannakoudakis, E.J., C.X. Tsionos, and C.A. Kapetis. 1999. A new framework for dynamically evolving database environments. *Journal of Documentation* 55 (2): 144–158.

Blocking for Entity Resolution in the Web of Data: Challenges and Algorithms

Kostas Stefanidis

Introduction

Over the past decade, numerous *knowledge bases* (KBs) have been built to power large-scale knowledge sharing, but also an entity-centric Web search, mixing both structured data and text querying (e.g., Hogan et al. 2011). These KBs offer comprehensive, machine-readable descriptions of a large variety of real-world entities (e.g., persons, places) published on the Web as *Linked Data* (LD). Traditionally, KBs are manually crafted by a dedicated team of knowledge engineers, such as the pioneering projects Wordnet and Cyc. Today, more and more KBs are built from existing Web content using information extraction tools (Cimiano et al. 2014). Such an automated approach offers an unprecedented opportunity to scale-up KBs construction and leverage existing knowledge published in HTML documents (Hovy et al. 2013).

Although KBs (e.g., DBpedia (Auer et al. 2007), Freebase (Bollacker et al. 2008)) may be derived from the same data source (e.g., Wikipedia), they may provide multiple descriptions of the same entities. This is mainly due to the different information extraction tools and curation policies (Deshpande et al. 2013) employed by KBs, resulting to complementary and sometimes conflicting descriptions. *Entity resolution* (ER) aims to identify descriptions that refer to the same entity within or across KBs (Christophides et al. 2015; Dong and Srivastava 2015). ER is essential in order to improve *interlinking* in the Web of data, even by third parties.[1] Compared to data warehouses, the new ER challenges stem from the *openness* of the Web of data in describing entities by an unbounded number of KBs, the *semantic and structural diversity* of the descriptions provided across domains even for the same entities, and

[1]For instance, the sameas.org service provides co-references of the same entities between different KBs that have been manually collected.

K. Stefanidis (✉)
University of Tampere, Tampere, Finland
e-mail: kostas.stefanidis@uta.fi

A. Kavoura et al. (eds.), *Strategic Innovative Marketing*, Springer Proceedings in Business and Economics, DOI 10.1007/978-3-319-56288-9_63

the *autonomy* of KBs in terms of adopted processes for creating and curating descriptions. In particular:

- The size of the Linking Open Data (LOD) cloud,[2] in which nodes are KBs (aka RDF datasets) and edges are links crossing KBs, has roughly doubled between 2011 and 2014 (Schmachtenberg et al. 2014), while data interlinking dropped by 30%. In general, the majority of the KBs are sparsely linked, while their popularity in links is heavily skewed.[3] Sparsely interlinked KBs appear in the periphery of the LOD cloud (e.g., Open Food Facts, Bio2RDF), while heavily interlinked ones lie at the center (e.g., DBpedia, GeoNames, FOAF). Encyclopaedic KBs, such as DBpedia, or widely used georeferencing KBs, such as GeoNames, are interlinked with the largest number of KBs both from the LOD center and the periphery.
- The descriptions contained in these KBs present a high degree of semantic and structural diversity, even for the same entity types. The former is due to the frequent creation of new names for entities that have been described in another KB (Hogan et al. 2012), as well as the simultaneous annotation of descriptions with semantic types not necessarily originating from the same vocabulary. The latter is due to the diverse sets of properties used to describe entities both in terms of types and number of occurrences, even within a KB.

The *scale*, *diversity* and *graph structuring* of entity descriptions in the Web of data challenge the way two descriptions can be effectively compared in order to efficiently decide whether they are referring to the same real-world entity. This clearly requires an understanding of the relationships among *somehow similar* entity descriptions that goes beyond duplicate detection without always being able to merge related descriptions in a KB and thus improve its quality. Furthermore, the *very large volume* of entity collections that we need to resolve in the Web of data is prohibitive when examining pairwise all descriptions.

In this context of big Web data, *blocking* is typically used as a preprocessing step for ER to reduce the number of unnecessary comparisons, i.e., comparisons between descriptions that do not match. After blocking, each description can be compared only to others placed within the same block and thus disregard comparisons between descriptions that are unlikely to be matches. The desiderata of blocking are to place (i) similar descriptions in the same block (*effectiveness*), and (ii) dissimilar descriptions in different blocks (*efficiency*). However, efficiency dictates skipping many comparisons, possibly leading to many missing matches, which in turn implies low effectiveness. This is even more critical in the context of the Web of data, in which we do not know which pieces of the descriptions are the most appropriate to consider for computing the similarities. Thus, the main objective of blocking is to achieve a trade-off between the number of comparisons suggested and the number of missed matches.

Most of the blocking algorithms proposed in the literature (for a survey, refer to Christen 2012) assume both the availability and knowledge of the schema of the

[2]http://lod-cloud.net.

[3]http://linkeddata.few.vu.nl/wod_analysis.

input data, i.e., they refer to relational databases. To support a Web-scale resolution of heterogeneous and loosely structured entities across domains, recent blocking algorithms (e.g., Papadakis et al. 2013; Efthymiou et al. 2015, 2017) disregard strong assumptions about knowledge of the schema of data and rely on a minimal number of assumptions about how entities match (e.g., when they feature a common token in their description or URI) within or across sources.

In this talk, we will focus on the behavior of such blocking algorithms for datasets exhibiting different semantic and structural characteristics. Specifically, we are interested in quantifying the factors that make blocking algorithms take different decisions on whether two descriptions from real LOD sources potentially match or not. Moreover, we will investigate typical cases of missed matches of existing blocking algorithms and examine alternative ways for them to be retrieved.

To further improve the efficiency of blocking, several approaches (e.g., Papadakis et al. 2013) focus on different ways for discarding comparisons that do not lead to (new) matches. More recently, (Efthymiou et al. 2015, 2017) propose to reconstruct the blocks of a given blocking collection in order to more drastically discard redundant comparisons, as well as comparisons between descriptions that are unlikely to match. Meta-blocking essentially transforms a given blocking collection B into a blocking graph. Its nodes correspond to the descriptions in B, while its undirected edges connect the co-occurring descriptions. No parallel edges are allowed, thus eliminating all redundant comparisons. Every edge is associated with a weight, representing the likelihood that the adjacent entities are matching candidates. The low-weighted edges are pruned, so as to discard comparisons between unlikely-to-match descriptions.

References

Auer, S., C. Bizer, G. Kobilarov, J. Lehmann, R. Cyganiak, and Z.G. Ives. 2007. Dbpedia: A nucleus for a web of open data. In *ISWC*.

Bollacker, K.D., C. Evans, P. Paritosh, T. Sturge, and J. Taylor. 2008. Freebase: A collaboratively created graph database for structuring human knowledge. In *SIGMOD*.

Christen, P. 2012. *Data matching—Concepts and techniques for record linkage, entity resolution, and duplicate detection*. Data-centric systems and applications. Berling: Springer.

Christophides, V., V. Efthymiou, and K. Stefanidis. 2015. *Entity resolution in the web of data*. Synthesis lectures on the semantic web: Theory and technology. Morgan & Claypool Publishers.

Cimiano, P., C. Unger, and J. McCrae. 2014. *Ontology-based interpretation of natural language*. Synthesis lectures on human language technologies. Morgan & Claypool Publishers.

Deshpande, O., D.S. Lamba, M. Tourn, S. Das, S. Subramaniam, A. Rajaraman, V. Harinarayan, and A. Doan. 2013. Building, maintaining, and using knowledge bases: A report from the trenches. In *SIGMOD*.

Dong, X.L., and D. Srivastava. *Big data integration*. Synthesis lectures on data management. Morgan & Claypool Publishers.

Efthymiou, V., G. Papadakis, G. Papastefanatos, K. Stefanidis, and T. Palpanas. 2015. Parallel meta-blocking: Realizing scalable entity resolution over large, heterogeneous data. In *IEEE big data*.

Efthymiou, V., G. Papadakis, G. Papastefanatos, K. Stefanidis, and T. Palpanas. 2017. Parallel meta-blocking for scaling entity resolution over big heterogeneous data. *Information Systems* 65: 137–157.

Efthymiou, V., K. Stefanidis, and V. Christophides. 2015. Big data entity resolution: From highly to somehow similar entity descriptions in the web. In *IEEE big data*.

Efthymiou, V., K. Stefanidis, and V. Christophides. 2017. Benchmarking blocking algorithms for web entities. *IEEE Transactions on Big Data* 3.

Hogan, A., A. Harth, J. Umbrich, S. Kinsella, A. Polleres, and S. Decker. 2011. Searching and browsing linked data with SWSE: The semantic web search engine. *Journal of Web Semantics* 9 (4): 365–401.

Hogan, A., J. Umbrich, A. Harth, R. Cyganiak, A. Polleres, and S. Decker. 2012. An empirical survey of linked data conformance. *Web Semantics* 14: 14–44.

Hovy, E.H., R. Navigli, and S.P. Ponzetto. 2013. Collaboratively built semi-structured content and artificial intelligence: The story so far. *Artificial Intelligence* 194: 2–27.

Papadakis, G., E. Ioannou, T. Palpanas, C. Niederée, and W. Nejdl. 2013. A blocking framework for entity resolution in highly heterogeneous information spaces. *IEEE Transactions on Knowledge and Data Engineering* 25 (12): 2665–2682.

Schmachtenberg, M., C. Bizer, and H. Paulheim. 2014. Adoption of the linked data best practices in different topical domains. In *ISWC*.

Analysis of GWAP Collected Tags in the Description of Heritage Materials

Tomislav Ivanjko and Sonja Špiranec

Introduction

Following the development of World Wide Web and especially with the rise of Web 2.0, a new wave of user participation in creating online resources started. Services such as Flickr, Delicious or YouTube emerged basing their entire business model on user-generated content. Apart from uploading content, users were encouraged to describe it by using keywords or labels added to the resource called tags. This process, where users add tags to shared content was gathered under the notion of social tagging (Golder and Hubermann 2006) and instigated a new approach in knowledge representation—folksonomies (Mathes 2004). The term itself was coined from the words folk and taxonomy denoting the aspect of user participation in the knowledge organization process, but the adequacy of the term is still a subject of debate (Peters 2009). Following the development of the research field, much effort was put into defining its structure and the characteristics of tags (Golder and Hubermann 2006; Heckner et al. 2008) where model of analysis and research framework were established. When researching tag characteristics in Croatian language Špiranec and Ivanjko (2012) showed that tags show many characteristics similar to those found in traditional indexing languages (noun, singular), but indicated that more research is needed in researching different environments (education, scientific, heritage) and on a larger tag corpus both on statistic, linguistic and functional levels.

T. Ivanjko (✉) · S. Špiranec
Faculty of Humanities and Social Sciences, Department of Information and Communication Sciences, University of Zagreb, Zagreb, Croatia
e-mail: tivanjko@ffzg.hr

A. Kavoura et al. (eds.), *Strategic Innovative Marketing*, Springer Proceedings in Business and Economics, DOI 10.1007/978-3-319-56288-9_64

Research

This research aims to shed additional light on the characteristic of tags in Croatian language when users are describing heritage materials. First step of the research was selecting 80 digitized heritage objects for description divided into four categories: archival materials (20), library materials (20), museum exhibits (20) and photographs (20). The segmenting was done in order to create additional points for comparison. The materials were selected from the exhibition catalogue of the exhibition “Croatian Homeland War” held at the Croatian History Museum, so they were all thematically based on the same topic that enabled analysis on the general as well as collection-level description. Since there was a large number of materials that needed to be tagged, an application that uses a Game With a Purpose (GWAP) approach was implemented. The open-source application Metadata Games (http://www.metadatagames.org) developed by Dartmouth College was implemented and localized for Croatian language. As authors describe it: “…games and game like activities can be used to attract the public to participate in providing valuable descriptive metadata… [by providing] a game approach that attracts participants to a site and facilitates tagging in an enjoyable way” (Flanagan and Carini 2012). This approach gave us the opportunity to collect large corpora of tags in a way that users may find enjoyable.

After the materials and the application were ready, a public call was sent through different mailing lists and other means of communication for participants. The application was active from June 1 to July 1 of 2014 and a total of 14,402 tags were submitted to the application. Figure 1 shows the distribution of tags according to different types of materials.

When describing each object users could either add a new tag that none of the other users added before them (increase the vocabulary) or add the same tag as any

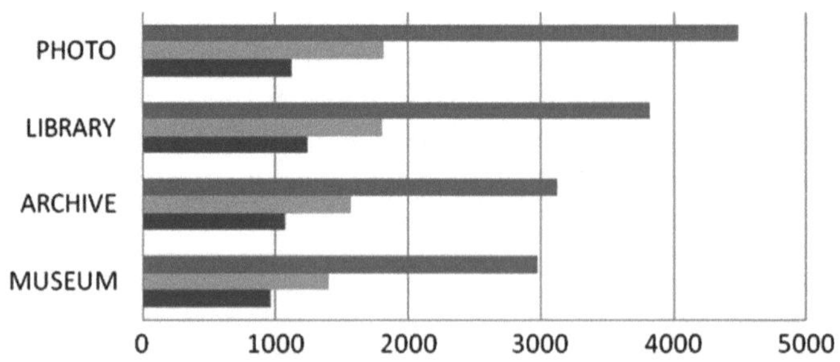

	MUSEUM	ARCHIVE	LIBRARY	PHOTO
SUBMITTED TAGS	2976	3124	3818	4484
ADDED TAGS	1403	1571	1803	1811
UNIQUE TAGS	959	1071	1238	1123

Fig. 1 Distribution of submitted, added and unique tags

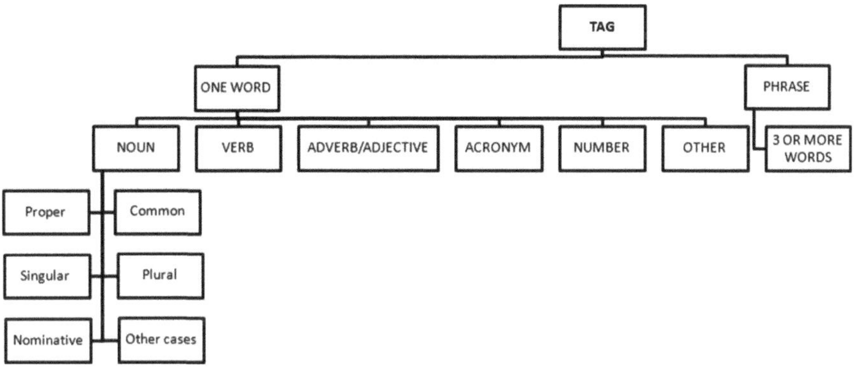

Fig. 2 Adapted categories of linguistic analysis based on the work Špiranec and Ivanjko (2012)

of the users before (increase frequency). In order to examine the difference between those approaches, tags were divided into 3 categories: submitted tags (all the tags including their frequencies), added tags (submitted tags without frequencies) and unique tags (tags with frequency 1). In order to see the connection between those three tag categories a correlation analysis was conducted. It was shown that there is a strong connection between submitted and added tags (+0.613) and especially between added tags and unique tags (+0.888), but there was a weak connection between submitted tags and unique tags (+0.237). Given the data we can conclude that, based on our sample, after around 1800 added tags to a single collection only the frequencies of tags started increasing but the vocabulary remained the same size. This shows that when collecting user tags for 20 objects of the same topic, one should stop when the threshold of 1,800 added tags is reached, because further tags will only increase frequency but the vocabulary base will not change. Second level of tag analysis was concerned with linguistic characteristics of the gathered tag corpora. The analysis was conducted using the tag categories originally suggested by Heckner et al. (2008), adapted for Croatian language based on the work of Špiranec and Ivanjko (2012) (Fig. 2).

It was shown that a typical tag consists from either one or two words (91%), is a noun (82%), common noun (91%), in singular (78%) and in its nominative form (99%). This part of the analysis showed that a typical tag does not differ from linguistic characteristics of a classic descriptor used for subject indexing. The final part of the research was concerned with content analysis of tags added to visual resources (photographs and museum materials), i.e. analyzing which level of meaning the tags are added on. These approaches to indexing visual resources stem from the work of Panofsky enriched by Shatford who also applied her ideas to image indexing (Fig. 3a, examples from Klenczon and Rygiel 2014). Combining those two approaches, a model of analysis was constructed to encompass all the levels presented in both models (Fig. 3b).

The first level of the proposed model identifies the type of material (*isness*), second level identifies both generic meaning (pre-iconographic) and specific

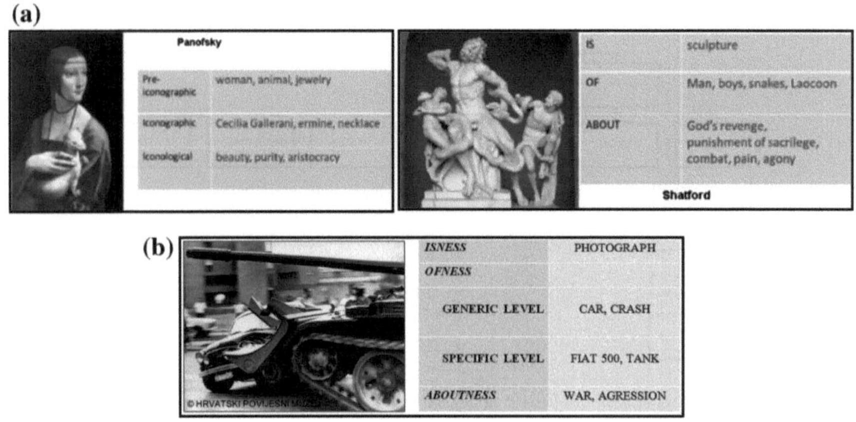

Fig. 3 Categories of indexing visual resources based on the work of Panofsky and Shatford

meaning (iconographic), while the third level analyzes the meaning on an abstract level (*aboutness*). Based on these categories, an analysis of a total of 3,214 submitted tags on 20 photographs and 20 museum exhibits (visual resources) was conducted. The results showed that the vast majority of tags were added on a general ofness level (80%) with little meaning added on a specific or abstract level.

Conclusion

This paper analyzed corpora of 14,402 submitted tags on selected 80 heritage objects divided into 4 categories (library, archive, museum and photographs) gathered using a crowdsourcing method, namely Game With a Purpose. Statistical analysis of gathered corpora has shown that after a certain threshold is achieved, vocabulary base remains steady with only frequencies increasing. Linguistic analysis showed that a typical user tag consists of one word or phrase in singular, while content analysis identified most user tags as generic descriptors without added specific knowledge.

References

Flanagan, M., and P. Carini. 2012. How games can help us access and understand archival images. *American Archivist* 75 (2): 514–537.

Golder, S.A., and B.A. Huberman. 2006. Usage patterns of collaborative tagging systems. *Journal of Information Science* 32 (2): 198–208.

Heckner, M., S. Mühlbacher, and C. Wolff. 2008. Tagging: Analysing user keywords in scientific bibliography management systems. *Journal of Digital Information* [e-journal] 9 (2). https://journals.tdl.org/jodi/index.php/jodi/article/view/246/208. Accessed 8 Aug 2016.

Klenczon, W., and P. Rygiel. 2014. Librarian cornered by images, or how to index visual resources. *Cataloging and Classification Quarterly* 52 (1): 42–61.

Mathes, A. 2004. *Folksonomies—cooperative classification and communication through shared metadata.* http://www.adammathes.com/academic/computer-mediated-communication/folksonomies.html. Accessed 8 Aug 2016.

Peters, I. 2009. *Folksonomies: Indexing and retrieval in Web 2.0.* Berlin: De Gruyter.

Špiranec, S., and Ivanjko, T. 2012. Predmetni jezici s korisničkim jamstvom: što možemo naučiti od folksonomija? In *15. seminar Arhivi, knjižnice, muzeji: mogućnosti suradnje u okruženju globalne informacijske infrastrukture*, ed. D. Hassenay, and M. Krtalić. Poreč, 23–25 November 2011. Zagreb: Hrvatsko knjižničarsko društvo.

Selective Monitoring of the Safety of Railway Buildings

Paolino Di Felice

Introduction

The solution to many problems of real interest requires an appropriate integration of descriptive data with geographic data. This class of problems includes the computation of the ranking of railway stations according to their degree of exposure to the landslide hazard. Such buildings are a relevant category of elements exposed to geo-hazards because of their intrinsic value and also because their damage may cause human casualties as well. The ranking we are talking about is the starting point to implement a selective monitoring of those assets in order to protect their safety.

The present work: (a) adopts the general method proposed by Di Felice (2015a) (and validated over 1,140 school buildings present in the Abruzzo region, central Italy, Di Felice 2015b) to calculate the ranking of the railway stations according to the landslide hazard they are exposed to; (b) describes the structure of the Geographical DataBase (Geo-DB in the following) suitable to store the data of the problem and facilitate its solution. The effectiveness of a Geo-DB as a tool for the management of the geo-hazard has been already testified (see, for example, Morelli et al. 2012); (c) reports the numerical results we got through a campaign of experiments carried out by taking into account the railway stations located within the Abruzzo region.

P. Di Felice (✉)
Department of Industrial and Information Engineering and Economics,
University of L'Aquila, L'Aquila, Italy
e-mail: paolino.difelice@univaq.it

A. Kavoura et al. (eds.), *Strategic Innovative Marketing*, Springer Proceedings in Business and Economics, DOI 10.1007/978-3-319-56288-9_65

Materials and Methods

Notations

Hereafter, we use the following notations.

GeoArea is a portion of land globally affected by a hazard caused, for example, by a prolonged and heavy period of rainfall. *GeoArea* is defined as the pair <*description, geometry of its boundary*>, where *description* is a string;

$DZ = \{z_k$ (k = 1, 2,...) | z_k is a danger zone}. By *danger zone,* we mean a portion of land characterized by a set of ground conditions. The elements in *DZ* make a full partition of *GeoArea*. In other words, knowing set *DZ* for a given area is equivalent to have built a map like that prepared by Guzzetti et al. (2006) for the Collazzone area (central Umbria, Italy). The generic element of *DZ* (i.e., z_k) is defined as the tuple <*ID*, Sz_k, *boundary*>, being *ID* an identifying code. Sz_k is a numerical value that quantifies the *(spatial) probability* that z_k produces landslides. Le danger zones we refer to in our study are *simple polygons*, as defined in the Open GISs Implementation Specification (2005).

$B = \{b_i$ (i = 1, 2,...) | b_i denotes a station building, expressed by a pair of coordinates, contained in the boundary of *GeoArea*}. Exp_b_i is a positive numeric value denoting the degree of (spatial) exposure of b_i to the landslide hazard caused by *all* the z_k in *DZ*; while Exp_b_i, z_k denotes the degree of exposure of b_i to the hazard caused by zone z_k. Each building in *B* is defined as the tuple <*ID*, *name*, *position*, Exp_b_i>, being *ID* an identifying code.

As emerged from definitions above, the full description of *GeoArea*, *DZ* and *B* is obtained by integrating descriptive data with geographical data.

A Method for Ranking the Railway Stations

The method in (Di Felice 2015a) takes as input the sets *B* and *DZ* and outputs a ranking about the buildings in the *GeoArea*, according to their degree of exposure to the landslide hazard. Such a method can be applied to the railway stations as well simply by interpreting element b_i as the centroid of the building that denotes the generic railway station. Hence, the computation of parameter Exp_b_i can be carried out through Eqs. (1)–(3):

$$Exp\_b_i = \sum_{k=1}^{n} Exp\_b_{i,k} \qquad (1)$$

$$Exp\_b_{i,k}(d) = Size \times Sz_k \times \begin{cases} 1 & \text{if } b_i \text{ is contained in } z_k \text{ or } d \leq d_0 \\ \left(\frac{d_0}{d}\right)^3 & \text{otherwise} \end{cases} \qquad (2)$$

$$Size = \frac{\text{area of } z_k}{\text{the average of the values of } all \text{ the areas of zones in DZ}} \quad (3)$$

where:

- n is equal to the cardinality of set DZ;
- d_0 is the radius of the circle centred on the centroid of building b_i, circle that approximates the area of b_i;
- d denotes the minimum distance between b_i and the boundary of zone z_k.

From the previous equations, we understand that the value of Exp_b_i is determined by three factors: (a) the distance of the buildings from the neighbouring danger zones, (b) the size of the zones, and (c) the spatial probability (Sz_k) that they produce a landslide.

A Case Study

The Input Data

GeoArea

GeoArea coincides with the boundary of the Abruzzo region. This is an area of 10,800 km^2 and 1,330,000 inhabitants divided into four provinces and 305 municipalities.

Set *B*

Figure 1 shows the 114 railway stations present over the Abruzzo region.

Set *DZ*

For the Abruzzo region a dataset with the characteristics of set *DZ* is not available. What we could find was a shapefile about the *landslide inventory* of the region. The limit of this dataset is that it does not achieve a complete partition of the region. This (real) dataset coincides with the "theoretical one" setting $Sz_k = 0$ for the portions of land not surveyed.

The Abruzzo landslide inventory is structured as three shapefiles whose elements belong to, respectively, the susceptibility classes called *S*1 (*low* susceptibility), *S*2 (*high* susceptibility) and *S*3 (*very high* susceptibility). Overall the inventory is composed of 4,425 elements in *S*1, 8,886 elements in *S*2 and 3,959 elements in *S*3.

Values of the Parameters Used in the Experiments

The position of elements of set B is described by a point denoting their centroid, while there is no data about the actual extension at ground of railway stations. Following feedback from the field about the average size of such a category of buildings, it was decided to set $d_0 = 50$ m (see Eq. 2). Moreover, we set

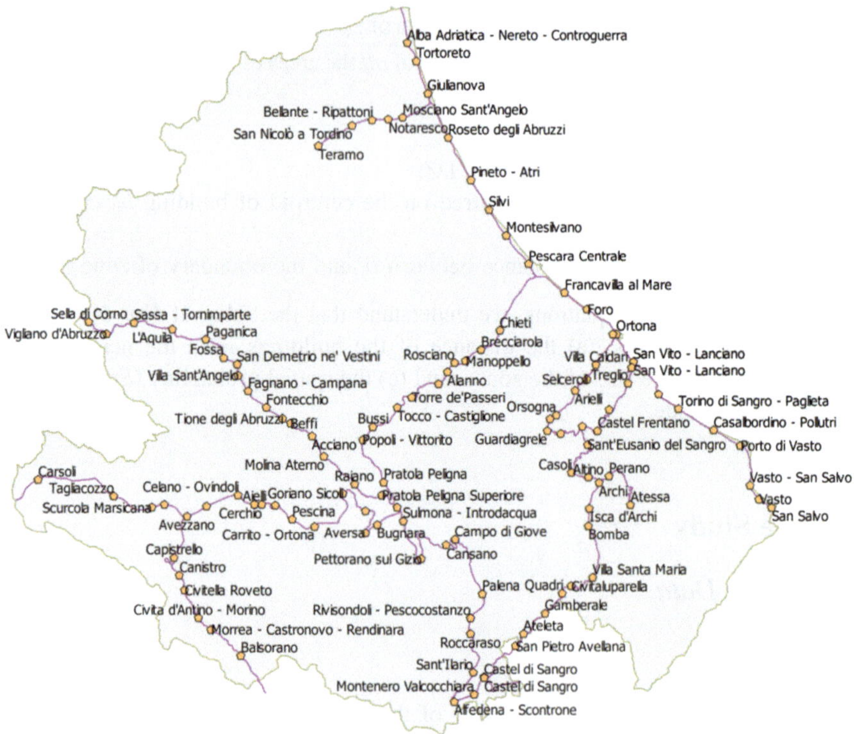

Fig. 1 The railway stations of the Abruzzo region together with the railway lines

$d = 500$ m; this is equivalent to assume 500 m as the limit beyond which it is unlikely that a landslide represents a tangible hazard to buildings. We set the following values for parameter Sz_k for the three susceptibility classes, $Sz_k = 0.25$ (class $S1$), $Sz_k = 0.50$ (class $S2$), $Sz_k = 1.00$ (class $S3$).

The Geographical DataBase

It has been made recourse to a Geo-DB in order to implement Eqs. 1–3 and store the records of the input shapefiles, as well as the results of the experiments to be performed. Figure 2 shows the overall structure of the Geo-DB.

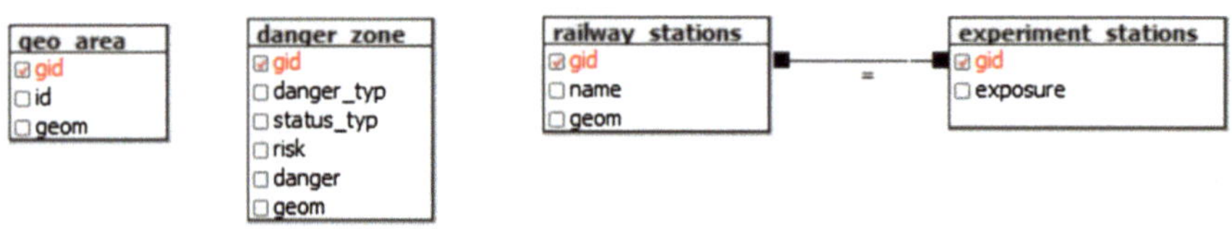

Fig. 2 A graphical view of the implemented Geo-DB

Tables **geo_area**, **danger_zone**, and **railway_stations** store data about sets *GeoArea*, *SZ*, and *B*, respectively. Table **experiment_stations** collects the results of the different experiments we carried out; in particular attribute **exposure** stores the value of parameter Exp_b_i (Eq. 1) for a specific building (**gid**).

Results and Discussion

Table 1 summarizes the results returned by the experiments carried out. It aggregates the values of the exposure (ranging from 0 up to 1318) for the 114 stations in four groups having decreasing values. For each group, the table explicits, also, the number and the percentage of the stations that are part of it.

Table 1 brings out the fact that only a very small number of the 114 railway buildings located in Abruzzo (7, equal to 6.1%) has to be considered "*unsafe*". This result confirms the validity of the idea behind our study, namely the need of providing local administrators with a software tool through which they can build a campaign of selective monitoring of the railway stations located inside the territory of their competence, thus limiting the time needed for the implementation, as well as the staff to be involved, and ultimately, the budget to be allocated without, however, lowering the level of security of the such relevant category of public buildings (Table 2).

Figure 3 shows the seven unsafe railway stations of Table 1 over a map.

The developed software tool makes use of a Geo-DB enriched with a large number of user defined functions through which it is easy to perform complex calculations by writing simple SQL queries.

Table 1 Summary of the ranking of the railway stations

Exp_b_i	$\#b_i$	%	Level of exposure to the landslide hazard
>501	5	4.4	High
101–500	2	1.7	Moderate
11–100	8	7.0	Low
0–10	99	86.9	Null

Table 2 The seven *unsafe* stations

#	Station name	Exposure
1	Quadri	1318
2	San Vincenzo	836
3	Sant'Ilario	772
4	Torino di Sangro-Paglieta	748
5	Bomba	721
6	Civitaluparella	253
7	Villa Santa Maria	133

Fig. 3 A map showing the unsafe railway stations along the railway lines of Abruzzo region

References

Di Felice, P. 2015a. Integration of descriptive and spatial data to rank public buildings according to their exposure to landslide hazard. In *5th International Conference on Integrated Information* (IC-ININFO), September 21–24, 2015, Mykonos, Greece.

Di Felice, P. 2015b. Integration of descriptive and spatial data to rank public buildings according to their exposure to landslide hazard: a case study. In *5th International Conference on Integrated Information* (IC-ININFO), September 21–24, 2015, Mykonos, Greece.

Guzzetti, F., P. Reichenbach, F. Ardizzone, M. Cardinali, and M. Galli. 2006. Estimating the quality of landslide susceptibility models. *Geomorphology* 81: 166–184.

Morelli, S., et al. 2012. Urban planning, flood risk and public policy: The case of the Arno River, Firenze, Italy. *Applied Geography* 34: 205–218.

Open GISs Implementation Specification. 2005. *Open GISs Implementation Specification for Geographic information—Simple Feature Access – Part2: SQL Option,* ed. Keith Ryden, Document: OGC05-134, 74 pp.

Group Recommendations in MapReduce

Vasilis Efthymiou, Petros Zervoudakis, Kostas Stefanidis and Dimitris Plexousakis

Introduction

Efficient top-k processing is a crucial requirement in many interactive environments, such as the Web, that involve huge amounts of data (for surveys on top-k computations, see Ilyas et al. 2008; Stefanidis et al. 2011). As an instance, consider that with the growing complexity of the Web (Christophides et al. 2015), users often find themselves overwhelmed by the mass of choices available. To facilitate users in their selection process, recommender systems offer suggestions of potential interest on items (Ricci et al. 2011). In particular, recommender systems aim at providing recommendations to users or groups of users by estimating their preferences and recommending those items featuring the maximal predicted preference. A prerequisite for determining such recommendations is historical data on the users' interests, e.g., their purchase history.

Collaborative filtering (Sandvig et al. 2008) is a widely used recommendations technique, in which the key concept is to locate users with similar rating behavior to the query user; the preferences of these users are employed then for issuing recommendations for the query user. The simplest, naïve approach for finding similar users is by linearly scanning the whole user base. Clearly, this is a costly process

V. Efthymiou (✉) · P. Zervoudakis
University of Crete, Rethimno, Greece
e-mail: vefthym@csd.uoc.gr

P. Zervoudakis
e-mail: zervoudak@csd.uoc.gr

K. Stefanidis
University of Tampere, Tampere, Finland
e-mail: kostas.stefanidis@uta.fi

D. Plexousakis
ICS-FORTH, Heraklion, Greece
e-mail: dp@ics.forth.gr

A. Kavoura et al. (eds.), *Strategic Innovative Marketing*, Springer Proceedings in Business and Economics, DOI 10.1007/978-3-319-56288-9_66

for large recommender systems with millions of users. More efficient approaches for identifying users sharing similar preferences build user models and employ these models for rating prediction. User models might be derived through clustering users into groups of similar users (e.g., Ntoutsi et al. 2012, 2014).

Based on recent studies (Ntoutsi et al. 2014), although a clustering approach is much faster than the naïve approach, the naïve is superior in terms of quality. Luckily, nowadays, even the naïve approach of linearly scanning the database to locate similar users might be implemented efficiently through distributed computing, allowing exact solutions. In this paper, we propose a distributed approach for computing recommendations using MapReduce. Specifically, we consider group recommendations (e.g., Roy et al. 2010; Ntoutsi et al. 2012), i.e., recommendations for groups of users instead of single users.

Group Recommendations Model

Assume a recommender system, where I is the set of items to be rated and U is the set of users in the system. A user $u \in U$ might rate an item $i \in I$ with a score $rating(u, i)$ in $[0, 1]$; let R be the set of all ratings recorded in the system. Typically, the cardinality of the item set I is high and users rate only a few items. The subset of users that rated an item $i \in I$ is denoted by $U(i)$, whereas the subset of items rated by a user $u \in U$ is denoted by $I(u)$.

For the items unrated by the users, recommender systems estimate a relevance score, denoted as $relevance(u, i)$, $u \in U$, $i \in I$. There are different ways to estimate the relevance score of an item for a user. In the content-based approach (e.g., Mooney and Roy 2000), the estimation of the rating of an item is based on the ratings that the user has assigned to similar items, whereas in collaborative filtering systems (e.g., Konstan et al. 1997), this rating is predicted using previous ratings of the item by similar users. In this work, we follow the collaborative filtering approach. Similar users are located via a *similarity function* $simU(u, u')$ that evaluates the proximity between $u, u' \in U$.

We define the distance between two users $u, u' \in U$ as the Euclidean distance over the items rated by both:

$$distU(u, u') = \left(\sqrt{\sum_{i \in \mathscr{I}(u) \cap \mathscr{I}(u')} (rating(u, i) - rating(u', i))^2} \right) / |\mathscr{I}(u) \cap \mathscr{I}(u')|. \quad (1)$$

Then, $simU(u, u') = 1 - distU(u, u')$.

We use F_u to denote the set of the most similar users to u, hereafter referred to as the *friends* of u.

Definition 1 Let $\mathscr{U}$ be a set of users. The friends $\mathscr{F}_u \subseteq \mathscr{U}$ of a user $u \in \mathscr{U}$ consist of all those users $u' \in \mathscr{U}$ that are similar to u with respect to a similarity threshold δ, i.e., $\mathscr{F}_u = \{u' \in \mathscr{U} : simU(u, u') \geq \delta\}$.

Clearly, one could argue for other ways of selecting $\mathscr{F}_u$, e.g., by selecting the k most similar users to u. Our main motivation is that we opt for selecting only highly connected users. Given a user u and his friends $\mathscr{F}_u$, if u has expressed no preference for an item i, the relevance of i for u is estimated as:

$$relevance_{\mathscr{F}_u}(u, i) = \frac{\sum_{u' \in (\mathscr{F}_u \cap U(i))} simU(u, u') rating(u', i)}{\sum_{u' \in (\mathscr{F}_u \cap U(i))} simU(u, u')}. \tag{2}$$

After estimating the relevance scores of all unrated user items, the top-k rated items are recommended to the user.

Since recommendations are typically personalized, different users receive different suggestions. However, there are cases where a group of people participates in a single activity. For instance, visiting a restaurant or a tourist attraction, watching a movie or a TV program, and selecting a holiday destination are examples of recommendations well suited for groups of people. For this reason, recent studies (e.g., Roy et al. 2010; Baltrunas et al. 2010; Ntoutsi et al. 2012) have focused on group recommendations, trying to satisfy the preferences of all the group members.

In general, we consider two different ways to produce recommendations for groups: (i) the *multi-users group* approach, and (ii) the *single-user group* approach. In the multi-users group approach, we first estimate the relevance scores of the unrated items for each user in the group, and then, aggregate these predictions to compute the suggestions for the group. Specifically, let $\mathscr{U}$ be a set of users and $\mathscr{I}$ be a set of items. Then, given a group of users $\mathscr{G} \subseteq \mathscr{U}$, the group relevance of an item $i \in \mathscr{I}$ for $\mathscr{G}$, such that, $\forall u \in \mathscr{G}, i \notin I(u)$, is:

$$relevance^m(\mathscr{G}, i) = Aggr_{u \in \mathscr{G}}(relevance_{\mathscr{F}_u}(u, i)). \tag{3}$$

As in Ntoutsi et al. (2012), we consider three different designs regarding the aggregation method *Aggr*: (i) the *least misery design*, capturing cases where strong user preferences act as a veto (e.g., do not recommend steakhouses to a group when a member is vegetarian), (ii) the *fair design*, capturing more democratic cases where the majority of the group members is satisfied, and (iii) the *most optimistic design*, capturing cases where the most satisfied member of the group acts as the most influential one (e.g., recommend a movie to a group when a member is highly interested in it and the rest have reasonable satisfaction). In the least misery (resp., most optimistic) design, the predicted relevance score of an item for the group is equal to the minimum (resp., maximum) relevance score of the item scores of the members of the group, while the fair design, that assumes equal importance among all group members, returns the average score.

In the single-user group approach, intuitively, we consider the group as a single user, search for the friends of this user, and based on their ratings, compute the group recommendations. This way, $\mathcal{F}_{\mathcal{G}} = \{u' \in \mathcal{U} : sim\mathcal{G}(\mathcal{G}, u') \geq \delta\}$, where $sim\mathcal{G}(\mathcal{G}, u') = f_{u \in \mathcal{G}}(simU(u, u'))$ and f is an aggregated function, e.g., the *minimum* or *average* function. Then, as above:

$$relevance^s(\mathcal{G}, i) = \frac{\sum_{u' \in (\mathcal{F}_{\mathcal{G}} \cap U(i))} sim\mathcal{G}(\mathcal{G}, u') rating(u', i)}{\sum_{u' \in (\mathcal{F}_{\mathcal{G}} \cap U(i))} sim\mathcal{G}(\mathcal{G}, u')}. \quad (4)$$

Implementation in MapReduce

In this section, we present the implementation of our recommender system in MapReduce.[1] First, we describe the implementation of the multi-user approach, and then we continue with the single-user approach. In both cases, we assume that our input consists of a set of user rating triples $R = \{(u, i, rating(u, i)) | u \in U, i \in I\}$, and a set of user ids $\mathcal{G} \subseteq U$, composing the group of interest. We conclude this section with a set of preliminary experiments, comparing the two approaches.

Multi-user Group Approach

In the multi-user approach, we compute the list of friends for each member of the group (Definition 1), the relevance of every item to each member of the group (Eq. 2), and, finally, aggregate those scores to get the final relevance of each item for the group (Eq. 3). In order to identify the friends of each member, we compute the similarity between each member of the group and every other user, outside the group. The implementation of this approach consists of three MapReduce jobs.

Job 1—Partial distances and unrated items. We group the input ratings by item id in the map phase, emitting $(i, < u, rating(u, i) >)$ pairs. The reduce phase produces two different outputs. If one (or more) member(s) of the group $\mathcal{G}$ is (are) among the users who have rated an item i, then, we compute a so-called *partial* distance between each member u and each non-member u' who have rated this item $part(u, u') = (rating(u, i) - rating(u', i))^2$, and emit a pair of the form $(< u, u' >, part(u, u'))$. We will need this partial distance later, to compute the value of Eq. 1. If none of the members of the group $\mathcal{G}$ have rated an item i, then i is one of the candidate items for recommendation, and we simply emit a pair of the form $(i, < u, rating(u, i) >)$ in a different path than the previous output.

Job 2—User similarities. This job forwards the partial distances from Job 1 to the reducers, grouping those distances by pairs of users. The reducers then, having all the partial distances for each user pair $u, u' \in U$, where $u \in \mathcal{G}$, compute the value of Eq. 1 and emit a pair $(< u, u' >, simU(u, u'))$. Based on Definition 1, we can filter

[1] Source code available at: https://github.com/vefthym/GroupRecsMR.

the emitted results to only those whose similarity value is above a certain threshold δ, i.e., emit only the similarity of u to each of his/her friends $u' \in \mathscr{F}_u$.

Job 3—Final relevance. The final job forwards a list of unrated items and the ratings of those items from the non-members of $\mathscr{G}$ from Job 1, grouped by item id, to the reducers. To reduce the network traffic, the emitted ratings are filtered to keep only those given by friends of a group member, i.e., from $u' \in \bigcup_{u \in \mathscr{G}} \mathscr{F}_u$. Having the similarities of group members to their friends from Job 2 loaded in memory, the reducers then compute the relevance score of each unrated item for every group member (Eq. 2), and aggregate those scores to produce the final group relevance values of Eq. 3. The final sorting and top-k selection of those relevance values is trivial when k elements are small enough to fit in memory. When this is not the case, we can use the top-k MapReduce algorithm suggested in Efthymiou et al. (2015).

Single-User Group Approach

The MapReduce algorithm for the single-user group approach is similar to the multi-user approach. This time, four MapReduce jobs are required, as explained next.

Job 1—Partial distances and unrated items. Identical to the multi-user approach.

Job 2—User similarities. The only difference to Job 2 of the multi-user approach, is that we cannot filter the results, based on the given similarity threshold, as an aggregated similarity is required to identify the friends of the group.

Job 3—Friends of the group. This job groups the similarity results of Job 2 by non-member user, to get, in the reduce phase, only the users with an aggregated similarity score above the similarity threshold.

Job 4—Final relevance. Same as the multi-user approach, without the aggregation.

Comparison

To compare the two approaches, we present our experimental results over the MovieLens datasets,[2] with 100K and 1M movie ratings. Our experiments were performed on a cluster of 15 virtual machines, each having 8 CPUs and 8 GB of RAM.

The execution times are presented in Fig. 1, showing that the multi-user group model is faster than the single-user group model, due to having one MapReduce job less. We plan to evaluate our approach on larger datasets and evaluate the quality of the recommendations with user studies.

[2]http://grouplens.org/datasets/movielens/.

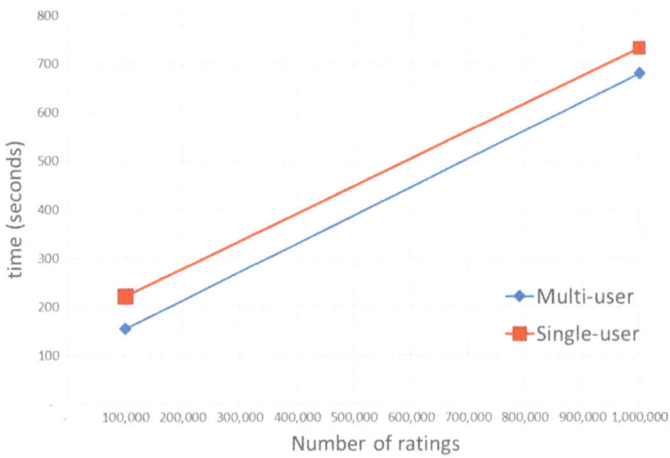

Fig. 1 Execution times (in seconds) of the two approaches over 100K and 1M ratings

References

Baltrunas, L., T. Makcinskas, and F. Ricci. 2010. Group recommendations with rank aggregation and collaborative filtering. In *RecSys*, 119–126.

Christophides, V., V. Efthymiou, and K. Stefanidis. 2015. *Entity resolution in the web of data*. Synthesis lectures on the semantic web: Theory and technology. Morgan & Claypool.

Efthymiou, V., K. Stefanidis, and E. Ntoutsi. 2015. Top-k computations in mapreduce: A case study on recommendations. In *IEEE big data*, 2820–2822.

Ilyas, I.F., G. Beskales, and M.A. Soliman. 2008. A survey of top-*k* query processing techniques in relational database systems. *ACM Computing Surveys* 40 (4).

Konstan, J.A., B.N. Miller, D. Maltz, J.L. Herlocker, L.R. Gordon, and J. Riedl. 1997. Grouplens: Applying collaborative filtering to usenet news. *Communications of the ACM* 40 (3): 77–87.

Mooney, R.J., and L. Roy. 2000. Content-based book recommending using learning for text categorization. In *ACM DL*, 195–204.

Ntoutsi, E., K. Stefanidis, K. Nørvåg, and H. Kriegel. 2012. Fast group recommendations by applying user clustering. In *ER*, 126–140.

Ntoutsi, E., K. Stefanidis, K. Rausch, and H. Kriegel. 2014. Strength lies in differences: Diversifying friends for recommendations through subspace clustering. In *CIKM*, 729–738.

Ricci, F., L. Rokach, B. Shapira, and P.B. Kantor (eds.). 2011. *Recommender systems handbook*. Springer.

Roy, S.B., S. Amer-Yahia, A. Chawla, G. Das, and C. Yu. 2010. Space efficiency in group recommendation. *VLDB Journal* 19 (6): 877–900.

Sandvig, J.J., B. Mobasher, and R.D. Burke. 2008. A survey of collaborative recommendation and the robustness of model-based algorithms. *IEEE Data Engineering Bulletin* 31 (2): 3–13.

Stefanidis, K., G. Koutrika, and E. Pitoura. 2011. A survey on representation, composition and application of preferences in database systems. *ACM Transactions on Database Systems* 36 (3): 19.

APANTISIS: A Greek Question-Answering System for Knowledge-Base Exploration

Emmanouil Marakakis, Haridimos Kondylakis and Papakonstantinou Aris

Introduction

The exponential growth of the web and the development of new scientific techniques have led to an information explosion. According to the 2011 Gartner Group Report,[1] the worldwide information volume is growing annually at a minimum rate of 59%. A prime obstacle for nontechnical people who wish to exploit the aforementioned information has been the need to either learn a special language for communicating with the machine or communicate via an intermediary.

To this direction, there is an ever growing interest in allowing users to ask questions using natural language in the hope of improving the usability of information systems. This need has already been recognized by many commercial vendors such as Microsoft, Apple, Amazon, and Google which are currently providing prominent question answering systems. Microsoft Cortana, Apple Ciri, Amazon Echo, and Google Now are being rapidly developed and updated daily

This work was partially support by the iManageCancer (H2020-643529) EU project.

[1]http://web.archive.org/web/20110710043533/, http://www.gartner.com/it/page.jsp?id=1731916.

E. Marakakis · P. Aris
Department of Informatics Engineering, Technological Educational Institute of Crete, 71410 Heraklion, Greece
e-mail: mmarak@cs.teicrete.gr

P. Aris
e-mail: aris.papakonstantinou@outlook.com

H. Kondylakis (✉)
Computational Biomedicine Laboratory, FORTH-ICS, N. Plastira 100, 70013 Heraklion, Greece
e-mail: kondylak@ics.forth.gr

A. Kavoura et al. (eds.), *Strategic Innovative Marketing*, Springer Proceedings in Business and Economics, DOI 10.1007/978-3-319-56288-9_67

showing the renewed increasing interest on efficient and effective question answering systems.

In this paper, we use the notions of *database* and *knowledge-base* interchangeably referring to systems adopting the entity relationship (ER) model (Chen 1976), assuming that our data conform to the aforementioned model. The reason for this assumption is that there is a well-defined mapping between a natural language sentence in English and the ER model (Chen 1983). We considered and applied the corresponding mapping for the Greek language and the ER model as well. The benefit of this approach is that users of a database can make their queries directly in the Greek language rather than in formal languages like SQL. The system *Apantisis* automatically transforms the Greek question into the corresponding Prolog query for retrieving the requested data. The answer is also given in Greek rather than in the form of tuples. More specifically the contributions of this paper are the following:

- We present Apantisis, a novel platform that accepts a user's natural Greek language input and provides explicit answers to questions. The system is composed of three main modules, the *question*, the *answer,* and the *ingestion* modules.
- The *question* module accepts user's question and converts it into an equivalent relational algebra expression. The query is then forwarded to the database to be answered (Varouxis 2007).
- The *answer* module accepts user's question and the results from the database and formulates the appropriate answer which is presented to the user (Antalis 2008).
- To enable effective question answering a data dictionary should be available at setup time for the external database. This data dictionary can be manually created and provided by the users or automatically extracted using the *ingestion* module.

Our system is unique in the sense that it exploits the unique characteristics of the Greek language to enable rapid and effective database exploration for the users not possessing technical skills.

The remaining of this paper is structured as follows: A running example is shown in section "Running Example". Then the architecture of our system and the different components are described in section "Architecture". Related work is reported in section "Related Work". Finally, section "Conclusion and Preliminary Evaluation" concludes this paper and presents a preliminary evaluation.

Running Example

The most common questions to a QA system can be separated in three basic categories:

- Factual or interrogative Questions: These questions have only one correct answer. For example, "`Which lessons does professor Marakakis teach?`"

Professors

ProfessorID	Surname	Name	Phone	e-mail
643	Marakakis	Emmanouil	2810379748	mmarak@cs.teicrete.gr
644	Papadakis	Nikolaos	2810379196	npapadak@cs.teicrete.gr
645	Haridimos	Kondylakis	2810391449	kondylak@ics.forth.gr

Teach

ProfessorID	LessonID	Semester	Year
643	CS404	Spring	2015
644	CS405	Fall	2015
644	CS404	Spring	2015

Lessons

LessonID	Name	Type	ECTS
CS404	Artificial Intelligence	C	8
CS405	Semantic Web	C	8

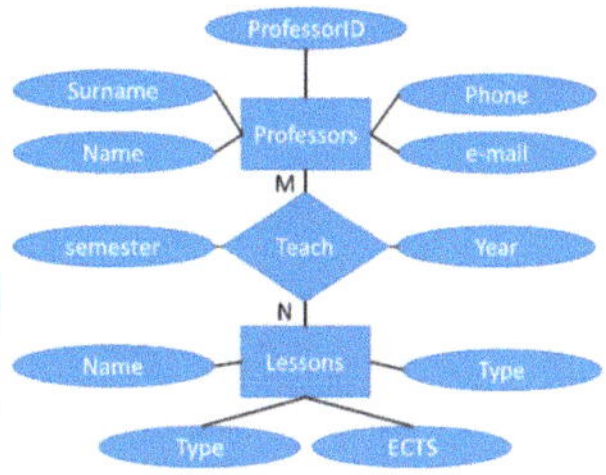

Fig. 1 An example database (*right*) and the corresponding ER model (*left*)

- Opinion or declarative Questions: These questions ask for some kind of opinion, belief or point of view, so they have yes or no answer. For example, "`Professor Marakakis teaches Artificial Intelligence`". This declarative statement may be correct or wrong.
- Summary or imperative Questions. These questions have more than one answer, but they still must be supported with evidence. For example, "`List all lecturers of Informatics Engineering Department for academic year 2015-16.`"

In this work we focus only on these three basic categories of questions. Consider, for example, the toy schema shown in Fig. 1 containing professors and the lessons they teach. In order to identify the courses taught by professor Marakakis, an experienced user should know the schema and he should formulate the following query-expressed in SQL:

```
SELECT Lessons.Name FROM Lessons, Teach, Professors
WHERE Lessons.LessonID=Teach.LessonID AND Teach.ProfessorID=Professors.Professc
  AND Professors.surname="Marakakis"
```

On the other hand, it would be a lot easier for an unexperienced user just to use the following natural language query: "`Which lessons does professor Marakakis teach?`"

Architecture

APANTISIS is composed of six individual modules which can be attached to any existing database enabling natural language query answering using the Greek language. The six modules are shown in Fig. 2 and they are *(a) the GUI*, *(b) the question*, *(c) the answer*, *(d) the ingestion*, the *(e) Greek Language Lexicon, Syntactic and Semantic rules*, and *(f) the data dictionary*. Below we will describe in detail each one of the aforementioned modules.

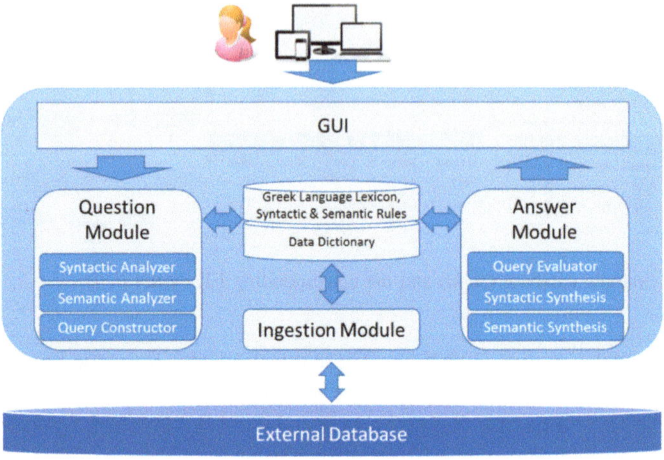

Fig. 2 The high level architecture of our system

The Ingestion Module

Before actually using the system the necessary data dictionary should be in place. The ingestion module connects to the external database and retrieves all relevant meta-data required for constructing the data dictionary. This data dictionary records various meta-data about the database such as the table and the column names and types and the foreign key constraints. In our example of Fig. 2 the names of the tables, the names, and types of their corresponding fields and the foreign key constraints are extracted and saved at the data dictionary as shown in Fig. 3. In case that the database tables and fields use abbreviations, the administrator is allowed to assign proper, meaningful names to those by annotating the corresponding fields. For example, for the field "ECTS," the administrator can add the annotation "European Credit Transfer and Accumulation System." Finally, synonyms can be added to the identified terms as well. For example, in our example the administrator can indicate in the data dictionary that "lecturer" is synonym to "teacher."

The GUI

The GUI is shown in Fig. 4 and is developed using JAVA. The Jasper library is used to communicate with the rest of the system which is developed in Prolog. As shown, a user can specify a question using the corresponding text area field and submit his question. The system transforms the natural language question to the corresponding query using the question module and retrieves the results from the database. Finally, the results are transformed to a natural language sentence by the

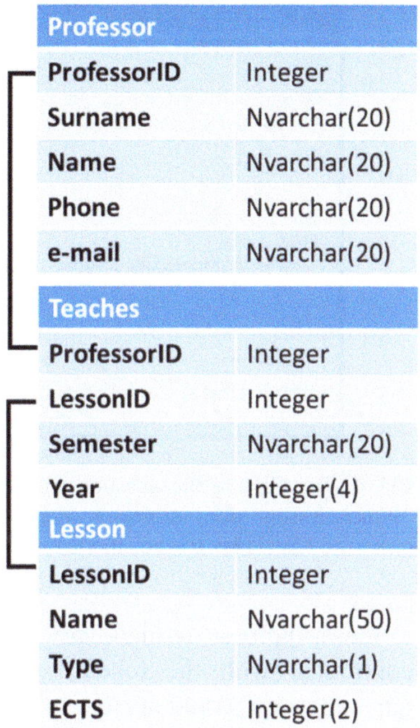

Fig. 3 The extracted meta-data

answer module and they are shown to the user. In our running example, the user issues the following question "*Which lessons does professor Marakakis teach?*" shown in Greek language in Fig. 4.

The Query Module

As soon as the question of the user is received, the syntactic analyser parses the query and constructs the parse tree of each sentence. To do that, initially, the syntactic analyser exploits *the Greek language dictionary* as shown in Fig. 2. In this step tokenization, stemming, and lemmatization is performed in order to reduce inflectional and derivationally related forms of a word to a common base form.

Tokenization is the recognition of word and punctuation boundaries inside the text. This involves an initial split at obvious points (spaces and punctuation marks) followed by post processing to avoid, for example, the separation of the relative indefinite pronoun "*ό,τι*" into two different tokens. Then stemming and lemmatization is following. Stemming usually refers to a crude heuristic process that chops off the ends of words in the hope of achieving this goal correctly most of the time, and often includes the removal of derivational affixes. Lemmatization, on the other hand, refers to doing things properly with the use of a vocabulary and morphological analysis of words, normally aiming to remove inflectional endings only and

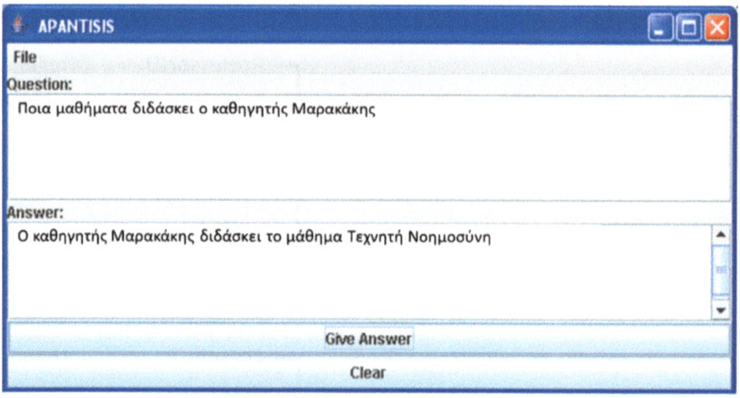

Fig. 4 The GUI of the question answering prototype. The query corresponds to the sentence "Which lessons does professor Marakakis teach?" and the answer corresponds to the "The professor Marakakis teaches the lesson of Artificial Intelligence"

to return the base or dictionary form of a word, which is known as the lemma. If confronted with the token "*saw,*" stemming might return just "*s,*" whereas lemmatization would attempt to return either "*see*" or "*saw*" depending on whether the use of the token was as a verb or a noun.

The Greek language, like many others, uses extensive inflection and therefore semantic relations between words cannot be detected unless those words are stemmed. Stemming Greek words is much harder than stemming words of other European languages because of the number of possible suffixes, many of which cannot be properly separated from the word stem without knowing the grammatical type of the word. Moreover, stemming of words with different meaning may lead to the same stem. In addition, although for the English language there are already established many approaches and heuristics with respect to stemming and lemmatization, for the Greek language we had to design and implement all of them from scratch. Then the syntactic analyzer constructs the parse tree of the sentence exploiting *the grammar rules of the Greek language* and then the semantic analyser identifies the elements of the query that correspond of the data dictionary and ascertains the correct usage of each. Synonyms can be identified and the correspondences between the user's query and the names of the tables and fields are matched. In our running example, the parse tree shown in Fig. 5a will be constructed.

After the syntactic and the semantic analysis of the question of user, the *query constructor* generates the corresponding query in relational algebra. The steps for creating the corresponding query are the following: *(a) Identify Tables*: To construct the corresponding query initially the query module tries to identify the tables involved in the query. In our running example, the words of the query are grammatically classified in the parse tree and then the data dictionary is used to match with specific DB elements. In our example, the words "καθηγητής," "διδάσκει,"

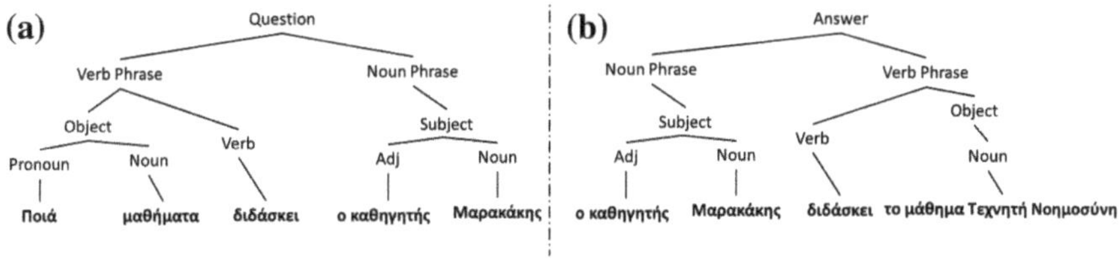

Fig. 5 The parse tree of the question (**a**) and the corresponding answer (**b**)

and "μαθήματα" of the analyzed question correspond to the database relations "*Professor*", "Teaches", and *"Lessons"*, respectively. Note that in this stage we exploit the entity relationship model in the sense that we try to correlate verbs with relationships and nouns with entities. *(b) Construct Join Path*: Next we try to identify the paths joining those tables using the foreign key constraints identified in the ingestion phase. If there are multiple paths joining the identified tables, the one with the minimum length is used. In our case, for example, the *"Professor"* table is joined with the *"Teaches*" table using the *"ProfessorID"* field, and the *"Lesson"* table is joined with the "*Teaches*" table using the *"LessonID"* field. To identify the proper join path our system exploits the entity relationship model. *(c) Identify Selections and Projection*: Then the query module tries to identify the projection part of the query exploiting the Greek Language Syntax and Semantic rules. In our case, the projection will be on the field "*Name*" of the lesson table. Finally, it will try to identify the selections of the query. In order to do that it searches all field of the table professor to identify records with the "*Marakakis*" value. Of course since we know the datatypes of the fields we are looking only at the fields with the correct datatypes—(Nvarchar in our case). Since the specific value is the "*Surname*" field the corresponding condition is added to the query.

The query can be directly translated into the corresponding SQL/relational algebra query and sent to the database. In our case it is translated to the following Prolog query: `Q(L):-Professors(P, Marakakis, N, P, E), Teach(P, L, S, Y), Lessons(L, Y, T, C).`

The Answer Module

This module is responsible for executing the query and transforming the results into a natural language expression. As such, the Answer module receives the parse tree of the question and the query as input. The corresponding algorithm proceeds as follows: Initially the Query Evaluator component of the Answer module sends the constructed query to the external database and collects the results. In our case the Prolog query returns the *"Artificial Intelligence.*" The second step of the corresponding algorithm constructs the parse tree of the answer using the parse tree of the question, the results of the knowledge base, the Greek language lexicon and the data dictionary. The noun phrase and the verb of the question are transferred directly to the noun phrase and the verb of the answer as shown in Fig. 5b. The remaining answer is constructed using the query results and the various phrase structure rules of the Greek language. Finally, in the last step of the corresponding algorithm the parse tree of the answer is checked and creates the final answer. In our running example the answer would be "*Professor Marakakis teaches the lesson of Artificial Intelligence.*"

Related Work

Work on question answering systems as front-ends to databases has been going on since the 1970s; however, the systems there where limited only to a narrow domain. More recent works include systems that use NLP for accessing databases using the ER model (Chen 1983) or try to transform a natural language question into a corresponding logical form by leveraging semantic associations between lexical representation and database properties in the latent space (Yang et al. 2014). In the same direction Badia (2007) introduces a query language with generalized quantifiers to bridge the gap between natural language queries and database querying. However, despite the fact that questions are transformed to a logic form equivalent to a relational query language they do not offer natural language answers as well. In addition, there is a strong community behind question answering systems using the English language with several tracks on well-respected conferences. For example, the CLEF question answering track (Peñas et al. 2015) benchmarks related systems allowing access over information using natural language questions. However, there is no corresponding Greek language benchmark to evaluate our system.

For the Greek language, there already have been some preliminary approaches on Natural Language Processing. For example, the Institute for Language and Speech Processing have created a set of tools (Papageorgiou et al. 2002; Prokopidis et al. 2011) based on both machine learning and rule-based algorithms for natural language processing tools for Greek. However, the aforementioned tools do not support query answering and are used mainly for whole text summarization. Adam et al. (2010) implement stemming and tagging for the Greek language based on word tagging techniques, whereas Ntais (2006) uses the Porter Stemmer (Porter 1980) to achieve stemming for the Greek language. Approaches like (Lyras et al. 2009) have created a large Greek–English dictionary with incorporated speech and language processing tools implementing lemmatizer for Greek and Text to Speech synthesizers for Greek. Although these tools contribute to the stemming and tagging of the Greek language still they only cover specific sub-modules of our system.

Conclusion and Preliminary Evaluation

To our knowledge, our approach is the only approach combining both question and answering in natural language in the Greek language. The system enables the specification of natural language questions, finds the corresponding answers and presents them using natural language as well. The combination of natural language processing for both the question and answer part and the Greek language implementation make the system unique. Its generality and modularity along with the ingestion module allow the quick deployments of the system on various databases with minor effort.

To evaluate our system, since there is no question answering evaluation benchmark available for the Greek language, we conducted a preliminary evaluation using available course data from the department of Informatics Engineering at the Technological Educational Institute of Crete. The benchmark is consisted of 14 tables published with the corresponding data from the department and 11 relevant query templates corresponding to hundreds of similar queries. The generated benchmark can be found online[2] along with the results from our system allowing other future systems to be evaluated using the aforementioned benchmark. All queries were successfully answered returning the expected results from the system. In addition, we tried to issue questions where the syntax was not correct and our system was able to identify the erroneous syntax and to notify the user. In the case that we are searching for tuples where there is no corresponding information in the database the system was able to correctly identify that there is no relevant information in the database.

As future work, we intend to conduct a thorough evaluation and go beyond these three simple types of questions. That is questions can be more complex to include multiple anaphoras. For example, "Which course is taught by professor Marakakis which has more than 100 students and which is given in Spring semester?" In addition, we would like to support more complex queries like why-not types of queries. Moreover, we would like to focus on correcting syntax and gramma errors of the input questions. Finally, building a combined portfolio of structured, semi-structured, and unstructured knowledge bases is an obvious extension we already started to explore (Kondylakis et al. 2015a, b).

References

Adam, G., K. Asimakis, C. Bouras, and V. Poulopoulos. 2010. An efficient mechanism for stemming and tagging: The case of Greek language. *KES* 3: 389–397.

Antalis, G. 2008. Development of a system which generates sentences in Greek language as answers from processing queries in a relational database. Department of Applied Informatics and Multimedia, TEI of Crete.

[2]http://users.ics.forth.gr/~kondylak/Benchmark.rar.

Badia, A. 2007. Question answering and database querying: Bridging the gap with generalized quantification. *Journal Applied Logic* 5 (1): 3–19.

Chen, P. 1976. The entity-relationship model-toward a unified view of data. *ACM TODS* 1 (1): 9–36.

Chen, P. 1983. English sentence structure and entity-relationship diagram. *IS Journal* 1 (1): 127–149.

Kondylakis, H., L. Koumakis, E. Kazantzaki, M. Chatzimina, M. Psaraki, K. Marias, and M. Tsiknakis. 2015a. Patient empowerment through personal medical recommendations. *MEDINFO* 216: 1117.

Kondylakis, H., L. Koumakis, M. Psaraki, G. Troullinou, M. Chatzimina, E. Kazantzaki, K. Marias, and M. Tsiknakis. 2015b. Semantically-enabled personal medical information recommender. ISWC.

Lyras, D.P., G.K. Kokkinakis, A. Lazaridis, K.N. Sgarbas, and N. Fakotakis. 2009. A large Greek-English dictionary with incorporated speech and language processing tools. *INTERSPEECH*, 1891–1894.

Ntais, G. 2006. Development of a stemmer for the Greek language, MSc Thesis, Stockholm University.

Papageorgiou, H., P. Prokopidis, I. Demiros, V. Giouli, A. Konstantinidis, and S. Piperidis. 2002. Multi-level XML based corpus annotation. In *Language resources and evaluation conference*. Las Palmas.

Peñas, A., C. Unger, G. Paliouras, and I.A. Kakadiaris. 2015. Overview of the CLEF. *QA Track*. 539–544.

Porter, M.F. 1980. An algorithm for suffix stripping. *Program* 14 (3): 130–137. Automated library and information systems.

Prokopidis, P., B. Georgantopoulos, and H. Papageorgiou. 2011. A suite of natural language processing tools for Greek. In *The 10th international conference of Greek linguistics*.

Varouxis, K. 2007. Development of a system which analyses queries in Greek language and transforms them into prolog goals. Department of Applied Informatics and Multimedia, TEI of Crete.

Yang, M.C., N. Duan, M. Zhou, and H.C. Rim. 2014. Joint relational embeddings for knowledge-based question answering. *EMNLP*, 645–650.

News Articles Platform: Semantic Tools and Services for Aggregating and Exploring News Articles

Koralia Papadokostaki, Stavros Charitakis, George Vavoulas, Stella Panou, Paraskevi Piperaki, Aris Papakonstantinou, Savvas Lemonakis, Anna Maridaki, Konstantinos Iatrou, Piotr Arent, Dawid Wiśniewski, Nikos Papadakis and Haridimos Kondylakis

Introduction

Internet is prevalent in our lives nowadays; access to it, is now easy and at high speeds and the availability of small portable devices has made it an integral part of our everyday life. It constitutes a basic medium for keeping ourselves updated. To this direction, following the news on the internet is gaining ground every day. Moreover, thousands of news items are produced everyday across the earth; whether important or trivial, they need to be saved, archived, searched and indexed. Information does not only involve pieces of text, but also images, video and audio files that complement the news articles and make their impact more significant. Lately, with the rise of social platforms, news articles can be shared through social networks, commented or even "followed" by external users.

In this exploding and demanding landscape, numerous research works focus on managing news articles. For modelling news articles for example BBC created its own ontology.[1] IPTC on the other hand, the global standards body of the news media, generated some widely used mark-up languages[2] such as NewsML and

[1]http://www.bbc.co.uk/ontologies/storyline.
[2]https://iptc.org/standards/.

K. Papadokostaki · S. Charitakis · G. Vavoulas · S. Panou · P. Piperaki · A. Papakonstantinou · S. Lemonakis · A. Maridaki · K. Iatrou · P. Arent · D. Wiśniewski · N. Papadakis
Department of Informatics Engineering, Technological Educational Institute of Crete, 71410 Heraklion, Greece

H. Kondylakis (✉)
Institute of Computer Science, FORTH-ICS, N. Plastira 100, V. Vouton, 70013 Heraklion, Greece
e-mail: kondylak@ics.forth.gr

A. Kavoura et al. (eds.), *Strategic Innovative Marketing*, Springer Proceedings in Business and Economics, DOI 10.1007/978-3-319-56288-9_68

rNews. In addition, the Schema.Org provides a well-known semantic vocabulary for modelling news articles.[3] Although those models are commonly used, a common data model integrating them all, linking them also with the emerging social media websites is still missing. Besides modelling news articles, web sites like NewsExplorer[4] and Event Registry[5] try to collect and annotate in real-time news articles. However, they provide limited APIs for importing and exporting articles, they do not expose the collected information as linked data limiting their potential and they miss linking the news articles with social media. Other approaches, assume that news articles are collected only through RSS feeds (Neptuno,[6] NEWS Fernández et al. 2010 and Hermes[7]) or they are submitted via email (like myPlanet Kalfoglou et al. 2001) and others lack a central storage mechanism (using big files (Mohirta et al. 2011) to store articles) or miss a common data model (like SemNews Java et al. 2006).

As a consequence, a new approach is required, unifying and linking the various data models and standards developed for modelling news articles, adding also the social dimension. In addition, the proper infrastructure should be in place offering flexible APIs and mechanisms for collecting, annotating, publishing, exploring and sharing of various news articles. To this direction, in this paper, we present *the News Article Platform* which aims to enable effective and efficient management of new articles using semantic web technologies and services. More specifically our contributions are the following:

- A novel ontology, named *News Articles Ontology*, to represent the required information and relationships among news articles integrating and linking all previous approaches adding also the social dimension.
- The necessary *APIs to enable pushing and pulling information* from a linked data repository publishing all relevant information as *Linked Open Data.*
- Besides programmatically interacting with the repository, our platform provides *an app with a friendly graphical user interface* (GUI) for *manually pushing news articles* and the relevant information to the repository and two easy ways to *automatically* insert new articles into it: (i) via a *news wrapper tool* which allows the bulk insertion of articles from selected webpages; (ii) via an *RSS crawler* which, given an RSS channel, allows the selective insertion of news articles into the repository.
- In addition, a search engine is provided, allowing the faceted search and exploration of all relevant information.
- A preliminary evaluation of the whole platform by 70 postgraduate students from the Department of Informatics Engineering at Technological Educational

[3]https://schema.org/NewsArticle.

[4]http://emm.newsexplorer.eu/NewsExplorer/home/en/latest.html.

[5]http://eventregistry.org/.

[6]http://ir.ii.uam.es/neptuno/.

[7]http://hermesportal.sourceforge.net/.

Institute of Crete shows the overall effectiveness of our platform and verifies the advantages of our approach.

To the best of our knowledge, the News Articles Platform is the only platform with an ontology representing all relevant information, and services to implement storing into and retrieval from a central repository, aggregators for the bulk insertion of data and a search engine. After the insertion of the articles into the repository, all data are made available as Linked Open Data, enabling their effective and efficient sharing and reuse. The rest of the paper is structured as follows: section "Architecture" elaborates on the architecture and the different components of our platform and section "Preliminary Evaluation" presents the preliminary evaluation performed. Finally, section "Conclusion" concludes this paper and presents directions for future work.

Architecture

A three-tier architecture was used for the implementation of the platform. It is illustrated in Fig. 1a and is consisted of the Data Layer, the Service Layer, and the GUI:

- **The Data Layer**: In the data layer, which is the lowest in the architecture, a Virtuoso[8] triple store is used to store the ontology and the collected data. Virtuoso is a multiprotocol server, enabling data integration, publishing linked data and managing RDF databases. Virtuoso offers an ideal solution for the data management layer of our project as it can handle massive RDF data and it is free and open source. Although the use of GraphDB (formerly known as OWLIM, which used to be open source) was at first considered as a candidate solution for data management, the fact that it is now a commercial product played an important role adopting Virtuoso.

In order to model all relevant information in the domain, we created an RDF/S ontology named *News Articles Ontology*. RDF is among the most widely used standards for publishing and representing data on the Web (Troullinou et al. 2016). The representation of knowledge in RDF is based on triples of the form (*subject*, *predicate*, *object*), whereas RDF datasets have attached semantics through RDFS,[9] a vocabulary description language. The main purpose of the designed ontology is to be used as the core data model for creating, publishing, storing, indexing, and retrieving news articles integrating all previous models and approaches. To generate the ontology we carefully considered (a) the fundamental classes exemplified in Schema.org, (b) associations described in FOAF[10] (c) the BBC ontology and

[8]http://virtuoso.openlinksw.com/.

[9]https://www.w3.org/TR/rdf-schema/.

[10]http://xmlns.com/foaf/spec.

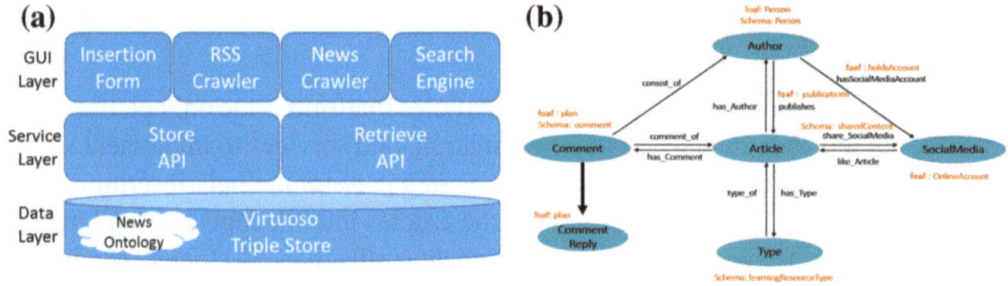

Fig. 1 The three-tier architecture of our platform (**a**) and the core classes of the News Articles Ontology and their equivalences with Schema.org and FOAF (**b**)

(d) the schema of the NewsML and rNews mark-up languages. As such, we reused the core classes specified in past approaches such as *"Article"*, *"Author"*, *"Type"*, and *"Comment"* and their corresponding properties identifying their equivalences with the Schema.org, the FOAF and the BBC ontology (for reasons of readability in Fig. 1b we only demonstrate equivalences with the first two ontologies). In addition, among other extensions and additions, we added classes and properties modelling social media and now an author might be a member of a social media website and an article can be "shared", "liked" or "commented" using one or multiple social media accounts (Facebook, Twitter, LinkedIn, Google+).

- **The Service Layer**: The service layer consists of two individual APIs one for storing information and one for retrieving. Both the APIs are developed as web services and adhere to the REST architectural design with constraints, namely RESTful APIs. Currently only the Retrieve API is publicly available.

The Store API: The Store API is a set of web services. Those services receive requests from any application for data insertion, they create and execute the corresponding SPARQL queries to the Virtuoso triple store and they return the proper messages according to the server response. SPARQL[11] is the official W3C Recommendation for querying linked data. Most forms of SPARQL queries contain a set of triple patterns called a basic graph pattern. Triple patterns are like RDF triples except that each of the subject, predicate and object may be a variable. A basic graph pattern matches a subgraph of the RDF data when RDF terms from that subgraph may be substituted for the variables. Besides SELECT SPARQL queries for selecting data INSERT SPARQL queries are used to add triples and DELETE SPARQL queries to delete specific triples from the triple store. The implemented API has the capability to check for duplicates returning the proper warning messages. The Store API is developed using PHP, accepts http POST and GET requests and communicates with the Virtuoso triple store using SPARQL queries using a PHP library, named SPARQLib. All web applications developed on top of the service layer such as the web tool for the manual insertion, the RSS

[11]https://www.w3.org/TR/rdf-sparql-query/.

crawler and the news wrapper use the corresponding functions from the store API to achieve data storage.

The Retrieve API: The Retrieve API on the other hand is a set of web services that receive requests for data retrieval, create and execute the proper SELECT SPARQL queries to the Virtuoso triple store and return the results in JSON-LD format. JSON (JavaScript Object Notation) is an open standard format that uses human-readable text to transmit data objects consisting of attribute–value pairs. It is the most common data format used for asynchronous browser/server communication, largely replacing XML which is used by AJAX. JSON-LD is a lightweight Linked Data format. Linked Data empowers people that publish and use information on the Web and is a way to create a network of standards-based, machine-readable data across Websites. It is easy for humans to read and write, based on JSON format and provides a way to help JSON data interoperate at Web-scale.[12]

- **The GUI Layer**: This layer contains a *search engine*, a *web app for the manual insertion* of articles, authors and all relevant information, an *RSS crawler* and a *news wrapper*. All applications have been developed using HTML5, Bootstrap, JQuery, and PHP in order to be user-friendly and up to date, and they rely on the APIs provided by the service layer. A short description of each app is provided below.

The web app for the manual insertion of articles: The web tool for the manual insertion of the articles comprises of an interactive, user-friendly form, which implements the insertion of articles into two steps. It contains the most important fields of the ontology and is also equipped with validation rules, thus allowing the error-free insertion of the corresponding information. A screenshot of the interface is shown in Fig. 2a. Using the form, articles, authors, comments, rating, images, videos, etc. can be inserted whereas the inserted information is automatically linked to relevant information already existing in the Virtuoso triple store. Additionally, the insertion of duplicate articles or authors is not allowed. The web tool posts the relevant information to the proper API calls and visualizes the returned messages.

The RSS crawler: Besides manually inserting news articles we have also implemented an RSS crawler which crawls existing RSS feeds, retrieves the corresponding news items, and uses the API for inserting and storing the extracted information to our repository. RSS (Rich Site Summary) is a format for delivering regularly changing web content. Many news-related sites, weblogs, and other online publishers syndicate their content as an RSS Feed to whoever wants it. RSS provides a standard easy method to retrieve the latest content from selected sites. The number of sites offering RSS feeds is growing rapidly and includes big names like Yahoo News. As such, the RSS crawler reads and displays initially one or multiple RSS channels and allows the selection of news items to be further saved into our database. As soon as an article is selected, the relevant parts are exported,

[12]http://json-ld.org/.

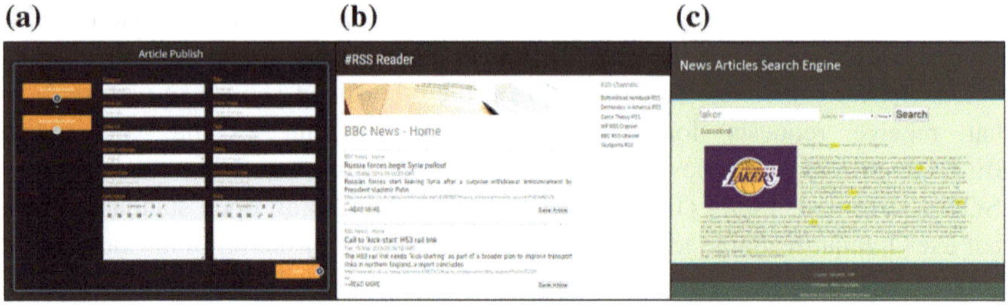

Fig. 2 The web app for the manual insertion of articles (**a**) the RSS reader (**b**) and the search engine (**c**)

and the corresponding calls to the Store API are issued. The interface of the RSS crawler is as simple as possible and a screenshot is shown in Fig. 2b.

The news wrapper: The news wrapper is an app which allows the retrieval of news items from sites that do not offer RSS feeds. It uses the FiveFilters library[13] to parse articles out of news sites and blogs, and stores them in the Virtuoso triple store calling the appropriate Store API calls. Currently the generated app is called through the command line, getting as input a list of URLs, but soon a new updated version will be released with a fully fledged web graphical user interface.

The search engine: The search engine of our platform is the app that allows searching into the Virtuoso triple store and visualizes the returned results. More specifically, users provide keywords and select the ordering of the results. The corresponding API calls are issued then using the Retrieve API. The Retrieve API accepts the request, formulates the correct SPARQL queries and returns the selected result to be visualized by the interface of the search engine. The results of the search can be ordered by various fields selected by the user interface whereas the faceted search is also possible searching in specific information types. For ranking the results of the search engine a variation of the vector space model is implemented and used (Kondylakis et al. 2015) calculating the cosine of the angle between the document vectors and the query vector—each vector contains the terms appearing in documents/queries. For the implementation of the search engine Html, JavaScript, PHP and CSS were used. The search engine receives a JSON-LD and shows the results of the query specified by the user. A screenshot of the first version of the interface is shown in Fig. 2c.

Preliminary Evaluation

Deploying a platform which meets our initial objectives along with user satisfaction, ease of use and absence of defects was our target throughout the whole life cycle of our software. In order to achieve it, norms such as the Software Product

[13]http://fivefilters.org/.

Quality Requirements and evaluation (SQUARE) (ISO/IEC 42010:2007 2007), defined from the International Organization for Standardization (ISO), have been used as a reference model As a result, the applicable functional and non-functional requirements according to ISO/IEC 25023 (2016) had been defined in the early stages of the project and monitored by the developers during the whole software life cycle.

For the evaluation, the quality features from the product quality model of the ISO/IEC 25000 series together with the System Usability Scale (SUS) (Brooke 1996) for global assessment of systems usability were used. At the evaluation stage 70 undergraduate students of the Department of Informatics Engineering, Technological Educational Institute of Crete were asked to complete a questionnaire with simple, accurate, non-time consuming, set of questions.

Still, the questions had to be without loss of functionality/quality, so the crucial sub-features of software quality measures from ISO/IEC 25000 series have been formed into simple questions in natural language. The evaluation form of the platform was a set of questions where the evaluator had to answer within a degree of satisfaction using Likert scale (Likert 1932).

Table 1 The results for the various evaluation categories

Functionality	Suitability	3.98	4.01
	Accurateness	3.83	
	Compliance	4.21	
Efficiency	Time behaviour	4.27	4.14
	Resource utilization	4.00	
Compatibility	Coexistence	4.19	4.17
	Interoperability	4.15	
Usability	Understandability	3.75	3.94
	Learnability	4.04	
	Operability	4.02	
	Attractiveness	3.96	
Reliability	Fault tolerance	3.71	3.70
	Recoverability	3.69	
Maintainability	Analyzability	3.92	3.99
	Changeability	4.13	
	Stability	3.94	
	Testability	4.00	
Portability	Adaptability	4.00	3.99
	Installability	4.00	
	Conformance	3.94	
	Replaceability	4.04	
Quality of use	Effectiveness	3.83	3.86
	Efficiency	3.85	
	Satisfaction	3.90	
SUS	79.18/100		

The results of our evaluation are illustrated in Table 1. Values greater than three represent high level of the specific software feature; values between 2.5 and 3 are at low risk, whereas values below 2.5 are considered of high risk. In our case, all were graded with a satisfactory average above 3.7 showing the high quality of the software. The lowest average score was for the reliability (3.7/5) since in some cases, errors appeared when inserting documents without allowing a proper recovery. User feedback was used to correct all errors. The highest average score for compatibility (4.27/5) shows that the system adopts state of the art interoperability standards, and modules can be replaced at will without affecting the behaviour of the entire system. When it comes to functionality, efficiency and compatibility our system receives high values, thus confirming its quality and high performance.

The SUS usability score was 79.18 on a scale of 0–100. The average SUS score from published studies has been measured by Sauro (2009) as the 62.1 but as a gold standard is often used the 68. Therefore, SUS score exceeding 68 are considered above average, while SUS scores below 68 are below average. Our SUS score of 79.18 exceeds by far the reference point of 68, yet future improvements can be made to provide even higher levels of understandability and fault tolerance.

The evaluation provided us with valuable feedback on the current state and with suggestions towards its improvement. For instance, minor problems regarding the search engine were located and were improved.

Conclusion

This paper presents a novel platform for aggregating, indexing and searching news articles as Linked Open Data. The platform consists of web service APIs to allow seamless integration of the GUI with the repository, an open source repository with SPARQL capabilities allowing the data to be stored as instances of our ontology. Moreover, an RSS crawler allows the uninterrupted insertion of articles and a news wrapper automatically parses articles from sites that do not expose RSS capabilities. The manual insertion of authors and articles is also possible through a user-friendly GUI. Finally, we enable effective and efficient search to the contents of our repository through a powerful search engine.

Currently we are experimenting with NLP solutions to understand the content of the articles and to be able to provide not only keyword search but semantically enabled answers to user questions. In addition, we plan to release soon all tools and services in an open source repository to be publicly available as well.

In an era where the information is generated at tremendous rates, platforms for effective and efficient aggregating and searching news articles are of utmost importance.

References

Brooke, J. 1996. SUS-A quick and dirty usability scale, usability evaluation in industry 189 (194): 4–7.

Fernández, N., D. Fuentes, L. Sánchez, and J.A. Fisteus. 2010. The NEWS ontology: Design and applications. *Expert Systems with Applications* 37 (12): 8694–8704.

ISO/IEC 42010:2007. 2007. Systems and software engineering—Recommended practice for architectural description of software-intensive systems.

ISO/IEC DIS 25023:2016. 2016. Systems and software engineering—Systems and software Quality Requirements and Evaluation (SQuaRE)—Measurement of system and software product quality.

Java, A., T. Finin, and S. Nirenburg. 2006. SemNews: A semantic news framework. In *Proceedings of the twenty-first national conference on artificial intelligence (AAAI)*, 1939–1940.

Kalfoglou, Y., J. Domingue, M. Enrico, M. Vargas-Vera, and S. Buckingham-Shum. 2001. MyPlanet: An ontology-driven Web-based personalised news service. In *IJCAI workshop on ontologies and information sharing*, Seatle, WA, USA.

Kondylakis, H., L. Koumakis, E. Kazantzaki, M. Chatzimina, M. Psaraki, K. Marias, and M. Tsiknakis. 2015. Patient empowerment through personal medical recommendations. In *MEDINFO* 216, 1117.

Likert, R. 1932. A technique for the measurement of attitudes. *Archives of Psychology* 140: 1–55.

Mohirta, M., A.S. Cernian, D. Carstoiu, A.M. Vladu, A. Olteanu, and V. Sgarciu. 2011. A semantic web based scientific news. In *6th IEEE international symposium on applied computational intelligence and informatics*, 285–289.

Sauro, J.R.L. 2009. Correlations among prototypical usability metrics: Evidence for the construct of usability. In *Proceedings of the SIGCHI conference on human factors in computing systems*, 1609–1618. ACM.

Troullinou, G., G. Roussakis, H. Kondylakis, K. Stefanidis, and G. Flouris. 2016. Understanding ontology evolution beyond deltas. EDBT/ICDT Workshops.

Data Mining of World Bank Indicators

Maha A. Hana

Introduction

This research aims to use data mining techniques specifically clustering techniques to understand and assess current status of different sectors in Egypt using World Bank Indicators. World Bank (WB) issues annual world development indicators for many countries, which denote the status of different sectors in a country. They are represented as 1300 time series for over 50 years (World Bank Group 2015). Researchers have been using WB data to analysis and forecast country's status in economic, social and political bases (Korotayev and Zinkina 2011; Ranganathan et al. 2015; World Bank's Egypt MFM Team 2015). Also, it is used to study scientific problems (Muhammad et al. 2011; Shaheen et al. 2012). Clustering is a multi-objective optimization problem that groups similar objects together in one well-separated cluster (Tan et al. 2006; Wagner and Wagner 2007; Jain 2010). The boundaries of the cluster are hypothetical and are affected by the data samples, the used clustering algorithm and the learning process (Tan et al. 2006; Jain 2010). Cluster results may be exclusive/hard clustering, overlapping/nonexclusive/soft cluster or fuzzy clustering. Clusters are characterized by cluster cohesion/compactness/tightness and cluster separation/isolation (Tan et al. 2006; Zaki and Meira 2014). Cohesion determines how close the members of one cluster are. Cluster separation determines how distinct the clusters are from each other. The aim of this research is to better understand Egypt's WB indicator using clustering techniques. The paper proceeds by a review in section "Related Work". Section "EGY_WBD Clustering System" explains EGY_WBD Clustering system. Section "Experiment"

M.A. Hana (✉)
Engineering Institute Zayed Branch, Canadian International College
(deputed from Department of Information Systems, Faculty of Computers
and Information, Helwan University), Cairo, Egypt
e-mail: maha_attia@cic-cairo.com; maha_hana_eg@yahoo.com

A. Kavoura et al. (eds.), *Strategic Innovative Marketing*, Springer Proceedings
in Business and Economics, DOI 10.1007/978-3-319-56288-9_69

demonstrates the conducted experiment. Section "Results" states the results. Section "Conclusion" concludes the results.

Related Work

Different clustering models are the connectivity models, centroid models, distribution models, density models, subspace models, group models and graph models (Tan et al. 2006; Jain 2010). Centroid-based clustering represents clusters by a central vector. A typical example is K-means algorithm and its variants. It starts by random assignment of the cluster centroid, assign objects as a member to the closet cluster and repeatedly modify the cluster centroid until no clusters changes occur. Variants of K-means are K-medians (Kaufman and Rousseeuw 1987) clustering, K-means++ (Arthur and Vassilvitskii 2007), Bisecting K-means (Bradley et al. 1998; Steinbach et al. 2000) and fuzzy c-means (Bezdek et al. 1984). K-medians use the medians instead of the mean. K-means++ starts with a selected K-centroids. Bisecting K-means uses traditional K-means and then improves clustering by splitting the most appropriate cluster into two clusters. Fuzzy c-means assign an object to more than one class and the clusters centroids are calculated accordingly. A clustering algorithm is evaluated by one or more of the three available evaluations (Brun et al. 2007; Jain 2010; Tan et al. 2006; Zaki and Meira 2014). External evaluation indices are used in supervised clustering. Relative indices are used to compare different clusters in supervised or unsupervised learning which are Figure of merit and stability (Brun et al. 2007). Internal indices are used in unsupervised clustering when the data set is unlabelled. The most common external evaluation metrics are sum of squared error (Zaki and Meira 2014), confusion matrix (Zaki and Meira 2014; Wagner and Wagner 2007), Rand measure (Rand 1971), F-measure (Davies and Bouldin 1979), Jaccard index (Jaccard 1912), normalized mutual information (Wagner and Wagner 2007) and Fowlkes–Mallows index (Fowlkes and Mallows 1983). The most common internal evaluation metrics are Dunn index (Rand 1971), Davis–Bouldin index (Davies and Bouldin 1979) and Silhouette (Rousseeuw 1987), and Hubert's correlation (Zaki and Meira 2014). Silhouette for an object is the ratio of the difference between the separation and cohesion of an object to the maximum value of either one of them. The average of Silhouette of a cluster estimates the cohesion while for the data set indicates intra-cluster Silhouette value. A positive high value indicates better clustering.

EGY_WBD Clustering System

EGY_WBD Clustering system consists of three phases; preprocessing, clustering and result analysis phases, Fig. 1. Data preprocessing phase performs two tasks; data consolidation and preparation. Data consolidation is an iterative task that

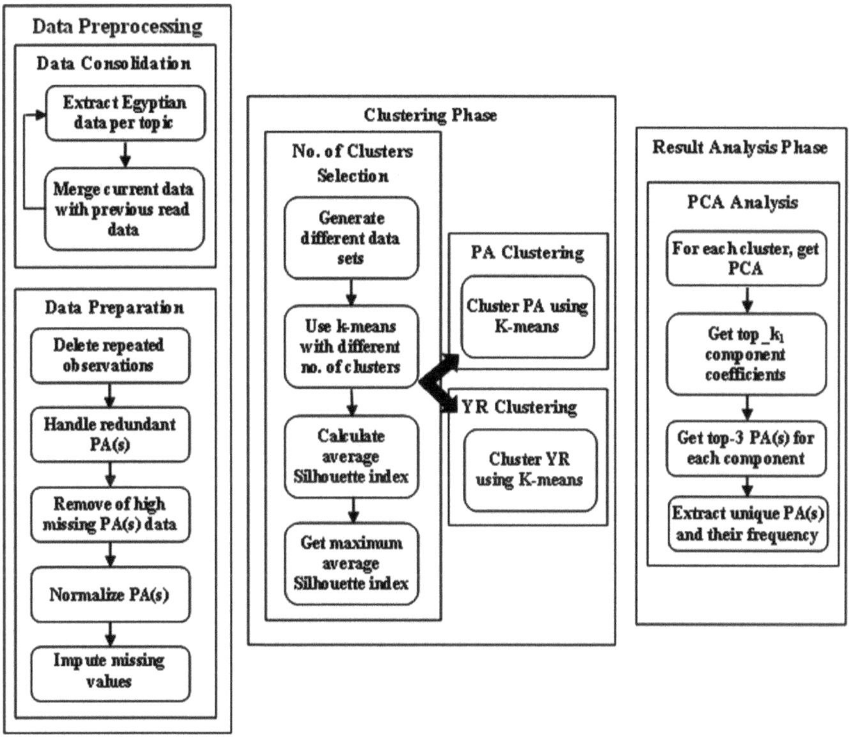

Fig. 1 EGY_WBD clustering system

extracts and merges Egypt's data from each topic's file. Data preparation first deletes replicate years (observations). Then, it replaces redundant parameters' data by their average data values. Next, it deletes parameters whose missed data values percent exceeds a certain threshold. The fourth step normalizes data using a linear scale. The last step is to impute missing data values with a parameter using Euclidian distance (Hana 2016). Clustering phase groups both observations (*YR Clstr*) and parameters' values (*PA Clstr*). As there is no prior information of the appropriate number of cluster (*K*), knowledge in clustering analysis is acquired. The steps to select *K* are to generate *n* data subsets using *n*-fold cross validation, to use k-means algorithm with different *K* values and to calculate the Silhouette index for each datum. The selected *K* corresponds to the highest average of Silhouette (*Avg_S*) for the entire data set. In the third phase, the results are further analyzed using principle component analysis (*PCA*) for both clusters. It gets the top-k_1 components coefficients that results in a total variance explained above a certain threshold (τ_2). Then, each component coefficient is approximated by top-3 parameters. Finally, unique and replicated parameters are identified.

Experiment

Data used in EGY_WBD Clustering system is an open source from officially recognized international data of development countries. The data values are extracted from twenty topics. Data starts from year 1960 to 2015 with a size of 119 Megabytes. The threshold value (τ_1) is selected to be 50%. To choose the appropriate value of *K* for *YR Clstr* and *PA Clstr*, K-means algorithm is tested with the range [3, 14] and [8, 15], respectively. In PCA, the threshold for explained variability (τ_2) is chosen to be 80%. The used platform is HP Pavlion DV2000 Notebook PC. CPU is Intel(R) Core(TM) with 2 GHz and 4 GB RAM. Code is written in MATLAB.

Results

EGY_WBD Clustering system uses 0.76% of the original data size with no redundant observation. The initial number of parameters is 1878 which is reduced to 1264 (32.69%) after handling the parameter duplication. The number is further reduced to 654 (48.26%) after the removal of highly missed parameters' data values. Figure 2 lists the *Avg_S* values for different *K* values for both clusters. The selected *K* for *YR Clstr* is 8 and for *PA Clstr* is 14. Table 1 shows *YR Clstr*

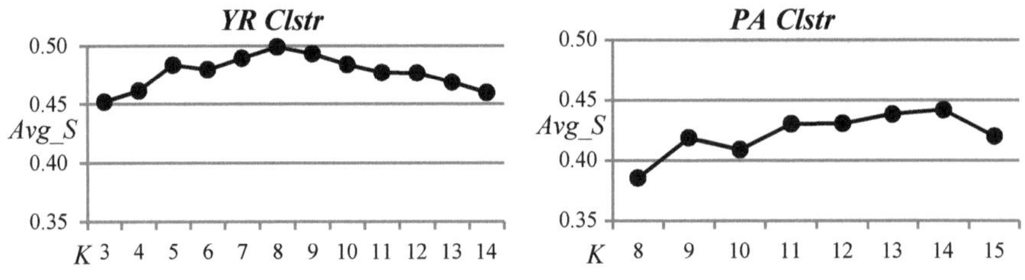

Fig. 2 *Avg_S* values for both clusters

Table 1 Observations clusters

Cluster #	K-means clusters for years 1960–2015										
1	1960	1961	1962	1963	1964	1965	1966	1967	1968	1969	2015
2	1970	1971	1972	1973	1974	1975	1976				
3	1977	1978	1979	1980	1981	1982					
4	1983	1984	1985	1986	1987	1988	1989				
5	1990	1991	1992	1993	1994	1995	1996				
6	1997	1998	1999	2000	2001	2002	2003	2004			
7	2005	2006	2007	2008							
8	2009	2010	2011	2012	2013	2014					

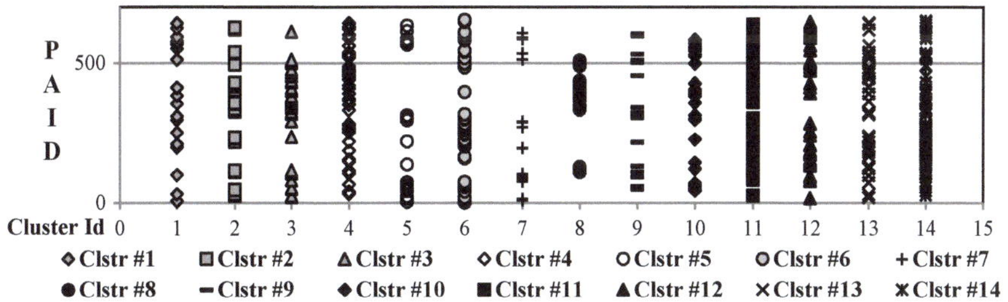

Fig. 3 Parameters data value clusters

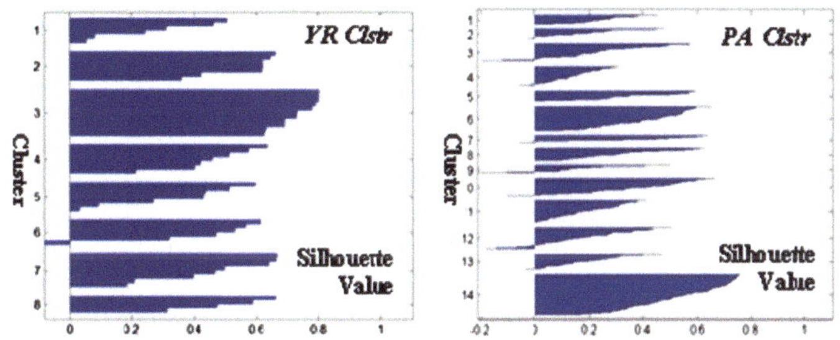

Fig. 4 *YR Clstr* and *PA Clstr* Silhouette values

Table 2 Explained variance statistics

Cluster	Mean	Standard deviation
YR	86.38	1.96
PA	82.62	1.82

members with range equals to [4, 11]. Figure 3 shows *PA Clstr* members with range equal to [18, 110]. Figure 4 shows that *Avg_S* values and average intra-cluster silhouette value for *YR Clstr* and *PA Clstr* are (0.493, 0.306) and (0.471, 0.278), respectively. The number of component coefficients range for *YR Clstr* and *PA Clstr* are [2, 4] and [1, 13], respectively. *YR Clstr* has higher explained variability mean value with slightly higher standard deviation value than *PA Clstr*, Table 2. Analysis is carried on to identify frequencies of parameters that compose the coefficient components. The number of parameters and unique parameters (UPA) of component coefficients for *YR Clstr* and *PA Clstr* are (72, 129) and (69, 58), respectively. The number of parameters with one occurrence in *YR Clstr* is slightly more than six times in *PA Clstr*. Table 4 lists nine UPA that are common in *YR Clstr* and *PA Clstr*. Most of the nine UPA are from Agricultural and Rural Development and Aid Effectiveness topics (Table 3).

Table 3 Parameters' frequencies and their percentages for *YR Clstr* and *PA Clstr*

Cluster	Freq.	1	2	3	4	5	6	7	8	9
YR	No. of PA	67	1	1						
	%	97.10	1.45	1.45						
PA	No. of PA	11	20	5	6	4	6	3	2	1
	%	19	34	9	10.3	7	10.3	5	3.4	2

Table 4 Common UPA between *YR Clstr* and *PA Clstr*

#	WB indicator	(*YR Clstr*, *PA Clstr*) Freq.
1	Agricultural raw materials exports	(1, 2)
2	Agriculture, value added (% of GDP)	(1, 7)
3	Arable land (% of land area)	(1, 6)
4	Arable land (hectares)	(1, 5)
5	Net ODA received (% of GNI)	(1, 2)
6	Net official development assistance and official aid received	(1, 2)
7	Net official development assistance received	(1, 4)
8	Net official flows from UN agencies, UNDP	(1, 1)
9	Net official flows from UN agencies, UNHCR	(1, 3)

Conclusion

EGY_WBD Clustering system aims to provide useful information about Egypt critical aspects during the past 56 years. Data collection methodology needs to be revised and enhanced as quarter of the parameters is redundant and more than half of the data have missing values. Silhouette values show that observations clusters is more compact and separated than parameter one. This result is supported by PCA as number of coefficients components is concise in observations clustering rather than in parameter one. There is great variability in number of WB Indicators used to explain variance in parameter clustering. Unique WB Indicators in parameter data clustering are more frequent than in observations one. It is of interest for field experts to examine the paper's finding. Also, it is recommended to use association rules and prediction.

References

Arthur, D., and S. Vassilvitskii. 2007. K-means++: The advantages of careful seeding. In *Proceedings of the eighteenth annual ACM-SIAM symposium on discrete algorithms*, 1027–1035.

Bezdek, J., R. Ehrlich, and W. Full. 1984. FCM: The fuzzy c-means clustering algorithm. *Computers & Geosciences* 10 (2): 191–203.

Bradley, P.S., U. Fayyad, and C. Reina. 1998. Scaling clustering algorithms to large databases. In *KDD*, 9–15.

Brun, M., C. Sima, J. Hua, J. Lowey, B. Carroll, E. Suh, and E.R. Dougherty. 2007. Model-based evaluation of clustering validation measures. *Pattern Recognition* 40: 807–824.

Davies, D., and D. Bouldin. 1979. A cluster separation measure. *IEEE Transactions on Pattern Analysis and Machine Intelligence* PAMI-1 (2):224–227.

Fowlkes, E.B., and C.L. Mallows. 1983. A method for comparing two hierarchical clustering. *Journal of the American Statistical Association* 78 (383): 553–569.

Hana, M. 2016. Handling of missing data. *Egyptian Computer Science Journal* 40 (3): 34–47.

Jaccard, P. 1912. The distribution of the flora in the alpine zone. *New Phytologist* 11 (2): 37–50.

Jain, A.K. 2010. Data clustering: 50 years beyond K-means. *Pattern Recognition Letters* 31 (2010): 651–666.

Kaufman, L, and P.J. Rousseeuw. 1987. Clustering by means of medoids. In *Statistical data analysis based on the Ll norm*, ed. Y. Dodge, 405–416.

Korotayev, A.V., and J.V. Zinkina. 2011. Egyptian revolution: A demographic structural analysis. *Entelequia Revista Interdisciplinar* 13: 139–169.

Muhammad, S., M. Shahbaz, A. Guergachi, and Z. Rehman. 2011. Mining sustainability indicators to classify hydrocarbon development. *Knowledge-Based Systems* 24 (8): 1159–1168.

Rand, W. 1971. Objective criteria for the evaluation of clustering methods. *Journal of the American Statistical Association* 66 (336): 846–850.

Ranganathan, S., S.C. Nicolis, V. Spaiser, and D.J.T. Sumpter. 2015. Understanding democracy and development traps using a data-driven approach. *Big Data* 3 (1): 22–33.

Rousseeuw, P. 1987. Silhouettes: A graphical aid to the interpretation & validation of cluster analysis. *Journal of Computational and Applied Mathematics* 20 (1987): 53–65.

Shaheen, M., M. Shahbaz, S. Ahsan, and S. Masood. 2012. Integrated data mining framework for natural resource exploration. *Life Science Journal* 9 (1): 314–316.

Steinbach, M., G. Karypis, and V. Kumar. 2000. A comparison of document clustering techniques. *KDD Workshop on Text Mining* 400 (1): 525–526.

Tan, P., M. Steinbach, and V. Kumar. 2006. *Introduction to data mining*. Boston: Pearson Addison Wesley.

Wagner, S., and D. Wagner. 2007. *Comparing clusterings: An overview*. Karlsruhe: Universität Karlsruhe, Fakultät für Informatik.

World Bank Group (ed.). 2015. *World development indicators 2015*. WB Publications.

World Bank's Egypt Macroeconomic and Fiscal Management (MFM) Team. 2015. Egypt economic monitor: Paving the way to sustained recovery. *Global Practice for Macroeconomics & Fiscal Management* 1.

Zaki, M.J., and W. Meira. 2014. *Data mining and analysis: Fundamental concepts and algorithms*. Cambridge University Press.

Why Today's Marketers Are Getting It Wrong

Michael A. Belch

Introduction

Marketers are often a reactive lot, jumping on the latest bandwagon of what is trending at the moment. Unfortunately, these knee jerk moves are often not thought out or supported by sound reasoning. Take the introduction of the Internet to marketing in the 1990s for example. All of a sudden the only medium that mattered was the Internet. Articles appeared forecasting the end of shopping malls, traditional media were all going to die, and even some of my own colleagues told me I was unlikely to have a job in the future as all marketing would center around the new digital medium. Well I still have a job, shopping malls still exist, and though not thriving, traditional media still exist. While the Internet frenzy declined, it has never died, and my treatise is that too many marketers are still too fascinated by digital media and, as a result, are not making optimal decisions.

Why the Fascination?

Let us go back a few decades to the introduction of VALS. The ability to now group individuals based on their values and lifestyles immediately became the de jour basis for segmentation strategies that resulted in target market labels like Baby Boomers, Gen X, Gen Y, etc. Each of these segments was supposedly different from the others, requiring marketers to develop different products, pricing and distribution strategies and advertising and promotion programs for each that addressed their specific needs and wants. The focus has continued into the present

M.A. Belch (✉)
Marketing Department, San Diego State University, San Diego, CA, USA
e-mail: mbelch@mail.sdsu.edu

A. Kavoura et al. (eds.), *Strategic Innovative Marketing*, Springer Proceedings in Business and Economics, DOI 10.1007/978-3-319-56288-9_70

day, with the center of attraction being Millennials. This generation, born in 1980 or later is estimated to be about 91 million with a strong buying power expected to exceed $200 billion in the U.S. by 2017. And, of course, they have become the center of marketers' efforts—just pick up any marketing focused business medium and you will see what I mean. All those other generations—forget about them!

The Millennial

How do we profile the Millennial? A review of numerous articles would lead one to conclude that they are: (1) hyper-connected digital extroverts, (2) trendsetters, (3) optimistic, (4) entrepreneurs who are (5) brand savvy. Many marketers consider them to be the future so far as targeting goes, thus the obsession with marketing to them. Their strategies are developed and/or changed to target them as effectively as they can based on these profiles.

In fact, there are numerous studies that show that these attributes are really not an accurate reflection of the Millennial. These studies indicate that the Millennial is more likely to be saddled with debt, and as a result are very unlikely to own a home—often living with their parents—or renting. They are much less likely to purchase a new car, or buy a product to reward themselves or on a whim. Most of them are not hyper-connected or trendsetters (only 42% are either) and less than 20% consider themselves to be entrepreneurial. They share many things with others in their cohorts including bikes, cars (if they own one), and even clothing. While they are still optimistic about their futures, they are much more skeptical than those of previous generations. The fact is, they are tight with their money, and may be less purchase prone due to their financial status.

Now compare this to the groups marketers are paying less attention to while they spend their time focusing on the "future". Again, studies show these older groups are more affluent, having more wealth and more disposable income. There are more of them (138 million) and are more willing to spend. Perhaps even more importantly, they are more likely to be brand loyal—a concept Millennials have seemingly failed to grasp. So, if you think about, which group holds the most potential for marketers?

Millennial Myths and Their Consequences

So, by not recognizing that they are may not be understanding Millennials, marketers may be developing potentially ineffective marketing strategies that they feel are necessary to reach them. The thinking that "if you get them now, you will have them for life" likely will not work with a target market that is not brand loyal and is driven by price. Are they always going to be this way? Previous generations all had their own idiosyncrasies but as they matured, their behaviors changed with them.

One has to ask if it is a smart strategy to bet on the future while ignoring the present, but that is exactly what marketers appear to be doing. For example, marketers are being mislead by a number of myths:

Myth 1: Millennials only shop online. In fact, more than one study has proven this wrong, showing that they continue to shop at stores for the same reasons everyone else does.

Myth 2: Their media habits are different. In fact, most Millennials spend half of their free time engaged with traditional media. They still watch TV (though the programs they watch maybe different), and still listen to the radio. They still get information about new products from TV, magazines, and social others.

Myth 3: Opinion leaders have significant influence over them. Of course they do. Studies from the sociology literature have shown that opinion leaders have a strong influence for the past 50 years or more.

I could go on, but the bottom line is that we don't really understand Millennials' media habits. We just think we do. And that is exactly why I say that marketers are making wrong judgments.

What Are We Doing Wrong?—The Obsession with Digital

It seems like the only medium that now exist is digital. We constantly read of companies making major shifts in spending from traditional media to digital and social. There is pressure on textbook writers to focus much more on digital to the expense of traditional media. There is a never-ending stream of articles on how to improve one's digital and social strategies and very few on how to improve our traditional strategies and tactics.

My contention is that we are spending too much time and effort on focusing on new media while ignoring the old in spite of the following:

- Mobile expenditures continue to grow at an almost astronomical rate even though the veracity of data reported in this area is questionable, and the effectiveness of this medium has been shown to be minimal
- Media expenditures in Twitter are up 62% even though multiple studies have indicated that consumers consider the ads there irrelevant
- Digital ad blocking—now estimated to be costing advertisers $22 billion a year—is expected to become even more prevalent in the future
- Social engagement rates are on the decline
- Personalization has been ineffective
- Retargeting leads to much less reach
- Issues with technology and fraud result in a significant number of ads never being seen.

And, perhaps most consequential of all, many studies have shown that every age group—including Millennials—find ads in digital media to be annoying.

Despite all this, marketers say they are less optimistic about digital than they were in the past but will continue to increase spending in this medium, and would spend even more if the effectiveness metrics were improved.

So What Needs to Be Done?

A required course in almost every college marketing program I am familiar with is consumer behavior. For decades we have recognized the need to understand the consumer if we want to develop effective marketing strategies. Two other courses that have grown in popularity in recent years are Integrated Marketing Communications and Marketing Analytics. Yet it seems that while academics recognize the importance of these practices, practitioners pay little attention to them. Their extreme focus on Millennials and the "new media" they think must be used to reach them has led them astray. In my opinion, if the course is to be righted, marketers must focus in these three areas. The data being relied upon now is primarily at the behavioral level only due to our fascination with technology. We know where the consumer goes, and what they buy, but we don't know why they buy. The reliance on cookie-level data provides us with analytics that yields metrics that are of minimal value in understanding the effectiveness of our programs. Finally, the obsession with digital and lack of attention paid to traditional media leads to less than effective media strategies. An integrated approach is still required.

In a sense we have returned to the 1990s. As the saying goes, "those who ignore history are doomed to repeat it."

Ontology-Based Term Matching Approaches in Social Media

Mariam Gawich, Marco Alfonse, Mostafa Aref and Abdel-Badeeh M. Salem

Introduction

The growth of World Wide Web and its users as well as the emergence of social web have led to the need to analyze the huge amount of data that are generated by the users. Data are presented in the form of informal text that is written in tweet messages, blogs, and web forums. Informal text (Alt 2014) reflects the opinions, complaints, emotions, and suggestions about products or services. The analysis of informal text can help companies to understand the customer behavior and measure the customer satisfaction.

Ontology is derived from philosophy which means the science of existence. In semantic web context, ontology (Gruber 1994) is defined as formal explicit specification of a shared conceptualization, where "formal" means that the ontology should be understandable by the machines and "shared" implies that it is validated by a group or a community. It is some kind of knowledge representation. Ontology presents the domain of interest as a hierarchy of classes and subclasses that are linked together by semantic relationships. Ontology can serve as an intermediate dictionary that can be used to determine the semantic matching between terms that come from structured or unstructured forms. The ontology can reflect terms that are generally used in social media. The matching between the ontology and social

M. Gawich (✉) · M. Alfonse · M. Aref · A.-B.M. Salem
Faculty of Computer and Information Science, Ain Shams University, Cairo, Egypt
e-mail: mariamjawich@gmail.com

M. Alfonse
e-mail: marco@fcis.asu.edu.eg

M. Aref
e-mail: mostafa.aref@fcis.asu.edu.eg

A.-B.M. Salem
e-mail: abmsalem@cis.asu.edu.eg

A. Kavoura et al. (eds.), *Strategic Innovative Marketing*, Springer Proceedings in Business and Economics, DOI 10.1007/978-3-319-56288-9_71

media text can help organizations to understand the meaning of informal text written by users. The objective of this paper is the investigation of ontology-based term matching approaches applied in social media. This paper is organized as follows: section "Introduction" introduces ontology-based term matching approaches in social media, section "Social Media Ontology-Based Term Matching Approaches" presents a framework proposal for comparative study, and the last section contains the conclusion.

Social Media Ontology-Based Term Matching Approaches

There are four ontology-based approaches for social media analysis; emotive ontology approach, ontology-based approach for social media analysis, methodological framework for semantic comparison of emotional values, and PREDOSE platform. This section discusses in details the four approaches.

Emotive Ontology Approach

Sykora and colleagues proposed this approach (2013) to analyze the emotional reactions of users regard to events, products, or services. These emotions are located in short text and informal messages that are disseminated in social media websites. The analysis and the classification of the emoticons are useful to build ontology of emotions that will be used to identify the most common human emotions. Emotive approach involves the matching of emotional ontology with sparse and informal messages. Emotive ontology involves eight fundamental emotions (Anger, Confusion, Disgust, Fear, Happiness, Sadness, Shame, and Surprise) as well as negations, intensifiers, conjunctions, injections, and perceived strength of individual emotions. The ontology takes into consideration slang terms and their related Part Of Speech (POS) tags. The emotions are extracted from twitter search Application Programming Interface (API). Out of Vocabulary (OOV) terms are used to identify the slang terms. Wordnet (Miller 1995), dictionary.com, thesaurus.com, Oxford English dictionary, and Merriam webster dictionaries are manually examined to identify the strength of words that reflect emotional intensity. Ontology is represented in python with customized hash tables and Trie wrapper objects that are connected with the details of valid intensifiers, conjunctions, negations, injections, and appropriate POS tags. The following pipeline in Fig. 1 demonstrates the matching between tweet and emotional ontology.

The input of the pipeline is the twitter messages that are broken into sentences. A customized tweaked version of Potts regex-based tokenizer and emoticon matching rules defined by O'Connor et al. (2010) are used to determine the matched emoticons. Tokenization process can break down the tokens according to their

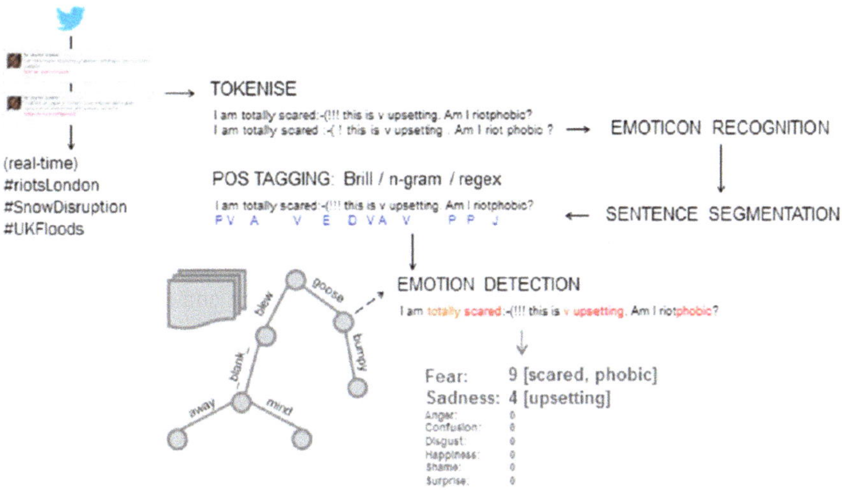

Fig. 1 EMOTIVE's NLP pipeline: incoming tweets; tokenization; emoticon recognition; sentence segmentation; POS tagging; Hashtables/Tries of emotions, negators; etc. are matched against tweets (Sykora 2013)

prefixes and suffixes that can be used for the substring matching with the ontology terms.

Ontology is represented in a set of Hashtable and Trie (prefix tree). Prefix tree is employed to save phrases provided by the ontology. The extracted token from tweet message is checked in the hash table. If there is no match detected, the token and the following tokens of the message will be compared with Trie. If an emotion was matched, the intension, negators, and conjunctions that appear before the matched token will be checked too. For each matched emotion, its strength scores are calculated. A general emotionally strength score is calculated taking into consideration the sum, average, and maximum score for the tweet (Sykora 2013).

Concerning the evaluation, Emotive ontology was evaluated by the use of a golden dataset that contains 150 tweets that are annotated independently by two Research Associates. Moreover, Emotive ontology-based matching is compared to an approach mentioned in CoNNL-2003 shared task (Tjong Kim Sang 2003). As Table 1 shows, the ontology-based matching approach achieves the highest f

Table 1 Performance of ontology matching (ablation tests) (Sykora 2013)

Matching	F measure	Precision	Recall
Sent.Seg + POS + Rules	0.962	0.927	1
Sent.Seg + Rules	0.952	0.909	1
POS + Rules	0.935	0.879	1
Sent.Seg + POS	0.929	0.868	1

measure (0.962) and recall (1) which means that the Emotive ontology matches the expressions and terms that are provided by the dataset.

Ontology-Based Approach for Social Media Analysis

Rainer Alt and colleagues (2014) proposed a framework for social media analysis based on the use of ontology. Its objective is to rev the social media analyses through a created dictionary, an ontology and social search and analysis concepts. This approach aims at improving the ontology building process through the use of extracted knowledge from various enterprise systems such as Customer Relationship Management (CRM) and Enterprise Resource planning (ERP). Figure 2 shows the framework components which are business databases, ontology builder, text mining, and social media.

Business databases component provide the major information of the business processes, products, and structure. Ontology builder component is employed to construct the ontology, and the component enables the extraction of data from structured and unstructured sources. Java Database Connectivity (JDBC) or Open Database Connectivity (ODBC) is applied to convert databases into ontology. Text mining component involves the analysis of unstructured text provided by forums and social websites. The use of the constructed ontology will help the text mining application to determine pertinent content and relations between different items. In social media component, social data that are extracted from different APIs (Facebook or Twitter) can be saved in the appropriate dataset in ERP database.

The framework supposes that the ontology is constructed from ERP database. Constructed ontology will be used by text mining component which receives data

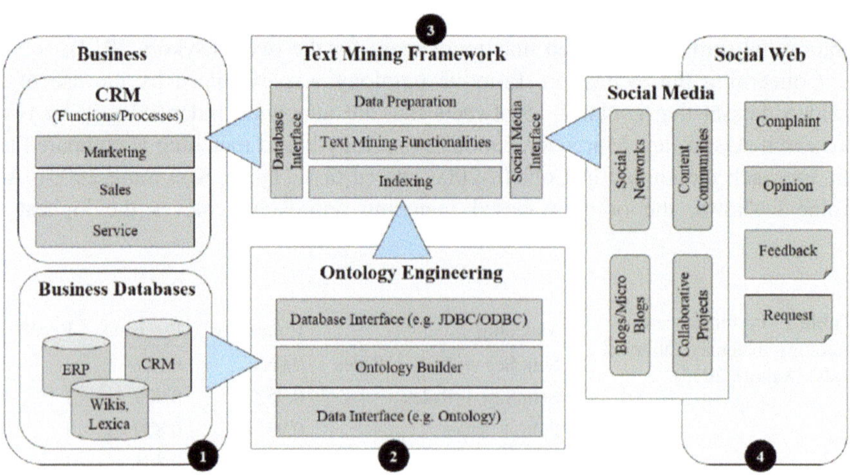

Fig. 2 Proposed framework of an ontology-based social media analysis (Alt 2014)

from social media component. The ontology plays the role of the dictionary that helps the text mining component to determine pertinent keywords and relations between concepts. Algorithms for ontology creation and algorithms that map the relational database to ontology can be used in text mining application. Examples of these mapping algorithms are as follows: DB2OWL (Cullot et al. 2007), R2O (Barrasa Rodríguez et al. 2004), RDB2ONT (Trinh et al. 2006), and RONTO (Papapanagiotou et al. 2006)

Methodological Framework for Semantic Comparison of Emotional Values

This framework (Jabreel 2016) was proposed by Mohammed Jabreel and colleagues. Its objective is to analyze large amount of tweet collected by the Destination Management Organizations (DMO). DMO is defined by the world tourism organization as coordinated management of all the elements that make up a destination (attractions, access, marketing, human resources, image, and pricing). It takes a strategic approach to link-up very separate entities for the better management of the destination. As Fig. 3 illustrates, the components of the framework involve the definition of emotional values, Tweet preprocessing, and semantic content analysis.

- **Definition of the Emotional Values**
  Human emotional values reflect the destinations personality (Henderson 2000; Morgan 2002). Therefore, emotional values that can depict destinations are classified as sincerity, excitement, competence, sophistication, and ruggedness dimensions. Each dimension involves a set of category which has a set of subcategories.

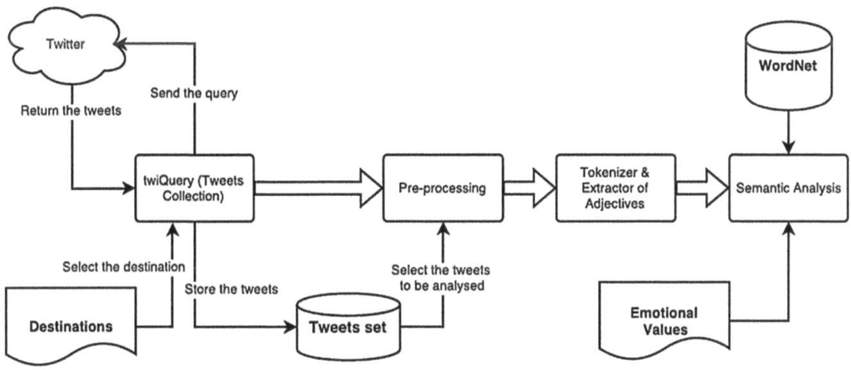

Fig. 3 Architecture of the methodological framework of analysis (Jabreel 2016)

- **Preprocessing of the Tweets**
  Tweet messages may include misspelling, slang terms, emoticons, URLS usernames, stopwords, and abbreviation that will be deleted. Wordnet can be used in this component for the words correction.
- **Semantic Content Analysis**
  This component focuses on the relationships between the tweets and emotional values. The analysis concerns about the adjectives expressed by the destinations and visitors. Therefore, an algorithm is applied to detect the semantic similarity between the adjectives provided by the tweet messages, categories, and sub-categories of emotional values. A parser is used to extract the adjectives and their frequency. The semantic similarity is applied by the use of knowledge sources such as Wordnet and ontology. Ontology-based similarity measure defined by Wu and Palmer (1994) can be applied to detect similarity between terms located in the ontology, as shown in Eq. 1:

$$\text{Sim W\&P}(c1, c2) = \frac{2 * N3}{N1 + N2 + 2 * N3}, \qquad (1)$$

  where N1 and N2 refer to the number of hypernym edges that start from terms c1 and c2 to the Least Common Subsumer (LCS). N3 refers to the number of hypernym edges that start from the LCS to the ontology root.
  If similarity measure equals one, which means the concepts are identical, 0 indicates that the ontology root is the LCS. Moreover, a semantic similarity algorithm (shown in Fig. 4) is applied to detect the semantic similarity between

Fig. 4 The semantic similarity algorithm (Jabreel 2016)

```
Function GetSemanticSimilarity (word1, word2)
  synsets1← getSynsets (word 1)
  synsets2← getSynsets (word2)
  if synsets1 is empty or synsets2 is empty then
    return 0
  else
    max_sim ← 0
    for each syns1 ∈ synsets1 do
      for each syns2 ∈ synsets2 do
        if pos (syns1) = pos (syns2) then
           sim ← Sim_W&P(syns1, syns2)
           max_sim← max (max_sim, sim)
        end if
      end for
      end for
      return max_sim
    end if
end function
```

emotional values and the adjectives. As Fig. 4 demonstrates, semantic similarity depends on the use of GETSynSets and POS functions. GETSynSets function detects the synset of each word provided by Wordnet. POS function is used to associate the synset with the suitable POS tag.

PREDOSE Platform

Derloy Cameron and colleagues proposed PREscription Drug abuse Online Surveillance and Epidemiology (PREDOSE) (Cameron et al. 2013), a semantic web platform that enables user to express their opinions about drugs through web forum posts. The analysis of these opinions can support the epidemiologic study of prescription. As Fig. 5 demonstrates, PREDOSE platform involves three modules; data collection, automatic coding, and data analysis and interpretation.

- **Collection Module**

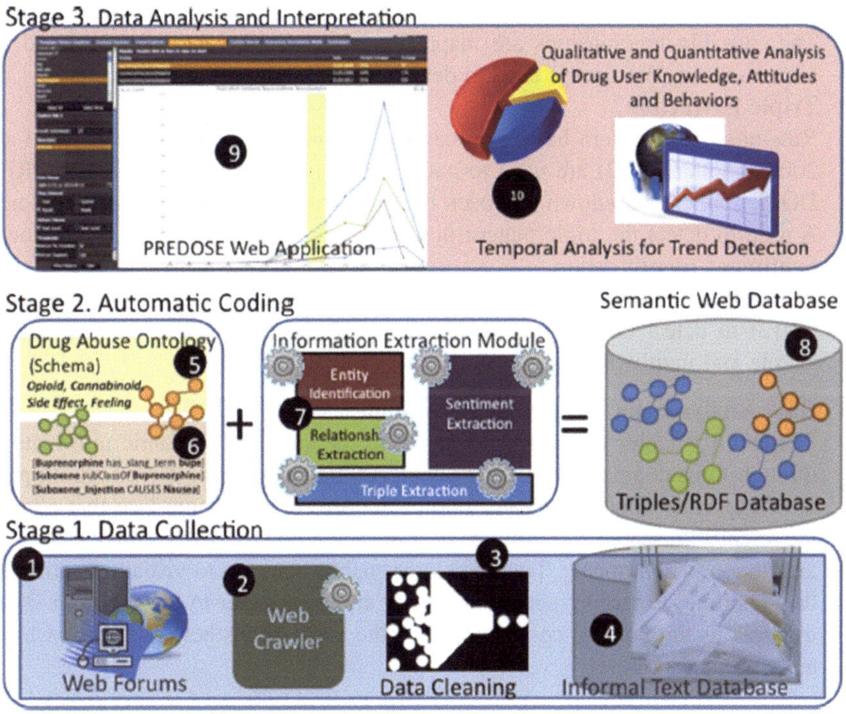

Fig. 5 The PREDOSE platform (Cameron et al. 2013)

Collection module relies on custom web crawlers that are used to bring data from web forum and save them in informal text database. Data involve the content of actual posts and metadata such as post identifier and user identifier.

- **Automatic Qualitative Coding Module**
  The module consists of five components which are Drug Abuse Ontology (DAO), entity identification, relationship extraction, triple extraction, and sentiment identification.

  Drug Abuse Ontology
  It involves 43 classes and 20 properties and links to other concepts located in other ontologies. Eleven classes of 43 classes are matched to URIs of Drug bank, Freebase, DBpedia, and Cyc.
  Entity Identification
  A lexical entity spotter and DAO are employed to detect the standard drugs of the slang terms provided by the corpus. The spotter involves the implementation of a tree data structure called prefix Trie (Cameron et al. 2010; Kavuluru et al. 2012). Spotter depends on term mapping established in DAO for spotted entity.
  Relationship Extraction
  It involves the extraction of relationships in the corpus. A set of target lexicon for relationship is created by the use of 54 unique predicates provided by the Unified Medical Language System (UMLS) which include biomedical formal relations. The causality relationships are mapped to the suitable relationships found in target lexicon. Wordnet is used to detect the synonym of the expression.
  Triple Extraction
  Rule-based and Pattern-based approaches (Ramakrishnan 2008; Suchanek et al. 2006; Thomas 2012) are used to extract the triple from the forum text. PREDOSE applies a top-down approach for triple extraction and the DOA ontology is used to detect the triple pattern that can be occurred between two concepts.
  Sentiment Identification
  PREDOSE implies the use of a technique proposed by Chen and colleagues (2012) to detect the triggers of sentiments. Chen technique is able to detect simple and multiwords.

- **Data Analysis and Interpretation Module**
  PREDOSE enables the scientist to analyze the extracted semantic information through three components: content explorer, trend explorer, and emerging patterns explorer. Content explorer implies the use of query interface that allows the scientist to search and browse the posts according to triples, entities, and the annotation of sentiments. Trend explorer enables the user to visualize statistical data charting. Emerging patterns explorer allows the user to browse drug–drug discussions through the co-occurence of the associations between drugs which are presented in posts.

Framework Proposal for Comparative Study

The points of comparison that are used to point out differences between term matching approaches are as follows:

- **Input**
- **Use of ontology in social media**
  The ontology can be used in social media to detect the matched slang terms, adjectives, emoticons, or to recommend related terms with informal medial text.
- **Social media analysis**
  Social media text analysis can involve the analysis of emoticons, slang terms, adjectives, or sentiments.
- **Output**

Table 2 demonstrates the comparison between the ontology-based term matching approaches.

First for the Emotive ontology approach, its inputs are tweet messages. The emotive ontology is used with rule-based matching approach to detect the emoticons in text. The social media analysis focuses on the extraction of emoticons from tweet messages. The output of this approach is the emoticons and their strength scores.

Second for the ontology-based approach for social media analysis, its inputs are business databases and social media text. Ontology is used to be matched with the social media text and to provide the related terms for a matched term. The social media analysis is not specific for certain entities in the text. The output is new

Table 2 A comparison between ontology-based term matching approaches

Approach Name	Input	Use of ontology in social media	Social media analysis	Output
Emotive ontology approach	Tweet messages	Matching between emoticons and emotive ontology	Emoticons extraction and mining	Emoticons and their strength scores
Ontology-based approach for social media analysis	Business databases and social media text	Matching between social text and ontology to detect the related terms	Text analysis	Created ontology and new information extracted from social media
Methodological framework for semantic comparison of emotional values	English language tweets	Used to match between emotional values and tweet adjectives	Adjectives extraction	Common terms between emotional values and tweet adjectives
PREDOSE	Text provided by web forums	Matching between slang terms and DAO ontology	Entity identification, sentiment extraction, and triplet extraction	Extracted semantic information

information provided by social media text; these information will be stored in ERP database.

Third for the methodological framework for semantic comparison of emotional values, its inputs are English language tweets. The ontology is used to detect the semantic similarity between emotional values and the adjectives. Social media analysis focuses on the adjectives provided by the tweets. The output is a set of common terms between emotional values and tweet adjectives.

Fourth for the PREDOSE approach, its inputs are texts collected from web forums. DAO ontology is used to normalize the drugs written in slang terms to standard terms. Moreover, DAO is used to extract the triple pattern that can be occurred between two concepts. Social media analysis relies on the extraction of entity (drug), sentiment, and triplets. The output is the extracted semantic information composed from extracted drugs, sentiment, and triplets. These information will be used in epidemiologic study.

Conclusion and Future Work

All approaches mention their use of ontology to match or extract specific set (entities) from text. The set could be emotions, sentiments, drugs, or adjectives. None of the approaches mentions how the semantic of a phrase can be analyzed. Only the ontology-based approach for social media mentions that its use for the ontology is not for the matching only but the ontology can recommend the related terms for a matched term. The creation of ontology is based on the goal of social media analysis. If the goal of social media analysis focuses on the emotion extraction, an emotive ontology will be created for this purpose. One of the interesting issues remaining for future work is to consider application of ontologies for sentiment analysis.

References

Alt, R., and M. Wittwer. 2014. Towards an ontology-based approach for social media analysis, In *Proceedings of 22 European conference on information systems (ECIS 2014).*

Barrasa Rodríguez, J., Ó. Corcho, and A. Gómez-Pérez. 2004. R2O, an extensible and semantically based database-to-ontology mapping language, In *Proceedings of the 7th international workshop on the web and databases (WebDB 2004).*

Cameron, D., P.N. Mendes, A.P. Sheth, and V. Chan. 2010. Semantics-empowered text exploration for knowledge discovery. In *ACM southeast regional conference*, 14.

Cameron, D., G.A. Smith, R. Daniulaityte, and A.P. Sheth. 2013. PREDOSE: A semantic web platform for drug abuse epidemiology using social media. *Journal of Biomedical Informatics* 46 (6): 985–997.

Chen, L., W. Wang, M. Nagarajan, S. Wang, and A.P. Sheth. 2012. Extracting diverse sentiment expressions with target-dependent polarity from Twitter. In *Proceedings of the sixth international AAAI conference on weblogs and social media (ICWSM'12)*, 50–57.

Cullot, N., R. Ghawi, and K. Yétongnon. 2007. A tool for automatic database-to-ontology mapping. In *SEBD*, 491–494.
Cyc ontology. http://en.wikipedia.org/wiki/Cyc. Accessed 06 Nov 2016.
DBpedia knowledge base. http://dbpedia.org/About. Accessed 06 Nov 2016.
Dictionary. http://www.dictionary.com/. Accessed 13 June 2016.
DrugBank database. http://www.drugbank.ca/. Accessed 06 Nov 2016.
EMOTIVE ontology paper material. http://emotive.lboro.ac.uk/resources/IJCSIS.html. Accessed 10 June 2016.
Freebase knowledge base. http://www.freebase.com/. Accessed 06 Nov 2016.
Gruber, T. 1994. Towards principles for the design of ontologies used for knowledge sharing. *International Journal of Human and Computer Studies* 43: 907–928.
Henderson, J.C. 2000. Selling places: The new Asia-Singapore brand. *Journal of Tourism Studies* 11 (1): 36–44.
Jabreel, M., A. Moreno, and A. Huertas. 2016. Semantic comparison of the emotional values communicated by destinations and tourists on social media. *Journal of Destination Marketing and Management*. http://dx.doi.org/10.1016/j.jdmm.2016.03.004.
Java database connectivity. http://www.oracle.com/technetwork/java/overview-141217.html. Accessed 13 June 2016.
Kavuluru, R., C. Thomas, A.P. Sheth, V. Chan, W. Wang, and A. Smith. 2012. An up-to-date in extracting, representing and mining semantic metadata from text; facilitating knowledge discovery in biomedicine. Day to knowledge-based literature search and exploration framework for focused bioscience domains. In *International health informatics symposium*, 275–284.
Merriam webster. http://www.merriam-webster.com/. Accessed 13 June 2016.
Miller, G.A. 1995. WordNet: A lexical database for English. *Communications of the ACM* 38 (11): 39–41.
Morgan, N., A. Pritchard, and R. Piggott. 2002. New Zealand, 100% pure. The creation of a powerful niche destination brand. *The Journal of Brand Management* 9 (4): 335–354.
O'Connor, B., M. Krieger, and D. Ahn. 2010. TweetMotif: Exploratory search and topic summarization for twitter. In *Proceedings of the international AAAI conference on weblogs and social media*, 384–386, Washington DC (USA).
Open database connectivity. https://dev.mysql.com/downloads/connector/odbc/. Accessed 13 June 2016.
Oxford English dictionary. http://www.oed.com/. Accessed 13 June 2016.
Papapanagiotou, P., P. Katsiouli, and V. Tsetsos. 2006. AIS Sigsemis. RONTO: Relational to ontology schema matching. *AIS Sigsemis Bulletin* 3 (3–4): 32–36.
Potts tokenizer. http://sentiment.christopherpotts.net/code-data/happyfuntokenizing.py. Accessed 12 June 2016.
Ramakrishnan, C. 2008. *Extracting, representing and mining semantic metadata from text; facilitating knowledge discovery in biomedicine*. Dayton (OH): Wright State University.
S&T Med Project. http://stmedproject.eu/what-we-do/destination-management-organization-dmo/. Accessed 14 June 2016.
Suchanek, F.M., G. Ifrim, and G. Weikum. 2006. Combining linguistic and statistical analysis to extract relations from web documents. In *Proceedings of the 12th ACM SIGKDD international conference on knowledge discovery and data mining ACM 2006*, 712–717.
Sykora, M.D., A. O'Brien, and S. Elayan. 2013. Emotive ontology: Extracting fine-grained emotions from terse, informal messages. *Computer Science and Information Systems Journal*.
Thesaurus. http://www.thesaurus.com/. Accessed 13 June 2016.
Thomas C.J. 2012. Knowledge acquisition in a system. Dayton (OH): Wright State University.
Tjong Kim Sang, E.F., and F. De Meulder. 2003. Introduction to the CoNLL-2003 shared task: Language-independent named entity recognition. In *Proceedings of the ACL seventh conference on Natural language learning*, 142–147.

Trinh, Q., K. Barker, and R. Alhajj. 2006. RDB2ONT: A tool for generating OWL ontologies from relational database systems. In *Proceedings of the advanced int'l conference on telecommunications and int'l conference on internet and web applications and services*, 170, Feb 19–25.

Unified medical language system. https://www.nlm.nih.gov/research/umls/. Accessed 12 June 2016.

Wu, Z., and M. Palmer. 1994. Verbs semantics and lexical selection. In *Proceedings of the 32nd annual meeting on linguistics*, 133–138. Association for Computational Linguistics.

Erratum to: Strategic Innovative Marketing

Androniki Kavoura, Damianos P. Sakas and Petros Tomaras

Erratum to:
A. Kavoura et al. (eds.), *Strategic Innovative Marketing*, Springer Proceedings in Business and Economics, DOI 10.1007/978-3-319-56288-9

In the original version of the book, the following belated corrections to change the order of First name and Family name of chapter authors have to be incorporated:

In Chapter 19, Platis Charalampos and Papadaki Maria have to be changed to read as Charalampos Platis and Maria Papadaki.
In Chapter 21, Zoulias Emmanouil has to be changed to read as Emmanouil Zoulias.
In Chapter 23, Papadimitriou Athanasia has to be changed to read as Athanasia Papadimitriou.
In Chapter 32, Kontis Alexios-Patapios and Gkoumas Aristeidis have to be changed to read as Alexios-Patapios Kontis and Aristeidis Gkoumas.
In Chapter 56, Apostolos P. Sarlis has to be changed to read as Apostolos S. Sarlis.

The erratum book has been updated with the changes.

The updated online version of this book can be found at

http://dx.doi.org/10.1007/978-3-319-56288-9
http://dx.doi.org/10.1007/978-3-319-56288-9_19
http://dx.doi.org/10.1007/978-3-319-56288-9_21
http://dx.doi.org/10.1007/978-3-319-56288-9_23
http://dx.doi.org/10.1007/978-3-319-56288-9_32
http://dx.doi.org/10.1007/978-3-319-56288-9_56

A. Kavoura et al. (eds.), *Strategic Innovative Marketing*, Springer Proceedings in Business and Economics, DOI 10.1007/978-3-319-56288-9_72

Index

A. Kavoura et al. (eds.), *Strategic Innovative Marketing*, Springer Proceedings in Business and Economics, DOI 10.1007/978-3-319-56288-9

MIX
Papier aus verantwortungsvollen Quellen
Paper from responsible sources
FSC® C105338

If you have any concerns about our products,
you can contact us on
ProductSafety@springernature.com

In case Publisher is established outside the EU,
the EU authorized representative is:
Springer Nature Customer Service Center GmbH
Europaplatz 3, 69115 Heidelberg, Germany

Printed by Libri Plureos GmbH
in Hamburg, Germany